Lecture Notes in Computer Science

Lecture Notes in Artificial Intelligence   14119

Founding Editor

Jörg Siekmann

Series Editors

Randy Goebel, *University of Alberta, Edmonton, Canada*
Wolfgang Wahlster, *DFKI, Berlin, Germany*
Zhi-Hua Zhou, *Nanjing University, Nanjing, China*

The series Lecture Notes in Artificial Intelligence (LNAI) was established in 1988 as a topical subseries of LNCS devoted to artificial intelligence.

The series publishes state-of-the-art research results at a high level. As with the LNCS mother series, the mission of the series is to serve the international R & D community by providing an invaluable service, mainly focused on the publication of conference and workshop proceedings and postproceedings.

Zhi Jin · Yuncheng Jiang ·
Robert Andrei Buchmann · Yaxin Bi ·
Ana-Maria Ghiran · Wenjun Ma
Editors

Knowledge Science, Engineering and Management

16th International Conference, KSEM 2023
Guangzhou, China, August 16–18, 2023
Proceedings, Part III

 Springer

Editors
Zhi Jin ⓘ
Peking University
Beijing, China

Robert Andrei Buchmann ⓘ
Babeş-Bolyai University
Cluj-Napoca, Romania

Ana-Maria Ghiran ⓘ
Babeş-Bolyai University
Cluj-Napoca, Romania

Yuncheng Jiang ⓘ
South China Normal University
Guangzhou, China

Yaxin Bi ⓘ
Ulster University
Belfast, UK

Wenjun Ma ⓘ
South China Normal University
Guangzhou, China

ISSN 0302-9743   ISSN 1611-3349 (electronic)
Lecture Notes in Artificial Intelligence
ISBN 978-3-031-40288-3   ISBN 978-3-031-40289-0 (eBook)
https://doi.org/10.1007/978-3-031-40289-0

LNCS Sublibrary: SL7 – Artificial Intelligence

This Springer imprint is published by the registered company Springer Nature Switzerland AG
The registered company address is: Gewerbestrasse 11, 6330 Cham, Switzerland

Preface

We are extremely pleased to introduce the Proceedings of the 16th International Conference on Knowledge Science, Engineering and Management (KSEM 2023), this is a four-volume set containing the papers accepted for this year's conference, which was organized by and hosted at the South China Normal University, Guangzhou, China during August 16–18, 2023.

Since its inaugural conference back in 2006, KSEM has accumulated great success under the immense efforts from each year's organizing committee and beyond. Previous years' events were held in Guilin, China (KSEM 2006); Melbourne, Australia (KSEM 2007); Vienna, Austria (KSEM 2009); Belfast, UK (KSEM 2010); Irvine, USA (KSEM 2011), Dalian, China (KSEM 2013); Sibiu, Romania (KSEM 2014); Chongqing, China (KSEM 2015); Passau, Germany (KSEM 2016); Melbourne, Australia (KSEM 2017); Changchun, China (KSEM 2018); Athens, Greece (KSEM 2019). Even during the COVID pandemic, KSEM was continued and held in Hangzhou, China (KSEM 2020); Tokyo, Japan (KSEM 2021) and Singapore (KSEM 2022), respectively.

The objective of KSEM is to create a forum that gathers researchers and practitioners from academia, industry, and government around the globe to present advancements in theories and state-of-the-art technologies in the field of knowledge science, engineering, and management. Attendees were encouraged to present prototypes and deploy knowledge-based systems, discuss and debate practical challenges as well as opportunities for the research community. With its interdisciplinary nature, KSEM 2023 focused on four broad areas: Knowledge Science with Learning and AI (KSLA), Knowledge Engineering Research and Applications (KERA), Knowledge Management Systems (KMS), and Emerging Technologies for Knowledge Science, Engineering and Management (ETKS).

In this year's conference, we received 395 submissions. Single-blind review was adopted for the conference review process. Each submission was peer reviewed by 2 to 4 reviewers from the program committee members and external reviewers. Among them, 114 regular papers (28.8% acceptance rate) and 30 short papers were selected, giving a total of 144 papers. We have separated the proceedings into four volumes: LNCS 14117, 14118, 14119, and 14120. The collection of papers represents a wide range of research activities, covering knowledge representation and reasoning, knowledge extraction, knowledge integration, data mining and knowledge discovery, and beyond.

In addition to the regular sessions, this year's event featured the following keynote speakers:

- Witold Pedrycz, University of Alberta, Canada, with the presentation titled *Credibility of Machine Learning Through Information Granularity*;
- Zhi-Hua Zhou, Nanjing University, China, with the presentation titled *A New Paradigm to Leverage Formalized Knowledge and Machine Learning*;

- Geoff Webb, Monash University, Australia, with the presentation titled *Recent Advances in Assessing Time Series Similarity Through Dynamic Time Warping*;
- Jie Tang, Tsinghua University, China, with the presentation titled *ChatGLM: Run Your Own "ChatGPT" on a Laptop.*

We would like to express our sincere gratitude to the many contributors who were steadfast supporters and made KSEM 2023 a great success. First of all, we would like to thank the KSEM 2023 Organizing Committee, the School of Computer Science at South China Normal University, Sun Yat-sen University, and our publisher Springer, without their crucial support the conference would not have been possible. Secondly, we would like to thank the members of our Steering Committee (Honorary General Chairs), Ruqian Lu from the Chinese Academy of Sciences, and Dimitris Karagiannis from the University of Vienna, Austria, for their invaluable guidance throughout the event; the General Co-chairs, Zhi Jin from Peking University, Christos Douligeris from the University of Piraeus, Daniel Neagu from the University of Bradford, and Weihua Ma from South China Normal University. They were involved in the whole process of the organization efforts, and provided various critical resources, including but not limited to connections to external reviewers and professional advice. Last but not least, we would like to thank the authors who submitted their papers to this year's conference, the Program Committee and the external reviewers, without whom the daunting tasks of paper reviews would not have been accomplished in time.

We hope that the reader finds the results of the conference program valuable and thought-provoking, and we hope attendees had a valuable opportunity to share ideas with other researchers and practitioners from institutions around the world.

August 2023   Zhi Jin
                                                                  Yuncheng Jiang
                                                          Robert Andrei Buchmann
                                                                      Yaxin Bi
                                                              Ana-Maria Ghiran
                                                                     Wenjun Ma

Organization

Honorary General Chairs

Ruqian Lu   Chinese Academy of Sciences, China
Dimitris Karagiannis   University of Vienna, Austria

General Chairs

Zhi Jin   Peking University, China
Christos Douligeris   University of Piraeus, Greece
Daniel Neagu   University of Bradford, UK
Weihua Ma   South China Normal University, China

Program Chairs

Yuncheng Jiang   South China Normal University, China
Robert Buchmann   Babeş-Bolyai University, Romania
Yaxin Bi   Ulster University, UK

Publication Chairs

Ana-Maria Ghiran   Babeş-Bolyai University, Romania
Wenjun Ma   South China Normal University, China

Publicity Chairs

Ye Zhu   Deakin University, Australia
Jieyu Zhan   South China Normal University, China

Steering Committee

Ruqian Lu (Honorary Chair)   Chinese Academy of Sciences, China
Dimitris Karagiannis (Chair)   University of Vienna, Austria

Bo Yang	Jilin University, China
Chengqi Zhang	University of Technology, Sydney, Australia
Christos Douligeris	University of Piraeus, Greece
Claudiu Kifor	Lucian Blaga University of Sibiu, Romania
Gang Li	Deakin University, Australia
Hui Xiong	State University of New Jersey, USA
Jörg Siekmann	German Research Centre of Artificial Intelligence, Germany
Martin Wirsing	Ludwig-Maximilians-Universität München, Germany
Meikang Qiu	Texas A&M University-Commerce, USA
Xiaoyang Wang	Zhejiang Gongshang University, China
Yaxin Bi	Ulster University, UK
Yoshiteru Nakamori	Japan Advanced Institute of Science and Technology, Japan
Zhi Jin	Peking University, China
Zili Zhang	Southwest University, China

Technical Program Committee

Achim D. Brucker	University of Exeter, UK
Achim Hoffmann	University of New South Wales, Australia
Agostino Cortesi	Universita' Ca' Foscari di Venezia, Italy
Andrea Polini	University of Camerino, Italy
Ben Roelens	Open Universiteit, Netherlands
Bo Luo	University of Kansas, USA
Bowen Zhao	Singapore Management University, Singapore
Chaobo He	South China Normal University, China
Chenyou Fan	South China Normal University, China
Cheng Huang	Sichuan University, China
Chunxia Zhang	Beijing Institute of Technology, China
Claudiu Kifor	Lucian Blaga University of Sibiu, Romania
Cungen Cao	Chinese Academy of Sciences, Beijing, China
Dan Oleary	University of Southern California, USA
Daniel Volovici	Lucian Blaga University of Sibiu, Romania
Dantong Ouyang	Jilin University, China
Dimitris Apostolou	University of Piraeus, Greece
Dongning Liu	Guangdong University of Technology, China
Florin Leon	Gheorghe Asachi Technical University of Iasi, Romania
Haibo Zhang	University of Otago, New Zealand

Hans Friedrich Witschel	Fachhochschule Nordwestschweiz, Switzerland
Hansi Jiang	SAS Institute, USA
Hao Tang	City University of New York, USA
Hechang Chen	Jilin University, China
Jiahao Cao	Tsinghua University, China
Jan Vanthienen	KU Leuven, Belgium
Jia-Huai You	University of Alberta, Canada
Jianfei Sun	University of Science and Technology of China, China
Jiangning Wu	Dalian University of Technology, China
Jianquan Ouyang	Xiangtan University, China
Jianting Ning	Singapore Management University, Singapore
Jiaqi Zhu	Chinese Academy of Sciences, China
Juan Manuel Vara	University Rey Juan Carlos, Spain
Jue Wang	Chinese Academy of Sciences, China
Jun Zheng	New Mexico Institute of Mining and Technology, USA
Junwei Zhang	Xidian University, China
Krzysztof Kluza	AGH University of Science and Technology, Poland
Leilei Sun	Beihang University, China
Lihua Cai	South China Normal University, China
Liang Chang	Guilin University of Electronic Science and Technology, China
Luca Cernuzzi	Universidad Católica, Chile
Man Zhou	Huazhong University of Science and Technology, China
Marite Kirikova	Riga Technical University, Latvia
Md Ali	Rider University, USA
Meiyong Liu	Sun Yat-sen University, China
Meng Li	Hefei University of Technology, China
Mengchi Liu	South China Normal University, China
Naveed Khan	Ulster University, UK
Nick Bassiliades	Aristotle University of Thessaloniki, Greece
Norbert Pataki	Eötvös Loránd University, Hungary
Pengfei Wu	National University of Singapore, Singapore
Pietro Ferrara	Ca' Foscari University of Venice, Italy
Priscila Cedillo	Universidad de Cuenca, Ecuador
Qiang Gao	Southwestern University of Finance and Economics, China
Qianli Ma	South China University of Technology, China
Qingtian Zeng	Shandong University of Science and Technology, China

Qingzhen Xu	South China Normal University, China
Radu Tudor Ionescu	University of Bucharest, Romania
Remus Brad	Lucian Blaga University of Sibiu, Romania
Ruisheng Shi	Beijing University of Posts & Telecommunications, China
Shaojing Fu	National University of Defense Technology, China
Songmao Zhang	Chinese Academy of Sciences, China
Suqin Tang	Guangxi Normal University, China
Takeshi Morita	Aoyama Gakuin University, Japan
Wei Luo	Deakin University, Australia
Weina Niu	UESTC, China
Weipeng Cao	Guangdong Laboratory of Artificial Intelligence and Digital Economy (Shenzhen), China
Xiang Zhao	National University of Defense Technology, China
Xiangyu Wang	Xidian University, China
Xiangru Li	South China Normal University, China
Xingfu Wu	Argonne National Laboratory, USA
Ye Zhu	Deakin University, Australia
Yiming Li	Tsinghua University, China
Yong Tang	South China Normal University, China
Yongmei Liu	Sun Yat-sen University, China
Yuxin Ye	Jilin University, China
Zehua Guo	Beijing Institute of Technology, China
Zengpeng Li	Lancaster University, UK
Zheng Wang	Northwestern Polytechnical University, China
Zhiping Shi	Capital Normal University, China
Zhiwen Yu	South China University of Technology, China
Zili Zhang	Deakin University, Australia
Zongming Fei	University of Kentucky, USA

Keynotes Abstracts

Credibility of Machine Learning Through Information Granularity

Witold Pedrycz Ⓘ

Department of Electrical and Computer Engineering, University of Alberta,
Edmonton, Canada
wpedrycz@ualberta.ca

Abstract. Over the recent years, we have been witnessing numerous and far-reaching developments and applications of Machine Learning (ML). Efficient and systematic design of their architectures is important. Equally important are comprehensive evaluation mechanisms aimed at the assessment of the quality of the obtained results. The credibility of ML models is also of concern to any application, especially the one exhibiting a high level of criticality commonly encountered in autonomous systems and critical processes of decision-making. With this regard, there are a number of burning questions: how to quantify the quality of a result produced by the ML model? What is its credibility? How to equip the models with some self-awareness mechanism so careful guidance for additional supportive experimental evidence could be triggered?

Proceeding with a conceptual and algorithmic pursuits, we advocate that these problems could be formalized in the settings of Granular Computing (GrC). We show that any numeric result be augmented by the associated information granules being viewed as an essential vehicle to quantify credibility. A number of key formalisms explored in GrC are explored, namely those involving probabilistic, interval, and fuzzy information granules. Depending on the formal settings, confidence levels and confidence intervals or coverage and specificity criteria are discussed in depth and we show their role as descriptors of credibility measures.

The general proposals of granular embedding and granular Gaussian Process models are discussed along with their ensemble architectures. In the sequel, several representative and direct applications arising in the realm of transfer learning, knowledge distillation, and federated learning are discussed.

A New Paradigm to Leverage Formalized Knowledge and Machine Learning

Zhi-Hua Zhou

Department of Computer Science and Technology, School of Artificial Intelligence,
Nanjing University, China
zhouzh@nju.edu.cn

Abstract. To develop a unified framework which accommodates and enables machine learning and logical knowledge reasoning to work together effectively is a well-known holy grail problem in artificial intelligence. It is often claimed that advanced intelligent technologies can emerge when machine learning and logical knowledge reasoning can be seamlessly integrated as human beings generally perform problem-solving based on the leverage of perception and reasoning, where perception corresponds to a data-driven process that can be realized by machine learning whereas reasoning corresponds to a knowledge-driven process that can be realized by formalized reasoning. This talk ill present a recent study in this line.

Recent Advances in Assessing Time Series Similarity Through Dynamic Time Warping

Geoff Webb

Department of Data Science and Artificial Intelligence, Monash Data Futures Institute,
Monash University, Australia
Geoff.Webb@monash.edu

Abstract. Time series are a ubiquitous data type that capture information as it evolves over time. Dynamic Time Warping is the classic technique for quantifying similarity between time series. This talk outlines our impactful program of research that has transformed the state of the art in practical application of Dynamic Time Warping to big data tasks. These include fast and effective lower bounds, fast dynamic programming methods for calculating Dynamic Time Warping, and intuitive and effective variants of Dynamic Time Warping that moderate its sometimes-excessive flexibility.

ChatGLM: Run Your Own "ChatGPT" on a Laptop

Jie Tang

Department of Computer Science, Tsinghua University, China
jietang@tsinghua.edu.cn

Abstract. Large language models have substantially advanced the state of the art in various AI tasks, such as natural language understanding and text generation, and image processing, multimodal modeling. In this talk, I am going to talk about how we build GLM-130B, a bilingual (English and Chinese) pre-trained language model with 130 billion parameters. It is an attempt to open-source a 100B-scale model at least as good as GPT-3 and unveil how models of such a scale can be successfully pre-trained. Based on GLM-130B, we have developed ChatGLM, an alternative to ChatGPT. A small version, ChatGLM-6B, is opened with weights and codes. It can be deployed with one RTX 2080 Ti (11G) GPU, which makes it possible for everyone to deploy a ChatGPT! It has attracted over 2,000,000 downloads on Hugging Face in one month, and won the trending #1 model for two weeks.

GLM-130B: https://github.com/THUDM/GLM-130B.
ChatGLM: https://github.com/THUDM/ChatGLM-6B.

Contents – Part III

Knowledge Management Systems

Explainable Multi-type Item Recommendation System Based on Knowledge Graph

Chao Chang[1,2] ⓘ, Junming Zhou[1] ⓘ, Weisheng Li[1,2] ⓘ, Zhengyang Wu[1,2] ⓘ, Jing Gao[3], and Yong Tang[1,2(✉)] ⓘ

[1] South China Normal University, Guangzhou 510631, Guangdong, China
{changchao,liws,wuzhengyang,ytang}@m.scnu.edu.cn
[2] Pazhou Lab, Guangzhou 510330, Guangdong, China
[3] Guangdong Hengdian Information Technology Co., Ltd., Guangzhou 510640, Guangdong, China

Abstract. Knowledge graphs and recommender systems have significant potential for improving recommendation accuracy and interpretability. However, most existing methods focus on single-type item recommendations and offer limited explainability of their recommendations. In this paper, we propose a novel framework knowledge graph transformer network (KGTN) for explainable multiple types of item recommendation, which aims to recommend items with different formats and categories to users simultaneously. Unlike previous methods that rely on predefined meta-paths, KGTN mines hidden path relationships in a collaborative knowledge graph. The KGTN integrates a transformer-based model with a meta-path-based graph convolutional network to effectively learn user-item representations and capture the complex relationships among users, items, and their corresponding attributes. Finally, we use the critical path in the learned useful meta-path graph as an explanation. Experimental results on two real-world datasets demonstrate KGTN's superiority over state-of-the-art methods in terms of recommendation performance and explainability. Furthermore, KGTN is shown to be effective at handling data sparsity and cold-start problems.

Keywords: multi-type item · recommender system · knowledge graph · explainable · graph transformer network

1 Introduction

With the development of society, the choice of goods and services has grown exponentially. Sometimes, the individual is not very clear about their needs in different scenarios. Recommender systems have played an increasingly important role in coping with the problem of information overload and personalized recommendations [1–3]. Traditional recommender systems rely on collaborative filtering [4], matrix factorization [5], etc. With the rapid development of deep

Z. Jin et al. (Eds.): KSEM 2023, LNAI 14119, pp. 3–15, 2023.
https://doi.org/10.1007/978-3-031-40289-0_1

learning and natural language processing, the recommendation has entered a period of booming [6–8]. Since Google proposed knowledge graph, as an important branch of artificial intelligence, knowledge graph has been widely studied and applied in the recommendation field [9,10]. Explaining along with the recommended item not only improves the transparency, persuasiveness, effectiveness, and trustworthiness of the recommender system but also improves user satisfaction [11]. Therefore, explanation recommendations have become a hot topic [12–14].

Despite the success, we notice that most existing methods focus only on recommending one product type [15,16]. That is, they are limited to providing a single type of item to users while failing to recommend multiple types simultaneously. However, it is very important to recommend multi-type items in real life. For example, as shown in Fig. 1 (a), on an e-commerce platform, there are various types of items that could be recommended, such as online stores, user evaluation feedback information, and different categories of merchandise. A single type of product recommendation has been unable to meet the needs of customers and businesses. Similarly, as shown in Fig. 1 (b), multi-type item recommendation is also necessary on academic social networks. Academic social networks contain a wealth of information, such as scholars, papers, and academic news. Recommending interested scholars, papers, academic news and other types of items could help users get effective information quickly and efficiently. At the same time, providing explanations of the multi-type recommending item could make them more convinced.

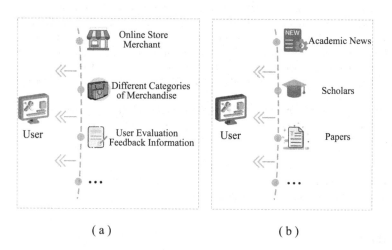

(a)   (b)

Fig. 1. Two examples illustrate the importance of item diversity in recommendation systems. (a) An example of item diversity in the E-commerce platform Taobao about personalized recommendations. (b) An example of item diversity on the academic social website Schoalt about information pushing.

However, multi-type item recommendation makes the recommended task more challenging because the different types of items have different attribute characteristics and data structures. Most existing neural networks learn node representations on fixed and homogeneous graphs [10,17,18]. Furthermore, as multi-type item recommendation item types, attributes, and data structures vary, it is difficult to find a unified standard to explain recommendation results. To address the above problem, we propose a novel method named Knowledge Graph Transformer Network (KGTN), which generalizes the previous state-of-the-art graph algorithm Graph Transformer Networks [19]. Through the graph transformer layer, the collaborative knowledge graph composed of the user, item, and other nodes enables the learning of useful hidden meta-path and multi-hop connections. This learning and training process does not need to define the meta-path in advance, nor any domain knowledge. Besides, the generation is interpretable. The graph convolutional layer aggregates the information of neighbor nodes to represent the vectors of users and items in different types of adjacency matrices. Then, we concatenate the user and item vectors from the different types of item adjacency matrices into a complete vector and get the list of items recommended to users by vector calculation. The critical path of the two nodes on the newly generated meta-path graph is recommended as an explanation.

The main contributions are three fold:

- We propose a novel deep learning approach Knowledge Graph Transformer Network (KGTN), which is a method designed to cope with the multi-type item explainable recommendation in an end-to-end manner based on knowledge graph.
- The KGTN directly mines the implicit relationships between items of different categories without relying on predefined meta-paths, which is able to effectively capture the complex semantic relationships between items of different categories, leading to improved recommendation performance.
- KGTN provides an innovative perspective on explainable multi-type item recommendations by generating item-level explanations. This allows users to understand why certain items are recommended to them, which increases user trust and satisfaction with the recommendation system.
- We conduct extensive experiments on two real-world datasets and demonstrate the superiority of our method.

2   Related Work

Leveraging knowledge graph as side information in recommendation systems not only mitigates the cold-start problem and improves recommendation accuracy but also provides explanations for the recommended items.

In 2017, Catherine et al. [15] used a Personalized PageRank algorithm to jointly rank both items and knowledge graph entities, which enables the model to produce personalized recommendations with explanations. In 2018, Lully et al. [20] presented an approach for explaining recommendations in the context of leveraging knowledge graphs with unstructured textual description data of items. They proposed three approaches to address the shortcomings of the state-of-the-art entity-based explanation approach: absence of entity filtering, lack of intelligibility, and poor user-friendliness. The first approach utilizes a DBpedia category tree to filter out irrelevant entities. The second approach integrates the classes of three ontologies to enhance the intelligibility of entities. The third approach uses the best sentences from the textual descriptions selected by means of the entities to explain recommendations. In 2019, Xian et al. [21] proposed a method called Policy-Guided Path Reasoning (PGPR) that combines recommendation and interpretability by providing actual paths in a knowledge graph. It highlights the importance of incorporating knowledge graphs into recommendation systems to formally define and interpret the reasoning process. In 2021, Huang et al. [22] proposed a model PeRN, which combines a recurrent neural network encoder with a meta-path-based entropy encoder to improve the explainability and accuracy of recommendations, as well as to address cold-start issues. The recurrent network encoder represents sequential path semantics in a knowledge graph, while the entropy encoder leverages meta-path information to distinguish paths in a single user-item interaction. To make the model more feasible, a bidirectional path extraction algorithm is also introduced. In 2023, Lyu et al. [23] proposed model Knowledge Enhanced Graph Neural Networks (KEGNN), which integrates semantic knowledge from an external knowledge base into representation learning of user, item, and user-item interactions. The knowledge enhanced semantic embedding is used to initialize the entities and relations of a user behavior graph. A graph neural network-based user behavior learning and reasoning model is developed to perform both semantic and relational knowledge propagation and reasoning over the user behavior graph. Hierarchical neural collaborative filtering layers are employed for precise rating prediction, and a combined generator with a copy mechanism is designed for human-like semantic explanation generation.

In general, the problem of efficiently recommending multiple types of items to users and providing explanations is still not completely solved. There is still significant room for research.

3   Methodology

Inspired by Graph Transformer Networks [19], in this paper, we design a novel method named Knowledge Graph Transformer Network (KGTN) to implement explainable multi-type recommendation, depicted in Fig. 2. It consists of three basic modules namely graph transformer layer, graph convolutional layer, and explainable recommender layer.

3.1   Graph Transformer Layer

In multi-type item recommendation, users, items, and the associated nodes form a collaborative knowledge $\mathcal{G}$. Due to the different types of nodes and attributes

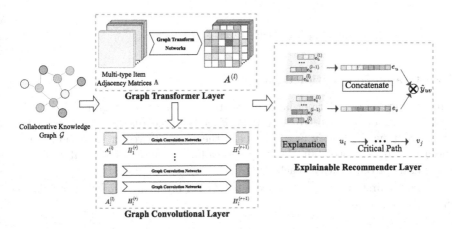

Fig. 2. The overview architecture of our proposed KGTN method is with three modules: graph transformer layer, graph convolutional layer, and explainable recommender layer. The input is a heterogeneous knowledge graph that includes users, multiple types of recommended items.

in $\mathcal{G}$, we can consider this knowledge graph as a heterogeneous network. Different from previous models, the graph transformer network does not need to define the original path in advance. Instead, it can learn the meta-path based on given data and tasks.

The main idea of original path generation is that a useful new meta-path $A_{\mathcal{P}}$ is obtained by multiplying the adjacency matrix as follows Eq. (1):

$$A_{\mathcal{P}} = A_{t_l} \dots A_{t_2} A_{t_1} \tag{1}$$

where $t_1, t_2 \dots t_l$ is a sequence of item type, $A_{t_1}, A_{t_2} \dots A_{t_l}$ is the adjacency matrix generated by different item types.

From the collaborative knowledge graph, $\mathcal{G}$ selects adjacency matrices $\mathbb{A}$ based on user and item type. The goal is to learn a new meta-path graph $A^{(l)}$.

First, we select two graphs A_1 and A_2 from the candidate adjacency matrix $\mathbb{A}$. Then calculate the convex combination of adjacency matrices by 1×1 convolution as in Eq. (1) with the weights from the softmax function as follows Eq. (2):

$$Q = \phi\left(\mathbb{A}; softmax\left(W_\phi\right)\right) \tag{2}$$

where $\emptyset$ is the convolution layer, $W_\emptyset$ is the parameter. Therefore, the meta-path adjacency matrix is obtained by matrix multiplication $Q_1 Q_2$. After the normalization operation, we get the $A^{(l)}$ as follows Eq. (3)

$$A^{(1)} = D^{-1} Q_1 Q_2 \tag{3}$$

Immediately after, repeat the above operation layer by layer for the graphs in the adjacency matrix $\mathbb{A}$. Finally, we obtain the learned adjacency matrix $A^{(l)}$ consisting of the useful meta-path as Eq. (4):

$$A^{(l)} = (\tilde{D}^{(l)})^{-1} A^{l-1} \phi \left(\mathbb{A}; \phi^{(l)} \right) \tag{4}$$

3.2 Graph Convolutional Layer

After the graph transformer layer, we learn a new meta-path graph $A^{(l)}$, which contains the newly generated meta-path. Each layer records the adjacency matrix of different types of node pairs. To learn the complete vector representation of the user and item, we train the graph convolutional network separately for the embedding of the nodes at each layer.

Take the first layer $A_1^{(l)}$ as an example. Other layers are similar in calculation principle as Eq. (5):

$$H_1^{(r+1)} = \sigma \left(\tilde{D}_1^{-\frac{1}{2}} \tilde{A}_1^l \tilde{D}_1^{-\frac{1}{2}} H_1^{(r)} W_1^{(r)} \right), \tag{5}$$

where σ is an activation function, $H_1^{(r)}$ is the feature representation of the rth layer in the graph convolutional network, $\tilde{A}_1^l = A_1^l + I$, $\tilde{D}_1$ is the degree matrix of $\tilde{A}_1^l$ and $W_1^{(r)}$ is a trainable weight matrix. By training, we obtain the vector representation of each node under the graph structure of the A_1^l.

3.3 Explainable Recommender Layer

After performing the graph transformer layer and the graph convolutional layer, we obtain multiple representations for user node $\left\{ e_u^1, \ldots e_u^{(l-1)}, e_u^l \right\}$ and analogous to item node $\left\{ e_v^1, \ldots e_v^{(l-1)}, e_v^l \right\}$. And then, we concatenate the representations into a single vector as follows Eq. (6):

$$e_u = e_u^1 || \ldots e_u^{(l-1)} || e_u^l, \qquad e_v = e_v^1 || \ldots e_v^{(l-1)} || e_v^l, \tag{6}$$

where $||$ is the concatenation operation. By concatenating vectors, we combine the user and item vector representations normalized under different adjacency matrices. Finally, we calculate the inner product of user and item vector representations to output the predicted clicking probability as Eq. (7):

$$\hat{y}_{uv} = \sigma \left(e_u^T e_v \right), \tag{7}$$

where $\sigma(x) = \frac{1}{1+exp(-x)}$ is the sigmoid function.

To explain why we recommend an item to a user, we provide the critical path $\mathcal{P} = E_u \xrightarrow{r_1} E_1 \xrightarrow{r_2} \ldots E_v$ on the adjacency matrix $A^{(l)}$ as the explanation for recommending this item to the user. This explanation is credible because we learn to obtain new graph structures through graph transformation networks and mine hidden relations during computation.

4 Experimental Evaluation

4.1 Experimental Setting

Data. We consider two field datasets including **Scholat**[1] and **UserBehavior**[2] [24] shown in Table 1. In these datasets, we filter out the active users and label the different types of items for experiments. In particular, the Scholat dataset is a multi-type item recommendation dataset that consists of user and item data from the scholar-centered academic social networking site, SCHOLAT. The UserBehavior dataset is a Alibaba user behavior dataset. After preprocessing and subset selection, it was designed for multi-type item recommendation purposes.

Table 1. Data statistics.

Dataset	Scholat	UserBehavior
User	7,833	1,891
Item	91,334	4,529
Item-type	9	20
Interaction	164,495	194,016
Entity	92,943	6,440
Relation	7	4
KG Triples	59,868	200,456

Baselines. We compare with state-of-the-art recommendation methods based on knowledge graph to demonstrate the superiority of our method **KGTN**.

- RippleNet [25][3] is designed for click-through rate prediction. The key idea is preference propagation based on knowledge graph.
- KARN [26][4] is a knowledge aware attentional reasoning network, which incorporates the user's click history sequences and path connectivity between users and items for recommendation.
- KGAT [27][5] recursively propagates the embeddings of neighboring nodes to update the embeddings of its nodes and uses an attention mechanism to distinguish the importance of neighboring nodes.
- LightGCN [28][6] includes the most basic component neighborhood aggregation for collaborative filtering in GCN.
- KGFER [10][7] samples 1-hop neighbors and relationships from the knowledge graph of items that interact with the user and feeds them to the TransR layer.

---

[1] https://www.scholat.com/.
[2] https://tianchi.aliyun.com/dataset/649.
[3] https://github.com/ZJJHYM/RippleNet.
[4] https://github.com/longzhen123/KARN.
[5] https://github.com/xiangwang1223/knowledge_graph_attention_network.
[6] https://github.com/kuandeng/LightGCN.
[7] https://github.com/fanhl/KGFER.

Implementation. We implement all the models using PyTorch, and run the codes on GPU machines of Tesla V100. All models are trained using Adam optimizer and the minibatch size is set to 1024. The learning rate is set to 0.02.

Evaluation. We choose truncated Hit Ratio (HR@k) and Normalized Discounted Cumulative Gain (NDCG@k) to measure ranking quality. A higher HitRatio implies that a greater number of users were able to locate their test items in the recommended list, indicating superior recommendation performance. Similar to HitRation, a higher NDCG score indicates superior ranking quality and, consequently, better recommendation algorithm performance.

4.2   Result Analysis

General Performance. In this section, we will report and analyze the comparison results on the two real-world datasets. The performance is evaluated using $HR@k$ and $NDCG@k$ metrics for different values of k (i.e., 5, 10, and 20). Results show that, in most cases, the proposed KGTN model outperforms the baselines on all two datasets, as indicated in the two Tables 2 and 3.

The performance of KGTN and baseline models on the Scholat dataset is shown in Table 2. From the comparison results, we could find that KGTN has shown more significant improvements compared to the UserBehavior dataset. Notably, the KGTN model has achieved the best performance in all HR and NDCG metrics on the Scholat dataset. This is due to the fact that the Scholat-MC dataset is more heavily impacted by user cold-start and data sparsity issues compared to the other dataset. Specifically, on the Scholat dataset, a majority of the nodes have a degree of less than 8, indicating a relatively sparse network. By identifying the hidden meta-path relationships between nodes, KGTN can effectively alleviate cold-start and data sparsity, resulting in more significant improvements.

Similar to the case of Scholat, on the UserBehavior dataset, KGTN achieves the best values for most indicators. In certain metrics, KGFER demonstrated superior performance to KGTN. This can be attributed to the fact that the nodes in the collaborative knowledge graph of the UserBehavior dataset possess rich attributes. KGFER utilizes pre-trained models and adaptive attention mechanisms to enhance knowledge graph representation, leading to improved model accuracy.

Table 2. Performance evaluation based on Scholat dataset.

Method	HR@5	HR@10	HR@20	NDCG@5	NDCG@10
RippleNet	0.3526	0.3852	0.4256	0.1505	0.0906
KARN	0.2702	0.3794	0.4311	0.1542	0.1039
KGAT	0.2013	0.3276	0.4366	0.1123	0.0917
LightGCN	0.2569	0.3599	0.3986	0.0960	0.1179
KGFER	0.3435	0.3752	0.4301	0.1638	0.0976
KGTN	**0.3810**	**0.4217**	**0.4572**	**0.1986**	**0.1298**

Table 3. Performance evaluation based on UserBehavior dataset.

Method	HR@5	HR@10	HR@20	NDCG@5	NDCG@10
RippleNet	0.4687	0.4789	0.4892	0.1700	0.1103
KARN	0.4523	0.4654	0.4782	0.1817	0.1089
KGAT	0.4289	0.4457	0.4613	0.1409	0.1056
LightGCN	0.3901	0.4055	0.4233	0.1550	0.1008
KGFER	0.4566	0.4732	0.4872	**0.2011**	**0.1207**
KGTN	**0.4965**	**0.5025**	**0.5035**	0.1704	0.1106

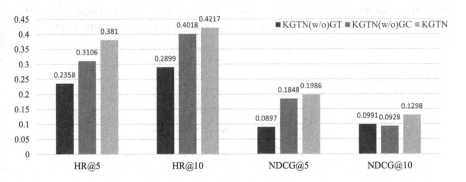

Fig. 3. Ablation Study on Scholat dataset.

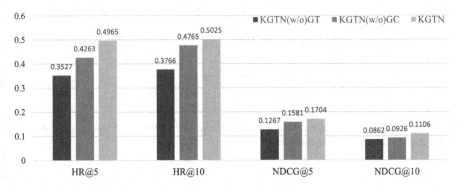

Fig. 4. Ablation Study on UserBehavior dataset.

Ablation Study. We conduct an ablation study to verify the effectiveness of the graph transformer layer and graph convolutional layer in the proposed KGTN model. As shown in Fig. 3 and Fig. 4, the evaluations on KGTN(w/o) graph transformer layer and graph convolutional layer achieve inferior values when compared with the KGTN.

The first simplified variant, KGTN(w/o) graph transformer layer, removes the graph transformer layer modules. This variant obtains user and item embedding representations directly using GCN on the original collaborative knowledge graph. The second simplified variant, KGTN(w/o) graph convolutional layer, removes the graph convolutional layer modules. After the graph transformation layer, embedding representations of users and items are generated directly through a general embedding method.

Figure 3 and Fig. 4 show the ablation study results. Our results indicate that KGTN significantly outperforms KGTN(w/o) graph transformer layer and KGTN(w/o) graph convolutional layer. Firstly, KGTN performs the best among the three models, indicating that the other two models cannot achieve optimal values without a specific evaluation metric. Secondly, comparing KGTN(w/o) graph transformer layer and KGTN(w/o) graph convolutional layer, KGTN(w/o) graph convolutional layer achieved a more significant improvement in terms of the improvement percentage compared to KGTN(w/o) graph transformer layer. This implies that mining hidden meta-paths in the collaborative knowledge graph is necessary and significant for multi-type item recommendation.

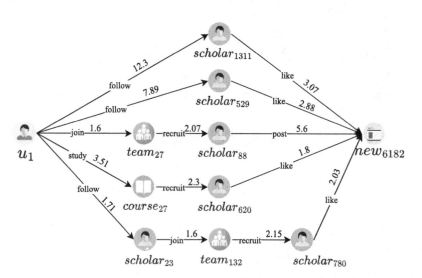

Fig. 5. Visualization of explanation paths between user u_1 and item new_{6182}. The case is selected from the Scholat dataset.

Case Study of Explainability. In the case study as shown in Fig. 5, we observe that there exist five distinct paths from user u_1 to item new_{6182}, each conveying a different semantic meaning. Among these paths, the one with the highest weight corresponds to u_1 traversing the path $u_1 \to scholar_{1311} \to new_{6182}$, with a weight of 15.37. Based on this observation, we can conclude that the most probable reason for recommending item new_{6182} to user u_1 is that u_1 followed the path via $scholar_{1311}$, and since $scholar_{1311}$ has a liking for new_{6182}, the recommendation system inferred that new_{6182} would likely be of interest to u_1. To further validate our conclusion, we may perform additional experiments and collect more data to verify the accuracy and reliability of the recommendation system. By adopting this approach, we can increase our confidence in the system and enhance its performance for future use.

5 Conclusion

In this paper, we propose a novel approach called Knowledge Graph Transformer Network (KGTN) for multi-type item explainable recommendation based on knowledge graph. Our approach directly mines the implicit relationships between items of different categories without relying on predefined meta-paths, leading to improved recommendation performance. Furthermore, KGTN provides an innovative perspective on explainable multi-type item recommendations by generating item-level explanations, which increases user trust and satisfaction with the recommendation system.

We have conducted extensive experiments on two real-world datasets and demonstrated the superiority of our method. Our results show that KGTN outperforms several state-of-the-art baselines in terms of various evaluation metrics, such as recall, precision, and NDCG. The experimental results also show that the generated explanations are interpretable and provide meaningful insights into the recommendation process.

In the future, we plan to explore the effectiveness of our approach on more diverse and larger-scale datasets. We will also investigate KGTN use for other recommendation tasks, such as sequential recommendation and group recommendation. Finally, we will continue to explore the semi-supervised and unsupervised recommendation methods when there is less annotation data. In addition, we will try to explain the recommendation in natural language.

Acknowledgements. This work was supported in part by the National Natural Science Foundation of China under Grant U1811263 and 62276277.

References

1. Himeur, Y., et al.: Blockchain-based recommender systems: applications, challenges and future opportunities. Comput. Sci. Rev. **43**, 100439 (2022)
2. Cai, Z., Cai, Z.: PEVAE: A hierarchical VAE for personalized explainable recommendation. In: SIGIR '22: The 45th International ACM SIGIR Conference on Research and Development in Information Retrieval, Madrid, Spain, July 11–15, 2022. pp. 692–702. ACM (2022)

3. Kompan, M., Gaspar, P., Macina, J., Cimerman, M., Bieliková, M.: Exploring customer price preference and product profit role in recommender systems. IEEE Intell. Syst. **37**(1), 89–98 (2022)
4. Adomavicius, G., Tuzhilin, A.: Toward the next generation of recommender systems: a survey of the state-of-the-art and possible extensions. IEEE Transactions on Knowledge and Data Engineering **17**(6), 734–749 (2005)
5. Koren, Y., Bell, R.M., Volinsky, C.: Matrix factorization techniques for recommender systems. Computer **42**(8), 30–37 (2009)
6. Chen, C., Zhang, M., Liu, Y., Ma, S.: Neural attentional rating regression with review-level explanations. In: Proceedings of the 2018 World Wide Web Conference on World Wide Web, WWW 2018, Lyon, France, April 23–27, 2018. pp. 1583–1592. ACM (2018)
7. Chen, X., Zhang, Y., Qin, Z.: Dynamic explainable recommendation based on neural attentive models. In: The Thirty-Third AAAI Conference on Artificial Intelligence, AAAI 2019, The Thirty-First Innovative Applications of Artificial Intelligence Conference, IAAI 2019, The Ninth AAAI Symposium on Educational Advances in Artificial Intelligence, EAAI 2019, Honolulu, Hawaii, USA, January 27 - February 1, 2019. pp. 53–60. AAAI Press (2019)
8. Guo, S., Wang, Y., Yuan, H., Huang, Z., Chen, J., Wang, X.: TAERT: triple-attentional explainable recommendation with temporal convolutional network. Inf. Sci. **567**, 185–200 (2021)
9. Guo, Q., et al.: A survey on knowledge graph-based recommender systems. IEEE Trans. Knowl. Data Eng. **34**(8), 3549–3568 (2022)
10. Fan, H., Zhong, Y., Zeng, G., Ge, C.: Improving recommender system via knowledge graph based exploring user preference. Appl. Intell. **52**(9), 10032–10044 (2022)
11. Zhang, Y., Chen, X.: Explainable recommendation: A survey and new perspectives. Found. Trends Inf. Retr. **14**(1), 1–101 (2020)
12. Cai, X., Xie, L., Tian, R., Cui, Z.: Explicable recommendation based on knowledge graph. Expert Syst. Appl. **200**, 117035 (2022)
13. Wei, T., Chow, T.W.S., Ma, J., Zhao, M.: Expgcn: review-aware graph convolution network for explainable recommendation. Neural Netw. **157**, 202–215 (2023)
14. Shimizu, R., Matsutani, M., Goto, M.: An explainable recommendation framework based on an improved knowledge graph attention network with massive volumes of side information. Knowl. Based Syst. **239**, 107970 (2022)
15. Catherine, R., Mazaitis, K., Eskénazi, M., Cohen, W.W.: Explainable entity-based recommendations with knowledge graphs. In: Proceedings of the Poster Track of the 11th ACM Conference on Recommender Systems (RecSys 2017), Como, Italy, August 28, 2017. CEUR Workshop Proceedings, vol. 1905. CEUR-WS.org (2017)
16. Ma, W., et al.: Jointly learning explainable rules for recommendation with knowledge graph. In: The World Wide Web Conference, WWW 2019, San Francisco, CA, USA, May 13–17, 2019. pp. 1210–1221. ACM (2019)
17. Duvenaud, D., et al.: Convolutional networks on graphs for learning molecular fingerprints. In: Advances in Neural Information Processing Systems 28: Annual Conference on Neural Information Processing Systems 2015, December 7–12, 2015, Montreal, Quebec, Canada. pp. 2224–2232 (2015)
18. Wu, Y., Liu, H., Yang, Y.: Graph convolutional matrix completion for bipartite edge prediction. In: Proceedings of the 10th International Joint Conference on Knowledge Discovery, Knowledge Engineering and Knowledge Management, IC3K 2018, Volume 1: KDIR, Seville, Spain, September 18–20, 2018. pp. 49–58. SciTePress (2018)

19. Yun, S., Jeong, M., Kim, R., Kang, J., Kim, H.J.: Graph transformer networks. In: Advances in Neural Information Processing Systems 32: Annual Conference on Neural Information Processing Systems 2019, NeurIPS 2019, December 8–14, 2019, Vancouver, BC, Canada. pp. 11960–11970 (2019)

20. Lully, V., Laublet, P., Stankovic, M., Radulovic, F.: Enhancing explanations in recommender systems with knowledge graphs. In: Proceedings of the 14th International Conference on Semantic Systems, SEMANTiCS 2018, Vienna, Austria, September 10–13, 2018. Procedia Computer Science, vol. 137, pp. 211–222. Elsevier (2018)

21. Xian, Y., Fu, Z., Muthukrishnan, S., de Melo, G., Zhang, Y.: Reinforcement knowledge graph reasoning for explainable recommendation. In: Proceedings of the 42nd International ACM SIGIR Conference on Research and Development in Information Retrieval, SIGIR 2019, Paris, France, July 21–25, 2019. pp. 285–294. ACM (2019)

22. Huang, Y., Zhao, F., Gui, X., Jin, H.: Path-enhanced explainable recommendation with knowledge graphs. World Wide Web **24**(5), 1769–1789 (2021). https://doi.org/10.1007/s11280-021-00912-4

23. Lyu, Z., Wu, Y., Lai, J., Yang, M., Li, C., Zhou, W.: Knowledge enhanced graph neural networks for explainable recommendation. IEEE Trans. Knowl. Data Eng. **35**(5), 4954–4968 (2023)

24. Zhu, H., et al.: Learning tree-based deep model for recommender systems. In: Proceedings of the 24th ACM SIGKDD International Conference on Knowledge Discovery & Data Mining, KDD 2018, London, UK, August 19–23, 2018. pp. 1079–1088. ACM (2018)

25. Wang, H., et al.: RippleNet: Propagating user preferences on the knowledge graph for recommender systems. In: Proceedings of the 27th ACM International Conference on Information and Knowledge Management, CIKM 2018, Torino, Italy, October 22–26, 2018. pp. 417–426. ACM (2018)

26. Zhu, Q., Zhou, X., Wu, J., Tan, J., Guo, L.: A knowledge-aware attentional reasoning network for recommendation. In: The Thirty-Fourth AAAI Conference on Artificial Intelligence, AAAI 2020, The Thirty-Second Innovative Applications of Artificial Intelligence Conference, IAAI 2020, The Tenth AAAI Symposium on Educational Advances in Artificial Intelligence, EAAI 2020, New York, NY, USA, February 7–12, 2020. pp. 6999–7006. AAAI Press (2020)

27. Wang, X., He, X., Cao, Y., Liu, M., Chua, T.: KGAT: knowledge graph attention network for recommendation. In: Proceedings of the 25th ACM SIGKDD International Conference on Knowledge Discovery & Data Mining, KDD 2019, Anchorage, AK, USA, August 4–8, 2019. pp. 950–958. ACM (2019)

28. He, X., Deng, K., Wang, X., Li, Y., Zhang, Y., Wang, M.: Lightgcn: Simplifying and powering graph convolution network for recommendation. In: Proceedings of the 43rd International ACM SIGIR conference on research and development in Information Retrieval, SIGIR 2020, Virtual Event, China, July 25–30, 2020. pp. 639–648. ACM (2020)

A 2D Entity Pair Tagging Scheme for Relation Triplet Extraction

Xu Liu[1,2(✉)], Ruiqi Cai[1,2], and Yonggang Zhang[1,2]

[1] College of Computer Science and Technology, Jilin University, Changchun 130012, China
{xuliu20,cairq21}@mails.jlu.edu.cn, zhangyg@jlu.edu.cn
[2] Key Laboratory of Symbolic Computation and Knowledge Engineering of Ministry of Education, Jilin University, Changchun 130012, China

Abstract. It is essential for large-scale knowledge graph construction to extract relation triplets composed of entity pairs and relations from unstructured texts. Although recent researches have made considerable progress in joint extraction of entities and relations, they are still confronted with some problems. Specifically, existing methods usually decompose the task of relation triplet extraction into several subtasks or different modules, which inevitably suffers from error propagation or poor information interaction. In this paper, a novel end-to-end relation extraction model named **2DEPT** is proposed, which can effectively address the problems mentioned above. The proposed model comprises a 2D entity pair tagging scheme that provides a simple but effective decoding method and a token-pair classifier based on scoring which determines whether a token pair belongs to the specific relationship. Besides, extensive experiments on two public datasets widely used by many researchers are conducted, and the experimental results perform better than the state-of-the-art baselines overall and deliver consistent performance gains on complex scenarios of various overlapping patterns and multiple triplets. The source code and dataset are available at: https://github.com/Oliverstars/Code42 DEPT.

Keywords: Knowledge Graph Construction · Relation Extraction · 2D Entity Pair Tagging · Biaffine Attention · Seq2table

1 Introduction

The end-to-end relation triplet extraction is an important and challenging task in natural language processing. It aims to jointly extract entity pairs and their relations from unstructured natural language texts. It is crucial for automatic construction of knowledge graph. As an important subtask of information extraction, this task is attracting more and more attention from researchers.

Previous studies [1, 2, 5] were devoted to extracting relation triplets with pipelined approaches, in which the task was often completed in two steps: named entity recognition [3, 4] and relation classification [6–8]. Although they could flexibly obtain relation triplets, these pipelined methods inevitably suffered from the error propagation problem.

© The Author(s), under exclusive license to Springer Nature Switzerland AG 2023
Z. Jin et al. (Eds.): KSEM 2023, LNAI 14119, pp. 16–29, 2023.
https://doi.org/10.1007/978-3-031-40289-0_2

Recently, a kind of end-to-end method [9–15] for relation triplet extraction has been proposed. These methods jointly extracted entity pairs and relations, which alleviated the impact of error propagation to some extent. The research of this kind of methods has made significant progress, where the seq2seq methods [9, 10, 13, 14] based on sequence tagging have become the mainstream. In essence, the seq2seq methods regarded the task of triplet extraction as three different modules, i.e. relation recognition, subject tagging and object tagging. Besides, they could not effectively avoid the adverse effects of different overlapping patterns which contained the cases of Single Entity Overlap (**SEO**), Entity Pair Overlap (**EPO**) and Subject-Object Overlap (**SOO**).

To consider the interaction among different subtasks while effectively mitigating the impact of error propagation, we propose a novel **2D Entity Pair Tagging** scheme (**2DEPT**) based on biaffine attention [16] in this paper. Our 2DEPT model can jointly extract entities and relations in a unified framework. Different from the previous entity tagging methods, our tagging scheme is a seq2table rather than seq2seq method that directly tags entity pairs through classifying the token pairs. Figure 1 describes the classical seq2seq annotation scheme. The sentence *"Beijing City is the capital of China."* contains a relation triplet (*"Beijing City"*, *"capital-of"*, *"China"*). For the relation *"capital-of"*, the seq2seq tagging scheme will obtain one sequence where both the subject *"Beijing City"* and the object *"China"* are tagged [9], or two sequences annotating the subject *"Beijing City"* and the object *"China"* respectively [10]. However, our seq2table tagging method will keep a table where the entity pair (*"Beijing City"*, *"China"*) is annotated without matching of subject and object.

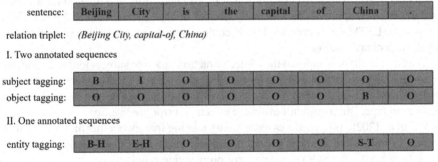

Fig. 1. The classical seq2seq annotation scheme.

In this paper, we conduct experiments on two public datasets to verify the performance of the proposed model. The results show that our 2DEPT model gains significant improvements over existing approaches and performs better than the state-of-the-art baselines overall. To sum up, our contribution is threefold as follows:

- We treat the relation triplet extraction task from a novel perspective and extract the relation triplets from the text directly in a unified framework, which can not only capture the interaction between subject and object but also effectively avoid the adverse effects of error propagation. At the same time, the complex cases of various overlapping patterns can be effectively solved.

- Following our perspective, we creatively propose a novel 2D entity pair tagging scheme and introduce a token-pair classifier based on scoring.
- Extensive experiments on two public datasets are conducted and the results show that our model gains significant improvements over existing approaches and performs better than the state-of-the-art baselines overall, especially for various complex scenarios.

2 Related Work

It is a significant and challenging task in information extraction to extract relation triplets from unstructured text. The early researches [1, 2, 5, 6] mainly focused on completing this task with pipelined methods, which implement relation classification after all entities are recognized. Although these approaches can extract the relation triplets flexibly through two independent steps, they have two unavoidable defects. Firstly, the correlation and interaction between relation and entity are ignored. Secondly, the error propagation problem is caused.

To effectively address the above problems, the joint extraction model of entity and relationship has attracted more and more attention. These joint extraction methods implement the end-to-end extraction of relation triplets by modeling entity and relationship in a single model.

Zheng et al. (2017) converted the joint extraction task into a sequence labeling task from a novel perspective and proposed a novel tagging scheme that unified the modeling of entity and relation, but it failed to solve the overlapping problems.

Fu et al. (2019) proposed GraphRel that propagated entity and relation information through a word graph with automatically learned linkage by applying 2nd-phase GCN on top of the LSTM-GCN encoder. However, this method ignored the interaction among subject, object and relation.

Yu et al. (2020) decomposed the triplet extraction task into subject identification and object-relation recognition with a span-based tagging scheme. The proposed model first labeled all subjects in the sentence with the entity type and then tagged the objects with the relation type. But it couldn't avoid the effects of error propagation.

Wei et al. (2020) proposed a cascade binary tagging framework that first extracted all subjects from text and then recognized objects for each subject and relation. However, it could not handle the **SOO** case and error propagation problem.

Zheng et al. (2021) obtained the potential relationships in the sentence with a relationship predictor while calculating the correspondence score between the start tokens of subject and object. Then they labeled the subjects and objects for each identified relationship. Although the proposed model effectively extracted relation triplets from a sentence, it still suffered from error propagation.

In a word, the classical joint entity and relationship extraction models almost have error propagation problems or poor entity-relationship interaction. In this paper, a novel 2D entity pair tagging scheme is proposed that can effectively solve the above problem. And it gains performance improvements even on complex scenarios of various overlapping patterns and multiple triples.

3 Methodology

In this section, we first give the definition of the end-to-end relation extraction task, then introduce the proposed 2D entity pair tagging scheme, and finally elaborate on the token-pair classifier based on scoring.

3.1 Task Definition

A sentence $S = w_1, w_2, \ldots\ldots, w_N$ that contains N words and a predefined relation set $R = \{r_1, r_2, \ldots\ldots, r_K\}$ where r_i indicates the i-th relation are given. In end-to-end relation extraction task, the relation triplet is in the format of (s, r, o), where s represents the subject, o indicates the object, and r represents the corresponding relation between s and o. It should be noted that both subject and object in a relation triplet can be called entities that are the concatenation of several consecutive tokens in the text. The purpose of the task is to extract the set of relation triplets $TS = \{(s, r, o)_i | r \in R\}_{i=1}^{M}$ from a given sentence, where M indicates the number of triplets in this sentence, and R is the set of relations mentioned above.

3.2 2D Entity Pair Tagging Scheme

For a given sentence S, our tagging scheme aims to model all triplets uniformly. For a sentence, we maintain a two-dimensional table $T^{N \times N}$ for each relation to hold the classification results of all token pairs under this relation, where N represents the sentence length. In the testing phase, we obtain all the triplets contained in a sentence by decoding the table under each relation. To facilitate the explanation of our 2D entity pair tagging method, we use $T^{(k)}$ to indicate the table corresponding to the k-th relation and $T^{(k)}[i, j]$ to denote the tag of the token pair composed of the i-th token and the j-th token. The token pair that consists of the i-th token and the j-th token is noted as (i, j). And each token pair in a sentence can be divided into three categories in our 2D tagging method as follows:

1) **BB**

If the token pair (i, j) belongs to this category, the i-th token and the j-th token are the Beginning of subject and object respectively. In this case, we set its tag to **BB**, i.e. $T^{(k)}[i, j] = $ **BB**. As shown in the Fig. 2(a), for the relation *"held-in"*, two entity pairs (*"2008 Olympic Games"*, *"Beijing City"*) and (*"2008 Olympic Games"*, *"China"*) can be extracted from the sentence *"The 2008 Olympic Games was held in Beijing City, China."*, where the token pairs (*"2008"*, *"Beijing"*) and (*"2008"*, *"China"*) belong to this category and their tags are both set to **BB**.

2) **IB**

This category contains two cases. The first case is that the i-th token is Inside a subject but not the beginning of this subject, while the j-th token is the Beginning token of an object. The second case is that the i-th token is the Beginning of a subject while the j-th token is Inside an object but not the beginning of this object. We set the tags of token pairs belonging to this category to **IB**, i.e. $T^{(k)}[i, j] = $ **IB**. For example, in Fig. 2(a), for the relation triplet (*"2008 Olympic Games"*, *"held-in"*, *"Beijing City"*), the words *"Olympic"* and *"Games"* are not the beginning of the subject, but *"Beijing"* is the beginning word of the object. Therefore, the word pairs (*"Olympic"*, *"Beijing"*) and (*"Games"*, *"Beijing"*) belong to the first case of this category. The word *"2008"* is the beginning of the subject, while *"City"* is not the beginning of the object. So the word pair (*"2008"*, *"City"*) belongs to the second case of this category. We set the tags of the above three word pairs to **IB**.

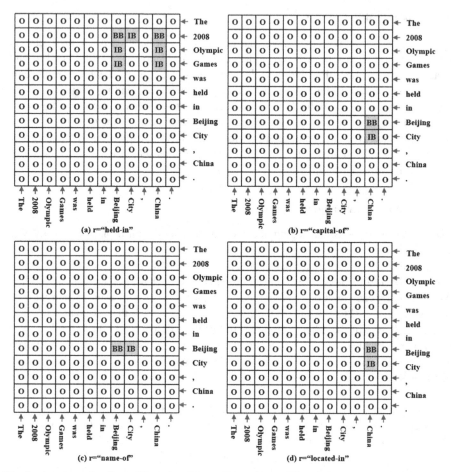

Fig. 2. An example of our 2D entity pair tagging scheme. The given sentence contains four relations: *"held-in"*, *"capital-of"*, *"name-of"* and *"located-in"*. For each relation, we present a table $T^{(k)}$.

3) Other

If a token pair (i, j) does not belong to any of the above two categories, we classify it into the category: **Other**, and its tag is set to **O**.

Furthermore, our 2D entity pair tagging scheme can naturally handle the complex scenarios with overlapping patterns. As shown in the Fig. 2, several triplets can be extracted from the sentence *"The 2008 Olympic Games was held in Beijing City, China."*

according to our tagging scheme. In the Fig. 2(a), ("*2008 Olympic Game*", "*held-in*", "*Beijing City*") and ("*2008 Olympic Games*", "*held-in*", "*China*") are two SEO (SingleEntityOverlap) triplets, whose entity pairs are tagged in a single table. For EPO (EntityPairOverlap) case, their relations are different. Thus, as shown in Fig. 2(b) and (d), the entity pairs from two EPO triplets ("*Beijing City*", "*capital-of*", "*China*") and ("*Beijing City*", "*located-in*", "*China*") are annotated in the tables corresponding to different relations. The seq2seq tagging methods (Zheng et al. 2017; Yuan et al. 2020) often have difficulty in handling the SOO (SubjectObjectOverlap) case, whereas our 2D tagging scheme has a natural advantage in tackling the SOO scenario. As shown in Fig. 2(c), the entity pair from the triplets ("*Beijing*", "*name-of*", "*Beijing City*") is the SOO case, which our 2D entity pair tagging scheme can address easily.

3.3 Token-Pair Classifier

Based on the above annotation method, we need to classify the token pairs, for which we introduce the biaffine-based [16] token-pair classifier in detail.

3.3.1 BERT-Based Encoder

To capture context feature information from a sentence, we use a BERT-based encoder [25], a multi-layer bidirectional Transformer based language representation model, to learn deep representation of each token. For an input sentence, the pre-trained BERT captures the d-dimensional embedding of each token:

$$X = \{x_1, x_2, \ldots \ldots, x_N\},$$

$$H = BERT(X) = \{h_1, h_2, \ldots \ldots, h_N\},$$

where x_i is the input representation of the i-th token that is the summation over the corresponding token embedding and positional embedding, $h_i \in R^{d_h}$ is the hidden state representation corresponding to the i-th token, and N is the length of the given sentence.

3.3.2 Representations for Subject and Object

In this paper, we argue that the information of subject and object has a positive impact on matching entity pair and relation. In other words, for a specific relation, the classification result of the token pair is associated with entity feature information. To this end, we capture the subject and object information from the input sentence by employing two MLPs (multi-layer perceptron), i.e. a subject MLP and an object MLP on each h_i as:

$$h_i^s = W^s h_i + b^s,$$

$$h_i^o = W^o h_i + b^o,$$

where $h_i^s \in R^{d_e}$ and $h_i^o \in R^{d_e}$ denote the representations of the i-th token in the input sentence with respect to subject and object respectively, $W^s \in R^{d_e \times d_h}$ and $W^o \in R^{d_e \times d_h}$ represent the trainable weights, and b^s and b^o are bias.

3.3.3 Biaffine Model

The deep biaffine attention mechanism was first proposed by Dozat and Manning [16], which aims to implement the dependency parsing task. In this paper, we use the biaffine model to implement our entity pair tagging task for each relation.

For the representation of the i-th token with respect to subject and the representation of the j-th token with respect to object, we calculate the scoring vector s(i, j) of each token pair through the biaffine model:

$$s(i,j) = Biaffine\left(h_i^s, h_j^o\right) = h_i^{sT} U^{(1)} h_j^o + U^{(2)} \left(h_i^s \oplus h_j^o\right) + b,$$

where $U^{(1)} \in R^{d_e \times |y| \times d_e}$ and $U^{(2)} \in R^{|y| \times 2d_e}$ represent trainable parameters, b is the bias and $\oplus$ indicates the concatenation operation. For a more comprehensive description of the deep biaffine attention mechanism, we refer readers to [16].

3.3.4 Training

For the k-th relation, we feed the scoring vector of each token pair into a softmax function to predict its tag:

$$P_{ij}^k = softmax(s(i,j)),$$

where P_{ij}^k denotes the probability distribution of tag for the token pair (i, j) under the k-th relation, and we choose the tag with the highest probability as the label of the token pair during inference.

Then the objective function of our proposed model is defined as:

$$L = -\frac{1}{N \times K \times N} \sum_{k=1}^{K} \sum_{i=1}^{N} \sum_{j=1}^{N} \left(y_{ij}^k log\left(P_{ij}^k\right) + \left(1 - y_{ij}^k\right) log\left(1 - P_{ij}^k\right)\right),$$

where y_{ij}^k is the gold tag, N is the length of an input sentence, and K is the number of pre-defined relations.

4 Experiments

In this section, we present the results of extensive experiments to validate the effectiveness of the proposed model. In addition, we will also analyze the properties of our model in this section.

4.1 Datasets and Evaluation Metrics

To enable a fair and comprehensive comparison with previous works, we follow [10, 14, 21] to evaluate our model on two widely used datasets: NYT [28] and WebNLG [26]. The NYT dataset that contains 56195 training sentences and 5000 test sentences is created by distant supervision. The WebNLG dataset that contains 5019 training sentences and

703 test sentences is initially generated for Natural Language Generation (NLG) task, which aims to generate the corresponding expressions according to the given triplet. Both NYT and WebNLG have two versions: one version denoted as NYT* and WebNLG* respectively only annotates the last word of entities in a sentence, and the other version which we denote as NYT and WebNLG, annotates the whole span of entities. Table 1 describes the number of samples in different datasets, including the numbers of triples and relations in the training set. Table 2 describes the statistical information on complex scenarios i.e. different overlapping patterns and triple numbers.

Table 1. The numbers of sentences, triples, and relations in NYT, NYT*, WebNLG and WebNLG*

Dataset	#Sentences			#Triples	#Rel
	Train	Dev.	Test		
NYT	56196	5000	5000	8120	24
NYT*	56195	4999	5000	8110	24
WebNLG	5019	500	703	1607	216
WebNLG*	5019	500	703	1591	171

Table 2. The number of samples on various complex scenarios. Normal means that there is no triplet with overlapping entities in one sample. SEO represents Single Entity Overlapping Pattern. EPO represents Entity Pair Overlapping Pattern. SOO represents Subject and Object Overlapping Pattern. N is the number of triples in a sample.

Dataset	Normal	SEO	EPO	SOO	N = 1	N = 2	N = 3	N = 4	N > = 5
NYT	3222	1273	969	117	3240	1047	314	290	109
NYT*	3266	1297	978	45	3244	1045	312	291	108
WebNLG	239	448	6	85	256	175	138	93	41
WebNLG*	245	457	26	84	266	171	131	90	45

In our experiment, we use three standard evaluation metrics i.e. micro Precision (Prec.), Recall (Rec.) and F1- score (F1). For different versions of the dataset, we use different matching criteria: Partial Match for NYT* and WebNLG* while Exact Match for NYT and WebNLG. Specifically, a Partial Match means an extracted triplet is considered to be correct if the relation is correct and the last token of subject and object are both correct, while an Exact Match refers to this triplet is regarded to be correct only if the whole span of two entities and their relation are all exactly matched with the ground truth.

4.2 Implementation Details

In our experiments, we employ Adam to train the proposed model, and we set the learning rate to 1e−5. The dimension d_h of token representation is set to 768. For the representations of the token with respect to subject and object, we set their dimension d_e to 3*768. In addition, different datasets have different batch size: 16 on NYT* and NYT, 10 on WebNLG* and WebNLG. We train the model with one RTX 3090 Ti GPU. In the experiment, all hyperparameters are determined on the development set, while the trained weight parameters are randomly initialized by the normal distribution. Following previous works [10, 14, 21], our model is run 5 times for each dataset and we take the averaged results as the final reported results.

4.3 Baselines

To prove the effectiveness of our model, our 2DEPT model is compared with the strong state-of-the-art baselines. For NYT* and WebNLG*, we choose CopyRE [20], GraphRel [17], CasRel [14], TPLinker [21], CasDE [22], RIFRE [23], PRGC [10], R-BPtrNet [24], BiRTE [11], DirectRel [15] as baselines. For NYT and WebNLG, we choose RSAN [13], TPLinker [21], CasDE [22], PRGC [10], BiRTE [11], DirectRel [15] as baselines. Following DirectRel [15], the reported results for all baselines are copied from the original literature.

Table 3. Comparison (%) of the proposed 2DEPT with other state-of-the-art baselines on NYT* and WebNLG*. Bold marks the highest score.

Model	NYT*			WebNLG*		
	Prec.	Rec.	F1	Prec.	Rec.	F1
CopyRE [20]	61.0	56.6	58.7	37.7	36.4	37.1
GraphRel [17]	63.9	60.0	61.9	44.7	41.1	42.9
CasRel [14]	89.7	89.5	89.6	93.4	90.1	91.8
TPLinker [21]	91.3	92.5	91.9	91.8	92.0	91.9
CasDE [22]	90.2	92.5	90.5	90.3	91.5	90.9
RIFRE [23]	93.6	90.5	92.0	93.3	92.0	92.6
PRGC [10]	93.3	91.9	92.6	94.0	92.1	93.0
R-BPtrNet [24]	92.7	92.5	92.6	93.7	92.8	93.3
BiRTE [11]	92.2	**93.8**	93.0	93.2	94.0	93.6
DirectRel [15]	93.7	92.8	93.2	94.1	**94.1**	94.1
ours	**94.2**	92.7	**93.4**	**94.4**	93.8	**94.1**

Table 4. Comparison (%) of the proposed 2DEPT with other state-of-the-art baselines on NYT and WebNLG. Bold marks the highest score.

Model	NYT			WebNLG		
	Prec.	Rec.	F1	Prec.	Rec.	F1
RSAN [13]	85.7	83.6	84.6	80.5	83.8	82.1
TPLinker [21]	91.4	92.6	92.0	88.9	84.5	86.7
CasDE [22]	89.9	91.4	90.6	88.0	88.9	88.4
PRGC [10]	93.5	91.9	92.7	89.9	87.2	88.5
BiRTE [11]	91.9	**93.7**	92.8	89.0	**89.5**	89.3
DirectRel [15]	**93.6**	92.2	92.9	91.0	89.0	89.0
ours	93.5	92.3	**92.9**	**91.9**	88.5	**90.2**

4.4 Overall Results

The overall results of the proposed 2DEPT compared to other baselines on NYT* and WebNLG* are shown in Table 3, from which we can observe that 2DEPT outperforms almost all the baselines and achieves the state-of-the-art performance in terms of Prec. and F1-score.

Table 4 shows the comparison of 2DEPT with other state-of-the-art baselines on NYT and WebNLG. In terms of F1-score, our 2DEPT reaches state of the art. In terms of Prec., our model preforms better than any other baseline on WebNLG, and achieves sub-optimal result on NYT.

Currently, BiRTE and DirectRel have the state-of-the art performance while our model achieves a comparable performance on all datasets, which demonstrates the effectiveness of our model for the joint entity and relationship extraction task. In terms of Prec., our 2DEPT outperforms BiRTE by 2.0, 1.2, 1.6, and 2.9 absolute gains on NYT*, WebNLG*, NYT, and WebNLG respectively. It outperforms DirectRel by 0.5 and 0.9 absolute gains on NYT* and WebNLG respectively while having comparable values on NYT and WebNLG*. Such results also demonstrate that our 2DEPT model can effectively address the error propagation problem and capture the interactivity between subject and object very well.

4.5 Detailed Results on Complex Scenarios

To further explore the capability of our 2DEPT in handling complex scenarios, we split the test set of NYT* and WebNLG* by overlapping patterns and triple numbers. Table 5 and Table 6 present the detailed extraction results of various complex scenarios on NYT* and WebNLG* respectively.

Table 5. F1-score (%) of various complex scenarios on NYT*. Bold marks the highest score.

Model	Normal	SEO	EPO	SOO	N = 1	N = 2	N = 3	N = 4	N > = 5
CasRel [14]	87.3	91.4	92.0	77.0	88.2	90.3	91.4	94.2	83.7
TPLinker [21]	90.1	93.4	94.0	90.1	90.0	92.8	93.1	96.1	90.0
PRGC [10]	91.0	94.0	94.5	81.8	91.1	93.0	93.5	95.5	93.0
DirectRel [15]	91.7	94.6	94.8	90.0	91.7	94.1	93.5	96.3	92.7
ours	**91.7**	**94.8**	**94.8**	**91.2**	**91.7**	**94.3**	**94.4**	**96.3**	**93.4**

Table 6. F1-score (%) of various complex scenarios on WebNLG*. Bold marks the highest score.

Model	Normal	SEO	EPO	SOO	N = 1	N = 2	N = 3	N = 4	N > = 5
CasRel [14]	89.4	92.2	94.7	90.4	89.3	90.8	94.2	92.4	90.9
TPLinker [2]	87.9	92.5	95.3	90.4	88.0	90.1	94.6	93.3	91.6
PRGC [10]	90.4	93.6	95.9	94.6	89.9	91.6	95.0	94.8	92.8
DirectRel [15]	**92.0**	94.5	**97.1**	94.6	**91.6**	92.2	96.0	95.0	94.9
ours	90.2	**94.8**	94.1	**95.5**	90.4	**92.2**	**96.0**	**96.4**	**95.0**

The experimental results in Table 5 show that our 2DEPT obtains the highest F1-score for all complex scenarios on NYT* dataset. From Table 6, we can see that our model achieves the state-of-the-art performance in the case of SEO and SOO on WebNLG* dataset and has highest F1-score for almost all triplet numbers.

Overall, the above experimental results adequately prove that our proposed 2DEPT is more consistent and robust than baselines when dealing with complex scenarios.

Table 7. The experimental results of entity pair recognition on NYT* and WebNLG*. Bold marks the highest score. The results of PRGC and DirectRel are copied from [15].

Model	NYT*			WebNLG*		
	Prec.	Rec.	F1	Prec.	Rec.	F1
PRGC	94.0	92.3	93.1	96.0	93.4	94.7
DirectRel	94.1	93.2	93.7	95.8	**95.9**	95.8
ours	**94.2**	**93.4**	**93.8**	**96.2**	95.8	**96.0**

Table 8. The experimental results of relation identification on NYT* and WebNLG*. Bold marks the highest score. The results of PRGC and DirectRel are copied from [15].

Model	NYT*			WebNLG*		
	Prec.	Rec.	F1	Prec.	Rec.	F1
PRGC	95.3	96.3	95.8	92.8	96.2	94.5
DirectRel	97.3	**96.4**	**96.9**	96.8	**96.7**	**96.7**
ours	**97.4**	94.7	96.1	**97.4**	94.7	96.1

4.6 Results for Different Subtasks

Following DirectRel [15], we further explore the performance of 2DEPT for entity pair recognition and relation identification on NYT* and WebNLG*, and the results are shown in Table 7 and Table 8 respectively.

From Table 7, we can observe that almost all experimental results on NYT* and WebNLG* datasets achieve the best performance for the subtask of entity pair recognition, which demonstrates the effectiveness and strength of our model for this subtask and further proves that our 2DEPT does capture the interaction between subject and object very well.

From Table 8, it can be observed that our 2DEPT only outperforms other baselines in terms of Prec. on two datasets for the subtask of relationship identification, one possible reason for which is the interference of redundant relations.

5 Conclusion

In this paper, we propose a 2D entity pair tagging scheme based on biaffine attention model named 2DEPT which can effectively address the error propagation problem and poor interaction between subject and object. We further conduct the experiments on two widely used datasets and the results perform better than the state-of-the-art baselines overall and deliver consistent performance gains on complex scenarios of various overlapping patterns and multiple triples.

It is worth noting that our model does not reach state of the art on Rec. In the future, we will improve our work in the following directions:

1) Our model annotates the entity pairs in a sentence for all relations in the relation set, which produces redundant information. Thus, we are going to reduce the redundant relation information to further improve the performance of the model.
2) The proposed model use biaffine attention model to calculate the scoring vector of token pair, a process that ignores the relation information. We will try to improve the performance of the model by incorporating relation feature information.

Acknowledgements. This work is supported by the Natural Science Foundation of Jilin Province, China (20210101172JC). We thank all anonymous reviewers for their constructive comments.

References

1. Mintz, M., Bills, S., Snow, R., Jurafsky, D.: Distant supervision for relation extraction without labeled data. In: Proceedings of the Joint Conference of the 47th Annual Meeting of the ACL and the 4th International Joint Conference on Natural Language Processing of the AFNLP, pp. 1003–1011 (2009)
2. Chan, Y.S., Roth, D.: Exploiting syntactico-semantic structures for relation extraction. In: Proceedings of the 49th Annual Meeting of the Association for Computational Linguistics: Human Language Technologies, pp. 551– 560 (2011)
3. Tjong Kim Sang, E.F., De Meulder, F.: Introduction to the CoNLL-2003 shared task: Language-independent named entity recognition. In: Proceedings of the Seventh Conference on Natural Language Learning at HLT-NAACL, pp. 142–147 (2003)
4. Ratinov, L., Roth, D.: Design challenges and misconceptions in named entity recognition. In: Proceedings of the Thirteenth Conference on Computational Natural Language Learning, pp. 147– 155 (2009)
5. Zelenko, D., Aone, C., Richardella, A.: Kernel methods for relation extraction. In: Proceedings of the Conference on Empirical Methods in Natural Language Processing, pp. 71–78 (2002)
6. Razvan, C., Bunescu, R., Mooney, R.: A shortest path dependency kernel for relation extraction. In: Proceedings of the Human Language Technology Conference and Conference on Empirical Methods in Natural Language Processing, pp. 724–731 (2005)
7. Pawar, S., Palshikar, G.K., Bhattacharyya, P.: Relation extraction: a survey. CoRR, abs/1712.05191 (2017)
8. Wang, Z., Wen, R., Chen, X., Huang, S.L., Zhang, N., Zheng, Y.: Finding influential instances for distantly supervised relation extraction. CoRR, abs/2009.09841 (2009)
9. Zheng, S., Wang,F., Bao, H., Hao, Y., Zhou, P., Xu, B.: Joint extraction of entities and relations based on a novel tagging scheme. In: Proceedings of the 55th Annual Meeting of the Association for Computational Linguistics, pp. 227–1236 (2017)
10. Zheng, H., et al.: PRGC: potential relation and global correspondence based joint relational triple extraction. In: Proceedings of the 59th Annual Meeting of the Association for Computational Linguistics, pp. 6225–6235 (2021)
11. Ren, F., Zhang, L., Zhao, X., Yin, S., Liu, S., Li, B.: A simple but effective bidirectional extraction framework for relational triple extraction. In: The 15th ACM Interntional Conference on Web Search and Data Mining (2022)
12. Sun, C., et al.: Joint type inference on entities and relations via graph convolutional networks. In: Proceedings of the 57th Conference of the Association for Computational Linguistics, pp. 1361–1370 (2009)
13. Yuan, Y., Zhou, X., Pan, S., Zhu, Q., Song, Z., Guo, L.: A relation-specific attention network for joint entity and relation extraction. In: Proceedings of the Twenty-Ninth International Joint Conference on Artificial Intelligence, pp. 4054– 4060 (2020)
14. Wei, Z., Su, J., Wang, Y., Tian, Y., Chang, Y.: A novel cascade binary tagging framework for relational triple extraction. In: Proceedings of the 58th Annual Meeting of the Association for Computational Linguistics, pp. 1476–1488 (2020)
15. Shang, Y.-M., Huang, H., Sun, X., Wei, W., Mao, X.-L.: Relational triple extraction: one step is enough. In: Proceedings of the Thirty-First International Joint Conference on Artificial Intelligence (IJCAI-22) (2022)
16. Dozat, T., Manning, C.D.: Deep biaffine attention for neural dependency parsing. arXiv preprint arXiv:1611.01734 (2016)
17. Fu, T-J., Li, P-H., Ma, W.H.: GraphRel: modeling text as relational graphs for joint entity and relation extraction. In: Proceedings of the 57th Annual Meeting of the Association for Computational Linguistics, pp. 1409–1418(2019)

18. Yu, B., et al.: Joint extraction of entities and relations based on a novel decomposition strategy. In: The 24th European Conference on Artificial Intelligence - ECAI 2020 (2019)
19. Bekoulis, G., Deleu, J., Demeester, T., Develder, C.: Joint entity recognition and relation extraction as a multi-head selection problem. Expert Syst. Appl. **114**, 34–45 (2018)
20. Zeng, X., Zeng, D., He, S., Liu, K., Zhao, J.: Extracting relational facts by an end-to-end neural model with copy mechanism. In: Proceedings of the 56th Annual Meeting of the Association for Computational Linguistics, 2018, pp. 506–514 (2018)
21. Wang, Y., Yu, B., Zhang, Y., Liu, T., Zhu, H., Sun, L.: TPLinker: single-stage joint extraction of entities and relations through token pair linking. In: Proceedings of the 28th International Conference on Computational Linguistics, pp. 1572–1582 (2020)
22. Ma, L., Ren, H., Zhang, X.: Effective cascade dual-decoder model for joint entity and relation extraction. CoRR, abs/2106.14163 (2021)
23. Zhao, K., Xu, H., Cheng, Y., Li. X., Gao, K.: Representation iterative fusion based on heterogeneous graph neural network for joint entity and relation extraction. Knowl.-Based Syst. **219**, 106888 (2021)
24. Chen, Y., Zhang, Y., Hu, C., Huang. Y.: Jointly extracting explicit and implicit relational triples with reasoning pattern enhanced binary pointer network. In: Proceedings of the 2021 Conference of the North American Chapter of the Association for Computational Linguistics, pp. 5694–5703(2021)
25. Devlin, J., Chang, M.-W., Lee, K., Toutanova, K.: BERT: pre-training of deep bidirectional transformers for language understanding. In: Proceedings of the 2019 Conference of the North American Chapter of the Association for Computational Linguistics, pp. 4171–4186 (2019)
26. Gardent, C., Shimorina, A., Narayan, S., Perez-Beltrachini, L.: Creating training corpora for NLG micro-planners. In:Proceedings of the 55th Annual Meeting of the Association for Computational Linguistics, pp. 179–188 (2017)
27. Ye, H., et al.: Contrastive triple extraction with generative transformer. In: The Thirty-Fifth AAAI Conference on Artificial Intelligence, pp. 14257–14265 (2021)
28. Riedel, S., Yao, L., McCallum, A.: Modeling relations and their mentions without labeled text. ML and KDD (2010)

MVARN: Multi-view Attention Relation Network for Figure Question Answering

Yingdong Wang ⓘ, Qingfeng Wu$^{(\boxtimes)}$ ⓘ, Weiqiang Lin, Linjian Ma, and Ying Li

Xiamen University, Xiamen, Fujian, China
{qfwu,wqlin,malinjian}@xmu.edu.cn

Abstract. **Figure Question Answering** (FQA) is an emerging multimodal task that shares similarities with Visual Question Answering (VQA). FQA aims to solve the problem of answering questions related to scientifically designed charts. In this study, we propose a novel model, called the Multi-view Attention Relation Network (MVARN), which utilizes key picture characteristics and multi-view relational reasoning to address this challenge. To enhance the expression ability of image output features, we introduce a **Contextual Transformer** (CoT) block that implements relational reasoning based on both pixel and channel views. Our experimental evaluation on the Figure QA and DVQA datasets demonstrates that the MVARN model outperforms other state-of-the-art techniques. Our approach yields fair outcomes across different classes of questions, which confirms its effectiveness and robustness.

Keywords: attention mechanism · multi-modal recognition · figure question answering · relation network · deep learning

1 Introduction

FQA represents an independent task from Visual Question Answering (VQA) [1], which is typically regarded as a classification problem for natural images. Unlike VQA, FQA is designed to make inferences and predictions for a given chart and a related question to derive the answer. A minor modification to the image in FQA may result in a complete change in the information conveyed by the chart, leading to disparate outcomes.

Several baseline models are also published for FQA. They are Text-only baseline [2], CNN + LSTM[13], CNN + LSTM on VGG-16 features [4], and Relation Network (RN) [5], of which RN has the best effect. Text-only baseline is a text-only model. CNN + LSTM uses the MLP classifier to connect the received LSTM to generate the problem code and the learned visual representation of the CNN with five convolutional layers. And CNN + LSTM on VGG-16 features extracts features from the fifth-layer pool of the ImageNet pre-trained VGG-16 network [4]. RN is currently the best baseline method, a simple and powerful neural module for relational reasoning. RN is proven to have the most advanced performance on a challenging data set called CLEVR [7]. The SANDY model proposed by Kushal et al. [6] adopts the attention mechanism of multiple iterations to capture the key areas of the image, which is matched with the proposed structure. Shen et al. [8] proposed a method for leveraging multi-modal data, including both text and images, to improve FQA performance on the DVQA dataset. Their approach, called CMM-Net, uses a cross-modal memory network to store and retrieve relevant information from both modalities, enabling effective reasoning about the relationship between textual and visual input. Their method achieved significant improvements over prior methods on the DVQA dataset.

It is well known that attention plays an important role in human perception [11]. The attention mechanism captures the key information that needs attention through certain calculation methods while ignoring other information. With the development of the computer field, attention mechanism has achieved good results in various fields, such as document classification and image classification. Transformer framework leads to the application of various attention mechanisms, which can be widely used in various fields. Hence, we introduce the attention mechanism into the original RN network to improve the accuracy of our model.

To address these challenges, recent research has focused on advancing the state of-the-art in FQA through diverse approaches. Such approaches include object-centric reasoning, multi-task learning, and the integration of multi-modal data. These stratgies have exhibited considerable promise in improving FQA performance and overcoming challenges related to understanding chart characteristics.

In this paper, we present a novel method named Multi-view attention relation network (MVARN) to improve the performance of the FQA task. We design a novel image encoder by CoT block to enrich the content of image features. Meanwhile, we also propose a multi-view relation module, which performs relational reasoning based on pixel and channel views and uses an attention mechanism for aggregation. The contribution of this paper can be summarized:

1. To obtain richer image representation features, we use the CoT block to design a new image encoder. To the best of our knowledge, it is the first time that the CoT block has been applied to FQA.
2. We propose a multi-view relation module to infer the relation reasoning, which pairs the objects from multiple views to make the relation features more concise.
3. We propose a wise aggregation submodule to give each relation feature a different weight to improve the reasoning accuracy.

2 Proposed Method

In this section, the framework of the proposed method will be introduced, as shown in image representation learning module, question representation learning module, andmulti-view relation module (Fig. 1).

2.1 Image Representation Learning

In the FQA tasks, the representative capacity of the feature map extracted from the image greatly affects the performance of the final model. Therefore, we apply the CoT block in the image representation learning module. The image representation learning module can be divided into five stages. We denote the output feature map from five stages as X_1,

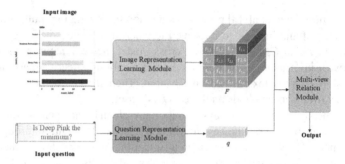

Fig. 1. The overall framework of MVARN.

$X_2, ..., X_5$. The first three stages uses the convolutional layers with 64 kernels of size 3×3, stride 2. The size of the feature map $X_i \in R^{\frac{W}{2} \times \frac{H}{2} \times C}$ is half of $X_{i-1} \in R^{W \times H \times C}$. The formula is as follows:

$$X_i = Conv(X_{i-1}), X_0 = I, i \in \{1, 2, 3\} \tag{1}$$

where X_0 is the original image I and $Conv$ represents the convolution layer.

Then, CoT block is used in the last two stages. Figure 2 depicts the detailed structures of the CoT block. Specifically, given the input feature map $X \in R^{W \times H \times C}$, the keys, queries, and values are denoted as $K = X$, $Q = X$, and $V = XW_v$, respectively. CoT block first employs 3×3 group convolution over all the neighbor keys within 3×3 grid spatially for contextualizing each key representation!. Then, K^1 is considered as the static context representation of X. After that, conditioned on the concatenation of K^1 and Q, the attention matrix is achieved through two convolution layers with 1×1 kernel (W_θ with ReLU activation function and W_δ without activation function):

$$A = \left[K^1, Q\right] W_\theta W_\delta \tag{2}$$

Next, depending on A, the attended feature map K^2 is calculated by aggregating all values V as in typical self-attention:

$$K^2 = V * A \tag{3}$$

K^2 is the dynamic contextual representation of inputs. The final output is measured as the fusion of K^1 and K^2 through attention mechanism. Then the last two stages can be formulated as:

$$X_i = CoTBlock(X_{i-1}), i \in \{4, 5\} \tag{4}$$

where $CoTBlock$ denotes as CoT block. Each stage is followed by a batch normalization layer. At last, we obtain the final feature map $F = X_5$.

2.2 Question Representation Learning

Like the RN model, we first combine all the existing words into a dictionary. Then each question can be expressed as $Q = [x_1, \ldots, x_T]$, where x_t Represents the vector after

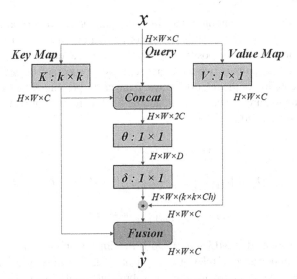

Fig. 2. The detailed structures of the CoT block

the one-hot encoding in the dictionary, and T is the length of the question. We apply the simple unidirectional LSTM with 512 hidden units to obtain the hidden state:

$$h_t = LSTM(x_t), 1 \le t \le T \tag{5}$$

We regard the hidden state in the last step as the question representation, i.e., $q = h_T \in R^{512}$.

2.3 Multi-view Relation Module

The original relational network takes the features of each pixel of the feature map F as a set of n "objects" and computes a representation of relations between objects. However, each channel of the feature map can be considered as the capture of a certain feature of the image. So we propose a multi-view relation module, that is, relationship pairing based on pixel and channel views.

In the pixel-based view, the object set can be denoted as $F_1 = \{f_{i,j} | 1 \le i, j \le n\} \in R^{(H*w) \times C}$, where $f_{i,j} \in R^C$ denotes the ith row and jth column of the feature map F, and $n = H = W = 8, C = 64$. Then the set of all object pairs is represented as:

$$P = \{p_{(i,j),(u,v)} | 1 \le i, j, u, v \le n\} \tag{6}$$

where $p_{(i,j),(u,v)}$ is the concatenation of the corresponding object vectors, their location information and the question vector q, i.e., $p_{(i,j),(u,v)} = [f_{i,j}, i, j, f_{u,v}, u, v, q]$. Each object is paired with all objects including itself, i.e., $p_{(1,1),(1,1)}, p_{(1,1),(1,2)}, \cdots, p_{(n,n),(n,n)}$.

In the channel-based view, the object set can be denoted as $F_2 = \{f_k | 1 \le k \le C\} \in R^{C \times (H*w)}$, where $f_k \in R^{h*w}$ denotes the features of kth channel of the feature map F after flattening. Then the set of all object pairs is represented as:

$$L = \{l_{(k),(w)} | 1 \le k, w \le C\} \tag{7}$$

where $l_{(k),(w)}$ is the concatenation of the corresponding object vectors and the question vector q, i.e., $l_{(k),(w)} = [f_k, f_w, q]$. It is worth noting that because there is no position in the features of the channel, the position information is not added in this view.

Then, every object pairs in two views are separately processed by MLPs to produce a feature representation of the relation between the corresponding objects, respectively, and combines the feature of two views to get the final features O of relation pairs. This process can be formulated as:

$$O_1 = \{o^1_{(i,j),(u,v)} = g_\theta\big(p_{(i,j),(u,v)}\big) | 1 \le i, j, u, v \le n\} \tag{8}$$

$$O_2 = \{o^2_{(k),(w)} = g_\theta\big(l_{(k),(w)}\big) | 1 \le k, w \le C\} \tag{9}$$

$$O = [O_1, O_2] \in R^{(n^4+C^2) \times d} \tag{10}$$

where g_θ is implemented as MLPs, $d = 256$ is the dimension of MLP.

Because the importance of relationship reasoning is different for each relation pair feature in O, we propose a wise aggregation submodule to give each feature a different weight to improve the reasoning accuracy.

In the wise aggregation submodule, firstly, max pooling and average pooling are used to compress the features set O, and get two descriptionectors F^c_{max} and $F^c_{avg} \in R^{(n^4+C^2) \times 1}$:

$$F^c_{max} = MaxPool(O) \tag{11}$$

$$F^c_{avg} = AvgPool(O) \tag{12}$$

Then, shared MLP is used to calculate the attention map $A \in R^{(n^4+C^2) \times 1}$, and O is multiplied by M_a to get the attention-based object pair features O_a. This process can be formulated as:

$$A = \sigma\Big(W_1\big(W_0(F^c_{max})\big) + W_1\big(W_0(F^c_{avg})\big)\Big) \tag{13}$$

$$O_a = O * A \tag{14}$$

where σ is the sigmoid function, and W_0 and W_1 is the weight matrixes of two MLPs. Next, we average O_a to get the middle features $F^M \in R^d$.

At last, two MLP layers are used to process the middle features F^M and get the final output, each with 256 ReLU units and using dropout with a rate of 25%.

3 Experiments

3.1 Dataset Description

In this paper, we perform experiments on the FigureQA [2] and DVQA [3] datasets. The FigureQA dataset is a synthetic corpus, which contains more than one million question-answer pairs of more than 100,000 images for visual reasoning. It contains 5 forms of charts: line plots, dot-line plots, vertical and horizontal bar graphs, and pie charts. In addition, the questions on the FigureQA data set consist of 15 question types, which include inference questions about the structure and details of various types of statistical graphs. The drawing elements of FigureQA are color-coded, with 100 unique colors. These colors are divided into two color schemes: scheme 1 and scheme 2. The dataset is divided into five separate packages, including one training set, two validation sets, and two testing sets.

The DVQA dataset is a large open source statistical graph question and answer data set proposed by Kushal Kafle and others in cooperation with the Adobe Research Laboratory. It contains a training set and two test sets (Test-Familiar and Test-Novel). The training set consists of 200,000 images and 2325316 questions, the Test-Familiar test set consists of 50,000 images and 580557 questions, and the Test-Novel test set consists of 50,000 images and 581321 questions. There are three types of questions in the DVQA data set: the first type is Structure Understanding, which is about the understanding of the overall structure of an image, the second type is Data Retrieval, and the third is reasoning. Reasoning is a type of reasoning problem about the relationship between elements in the image.

3.2 Experimental Setting

For FigureQA dataset, we verify the effectiveness of our model on validation1 and validation2 data because test sets are non-publicly available. For DVQA, we use two versions to verify our model: the method without dynamic dictionary (No OCR) and the method with Oracle Version (Oracle). The batch size is 80. We trained our model for 100 epochs. Our model is trained using the *Adam* optimizer with a learning rate of $2.5e-4$. And we use the binary cross-entropy loss as the loss function. The accuracy is adopted as the evaluation metric. We select the model with the best performance on the validation set.

3.3 Experimental Results and Analysis

In this section, we show the comparison of our model with other methods both on FigureQA and DVQA datasets. Table 1 and Table 2 show our comparison results with other methods on the FigureQA dataset. It notes that FigureNet carries out the experiments only on three types of charts, i.e., vBar, hBar, and Pie, in Validation1 data of FigureQA dataset. Then Table 3 shows the performance of our model compared with other methods on two versions of DVQA dataset, such as SANDY (No OCR + Oracle) [2], ARN (No OCR + Oracle) [8], and LEAF-Net (Oracle) [9].

On the FigureQA dataset, our proposed MVARN significantly outperforms the baseline method RN on each type of chart both on two validation sets, which demonstrates the effectiveness of our model. Specifically, compared with RN, our method obtains an accuracy promotion of approximately 2.13%, 10.80%, 7.29%, 15.93%, and 14.86% in the five types of charts of validation1 data and 6.84%, 13.17%, 12.57%, 12.55%, and 12.12% in the five types of charts of validation2 data, respectively. Overall, the accuracy of our model is improved by 10.77% on validation1 data and 11.70% on validation2

Table 1. Validation 1 -Same Colors

Method	vBar	hBar	Pie	Line	Dot-line	Overall
IMG + QUES [3]	61.98	62.44	59.63	57.07	57.35	59.41
RN [4],	85.71	80.60	82.56	69.53	68.51	76.39
FigureNet [7]	87.36	81.57	83.13	-	-	-
ARN [8]	**92.49**	91.20	84.25	81.31	81.03	85.48
MVARN (Ours)	87.84	**91.40**	**89.85**	**85.16**	**83.37**	**87.16**

Table 2. Validation 2 -Alternated Colors

Method	vBar	hBar	Pie	Line	Dot-line
IMG + QUES [3]	58.60	58.05	55.97	56.37	56.97
RN [4]	77.35	77.00	74.16	67.90	69.40
ARN [8]	**90.46**	89.56	80.29	77.60	78.28
MVARN (Ours)	84.19	**90.17**	**86.73**	**80.45**	**81.52**
LEF-Net [9]					81.15

data compared with the RN model. Then we compare our model with other state-of-the-art methods. FigureNet achieves an average accuracy of approximately 83.9% on three types of charts of validation1 data while our model reaches 89.68%. And MVARN obtains a promotion of about 3.09% on validation2 data compared with LEAF-Net. It is found that MVARN achieves about 1.68% and 1.29% higher accuracy compared with ARN on the validation1 and validation2 data respectively. In addition, we also found that the accuracy of our model in the bar and pie charts is significantly higher than that in the line charts. After analysis, this may be because line charts often contain more complex information and the questions are quite more difficult to answer, so the accuracy of line charts is relatively low.

On the DVQA dataset, first compare the performance of No OCR version, it can find that our method achieves the best results, which achieves higher accuracy of 14.11% and 13.90% than the IMG + QUES baseline and 1.62% and 1.40% higher than ARN on the two test sets, respectively. In the Oracle version, we also achieve the best performance compared with these three methods on both two test sets. Our model achieves higher accuracy of 1.42% and 1.53% than ARN on two test sets.

Table 3. Results Comparisons with Other Methods on DVQA Dataset

	Test-Familiar	Test-Novel
IMG + QUES	32.01	32.01
SANDY (No OCR)	36.02	36.14
ARN (No OCR)	44.50	44.51
MVARN (ours)	**46.12**	**45.91**
SANDY (Oracle)	56.48	56.62
LEAF-Net (Oracle)	72.72	72.89
ARN (Oracle)	79.43	79.58
MVARN (Oracle)	**80.85**	**81.11**

4 Conclusion

In this paper, we propose a multi-view attention relation network (MVARN) to improve the performance of FQA tasks. We device a new image encoder to extract more effective image features and a multi-view relation module to infer the relation reasoning, which pairs the objects from multiple views to make the relation features more concise. In experiments, MVARN is compared with other state-of-the-art methods and experimental results confirm that our algorithm can achieve good performance on both validation sets. In the future, we intend to improve the performance of these low-accuracy figure types and question types by capturing more useful inter-relation features between mages and questions.

Acknowledgments. This work was supported by the Key Project of National Key R&D Project (No. 2017YFC1703303); Industry University-Research Cooperation Project of Fujian Science and Technology Planning (No: 2022H6012); Industry University-Research Cooperation Project of Ningde City and Xiamen University (No. 2020C001); Natural Science Foundation of Fujian Province of China (No. 2021J011169, No. 2020J01435).

References

1. Zhou, B., Tian, Y., Sukhbaatar, S., Szlam, A., Fergus, R.: VQA: visual question answering. In: ICCV, pp. 2425–2433 (2015)
2. Kafle, K., Price, B., Cohen, S., Kanan, C.: Dvqa: Understanding data visualizations via question answering. In: CVPR, pp. 5648–5656 (2018)
3. Kahou, S.E., et al.: Figureqa: an annotated figure dataset for visual reasoning. arXiv preprint arXiv:1710.07300 (2017)
4. Simonyan, K., Zisserman, A.: Very deep convolutional networks for large-scale image recognition. In: ICLR (2015)
5. Johnson, J., Hariharan, B., van der Maaten, L., Fei-Fei, L.: CLEVR: A diagnostic dataset for compositional language and elementary visual reasoning. In: CVPR, pp. 1988–1997 (2017)

6. Kafle, K., Kanan, C.; Answer-type prediction for visual question answering. In: CVPR, pp. 4976–4984 (2016)
7. Reedy, R., Ramesh, R., Deshpande, A., and Khapra M.M.: FigureNet: a deep learning model for question answering on scientific plots. In: 2019 International Joint Conference on Neural Networks (IJCNN), pp. 1–8 (2019)
8. Zhu, J., Wu. G., Xue, T., Wu, Q.F.: An affinity-driven relation network for figure question answering. In: 2020 IEEE International Conference on Multimedia and Expo (ICME), pp. 1–6 (2020)
9. Chaudhry, R., Shekhar, S., Gupta, U., Maneriker, P, Bansal, P., Joshi, A.: LEAF-QA: locate, encode and attend for figure question answering. In: 2020 IEEE Winter Conference on Applications of Computer Vision (WACV), pp. 3501–3510 (2020)
10. Itti, L., Koch, C., Niebur, E.: A model of saliency-based visual attention for rapid scene analysis. IEEE Trans. Pattern Anal. Mach. Intell. (TPAMI), **20**, 1254 – 1259 (1998)
11. Rensink, R.A.: The dynamic representation of scenes. Visual Cog. **7** (2000)

MAGNN-GC: Multi-head Attentive Graph Neural Networks with Global Context for Session-Based Recommendation

Yingpei Chen⬛, Yan Tang$^{(\boxtimes)}$⬛, Peihao Ding⬛, and Xiaobing Li⬛

School of Computer and Information Science, Southwest University, Chongqing, China
{chenyingpei1,dph365475889,1597438586}@email.swu.edu.cn, ytang@swu.edu.cn

Abstract. Session-based recommendation aims to predict the final preference of anonymous users based on their current session and global context. However, integrating high-dimensional information such as the item features of the current session and global context can lead to insufficient information fusion and imbalanced positive and negative samples during model training. To address these issues, we propose Multi-Head Attentive Graph Neural Networks with Global Context for Session-based Recommendation (MAGNN-GC). We construct global and local session graphs based on all historical session sequences to fully represent the complex transition relationships between items in the session. We use graph convolutional networks to capture the item features in the global context and graph attention networks to capture the item features of the current session. We also integrate the position information of session items with the learned global-level and local-level item embeddings using the multi-head attention mechanism. Additionally, we use the focal loss as a loss function to adjust sample weights and address the problem of imbalanced positive and negative samples during model training. Our experiments on three real-world datasets consistently show the superior performance of MAGNN-GC over state-of-the-art methods.

Keywords: Recommender systems · Session-based recommendation · Graph neural networks · Information fusion · Multi-head attention mechanism

1 Introduction

Recommender systems are an integral part of online platforms that provide personalized suggestions to users based on their historical interactions with items. However, in scenarios where user identification is anonymous, such historical interactions are unavailable, making it challenging to provide relevant recommendations. To address this challenge, session-based recommendation (SBR) has emerged as a crucial task that predicts the user's interested items based on their limited and anonymous behavior during the current session. SBR methods use implicit user feedback to predict items and have shown better performance

Z. Jin et al. (Eds.): KSEM 2023, LNAI 14119, pp. 39–53, 2023.
https://doi.org/10.1007/978-3-031-40289-0_4

than conventional recommendation methods, especially when there is insufficient user-item interaction data [4]. As a result, SBR has gained extensive attention from researchers.

The rise of deep learning has facilitated the successful application of recurrent neural networks (RNN) and graph neural networks (GNN) in SBR. While RNN-based methods [4,5,8] view the session recommendation task as a natural language processing task, which improves interpretability, they only consider unidirectional transitions between adjacent items and ignore the influence of other items on the recommendation results. In contrast, GNN-based methods [18–20] construct the session graph from historical session sequences and use GNN for feature extraction and information aggregation on the session graph. Compared to RNN-based methods, GNN-based methods can better handle the complex transitions of user historical interaction data, thereby improving recommendation accuracy. Currently, GNN-based methods have become one of the research hotspots in SBR.

Despite their effectiveness, GNN-based methods have limitations that need to be addressed, including insufficient information fusion when integrating high-dimensional information and imbalanced positive and negative samples during model training.

To address the limitations, we propose a novel approach called Multi-Head Attentive Graph Neural Networks with Global Context for Session-based Recommendation (MAGNN-GC). Our approach constructs global and local graphs based on all training sequences and uses graph convolutional networks (GCNs) [7] with a session-aware attention mechanism to learn global-level item embeddings in all sessions. It also employs a graph attention networks (GATs) [16] module to learn local-level item embeddings in the current session. A multi-head attention mechanism [15] is used to enhance the fused information after learning global-level and local-level item embeddings, resulting in the final representation of a session sequence. Additionally, we apply focal loss [9] to balance positive and negative samples during model training.

The main contributions of our work are summarized as follows:

- We propose a novel multi-head attention mechanism to fuse the high-dimensional feature information, which helps learn the final representation of a session sequence.
- We apply the focal loss to address imbalanced positive and negative samples during model training.
- We conduct extensive experiments on three real-world datasets, demonstrating the superior performance of MAGNN-GC over state-of-the-art methods.

2 Related Work

This section reviews the related work on session-based recommendation (SBR), including RNN-based methods, MLP-based methods, and GNN-based methods.

2.1 RNN-Based or MLP-Based Methods

Hidasi et al. [4] proposed a recurrent neural network (RNN) approach for SBR for the first time. In the next year, they proposed a parallel RNN approach [5] that considers the basic information of clicked items and uses other features to improve the recommendation results. Building on this work, Tan et al. [14] enhanced the model's performance by incorporating data augmentation, pre-training, and temporal shifts in user behavior. Li et al. proposed NARM [8], a transformer-based model commonly used in natural language processing. It has an encoder-decoder neural network structure and uses an RNN approach with an attention mechanism to capture users' sequential behavioral features. Liu et al. proposed STAMP [10], which uses multilayer perceptron (MLP) networks and attention mechanisms to capture users' global and current preferences.

2.2 GNN-Based Methods

Recently, graph neural networks (GNN) have shown promise for SBR models. Most GNN-based methods construct session sequences as session graphs and use GNNs to aggregate information on adjacent nodes.

One such method is SR-GNN [18], which combines recurrent neural networks (RNN), gated graph neural networks, and an attention network. It converts user-item sequences into graph-structured data and captures the underlying transitions of the items in sessions. Similarly, Xu et al. proposed GC-SAN [19], which employs GNN and self-attention mechanisms to learn long-term dependencies between items in session sequences. Following SR-GNN, TAGNN [20] enhances the attentive module by considering the relevance of historical behaviors given a specific target item. Qiu et al. introduced FGNN [11], which uses the multi-weight graph attention layer to compute the information flow between items in the session, learn the item representation, and then aggregate it through the feature extractor to extract features. Wang et al. proposed GCE-GNN [17] to learn the complete transitions of items from current and historical sessions by enlarging the range of helpful information and achieving outstanding performance. More recently, Dong et al. presented GPAN [2], which employs the high-low order session perceptron to model directed and undirected graphs to obtain high-order and low-order item transitions in sessions and session position information to enhance the relevance of sequence order to user preferences.

Overall, GNN-based methods have shown great potential in SBR, and the methods described above have achieved impressive results in capturing complex dependencies between items in session sequences.

3 Proposed Method

This section defines the problem statement, introduces two graph construction approaches, and provides a detailed explanation of MAGNN-GC. The framework of MAGNN-GC is shown in Fig. 1, which consists of four parts: (a) Learning Global-level Item Embedding; (b) Learning Local-level Item Embedding; (c) Multi-Information Fusion; (d) Making Recommendations.

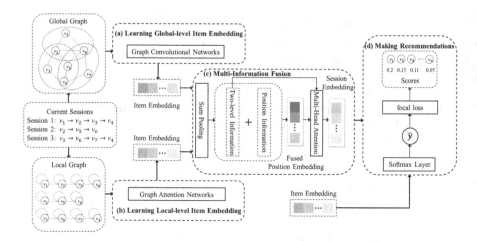

Fig. 1. Framework of MAGNN-GC.

3.1   Problem Statement

Session-based recommendation (SBR) aims to predict a user's next-click item based solely on their historical session sequences rather than their long-term preference profile. Let $V = \{v_1, v_2, \ldots, v_m\}$ denote all user-clicked items in the session. An anonymous session sequence $s = [v_1^s, v_{s,2}, \ldots, v_{s,n}]$ sorted by timestamp is used to represent the session, with length n. Let $v_{s,n+1}$ denote the next user-click item. Ultimately, a probability ranking list of all candidate items is generated, and the top-k items with the highest probabilities are recommended.

Three different session sequences labeled as Session 1, Session 2, and Session 3 are shown in Fig. 1. Each sequence includes all clicked items in the corresponding session, with arrows indicating the order of clicks.

3.2   Preliminaries

To describe the transitions between items in current sessions at different levels, we introduce two graph models, the global and the local graphs. An instance of the global and local graphs is shown in Fig. 2.

Global Graph. For SBR, RNN-based methods aim to capture the sequential patterns to learn session-specific item representations. In contrast, GNN-based methods learn item embeddings by constructing a session graph that represents the historical sequence of user interactions and captures information about neighboring nodes. Therefore, we choose to construct a global graph to model the global-level item transitions across all sessions.

We consider global-level item transitions for global-level item representation learning by integrating all pairwise item transitions over sessions. Referring to [17], we define a concept (i.e., ε-neighbor set) for modeling the global-level item

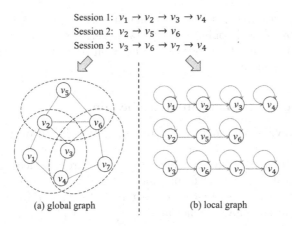

Session 1: $v_1 \to v_2 \to v_3 \to v_4$
Session 2: $v_2 \to v_5 \to v_6$
Session 3: $v_3 \to v_6 \to v_7 \to v_4$

(a) global graph   (b) local graph

Fig. 2. An instance of global graph and local graph.

transition. For each item v_i^p in session S_p, the ε-neighbor set of v_i^p denotes a set of items, as follows:

$$N_\varepsilon\left(v_i^p\right) = \left\{v_j^p \mid v_i^p = v_{i'}^p \in S_p \cap S_q; v_j^p \in S_q; \ j \in [i' - \varepsilon, i' + \varepsilon]; S_p \neq S_q\right\} \quad (1)$$

where v_i^p is the i'-th item in the session S_q, ε is the hyperparameter that controls the modeling scope of item transitions between v_i^p and other items in S_q. Besides, we use v_j^p to represent each item in ε-neighbor set $N_\varepsilon\left(v_i^p\right)$.

Based on ε-neighbor set, for item v_i global-level item transition is defined as $\{(v_i, v_j) \mid v_i, v_j \in V; v_j \in N_\varepsilon(v_i)\}$. Note that, to improve efficiency, we do not consider the direction of the global-level item transitions [17].

Next, the global graph is defined as $G_g = (V_g, E_g)$ which is an undirected weighted graph, where V_g represents the graph node set which has all items in V, and $E_g = \left\{e_{ij}^g \mid (v_i, v_j) \mid v_i, v_j \in V; v_j \in N_\varepsilon(v_i)\right\}$ represents the set of edges corresponding to two pairwise items in all sessions. Besides, we generate a weight for v_i's adjacent edges to emphasize the significance of its neighbors. The frequency of all the sessions is used as the weight of each corresponding edge, and we only keep top-k edges with the highest importance for each item v_i on graph G_g [17].

Local Graph. The target of constructing a local graph is to model the transitions of adjacent nodes in the current session to learn local-level item embedding. Following [18,20], we model each session sequence into a directed local graph, which describes the click order of nodes in the session. Specifically, it is defined as $G_l = (V_l, E_l)$, where V_l denotes the node set and E_l denotes the edge set. In other words, each node $v_i^s \in V_l$ in G_l represents an item, and each edge $\left(v_{i-1}^s, v_i^s\right) \in E_l$ denotes that the user clicks the item v_{i-1}^s and item v_i^s in sequence, which is called the local-level item-transition pattern. Similar to [11], each node has a self-loop to fuse its information in the following modeling process.

Inspired by [17], there are four types of edge connections in the local graph, which are represented as r_{in}, r_{out}, r_{in-out} and r_{self}. For example, in the edge

$\left(v_i^s, v_j^s\right)$, r_{in} denotes that there is only a single transition from v_j^s to v_i^s. Similarly, r_{out} means that there is only a single transition from v_i^s to v_j^s, and r_{in-out} indicates that there are both transitions between v_i^s and v_j^s. Finally, r_{self} the transition of the node itself.

3.3   Learning Global-Level Item Embedding

Referring to previous methods [7,16], this module is based on GCNs, and we calculate the attention weights according to the importance of each connection. Since a single item may involve multiple sessions, from which we can obtain useful item transitions that are helpful for subsequent recommendation task. By mean pooling to obtain the first-order neighbor's features of item v is a simple and effective solution. However, not all items in v's ε-neighbor set are related to the user preferences of the current session, so we consider using session-aware attention to emphasize the importance of items in its $N_\varepsilon(v)$ [17]. In terms of session-aware attention, each item in $N_\varepsilon(v)$ is linearly combined, which is as follows:

$$h_{N_{v_i}^g} = \sum_{v_j \in N_{v_i}^g} \pi\left(v_i, v_j\right) h_{v_j} \tag{2}$$

where $\pi\left(v_i, v_j\right)$ denotes the weight of different neighbors, and h_{v_j} denotes the representation of item v_j in the unified embedding space. The closer an item is to the preference of the current session, the greater the significance of the item is to the recommendation, which is consistent with empirical judgment. Hence, $\pi\left(v_i, v_j\right)$ is formulated as follows:

$$\pi\left(v_i, v_j\right) = \boldsymbol{q}_1^\top \text{LeakyReLU}\left(\boldsymbol{W}_1\left[\left(\boldsymbol{s} \odot \boldsymbol{h}_{v_j} \| w_{ij}\right)\right]\right) \tag{3}$$

Here $w_{ij} \in \mathbb{R}^1$ represents the weight of the edge v_1, v_2, $\odot$ denotes element-wise product, $\|$ represents the concatenation operation, $\boldsymbol{q}_1 \in \mathbb{R}^{d+1}$ and $\boldsymbol{W}_1 \in \mathbb{R}^{d+1 \times d+1}$ are trainable parameters. And we choose LeakyReLU as the activation function [17]. $\boldsymbol{s}$ represents the features of current sessions. And it can be obtained by calculating the mean value of the current session's item representation:

$$\boldsymbol{s} = \frac{1}{|S|} \sum_{v_i \in S} h_{v_i} \tag{4}$$

After that, the coefficients across $N_\varepsilon(v)$ connected with v_i are normalized by the softmax function:

$$\pi\left(v_i, v_j\right) = \frac{\exp\left(\pi\left(v_i, v_j\right)\right)}{\sum_{v_i \in N_{v_i}^g}^g \exp\left(\pi\left(v_i, v_k\right)\right)} \tag{5}$$

Finally, we aggregate the item representation h_v and its neighbor representation $h_{N_v}^g$, the k-th representation of multiple aggregator layers is implemented as follows:

$$h_v^{g,(k)} = \text{ReLU}\left(\boldsymbol{W}_2^{(k)}\left[h_v^{(k-1)} \| h_{N_v^g}^{(k-1)}\right]\right) \tag{6}$$

where ReLU is the activation function, $h_v^{(k-1)}$ is generated from previous $k-1$ steps, and the initial $h_v^{(0)}$ is the same as h_v when $k=1$. Besides, $W_2^{(k)} \in \mathbb{R}^{d \times 2d}$ is the k-th layer aggregation weight.

After applying these operations, each global-level item embedding representation becomes dependent on both itself and the representation of the current session's connectivity information.

3.4   Learning Local-Level Item Embedding

According to [16], we adopt GATs to learn the local-level item embedding representation. Specifically, the attention mechanism of GATs is used to compute the significant weights of different nodes. Given a node v_i, the significant weight of v_j on it can be calculated by element-wise product and non-linear transformation:

$$e_{ij} = \text{LeakyReLU} \left(a_{r_{ij}}^\top \left(h_{v_i} \odot h_{v_j} \right) \right) \tag{7}$$

where r_{ij} indicates the relationship between v_i and v_j, $a_* \in \mathbb{R}^d$ represent the weight vectors, and LeakyReLU is the activation function.

Referring to [17], according to the relationship of each node v_i, we train four weight matrices, a_{in}, a_{out}, a_{in-out} and a_{self} respectively, which can describe the impact of all nodes over v_i. And to make the weights of different nodes comparable, the softmax function is utilized to normalize them, and the attention weights coefficient α_{ij} is as follows:

$$\alpha_{ij} = \frac{\exp(e_{ij})}{\sum_{v_k \in N_{v_i}^S} \exp \left(\text{LeakyReLU} \left(a_{r_{ik}}^\top \left(h_{v_i} \odot h_{v_k} \right) \right) \right)} \tag{8}$$

Due to different neighbors, α_{ij} is asymmetric. Hence, we need to calculate a linear combination of features of each node v_i to get the feature representations:

$$h_{v_i}^l = \sum_{v_j \in N_{v_i}^S} \alpha_{ij} h_{v_j} \tag{9}$$

After aggregating the relevant information of each node and its neighboring nodes in the current session, we obtain the local-level item embedding representation for each node.

3.5   Multi-information Fusion

After obtaining the global-level and local-level item embedding representations, we need to fuse the information before making recommendation. With the dropout on the global-level item embedding, the two-level information is extracted by sum pooling, which is as follows:

$$h_{v_i}^* = \text{SumPooling} \left(\text{dropout} \left(h_v^{g,(k)} \right), h_{v_i}^l \right) \tag{10}$$

where $h_{v_i}^*$ is the item representation with two-level information in the session.

Considering noise filtering and the items clicked later in the session show the greater significance for the recommendation [18,20], we design a new position attention mechanism to compute soft-attention weights on all items in the session, which fuses two-level information with position information of items in the session.

Next, we can get the representations of items among the session, i.e., $H = \left[h_{v_1}^*, h_{v_2}^*, \ldots, h_{v_l}^*\right]$. We also employ reverse position embedding matrix $P = \left[p_1, p_2, \ldots, p_l\right]$ to reveal the position information embeddings for all the items involved in the session, where $p_1 \in \mathbb{R}^d$ is the first position vector, $p_l \in \mathbb{R}^d$ is the last position vector [17].After these operations above, we leverage concatenation and non-linear transformation to generate the fused position embedding:

$$f_i^* = \tanh\left(W_3\left[h_{v_l}^* \| p_{l-i+1}\right] + b\right) \tag{11}$$

where $W_3 \in \mathbb{R}^{d \times 2d}$ and $b \in \mathbb{R}^d$ are the trainable parameters and $\|$ denotes the concatenation operation. Referring to [17], the reversed position information can more accurately suggest the significance of each item than the forward position information. The two-level information of items in the session is averaged:

$$s^* = \frac{1}{l}\sum_{i=1}^{l} h_{v_i}^* \tag{12}$$

A single soft-attention mechanism has the problem of insufficient information fusion when integrating high-dimensional information. Therefore, different from previous work, we apply the multi-head attention mechanism [15] to calculate soft-attention weights. Compared to the single soft-attention mechanism, the multi-head attention mechanism can solve the problem of insufficient information fusion and is better suited for the current task. Specifically, high-dimensional information is reduced to its original dimension of $1/head$, and soft attention is calculated in parallel within subspaces of $head$:

$$\beta_i^{head} = q_2^{head\top} \text{ReLU}(W_4^{head} f_i^{*,head} + W_5^{head} s^{*,head} + c^{head}) \tag{13}$$

where $W_4^{head}, W_5^{head} \in \mathbb{R}^{d' \times d'}$ and $q_2^{head}, c^{head} \in \mathbb{R}^{d'}$ are learnable parameters. Exceptionally, to release the vanishing gradient problem [6], we choose ReLU as the activation function [3].

Next, it is normalized by a softmax function:

$$\alpha_i^{head} = \text{softmax}\left(\beta_i^{head}\right) = \frac{\exp\left(\beta_i^{head}\right)}{\sum_{i=1}^{n} \exp\left(\beta_i^{head}\right)} \tag{14}$$

Ultimately, the attention results of all subspaces are concatenated, and the final session embedding representation can be generated through linear combination operations, which comprehensively represents the features of the session:

$$F = \|_{head=1}^{H} \sum_{i=1}^{l} \alpha_i^{head} h_{v_i}^{*,head} \tag{15}$$

The session embedding representation F can effectively represent the session features by fusing both global-level and local-level information while considering the order and position of all involved items.

3.6 Making Recommendations

Based on the obtained session embedding representation F, let $\widehat{y_i}$ denote the final recommendation probability for each item v_i based on the original embedding representation and the current session embedding representation. We first take a dot product and next add a softmax function to get the results:

$$\widehat{y_i} = \text{softmax}\left(F^\top h_{v_i}\right) \tag{16}$$

Different from the previous work, to solve the problem of imbalanced positive and negative samples, the focal loss [9] is innovatively applied to replace the conventional cross-entropy loss for optimizing the model, which is defined as follows:

$$\mathcal{L}(\widehat{y}) = \begin{cases} -\alpha \sum_{i=1}^{m} (1 - \widehat{y_i})^\gamma \log \widehat{y_i}, \, y_i = 1 \\ -(1 - \alpha)\widehat{y_i}^\gamma \log (1 - \widehat{y_i}), \; y_i = 0 \end{cases} \tag{17}$$

where y is the one-hot vector, which denotes the ground truth of the target item, α is a factor that can balance the ratio of positive and negative samples, and γ is a factor that can solve the problem of imbalance between distinguishable and indistinguishable samples. Hence, it ensures that in the training process, the model will pay more attention to those small and indistinguishable samples, reducing the impact of the gradient superposition of a significant number of distinguishable samples on model training.

4 Experiments

To verify the validity of MAGNN-GC, we conducted a range of experiments by answering the following questions:

- RQ1: Can MAGNN-GC outperform state-of-the-art methods on real-world datasets?
- RQ2: Can the use of multi-head attention and focal loss for representing user interests improve the performance of MAGNN-GC?
- RQ3: How do different hyperparameter settings for multi-head attention impact the performance of MAGNN-GC?

4.1 Experimental Setup

Datasets. We conducted extensive experiments on three representative public datasets, i.e., Diginetica[1], Nowplaying[2], and Tmall[3]. Diginetica comes from

---

[1] https://competitions.codalab.org/competitions/11161.
[2] https://dbis.uibk.ac.at/node/263#nowplaying.
[3] https://tianchi.aliyun.com/dataset/42.

48   Y. Chen et al.

Table 1. Statistics of the datasets.

Dataset	Diginetica	Nowplaying	Tmall
total clicks	982961	1367963	818479
training sessions	719470	825304	351268
test sessions	60858	89824	25898
total items	43097	60417	40728
average session length	5.12	7.42	6.69

CIKM Cup 2016, and we only select the public transactional data. Nowplaying comes from Twitter, which contains users' music-listening behavior. Tmall comes from IJCAI-15 competition, which records the shopping logs of anonymous users on Tmall e-commerce platform.

Following previous methods [17], we conduct the same data preprocessing step on the datasets above to make it fair. Notably, we filter out the sessions with a length of 1 and items with less than five occurrences, and we choose the sessions of last week (latest data) as the test set. Besides, we split session data into a series of sequences and corresponding labels. After preprocessing, the statistics of the datasets are shown in Table 1.

Baselines. We compare MAGNN-GC with the following representative baselines, including three conventional and eight latest deep-learning-based recommendation methods.

- POP [4]: It always recommends the most popular items in the training set.
- Item-KNN [13]: It is a conventional recommendation method based on cosine similarity between session vectors.
- FPMC [12]: It is a Markov-based recommendation method.
- GRU4REC [4]: It is the first SBR method based on RNN that uses Gated Recurrent Units (GRUs).
- NARM [8]: It is a deep-learning-based method that extracts sequential action features of users by an attentive RNN-based network.
- STAMP [10]: It is an SBR method with short-term attention memory priority that effectively captures user preferences.
- SR-GNN [18]: It is the first GNN-based SBR method that captures the user's global and current preferences.
- GC-SAN [19]: It is an SBR method with self-attention networks to learn global and local dependency information between items in a session.
- FGNN [11]: It employs a weighted attention graph layer to learn the item representations and utilizes a graph feature encoder to extract the final representation of the session.
- GCE-GNN [17]: It utilizes GNN to learn two levels of item embeddings from global and session graphs, and next aggregates the learned item representations considering the position embeddings.

- GPAN [2]: It utilizes the high-low order session perceptron to model directed and undirected graphs respectively to obtain high and low order item transitions in session, and session position information to enhance the relevance of sequence order to user preferences.

Table 2. Comparisons of HR@20 and MRR@20 between MAGNN-GC and baselines.

Method	Diginetica		Nowplaying		Tmall	
	HR@20	MRR@20	HR@20	MRR@20	HR@20	MRR@20
POP	0.89	0.20	2.28	0.86	2.00	0.90
Item-KNN	35.75	11.57	15.94	4.91	9.15	3.31
FPMC	26.53	6.95	7.36	2.82	16.06	7.32
GRU4REC	29.40	8.31	7.92	4.48	10.93	5.89
NARM	49.70	16.17	18.59	6.93	23.30	10.70
STAMP	45.64	14.32	17.66	6.88	26.47	13.36
SR-GNN	50.77	17.62	18.87	7.47	27.57	13.72
GC-SAN	48.58	16.55	17.31	6.80	19.14	8.54
FGNN	50.58	16.84	18.78	7.15	25.24	10.39
GCE-GNN	54.22	19.04	22.37	8.40	33.42	15.42
GPAN	53.96	18.84	22.64	7.66	28.37	13.86
MAGNN-GC	**54.43**	**19.06**	**23.08**	**8.75**	**34.46**	**15.91**

Evaluation Metrics. Following previous methods [1], we adopt the commonly used HR@20 (Hit Rate)[4] and MRR@20 (Mean Reciprocal Rank) as evaluation metrics [1].

Parameter Settings. All the experiments below were run on the Ubuntu 16.04.6 LTS Docker system with PyTorch 1.10.1. The dimension of embedding vectors is set to 128, and the batch size is set to 128, the L2 penalty is set to 10^{-5}. The dropout ratio is set to 0.5 in Diginetica, 0.5 in Nowplaying, 0.7 in Tmall. The hyperparameter *head* of the multi-head attention mechanism is set to 4. The hyperparameters α and β of the focal loss are set to 0.9 and 2, respectively. Moreover, we select a random 10% subset of the training set as the validation set. All parameters are initialized using a Gaussian distribution with a mean value of 0 and a standard deviation of 0.1. After that, the mini-batch Adam optimizer with an initial learning rate of 0.001 is adopted, which will decay at a rate of 0.1 every three epochs. Besides, the number of neighbors and the maximum distance of items are set to 12 and 3, respectively.

[4] Note that [2,8,10,11,17,18] used different metric names for HR@20 (e.g., P@20 and Recall@20). However, they used the same formula to obtain the measurement (i.e., the proportion of cases when the desired item is among the top-20 items in all cases).

4.2   Comparison with Baselines (RQ1)

To verify the overall performance of MAGNN-GC, we compare it with existing representative baselines. The overall performance in HR@20 and MRR@20 is shown in Table 2, where the best results are highlighted in bold.

As presented in Table 2, MAGNN-GC achieves superior performance compared to the baselines across all three datasets, indicating its effectiveness in utilizing the multi-head attention mechanism to fuse high-dimensional information and enhance recommendation quality.

Table 3. The performance of MAGNN-GC and its variants.

Strategy	Diginetica		Nowplaying		Tmall	
	HR@20	MRR@20	HR@20	MRR@20	HR@20	MRR@20
MAGNN-GC-w/o-C	54.29	18.90	22.53	8.54	33.62	15.41
MAGNN-GC-C	54.34	**19.06**	22.93	8.58	34.10	15.83
MAGNN-GC-w/o-F	54.35	19.00	23.07	8.62	33.68	15.54
MAGNN-GC	**54.43**	**19.06**	**23.08**	**8.75**	**34.46**	**15.91**

In contrast, POP, Item-KNN, and FPMC are early conventional methods that do not adopt advanced deep neural networks, leading to lower recommendation performance on the three datasets.

RNN-based or MLP-based methods (GRU4REC, NARM, and STAMP) perform better than conventional methods, suggesting that neural networks can better capture complex user behaviors and improve recommendation performance.

GNN-based methods (SR-GNN, ACGNN, GC-SAN, FGNN, GCE-GNN, and GPAN) demonstrate significant performance improvements. This indicates that with the help of GNN, these methods can better capture complex item transitions in session sequences.

GCE-GNN and GPAN outperform other baselines on all three datasets, demonstrating the importance of extracting item features from diverse dimensions for information fusion.

4.3   Comparison with Variants of the Proposed Method (RQ2)

To verify the impact of multi-head attention and focal loss on the recommendation results, we compare MAGNN-GC on three datasets (Diginetica, Nowplaying, and Tmall) with its three variants: (1) relu-adding attention mechanism without multi-head structure for processing fused features, and conventional cross-entropy loss for training (MAGNN-GC-w/o-C), (2) multi-head attention mechanism for processing fused features and conventional cross-entropy loss for training (MAGNN-GC-C), (3) relu-adding attention mechanism without multi-head structure for processing fused features, and focal loss for training (MAGNN-GC-w/o-F). The evaluation metrics are HR@20 and MRR@20, respectively. The results are shown in Table 3.

It reveals that the proposed method MAGNN-GC outperforms the other approaches. Specifically, MAGNN-GC and MAGNN-GC-w/o-F outperform MAGNN-GC-w/o-C and MAGNN-GC-C on all three datasets. This suggests that incorporating focal loss during training improves the classification of positive samples and challenging samples. Moreover, our results show that MAGNN-GC outperforms MAGNN-GC-w/o-F, highlighting the effectiveness of the multi-head attention mechanism in the information fusion module for processing fused features.

4.4 Impact of Multi-head Attention Setting (RQ3)

From Fig. 3, it shows that choosing an appropriate value for *head* can enhance the performance of the proposed method. This finding indicates that incorporating the multi-head attention mechanism to combine session and item features has a positive impact on the proposed method. To reduce multiple high-dimensional information to their original dimension of $1/head$ in the information fusion module, *head* must be divisible by the embedding dimension. As a result, we selected *head* from $\{2, 4, 8, 16\}$. It achieves the highest HR@20 when *head* is set to 4, indicating that optimal fusion of session and item features is achieved across four subspaces.

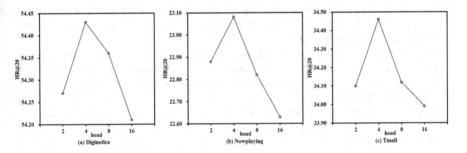

Fig. 3. Performance effects of varying *head* on three datasets.

5   Conclusion

This paper presents a novel approach for session-based recommendation based on graph neural networks. It first constructs global and local graphs based on all training sequences. Next, it learns global-level and local-level item embedding information and fuses them to enhance the feature presentations of items using a novel multi-head attention mechanism that can effectively fuse the high-dimensional information. Finally, it applies the focal loss to balance positive and negative samples during model training to achieve accurate predictions. Our experiments on three real-world datasets demonstrate the superiority of our method over most advanced methods.

References

1. Chen, T., Wong, R.C.W.: Handling information loss of graph neural networks for session-based recommendation. In: KDD'20: Proceedings of the 26th ACM SIGKDD International Conference on Knowledge Discovery & Data Mining (2020)
2. Dong, L., Zhu, G., Wang, Y., Li, Y., Duan, J., Sun, M.: A graph positional attention network for session-based recommendation. IEEE Access **11**, 7564–7573 (2023)
3. Glorot, X., Bordes, A., Bengio, Y.: Deep sparse rectifier neural networks. In: Proceedings of the Fourteenth International Conference on Artificial Intelligence and Statistics. pp. 315–323. JMLR Workshop and Conference Proceedings (2011)
4. Hidasi, B., Karatzoglou, A., Baltrunas, L., Tikk, D.: Session-based recommendations with recurrent neural networks. arXiv preprint arXiv:1511.06939 (2015)
5. Hidasi, B., Quadrana, M., Karatzoglou, A., Tikk, D.: Parallel recurrent neural network architectures for feature-rich session-based recommendations. In: Proceedings of the 10th ACM Conference on Recommender Systems. pp. 241–248 (2016)
6. Hochreiter, S.: The vanishing gradient problem during learning recurrent neural nets and problem solutions. Int. J. Uncertainty Fuzziness Knowl-Based Syst. **6**(02), 107–116 (1998)
7. Kipf, T.N., Welling, M.: Semi-supervised classification with graph convolutional networks. arXiv preprint arXiv:1609.02907 (2016)
8. Li, J., Ren, P., Chen, Z., Ren, Z., Lian, T., Ma, J.: Neural attentive session-based recommendation. In: Proceedings of the 2017 ACM on Conference on Information and Knowledge Management. pp. 1419–1428 (2017)
9. Lin, T.Y., Goyal, P., Girshick, R., He, K., Dollár, P.: Focal loss for dense object detection. In: Proceedings of the IEEE International Conference on Computer Vision. pp. 2980–2988 (2017)
10. Liu, Q., Zeng, Y., Mokhosi, R., Zhang, H.: Stamp: short-term attention/memory priority model for session-based recommendation. In: Proceedings of the 24th ACM SIGKDD International Conference on Knowledge Discovery & Data Mining. pp. 1831–1839 (2018)
11. Qiu, R., Li, J., Huang, Z., Yin, H.: Rethinking the item order in session-based recommendation with graph neural networks. arXiv preprint arXiv:1911.11942 (2019)
12. Rendle, S., Freudenthaler, C., Schmidt-Thieme, L.: Factorizing personalized markov chains for next-basket recommendation. In: Proceedings of the 19th International Conference on World Wide Web. pp. 811–820 (2010)
13. Sarwar, B., Karypis, G., Konstan, J., Riedl, J.: Item-based collaborative filtering recommendation algorithms. In: Proceedings of the 10th International Conference on World Wide Web. pp. 285–295 (2001)
14. Tan, Y.K., Xu, X., Liu, Y.: Improved recurrent neural networks for session-based recommendations. In: Proceedings of the 1st Workshop on Deep Learning for Recommender Systems. pp. 17–22 (2016)
15. Vaswani, A., et al.: Attention is all you need. Adv. Neural Inf. Proc. Syst. **30** (2017)
16. Veličković, P., Cucurull, G., Casanova, A., Romero, A., Lio, P., Bengio, Y.: Graph attention networks. arXiv preprint arXiv:1710.10903 (2017)
17. Wang, Z., Wei, W., Cong, G., Li, X.L., Mao, X.L., Qiu, M.: Global context enhanced graph neural networks for session-based recommendation. arXiv preprint arXiv:2106.05081 (2021)
18. Wu, S., Tang, Y., Zhu, Y., Wang, L., Xie, X., Tan, T.: Session-based recommendation with graph neural networks. In: Proceedings of the AAAI Conference on Artificial Intelligence. vol. 33, pp. 346–353 (2019)

19. Xu, C., Zhao, P., Liu, Y., Sheng, V.S., Xu, J., Zhuang, F., Fang, J., Zhou, X.: Graph contextualized self-attention network for session-based recommendation. In: IJCAI. vol. 19, pp. 3940–3946 (2019)
20. Yu, F., Zhu, Y., Liu, Q., Wu, S., Wang, L., Tan, T.: Tagnn: Target attentive graph neural networks for session-based recommendation. arXiv preprint arXiv:2005.02844 (2020)

Chinese Relation Extraction with Bi-directional Context-Based Lattice LSTM

Chengyi Ding[1], Lianwei Wu[2(✉)], Pusheng Liu[2], and Linyong Wang[3]

[1] School of Software, Northwestern Polytechnical University, Xian, China
_dcy@mail.nwpu.edu.cn
[2] School of Computer Science, Northwestern Polytechnical University, Xian, China
wlw@nwpu.edu.cn, lps@mail.nwpu.edu.cn
[3] School of Computer Science, Nanjing University of Posts and Telecommunications,
Nanjing, China
b19030610@njupt.edu.cn

Abstract. Chinese entity relation extraction (Chinese RE) is a crucial task for various NLP applications. It aims to automatically extract relationships between entities in Chinese texts, thereby enhancing the accuracy of natural language understanding. Although existing hybrid methods can overcome some of the shortcomings of character-based and word-based methods, they still suffer from polysemy ambiguity, which results in inaccuracy when representing the relationships between entities in text. To address the issue, we propose a Bi-directional Context-based Lattice (BC-Lattice) model for Chinese RE task. In detail, our BC-Lattice consists of: (1) A context-based polysemy weighting (CPW) module allocates weights to multiple senses of polysemous words from external knowledge base by modeling context-level information, thus obtaining more accurate representations of polysemous words; (2) A cross-attention semantic interaction-enhanced (CSI) classifier promotes exchange of semantic information between hidden states from forward and backward perspectives for more comprehensive representations of relation types. In experiments conducted on two public datasets from distinct domains, our method yields improved F1 score by up to 3.17%.

Keywords: Information extraction · Relation extraction · NLP · Polysemy disambiguation · Lattice architecture · External knowledge

1 Introduction

As a crucial subtask of information extraction (IE), the entity relation extraction (RE) task aims to identify semantic relations between entity pairs in unstructured text. Downstream applications can leverage this idea to extract rich semantic knowledge and enhance the efficiency of various tasks, including but not limited to text summarization, question-answering system [1], reading comprehension, and knowledge graph [2].

Except for a few methods that take Chinese documents and paragraphs as inputs, most existing methods for Chinese relation extraction (Chinese RE) rely

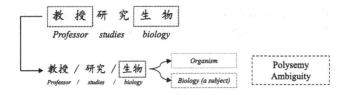

Fig. 1. Two main issues in Chinese RE. For polysemy ambiguity, the word "生物" means *Biology* in the context, but may be misunderstood as *Organism*.

on sentence-level datasets. They can be divided into three categories: character-based RE, word-based RE and hybrid RE models. For **character-based models** [3–6], character sequences are input into the models so that morphological information from characters of words is effectively extracted. Nevertheless, this approach has a limitation in that it cannot make full use of word-based semantic and grammatical information. To this end, **word-based models** [7–10] are introduced, which mainly segment input text into word sequences, so as to fully learn the contextual semantics of sequences. Theoretically, this type of model is more competent in Chinese RE task, its performance could be significantly affected by segmentation error. To overcome the shortcomings of the above two models, **hybrid models** [11–15] are proposed. Hybrid models are able to utilize both character-level and word-level information. More precisely, with the assistance of external knowledge, word-level information is dynamically integrated into character-level representation, thus effectively injecting segmentation knowledge into semantic representations. This makes them significantly more capable of dealing with segmentation issues than character-based and word-based methods. However, hybrid models still suffer from ambiguity caused by polysemous words, as shown in Fig. 1.

In order to alleviate polysemy ambiguity in Chinese RE, we introduce Bi-directional Context-based Lattice (BC-Lattice) model, an end-to-end method that integrates character-level, word-level and context-level knowledge. Concretely, we promote a context-based polysemy weighting (CPW) module that collects multiple senses of polysemous words from external knowledge base and then allocates weights to the senses by dynamically modeling the context, thus obtaining more accurate representations of polysemous words. We also devise a cross-attention semantic interaction-enhanced (CSI) classifier that exchanges and fuses semantics between bi-directional hidden states obtained from the encoding process. It improves the classification performance of our model.

We summarize our contributions as follows:

- The paper introduces a Bi-directional Context-based Lattice (BC-Lattice) model to ease polysemy ambiguity issue in Chinese RE.
- To obtain more accurate representations of polysemous words, we promote a CPW module. A CSI classifier is also put forward to achieve more accurate classification.

- Experimental results on two public Chinese RE datasets indicate that our model achieves a great improvement in evaluation metrics.

2 Related Work

Based on basic granularity of input sequences, recent Chinese RE models can be roughly classified into three categories: character-based models, word-based models, hybrid based models.

Character-Based Models. In character-based models, character sequences are input into the models. With the increasing importance of knowledge engineering, Han et al. [6] introduced an attention-based model utilizing the characters that compose the entities to eliminate the limitation of additional information provided by knowledge base, and Zhang et al. [16] took advantage of knowledge graph to solve the problems of knowledge related issues.

Word-Based Models. In this type of architecture, text sequences are first segmented into word-level. Then, the word sequences obtained are invoked as the direct input of the model. Chen et al. [17] introduced a multi-scale convolutional recurrent neural network to capture text features at a specific scale. Considering traditional RE methods extract relationships and entities in separate steps, Lv et al. [10] proposed the entity relation chain, implementing integrated identification of entities and relationships.

Hybrid Models. This type of architecture is able to integrate word-based and character-based semantics. To deal with segmentation and polysemy ambiguity issues, lattice architecture [13,14,18–20] was introduced. This architecture is capable of dynamically merging rich word-level knowledge into character-level representation. However, lattice-based models cannot meet the requirements of parallel computing. Thus, Zhao et al. [21] proposed polysemy rethinking mechanism for Chinese RE. To further improve hybrid models' ability to filter out noise of external knowledge, Yang et al. [15] devised a mixture-of-view-experts framework that learns multi-view features.

Unlike previous words, this paper propose to wrestle with polysemy ambiguity by modeling context of polysemous words. In addition, we devise a novel CSI classifier for bi-directional encoding process. Compared with unidirectional encoding methods, our model achieves more accurate relation classification.

3 Methodology

3.1 Input Representation

The input to our model is a Chinese sentence with two labeled entities. Since the model utilizes multi-granularity information, we utilize both character-level and word-level representations (Fig. 2).

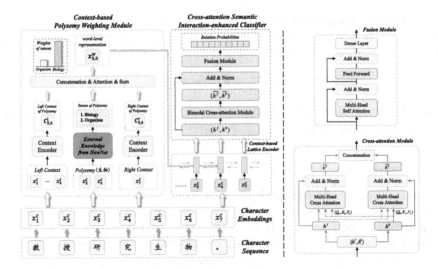

Fig. 2. Overall architecture of BC-Lattice model, consisting of input representation, context-based lattice encoder and cross-attention semantic interaction-enhanced classifier.

Character-Level Representation. The input sequence can be defined as $s = \{c_1, c_2, ..., c_M\}$, where s is a sentence containing M Chinese characters. We first map each character c_i to a dense vector x_i^{ce} of d^c dimensions.

In order to specify the head entity E^h and tail entity E^t of the relation tuple, we leverage positional embedding proposed by Zeng et al. [22]. The position is defined as the relative distances to the current character. For example, the relative distance from the i-th character to entity E^h and E^t are expressed as p_i^h and p_i^t respectively. The formula for p_i^h is as follows.

$$p_i^h = \begin{cases} i - b^h & i < b^h \\ 0 & b^h \le i \le e^h \\ i - e^h & i > e^h \end{cases} \tag{1}$$

where b^h and e^h are the beginning and end indices of the head entity. The formula for p_i^t is same to Eq. 1. Then, p_i^h and p_i^t are also mapped to vectors by looking up to embedding table, denoted as $x_i^{p^h} \in \mathbb{R}^{d^p}$ and $x_i^{p^t} \in \mathbb{R}^{d^p}$, where d^p stands for the dimension of positional embeddings.

In this way, we get the final representation of the i-th character $x_i^c \in \mathbb{R}^d (d = d^c + 2 \times d^p)$, where semicolons here represent concatenation.

$$x_i^c = [x_i^{ce}; x_i^{p^h}; x_i^{p^t}] \tag{2}$$

The embedding matrix of the input sentence is denoted as $x^c = \{x_1^c, x_2^c, ..., x_M^c\}$, where $x^c \in \mathbb{R}^{M \times d}$.

Word-Level Representation. For each potential polysemous word $w_{b,e}$ that starts from the b-th character and ends at the e-th character, we obtain all its N senses by retrieving the HowNet. The k-th sense of $w_{b,e}$ is denoted as follows.

$$x_{b,e,k}^{sen} \in e^{sen}(w_{b,e}) \tag{3}$$

where e^{sen} serves as the lookup table and $x_{b,e,k}^{sen} \in \mathbb{R}^{d^{sen}}$. Hence, the sense set of word $w_{b,e}$ is represented as $x_{b,e}^{sen} = \{x_{b,e,1}^{sen}, x_{b,e,2}^{sen}, ..., x_{b,e,N}^{sen}\}(x_{b,e}^{sen} \in \mathbb{R}^{N \times d^{sen}})$.

3.2   Context-Based Lattice Encoder

The direct input of the encoder is the final character-level representation mentioned above as well as sense sets of polysemous words. In this part, we propose a context-based polysemy weighting (CPW) module that models left and right context of a polysemous word to allocate weights to its multiple senses, so that senses with high relativity are enhanced and those irrelevant are weakened.

Context-Based Polysemy Weighting Module. For a specific word that starts from the b-th character and ends at the e-th character, we define the left context as $s_{b,e}^l = \{x_1^c, x_2^c, ..., x_{b-1}^c\}$ and right context as $s_{b,e}^r = \{x_{e+1}^c, x_{e+2}^c, ..., x_M^c\}$, where x_i^c is the representation of the i-th character in the sentence. The left context and right context would first go through a context encoder respectively. The representation obtained from the encoding process is denoted as $C_{b,e}^l$ and $C_{b,e}^r$. After the encoding process, the two parts of representation are concatenated as $C_{b,e}^c \in \mathbb{R}^{L \times d^{sen}}$, where L is total length of context. Besides, for convenience of calculation, dimension of context embeddings is set to be the same as that of sense embeddings.

The core of the context extractor is an attention layer. The overall framework of the attention layer can be expressed as follows.

$$x_{b,e}^w = Attn(C_{b,e}^c, x_{b,e}^{sen}) \tag{4}$$

where $x_{b,e}^w$ represents the final word-level representation, and $x_{b,e}^{sen} \in \mathbb{R}^{N \times d^{sen}}$ denotes the sense set mentioned in Sect. 3.1.

The details of the designed attention mechanism are as follows.

$$M = W_1 x_{b,e}^{sen} \odot (W_2 W_3 C_{b,e}^c \otimes E) \tag{5}$$

$$c = softmax(w_4^T M) \tag{6}$$

$$x_{b,e}^w = sum(c \odot x_{b,e}^{sen}) \tag{7}$$

where W_1, W_2, W_3 and w_4 are trainable parameters, and $\odot$ means dot product operation. W_3 extracts and fuses context knowledge to obtain a semantic feature vector. $W_3 C_{b,e}^c \in \mathbb{R}^{d^{sen}}$ denotes the central semantic representation. Parameter W_1 and W_2 project matrices into the same size. E is a N-dimensional matrix of ones, where N stands for the number of senses in the sense set. Given a matrix Ma, $Ma \otimes E$ means repeating the matrix for N times. Then, transposed parameter w_4 projects the matrix into a vector of size $N \times d^{sen}$, and the following softmax function is used to rescale the weight vector. Lastly, we perform dot product operation between normalized weight matrix c and sense set $x_{b,e}^{sen}$, then add together elements in the N-sized dimension. After that, we obtain the final word-level representation $x_{b,e}^{w} \in \mathbb{R}^{d^{sen}}$.

Context-Based Lattice Encoder. As mentioned before, our BC-Lattice Encoder is a Bi-LSTM-based architecture that dynamically integrates word-level representation into character-level representation. Specifically, there are two types of cell units: word-level cell and character level cell. The computation of character-level cell is similar to common LSTM cell.

$$i_j^c = \sigma(W_i^1 x_j^c + U_i^1 h_{j-1}^c + b_i^1) \tag{8}$$

$$o_j^c = \sigma(W_o^1 x_j^c + U_o^1 h_{j-1}^c + b_o^1) \tag{9}$$

$$f_j^c = \sigma(W_f^1 x_j^c + U_f^1 h_{j-1}^c + b_f^1) \tag{10}$$

$$\tilde{c}_j^c = \tanh(W_c^1 x_j^c + U_c^1 h_{j-1}^c + b_c^1) \tag{11}$$

where all variables with superscript c indicate character-level.
Word-level cells share similar structure with character-level ones.

$$i_{b,e}^w = \sigma(W_i^2 x_{b,e}^w + U_i^2 h_b^c + b_i^2) \tag{12}$$

$$f_{b,e}^w = \sigma(W_f^2 x_{b,e}^w + U_f^2 h_b^c + b_f^2) \tag{13}$$

$$\tilde{c}_{b,e}^w = \tanh(W_c^2 x_{b,e}^w + U_c^2 h_b^c + b_c^2) \tag{14}$$

$$c_{b,e}^w = f_{b,e}^w \odot c_b^c + i_{b,e}^w \odot \tilde{c}_{b,e}^w \tag{15}$$

where $c_{b,e}^w$ is word-level cell state and b, e denotes the index of starting and ending characters.
The cell state of the e-th character is calculated by incorporating the information of all the words that end in index e with that of the e-th character.

$$c_e^c = \sum_{b \in \{b' | w_{b',e} \in \mathbb{D}\}} a_{b,e}^2 \odot c_{b,e}^w + a_e^1 \odot \tilde{c}_e^c \tag{16}$$

The expression of hidden state is computed as follows.

$$h_e^c = o_e^c \odot \tanh(c_e^c) \tag{17}$$

The normalization factors $a_{b,e}^2$ and a_e^1 are defined in order to control the contribution of word-level and character-level information. They are computed by the following formulas, where $\mathbb{D}$ refers to the lexicon.

$$a_{b,e}^2 = \frac{\exp(i_{b,e}^w)}{\exp(i_e^c) + \sum_{b' \in \{b'' | w_{b'',e} \in \mathbb{D}\}} \exp(i_{b',e}^c)} \tag{18}$$

$$a_e^1 = \frac{\exp(i_e^c)}{\exp(i_e^c) + \sum_{b' \in \{b'' | w_{b''},_e \in \mathbb{D}\}} \exp(i_{b',e}^c)} \tag{19}$$

We carry out the encoding process from forward and backward directions, obtaining hidden state vectors $\overrightarrow{h^c}$ and $\overleftarrow{h^c}$ respectively, and we get the final hidden state representation h^c by concatenation operation.

$$h^c = [\overrightarrow{h^c} \oplus \overleftarrow{h^c}] \tag{20}$$

Eventually, the hidden state vector is fed into the classifier.

3.3   Cross-Attention Semantic Interaction-Enhanced Classifier

After the hidden state of an instance $h^c \in \mathbb{R}^{M \times 2d^h}$ is learned, we leverage a cross-attention semantic interaction-enhanced (CSI) classifier, so that we can learn the joint representation of bi-directional hidden state. The classifier can be divided into two parts: cross query module and fusion module. For the sake of convenience, we denote $\overrightarrow{h^c}$ and $\overleftarrow{h^c}$ as h^f and h^b.

For the cross-attention module, we modify the multi-head attention proposed by Vaswani et al. [23]. Here, we define query, key and value from h^f and h^b as (Q_f, K_f, V_f) and (Q_b, K_b, V_b). To better switch information between forward and backward process, we recombine the Q-K-V sets as (Q_b, K_f, V_f) and (Q_f, K_b, V_b). Then, each set is attached to one of the two multi-head attention sub-layers and we get the output expression: $(\tilde{h}^f, \tilde{h}^b)$.

After cross-attention, $(\tilde{h}^f, \tilde{h}^b)$ contains information from each other. Then, it goes through a fusion module to obtain a unified semantic vector. $(\tilde{h}^f, \tilde{h}^b)$ and (h^f, h^b) are concatenated, added and normalized. The result vector goes through a normalization sub-layer afterwards. Next, we pass the vector into a multi-head self-attention layer followed by a feed forward layer to obtain a feature vector U.

To compute the conditional probability of each relation, the feature vector is transformed into a Y-dimensional vector o, and then fed into a softmax layer.

$$o = WU + b \tag{21}$$

$$p(y|S) = softmax(o) \tag{22}$$

where W is the transformation matrix that transforms U into a Y-dimensional vector, and $b \in \mathbb{R}^Y$. Y indicates the number of candidate relations.

Finally, we define the loss function using cross-entropy method.

$$L(\theta) = \sum_{i=1}^{T} \log p(y^{(i)}|S^{(i)}, \theta) \tag{23}$$

where T is the number of examples in the datasets.

4   Experiments

4.1   Experimental Settings

Datasets. We carry out our experiments on two different datasets, including Chinese SanWen [24], and FinRE [13]. **Chinese SanWen dataset** is a discourse-level dataset created mainly for named entity recognition (NER) task and relation extraction (RE) task. It contains 9 identified entity relations among 837 articles. Among instances from the total 837 articles, 695 articles are chosen for training, 84 for testing and 58 for validating. **FinRE dataset** is a manually annotated dataset from 2,647 financial news in Sina Finance. The dataset contains 44 distinguished relationships, including a special class NA. For our experiments, 13,486, 3,727 and 1,489 relation instances are utilized for training, testing and validation respectively.

Evaluation Metrics. Several widely recognized evaluation metrics are applied in the experiments, including area under the curve (AUC) and F1 score (F1).

4.2   Evaluation Results

To establish a comprehensive comparison and analysis, we carry out experiments on several baselines. The selected baselines are as follows.

- **PCNN+ATT** [25]: A sentence-level attention-based model reduces noise in data by reducing the weights of noisy instances.
- **Bi-LSTM** [26]: Bi-directional RNN-based framework identifies long-distance dependency between nominal pairs by learning temporal features.
- **MG-Lattice** [13]: MG lattice model dynamically merges word-level knowledge into character-based LSTM encoder to alleviate segmentation ambiguity and polysemy ambiguity.
- **Flat-Lattice** [14]: Flat lattice method improves the performance by utilizing optimized position encoding scheme and pretrain-transfer strategy.
- **PRM-CNN-Rl** [21]: CNN-based polysemy rethinking mechanism continuously incorporates lexical and polysemous word information into CNN-based character-level model.

In addition, to verify the effectiveness of the modules designed, we conduct experiments for both CPW module and CSI classifier. For CPW, we replace the weighting method proposed by Li et al. in MG-Lattice model with our proposed context-based weighting method. For CSI, we apply it to LSTM, Bi-LSTM, and MG-Lattice encoder respectively.

We report the main results in Table 1, from which we can conclude that: (1) The performance of BC-Lattice model with CSI classifier and CPW module is notably better than the other Chinese RE baselines on both SanWen and FinRE dataset. Compared with PRM-CNN-Rl in FinRE, the F1 score of our model improves by 3.17%. (2) The CPW method proposed by us outperforms

Table 1. F1 score and AUC of baselines and our model

Models	SanWen		FinRE	
	F1	AUC	F1	AUC
PCNN+Att	60.55	50.41	46.13	31.89
Bi-LSTM	61.04	50.21	42.87	28.80
MG-Lattice	65.61	57.33	49.26	38.47
Flat-Lattice	68.35	59.14	50.60	40.03
PRM-CNN-Rl	67.72	59.67	52.97	41.32
LSTM+CSI	63.56	54.86	47.51	35.40
Bi-LSTM+CSI	64.77	55.34	50.10	39.03
MG-Lattice+CSI	67.47	61.84	55.06	43.97
MG-Lattice+CPW	66.23	57.16	52.75	40.95
Our Model	**68.38**	**62.65**	**56.14**	**45.87**

the weighting method of previous state-of-the-art MG-Lattice model in F1 score on two datasets, demonstrating the effectiveness of our weighting method. (3) The performances of Bi-LSTM and MG-Lattice significantly improve with CSI classifier. Besides, the F1 score of LSTM is lower than Bi-LSTM as it only provides single-directional encoding results. (4) The improvement of our method on the sentence-level dataset (FinRE) is greater than that on the discourse-level dataset (SanWen). We infer that there are semantic connections between sentences in discourse-level datasets thus requiring multi-level operations for contextual information extraction.

4.3 Ablation Study

We conduct ablation study on SanWen dataset to further investigate the effectiveness of main components in our mode, namely CSI classifier and CPW module. For BC-Lattice without CSI classifier, CSI is substituted with a classifier

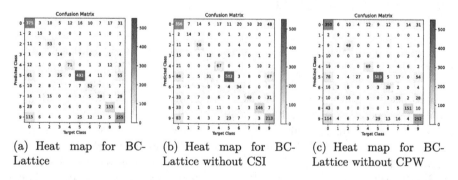

(a) Heat map for BC-Lattice

(b) Heat map for BC-Lattice without CSI

(c) Heat map for BC-Lattice without CPW

Fig. 3. Heat maps for ablation study, where classes 0 to 9 refer to Unknown, Create, Use, Near, Social, Located, Ownership, General-Special, Family, Part-Whole.

mainly consisting of one trainable attention matrix and bias matrix. For BC-Lattice without CPW module, CPW method is replaced by weighting method adopted by MG lattice. In addition, since CSI classifier is a relatively complex module, we conduct ablation study by discarding its sub-modules cross-attention module and fusion module respectively to validate their contributions.

Table 2. Ablation study on SanWen dataset. We get normalized prediction speed (NPS) by first computing the reciprocal of prediction time and then normalizing the obtained results.

Models	F1	AUC	NPS
BC-Lattice	**68.38**	**62.65**	0.86
w/o CSI	66.83	59.51	1.00
w/o CPW	67.47	61.84	**0.83**
w/o Cross-attention Module	66.87	58.95	-
w/o Fusion Module	66.12	58.97	-

Effect Against CSI Classifier and CPW Module. In this part, we mainly concentrate on the effectiveness of CPW module and CSI classifier. We consider two model settings: BC-Lattice without CSI (w/o CSI) and BC-Lattice without CPW (w/o CPW).

As shown in Table 2, we can discover that the F1 score drops by 1.55% and 0.91% without CSI classifier and CPW module respectively. This shows that both modules make contributions to the performance of BC-Lattice model. Although the contribution of CPW module is less than that of CSI classifier, we can observe from Fig. 2 that CPW module improves the normalized prediction speed in each iteration.

To further figure out the reasons, we plot heat maps in Fig. 3. From the figures we can observe that the number of correctly identified Unknown instances drops by 19 and 25, and that of labeled relation classes decreases by 49 and 28 without CSI classifier and CPW module respectively. Besides, for most labeled classes, the absence of CSI classifier and CPW leads to decline in accuracy, such as Part-Whole and Ownership. This verifies the conclusion that both CSI classifier and CPW module are effective components of BC-Lattice model.

Effect Against Sub-modules in CSI. CSI classifier is mainly composed of two sub-modules: a cross-attention module and a fusion module. In ablation study, we discard one of them at a time to validate their contributions. Referring to results in Table 2, we observe that the absence of any one of the two modules leads to decrease in performance. For model without cross-attention module, F1 score falls by 1.51%, from 68.38% to 66.87%, which demonstrates the significance of cross-attention between bi-directional semantic information.

For model without fusion module, F1 score declines by 2.26%, from 68.38% to 66.12%, indicating that the fusion operation fully integrates semantic information to more accurately model the context.

5 Conclusion

In this paper, we propose the BC-Lattice model for Chinese relation extraction. We propose a CPW module that alleviates the issue of polysemy ambiguity by utilizing context information. In addition, a CSI classifier is designed to promote exchange of semantic information between hidden states from bi-directional perspectives. Experiments on two public datasets demonstrate the superiority of our model compared with other baselines. In the future, we will further investigate paragraph-level and document-level Chinese RE.

Acknowledgements. This work was supported in part by the National Natural Science Foundation of China under Grants U22B2036, U19B2037, and 62202381, in part by Shenzhen Science and Technology Program and Guangdong Basic and Applied Basic Research Foundation (2021A1515110717), General Program of Chongqing Natural Science Foundation (No. CSTB2022NSCQ-MSX1284), the Fundamental Research Funds for the Central Universities (D5000220185), sponsored by CAAI-Huawei MindSpore Open Fund, the National Postdoctoral Innovative Talents Support Program for L. Wu. We would like to thank the anonymous reviewers for their constructive comments.

References

1. Xu, K., Reddy, S., Feng, Y., Huang, S., Zhao, D.: Question answering on freebase via relation extraction and textual evidence. arXiv preprint arXiv:1603.00957 (2016)
2. Ehrlinger, L., Wöß, W.: Towards a definition of knowledge graphs. SEMANTiCS (Posters Demos SuCCESS) **48**(1–4), 2 (2016)
3. Zhang, Z., Zhou, T., Zhang, Y., Pang, Y.: Attention-based deep residual learning network for entity relation extraction in Chinese EMRs. BMC Med. Inform. Decis. Making **19**, 171–177 (2019)
4. Guo, M., Zhang, J., Li, M., Geng, Y., Geng, N.: Chinese relation extraction of apple diseases and pests based on a dual-channel neural network. In: 2021 IEEE 23rd International Conference on High Performance Computing & Communications; 7th International Conference on Data Science & Systems; 19th International Conference on Smart City; 7th International Conference on Dependability in Sensor, Cloud & Big Data Systems & Application (HPCC/DSS/SmartCity/DependSys), pp. 1229–1236 (2021)
5. Lai, Q., Ding, S., Gong, J.W., Cui, J., Liu, S.: A Chinese multi-modal relation extraction model for internet security of finance. In: 2022 52nd Annual IEEE/IFIP International Conference on Dependable Systems and Networks Workshops (DSN-W), pp. 123–128 (2022)
6. Han, X., Zhang, Y., Zhang, W., Huang, T.: An attention-based model using character composition of entities in Chinese relation extraction. Information **11**, 79 (2020)

7. Ma, X., Hovy, E.: End-to-end sequence labeling via bi-directional LSTM-CNNs-CRF. In: Proceedings of the 54th Annual Meeting of the Association for Computational Linguistics (Volume 1: Long Papers), Berlin, Germany, pp. 1064–1074. Association for Computational Linguistics (2016)
8. Jia, S., Shijia, E., Li, M., Xiang, Y.: Chinese open relation extraction and knowledge base establishment. ACM Trans. Asian Low-Resource Lang. Inf. Process. (TALLIP) **17**, 1–22 (2018)
9. Pang, N., Tan, Z., Zhao, X., Zeng, W., Xiao, W.D.: Domain relation extraction from noisy Chinese texts. Neurocomputing **418**, 21–35 (2020)
10. Lv, C., Pan, D., Li, Y., Li, J., Wang, Z.: A novel Chinese entity relationship extraction method based on the bidirectional maximum entropy Markov model. Complexity **2021**, 6610965:1–6610965:8 (2021)
11. Wang, H., Qi, Z., Hao, H., Xu, B.: A hybrid method for Chinese entity relation extraction. In: Natural Language Processing and Chinese Computing (2014)
12. Zhang, Y., Yang, J.: Chinese NER using lattice LSTM. arXiv abs/1805.02023 (2018)
13. Li, Z., Ding, N., Liu, Z., Zheng, H., Shen, Y.: Chinese relation extraction with multi-grained information and external linguistic knowledge. In: Annual Meeting of the Association for Computational Linguistics (2019)
14. Zeng, X., Zhong, J., Wang, C., Hu, C.: Chinese relation extraction with flat-lattice encoding and pretrain-transfer strategy. In: Qiu, H., Zhang, C., Fei, Z., Qiu, M., Kung, S.-Y. (eds.) KSEM 2021, Part II. LNCS (LNAI), vol. 12816, pp. 30–40. Springer, Cham (2021). https://doi.org/10.1007/978-3-030-82147-0_3
15. Yang, J., Ji, B., Li, S., Ma, J., Peng, L., Yu, J.: Dynamic multi-view fusion mechanism for Chinese relation extraction. arXiv abs/2303.05082 (2023)
16. Zhang, W., et al.: Research on the Chinese named-entity-relation-extraction method for crop diseases based on BERT. Agronomy **12**(9), 2130 (2022)
17. Chen, T., Wu, X., Li, L., Li, J., Feng, S.: Extraction of entity relations from Chinese medical literature based on multi-scale CRNN. Ann. Transl. Med. **10** (2021)
18. Xu, C., Yuan, L., Zhong, Y.: Chinese relation extraction using lattice GRU. In: 2020 IEEE 4th Information Technology, Networking, Electronic and Automation Control Conference (ITNEC), vol. 1, pp. 1188–1192 (2020)
19. Zhang, Z., Yu, Q.: Chinese relation extraction based on lattice network improved with BERT model. In: Proceedings of the 2020 5th International Conference on Mathematics and Artificial Intelligence (2020)
20. Ran, X., Yang, F.: Chinese relation extraction with phrase component representations. In: 2021 IEEE 5th Information Technology, Networking, Electronic and Automation Control Conference (ITNEC), vol. 5, pp. 454–458 (2021)
21. Zhao, Q., Gao, T., Guo, N.: A novel Chinese relation extraction method using polysemy rethinking mechanism. Appl. Intell. **53**, 7665–7676 (2022)
22. Zeng, D., Liu, K., Lai, S., Zhou, G., Zhao, J.: Relation classification via convolutional deep neural network. In: International Conference on Computational Linguistics (2014)
23. Vaswani, A., et al.: Attention is all you need. arXiv abs/1706.03762 (2017)
24. Xu, J., Wen, J., Sun, X., Su, Q.: A discourse-level named entity recognition and relation extraction dataset for Chinese literature text. arXiv abs/1711.07010 (2017)
25. Lin, Y., Shen, S., Liu, Z., Luan, H., Sun, M.: Neural relation extraction with selective attention over instances. In: Annual Meeting of the Association for Computational Linguistics (2016)
26. Zhang, D., Wang, D.: Relation classification via recurrent neural network. arXiv abs/1508.01006 (2015)

MA-TGNN: Multiple Aggregators Graph-Based Model for Text Classification

Chengcheng Huang, Shiqun Yin$^{(\boxtimes)}$, Lei Li, and Yaling Zhang

Faculty of Computer and Information Science, Southwest University,
ChongQing 400715, China
{hcc044914,llandlmt,ruby0110}@email.swu.edu.cn, qqqq-qiong@163.com

Abstract. In recent years, graph neural network (GNN) has performed well in processing non-Euclidean structural data and saving global co-occurrence information. Researchers are exploring the application of GNN in the field of text classification. However, some existing GNN-based methods employ corpus-level graph structures, which can result in high memory consumption. Additionally, a single-node aggregation method may only partially extract semantic features. We propose a graph-based text classification model called the Multi-Aggregator GNN model to address these limitations. Specifically, we utilize multiple aggregation methods to obtain the distributional characteristics of the text comprehensively. And we incorporate dimensionality reduction pooling to preserve crucial information in the text representation. Finally, we use the updated node representations as document embeddings. Experimental results on seven benchmark datasets demonstrate that our proposed model significantly improves the performance of text classification tasks.

Keywords: Graph neural network · Text classification · Multiple aggregators · Mechanism of attention

1 Introduction

Text classification is a fundamental problem in natural language processing (NLP). Traditional machine learning methods such as support vector machine (SVM) [4] and Naive Bayes [17] are only suitable for small-scale text classification tasks. For datasets with large amounts of data, these methods require manual feature extraction, which can be time-consuming and resource-intensive.

Convolutional neural networks (CNN) [1] and recurrent neural networks (RNN) [3] are being used to extract semantic information from continuous word sequences. These models could be more extensive in capturing long-distance and global semantic information. TextGCN [18] utilizes nodes and edges in a graph structure to represent relationships between words and updates its text representation by considering neighboring nodes. To reduce memory consumption, Huang et al. construct text-level graphs for each text and propose a Text-level GNN model [6]. TextING [19] uses GNN for inductive learning in previous work.

© The Author(s), under exclusive license to Springer Nature Switzerland AG 2023
Z. Jin et al. (Eds.): KSEM 2023, LNAI 14119, pp. 66–77, 2023.
https://doi.org/10.1007/978-3-031-40289-0_6

The graph-based methods rely on a single aggregation model in the node update process, conveying insufficient neighborhood information.

In this research, we introduce a novel method for text classification using neural graph networks called MA-TGNN. Unlike previous GNN models, we construct individual graphs for each document using a sliding window. The word embeddings are propagated to neighboring nodes using a gated graph neural network, and we utilize four popular aggregation techniques (mean, max, standard deviation, and normalized moments). After dual pooling, nodes preserve the critical information through concatenation, and the resulting aggregates represent the text.

To validate the effectiveness of our proposed model, we conducted experiments on seven datasets commonly used in text classification research. Our model outperforms TextCNN, TextRNN, FastText, Transformer, Bert, TextGCN, TextlevelGCN, and TextING on most benchmark datasets. Our main contributions can be summarized as follows:

- We propose a GNN classification model based on a multi-aggregator. By utilizing multiple aggregation methods, our model can aggregate more comprehensive feature information from neighboring nodes to obtain a final node representation.
- We perform dimensionality reduction stitching on the aggregated values to mitigate the loss of critical information and enable accurate predictions.

2   Related Work

2.1   Machine Learning and Convolutional Neural Network

The researchers divided prevalent text classification methods into feature-based and neural network-based categories. The first category of models mainly uses feature extraction for text classification. Specifically, it allows the model to extract as much essential information from the text as possible and use machine learning algorithms [7] for sorting. At the same time, these methods require manual feature extraction, which is inefficient and time-consuming and cannot effectively utilize a large amount of data. The second category uses deep neural networks for classification. Text classification models based on CNN convert words into word vectors and perform feature extraction through CNN. Text classification based on RNN and their variants focuses on the semantic order between words. It proposes a hierarchical attention network, focusing on more critical parts when learning text representations.

2.2   Graph Neural Network

The graph structure contains a vast amount of information [11]. Wei et al. [16]first proposed the concept of GNN in text classification. At present, The researchers divided all methods into three types: graph convolutional network (GCN), graph attention network (GAT) [10], and gated graph neural network

(GGNN) [8]. In addition, GCN adopts the frequency-domain convolution method of the graph, and GraphSAGE [5] adopts the spatial convolution method of the chart to obtain the feature representation of this node by fusing the neighbor nodes of the current node. However, in the actual scenario, the importance of the neighbor node to the central node differs. GAT adaptively matches the weight of the neighbor node by introducing a self-attention mechanism. GGNN uses the Gated Recurrent Unit(GRU) to obtain the weight of neighboring nodes.

2.3   Neighbourhood Aggregation

An aggregator [2] is a continuous function that computes information from neighboring nodes, and a single aggregation method, such as mean or max, has traditionally been used. Each node is updated through the embedding of its neighborhood (which includes the node itself). Some aggregators cannot distinguish nearby messages for a single GNN layer and a continuous input feature space. Predecessors argue that multiple aggregators have complementary relationships and that using numerous aggregators can solve this problem.

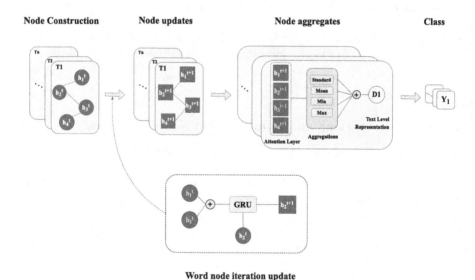

Fig. 1. The overall framework of the MA-TGNN model, this model contains three parts: node construction, node updates, and node aggregates. We create the graph with a sliding window, update the node itself, and aggregate the neighboring nodes into a text representation.

3   Model Structure

We propose a new text classification graph network consisting of three parts: node construction, node updates, and node aggregates. The overall framework of the model is illustrated in Fig. 1. This section will describe how the model achieves these three functions and how they work in detail.

3.1   Node Construction

This section will transform the entire text into a text-level graph based on the intrinsic relationships between words. This process is different from GCN, which constructs a corpus-level graph by processing all the words in the corpus. Specifically, we will follow these steps to create a text-level graph for a given text:

$$\mathcal{G} = (\mathcal{E}, \mathcal{N}) \tag{1}$$

In Eq. (1). $\mathcal{G}$ refers to a graph composed of a set of vertices $\mathcal{N}$ and edges $\mathcal{E}$. Co-occurrence describes the relationship between words within a sliding window of fixed size. We downplay the significance of long-range word relationships in the text, but this does not imply that we discard such relationships. In the node graph construction stage, we utilize GNN only for the initial node representation of words. In the subsequent node update and aggregation phase, we hierarchically combine the feature information of the word with the context information.

We preprocessed the text using standard techniques, including tokenization and removing stop words. The embeddings of vertices are initialized with the word features, represented as $\mathbf{h} \in \mathbb{R}^{|\mathcal{V}| \times d}$, where d denotes the size of the embedding.

3.2   Node Updates

Based on the node graph we constructed, we update the node representation using a gate graph neural network. This network uses a GRU to learn the information of neighboring nodes associated with the node and then merge with its representation to update its state. We illustrate the node update process, in which we superimpose t times to achieve high-order feature fusion as much as possible. The overall is as follows:

$$\mathbf{h}^t = \mathrm{GRU}\left(\mathbf{h}^{t-1}, \mathbf{x}^t\right) \tag{2}$$

In Eq. (2). x^t is the node representation after the dimension splicing of the adjacent node of the h^{t-1} node.

3.3   Node Aggregates

After updating the word nodes sufficiently, we combine them into a graphical representation of the document and predict the label it belongs to. This study defines an aggregator as a continuous function of multiple sets that calculates a statistic on adjacent nodes. We utilize four distinct independent aggregators: mean, maximum, minimum, and standard value aggregation functions.

The Mean Message Aggregator calculates the weighted mean or sum of incoming messages. It uses the weighted average node to compute the text representation, which gives more importance to valuable and meaningful words and learns the text representation for them. For clarity, we define the following:

$$\mu(X) = \mathbb{E}[X], \quad h_{mean} = \frac{1}{d_i} \sum_{j \in N(i)} X_j^l \tag{3}$$

The Eq. (3) presents the general average equation on the left-hand side and the direct domain formula on the right-hand side. X represents any multiset, X^l denotes the nodes' features at layer l. $N(i)$ denotes the neighborhood of node i. To ensure clarity, we define $\mathbb{E}[f(X)]$ as the expected value of a function f applied to a multiset X of size d, which can be expressed as $\mathbb{E}[f(X)] = \frac{1}{d} \sum_{x \in X} f(x)$.

The Maximum and Minimum aggregators are useful for discrete tasks and extrapolating unknown distributions onto graphs.

$$h_{max} = \max_{j \in N(i)} X_j^l \tag{4}$$

$$h_{min} = \min_{j \in N(i)} X_j^l \tag{5}$$

The Eq. (4) and Eq. (5) can preserve the most significant features of each node by utilizing the max-pooling and min-pooling operators.

Standard deviation aggregation is a statistical method used to measure the variability or spread of a set of data values. In the context of network analysis, it can quantify the diversity of signals that neighboring nodes send to a particular node. By calculating the standard deviation of the signals received from neighboring nodes, a node can understand how different or similar the signals are and use that information to make decisions or take action.

$$\sigma(X) = \sqrt{\mathbb{E}\left[X^2\right] - \mathbb{E}[X]^2} \tag{6}$$

$$h_{std} = \sqrt{\operatorname{ReLU}\left(\mu_i\left(X^{l2}\right) - \mu_i\left(X^l\right)^2\right) + \epsilon} \tag{7}$$

The Eq. (6) provides the formula for calculating the standard deviation, while the Eq. (7) provides the formula for calculating the standard deviation for the neighborhood of a node. The ReLU is a rectified linear unit used to prevent the generation of negative values.

We will combine the results obtained from various aggregations to create a comprehensive overview. The process is as follows:

$$h_{\mathcal{G}} = h_{mean} \oplus h_{max} \oplus h_{min} \oplus h_{std} \tag{8}$$

In Eq. (8), $\oplus$ represents dimensional stitching.

Finally, we predict the labels of the resulting graph vector using the softmax layer and minimize the loss using the cross-entropy function. The process is as follows:

$$\mathbf{Y} = \mathrm{softmax}\,(\mathbf{W}h_{\mathcal{G}} + \mathbf{b}) \tag{9}$$

$$\mathcal{L} = -\sum_i y_i \log\,(\mathbf{Y}_i) \tag{10}$$

In Eq. (9) and Eq. (10). The variables W and b are used as weights and biases, while y_i represents the one-hot encoding of the i-th text.

4 Experiment

This section focuses on training and evaluating the model's overall performance.

4.1 Dataset

The benchmark dataset consists of seven text corpora, which include two short text dichotomous datasets (MR and SST2), two short text multiclassification datasets (SST1 and TREC), and three long text multiclassification datasets (R8, R52, and Ohsumed).

- **MR**[1] [12]: A movie reviews dataset, primarily used for sentiment analysis, contains positive and negative reviews.
- **SST1**[2] [14]: An enhanced version of the MR dataset includes a more detailed sentiment polarity comprising five emotional categories.
- **SST2**: An expanded version of the MR dataset includes emotional polarity, divided into positive and negative categories.
- **TREC**[3]: The spam dataset is primarily categorized into six categories.
- **R8**[4]: They are primarily sourced from Reuters institutional news, including financial news, natural science, and eight other categories.
- **R52**: They are similar to R8, but contains 52 classes.
- **Ohsumed**[5]: The MEDLINE database is a bibliographic database of crucial medical literature maintained by the National Library of Medicine.

Table 1. Overview of Datasets

Dateset	Doc	Train	Test	Words	Classes	Avg_Length
MR	10661	9596	1065	18764	2	19.44
SST2	9612	8652	960	4516	2	19.62
SST1	11854	10670	1184	4683	5	19.17
TREC	5951	5357	594	1237	6	6.41
R8	7673	6907	766	7688	8	65.72
R52	9099	8190	909	8892	52	69.82
Ohsumed	7400	3357	4043	14157	23	121.59

We preprocess all datasets to remove non-English characters, stop words, and low frequencies that occur less than five times. However, due to their short text length, we abandon these methods for datasets SST1, SST2, MR, and TREC. The resulting processed dataset is presented in Table 1.

4.2 Baseline

We are comparing our MA-TGNN text classification model to several other baselines, including the Convolutional neural network model, Language representation pre-trained model, and Graph neural networks.

Convolutional neural network model:

- **TextCNN** embeds words into the convolutional network's training layer through the convolution operation and trains the output text representation using the softmax layer.
- **TextRNN** is achieved by using the hidden state of the last recurrent layer as the output representation of the text rather than simply outputting a prediction.
- **FastText** [9] extends CBOW by including subword n-gram features in the input and predicting document categories as output.

Language representation pre-trained model:

- **Transformer** [13] uses the Self-Attention structure to replace the RNN network structure in NLP tasks and connects encoders and decoders. Because we only need to implement the text classification task, we only use the encoder part.
- **Bert** [15]originates from Transformer. Bert's model has powerful language representation ability. We use Google open source pre-trained model – Bert Base model, which we directly followed by a softmax layer for text classification prediction.

---

[1] https://www.cs.cornell.edu/people/pabo/movie-review-data/.
[2] https://nlp.stanford.edu/sentiment/code.html.
[3] https://plg.uwaterloo.ca/~gvcormac/treccorpus06/about.html.
[4] https://martin-thoma.com/nlp-reuters/.
[5] http://disi.unitn.it/moschitti/corpora.htm.

Graph neural network model:

- **TextGCN** is the earliest graph convolutional network used for text classification, which establishes a corpus-level graph based on word co-occurrence, then learns the node text representation through a two-layer convolutional network.
- **TextLevelGCN**[6] no longer builds a corpus-level graph. It builds a graph for each text and updates the text.
- **TextING**[7] uses GNN to build graphics for each input text and updates nodes through GRU to realize inductive learning of new words.

4.3 Experimental Setting

To compare our work with previous researchers, we have split the training set into a ratio of 9:1 for validation and testing purposes. We have set the embedding node size to 300 and the hidden size to 96 and selected Adam as the optimizer. In line with standard practice, we have set the learning rate to 0.001 and the dropout rate to 0.5. If the loss does not decrease for ten consecutive cycles or after 200 cycles, we stop training the model.

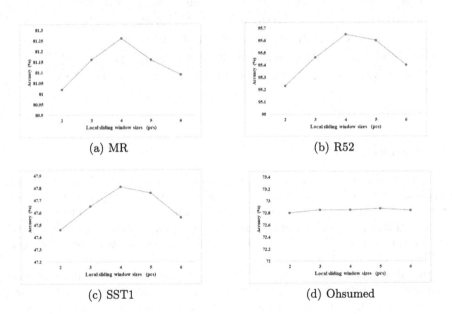

(a) MR

(b) R52

(c) SST1

(d) Ohsumed

Fig. 2. Test accuracy with different local sliding window sizes on datasets MR, SST1, R52, and Ohsumed. For fairness, our model performs best when the window size is 4.

All baseline models use the same Glove.6B.300d pre-trained word vectors for embedding to ensure a fair comparison.

---

[6] https://github.com/mojave-pku/TextLevelGCN.
[7] https://github.com/CRIPAC-DIG/TextING.

4.4 Dynamic Parameter Setting

Choosing the optimal sliding window size during the graph construction phase is crucial. Based on Fig. 2, a sliding window size of 4 is optimal for the short text dataset.

Additionally, the window size has minimal impact on the results for the Ohsumed dataset, which contains longer texts. We will use a default sliding window size of 4 for all experiments to ensure fairness in our experimental comparisons.

Table 2. Accuracy of different methods in all datasets

Model	MR	SST2	SST1	TREC	R8	R52	Ohsumed
TextCNN	78.03	82.92	<u>47.04</u>	93.43	95.56	87.59	51.27
TextRNN	77.65	81.25	42.48	88.05	93.08	90.54	49.24
FastText	74.55	75.36	36.44	88.89	94.65	92.81	52.34
Transformer	71.74	72.29	38.34	85.52	90.6	90.12	60.87
Bert	**85.26**	87.92	46.87	97.96	96.74	94.3	70.5
TextGCN	76.4	85.69	40.63	95.3	97.02	93.6	68.4
TextLevelGCN	72.84	83.56	44.65	93.46	96.1	91.7	54.1
TextING	80.4	**88.94**	46.73	<u>98.4</u>	<u>97.07</u>	<u>94.36</u>	<u>70.56</u>
MA-TGNN(ours)	<u>81.26</u>	<u>88.08</u>	**47.81**	**98.96**	**98.01**	**95.65**	**72.85**

4.5 Results

We give the test accuracy for each model in Table 2. Graph-based methods have advantages over traditional deep learning methods and can outperform language representation models on specific datasets. It indicates their superiority in text classification. Our model performs better than previous methods on the long text and multi-class classification tasks while achieving good results on the short text and binary classification tasks.

Specifically, on the MR and SST1 datasets, our approach maintains a top-tier accuracy, demonstrating its effectiveness in handling short text and two-class classification tasks. Our model improves the best baselines on other datasets by 1.08%, 0.56%, 1.01%, 1.29%, and 2.29% for SST1, TREC, R8, R52, and Ohsumed.

The effect on the TREC dataset is insignificant because of its short text length, which cannot fully leverage our model's capabilities. Our model shows the most remarkable improvement on the Ohsumed dataset, which has the longest text length.

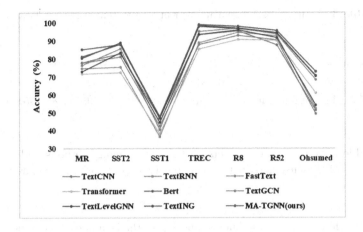

Fig. 3. The capability of model application.

Our model can extract more information for longer text through various aggregation methods. As shown in Fig. 3, multiple aggregation functions can provide more comprehensive feature information. Under mostly the same parameter settings, MA-TGNN outperforms previous works, which benefits text classification.

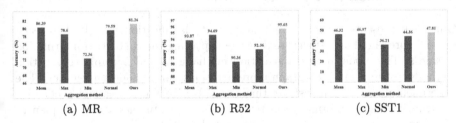

(a) MR   (b) R52   (c) SST1

Fig. 4. The text accuracy under different aggregation methods is in the MR, R52, and SST1 datasets.

4.6 Ablation Study

This part conducts the ablation experiment; the results are shown in Fig. 4. We tested various single aggregation functions and observed that they produced different results. In Table 3, we further explore the influence of the number of aggregators on classification accuracy. We noticed that the single aggregation function's performance decreased compared to the multiple aggregation functions. It shows that the aggregated features of the single aggregation function still need to be completed.

Table 3. Accuracy of different number of aggregators in partial datasets

Aggregator	MR	SST1	Ohsumed
Single (max)	78.6	46.97	94.69
Double+Dimension (max+mean) reduction splicing	79.32	47.22	94.88
Multiple+Dimension reduction splicing	**81.26**	**47.81**	**95.65**

In Table 4, we explore the effects of different splicing methods and find that the method of dimension reduction splicing is helpful to improve classification accuracy.

Table 4. Accuracy of different splicing methods in partial datasets

Aggregator	MR	SST1	Ohsumed
Multiple+Splicing	80.79	47.24	94.96
Multiple+Dimension reduction splicing	**81.26**	**47.81**	**95.65**

5 Conclusion and Future Works

Our work presents a novel graph-based text classification model where each text is represented as a structure diagram capturing the contextual information of words. The model uses self-attention mechanisms and multiple aggregation methods to learn node and graph representations during node aggregation. The experimental results demonstrate that the MA-TGNN model is highly effective in achieving high performance in text classification. In the future, we plan to add domain word prior information of related fields to improve the accuracy of the text classification task.

Acknowledgments. This work is supported by the Science &Technology project (4411700474, 441 1500476).

References

1. Ce, P., Tie, B.: An analysis method for interpretability of CNN text classification model. Future Internet **12**(12), 228 (2020)
2. Corso, G., Cavalleri, L., Beaini, D., Liò, P., Veličković, P.: Principal neighbourhood aggregation for graph nets. Adv. Neural. Inf. Process. Syst. **33**, 13260–13271 (2020)
3. Du, J., Vong, C.M., Chen, C.P.: Novel efficient RNN and LSTM-like architectures: recurrent and gated broad learning systems and their applications for text classification. IEEE Trans. Cybern. **51**(3), 1586–1597 (2020)

4. Goudjil, M., Koudil, M., Bedda, M., Ghoggali, N.: A novel active learning method using SVM for text classification. Int. J. Autom. Comput. **15**, 290–298 (2018)
5. Hamilton, W., Ying, Z., Leskovec, J.: Inductive representation learning on large graphs. In: Advances in Neural Information Processing Systems, vol. 30 (2017)
6. Huang, L., Ma, D., Li, S., Zhang, X., Wang, H.: Text level graph neural network for text classification. arXiv preprint arXiv:1910.02356 (2019)
7. Kadhim, A.I.: Survey on supervised machine learning techniques for automatic text classification. Artif. Intell. Rev. **52**(1), 273–292 (2019)
8. Li, Y., Tarlow, D., Brockschmidt, M., Zemel, R.: Gated graph sequence neural networks. arXiv preprint arXiv:1511.05493 (2015)
9. Liao, M., Shi, B., Bai, X., Wang, X., Liu, W.: Textboxes: a fast text detector with a single deep neural network. In: Thirty-First AAAI Conference on Artificial Intelligence (2017)
10. Linmei, H., Yang, T., Shi, C., Ji, H., Li, X.: Heterogeneous graph attention networks for semi-supervised short text classification. In: Proceedings of the 2019 Conference on Empirical Methods in Natural Language Processing and the 9th International Joint Conference on Natural Language Processing (EMNLP-IJCNLP), pp. 4821–4830 (2019)
11. Malekzadeh, M., Hajibabaee, P., Heidari, M., Zad, S., Uzuner, O., Jones, J.H.: Review of graph neural network in text classification. In: 2021 IEEE 12th Annual Ubiquitous Computing, Electronics & Mobile Communication Conference (UEMCON), pp. 0084–0091. IEEE (2021)
12. Pang, B., Lee, L.: Seeing stars: exploiting class relationships for sentiment categorization with respect to rating scales. arXiv preprint cs/0506075 (2005)
13. Raffel, C., et al.: Exploring the limits of transfer learning with a unified text-to-text transformer. J. Mach. Learn. Res. **21**(140), 1–67 (2020)
14. Socher, R., et al.: Recursive deep models for semantic compositionality over a sentiment treebank. In: Proceedings of the 2013 Conference on Empirical Methods in Natural Language Processing, pp. 1631–1642 (2013)
15. Tenney, I., Das, D., Pavlick, E.: Bert rediscovers the classical NLP pipeline. arXiv preprint arXiv:1905.05950 (2019)
16. Wei, K., Iyer, R., Bilmes, J.: Submodularity in data subset selection and active learning. In: International Conference on Machine Learning, pp. 1954–1963. PMLR (2015)
17. Xu, S.: Bayesian naïve bayes classifiers to text classification. J. Inf. Sci. **44**(1), 48–59 (2018)
18. Yao, L., Mao, C., Luo, Y.: Graph convolutional networks for text classification. In: Proceedings of the AAAI Conference on Artificial Intelligence, vol. 33, pp. 7370–7377 (2019)
19. Zhang, Y., Yu, X., Cui, Z., Wu, S., Wen, Z., Wang, L.: Every document owns its structure: inductive text classification via graph neural networks. arXiv preprint arXiv:2004.13826 (2020)

Multi-display Graph Attention Network for Text Classification

Xinyue Bao[1](✉), Zili Zhou[1](✉), Shiliang Gao[1], Zhaoan Dong[2], and Yuanyuan Lin[1]

[1] School of Cyber Science and Engineering, Qufu Normal University, Qufu 273165, Shandong, China
bxy156503917680163.com, zzl@qfnu.edu.cn
[2] School of Computer Science, Qufu Normal University, Qufu 273165, Shandong, China

Abstract. Text classification, a fundamental task in natural language processing, has been extensively studied by researchers worldwide. The primary focus of text classification is on extracting effective features from text, as accurate information extraction is crucial for the task. However, the current utilization of text information in text classification is not optimal, and thus, effective extraction of text information remains an important research topic. Graph attention networks (GATs) have gained popularity among researchers due to their excellent performance in various tasks, including text classification. Additionally, previous graph neural network-derived models only address the differences in importance of edges within nodes during the information aggregation process, but ignore the importance differences between different nodes. But, the correlation between nodes also needs to be exploited for a more comprehensive understanding of the text. In this paper, we propose a novel multi-display graph attention network (MDGAT)-based model to address the challenges of inadequate text information capture and higher-order interactions between words. Our approach involves fusing multiple display graphs to capture diverse features of the text, for comprehensive text information representation. Additionally, we introduce a new information aggregation method called multi-step information aggregation, which considers the importance within nodes and the correlation between nodes, leading to improved text representation learning. We validate the performance of our proposed method through extensive experiments on various benchmark datasets. The results demonstrate the superior performance of our approach in text classification tasks.

Keywords: Text classification · multi-display graph attention network · multi-step information aggregation

1 Introduction

Text classification is a critical task in natural language processing, involving the categorization of text into specific categories using predefined rules and algorithms [1]. It has garnered significant attention from scholars worldwide over the

© The Author(s), under exclusive license to Springer Nature Switzerland AG 2023
Z. Jin et al. (Eds.): KSEM 2023, LNAI 14119, pp. 78–93, 2023.
https://doi.org/10.1007/978-3-031-40289-0_7

past decade. Text classification finds applications in various domains, including sentiment analysis, news classification, medical diagnosis, question and answer systems, conversational behavior classification, natural language inference, and many others [2].

Text classification methods can be broadly categorized into two categories: those based on shallow learning, and those based on deep learning. Deep learning-based methods can be further subdivided into sequence-based methods and graph-based methods. Sequence-based methods, such as convolutional neural networks (CCN) [3], recurrent neural networks (RNN, LSTM, GRU) [4–6], etc., have been commonly used in the past few years for text classification. These methods are effective in capturing text features from local sequences of consecutive words. Recently, graph-based learning methods have gained wide attention in the field of text classification. Examples of such methods include graph neural networks (GNNs) [7,8], graph convolutional neural networks (GCNs) [9], and graph attention networks (GATs) [10]. These methods are capable of directly processing complex structured data, and numerous researchers have demonstrated that utilizing graph structures can lead to improved performance in text classification tasks.One notable graph-based model is the graph attention network (GAT) proposed by Yoshua Bengio's group [11]. The GAT model builds on GNN by aggregating edges into target nodes as information and introducing an attention mechanism to highlight the importance of neighboring nodes. Another notable model is TEXTGCN proposed by Yao et al. [12,13], which is a text graph-based neural network that achieves state-of-the-art performance in some benchmark datasets for text classification. In the TEXTGCN framework, text graphs are constructed based on sequential contextual relationships between words, followed by the use of a GCN to learn the text graph.

Despite achieving good results initially, there is still a limitation in capturing higher-order interactions between words in text classification tasks. For example, the surface meaning of a close combination of words, such as "let your hair down", may be misunderstood by traditional graph-based neural networks as "put your hair down" when the intended meaning is actually "relax", leading to misjudgment of the entire text. To address this issue, scholars in China and abroad have conducted a series of studies. However, it is important to note that existing GAT-based approaches do not fully exploit the syntactic information of the text and ignore the syntactic structure between words. In longer texts with more complex structures, richer information needs to be captured for better representation learning of the text. Therefore, it is necessary to consider more contextual information, such as syntactic, semantic, and thematic information, for improved performance. Additionally, previous graph neural network-derived models only address the differences in importance of edges within nodes during the information aggregation process, but ignore the importance differences between different nodes. Thus, the correlation between nodes also needs to be exploited for a more comprehensive understanding of the text.

To achieve this goal, we propose a new multi-display graph attention network (MDGAT) model that aims to fully extract multiple information from text, including syntactic, grammatical, semantic, and thematic information.

Evaluate our approach on five benchmark datasets and demonstrate that our model outperforms several baselines, achieving new state-of-the-art performance. Our contributions can be summarized as follows:

1. we construct multiple display graphs from different perspectives, such as syntactic, grammatical, semantic, and thematic perspectives, to comprehensively capture text information [14–16]. To highlight the importance of different information in the text, we assign different weights to each graph. These graphs are then fused using weighted accumulation to fully obtain syntactic, grammatical, semantic, topic, and other relevant information from the text.
2. The MDGAT model is proposed with the aim of efficiently aggregating graph structure information. The proposed multi-step aggregation method incorporates information for importance within nodes and correlation between nodes, which can perform better text representation learning and enhanced capture of higher-order interactions between words. Additionally, gated cyclic units are employed to aggregate contextual information, effectively transforming the graph structure into a sequence structure while preserving the sequential structure of the text. This approach contributes to better text representation and improved modeling of inter-word dependencies
3. Extensive experiments were conducted on multiple benchmark datasets to highlight the superior performance of MDGAT compared to other methods in text classification tasks.

2   Related Work

Recently, GNNs have gained significant attention and achieved remarkable success in various graph learning tasks. Most popular graph neural network models follow the neighborhood aggregation paradigm, which aims to learn node representations by exchanging messages among local neighbors in the graph. Yao et al. applied GCN to text classification tasks [12,13], using words as nodes and employing mean pooling for domain aggregation. GAT aggregated edge relations into nodes as information and combined trainable attention weights to focus on aggregating node information. The subsequent HyperGAT model [17], for the first time, combined hypergraphs [18,19] with GAT, using sentence-level structure as a cutoff for information aggregation. The BERTGCN model proposed by Shannon's team [20] fused BERT [21] and GAT to process text sequences and then selected the optimal output using valves, effectively combining the advantages of BERT and GAT. The DAGNN model proposed by Liu et al. [22] addressed the issue of interaction between distant words using the attention diffusion mechanism. Zheng Zhang et al. proposed the SSEGCN model [23] to obtain syntactic structure information of a sentence by constructing the syntactic mask matrix of the sentence. However, there are still challenges in preserving the text order when dealing with longer text data and fully capturing the underlying information of the text using graph structures. Our proposed model, MDGAT, is the first attempt to fuse multiple display graphs to fully capture richer information from different perspectives.

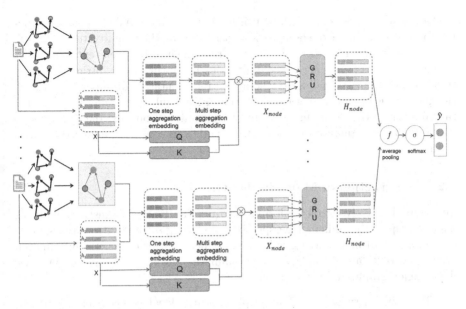

Fig. 1. The overall architecture of MDGAT.

3   Methods

In this study, we propose the MDGAT (Multi-Display Graph Attention Network) model, which utilizes the GAT as the base component. The general architecture of MDGAT is illustrated in Fig. 1. In this section, we will provide detailed explanations of MDGAT, including the GAT, construction of multi-display graphs, graph-level representation learning, and inductive text classification.

3.1   Application of Graph Attention Network on Text Classification

With the rapid advancement of deep learning techniques, graph structures have become increasingly popular for text representation learning. Many state-of-the-art graph-based models utilize the GNN aggregation approach, where node representations are updated by aggregating information from neighboring nodes in the graph. However, Graph Attention Network (GAT) introduces edge information by assigning different importance factors, or attention coefficients, to nodes in the aggregation process:

$$h_j^{'l-1} = \alpha_{ij} \cdot W h_j \tag{1}$$

$$h_i^l = Aggregate(h_i^{l-1}, h_j^{'l-1}) \tag{2}$$

where h_i^l is the node representation of the node at layer l, α_{ij} is the attention coefficient of node j, W is the weight matrix, $h_j^{'l-1}$ is the node representation at layer l-1 given different importance, and *Aggregate* is the aggregation function.

Graph structures, such as those utilized in GNN and GAT, have shown superior performance in text classification tasks due to their ability to model the connections between words and represent relationships between texts. However, simple graph structures may have limitations in capturing the intricate interactions between words, leading to incomplete representation of important syntactic, grammatical, and thematic information. As a result, it remains a challenging task to extract the maximum amount of information from text data in order to enhance the performance of graph-based models in capturing nuanced features of the text.

3.2   Construction of Multi-display Graph

To comprehensively extract information from the text, we construct multiple display graphs from different perspectives, including sentence structure, syntax, semantics, and topic. These graphs are designed to capture diverse information about the text, and include the text similarity graph, hypergraph, syntactic dependency graph, and topic graph.

(1) Text similarity graph: This graph captures local co-occurrence patterns between neighboring words in the text. We use a sliding window of fixed size to collect co-occurrence statistics, and calculate the weight between two word nodes using point-wise mutual information (PMI). The text similarity graph is denoted as $G1 = (V, E)$, where $V = v_1, v_2, ..., v_n$ represents the nodes representing words, and $E = e_1, e_2, ..., e_n$ represents the similarity between two neighboring words. The weight between two word nodes is calculated using the formula:

$$e_{ij} = \log \frac{p(i, j)}{p(i)p(j)} \tag{3}$$

$$p(i, j) = \frac{\#w(i, j)}{\#w} \tag{4}$$

$$p(i) = \frac{\#w(j)}{\#w} \tag{5}$$

where $\#W(i)$ is the number of sliding windows containing word i in the corpus; $\#W(i, j)$ is the number of sliding windows containing both word i and j; $\#W$ is the total number of sliding windows in the corpus

(2) Text hypergraph: This graph captures the relationships between words and sentences in the text. We construct the text hypergraph denoted as $G2 = (V, \varepsilon)$ to consider both the sentence structure and the word-sentence relationships. Here, $V = v_1, v_2, ..., v_n$ represents the nodes representing words, and $\varepsilon = e_1, e_2, ..., e_n$ represents the hyperedges, which are represented by the sentences where the words are located.

$$e_{ij} = \begin{cases} 1 & \text{if} \quad v_i \in e_j \\ 0 & \text{if} \quad v_i \notin e_j \end{cases} \tag{6}$$

(3) Syntactic dependency graph: We construct the syntactic dependency graph denoted as $G3 = (V, E)$ by extracting the syntactic dependencies of the text, which allows us to capture the syntactic information of the text. In this graph, nodes $V = v_1, v_2, ..., v_n$ are represented by words, and edges $E = e_1, e_2, ..., e_n$ represent the word-to-word dependencies.

$$e_{ij} = \frac{N_{syn}(i, j)}{N_{total}(i, j)} \tag{7}$$

where $N_{total}(i, j)$ denotes the number of times word i and word j are present in the same sentence in the entire corpus; $N_{syn}(i, j)$ denotes the number of times word i and word j have syntactic dependencies on all sentences in the corpus.

(4) Topic graph: To improve the accuracy of text topic prediction, we construct a topic graph. First, we employ the LDA model to mine the probability distribution of relevant topic words in the text data. Then, for each topic, we select the top k words with the highest probability as the set of topic candidates denoted as $T = t_1, t_2, ..., t_k$. These topic candidates are used to construct the nodes in the topic graph $G4 = (V, E)$.

For ease of use, we define the topology of the graph in the form of an adjacency matrix.

$$A_{ij} = \begin{cases} 1 & if e_{ij} \in \delta \\ 0 & if e_{ij} \notin \delta \end{cases} \tag{8}$$

where δ is a specific condition satisfied by different graphs. Since different information has different importance to the sentence, we make the graphs multiply with different weight matrices separately in order to distinguish the importance of each graph, and then accumulate them for the purpose of fusion:

$$A = \sum_{i=0}^{N} W_i A_i \tag{9}$$

where N is the number of graphs, A_i denotes the ith display graph, W_i and denotes the weight matrix of the ith display graph.

In general, each node in the graph is associated with a d-dimensional attribute vector denoted by $X = x_1, x_2, ..., x_n \in R^{n \times d}$. This attribute vector allows us to represent the entire graph $G = (A, X)$, where A is the adjacency matrix representing the connections between nodes, and X is the node attribute matrix representing the features of the nodes.

3.3 Graph-Level Representation Learning

To enhance the representation learning on the constructed fusion graph, we propose an improved information aggregation mechanism called multi-step information aggregation, building upon the aggregation method of GAT.

The multi-step information aggregation process involves several steps. Firstly, for each node i in the graph, the neighbor nodes k of all nodes j that are connected to i through edges are aggregated into node j, resulting in multi-step neighbor node information. Next, the multi-step neighbor node information is combined with the upper layer information of the target node i. Finally, the combined information is aggregated into the target node i, incorporating information from multiple steps of neighbor nodes. This multi-step information aggregation mechanism allows for more comprehensive and refined information integration during the graph neural network learning process.

$$f_j^l = Aggregate1^l(h_k^{l-1}|\forall v_k \in \delta_j) \qquad (10)$$

$$h_j^l = Aggregate2^l(h_i^{l-1}|\forall v_j \in \varepsilon_j) \qquad (11)$$

where δ_j is the set of neighbor nodes of node j and ε_j is the set of neighbor nodes of node i. And $Aggregate1^l$ and $Aggregate2^l$ are the aggregation functions for multi-step neighbor node aggregation and neighbor node aggregation, respectively, which are implemented as follows:

$$u_k = LeakyReLU(W_i h_k^{l-1}) \qquad (12)$$

$$p(i) = \frac{\exp(a_1^T \mu_k)}{\sum_{v_k \in \Delta_j} \exp(a_q^T \mu_p)} \qquad (13)$$

$$f_j^l = \sigma(\sum_{v_k \in \Delta_j} \alpha_{jk} W_1 h_j^{l-1}) \qquad (14)$$

where W_1 is the weight matrix, h_k^{l-1} is the upper layer information of neighbor node k, a_1^T is the weight vector used to measure the importance of neighbor nodes, and σ is a nonlinear function.

$$v_j = LeakyReLU([W_2 f_j^l || W_1 h_i^{l-1}]) \qquad (15)$$

$$p(i) = \frac{\exp(a_2^T v_j)}{\sum_{v_j \in \varepsilon_i} \exp(a_2^T v_p)} \qquad (16)$$

$$h_i^l = \sigma(\sum_{v_j \in \varepsilon_i} \beta_{ij} W_2 f_j^l) \qquad (17)$$

where W_2 is the weight matrix, h_i^{l-1} is the upper layer information of node i, and a_2^T is the weight vector used to measure the importance of neighboring nodes.Get the set of nodes $H = \{h_1, h_2, ..., h_n\}$.

We have obtained the nodes after aggregating the information. However, considering that there may be differences in importance among nodes, we can now use self-attention to highlight the relevance of different nodes. One small change in the application of self-attention is that we use the node vector X, which contains unaggregated information, as input to calculate the attention coefficient. We then assign the resulting attention coefficient to the node vector H, which contains the aggregated information. This can be done as follows:

$$Q = XW^Q \tag{18}$$

$$K = XW^K \tag{19}$$

$$A_{self} = softmax\left(\frac{QK^T}{\sqrt{d_k}}\right) \tag{20}$$

$$X_{node} = A_{self}V \tag{21}$$

where X is the encoded vector, V is equal to the node H after information aggregation, $W^Q \in R_{d_x \times d_k}$ and $W^K \in R_{d_x \times d_k}$ are learnable weights. Finally, we get the node information $X_{node} = \{x_{node_1}, x_{node_2}, ..., x_{node_n}\}$ with correlation.

3.4 Inductive Text Classification

To preserve the sequential structure of the text and effectively capture contextual information, we utilize GRU (Gated Recurrent Unit) as loop units. This helps us consolidate the sequential relationships and successfully convert the graph structure into a sequential structure, resulting in the final word-level vector representation. The process can be described as follows:

$$z^t = \sigma(W_z \cdot [h^{t-1}, x_{node^t}]) \tag{22}$$

$$r^t = \sigma(W_r \cdot [h^{t-1}, x_{node^t}]) \tag{23}$$

$$\tilde{h}^t = \tanh(W \cdot [r^t * h^{t-1}, x_{node^t}]) \tag{24}$$

$$h^t_{node} = z^t * \tilde{h}^t + (1 - z^t) * h^{t-1} \tag{25}$$

where z^t is the update gate and r^t is the forget gate; $\tilde{h}^t$ is the new memory; x_{node} is the node vector output from GAT.

The document-level vector representation is obtained through the averaging pooling operation, which is implemented as follows:

$$h_{document} = avg - pooling(h_{node}) \tag{26}$$

Finally, the document-level vector representation is fed into a softmax layer for classification, resulting in the final label vector $\hat{y}$.

$$\hat{y} = sofemax(W_c h_{document} + b_c) \tag{27}$$

where $\hat{y}$ is the final predicted label; W_c is the parameter matrix that maps the document representation to the output space; and b_c is the bias.

3.5   Training

As our objective function, we utilize the cross entropy loss function.

$$L = -\sum_{d} log(\hat{y_j}^d) \tag{28}$$

where d denotes the document and j denotes the real tag.

4   Experiments

4.1   Datasets

We have chosen two types of datasets, namely long document and short document, as the benchmark corpus for our text classification task. The summary statistics of these datasets are provided in Table 1.

Table 1. Summary statistics of the evaluation datasets.

Dataset	20ng	R8	R52	ohsumed	MR
#Doc	18846	9100	7674	7400	10662
#Train	11314	6532	5485	3357	7108
#Test	7532	2568	2189	4043	3554
#Word	42757	8892	7688	14157	19764
#Avg Len	221.26	69.82	65.72	135.82	20.39
#Class	20	52	8	23	2

4.2   Baselines

To ensure a comprehensive evaluation of our model's performance, we compare our MDGAT model with three types of baseline models.

1. Word embedding-based approaches
   - **fastText** [24] treats text as a bag of words and incorporates n-gram features to capture word sequence information.
   - **SWEM** [25] pooling directly on word vectors.
2. Sequence-based approaches
   - **CNN** [3] proposes the use of convolutional neural networks for text classification, aiming to capture local relevance more effectively.
   - **LSTM** [26] controls the transmission state using gating mechanisms, which allows for effective capture of contextual information in the text.

- **Bi-LSTM** [27] combines the information of the input sequence in both forward and backward directions for bidirectional transmission, based on the LSTM architecture.
- **Graph-CNN** [13] converts text into a graph-of-words representation and applies graph convolution operation to convolve the word graph, capturing contextual information in the text.
3. Graph-based approaches
    - **Text-level GNN** [13] uses convolutional neural networks for text classification, aiming to capture local relevance more effectively.
    - **TextGCN** [12] controls the transmission state by gating the state, effectively capturing the contextual information of the text.
    - **HETEGCN** [28] proposes a heterogeneous graph convolutional network that combines the ideas of predictive text embedding and TextGCN. It splits the adjacency matrix into word-document and word-sub-matrices and fuses the representations of different layers when needed.
    - **TensorGCN** [29] constructs text tensor graphs to capture textual information and integrate heterogeneous information. It leverages the power of tensor operations for graph convolution to handle multi-modal data and capture higher-order interactions among text data.
    - **HyperGAT** [17] combines hypergraphs with GAT to capture higher-order interactions between words. Capturing complex dependencies and interactions that may not be effectively represented by traditional graphs.
    - **DADGNN** [22] addresses the long-range word interaction problem by widening the sensory domain using deep diffusion techniques. It also solves the oversmoothing problem of Graph Neural Networks by using decoupling techniques.
    - **BC+BL** [30] considers the text as a superposition of words, derives the wave function of the document, and calculates the transition probability from the document to the target class based on Born's rule.

4.3   Implementation Details

The experimental environment consisted of an Intel(R) Xeon(R) Gold 6254 CPU running at 3.10GHz, with PyTorch version 1.11.0, and optimized using the Adam optimizer. Five datasets, namely 20ng, R8, R52, ohsumed, and mr, were used in the experiments, and preprocessing operations were performed on the data. These operations included data cleaning, sentence splitting, and removal of words with less than 5 occurrences. The training set was further divided into a training set and a validation set with a ratio of 9:1. In this experiment, a batch size of 8, a learning rate of 0.001, and a dropout rate of 0.3 were set to achieve optimal accuracy.

To obtain word embeddings of dimension 300, pre-trained Glove embeddings were used. For constructing multi-display graphs, Stanford's coreNLP toolkit was utilized to extract text dependencies and construct syntactic dependency graphs. The training dataset was used to train LDA models, and the top 10 words with the highest probability from each topic were selected to form a candidate topic

Table 2. The result of test accuracy on document classification with different models.

Model	20ng	R8	R52	ohsumed	MR
TextCNN	0.8215 ± 0.0052	0.9571 ± 0.0052	0.8759 ± 0.0048	0.5833 ± 0.0106	0.7775 ± 0.0072
LSTM	0.6571 ± 0.0152	0.9368 ± 0.0082	0.8554 ± 0.0113	0.4114 ± 0.01117	0.7506 ± 0.0044
Bi-LSTM	0.7318 ± 0.0185	0.9631 ± 0.0033	0.9054 ± 0.0091	0.4927 ± 0.0107	0.7768 ± 0.0086
fastText	0.7938 ± 0.0030	0.9613 ± 0.0021	0.9281 ± 0.0009	0.5770 ± 0.0059	0.7514 ± 0.0020
Graph-CNN	0.8142 ± 0.0032	0.9699 ± 0.0012	0.9275 ± 0.0030	0.6386 ± 0.0053	0.7722 ± 0.0027
Text-level GNN	0.8416 ± 0.0025	0.9789 ± 0.0020	0.9460 ± 0.0030	0.6940 ± 0.0060	0.7547 ± 0.0006
HETEGCN	0.8715 ± 0.0015	0.9724 ± 0.0051	0.9435 ± 0.0025	0.6811 ± 0.0019	0.7671 ± 0.0033
HyperGAT	0.8662 ± 0.0016	0.9797 ± 0.0023	0.9498 ± 0.0027	0.6990 ± 0.0034	0.7832 ± 0.0027
TensorGCN	0.8774 ± 0.0005	0.9804 ± 0.0008	0.9505 ± 0.0011	0.7011 ± 0.0024	0.7791 ± 0.0007
DADGNN	-	0.9815 ± 0.0036	0.9516 ± 0.0022	-	**0.7864 ± 0.0029**
BL+BC	0.8740 ± 0.0001	0.9720 ± 0.0050	0.9440 ± 0.0080	-	-
MDGAT(our)	**0.9089 ± 0.0058**	**0.9904 ± 0.0035**	**0.9568 ± 0.0045**	**0.7628 ± 0.0036**	0.7808 ± 0.0012

Table 3. Experimental results of ablation study

Model	20ng	R8	R52	ohsumed	MR
w/o multi-display	0.8891	0.9735	0.9424	0.6973	0.7611
w/o GRU	0.7967	0.9640	0.9436	0.6604	0.7392
w/o attention	0.8814	0.9826	0.9245	0.6237	0.7676
MDGAT(1 layer)	0.9087	0.9852	0.9545	0.7289	0.7801
MDGAT	0.9089	0.9904	0.9568	0.7628	0.7808

set for constructing text topic graphs. For text similarity graphs, a window size of 8 was set for sliding window operation, and PMI was used to calculate similarity.

For the representation learning part, the hyperparameters of the MDGAT model were set as follows: initial size of 300, hidden size of 100, number of GAT layers of 2, and number of GRU layers of 1. Baseline models were compared with the results reported in the original paper and previous studies.

5   Results and Analysis

5.1   Experimental Results

To demonstrate the effectiveness of our MDGAT model, we conducted a comparison with previous works, and the results are presented in Table 2. The experimental findings indicate that our model outperforms other models on all datasets. The notable improvement of our model can be attributed to its capability to capture multiple perspectives, including grammar, semantics, syntax, and theme, to obtain multifaceted information from the text. This validates the effectiveness of our approach in gaining comprehensive access to information.

Furthermore, our model incorporates information acquisition based on sentence structure, which proves to be particularly beneficial for handling long documents. It is concluded for a large number of MR dataset-based methods

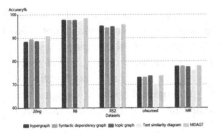

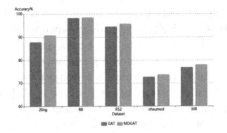

Fig. 2. Influence of different display layers on model accuracy

Fig. 3. Comparison of effects of multi-step polymerization, GAT and inattention on model accuracy.

that sequence-based approaches exhibit robust performance in sentiment classification tasks. Our model introduces gated cyclic units to capture sequential contextual information that may be overlooked by the graph structure, enabling efficient conversion from graph to sequence representation. As a result, our model achieves excellent performance in sentiment classification tasks as well.

5.2 Ablation Study

To investigate the effectiveness of each module in our MDGAT model, we conducted ablation experiments and the results are presented in Table 3. Using MDGAT as the control, we observed that reducing the multi-display graph to a single text similarity graph significantly degraded the model's performance, confirming the importance of rich text information for text classification tasks. Moreover, removing the GRU gating loop unit resulted in lower performance, highlighting the significance of aggregating sequential contextual information to enhance the performance of graph structured networks. Similarly, comparing the results of removing the attention module with our MDGAT results demonstrated the effectiveness of our proposed multi-step information aggregation attention mechanism for node representation learning. Lastly, reducing the number of model layers to 1 for comparison revealed that stacking more layers generally improved the model's performance for most datasets. These ablation experiments collectively emphasize the criticality of each module in our MDGAT model.

5.3 Analysis of Each Layer of the Module

Effect of Multi-display Graphs. In order to showcase the advantages of our multiple display graph energy module, we conducted experiments using five datasets and evaluated the impact of individual graphs as well as all possible combinations of them on the model's accuracy. The experimental results clearly demonstrate that our MDGAT model outperforms the other cases. As a visual representation of the experimental results, we selected the most representative single graph as the control, as depicted in Fig. 2. It can be observed that the text similarity graph only captures word co-occurrence relationships between neighboring words, the text hypergraph only captures the belonging relationships between sentences and words, and the syntactic dependency graph only captures the syntactic information of sentences. However, by utilizing the fusion of multiple display graphs, our model is able to comprehensively capture the intrinsic information of the text, resulting in significant improvements in model performance.

Effect of Multi-step Information Aggregation. In order to assess the effectiveness of our multi-step aggregation. We conducted a comparative analysis by comparing our MDGAT model with a baseline model that uses the traditional GAT (Graph Attention Network) aggregation approach, replacing our multi-step information aggregation approach. We evaluated the performance of both models on five different datasets, and the results are presented in Fig. 3. The results clearly indicate that using the original aggregation approach of traditional GAT for representation learning is not effective in capturing higher-order word interactions in the text. On the other hand, our MDGAT model outperforms both the traditional GAT and the baseline model in terms of performance. This demonstrates the superiority of our multi-step aggregation approach in improving the performance of our MDGAT model.

5.4   Visualization

In order to further highlight the superiority of our model, we used HyperGAT as the baseline for comparison with our MDGAT model. We visualized both models using t-SNE for the test set and the results are presented in Fig. 4. In the visualization, different colors represent different categories, and it is evident that our MDGAT model performs better in terms of separating different categories compared to the other models. This visual representation effectively demonstrates the superior performance of our MDGAT model in comparison to the baseline model.

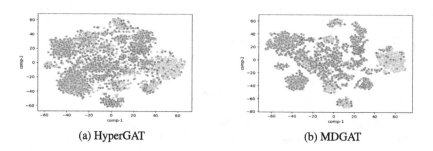

(a) HyperGAT   (b) MDGAT

Fig. 4. The t-SNE visiualization of difference for test documents on ohsumed.

6   Conclusion

In this paper, we propose the MDGAT model for text classification, which effectively captures multiple dimensions of textual information and performs robust representation learning. Our model includes several key components. Firstly, we introduce a multi-display graph fusion module that captures textual information from multiple perspectives, including syntax, semantics, syntax, and topic, to comprehensively represent the text. Secondly, we design a multi-step information aggregation approach for improved textual representation learning. Additionally, we incorporate the GRU (Gated Recurrent Unit) to bridge the gap between graph structure and sequential structure of text sequences, thereby enhancing the model's ability to capture contextual information. Finally, extensive experimental results demonstrate the effectiveness of our approach in achieving state-of-the-art performance in text classification tasks.

Acknowledgements. This work was supported in part by the Shandong Provincial Natural Science Foundation (No. ZR2020MF149) and (No. ZR2021MD115), in part by the Science and Technology Commission of Shanghai Municipality (21511100302).

References

1. Minaee, S., Kalchbrenner, N., Cambria, E., et al.: Deep learning-based text classification: a comprehensive review. ACM Comput. Surv. (CSUR) **54**(3), 1–40 (2021)
2. Marelli, M., Bentivogli, L., Baroni, M., Bernardi, R., Menini, S., Zamparelli, R.: Semeval-2014 task 1: evaluation of compositional distributional semantic models on full sentences through semantic relatedness and textual entailment. In: Proceedings of the 8th International Workshop on Semantic Evaluation (SemEval 2014), pp. 1–8 (2014)
3. Kim, Y.: Convolutional neural networks for sentence classification. In: Proceedings of the 2014 Conference on Empirical Methods in Natural Language Processing, pp. 1746–1751 (2014)
4. Liu, P., Qiu, X., Huang, X.: Recurrent neural network for text classification with multi-task learning. In: Proceedings of the Twenty-Fifth International Joint Conference on Artificial Intelligence, pp. 2873–2879 (2016)
5. Tai, K.S., Socher, R., Manning, C.D.: Improved Semantic Representations From Tree-Structured Long Short-Term Memory Networks: Association for Computational Linguistics (ACL) (2015). https://doi.org/10.3115/v1/P15-1150
6. Cho, K., Van Merriënboer, B., Gulcehre, C., et al.: Learning phrase representations using RNN encoder-decoder for statistical machine translation. arXiv preprint arXiv:1406.1078 (2014)
7. Kipf, T.N., Welling, M.: Graph neural networks: a review of methods and applications. AI Open **1**, 57–81 (2020)
8. Wu, Z., Pan, S., Chen, F., Long, G., Zhang, C., Yu, P.S.: A comprehensive survey on graph neural networks. IEEE Trans. Neural Netw. Learn. Syst. **32**(1), 4–24 (2021). https://doi.org/10.1109/TNNLS.2020.2978386
9. Kipf, T.N., Welling, M.: Semi-supervised classification with graph convolutional networks. In: NeurIPS (2017)

10. Brody, S., Alon, U., Yahav, E.: How attentive are graph attention networks? arXiv preprint arXiv:2105.14491 (2021)
11. Veličković, P., Cucurull, G., Casanova, A., et al.: Graph attention networks. arXiv preprint arXiv:1710.10903 (2017)
12. Yao, L., Mao, C., Luo, Y.: Graph convolutional networks for text classification. In: Proceedings of the AAAI Conference on Artificial Intelligence, vol. 33, no. 1, pp. 7370–7377 (2019)
13. Huang, L., Ma, D., Li, S., Zhang, X., Wang, H.: Text level graph neural network for text classification. In: Proceedings of the 2019 Conference on Empirical Methods in Natural Language Processing and the 9th International Joint Conference on Natural Language Processing, pp. 3435–3441 (2019)
14. Sun, K., Zhang, R., Mensah, S., et al.: Aspect-level sentiment analysis via convolution over dependency tree. In: Proceedings of the 2019 Conference on Empirical Methods in Natural Language Processing and the 9th International Joint Conference on Natural Language Processing (EMNLP-IJCNLP), pp. 5679–5688 (2019)
15. Wang, Z., Wang, C., Zhang, H., et al.: Learning dynamic hierarchical topic graph with graph convolutional network for document classification. In: International Conference on Artificial Intelligence and Statistics, pp. 3959–3969. PMLR (2020)
16. Tang, H., Ji, D., Li, C., et al.: Dependency graph enhanced dual-transformer structure for aspect-based sentiment classification. In: Proceedings of the 58th Annual Meeting of the Association for Computational Linguistics, pp. 6578–6588 (2020)
17. Ding, K., Wang, J., Li, J., Li, D., Liu, H.: Be more with less: hypergraph attention networks for inductive text classification. In: Proceedings of the 2020 Conference on Empirical Methods in Natural Language Processing, pp. 4927–4936 (2020)
18. Bai, S., Zhang, F., Torr, P.H.S.: Hypergraph convolution and hypergraph attention. Pattern Recogn. **110**, 107637 (2021)
19. Feng, Y., You, H., Zhang, Z., et al.: Hypergraph neural networks. In: Proceedings of the AAAI Conference on Artificial Intelligence, vol. 33, no. 1, pp. 3558–3565 (2019)
20. Lin, Y., Meng, Y., Sun, X., et al.: BertGCN: transductive text classification by combining GCN and BERT. arXiv preprint arXiv:2105.05727 (2021)
21. Devlin, J., Chang, M.W., Lee, K., Toutanova, K.: BERT: pre-training of deep bidirectional transformers for language understanding. In: Proceedings of the 2019 Conference of the North American Chapter of the Association for Computational Linguistics: Human Language Technologies, Volume 1 (Long and Short Papers), Minneapolis, Minnesota, pp. 4171–4186. Association for Computational Linguistics (2019)
22. Liu, Y., Guan, R., Giunchiglia, F., Liang, Y., Feng, X.: Deep attention diffusion graph neural networks for text classification. In: Proceedings of the 2021 Conference on Empirical Methods in Natural Language Processing, pp. 8142–8152 (2021)
23. Zhang, Z., Zhou, Z., Wang, Y.: SSEGCN: syntactic and semantic enhanced graph convolutional network for aspect-based sentiment analysis. In: Proceedings of the. Conference of the North American Chapter of the Association for Computational Linguistics: Human Language Technologies, pp. 4916–4925 (2022)
24. Joulin, A., Grave, E., Bojanowski, P., Mikolov, T.: Bag of tricks for efficient text classification. In: Proceedings of the 15th Conference of the European Chapter of the Association for Computational Linguistics, pp. 427–431 (2017)
25. Shen, D., Wang, G., Wang, W., et al.: Baseline needs more love: on simple word-embedding-based models and associated pooling mechanisms. arXiv preprint arXiv:1805.09843 (2018)

26. Huang, Z., Xu, W., Yu, K.: Bidirectional LSTM-CRF models for sequence tagging. arXiv preprint arXiv:1508.01991 (2015)
27. Peng, H., Li, J., He, Y., et al.: Large-scale hierarchical text classification with recursively regularized deep graph-CNN. In: Proceedings of the 2018 World Wide Web Conference, pp. 1063–1072 (2018)
28. Ragesh, R., Sellamanickam, S., Iyer, A., et al.: HeteGCN: heterogeneous graph convolutional networks for text classification. In: Proceedings of the 14th ACM International Conference on Web Search and Data Mining, pp. 860–868 (2021)
29. Liu, X., You, X., Zhang, X., et al.: Tensor graph convolutional networks for text classification. In: Proceedings of the AAAI Conference on Artificial Intelligence, vol. 34, no. 05, pp. 8409–8416 (2020)
30. Guidotti, E., Ferrara, A.: Text classification with Born's rule. Adv. Neural. Inf. Process. Syst. **35**, 30990–31001 (2022)

Debiased Contrastive Loss
for Collaborative Filtering

Zhuang Liu[1], Yunpu Ma[2], Haoxuan Li[3], Marcel Hildebrandt[4],
Yuanxin Ouyang[1]([✉]), and Zhang Xiong[3]

[1] State Key Laboratory of Software Development Environment, Beihang University,
Beijing, China
{liuzhuang,oyyx}@buaa.edu.cn
[2] Lehrstuhl für Datenbanksysteme und Data Mining,
Ludwig-Maximilians-Universität München, Munich, Germany
[3] Engineering Research Center of Advanced Computer Application Technology,
Ministry of Education, Beihang University, Beijing, China
xiongz@buaa.edu.cn
[4] University of Munich and Siemens AG, Munich, Germany
Marcel.hildebrandt@Siemens.com

Abstract. Collaborative filtering (CF) is the most fundamental technique in recommender systems, which reveals user preference by implicit feedback. Generally, binary cross-entropy or bayesian personalized ranking are usually employed as the loss function to optimize model parameters. Recently, the sampled softmax loss has been proposed to enhance the sampling efficiency, which adopts an in-batch sample strategy. However, it suffers from the sample bias issue, which unavoidably introduces false negative instances, resulting inaccurate representations of users' genuine interests. To address this problem, we propose a debiased contrastive loss, incorporating a bias correction probability to alleviate the sample bias. We integrate the proposed method into several matrix factorizations (MF) and graph neural network-based (GNN) recommendation models. Besides, we theoretically analyze the effectiveness of our methods in automatically mining the hard negative instances. Experimental results on three public benchmarks demonstrate that the proposed debiased contrastive loss can augment several existing MF and GNN-based CF models and outperform popular learning objectives in the recommendation. Additionally, we demonstrate that our method substantially enhances training efficiency.

Keywords: collaborative filtering · debiased contrastive learning · sample bias · matrix factorization · graph neural network

This work was partially supported by the National Natural Science Foundation of China (No. 61977002), the German Federal Ministry of Education and Research (BMBF) under Grant No. 01IS18036A and the State Key Laboratory of Software Development Environment of China (No. SKLSDE-2022ZX-14).

Z. Jin et al. (Eds.): KSEM 2023, LNAI 14119, pp. 94–105, 2023.
https://doi.org/10.1007/978-3-031-40289-0_8

1   Introduction

Recommender system plays an essential role in helping users filter information. Collaborative filtering (CF) is the most popular recommendation technique, which assumes that similar users would exhibit similar preference on items [1]. Many classical CF algorithms employ matrix factorizations (MFs) corresponding to scoring user-item interactions via inner products. In turn, MFs exhibit rather limited expressiveness and the inability to capture complex patterns. As a potential remedy, graph neural networks (GNNs) are nowadays widely employed for the recommendation task. GNNs have the ability to create comprehensive representations of users and items, enabling accurate predictions of new interactions and raising the bar on different benchmark measures [1–4].

To train and optimize the model parameters, most recommendation algorithms adopt binary cross-entropy (BCE) [5] or bayesian personalized ranking (BPR) [6] as the loss function. They are both based on random sample strategies. With the success of contrastive learning [7], sampled softmax (SSM) loss [8,9] is proposed, which adopts the in-batch sample strategy and regards the other instances in the same batch as negatives of the current instance. It significantly improves the sampling efficiency and brings better recommendation performance.

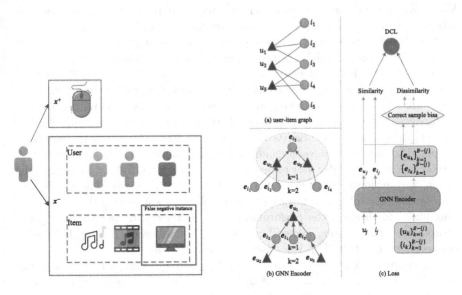

Fig. 1. An example of the sample bias.

Fig. 2. The architecture of the proposed method.

However, the in-batch sample strategy does not consider that negative instances may be consistent with the users' interests. This phenomenon, which we refer to as *sample bias*, can cause a significant performance drop [10]. As shown in Fig. 1, a user is keen on electronic products, and items like the monitor in the red box are consistent with the user's genuine interests. They will likely be sampled as negatives in the same batch and, thus, are described as false negative instances.

In this paper, we propose a debiased contrastive loss (DCL) for the CF model to alleviate the sample bias. In particular, given a user-item pair in a batch, we consider all other instances in the current batch as negatives and then incorporate an explicit correction probability τ^+ to correct the negative scores. Here, τ^+ denotes the proportion of false negatives. We verify the effectiveness of DCL in three public datasets.

To summarize, our main contributions are as follows:

- We propose DCL, a debiased contrastive loss for the general CF model, which can alleviate the sample bias and brings better performance.
- We theoretically analyze that DCL could automatically mine the hard negative instances for users.
- Experimental results on three public datasets demonstrate that our method augments several CF models by a significant margin and outperforms several existing representative loss functions in recommendation while being computationally efficient.

2   Related Work

We briefly review some works closely related to ours, including collaborative filtering and corresponding learning objectives.

Collaborative filtering is the most popular recommendation technique. Many CF algorithms employ MFs corresponding to scoring user-item interactions via products [6,11]. The recent neural recommender models like DMF [12] and NCF [13] enhance the interaction modeling with neural networks. Moreover, formed by user-item interactions, bipartite graphs often serve as a common representation, with edges representing the connections between users and items. With the success of graph neural networks (GNNs), various GNN-based methods have been proposed to improve the recommendation performance, exploiting the user-item interaction graph to infer user preferences. For example, GC-MC [14] applies the graph convolution network (GCN) [15] on the user-item graph. However, it only employs one convolutional layer to exploit the direct connections between users and items. To obtain better performance, NGCF [1] exploits the user-item graph structure by propagating embeddings on it, which allows capturing high-order connectivity. LightGCN [4] is a trimmed-down version of NGCF.

The popular objectives for the CF model mainly consist of BCE loss [5,16], BPR loss [4,6] , and softmax loss [8,9]. BCE loss considers the recommendation task as a binary classification problem. It treats the observed interactions as positives and unobserved interactions as negatives. Instead of scoring the interactions strictly positive or negative, BPR loss aims to encourage the score of an observed interaction to be higher than its unobserved counterparts. To improve the sampling efficiency, [8] proposes CLRec, a cached-batch contrastive loss for recommendation. It designs a first-in-first-out queue to store the instances and fetches those in the queue as negatives. SSM loss [9] is a special version of CLRec, which treats the other instances in the same batch as negatives.

3   Methodology

3.1   Problem Setup

Consider the indexed set of n users $\mathcal{U} = \{u_1, u_2, \cdots, u_n\}$ and m items $\mathcal{I} = \{i_1, i_2, \cdots, i_m\}$, respectively. We assume that $\mathcal{G} = (\mathcal{V}, \mathcal{E})$ is the undirected user-item interaction graph. The vertex set is given by $\mathcal{V} = \mathcal{U} \cup \mathcal{I}$. Moreover, we draw an edge $\{u, i\} \in \mathcal{E}$ if and only if the user $u \in \mathcal{U}$ has interacted with item $i \in \mathcal{I}$. An example of a user-item interaction graph is shown in Fig. 2(a). To ease the notation, we denote with $\mathbf{e}_u \in \mathbb{R}^d$ the embedding of a generic user $u \in \mathcal{U}$ and use $\mathbf{e}_i \in \mathbb{R}^d$ to represent the embedding of an item $i \in \mathcal{I}$, where d is the dimension of embedding vector. Then, the recommendation task consists of predicting the users' preferences towards new items given the user-item interaction graph $\mathcal{G}$. In this paper, we mainly focus on MF and GNN-based CF methods.

3.2   An Overview of the Proposed Method

The architecture of the proposed method is shown in Fig. 2. First, we construct an undirected bipartite user-item graph based on the historical interactions of the users. Then, we use MFs or GNNs to encode the users' behaviors and items, and the GNN encoder is shown in Fig. 2(b). Finally, to boost the performance of various MF and GNN-based CF models, we propose a debiased contrastive loss to learn the embeddings of users and items, as shown in Fig. 2(c). Specifically, given a user-item pair, we treat the instances in the same batch as negatives and propose bias correction probability τ^+ to alleviate the sample bias to maintain state-of-the-art performance.

3.3   Debiased Contrastive Loss

To solve the problems of sample bias, we propose a debiased contrastive loss for CF models, as illustrated in Fig. 2(c). Given an arbitrary user u (an item i), we can obtain its embedding $\mathbf{e}_u$ (or $\mathbf{e}_i$) based on MF or GNN models. The recommender system is supposed to retrieve the top k items relevant to the user u by retrieving the top k candidate $\{\mathbf{e}_i\}_{i \in I}$ similar to $\mathbf{e}_u$. Most implementations use the inner product or the cosine similarity $\phi(u, i) = < \mathbf{e}_u, \mathbf{e}_i >$ as the similarity score. Considering the efficiency of sampling, the SSM loss emerges as a special softmax loss, which samples a subset of unobserved items as negatives, and further leading to

$$\mathcal{L}_{SSM} = \frac{1}{|\mathcal{D}|} \sum_{(u,i) \in \mathcal{D}} - \log \frac{e^{\phi(u,i)}}{e^{\phi(u,i)} + \sum_{l=1}^{L} e^{\phi(u,i_l)}}, \qquad (1)$$

where $\mathcal{D} = \{(u, i) : u \in \mathcal{U}, i \in \mathcal{I} \quad \text{and} \quad g_{ui} = 1\}$ denotes the training set, $\{i_l\}_{l=1}^{L}$ are negative items that the user u has not interacted with, and L denotes the number of negative items for u.

Among the negative instances $\{i_l\}_{l=1}^L$, false negative items may fall into the user's area of interest. To address the sample bias, we develop a debiased contrastive loss. We assume a negative item in $\{i_l\}_{l=1}^L$ is actually a false negative with probability τ^+. Therefore, we can re-write the negative score $e^{\phi(u,i_l')} = \tau^+ e^{\phi(u,i)} + (1-\tau^+)e^{\phi(u,i')}$, where i' is the true negative item for user u. Here, we equally treat each negative item and employ the average score of all L negatives to approximate $e^{\phi(u,i_l')}$, namely, $e^{\phi(u,i_l')} = \frac{1}{L}\sum_{l=1}^L e^{\phi(u,i_l)}$. In this way, for each item i_l in $\{i_l\}_{l=1}^L$, we can obtain the corrected negative score for a user-item pair (u,i) as follows

$$g\left(u,i,\{i_l\}_{l=1}^L\right) = \frac{1}{1-\tau^+}\left(\frac{1}{L}\sum_{l=1}^L e^{\phi(u,i_l)} - \tau^+ e^{\phi(u,i)}\right), \qquad (2)$$

where the second term in brackets can be regarded as the positive score for user u. We basically reduce the energy of negative samples by the false negative rate τ^+ times the energy of the positive sample. Note that we further scale the negative score by the inverse of $1-\tau^+$ (i.e., the probability of sampling a true negative example). Therefore, the debiased contrastive loss is given by

$$\mathcal{L}_{DCL} = \frac{1}{|\mathcal{D}|}\sum_{(u,i)\in\mathcal{D}} -\log\frac{e^{\phi(u,i)}}{e^{\phi(u,i)} + Lg\left(u,i,\{i_l\}_{l=1}^L\right)}. \qquad (3)$$

Following the sampling strategy in [9], we consider the other (2B-2) instances in the current minibatch as negatives. Here, we treat users and items in the current minibatch as negative instances for the following reason: GNN models treat users and items equally in the sense that both of them are processed by fusing embeddings from their high-order neighbors. Therefore, users and items can be selected equally in the negative sampling process. Thus, we can modify Eq. (2) so that

$$g\left(u_j,i_j,\{u_k\}_{k=1}^{B-\{j\}},\{i_k\}_{k=1}^{B-\{j\}}\right) =$$

$$\frac{1}{1-\tau^+}\left[\frac{\sum_{k=1}^{B-1}\left(e^{\phi(u_j,u_k)} + e^{\phi(u_j,i_k)}\right)}{2B-2} - \tau^+ e^{\phi(u_j,i_j)}\right], \qquad (4)$$

where j is the index of the user or item in a minibatch. $\{u_k\}_{k=1}^{B-\{j\}}$ and $\{i_k\}_{k=1}^{B-\{j\}}$ denote the other $B-1$ instances in a minibatch for a user and an item.

In this work, we use the cosine similarity with temperature $t > 0$ as the similarity function, i.e., $\phi(u,i) = \frac{f(u,i)}{t}$, where $f(u,i)$ denotes the cosine similarity. In addition, the value of $f(u,i)$ change in range $[-1,1]$, so Eq. (4) attains its theoretical minimum at $e^{-1/t}$ [17]. Therefore, in implementation, we constrain Eq. (4) to be greater than $e^{-1/t}$ to prevent calculating the logarithm of a negative number. Finally, the debiased contrastive loss for recommendation algorithm in this work is defined as

$$\mathcal{L}_{DCL} = \frac{1}{|\mathcal{D}|}\sum_{(u_j,i_j)\in\mathcal{D}} -\log\frac{e^{\phi(u_j,i_j)}}{e^{\phi(u_j,i_j)} + (2B-2)g}. \qquad (5)$$

3.4 Theoretical Analysis

Proposition 1. *DCL can automatically mine the hard negative instance, where the hardness level for each negative instance adaptively depends on the predicted score and can also be controlled by the temperature t.*

Proof. To analyze the ability of mining hard negative instances for DCL, we resort the gradient with respect to negative instances. First, we re-write the $\mathcal{L}_{DCL}$:

$$
\begin{aligned}
\mathcal{L}_{DCL} &= \frac{1}{|\mathcal{D}|} \sum_{(u_j, i_j) \in \mathcal{D}} - \log \frac{e^{\phi(u_j, i_j)}}{e^{\phi(u_j, i_j)} + (2B - 2)g} \\
&= \frac{1}{|\mathcal{D}|} \sum_{(u_j, i_j) \in \mathcal{D}} \log \left[1 + \frac{(2B - 2)g}{e^{\phi(u_j, i_j)}} \right].
\end{aligned}
\tag{6}
$$

The gradients *w.r.t.* $f(u_j, i_k)$ and $f(u_j, u_k)$ are respectively computed as

$$
\frac{\partial \mathcal{L}_{DCL}}{\partial f(u_j, i_k)} = \frac{1}{|\mathcal{D}|} \sum_{(u_j, i_j) \in \mathcal{D}} \frac{1}{t} \frac{e^{f(u_j, i_k)}}{(1 - \tau^+) \left[e^{\phi(u_j, i_j)} + (2B - 2)g \right]}
\tag{7}
$$

$$
\frac{\partial \mathcal{L}_{DCL}}{\partial f(u_j, u_k)} = \frac{1}{|\mathcal{D}|} \sum_{(u_j, i_j) \in \mathcal{D}} \frac{1}{t} \frac{e^{f(u_j, u_k)}}{(1 - \tau^+) \left[e^{\phi(u_j, i_j)} + (2B - 2)g \right]}
\tag{8}
$$

Therefore, for each negative instance, the gradient is proportional to the predicted score $f(u_j, i_k)$ or $f(u_j, u_k)$. A harder negative instance with larger predicted score has larger gradient, which indicates that DCL aims to optimize harder negative instance. Moreover, the larger the predicted score, the larger the gradient, and the harder the negative instance. In addition, we can tune the temperature t to control the gradient and further control the hardness level of negative instances, which is consistent with [18].

3.5 Model Training

To effectively learn the parameters of our method, we train the debiased contrastive loss $\mathcal{L}_{DCL}$ with regularization in an end-to-end fashion as follows

$$
\mathcal{L} = \mathcal{L}_{DCL} + \lambda \left(||\mathbf{e}_u||_2^2 + ||\mathbf{e}_i||_2^2 \right),
\tag{9}
$$

where β is a coefficient that balances between the two losses. λ controls the L_2 regularization strength.

4 Experiments

4.1 Experimental Settings

Datasets. We conduct experiments on three real-world datasets: **Yelp2018** is adopted from the 2018 edition of the Yelp challenge. Local businesses like restaurants and bars are considered as items. **Amazon-Book** consists of book review data crawled from Amazon.com. **Steam** is a video game dataset collected from Steam, where items correspond to video games. We apply the preprocessing to Yelp2018 and Amazon-Book detailed in [1]. Concerning the Steam dataset, we follow the common practice detailed in [19]. The statistics of the processed datasets are summarized in Table 1. These datasets vary significantly in their domains, size, and sparsity. Following [1], we randomly select 80% of historical interactions of each user and assign them to the training set. The remainder comprises the test set.

Table 1. Statistics of the datasets.

Dataset	Yelp2018	Amazon-Book	Steam
#Users	31668	52643	281428
#Items	38048	91599	13044
#Interactions	1561406	2984108	3488885
Density	0.00130	0.00062	0.00095

Evaluation Metrics. To evaluate the quality of the recommendation algorithms, we adopt two ranking-based metrics: (1) recall@K measures the average number of items that the users interact with that are ranked among the top-K candidates. (2) ndcg@K is a precision-based metric that accounts for the predicted position of the ground truth instance. Thereby, all items, except for the ones with which the user has interacted, are considered for the ranking. Following [1,4], we set $K = 20$ and report the average metrics for all users in the test set. Concerning both metrics, larger values indicate better performances.

Baselines. We first verify whether our proposed DCL can augment existing MF-based or GNN-based recommendation methods: **MF** [6], **DMF** [12], **GCN** [15], **GC-MC** [14], **Pinsage** [2], **NGCF** [1], **LR-GCCF** [3], **LightGCN** [4], and **LightGCN-single** [4]. The detail of all baselines can be found in the original publications. For a fair comparison, all baselines optimize the BPR loss. For each baseline, we retain the base model to encode the user behaviors and items and change the loss function to DCL. We append ++ to the name of each method to indicate that the results are obtained with our proposed DCL (e.g., NGCF++). Then, we choose LightGCN-single as the backbone and compare DCL with several popular loss functions for recommendation: **BCE** [5], **BPR** [6], **SSM** [9].

Parameter Settings. We optimize all models using Adam and employ Xavier initializations. The embedding size is fixed to 128 and the batch size to 2048 for all methods. Grid search is applied to choose the learning rate and the L_2 regularization coefficient λ over the ranges $\{10^{-4}, 10^{-3}, 10^{-2}\}$ and $\{10^{-6}, 10^{-5}, \cdots, 10^{-2}\}$. We set the number of layers $K = 1$ for GC-MC, and

$K = 2$ for other GNN-based methods. We use the cosine similarity with temperature as the similarity function, and set $t = 0.07$ for the Amazon-Book and $t = 0.1$ for both Yelp2018 and Steam. We use normalizations to stabilize debiased contrastive learning. The bias correction probability τ^+ is tuned on the sets $\{0, 0.1, 0.01, 0.001, 0.0001, 0.00001\}$. All other hyperparameters are set according to the suggestions from the settings specified in the original publications. All models are trained on a single NVIDIA GeForce GTX TITAN X GPU.

4.2 Overall Performance Comparison

Combine Our Method into Several Existing Recommendation Baselines. Table 2 summarizes the best results of all considered methods with (indicated by ++) and without our proposed DCL on the three benchmark datasets. The percentages in right corners indicate the relative improvements of our methods compared to each baseline. Bold scores indicate the best performance in each column; Bold percentages in right corners indicate the most significant relative improvements.

Table 2. A comparison of the overall performance among all considered baseline methods with (indicated by ++) and without our proposed DCL.

Methods	Dataset					
	Yelp2018		Amazon-Book		Steam	
	recall@20	ndcg@20	recall@20	ndcg@20	recall@20	ndcg@20
MF	0.0445	0.0361	0.0306	0.0231	0.0632	0.0303
MF++	$0.0502_{+12.81\%}$	$0.0403_{+11.63\%}$	$0.0489_{+\mathbf{59.80\%}}$	$0.0386_{+\mathbf{67.10\%}}$	$0.0759_{+20.09\%}$	$0.0390_{+28.71\%}$
DMF	0.0419	0.0347	0.0268	0.0215	0.0877	0.0441
DMF++	$0.0615_{+\mathbf{46.78\%}}$	$0.0507_{+\mathbf{46.11\%}}$	$0.0408_{+52.24\%}$	$0.0333_{+54.88\%}$	$0.1063_{+21.21\%}$	$0.0547_{+24.04\%}$
GCN	0.0457	0.0371	0.0312	0.0242	0.0866	0.0435
GCN++	$0.0649_{+42.01\%}$	$0.0533_{+43.67\%}$	$0.0486_{+55.77\%}$	$0.0381_{+57.44\%}$	$0.1089_{+\mathbf{25.75\%}}$	$0.0568_{+\mathbf{30.57\%}}$
GC-MC	0.0498	0.0411	0.0346	0.0258	0.1023	0.0518
GC-MC++	$0.0622_{+24.90\%}$	$0.0504_{+22.63\%}$	$0.0457_{+32.08\%}$	$0.0360_{+39.53\%}$	$0.1161_{+13.49\%}$	$0.0605_{+16.80\%}$
PinSage	0.0458	0.0369	0.0403	0.0309	0.0849	0.0455
PinSage++	$0.0479_{+4.59\%}$	$0.0392_{+6.23\%}$	$0.0469_{+16.38\%}$	$0.0369_{+19.42\%}$	$0.1044_{+22.97\%}$	$0.0540_{+18.68\%}$
NGCF	0.0584	0.0489	0.0365	0.0271	0.1129	0.0597
NGCF++	$0.0646_{+10.62\%}$	$0.0532_{+8.79\%}$	$0.0452_{+23.84\%}$	$0.0348_{+28.41\%}$	$0.1149_{+1.77\%}$	$0.0597_{+1.51\%}$
LR-GCCF	0.0602	0.0493	0.0373	0.0283	0.1035	0.0534
LR-GCCF++	$\mathbf{0.0711}_{+18.11\%}$	$0.0558_{+13.18\%}$	$0.0460_{+23.32\%}$	$0.0340_{+20.14\%}$	$0.1086_{+4.93\%}$	$0.0565_{+5.81\%}$
LightGCN	0.0630	0.0519	0.0453	0.0346	0.1159	0.0611
LightGCN++	$0.0677_{+7.46\%}$	$\mathbf{0.0562}_{+8.29\%}$	$\mathbf{0.0537}_{+18.54\%}$	$\mathbf{0.0424}_{+22.54\%}$	$0.1185_{+2.24\%}$	$0.0622_{+1.80\%}$
LightGCN-single	0.0633	0.0506	0.0466	0.0358	0.1246	0.0650
LightGCN-single++	$0.0680_{+7.42\%}$	$0.0556_{+9.88\%}$	$0.0532_{+14.16\%}$	$0.0418_{+16.76\%}$	$\mathbf{0.1369}_{+9.87\%}$	$\mathbf{0.0704}_{+8.31\%}$

On the one hand, DCL exhibits the largest performance gains when combined with the most basic model, such as MF, DMF, and GCN. Especially on Yelp2018, DMF++ exhibits a performance increase of 46.78% recall@20 and 46.11% ndcg@20. On Amazon-Book, MF++ outperforms MF with 59.80% recall@20 and 67.10% ndcg@20, respectively. On Steam, compared with GCN,

GCN++ obtains relative performance gains of 25.75% and 30.57% concerning recall@20 and ndcg@20, respectively. On the other hand, DCL shows the best performance in some state-of-the-art models. For example, on Yelp2018, LR-GCCF++ reaches 0.0711 concerning recall@20, and LightGCN++ reaches 0.0562 concerning ndcg@20. On Amazon-Book, LightGCN++ shows the best performance, and on Steam, LightGCN-single++ consistently outperforms all the other baselines.

GCN and GC-MC indicate their superior capabilities to incorporate information from the user-item graph compared to MF and DMF. By correcting sampling bias, GCN++ and GC-MC++ consistently outperform GCN and GC-MC, respectively. Compared to GCN and GC-MC, PinSage and NGCF further consider higher-order neighborhoods. Moreover, PinSage++ and NGCF++ consistently outperform PinSage and NGCF, but the relative improvements are slightly worse than the ones of GCN++ and GC-MC++.

These results show that debiased contrastive learning positively affects recommendation performances. In the following subsections, we focus on LightGCN-single++ and analyze its performance in greater detail.

Compare with Different Loss Functions. Table 3 summarizes the best results of all considered loss functions on three benchmark datasets *w.r.t.* LightGCN-single. Bold scores are the best in each column, while underlined scores are the second best. The last row shows the improvements in our DCL relative to the best baseline.

Table 3. A comparison of the overall performance among different loss functions.

Methods	Dataset					
	Yelp2018		Amazon-Book		Steam	
	recall@20	ndcg@20	recall@20	ndcg@20	recall@20	ndcg@20
BCE	0.0591	0.0482	0.0437	0.0335	0.1134	0.0581
BPR	0.0633	0.0506	0.0466	0.0358	0.1246	0.0650
SSM	0.0673	0.0542	0.0511	0.0405	0.1328	0.0689
DCL	**0.0680**	**0.0556**	**0.0532**	**0.0418**	**0.1369**	**0.0704**
Improv	1.04%	2.58%	4.11%	3.21%	3.09%	2.18%

Table 3 shows that the model with BCE loss achieves the worst performance on all three datasets, indicating that it is unsuitable to take the top-k recommendation as a classification problem. In particular, it may introduce noise when fitting the exact value of ratings. BPR loss outperforms BCE loss, verifying the effectiveness of capturing relative relations among items. While SSM loss further outperforms BCE and BPR loss, indicating that it conducts in-batch sampling and efficiently uses negative instances. However, a few negative instances may constitute false negatives. Thus, we apply the bias correction probability τ^+ to control sample bias and define it as DCL. We find that DCL loss further improves the performance of the recommendation compared to SSM loss. Specifically, on the Amazon-Book dataset, DCL achieves 4.11% improvement for recall@20 and 3.21% improvement for ndcg@20. In summary, adequate negative instances and an effective sample bias control are essential to improve the performance of recommendation algorithms.

4.3 Effectiveness Analysis

Figure 3 shows the test performance regarding recall@20 for each epoch of LightGCN-single and LightGCN-single++. Due to the space limitation, we omit the performance concerning ndcg@20, which has a similar trend as recall@20. Since the convergence speed of the LightGCN-single is relatively slow, we include a small sub-figure in the lower right corner of each figure.

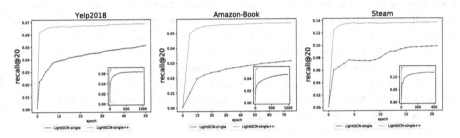

Fig. 3. The test performance after each training epoch of LightGCN-single and LightGCN-single++.

We observe that LightGCN-single++ exhibits faster convergence than LightGCN-single on all three datasets. Specifically, to achieve the best performance, LightGCN-single requires thousands of epochs on Yelp2018 and Amazon-Book and about 400 epochs on Steam. While LightGCN-single++ only requires 50–70 epochs to achieve the best performance on Yelp2018 and Amazon-Book dataset. Moreover, it only requires 18 epochs to converge on the Steam dataset. It is reasonable that even though we sample thousands of negatives for each user, this does not increase the memory overhead due to the reuse of the instances in the current minibatch. These results indicate that a debiased sampling strategy not only improves training efficiency but also improves the recommendation performance. This finding provides a new optimization perspective for the design of future recommendation algorithms.

4.4 Parameter Sensitivity Analysis

In this subsection, we examine the robustness with respect to the bias correction probability τ^+. We analyze this hyperparameter by fixing the remaining hyperparameters at their optimal value. Figure 4 shows the recall@20 and ndcg@20

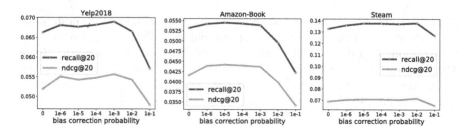

Fig. 4. Performance of LightGCN-single++ obtained with different bias correction probabilities τ^+.

for LightGCN-single++ with the bias correction probability τ^+ varying from 0 to 0.1 while keeping other optimal hyper-parameters unchanged.

The most obvious observation from Fig. 4 is that the recall@20 and ndcg@20 have the same trend: they both increase first and then decrease as τ^+ increases. On Yelp2018 and Amazon-Book, recall@20 and ndcg@20 increase steadily to specific high values of τ^+. If we continue to increase τ^+ further, the performance drops suddenly. Moreover, on the Steam dataset, when we vary τ^+ from 0.01 to 0.1, the performance starts to drop. It shows we can correct the sample bias by carefully selecting τ^+ in an appropriate interval. Empirically, we find that when the hyperparameter τ^+ exceeds a specific range, the performance will deteriorate since more samples are considered false negative.

For a more fine-grained analysis, when setting $\tau^+ = 0$, we do not correct the sample bias and treat the other $(2B - 2)$ users and items in the current minibatch as true negative instances. We find that the performance is relatively weak across all three datasets. It indicates that among these negative samples, false negative instances need to be taken into account. When we set τ^+ to a small value to correct the sample bias, recall@20 and ndcg@20 improve. We can obtain the best performance when setting τ^+ to $1e^{-3}$, $1e^{-5}$, and $1e^{-2}$ on Yelp2018, Amazon-Book, and the Steam datasets, respectively.

5   Conclusion

In this work, we presented a general debiased contrastive loss for collaborative filtering, aiming to alleviate the sample bias. Concretely, we treat the other users and items in the current minibatch as negative instances and employ a bias correction probability τ^+ to control the proportion of false negative samples. Experimental results on three real-world datasets showed that our method significantly augments several MF and GNN-based CF models and outperforms popular learning objectives. In addition, we also find that our method improves training efficiency significantly. In future works, we plan to explore personalized τ^+ for different users to adaptively alleviate sample bias and examine whether the proposed method can be extended to different recommender settings, such as sequential recommendation tasks.

References

1. Wang, X., He, X., Wang, M., Feng, F., Chua, T.S.: Neural graph collaborative filtering. In: The 42nd International ACM SIGIR Conference (2019)
2. Ying, R., He, R., Chen, K., Eksombatchai, P., Hamilton, W.L., Leskovec, J.: Graph convolutional neural networks for web-scale recommender systems. In: KDD, pp. 974–983. ACM (2018)
3. Chen, L., Wu, L., Hong, R., Zhang, K., Wang, M.: Revisiting graph based collaborative filtering: a linear residual graph convolutional network approach. In: AAAI, pp. 27–34. AAAI Press (2020)
4. He, X., Deng, K., Wang, X., Li, Y., Zhang, Y., Wang, M.: Lightgcn: simplifying and powering graph convolution network for recommendation. In: SIGIR, pp. 639–648. ACM (2020)
5. He, X., Liao, L., Zhang, H., Nie, L., Hu, X., Chua, T.-S.: Neural collaborative filtering. In: Proceedings of the 26th International Conference on World Wide Web, pp. 173–182 (2017)
6. Rendle, S., Freudenthaler, C., Gantner, Z., Schmidt-Thieme, L.: BPR: Bayesian personalized ranking from implicit feedback. CoRR, abs/1205.2618 (2012)
7. Barbano, C.A., Dufumier, B., Tartaglione, E., Grangetto, M., Gori, P.: Unbiased supervised contrastive learning. In: The Eleventh International Conference on Learning Representations (2023)
8. Zhou, C., Ma, J., Zhang, J., Zhou, J., Yang, H.: Contrastive learning for debiased candidate generation in large-scale recommender systems (2021)
9. Wu, J., et al.: On the effectiveness of sampled softmax loss for item recommendation. arXiv preprint arXiv:2201.02327 (2022)
10. Chuang, C.-Y., Robinson, J., Lin, Y.-C., Torralba, A., Jegelka, S.: Debiased contrastive learning. CoRR, abs/2007.00224 (2020)
11. Koren, Y., Bell, R.M., Volinsky, C.: Matrix factorization techniques for recommender systems. Computer $42(8)$, 30–37 (2009)
12. Xue, H.-J., Dai, X., Zhang, J., Huang, S., Chen, J.: Deep matrix factorization models for recommender systems. In: IJCAI, Melbourne, Australia, vol. 17, pp. 3203–3209 (2017)
13. He, X., Liao, L., Zhang, H., Nie, L., Hu, X., Chua, T.-S.: Neural collaborative filtering. CoRR, abs/1708.05031 (2017)
14. van den Berg, R., Thomas, N.K., Welling, M.: Graph convolutional matrix completion. CoRR, abs/1706.02263 (2017)
15. Kipf, T.N., Welling, M.: Semi-supervised classification with graph convolutional networks. In: ICLR (Poster). OpenReview.net (2017)
16. Shan, Y., Hoens, T.R., Jiao, J., Wang, H., Yu, D., Mao, J.C.: Deep crossing: web-scale modeling without manually crafted combinatorial features. In: Proceedings of the 22nd ACM SIGKDD International Conference on Knowledge Discovery and Data Mining, pp. 255–262 (2016)
17. Chuang, C.-Y., Robinson, J., Lin, Y.-C., Torralba, A., Jegelka, S.: Debiased contrastive learning. Adv. Neural. Inf. Process. Syst. **33**, 8765–8775 (2020)
18. Wang, F., Liu, H.: Understanding the behaviour of contrastive loss. In: Proceedings of the IEEE/CVF Conference on Computer Vision and Pattern Recognition, pp. 2495–2504 (2021)
19. Sun, F., et al.: BERT4Rec: sequential recommendation with bidirectional encoder representations from transformer. In: Proceedings of the 28th ACM International Conference on Information and Knowledge Management, pp. 1441–1450 (2019)

ParaSum: Contrastive Paraphrasing for Low-Resource Extractive Text Summarization

Moming Tang[1], Chengyu Wang[2], Jianing Wang[1], Cen Chen[1(✉)], Ming Gao[1], and Weining Qian[1]

[1] School of Data Science and Engineering, East China Normal University, Shanghai, China
cecilia.cenchen@gmail.com
[2] Alibaba Group, Hangzhou, China

Abstract. Existing extractive summarization methods achieve state-of-the-art (SOTA) performance with pre-trained language models (PLMs) and sufficient training data. However, PLM-based methods are known to be data-hungry and often fail to deliver satisfactory results in low-resource scenarios. Constructing a high-quality summarization dataset with human-authored reference summaries is a prohibitively expensive task. To address these challenges, this paper proposes a novel paradigm for low-resource extractive summarization, called ParaSum. This paradigm reformulates text summarization as textual paraphrasing, aligning the text summarization task with the self-supervised Next Sentence Prediction (NSP) task of PLMs. This approach minimizes the training gap between the summarization model and PLMs, enabling a more effective probing of the knowledge encoded within PLMs and enhancing the summarization performance. Furthermore, to relax the requirement for large amounts of training data, we introduce a simple yet efficient model and align the training paradigm of summarization to textual paraphrasing to facilitate network-based transfer learning. Extensive experiments over two widely used benchmarks (i.e., CNN/DailyMail, Xsum) and a recent open-sourced high-quality Chinese benchmark (i.e., CNewSum) show that ParaSum consistently outperforms existing PLM-based summarization methods in all low-resource settings, demonstrating its effectiveness over different types of datasets.

Keywords: low-resource scenarios · extractive summarization · textual paraphrasing · transfer learning · pre-trained language model

1 Introduction

The exponential proliferation of information on the Internet has created an urgent need for industrial scenarios to extract knowledge from vast amounts of documents. Extractive summarization aims at reducing information acquisition costs while preserving the key information of the document, which leads to a significant surge in interest in text summarization from both academic

Z. Jin et al. (Eds.): KSEM 2023, LNAI 14119, pp. 106–119, 2023.
https://doi.org/10.1007/978-3-031-40289-0_9

and industrial communities [1,2]. Most extractive summarization methods are implemented in a supervised fashion, which can be categorized into two classes, i.e., ranking-based summarization and auto-regressive summarization. Ranking-based methods are designed to assign a numerical score to each sentence in a given document and subsequently select the top K sentences that achieve the highest scores to form a summary [1,3], while auto-regressive summarization methods usually employ the Seq2Seq architecture and extracts summaries on a sentence-by-sentence basis during the decoding phase, with each sentence being selected based on the summary that has been produced up to that point [4,5].

In recent times, pre-trained language models (PLMs) have emerged as an essential infrastructure for a wide range of downstream natural language understanding (NLU) tasks [6,7]. These models are fully pre-trained on large-scale corpora through well-designed self-supervised learning techniques. Recent methods have incorporated the PLM-based fine-tuning paradigm into either ranking-based [3,8] or auto-regressive summarization [9] approaches and successfully achieve much better summarization performance through the use of fully-supervised labeled data. However, the conventional fine-tuning frameworks heavily depend on the time-consuming and labor-intensive process of data annotation[1], which may be bothersome in real-world low-resource scenarios (e.g., having only 200 labeled samples for model training). In addition, there is a large gap between the pre-training objective of PLMs, i.e., NSP and the fine-tuning objective of extractive summarization, which hinders the transfer and adaptation of knowledge in PLMs to summarization tasks. Fortunately, PLMs have demonstrated remarkable ability in few-shot learning by redefining the downstream tasks' formats similar to their pre-training objectives [10]. To this end, the rich knowledge encoded in PLMs can be better probed through specific patterns to facilitate downstream NLP tasks even when there is a scarcity of labeled data available. Therefore, a natural question arises: *how can we employ text paraphrasing in PLMs to boost the model performance for low-resource extractive summarization?*

In order to effectively probe the knowledge of PLMs to improve extractive summarization, this paper presents a novel paradigm called ParaSum. The primary objective of this approach is to reformulate the extractive summarization task as text paraphrasing. Textual paraphrasing that determines whether given sentence pairs are paraphrases of one another, has a latent connection to extractive summarization which aims to extract a summary that paraphrases the gist of the document. To support this reformulation, we obey two principles:

a) The training paradigm gap between extractive summarization and PLMs should be minimized.

b) The model's backbone architecture should be simple enough to facilitate network-based transfer learning to relax the requisition of training data and achieve satisfactory performance.

---

[1] Existing mainstream summarization datasets typically contain at least 100,000 news articles with corresponding human-authored reference summaries [11–13].

This paper proposes a novel paradigm for extractive summarization in low-resource scenarios, which is referred to as ParaSum. The approach involves reformulating extractive summarization as a textual paraphrasing task between the original document and candidate summaries. This paradigm is aligned with the self-supervised task (NSP) of BERT, thereby enabling the leveraging of knowledge from both textual paraphrasing and PLMs to guide the model in distinguishing semantically salient summaries. Extensive experiments were conducted in this study on two commonly used benchmarks (CNN/DailyMail, Xsum) and a recently released high-quality Chinese benchmark (CNewSum). The results indicate that ParaSum consistently outperforms the baseline models with scarcity available labeled data.

2   Related Work

Incorporating PLMs-based fine-tuning paradigm into extractive summarization methods significantly improves their results on large-scale, high-quality, open-source summarization datasets. However, as the parameter size of PLMs increases, the fine-tuning paradigm increasingly relies on a substantial amount of labor-intensive annotation. In many real-world application scenarios, only small-scale datasets are available, rendering existing data-hungry methods impractical to apply. While some researchers have been studying low-resource abstractive summarization [14–16], it is important to note that summaries generated by such methods may deviate from documents' main information. Therefore, this paper mainly focuses on extractive summarization. To the best of our knowledge, this study represents the first investigation of low-resource extractive summarization.

Another thread of related work is few-shot Natural Language Understanding (NLU). Here, we briefly summarize few-shot NLU in the following topics. i) Partial-parameter fine-tuning paradigms only tune a subset parameters of PLMs during training aiming to preserve most pre-trained knowledge of PLMs while reducing the magnitude of tunable parameters [17,18]. ii) Prompt Engineering [19] reformulates visual grounding and visual question answering as a "fill-in-blank" problem by hand-crafted prompts. iii) Adapter-based paradigms [20,21] utilize a lightweight adapters module to learn from downstream small-scale training datasets during training, while combining the knowledge of both PLMs and downstream tasks through residual functions during inference to complete downstream tasks [22]. iv) Transfer learning [23,24] is employed to overcome the constraint that training and testing data must be independent and identically distributed, thereby alleviating the scarcity of supervisory signals caused by small-scale training datasets. Drawing inspiration from prompt learning and transfer learning, this paper aims to alleviate the issue of sparse supervisory signals in low-resource scenarios by leveraging knowledge from relevant NLU tasks and PLMs for extractive summarization.

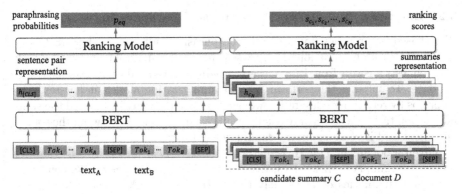

Fig. 1. Model architecture and transfer learning procedure of ParaSum.

3 Method

This paper dispenses with data-hungry summarization paradigms (ranking-based [3] and auto-regressive [4,9]). Since PLMs are few-shot learners [25], this paper aims to minimize the training gap between extractive summarization and PLM in order to leverage the knowledge of PLMs for downstream summarization. Additionally, network-based transfer learning is employed to alleviate the issue of sparse supervisory signals. To achieve these objectives, extractive summarization is reformulated as textual paraphrasing. Specifically, the method distinguishes the most salient summary from candidate summaries of the document. The model architecture and the transfer learning process are illustrated in Fig. 1.

3.1 PLM-Based Textual Paraphrasing

Given the textual paraphrasing sentence pairs, namely $\{(s_1^t, s_2^t), y_t\}_{t=1}^T$, where (s_1^t, s_2^t) indicates the t-th sentence pair, and y_t is the corresponding binary label. The sentence pair (s_1^t, s_2^t) is concatenated as: $x_{in} = $ [CLS] s_1^t [SEP] s_2^t [SEP]. The PLM, parameterized by $\mathcal{M}$, takes x_{in} as input and maps x_{in} to a sequence of hidden representations. The representation located at position [CLS], denoted as $h_{\text{[CLS]}}$, is used as input to a ranking model, which computes the probability p_{eq}. This probability indicates the extent to which s_1^t and s_2^t are paraphrases of each other. The ranking model typically consists of a single-layer feed-forward network (FFN) and a sigmoid function. The computation proceeds as follows:

$$h_{\text{[CLS]}} = \mathcal{M}(x_{in})_{\text{[CLS]}} \qquad (1)$$

$$p_{eq} = \text{sigmoid}(W^\top h_{\text{[CLS]}} + b) \qquad (2)$$

where W and b are learnable parameters of FFN.

3.2 Extractive Summarization as Textual Paraphrasing

PLM-based approaches for textual paraphrasing adhere to the NSP self-supervised task of PLMs [6] which transforms textual paraphrasing into a task that requests answers from PLMs, thereby reducing the need for large-scale training data. To enhance the performance of summarization models in low-resource scenarios by retrieving relevant knowledge from PLMs, we reformulated the summarization task as a series of textual paraphrasing operations between the source document and its corresponding candidate summaries.

Given a document D with L sentences, namely $D = \{s_i | i = 1 \cdots L\}$, and its reference summary R_D, where s_i denotes the i-th sentence of D. We construct candidate summaries of D, namely $C_D = \{c_j | j = 1 \cdots N\}$, where N denotes the number of candidate summaries. The candidate summary $c_j = \{s_k^j | k = 1 \cdots I, s_k^j \in D\}$ consists of I sentences from D, where s_k^j denotes the k-th sentence of c_j. Sentences in c_j are sorted according to their position in D. Candidate summaries in C_D are sorted in descending order according to their ROUGE score [26], namely $R(\cdot)$, with the reference summary R_D, in other words:

$$R(c_m) > R(c_n); \forall c_m, c_n \in C_D \text{ and } m < n \qquad (3)$$

The first step in our approach is concatenating the candidate summary c_j with the source document D, just as $x_{c_j} = [\text{CLS}] \ c_j \ [\text{SEP}] \ D \ [\text{SEP}]$. Next, we input x_{c_j} into PLM $\mathcal{M}$ and utilize the output representation at the [CLS] position to compute the ranking score s_{c_j} for c_j. This score is computed using the same ranking model employed in the textual paraphrasing step. Subsequently, we obtain ranking scores for the candidate summaries in C_D, which are represented as $S_D = \{s_{c_j} | j = 1 \cdots N\}$. Furthermore, we compute the ranking score of the reference summary R_D, denoted as s_{R_D}, using the same calculation procedure.

3.3 Training Paradigm

Supervised Training Paradigm. In order to ensure that the model assigns the highest probability to the candidate summary with the highest ROUGE score, denoted as c_1, we employ the cross-entropy loss (CE). Specifically, we set the ground-truth label for c_1 to 1, and 0 for the remaining summaries:

$$L_{CE} = \sum_{j=1}^{N} -l_j \cdot \log s_{c_j}; \quad l_1 = 1 \text{ and } \{l_j\}_{j=2}^{N} = 0 \qquad (4)$$

where l_j denotes the ground-truth label for c_j. However, in the case of low-resource datasets, the supervised information provided by the CE loss is insufficient to train the model to achieve satisfactory performance. The sorting information of the candidate summaries can be employed by the contrastive learning paradigm to guide the model in distinguishing salient summaries. Contrastive learning allows for the definition of positive and negative samples based on the specific application scenarios, while ensuring that negative samples are kept distinct from positive samples [27]. Given any candidate summary pair $c_m, c_n \in C_D$

where $m < n$, we define c_m with a higher ROUGE score as a positive sample and c_n with lower ROUGE score as a negative sample. The contrastive loss for any summary pair of C_D is computed following [28,29], as:

$$L_{C_D} = \sum_{i=1}^{N} \sum_{j=i}^{N} \max(0, s_{c_j} - s_{c_i}) \tag{5}$$

Moreover, it is essential to make sure that the reference summary is ranked higher than all the candidate summaries:

$$L_{R_D} = \sum_{i=1}^{N} \max(0, s_{c_i} - s_{R_D}) \tag{6}$$

Finally, the loss function for extractive summarization, namely L_{ext}, is defined as follows:

$$L_{ext} = L_{C_D} + L_{R_D} + L_{CE} \tag{7}$$

Knowledge Transfer. Initially, the summarization model is pre-trained using a textual paraphrasing dataset. However, conventional PLM-based textual paraphrasing methods only employ the CE loss during the training phase. To facilitate better knowledge transfer, the training paradigm of textual paraphrasing must be aligned with that of extractive summarization. We define the calculated probability of the ground-truth paraphrasing label, denoted as p_g, as the positive sample, and $1 - p_g$ as the negative sample. We then use the contrastive loss to maximize the likelihood of the ground-truth sample. The contrastive loss, denoted as L_{CL}, the BCE loss, denoted as L_{BCE}, and the final loss function of textual paraphrasing, denoted as L_{para}, are defined as follows:

$$L_{CL} = \max(0, (1 - p_g) - p_g) \tag{8}$$

$$L_{BCE} = -l_t \log p_{eq} - (1 - l_t) \log(1 - p_{eq}) \tag{9}$$

$$L_{para} = L_{CL} + L_{BCE} \tag{10}$$

where l_t indicates the ground-truth label for the textual paraphrasing dataset. Subsequently, the pre-trained model is fine-tuned with the small-scale summarization dataset using the extractive loss, namely L_{ext}.

The whole training algorithm for ParaSum is listed in Algorithm 1. For a document D that contains L sentences, the number of its candidate summaries, denoted as N, is equal to $\binom{L}{I}$. This value is typically much larger than L, and computing ranking scores for all candidate summaries can be time-consuming. Therefore, it is necessary to exclude trivial candidate summaries in advance. To address this issue, we employ a straightforward yet effective heuristic approach [8] that utilizes a ranking-based method [3] to pre-select the top K sentences ($K \ll L$), and then enumerate all combinations of the K sentences according to I to generate candidate summaries. It should be noted that the ranking-based method [3] is trained using the same data as ParaSum.

Algorithm 1: Training Paradigm of ParaSum

Input: learning rate α; number of epochs for transfer learning and summarization M,N; number of training steps per epoch for transfer learning and summarization Q, S

1   Initialize parameters of the ranking model, namely, W and b;

2   **for** $i \leftarrow 1$ **to** M **do**

3   **for** $q \leftarrow 1$ **to** Q **do**

4       $W_{i,q}, b_{i,q}, \mathcal{M}_{i,q} \leftarrow$

        $W_{i,q-1} + \alpha_{i,q}\nabla_W L_{para}, \ b_{i,q-1} + \alpha_{i,q}\nabla_b L_{para}, \ \mathcal{M}_{i,q-1} + \alpha_{i,q}\nabla_{\mathcal{M}} L_{para}$

5   update learning rate $\alpha_{i,q}$

6   **end**

7   **end**

8   **for** $j \leftarrow 1$ **to** N **do**

9   **for** $s \leftarrow 1$ **to** S **do**

10      $W_{j,s}, b_{j,s}, \mathcal{M}_{j,s} \leftarrow$

        $W_{j,s-1} + \alpha_{j,s}\nabla_W L_{ext}, \ b_{j,s-1} + \alpha_{j,s}\nabla_b L_{ext}, \ \mathcal{M}_{j,s-1} + \alpha_{j,s}\nabla_{\mathcal{M}} L_{ext}$

11   update learning rate $\alpha_{j,s}$

12   **end**

13 **end**

---

4 Experiments

4.1 Experimental Settings

Summarization Datasets. Three widely-used datasets are adopted for evaluation, including two mainstream English news datasets and one Chinese news dataset:

- CNN/DailyMail [11] consists of news articles and corresponding multi sentences summaries from news stories in CNN and Daily Mail websites.
- Xsum [12] is more abstractive with only single-sentence summaries that answers the question "What is the article about?".
- CNewSum [30] is a high-quality Chinese news dataset collected from hundreds of thousands of news publishers with human-authored summaries.

Paraphrasing Datasets. The present study reports on the adoption of two commonly utilized textual paraphrasing datasets for the purpose of transfer-learning in the context of English and Chinese text summarization tasks:

- Quora Question Pairs (QQP) [31] consists of over 400,000 question pairs, and each question pair is annotated with a binary value indicating whether the two questions are paraphrases of each other.
- LCQMC [32] consists of Chinese question pairs with manual annotations.

Evaluation Metrics. The model performance on English datasets i.e., Xsum and CNN/DailyMail, are evaluated on ROUGE [26,33]. We compute the ROUGE

Table 1. ROUGE evaluations and their average on CNN/DailyMail dataset with 200, 500, 1000, 2000 training samples. Here, R-1/2/L stands for ROUGE-1/2/L, ParaSum^{-p} for ParaSum w/o para. Best results are in bold, and second best results are underlined.

Model	200			500			1000			2000		
	R-1	R-2	R-L	R-1	R-2	R-L	R-1	R-2	R-L	R-1	R-2	R-L
rnn-ext+rl [4]	40.13	<u>17.73</u>	36.36	40.20	17.76	36.42	40.23	17.76	36.46	40.30	17.77	36.51
MemSum [5]	35.30	15.10	32.44	37.05	16.10	33.87	37.11	16.12	33.92	39.14	17.45	35.65
PNBert [9]	40.18	17.58	36.32	40.42	17.95	36.60	40.54	17.96	36.69	40.56	18.06	36.80
BertSumExt [3]	40.34	17.41	<u>36.57</u>	40.45	17.51	36.68	40.48	17.59	36.72	40.49	17.56	36.72
MatchSum [8]	39.75	17.09	36.04	40.50	17.79	36.79	40.98	18.10	37.23	41.45	<u>18.56</u>	<u>37.68</u>
ParaSum^{-p}	<u>40.49</u>	17.53	36.56	<u>41.10</u>	<u>18.26</u>	<u>37.22</u>	<u>41.56</u>	<u>18.44</u>	<u>37.63</u>	<u>41.58</u>	18.51	37.62
ParaSum	**40.81**	**17.78**	**36.94**	**41.28**	**18.31**	**37.42**	**41.76**	**18.70**	**37.86**	**41.86**	**18.62**	**37.91**

scores using the standard pyrouge package, and report the F1 scores of ROUGE-1, ROUGE-2, and ROUGE-L. These metrics measure the uniform, bigram, and longest common subsequence overlapping between the candidate summaries generated by different methods and the corresponding reference summaries.

Baselines: rnn-ext+rl [4] is a reinforcement learning (RL) based autoregressive summarization method; **PNBert** [9] is a RL-based extractive summarization method that utilizes BERT as its base model, with ROUGE-based rewards; **BertSumExt** [3] is a ranking-based method that performs binary classification on each sentence based on its contextual representation from BERT; **MatchSum** [8] is the current state-of-the-art method that formulates summarization as a text-matching task, and employs a two-stage approach based on BertSumExt [3]. **MemSum** [5] is a recently proposed method that is specifically designed for summarizing long documents. This approach views extractive summarization as a multi-step episodic Markov Decision Process (MDP) that is aware of the extraction history.

Implementation Details: For the CNewSum dataset, ParaSum, PNBert, BertSumExt, and MatchSum employ the "bert-base-chinese" version of BERT, while rnn-ext+rl utilizes Chinese word embeddings [34]. We set $K = 5$ and $I = 2, 3$ for CNN/DailyMail, $I = 1$ for Xsum, and $I = 2$ for CNewSum. The reported best experimental results are obtained through multiple rounds of experiments, with concurrent grid search for the number of QQP sentence pairs used in textual paraphrasing transfer learning.

4.2 Experimental Results

Results in Different Low-Resource Settings: We evaluate the performance of ParaSum and baseline methods under various low-resource settings. Table 1 presents ROUGE evaluations of ParaSum and baselines trained with 200, 500, 1000, and 2000 samples of CNN/DailyMail. ParaSum^{-p} refers to ParaSum without textual paraphrasing transfer learning, and it consistently outperforms the baselines on all ROUGE metrics when trained with 500 and 1000 samples. Additionally, it outperforms the baselines on the ROUGE-1 metric when trained with

Table 2. Ablation study on CNN/DailyMail dataset with 1000 training samples.

Model	R-1	R-2	R-L
Full implement.	41.76	18.70	37.86
w/o. Para	41.56 (−0.20)	18.44 (−0.26)	37.63 (−0.23)
w/o. CE	41.65 (−0.11)	18.59 (−0.11)	37.76 (−0.10)
w/o. CL	40.18 (−1.58)	17.45 (−1.25)	36.21 (−1.60)

200 and 2000 samples. The results of this study indicate that conventional summarization paradigms are optimized for scenarios where there is an abundance of training instances. Consequently, these paradigms may demonstrate suboptimal performance in low-resource settings. In contrast, the ParaSum approach reframes summarization tasks as textual paraphrasing, which shares similarities with BERT's NSP self-supervised task. As a result, ParaSum is better equipped to leverage pertinent knowledge from BERT, thereby enhancing its performance in the context of summarization. ParaSum exhibits further enhancements over ParaSum^{-p}, and it significantly outperforms the baseline models across all low-resource scenarios. These findings provide compelling evidence that the knowledge obtained from textual paraphrasing can effectively assist the model in distinguishing between salient and trivial summaries, while simultaneously reducing the method's reliance on a large number of training instances.

Ablation Studies: To evaluate the potential advantages of utilizing knowledge from textual paraphrasing for text summarization, we remove the textual paraphrasing transfer learning stage from ParaSum (referred to as ParaSum w/o. Para) and train the model from scratch using randomly initialized parameters. To further investigate the effectiveness of the contrastive learning paradigm in providing high-quality supervision signals, we conducted an additional experiment in which we removed either the cross-entropy loss (referred to as ParaSum w/o. CE) or the contrastive loss (referred to as ParaSum w/o. CL) from ParaSum during the training phase. Table 2 presents the ROUGE evaluations of ParaSum and its ablations, trained with 1000 samples of CNN/DailyMail. Our experimental results indicate that removing the contrastive loss from ParaSum (ParaSum w/o. CL) results in a significant decrease in performance. This finding aligns with the theoretical foundations of contrastive learning, which posit that it can effectively guide the model to differentiate between the most important summary among any given pair of candidate summaries, thus providing more supervised signals to the model. In contrast, removing the cross-entropy loss from ParaSum (ParaSum w/o. CE) leads to a modest reduction in model performance. This is likely because the cross-entropy loss encourages the model to assign a high probability to the most optimal summary, thereby enhancing the overall quality of the summarization output. Furthermore, removing the textual paraphrasing pre-training stage from ParaSum (ParaSum w/o. Para) results in a significant decrease in model performance. This finding provides compelling evidence that the knowledge acquired through textual paraphrasing can effectively aid ParaSum in distinguishing between crucial and non-essential summaries.

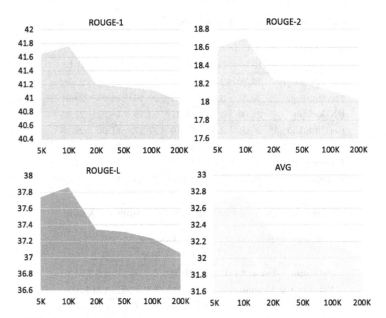

Fig. 2. Evaluations of ParaSum pre-trained with different amount of QQP sentence pairs and trained with 1000 samples of CNN/DailyMail. Avg stands for average results.

Impact of the Quantity of QQP Data: In this study, we carried out an evaluation to examine the effect of the number of QQP sentence pairs used in the transfer learning stage on ParaSum. Following the transfer learning stage, we trained ParaSum using 1000 samples of CNN/DailyMail. The results concerning the influence of varying the number of QQP sentence pairs on model performance are presented in Fig. 2. The experimental results reveal that Para-Sum attains optimal performance when pre-trained using 10,000 Quora Question Pairs (QQP) sentence pairs in transfer learning stage. The performance of Para-Sum tends to degrade as the number of QQP sentence pairs increases. This is likely due to the fact that an excessive number of QQP pairs can cause ParaSum to deviate from extractive summarization and overfit to the QQP dataset. Conversely, decreasing the quantity of QQP sentence pairs also leads to a decrease in performance, as the model may not acquire sufficient knowledge to improve extractive summarization.

Generalization Studies: To evaluate the generalizability of ParaSum, we conducted an assessment on two additional datasets: Xsum, which is an abstractive summarization dataset, and CNewSum, which is a high-quality Chinese summarization dataset. For this evaluation, we utilized a training set comprising of 1000 samples for each dataset. Table 3 presents the results of our evaluation of ParaSum and the baseline models on Xsum and CNewSum. Our results demonstrate that although ParaSum outperforms the baseline models on the Xsum dataset, it only exhibits a minimal improvement over MatchSum, and slightly underperforms MemSum on the ROUGE-2 evaluation metric. This finding may

Table 3. ROUGE evaluations on Xsum and CNewSum.

Model	Xsum			CNewSum		
	R-1	R-2	R-L	R-1	R-2	R-L
rnn-ext+rl [4]	19.70	2.41	14.85	30.12	17.28	25.02
MemSum [5]	20.32	**3.26**	15.84	29.26	14.99	23.91
PNBert [9]	21.06	3.06	15.87	33.18	18.22	27.85
BertSumExt [3]	20.01	2.61	15.16	31.17	17.00	26.25
MatchSum [8]	21.12	3.03	15.74	32.48	18.22	27.05
ParaSum^{-p}	20.97	3.04	15.72	33.09	18.46	27.47
ParaSum	**21.15**	3.08	**15.91**	**33.76**	**19.22**	**28.26**

Table 4. T-Test of ParaSum and baselines on Xsum.

Method Comparison	Xsum P-Value		
	R-1	R-2	R-L
ParaSum & rnn-ext+rl	1.22E-09	7.33E-11	4.87E-12
ParaSum & MemSum	4.92E-11	3.04E-08	1.50E-02
ParaSum & PNBert	8.61E-06	1.00E-03	6.00E-03
ParaSum & BertSumExt	5.94E-12	9.26E-09	1.66E-10
ParaSum & MatchSum	2.70E-02	2.01E-05	8.05E-07

be attributed to the fact that Xsum imposes strict limitations on the methods, allowing them to select only a single sentence to create the summary. As a result, the potential performance gains offered by ParaSum are limited. To further analyze the performance of ParaSum and the baseline models on Xsum, we conducted T-tests with a confidence level of 0.95, and the results are presented in Table 4. The results of the T-tests reveal that the P-Values of ParaSum and the baseline models on the ROUGE-1, ROUGE-2, and ROUGE-L metrics are below the threshold of 0.05. This suggests that the observed differences in performance are statistically significant, thereby providing further support for the superior performance of ParaSum over the baseline models. In contrast, evaluations on CNewSum dataset demonstrated that ParaSum significantly outperformed the baseline models. This finding emphasizes the importance of utilizing knowledge acquired from textual paraphrasing and pre-trained language models in low-resource scenarios, especially when summarizing a document whose reference summary comprising multiple sentences.

Case Study: Table 5 illustrates a use case of ParaSum and various baselines, with models trained using 1000 CNN/DailyMail samples. The first and second sentences extracted by BertExtSum contain similar content, whereas the third summary sentence deviates from the reference summary by providing additional details. In contrast, the third sentence extracted by MatchSum presents content conveyed in the first summary sentence, thus demonstrating a level of semantic redundancy. Based on the subjective analysis, the summary extracted by ParaSum is superior to the summaries generated by the baseline methods.

Table 5. Use case study of ParaSum and baselines, all of which are trained using 1000 samples from CNN/DailyMail.

Ref. Summary	1. american women look to celebrities for hair inspiration, often uneducated about the potential dangers of beauty procedures 2. many celebrities who wear weaves, such as beyonce, selena gomez and paris hilton, could be doing serious damage to their hair 3. jennifer aniston, sandra bullock and jennifer lopez were revealed as having the three most popular celebrity hairstyles
ParaSum	1. one in five american women are willing to undergo dangerous beauty treatments in order to achieve the ideal look, despite the risks that these procedures pose to their health. 2. the survey, conducted by beauty research organization lqs and associates, looked at the lengths 1,000 american women go to in order to enhance their appearances or copy a celebrity, and the potentially disastrous consequences they might face in doing so, including hair loss, skin swelling, and overly painful procedures.
BertExtSum	1. one in five american women are willing to undergo dangerous beauty treatments in order to achieve the ideal look, despite the risks that these procedures pose to their health. 2. according to a new study, while just over half of women worry about the long term damage of beauty treatments, nearly a fifth would still pursue a treatment to get the right look - even if it proved hazardous to their health. 3. seven per cent, meanwhile, have actually had allergic reactions.
MatchSum	1. according to a new study, while just over half of women worry about the long term damage of beauty treatments, nearly a fifth would still pursue a treatment to get the right look - even if it proved hazardous to their health. 2. the survey, conducted by beauty research organization lqs and associates, looked at the lengths 1,000 american women go to in order to enhance their appearances or copy a celebrity, and the potentially disastrous consequences they might face in doing so, including hair loss, skin swelling, and overly painful procedures. 3. the cost of beauty: women often do n't realize the dangers of salon treatments before sitting in the styling chair

5   Conclusion

To address the issue of limited supervised signals arising from small-scale training datasets, this paper proposes a novel paradigm for extractive summarization called ParaSum, which is tailored for low-resource scenarios. ParaSum reframes extractive summarization as textual paraphrasing between the candidate summaries and the document. This approach helps to reduce the training gap between the summarization model and PLMs, thereby enabling the effective retrieval of relevant knowledge from PLMs to enhance summarization performance. In addition, ParaSum utilizes the knowledge acquired from textual paraphrasing to guide the summarization model in distinguishing high-quality summaries among the candidate summaries. Furthermore, ParaSum takes advantage of contrastive learning to provide additional supervised signals for model training. The experimental results indicate that ParaSum consistently outperforms conventional summarization paradigms in low-resource scenarios.

Acknowledgments. This work was supported by the National Natural Science Foundation of China under Grant No. 62202170 and Alibaba Group through the Alibaba Innovation Research Program.

References

1. Xu, J., Gan, Z., Cheng, Y., Liu, J.: Discourse-aware neural extractive text summarization. In: ACL (2020)
2. Quatra, M., Cagliero, L.: End-to-end training for financial report summarization. In: COLING, pp. 118–123 (2020)
3. Liu, Y., Lapata, M.: Text summarization with pretrained encoders. In: EMNLP-IJCNLP, pp. 3730–3740 (2019)
4. Chen, Y.-C., Bansal, M.: Fast abstractive summarization with reinforce-selected sentence rewriting. In: ACL (2018)
5. Gu, N., Ash, E., Hahnloser, R.: MemSum: extractive summarization of long documents using multi-step episodic Markov decision processes. In: ACL, Ireland, Dublin, pp. 6507–6522 (2022)
6. Devlin, J., Chang, M.W., Lee, K., Toutanova, K.: BERT: pre-training of deep bidirectional transformers for language understanding. In: NAACL, pp. 4171–4186 (2019)
7. Liu, Y., Ott, M., Goyal, N., et al.: Roberta: a robustly optimized BERT pretraining approach, arXiv, vol. abs/1907.11692 (2019)
8. Zhong, M., Liu, P., Chen, Y., Wang, D., Qiu, X., Huang, X.: Extractive summarization as text matching. In: ACL, pp. 6197–6208 (2020)
9. Zhong, M., Liu, P., Wang, D., Qiu, X., Huang, X.: Searching for effective neural extractive summarization: what works and what's next. In: ACL, pp. 1049–1058 (2019)
10. Schick, T., Schütze, H.: It's not just size that matters: small language models are also few-shot learners. In: NAACL, pp. 2339–2352 (2021)
11. Hermann, K.M., et al.: Teaching machines to read and comprehend. In: NeuralIPS, pp. 1693–1701 (2015)
12. Narayan, S., Cohen, S.B., Lapata, M.: Don't give me the details, just the summary! Topic-aware convolutional neural networks for extreme summarization. In: EMNLP (2018)
13. Chen, K., Fu, G., Chen, Q., Hu, B.: A large-scale Chinese long-text extractive summarization corpus. In: ICASSP, pp. 7828–7832 (2021)
14. Shafiq, N., et al.: Abstractive text summarization of low-resourced languages using deep learning. PeerJ Comput. Sci. 9, e1176 (2023)
15. Chen, Y.-S., Song, Y.-Z., Shuai, H.-H.: SPEC: summary preference decomposition for low-resource abstractive summarization. IEEE/ACM Trans. Audio Speech Lang. Process. 31, 603–618 (2022)
16. Huh, T., Ko, Y.: Lightweight meta-learning for low-resource abstractive summarization. In: SIGIR, pp. 2629–2633 (2022)
17. Zaken, E.B., Ravfogel, S., Goldberg, Y.: BitFit: simple parameter-efficient fine-tuning for transformer-based masked language-models. In: ACL, pp. 1–9 (2022)

18. Song, H., Dong, L., Zhang, W., Liu, T., Wei, F.: CLIP models are few-shot learners: empirical studies on VQA and visual entailment. In: ACL, pp. 6088–6100 (2022)
19. Wang, S., Fang, H., Khabsa, M., Mao, H., Ma, H.: Entailment as few-shot learner, CoRR (2021)
20. Gao, P., et al.: CLIP-Adapter: Better Vision-Language Models with Feature Adapters, arXiv (2021)
21. Zhang, R., et al.: Tip-adapter: training-free adaption of CLIP for few-shot classification. In: Avidan, S., Brostow, G., Cissé, M., Farinella, G.M., Hassner, T. (eds.) ECCV 2022. LNCS, vol. 13695, pp. 493–510. Springer, Cham (2022). https://doi.org/10.1007/978-3-031-19833-5_29
22. Houlsby, N., et al.: Parameter-efficient transfer learning for NLP. In: ICML, pp. 2790–2799 (2019)
23. Ganin, Y., et al.: Domain-adversarial training of neural networks. J. Mach. Learn. Res. **17**, 2096-2030 (2016)
24. Yosinski, J., Clune, J., Bengio, Y., Lipson, H.: How transferable are features in deep neural networks? In: NeurIPS (2014)
25. Gao, T., Fisch, A., Chen, D.: Making pre-trained language models better few-shot learners. In: ACL, pp. 3816–3830 (2021)
26. Lin, C.-Y.: ROUGE: a package for automatic evaluation of summaries. In: Text Summarization Branches Out, pp. 74–81 (2004)
27. Radford, A., et al.: Learning transferable visual models from natural language supervision. In: ICML, pp. 8748–8763 (2021)
28. Liu, Y., Liu, P.: SimCLS: a simple framework for contrastive learning of abstractive summarization. In: ACL, pp. 1065–1072 (2021)
29. Liu, Y., Liu, P., Radev, D., Neubig, G.: BRIO: bringing order to abstractive summarization. In: ACL, pp. 2890–2903 (2022)
30. Wang, D., Chen, J., Wu, X., Zhou, H., Li, L.: CNewSum: a large-scale summarization dataset with human-annotated adequacy and deducibility level. In: Wang, L., Feng, Y., Hong, Yu., He, R. (eds.) NLPCC 2021. LNCS (LNAI), vol. 13028, pp. 389–400. Springer, Cham (2021). https://doi.org/10.1007/978-3-030-88480-2_31
31. Sharma, L., Graesser, L., Nangia, N., Evci, U.: Natural language understanding with the quora question pairs dataset, arXiv (2019)
32. Liu, X., et al.: LCQMC: a large-scale Chinese question matching corpus. In: COLING, pp. 1952–1962 (2018)
33. Hu, B., Chen, Q., Zhu, F.: LCSTS: a large scale Chinese short text summarization dataset. In: EMNLP, pp. 1967–1972 (2015)
34. Li, S., Zhao, Z., Hu, R., Li, W., Liu, T., Du, X.: Analogical reasoning on Chinese morphological and semantic relations. In: ACL, pp. 138–143 (2018)

Degree-Aware Embedding and Interactive Feature Fusion-Based Graph Convolution Collaborative Filtering

Chao Ma[1,2], Jiwei Qin[1,2(✉)], and Aohua Gao[1,2]

[1] School of Information Science and Engineering, Xinjiang University,
Urumqi 830046, China
{chao,gaoaohua}@stu.xju.edu.cn, jwqin_xju@163.com
[2] Key Laboratory of Signal Detection and Processing, Xinjiang Uygur Autonomous
Region, Xinjiang University, Urumqi 830046, China

Abstract. The graph convolution network(GCN), as an advanced deep learning technique, has been effectively implemented in the collaborative filtering recommendation system. However, existing graph convolution-based collaborative filtering models neglect a pervasive issue, which is the distinction between users' activity and sensitivity for items' popularity, while the traditional neighbor aggregations in GCN have addressed this issue through Graph Laplacian Normalization, which produces suboptimal personalized outcomes. To solve this problem, this paper proposes a Degree-aware embedding and Interaction feature fusion-based Graph Convolution Collaborative Filtering (Di-GCCF). Firstly, the degree-aware embedding utilizes the degree of nodes in the user-item graph to reflect users' activity and items' popularity. Moreover, it combines users' activity and popularity preferences to generate feature representations of users and items, which enables the model to capture their personalized preferences better. Secondly, the interaction feature fusion merges shallow and high-order features during propagation to improve the representation ability of high-order GCN. Finally, this paper performs comprehensive experiments on four public datasets to validate the effectiveness of our proposed model, and the results demonstrate the superior performance of our model from both analytical and empirical perspectives.

Keywords: Collaborative filtering · Degree-aware · Feature fusion · Graph convolutional network · Recommender system

1 Introduction

Nowadays, recommender systems have gained widespread implementation in various domains to predict personalized preferences [1]. Collaborative filtering [2], a simple and effective technique, is frequently employed as a basic component of various recommender systems [3]. It takes into account the interaction history between users and items, and draws inferences about users' preferred items based on the premise that users with similar interests also exhibit similar patterns of behavior in their interactions with items [4].

Recently, with the great success of graph convolutional network (GCN) in graph-structured data modeling [5], GCN is considered to have tremendous potential in improving recommendation performance [6,7]. This can be attributed to the preponderance of data in recommendation systems exhibiting a graph structure [8], such as the historical interactive data of users can be characterized by the user-item bipartite graph, where edges represent interactions. Additionally, graph structures can combine structured exterior information, such as the social connection between users and the knowledge graphs connected to items [9]. Therefore, it is highly rational to consider transforming the collaborative filtering task in recommendation systems into a graph-based task [10].

Specifically, the critical idea of GCN is that aggregating neighborhood embeddings across uses embedding propagation. Then through stacking multiple layers of propagation, each user and item can obtain information about higher-order neighbors. In earlier studies on graph convolutional collaborative filtering, such as GC-MC [11] can effectively extract the feature representation by utilizing graph convolution network to the users' history interaction graph. However, it only considers first-order neighbors in its feature propagation, which prevents it from capturing higher-order collaborative relationships between users and items. To solve this limitation, NGCF [12] learns high-order collaboration signals by iteratively stacking multi-layer graph convolutions. While the feature propagation and nonlinear transformation operations in NGCF significantly increased training difficulty. Later, LightGCN [13] immensely simplified the training difficulty of NGCF, which produced a better performance.

Although the previously mentioned models have achieved significant success, there remains a primary limitation in GCN. Traditional neighbor aggregation methods capture users' activity and preference differences for items' popularity at a fixed granularity [13,14], which deviates from reality. For instance, a highly active user may have purchased the majority of books in a bookstore, while another user with low activity may have only bought two books. In contrast, the low-activity users' similarity to these two books can better illustrate their relationship. Furthermore, as shown in Fig. 1, users' preferences for item popularity also exhibit significant differences [15]. Existing methods [16,17] have failed to alleviate this inevitable problem, consequently impeding the achievement of excellent personalized preference. In addition, GCN is still constrained by the smoothing problem, that is, with the increase of propagation layers, the learned node embeddings converge towards a constant value. Therefore, existing GCN-based recommendation models are only capable of aggregating low-order relationships to attain optimal performance, which impedes their ability to utilize higher-order relationships.

To solve these issues, this paper proposes a novel model named Di-GCCF, which consists of two components: degree-aware embedding and interactive feature fusion. Specifically, we utilize the degree of nodes in users' history interaction graph to reflect the users' activity and the popularity of items, Subsequently, degree-aware embedding is applied to produce feature representations for users and items. In contrast to previous approaches that capture users' activity and preference for item popularity differences using fixed granularity, our method reduces the influence of active users on the central node and produces feature representations for users and items based on dynamic granularity in accordance with users' preference for item popularity. Furthermore, we propose interactive feature fusion, which fuses shallow and high-order features in the propagation layer, thereby augmenting the models' capacity for feature representation and facilitating the discovery of deeper connections. Finally, we perform comprehensive experiments on four public datasets and validate the efficacy of our model. The findings demonstrate that our model not only surpasses existing methods but also maintains strong performance even with a larger number of stacked layers. In conclusion, this work makes the following significant contributions:

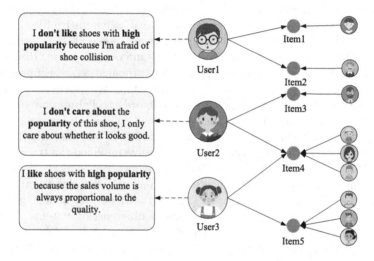

Fig. 1. Illustration of Variations in User Preferences for Item Popularity, illustrates the differences in users' preferences for item popularity. User1 tends to purchase items with low popularity, resulting in a lack of interaction with other users in the right half of the graph. In contrast, User3 favors popular items and has purchased many of them, resulting in high levels of interaction in the interaction graph. User2 is not particularly sensitive to item popularity and has purchased both popular and unpopular items.

- Introducing the degree-aware embedding method to produce feature representations for users and items. This embedding approach reduces the impact of active users on the central node while generating feature representations at a dynamic granularity based on users' preferences for items' popularity.
- Proposing an interaction feature fusion method that combines shallow and high-order features to fully leverage the representational power of deep GCN,

while maintaining good performance at higher levels. This method effectively alleviates the over-smoothing issue in GCN.

- Perform comprehensive experiments on four public datasets to validate the efficacy of the Di-GCCF model. Compared to other existing methods, Di-GCCF demonstrates better performance. Moreover, the experimental results also show that Di-GCCF can consistently achieve promising performance when stacking more layers.

2 Related Work

In early research, for instance, SpectralCF [18] employed spectral convolution operations to define user-item interactions as bipartite graphs to mine the full possible link between users and items. However, using spectral convolution requires feature decomposition, which results in significant time consumption, thus seriously restricting the application scenarios and scope of spectral graph convolution. Later, GCN models used efficient hierarchical propagation rules [5,7,19], which was in view of the first-order approximation of the spectral convolution; that is, the computational complexity is reduced by using spectral graph convolution to simplify the computation. GC-MC [11] was one of the first endeavors to apply graph convolution to user-item interaction graphs directly. However, the message propagation mechanism of GC-MC solely takes into account the immediate neighbors, which makes it unable to gain high-order collaboration relationships between users and items. PinSage [8] combined efficient random walks and GCN operations to obtain user and item features. Later, NGCF [12] learned high-order collaborative signals by iterative stacking of graph convolution. Nevertheless, the feature propagation and nonlinear transformation operations greatly increase the training difficulty. To break the limitations brought by non-linear operations, LR-GCCF [14] eliminates non-linear operations, which makes it much more capable of training models for complex graphs. More importantly, to mitigate the issue of over-smoothing, it also designed a residual structure. LightGCN [13] substantially simplified NGCF by eschewing its transformation function and non-linear activation, leading to superior performance. HMLET [20] incorporates linear and non-linear propagation steps during the processing of each user or item node, where the gating module selectively chooses between the two to create a hybrid GCN-based collaborative filtering model.

However, these graph-based collaborative filtering models have not fully addressed differences in users' activity and preference for item popularity, as well as the issue of over-smoothing in recommendations. In contrast, we endeavor to apply degree-aware embedding to reduce the influence of active users on the central node, and generates feature representations at a dynamic granularity based on user preferences for item popularity. Furthermore, we employ interactive feature fusion to alleviate over-smoothing, thereby enabling the model to explore deeper connections.

3   Methodology

In this section, we will offer an elaborate exposition of various pivotal con-
stituents of our model, as illustrated in Fig. 2. The critical elements of the
framework include (1) degree-aware embedding, which provides an initialization
approach for user and item embeddings and generates feature representations for
users and items; (2) feature propagation, which processes the user-item bipartite graph to obtain relationships between nodes and perform interaction feature
fusion, integrating shallow and high-order features in the propagation layer; (3)
model prediction, which is applied to obtain the interaction probability of user-
item pairs.

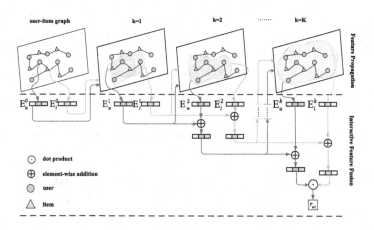

Fig. 2. Overall architecture of Di-GCCF.

3.1   Degree-Aware Embedding

We represent the interaction between users and items using the sparse matrix
$R \in R^{m \times n}$, where m and n denote the number of users and items, respectively.
Specifically, if $r_{ui} = 1$ indicates a prior interaction between u and i, while $r_{ui} = 0$
otherwise. Upon obtaining R, the user-item bipartite graph $G = < U \cup I, A >$ can
be constructed, which comprises two distinct sets of nodes, i.e., user and item
nodes. The adjacency matrix $A \in R^{(m+n) \times (m+n)}$, which is constructed from the
interaction matrix R,

$$A = \begin{pmatrix} 0 & R \\ R^T & 0 \end{pmatrix}.$$ (1)

In Eq. 1, where $0 \in R^{m \times n}$ is a null matrix, the adjacency matrix $\tilde{A}$ can be
gained by adding the identity matrix I to the adjacency matrix A.

Traditional GCN-based methods use Laplacian normalization to fix the differences in users' activity and preference for items' popularity, which deviates from the actual situation. For example, a highly active user may have purchased a majority of the books in a bookstore, while another less active user may have only purchased two books, indicating that the similarity between these two books is more significant for the less active user. Therefore, when dealing with highly active users, their weight towards the central node should be appropriately reduced. At the same time, to enhance the sensitivity to item popularity, nodes with higher item popularity should receive increased weights. To obtain a normalized adjacency matrix that incorporates varying levels of activity and popularity features, we propose a method of fine-tuning the adjacency matrix exponent, which is implemented as follows:

$$L_i = (D + I)^{-\frac{1}{2}} \tilde{A} (D + I)^{(P_1 - 1)}, \tag{2}$$

$$L_u = (D + I)^{(P_2 - 1)} \tilde{A} (D + I)^{-\frac{1}{2}}, \tag{3}$$

$$L = \alpha L_i + (1 - \alpha) L_u. \tag{4}$$

Where, D represents the degree matrix of adjacency matrix A. In Eq. 4, L is the Laplacian matrix obtained by merging two different aggregators. Specifically, when considering user preference for item popularity, we set P_1 as the granularity of popularity, indicating the extent to which embeddings are adjusted based on changes in popularity. As P_1 increases, the weight of node popularity increases, forcing the model to more easily recommend more popular items to users. When $P_1 = 0.5$, Eq. 2, is the same as traditional graph convolutional operations, considering only the CF signal modeling. When $P_1 = 0.6$, the model begins incorporating larger popularity features and appropriately upgrades embedding values. When $P_1 = 0.7$ or bigger, the models' popularity granularity is larger and the embedding values are higher, making the model more sensitive to the popularity level. We consider that users have different preferences for popularity features, so when generating item embeddings, we set different popularity granularities P_1 for each node, enabling the model to encompass products with varying degrees of popularity to the greatest extent feasible and thereby increasing user satisfaction. Secondly, when considering users' activity, we set P_2 as the granularity of activity, indicating the degree to which embeddings are adjusted based on changes in activity. The smaller P_2, the lower the weight of nodes with respect to activity, compelling the model to decrease the weight of users with high activity, where when $P_2 = 0.5$, Eq. 3 is equivalent to traditional graph convolutional operation, considering only the CF signal. When $P_2 = 0.4$, the model starts to incorporate finer-grained activity features and appropriately decrease embedding values. When $P_2 = 0.3$ or smaller, the model is less sensitive to activity, with lower embedding values corresponding to less weight on user activity. Due to variations in user activity, we set a different activity granularity P_2 for each node when generating user embeddings, to maximize the model's ability to cover users with different activity levels and thereby increase user satisfaction.

3.2   Interaction Feature Fusion

With the increased number of propagation layers in GCN, the learned embeddings of individual nodes become less distinctive, rendering discernment between the nodes more challenging. Existing GCN-based recommendation models are limited to aggregating shallow relationships, achieving at most a performance peak of three or four layers. This constraint restricts their ability to utilize higher-order relationships to enhance performance. To address this issue, we propose an interaction feature fusion module, which fuses shallow and high-order features at the propagation layer. Specifically:

$$E^{(0)} = \left[\underbrace{e_{u_1}^{(0)}, \cdots, e_{u_m}^{(0)}}_{user\,embeddings}, \underbrace{e_{i_1}^{(0)}, \cdots, e_{i_n}^{(0)}}_{item\,embeddings} \right], \tag{5}$$

$$E^{(1)} = L \times E^{(0)}, \tag{6}$$

$$E^{(2)} = L \times E^{(1)} + E^{(1)}. \tag{7}$$

In Eq. 5, where $E^{(0)}$ represents the embedding matrix of the 0th layer for users and items. In Eq. 6, $E^{(1)}$ represents the feature representation generated after aggregating the first layer of graph convolutional networks. While computing the second layer feature $E^{(2)}$, we integrate the feature representation $E^{(1)}$ generated from the first layer, in order to enhance the capability of the $E^{(2)}$ feature representation. Subsequently, we fuse the second-order features $E^{(2)}$ into the calculation of higher-order features. Specifically:

$$E^{(k+1)} = L \times E^{(k)} + E^{(2)} (k \geq 3). \tag{8}$$

In Eq. 8, where $E^{(k+1)}$ represents the feature representation of the $k+1$ layer, which is formed by merging the aggregated features of the kth layer and the second layer's features. This approach enables the preservation of low-order feature information while also exploring high-order information. It is necessary to explain why the second layer features are fused instead of the initial feature or first layer features. Firstly, both $E^{(0)}$, $E^{(1)}$ and $E^{(2)}$ belong to low-order features, but $E^{(2)}$ contains more abundant feature information than $E^{(0)}$ and $E^{(1)}$. Secondly, in the propagation process of GCN, the user's direct neighbors are items and the 2-hop neighbors are users. Adding second-order neighbors allows users to obtain isomorphic node information from similar users directly and enables items to obtain similar information directly. Finally, we have also validated the advantage of adding $E^{(2)}$ features in the experimental section.

To alleviate the issue of over-smoothing, we fuse low-order and high-order features. Furthermore, to further mitigate this problem and draw inspiration from the adaptive combination approach mentioned in LaGCF [21], we introduce weight parameters $W^{(k)} \in R$ in the linear aggregation. Specifically:

$$E^{(k+1)} = L(E^{(k)} + E^{(2)})(\frac{\beta}{k}W^{(k)} + (1 - \frac{\beta}{k})I^{(k)}). \tag{9}$$

3.3   Feature Representation

User u and item i can gain numerous features through k layers feature propagation, which are respectively represented as $\{E_u^{(1)}, E_u^{(2)}, ..., E_u^{(k)}\}$ and $\{E_i^{(1)}, E_i^{(2)}, ..., E_i^{(k)}\}$, respectively. It is noteworthy that the features obtained from various layers stem from diverse connections, which can supplement each other, so a more true representation of both users and items is reflected. Therefore, a commonly used method is to fuse these representations to obtain the ultimate representation of user and item. Specifically:

$$E_u = \frac{1}{(K+1)} \sum_{k=0}^{k} E_u^{(k)}, \qquad (10)$$

$$E_i = \frac{1}{(K+1)} \sum_{k=0}^{k} E_i^{(k)}. \qquad (11)$$

3.4   Model Training

The loss function is a pivotal element in the training of deep learning. It facilitates the precise update of model parameters through the computation of gradient values, thus directing the training process toward accuracy. In recommendation systems, various loss functions are commonly utilized for different usage scenarios, including pairwise, pointwise, and listwise loss functions. In this paper, we employ the pairwise loss function Bayesian Personalized Ranking (BPR) [22].

Specifically, BPR presumes that compared with unobserved interactions, the interaction of observation items should be given a higher predictive score. This can be described as:

$$Loss = - \sum_{(u,i,j) \in O} -\ln \sigma(eu \bullet ei - eu \bullet ej) + \lambda \|\theta\|_2^2. \qquad (12)$$

Where $O = \{(u,i,j)|(u,i) \in R^+, (u,j) \in R^-\}$ denotes the paired training data, R^+ denotes the set of observed interactions, R^- denotes the set of unobserved interactions. Function $\sigma(\bullet)$ denotes the sigmoid function, $\theta = \left\{ E^{(0)}, \left\{ W^{(k)} \right\}_{k=1}^{K} \right\}$ denotes the trainable parameters of the model. To prevent overfitting, λ is utilized to restrict the strength of L_2 regularization.

4   Experimental Evaluation

4.1   Datasets and Evaluation Metrics

In this paper, we conducted a series of experiments on four real-world datasets to demonstrate the efficacy of our proposed model: Ciao DVD[1] (Ciao for short),

---

[1] http://www.ciao.co.uk.

Movielens-1M[2] (ML-1M for short), Yelp[3], and Gowalla[4]. All of these datasets are publicly available. We excluded users and items with fewer than 10 interactions from all datasets. The statistical data of these datasets is presented in Table 1. To conduct model training and evaluation, we partitioned the items in each users' interaction history into a training set and a testing set, with 80% randomly selected for training and the remaining 20% reserved for testing. For pairwise learning, every user-item interaction observed is regarded as a positive example, while a randomly chosen unobserved interaction is considered a negative example.

Table 1. Statistics of the experimented data

Dataset	#User	#Item	#Interaction	Sparsity
Ciao	442	534	9822	95.839%
ML-1M	6040	3706	1000209	95.532%
Yelp	7062	7488	167456	99.683%
Gowalla	29858	40988	1027464	99.916%

For all experiments, this paper employs the following two metrics to evaluate our model and baseline: Recall@20 and NDCG@20. Recall@k denotes the scope of authentic items for top-k recommendations, whereas NDCG@k functions as a gauge for the standard of ranking.

4.2 Baseline Algorithms

This paper presents a comparative analysis between the proposed model and the following existing methods:

- **MF [23]:** This model is a matrix factorization approach widely used as a baseline for recommendation systems, which adopts the Bayesian personalized ranking loss function.
- **NeuMF [24]:** This model is a hybrid model that integrates matrix factorization with neural networks for collaborative filtering. By fusing the results of the MF model and MLP model and simultaneously learning low-order and high-order representations of latent vectors, it improves the model's predictive accuracy.
- **GC-MC [11]:** This model is a GCN-based matrix completion approach, which combines graph convolution and matrix factorization. By utilizing the graph structure information to embed representations of users and items and using the embedded vectors as input for matrix factorization, it improves the accuracy and stability of recommendation.

---

[2] https://github.com/familyld/DeepCF.
[3] https://www.yelp.com/dataset.
[4] https://snap.stanford.edu/data/loc-gowalla.html.

- **NGCF** [12]: This model is a collaborative filtering method make use of GCN that refines user feature and item feature by putting user-item interaction data into multiple embedding propagation layers. And the obtained multiple layers of embeddings are connected together to get the complete feature.
- **LR-GCCF** [14]: This model can be seen as a linear GCN-based recommender model, which simplifies the NGCF model, resulting in a straightforward yet effective recommendation model.
- **LightGCN** [13]: This model is the most advanced collaborative filtering model achieved by using graph convolution network, which is developed by simplifying and eliminating some unnecessary operations in the NGCF model and gets good performance.
- **HMLET** [20]: This model incorporates linear and non-linear propagation steps during the processing of each user or item node, where the gating module selectively chooses between the two to create a hybrid GCN-based collaborative filtering model.

4.3   Parameter Settings

For all baseline models that we compared, including MF, GC-MC, NeuMF, LR-GCCF, NGCF, LightGCN and HMLET, we used the publicly available code published by the respective authors. To ensure fairness in our experiments, we set the embedding size of all models to the optimal value of 64 provided in the papers, where GC-MC utilized a single graph convolutional layer, while NGCF and LightGCN used 3 layers of graph convolution. The learning rate of Adam was set to 0.001, mini-batch size was 2048, and the L_2 regularization coefficient λ was set to $1e^{-4}$. In our model, we adjusted the L_2 regularization coefficient λ within the range of $\left\{1e^{-5}, 1e^{-4}, ..., 1e^{-1}\right\}$ and the parameter β within the range of $\{0.0001, 0.001, 0.005, 0.01, 0.5, 1.0\}$. The number of graph convolutional layers was set to 7.

Table 2. Experimental results of different models on Ciao, ML-1M, Yelp, and Gowalla. The best results of the model are shown in bold, and the second-best result is underlined. The evaluation metrics are recall@20 and ndcg@20 by default.

Dataset	Ciao		ML-1M		Yelp		Gowalla	
Model	recall	ndcg	recall	ndcg	recall	ndcg	recall	ndcg
MF	0.2467	0.1600	0.2023	0.2971	0.0833	0.0575	0.1536	0.1224
NeuMF	0.2419	0.1539	0.2259	0.3424	0.0803	0.0556	0.1266	0.1007
GC-MC	0.2168	0.1300	0.2290	0.3452	0.0860	0.0585	0.1758	0.1378
NGCF	0.2419	0.1489	0.2332	0.3506	0.0928	0.0623	0.1785	0.1401
LR-GCCF	0.2537	0.1692	0.2258	0.3441	0.1020	0.0692	0.1485	0.1164
LightGCN	<u>0.2635</u>	<u>0.1743</u>	0.2434	0.3644	<u>0.1112</u>	<u>0.0760</u>	0.1984	0.1607
HMLET	0.2610	0.1705	<u>0.2461</u>	<u>0.3660</u>	0.1084	0.0740	<u>0.2012</u>	<u>0.1622</u>
Di-GCCF	**0.2796**	**0.1812**	**0.2587**	**0.3841**	**0.1209**	**0.0829**	**0.2090**	**0.1677**

4.4   Performance Comparison

Table 2 exhibits a comprehensive evaluation and assessment of all comparative methodologies in regard to Recall@20 and NGCG@20. Furthermore, we have illustrated the progression curve of the training loss, test recall and ndcg in Fig. 3 to divulge the superiority of our model. According to the findings, we have noted the following observations:

(1) Compared with traditional models, GCN-based approaches demonstrate superior performance due to their ability to leverage graph convolutional networks for extracting higher-order neighbor information, thereby enhancing the model's representational capacity.

(2) LR-GCCF simplifies the NGCF model, leading to improved performance on Ciao and Yelp. However, LR-GCCF performs worse than NGCF on ML-1M and Gowalla, likely due to the existence of more intricate relationships in these two datasets. Without feature transformation, LR-GCCF cannot fully exploit its advantages. LightGCN outperforms both LR-GCCF and NGCF by removing self-connections and introducing layer combinations. HMLET uses linear and non-linear propagation to improve its performance on ML-1M and Gowalla. However, HMLET performs worse than LightGCN on Ciao and Yelp, likely owing to the sparse nature of the interaction data in the two datasets, the number of interactions is relatively low.

(3) The proposed model exhibits superior performance on all datasets, with Di-GCCF's Recall@20 improving by 6.11%, 5.12%, 8.72%, and 3.88%, respectively, over the best baseline on Ciao, ML-1M, Yelp, and Gowalla. This indicates the effectiveness of introducing degree-aware embeddings and interaction feature fusion. Di-GCCF is particularly suitable for practical applications with highly sparse interactions, as it can utilize high-order relationships when facing fewer interactions.

(4) Throughout the training process, Di-GCCF consistently attains a lower training loss compared to LightGCN, signifying that Di-GCCF is more closely with the training data. This lower training loss subsequently translates into superior test accuracy, corroborating the greater generalization ability of Di-GCCF.

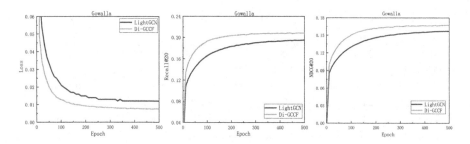

Fig. 3. Training curves of Di-GCCF and LightGCN were evaluated on the Gowalla dataset based on the training loss, testing recall, and ndcg per 10 epochs.

4.5   Ablation Analysis

Effect of Propagation Layers. GCN based models are often limited by the oversmooth problem, which makes rising the number of propagation layers unable to effectively improve the expression ability. To address this, we conducted experiments to compare GCN-based methods with various numbers of layers (k) and examined whether the introduction of degree-aware embeddings and interactive feature fusion can alleviate the smoothing problem. Figure 4 demonstrates the results for Recall@20 and NDCG@20 on Ciao and Yelp. According to the experimental findings, the following observations can be made:

(1) The problem of gradient disappearance hinders the effective training of LightGCN when the number of layers surpasses 8. After attaining the peak performance, the performance indicators of LightGCN precipitously deteriorate, resulting in suboptimal performance.

(2) The performance of Di-GCCF consistently outperforms other models with the rising of the k. Especially as the number of layers surpasses 7, the disparity in performance between our model and other approaches becomes increasingly pronounced. This further proves that our design of degree-aware embeddings and interactive feature fusion is effective in improving the expressive ability of GCN-based models.

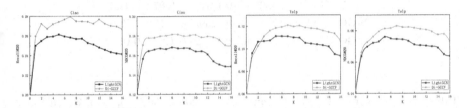

Fig. 4. The trend of Recall@20 and NDCG@20 of LightGCN, Di-GCCF with increased number of layers on Ciao and Yelp.

Effect of Different Components. To examine the impact of degree-aware embedding, interactive feature fusion (iff for short), and adaptive combination (ac for short) on performance, For conducting ablation studies, we evaluated several variations of Di-GCCF models, which are summarized in Table 3. Because of space constraints, we only reported the results of Di-GCCF on Ciao and Yelp, as Di-GCCF exhibited the performance trends observed on the other two datasets are similar. According to the obtained results, we have noted the following observations:

(1) For a fixed number of layers, the performance of the approach that lacks interactive feature fusion and adaptive combination is inferior to that of the approach that employs only one of these techniques, while the method with both interactive feature fusion and adaptive combination, Di-GCCF, always achieves the best results.

(2) Intuitively, Di-GCCF using L_i aggregated neighbors outperformed those using L_u aggregated neighbors. However, the combination of L_i and L_u achieved the best performance. It should be noted that we simply added L_i and L_u together and adjusted their weights to obtain superior results.

(3) By replacing $E^{(2)}$, we investigated the impact of the initial feature $E^{(0)}$ and the first-layer feature representation $E^{(1)}$ on the model's interaction feature fusion. It can be observed that if $E^{(0)}$ and $E^{(1)}$ and are used, the performance will decline, which further explains why we use $E^{(2)}$ for interaction feature fusion in the model.

Table 3. The effectiveness of different components in Di-GCCF.

Dataset	Ciao		Yelp	
Methods	recall	ndcg	recall	ndcg
Di-GCCF/L_u	0.2699	0.1775	0.1199	0.0821
Di-GCCF/L_i	0.2616	0.1701	0.1033	0.0692
Di-GCCF/$E^{(0)}$	0.2639	0.1755	0.1029	0.0720
Di-GCCF/$E^{(1)}$	0.2706	0.1786	0.1177	0.0806
Di-GCCF/iff	0.2643	0.1741	0.1177	0.0797
Di-GCCF/ac	0.2791	0.1812	0.1207	0.0827
Di-GCCF/iff+ac	0.2632	0.1739	0.1175	0.0798
Di-GCCF	**0.2796**	**0.1812**	**0.1209**	**0.0829**

Table 4. Performance of Recall@20 and NDCG@20 on the Ciao, Yelp, Gowalla and ML-1M dataset, different granularity of popularity and activity features.

Dataset	Ciao		ML-1M		Yelp		Gowalla	
Method	recall	ndcg	recall	ndcg	recall	ndcg	recall	ndcg
$P_1 = 0.7$, $P_2 = 0.4$	**0.2796**	**0.1812**	0.2380	0.3620	0.1206	0.0823	0.1997	0.1567
$P_1 = 0.7$, $P_2 = 0.1$	0.2753	0.1806	0.2450	0.3714	**0.1209**	**0.0829**	0.2034	0.1603
$P_1 = 0.6$, $P_2 = 0.4$	0.2725	0.1792	0.2571	0.3823	0.1172	0.0800	0.2075	0.1669
$P_1 = 0.6$, $P_2 = 0.1$	0.2732	0.1779	**0.2587**	**0.3841**	0.1170	0.0795	**0.2090**	**0.1677**
$P_1 = 0.5$, $P_2 = 0.5$	0.2727	0.1762	0.2570	0.3828	0.1146	0.0775	0.2055	0.1638

Effect of Using Popularity and Activate Integration. We employed sensitivity features, specifically $P_1 = 0.7$, $P_1 = 0.6$, $P_2 = 0.4$, and $P_2 = 0.1$, to model user activity and item popularity, and as a consequence, we developed four distinct levels of granularity in our features. Experimental outcomes, as demonstrated in Table 4, exhibit diverse effects at various levels of granularity across four datasets, highlighting the importance of modeling user preferences with activity and popularity characteristics, and confirming the existence of preferences disparity among users with regard to item popularity characteristics. Moreover, we have observed that integrating item popularity features yields more pronounced performance improvements in the Ciao and Yelp datasets, which could be attributed to the heightened sensitivity of users towards item popularity in these two scenarios. We also observed that decreasing the weight assigned to active users in the ML-1M and Gowalla datasets can significantly enhance the model's performance. Finally, we have observed that when simultaneously adjusting P_1 and P_2 to 0.5, resulting in the transformation of the model into a traditional aggregator, the performance of the model significantly deteriorates across the four datasets, thereby further substantiating the efficacy of the proposed multi-granularity embedding.

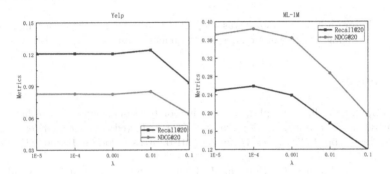

Fig. 5. Varying λ with 7-layer LaGCF on Yelp and ML-1M.

Hyper-Parameter Sensitivity. Further sensitivity analysis of the key parameter L_2 regularization coefficient λ was conducted, and the performance of the 7-layer Di-GCCF was studied. As shown in Fig. 5, different values of λ were tested. Our results were demonstrated on both the Yelp and ML-1M datasets.

(1) As depicted in Fig. 5, Di-GCCF achieved the highest performance on the Yelp dataset when λ was set to 0.01, and the highest performance on the ML-1M dataset was achieved when λ was set to $1e^{-4}$. It is worth noting that when λ was relatively small ($\lambda = 1e^{-3}$), there was no significant degradation in model performance on both datasets. This suggests that the Di-GCCF model is highly stable and less prone to overfitting. Conversely, when λ was set to a large value ($\lambda = 0.1$ or greater), the model exhibited unsatisfactory performance, potentially due to the excessive L_2 regularization that curtails the models' learning capacity. Therefore, it is recommended not to choose a too large L_2 regularization coefficient when applying Di-GCCF to new datasets.

5   Conclusion and Future Work

In this paper, we introduce a new approach to collaborative filtering based on GCN, which we refer to as Di-GCCF. It combines degree-aware embeddings and interaction feature fusion. In degree-aware embeddings, we utilize the users' activity and items' popularity to generate feature representations for users and items, thereby better capturing personalized preferences. In the interaction feature fusion, we enhance the capability of feature representation by fusing shallow features and higher-order features in the propagation layer. We have conducted comprehensive experiments on four public datasets, and the results have shown that our proposed model surpasses all baseline models. Furthermore, we have validated the effectiveness of each component through ablation experiments. In future studies, we intend to introduce adaptive attention mechanisms that adjust the weights of users' activity and users' preference differences for item popularity. Furthermore, we aim to propose a layer selection mechanism that allows the model to select the optimal graph convolutional layer for obtaining feature representations for users and items, rather than relying on weighted averages.

Acknowledgements. This work was supported by the Science Fund for Outstanding Youth of Xinjiang Uygur Autonomous Region under Grant No. 2021D01-E14.

References

1. Ricci, F., Rokach, L., Shapira, B.: Introduction to recommender systems handbook. In: Ricci, F., Rokach, L., Shapira, B., Kantor, P. (eds.) Recommender Systems Handbook, pp. 1–35. Springer, Boston (2010). https://doi.org/10.1007/978-0-387-85820-3_1
2. Sarwar, B., Karypis, G., Konstan, J., Riedl, J.: Item-based collaborative filtering recommendation algorithms. In: Proceedings of the 10th International Conference on World Wide Web, pp. 285–295 (2001). https://doi.org/10.1145/371920.372071
3. Hu, Y., Koren, Y., Volinsky, C.: Collaborative filtering for implicit feedback datasets. In: 2008 Eighth IEEE International Conference on Data Mining, pp. 263–272 (2008). https://doi.org/10.1109/ICDM.2008.22
4. Pujahari, A., Sisodia, D.S.: Preference relation based collaborative filtering with graph aggregation for group recommender system. Appl. Intell. **51**, 658–672 (2021). https://doi.org/10.1007/s10489-020-01848-4
5. Kipf, T.N., Welling, M.: Semi-supervised classification with graph convolutional networks. arXiv preprint arXiv:1609.02907 (2016)
6. Defferrard, M., Bresson, X., Vandergheynst, P.: Convolutional neural networks on graphs with fast localized spectral filtering. In: Advances in Neural Information Processing Systems 29 (2016). https://doi.org/10.48550/arXiv.1606.09375
7. Hamilton, W., Ying, Z., Leskovec, J.: Inductive representation learning on large graphs. In: Advances in Neural Information Processing Systems 30 (2017). https://doi.org/10.48550/arXiv.1706.02216
8. Ying, R., He, R., Chen, K., Eksombatchai, P., Hamilton, W.L., Leskovec, J.: Graph convolutional neural networks for web-scale recommender systems. In: Proceedings of the 24th ACM SIGKDD International Conference on Knowledge Discovery & Data Mining, pp. 974–983 (2018). https://doi.org/10.1145/3219819.3219890
9. Wu, S., Sun, F., Zhang, W., Xie, X., Cui, B.: Graph neural networks in recommender systems: a survey. ACM Comput. Surv. **55**(5), 1–37 (2022). https://doi.org/10.1145/3535101

10. Derr, T., Ma, Y., Tang, J.: Signed graph convolutional networks. In: 2018 IEEE International Conference on Data Mining (ICDM), pp. 929–934 (2018)
11. Berg, R.v.d., Kipf, T.N., Welling, M.: Graph convolutional matrix completion. arXiv preprint arXiv:1706.02263 (2017). https://doi.org/10.48550/arXiv. 1706.02263
12. Wang, X., He, X., Wang, M., Feng, F., Chua, T.-S.: Neural graph collaborative filtering, pp. 165–174 (2019). https://doi.org/10.1145/3331184.3331267
13. He, X., Deng, K., Wang, X., Li, Y., Zhang, Y., Wang, M.: LightGCN: simplifying and powering graph convolution network for recommendation. In: Proceedings of the 43rd International ACM SIGIR Conference on Research and Development in Information Retrieval, pp. 639–648 (2020). https://doi.org/10.1145/3397271. 3401063
14. Chen, L., Wu, L., Hong, R., Zhang, K., Wang, M.: Revisiting graph based collaborative filtering: a linear residual graph convolutional network approach. In: Proceedings of the AAAI Conference on Artificial Intelligence, vol. 34, no. 01, pp. 27–34 (2020). https://doi.org/10.1609/aaai.v34i01.5330
15. Liu, K., Xue, F., He, X., Guo, D., Hong, R.: Joint multi-grained popularity-aware graph convolution collaborative filtering for recommendation. IEEE Trans. Comput. Soc. Syst. **10**, 72–83 (2022)
16. Steck, H.: Item popularity and recommendation accuracy, In: Proceedings of the Fifth ACM Conference on Recommender Systems, pp. 125–132 (2011). https:// doi.org/10.1145/2043932.2043957
17. Li, H., Liu, J., Cao, B., Tang, M., Liu, X., Li, B.: Integrating tag, topic, cooccurrence, and popularity to recommend web APIs for mashup creation, pp. 84–91. IEEE (2017). https://doi.org/10.1109/SCC.2017.19
18. Lei, Z., Chun-Ta, L., Fei, J., Jiawei, Z.: Spectral collaborative filtering. In: Proceedings of the 12th ACM Conference on Recommender Systems, pp. 311–319 (2018). https://doi.org/10.1145/3240323.3240343
19. Xue, G., Zhong, M., Li, J., Chen, J., Zhai, C., Kong, R.: Dynamic network embedding survey. Neurocomputing **472**, 212–223 (2022). https://doi.org/10.1016/j. neucom.2021.03.138
20. Kong, T., et al.: Linear, or non-linear, that is the question! In: Proceedings of the Fifteenth ACM International Conference on Web Search and Data Mining, pp. 517–525 (2022). https://doi.org/10.1145/3488560.3498501
21. Guo, Z., Wang, C., Li, Z., Li, J., Li, G.: Joint locality preservation and adaptive combination for graph collaborative filtering. In: Bhattacharya, A., et al. (eds.) Database Systems for Advanced Applications. DASFAA 2022. LNCS, vol. 13246, pp. 183–198. Springer, Cham (2022). https://doi.org/10.1007/978-3-031-00126- 0_12
22. Rendle, S., Freudenthaler, C., Gantner, Z., Schmidt-Thieme, L.: BPR: Bayesian personalized ranking from implicit feedback. arXiv preprint arXiv:1205.2618 (2012)
23. Koren, Y., Bell, R., Volinsky, C.: Matrix factorization techniques for recommender systems. Computer **42**(8), 30–37 (2009). https://doi.org/10.1109/MC.2009.263
24. He, X., Liao, L., Zhang, H., Nie, L., Hu, X., Chua, T.-S.: Neural collaborative filtering. In: Proceedings of the 26th International Conference on World Wide Web, pp. 173–182 (2017). https://doi.org/10.1145/3038912.3052569

Hypergraph Enhanced Contrastive Learning for News Recommendation

Mankun Zhao[1,2,3], Zhao Liu[1,2,3], Mei Yu[1,2,3], Wenbin Zhang[1,2,4],
Yue Zhao[1,2,4], Ming Yang[5], and Jian Yu[1,2,3(✉)]

[1] College of Intelligence and Computing, Tianjin University, Tianjin, China
{zmk,lzhao,yumei,zhangwenbin,zhao_yue,yujian}@tju.edu.cn
[2] Tianjin Key Laboratory of Advanced Networking (TANK Lab), Tianjin, China
[3] Tianjin Key Laboratory of Cognitive Computing and Application, Tianjin, China
[4] Information and Network Center, Tianjin University, Tianjin, China
[5] College of Computing and Software Engineering, Kennesaw State University,
Marietta, GA, USA
ming.yang@kennesaw.edu

Abstract. With the explosion of news information, user interest modeling plays an important role in personalized news recommendation. Many
existing methods usually learn user representations from historically
clicked news articles to represent their overall interest. However, they
neglect the diverse user intents when interacting with items, which can
model accurate user interest. Moreover, GNN methods based on bipartite graph cause the over-smoothing effect when considering high-order
connectivity, which declines the news recommendation quality. To tackle
the above issue, we propose a novel **H**ypergraph **E**nhanced **C**ontrastive
Learning model, named HGCL, to incorporate the intent representation
and the hypergraph representation with a cross-view contrastive learning architecture. Specifically, we design an intent interaction learning
module, which explores user intents of each user-item interaction at a
fine-grained topic level and encodes useful information into the representations of users and items. Meanwhile, the designed hypergraph structure learning module enhances the discrimination ability and enriches
the complex high-order dependencies, which improves the presentation
quality of the recommendation system based on hypergraph enhanced
contrastive learning. Extensive experiments on two real-world datasets
demonstrate the superiority of our model over various state-of-the-art
news recommendation methods.

Keywords: Hypergraph · Graph Neural Networks · Contrastive
Learning

1 Introduction

The amount of news and articles on many news platforms, such as Google News
and Microsoft News have been growing constantly, making it difficult for users
to quickly find the content that they are interested in [1]. To meet the needs of

Z. Jin et al. (Eds.): KSEM 2023, LNAI 14119, pp. 136–147, 2023.
https://doi.org/10.1007/978-3-031-40289-0_11

users, news recommendation has been playing an increasingly important role in users' interest and personalized content.

Appropriate user interest modeling is crucial for news recommendation to learn better representations of users and news [2]. Earlier works usually build user representations from news content and use attention mechanism to capture user interests. More recently, a technical trend is to leverage graph neural networks (GNNs) [3], which model the user-news interactions as a bipartite graph and can effectively integrate multi-hop neighbors into representations. Benefiting from the integration of connectivity modeling and representation learning, these GNN-based models achieve promising performance for recommendation.

Despite their effectiveness, we argue that current graph-based methods remain two issues: (1) **User Intents.** The current GNN-based methods fail to identify user-item relation at a fine-grained level of intents, which can model accurate user interest. Taking Fig. 1 as an example, u_1 chooses to browse the i_2 may be because his friend u_2 has browsed the i_2, but the fine-grained intents relationship u_1-e_1-i_2 indicates the behavior that u_1 adopts i_2 is due to the user's intent towards sports topic. The informative intent representation can be more accurate for user modeling. (2) **Over-Smoothing Collaborative Effects.** In addition, for the method of applying graph neural network, the deeper embedding propagation layers will also lead to the problem of over-smoothing. With the increase of the graph propagation layer, different user embedding representations become more difficult to distinguish, which limits the expression of higher-order collaboration relationships. Hence, it is crucial to distinguish user preferences from distinguishable representations.

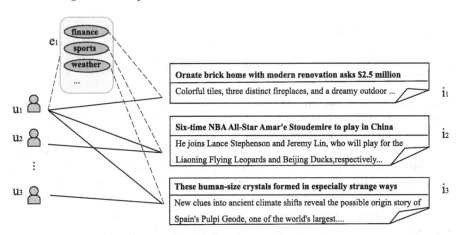

Fig. 1. An example of a user-item interaction graph, where the node viewed in green is the intent from the user to the news. (Color figure online)

In this paper, to address the above issues, we propose a novel **H**ypergraph **E**nhanced **C**ontrastive **L**earning model (HGCL), which consists of two components to capture the informative intents representations and the distinguishable hypergraph structure representations: (1) **Intent Interaction Learning**

Module. Considering the user-item interaction of graph convolution networks, we constructed intent nodes to extract users' attention weights on news topics based on different behavioral patterns. In this way, we construct a fine-grained user intent at the topic level and embed it into the representation of users and news, which can more accurately mine the motivation of users to click on news. And we further enhance news representations by utilizing both their semantic representations and ID embeddings via the multi-headed self-attention mechanism. (2) **Hypergraph Structure Learning Module.** Unlike the method of bipartite graph structure, we apply the hypergraph neural networks and design a hyperedge aggregation mechanism to handle the data correlation during representation learning, which can better represent the relationship between the underlying data to distinguish user preferences. Finally, the total representation is made by incorporating the representations of intent interaction and hypergraph structure as two contrastive views for contrastive learning. The contributions of this paper are summarized as follows:

- We propose a novel contrastive learning news recommendation approach HGCL which jointly models the user's intents and the hypergraph representations.
- In HGCL, to further improve representation learning, the informative intent interaction learning and the distinguishable hypergraph structure learning enriches user representations to improve recommendation.
- Extensive experiments on two benchmark datasets demonstrate the advantages of HGCL.

2   Related Work

In this section, we will review relevant research from three aspects: news recommendation, graph neural network and contrastive learning.

News Recommendation. At present, the existing news recommendation [4] mainly applies the traditional vector decomposition method and neural network. LSTUR [5] models short-term user interests from user's clicked news via a GRU network and long-term user interests from user-news interactions via user ID embeddings. KRED [6] proposing a knowledge graph attention network to learn news representations from texts and entities of news titles. GNewsRec [7] modeling short-term user interests from clicked news sequences via an attentive GRU network and long-term from user-news click graph via a graph neural network. However, these works seldom mine high-order structure information.

Graph Neural Networks. Recently, GCN [3], an approach for semi-supervised learning on graph-structured data, achieves good results in various recommendation systems. LightGCN [8] simplifies the design of GCN to make it more concise and appropriate for recommendation. HGNN [9] designs a hyperedge convolution operation to handle the data correlation during representation learning. Different from all these methods, we use contrastive learning to consider both the latent intent representation underlying the user-news interactions and rich hypergraph hidden layer representation.

Contrastive Learning. Since the success of contrastive learning in CV, contrastive learning has been widely applied on NLP, graph data mining and recommender systems. Existing studies [10] [11] extract self-supervised signals from the raw data is well-aligned with recommender systems' needs for tackling the data sparsity issue. NCL [12] explicitly incorporates the potential neighbors from graph structure and semantic space respectively into contrastive pairs. To the best of our knowledge [13], this is the first work to explore hypergraph contrastive learning in news recommendation.

3 Methodology

In this section, we will introduce the hypergraph enhanced contrast learning (HGCL) method shown in Fig. 2, which is composed of an intent interaction learning module and a hypergraph structure learning module. The intent interaction learning module represents the user's implicit interest in clicking on the item and encourages multiple potential intents to be independent of each other. The hypergraph structure learning module captures the influence of the collaborative filtering graph neural network paradigm globally.

3.1 Preliminary

We let the set $\mathbf{U} = \{u\}$ and $\mathbf{I} = \{i\}$ represent the set of users and items, respectively. The interaction matrix $\mathbf{A} \in \{0,1\}^{|U| \times |I|}$ indicates the interactions between each user in U and his/her browsing news. Each entry $A_{u,i} = 1$ if the user $\mathbf{u}$ has clicked this news $\mathbf{i}$, otherwise $A_{u,i} = 0$. In news recommendation, each news $\mathbf{i}$ has a title, a topic and the text. Specifically, we also build a clicked topic set $\mathbf{T} = \{t\}$ from topics of news clicked by users. The goal of recommender systems is to calculate the interest score of this user in the candidate news.

3.2 News Representation

We first describe how to obtain the news representation $\mathbf{i}$ from contexts of news texts and entity representation of news. We use two self-attention network to model news texts i_x and entities representation i_t, and build original representation news $\mathbf{i}$ as: $i^{(0)} = W_x \times i_x + W_t \times i_t$ with parameters W_x and W_t.

3.3 Intent Interaction Learning Module

We can express intents to represent users' interests via latent vectors, bus it is difficult to understand the specific meaning of each interest. We utilize intents representations behind a user-item interaction to form accurate user interest and propose fine-grained intent interaction learning. Assuming that the user's intent

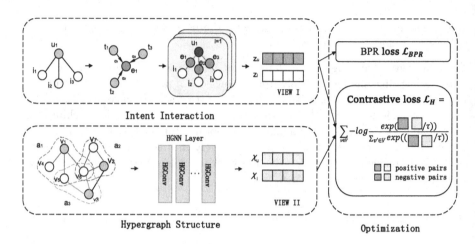

Fig. 2. Overall framework of our proposed hypergraph enhanced contrastive learning method. The well-defined intent e is colored in GREEN, a_1, a_2, a_3 are different hyperedges, and HGConv uses the robust hypergraph convolutional operation; Two representations of a node in VIEW I and VIEW II (colored in BLUE, AZURE) are regarded as positive sample pairs, and different node representations (colored in BLUE, PINK) are regarded as negative pairs. (Color figure online)

to $|T|$ interactive news topic type will affect the user's decision to interact with news. However, the solution only considers whether the topic has been clicked, thereby cannot get the user's high-level concept intent. Hence, our solution is to assign different weight proportions to each intent $p \in \mathcal{P}$ and focus on the interaction and combination of topics, which is extracted from each news article. More formally, the intent is to have an attention strategy on different topics, which can be formulated as:

$$e_p = \sum_{t \in T_u} \alpha\left(t, u\right) t_i, \tag{1}$$

where t_i is the ID embedding of topic t, which is assigned with an attention score $\alpha(t, u)$ to quantify its importance, formally:

$$\alpha(t, u) = \frac{exp(w_{t,u})}{\sum_{t' \in T} exp(w_{t'u})}, \tag{2}$$

where $w_{t,u}$ is a trainable parameter for topics and users.

In HGCL, we design a hybrid attention normalization layer in the process of GNN message passing, and flexibly model the importance of neighbors by integrating different normalization rules. Meanwhile, we integrate intent-aware information from historical news to represent user u as:

$$z_{N_u,LN}^{(l+1)} = \sum_{(i,t) \in N_u} \frac{1}{\sqrt{|N_u|}})e_p z_i^{(l)}, \tag{3}$$

$$z_{N_u,SN}^{(l+1)} = \sum_{(i,t)\in N_u} \frac{1}{\sqrt{|N_u||N_i|}})e_p z_i^{(l)}, \tag{4}$$

$$z_u^{(l+1)} = z_u^{(l)} + \alpha_{u,LN}^{(l+1)} z_{N_u,LN}^{(l+1)} + \alpha_{u,SN}^{(l+1)} z_{N_u,SN}^{(l+1)}, \tag{5}$$

Where $z_{N_u,LN}^{(l+1)}$ and $z_{N_u,SN}^{(l+1)}$ represent the left normalization and symmetric normalization of user's neighbor representation at l-th layer, N_u and N_i are the degrees of vertex u and i in the adjacency matrix, where symmetric normalization in Eq. 4 mitigate the weight of popular items, $\alpha_{(u,*)}^{(l)}$ indicates the normalized attention scores of neighbor representations. Here the attention network which uses a simple average aggregation operation is normalized by a Softmax function:

$$\alpha_{(u,*)}^{(l)} = \frac{exp(h_{u,*}^{(l)})}{\sum_{k\in\{LN,SN\}} exp(h_{u,k}^{(l)})}. \tag{6}$$

$$h_{(u,*)}^{(l+1)} = ave(z_{N_u,LN}^{(l+1)} + z_{N_u,LN}^{(l+1)} \cdot z_u^{(l)}), \tag{7}$$

After propagating with L layers, we average the representations of all layers and obtain the final representations of user u and item i as follows:

$$z_u = \frac{1}{L+1}\sum_{k=0}^{L} z_u^{(k)}, \qquad z_i = \frac{1}{L+1}\sum_{k=0}^{L} z_i^{(k)}, \tag{8}$$

Where z_u and z_i are the final representations of user u and item in intent interaction learning module, and we employ the inner product on the user and item representations to predict how likely the user would adopt the item:

$$\hat{y}_{u,i} = \mathbf{z_u}^\mathsf{T} z_i. \tag{9}$$

Given these notations, we define our Bayesian Personalized Ranking (BPR) loss as:

$$\mathcal{L}_{BPR} = \sum_{u,i,j\in\mathcal{O}} -ln\sigma(\hat{y}_{u,i} - \hat{y}_{u,j}) \tag{10}$$

Where $\sigma(\cdot)$ is the sigmoid function, $\mathcal{O} = \{(u,i,j)|A_{u,i} = 1, A_{u,j} = 0\}$ is the training dataset which denotes the user u has interacted with new i and not interacted with new j.

3.4   Hypergraph Structure Learning Module

In the traditional graph neural network, when the number of convolution layers is too many, it will inevitably lead to the problem of overs-smoothing. We use another hypergraph perspective to alleviate this problem, and at the same time, we can explore more favorable information from the data. In the face of the recommended complex scenario, we construct a hypergraph to model multiple information.

Hypergraph G can be expressed as $\mathcal{G} = (\mathcal{V}, \mathcal{E})$, where $\mathcal{V} = \{v_1, ..., v_n\}$ represents the set of n nodes including users and news in the hypergraph, and $\mathcal{E} = \{a_1, ..., a_m\}$ represents m hyperedges in the hypergraph. Hyperedges can connect multiple nodes, which is different from traditional graphs where edges can only connect two nodes. As show in Fig. 2, nodes$\{v_1, v_4, v_5, v_6\}$ belongs to hyperedge a_1. The $m \times n$ incidence matrix $\mathcal{H}$ of hypergraph is defined as follows:

$$h(v, a) = \begin{cases} 1, & if \quad v \in a \\ 0, & if \quad v \notin a \end{cases}, \qquad (11)$$

The message transmission is changed from point-to-point to point-edge-point, which makes more use of data utilization and neural network parameter training. It can effectively model higher-order relationships while ensuring information integrity, thus realizing information fusion more fully.

Then, we input the hypergraph adjacency matrix H and node characteristics into hypergraph neural networks to obtain the node output labels of users and news, the convolution operation (HGConv) can be simplified to the following expression:

$$\chi^{(l+1)} = \sigma \left(D_v^{-\frac{1}{2}} HWD_a^{-1} H^\mathsf{T} D_v^{-\frac{1}{2}} \chi^{(l)} \hat{\Theta}^{(l)} \right), \qquad (12)$$

where $\chi^{(l)}$ denotes the nodes representation of hypergraph int at l-th layer, W is the trainable parameters matrices of hyperedge and $\hat{\Theta}$ for hypergraph convolutional network, D_a and D_v denote the diagonal matrices of the edge degrees and the vertex degrees, and σ denotes the nonlinear activation function.

3.5 Optimization

In this section, we introduce the overall loss and the optimization of the proposed hypergraph enhanced contrastive learning.

To combine the representations of intent interaction learning module and hypergraph structure learning module, we apply them from these two views for contrastive learning. To be specific, we regard (z_v, χ_v) obtained by different methods as positive sample pairs, and view different users/news as negative pairs. In this way, our model generates positive and negative examples for comparison. We employ **contrastive learning objectives** with the InfoNCE to minimize the distance between positive sample pairs and maximize the distance between negative sample pairs:

$$\mathcal{L}_H = \sum_{v \in \mathcal{V}} -log \frac{exp\left((z_v \cdot \chi_v/\tau)\right)}{\sum_{v' \in \mathcal{V}} exp\left((z_v \cdot \chi_v'/\tau)\right)}, \qquad (13)$$

where τ denotes the temperature hyper-parameter of softmax. We combine intent interaction learning embedding and hypergraph structure learning representation. This allows intent-aware view and hypergraph structure view to cooperate and supervise each other, thus enhancing users and news representation.

Since the main goal of the intent interaction module is to model the interaction between users and news, we will complement the proposed hypergraph structure module with its contrastive learning loss, and use the multi-task learning strategy to jointly train the traditional ranking loss and the proposed contrastive loss as:

$$\mathcal{L} = \mathcal{L}_{BPR} + \lambda_1 \cdot \mathcal{L}_H + \lambda_2 \cdot ||\Theta||_2, \tag{14}$$

Where $\Theta = \{z_u, z_i, e_p, \chi_v, w, W | u \in U, i \in I, p \in P, \chi_v \in \chi\}$ is the set of model parameters, λ_1, λ_2 are the super parameter that controls the weight of the proposed objective and L2 regularization terms, which control the loss of independence, We minimize $\mathcal{L}$ using the Adam optimizer.

4 Experiments

4.1 Experimental Settings

Evaluation Datasets. We conducted extensive experiments on two real-world datasets to evaluate the effectiveness of HGCL. The first is the public MIND dataset [14]. The user data in the first four weeks is used to build user reading history, the user data in the penultimate week is used for model training, and the user data in the last week is used for evaluation. In addition, MIND provides existing topic tags for each news item. The second (named Feeds) is built from user behavior data sampled from a Microsoft business news feed application, training and validation set is randomly selected from the first ten weeks, and test data from the next three weeks (Table 1).

Table 1. Statistics of the experimental datasets.

	#Users	#News	#Topics	#Clicks
MIND	94,057	65,238	18	347,727
Feeds	50,605	1,126,508	28	473,697

Compared Models. We compare HGCL with 12 baselines **EBNR** [2], **DKN** [15], **DAN** [16], **NAML** [17], **NPA** [1], **LSTUR** [5], **NRMS** [18], **KRED** [6], **GNewsRec** [7], **FIM** [4], **HieRec** [19], **NCL** [12] various recommendation paradigms.

Evaluation Metrics. To mitigate the sampling bias, we evaluate the prediction accuracy using the all-ranking protocol over all items. We use four ranking metrics to evaluate the recommended performance, i.e., AUC, MRR, nDCG@5 and nDCG@10, which are widely used in recommendation [20].

Hyperparameter Settings. Next, we will introduce the experimental settings and hyper-parameters of HGCL. The embedding size is initialized to 64. The batch size is set to 4096, and the parameters are initialized by the default Xavier distribution. We adjust the number of convolution layers of the hyper-parameter to 3. We set the dropout rate to 0.5, the batch size to 128, λ_1 in [1e−10, 1e−6], and τ in [0.01, 1]. These parameters are selected and adjusted according to the results of the validation set.

4.2   Performance Evaluation

We compare with the baseline methods, and all baselines are initialized as corresponding papers. We carefully adjust them to achieve the best performance and We independently repeated each experiment 10 times and reported the average performance in Table 2.

Table 2. Performance of different methods. The improvement of HGCL over the best baseline method.

	MIND				Feeds			
	AUC	MRR	nDCG@5	nDCG@10	AUC	MRR	nDCG@5	nDCG@10
EBNR	61.62	28.07	30.55	37.07	63.48	28.01	32.05	37.64
DKN	63.99	28.95	31.73	38.38	62.94	28.05	32.15	37.68
DAN	64.68	29.78	32.63	39.27	62.67	27.75	31.74	37.42
NAML	64.30	29.81	32.64	39.11	64.48	28.99	33.37	38.90
NPA	64.28	29.64	32.28	38.93	64.02	28.71	33.01	38.55
LSTUR	65.68	30.44	33.49	39.95	65.01	29.28	33.74	39.16
NRMS	65.43	30.74	33.13	39.66	65.27	29.40	33.89	39.34
KRED	65.89	30.80	33.78	40.23	65.51	29.57	34.04	39.60
GNewsRec	65.91	30.50	33.56	40.13	65.23	29.36	33.87	39.44
FIM	64.65	29.70	32.51	39.30	65.41	29.57	34.08	39.56
HieRec	67.95	32.87	36.36	42.53	66.23	29.82	34.42	39.94
NCL	69.02	69.73	55.32	53.87	68.71	67.18	56.25	52.86
HGCL	**69.12**	**69.89**	**56.70**	**55.13**	**68.92**	**67.34**	**56.40**	**53.21**

Overall Performance Validation. As shown in Table 2, we can see that the proposed HGCL method always performs better than the baseline in all evaluation metrics. This observation verifies the advantages of our HGCL method, which can be summarized as follows: i) Benefiting from intent interaction learning schema, HGCL can not only model the intent tendency of users when choosing news but also have better overall dependence on higher-order neighbor information. ii) Through our hypergraph structure contrastive learning mode, HGCL has realized data augmentation of sparse user-news interaction, with cross-views (from ordinary graph to hypergraph) contrastive learning.

Effectiveness of Intent Interaction Learning. We can also see that our methods are better than those of single user embedding to model the overall user interest, such as NRMS, NPA, and NAML. This is because users' interests are usually complex and fine-grained. We propose a user intent interaction modeling framework, which can express complex and fine-grained user interests by constructing attention intent representation.

Effectiveness of Hypergraph Structure Learning. We can see that HGCL always performs better than the method based on graph neural network, which benefits from rich contrastive learning objectives. In addition, we choose intent interaction and hypergraph structure on the view of contrastive, which is superior to NCL [12] that only compares views on the traditional graph. It indicates that hypergraph constitutes great promotion in the representation of complex data, which enhances the discrimination ability of GNN-based paradigm and captures the complex high-order dependencies among users.

4.3   Ablation Study

The HGCL method we proposed utilizes neighbor information in two aspects. To verify the effectiveness of each modeling method, we conducted ablation experiments to analyze their contributions. Table 3 reports the results, where "w/o I&H" and "w/o I" represent variables by deleting hypergraph structure contrastive learning and intent interaction learning, respectively. From the table, we can observe that deleting each module will cause performance degradation, which proves the rationality and effectiveness of HGCL. We attribute these improvements to the effective modeling of HGCL: (1) By revealing user intents, HGCL can better describe the relationship between users and news, and generate stronger user and news representation. In contrast, all baselines ignore hidden user intents and focus more on news content to collect information; (2) Thanks to our hypergraph structure contrastive learning scheme, compared with content-based news representation (i.e., NRMS, NPA, and NAML), HGCL can retain the overall semantics of news and collect different attention information from news topics to obtain user intents. Different aggregation schemes are applied on the hypergraph to enable HGCL to better represent the collaborative signals and hypergraph signals for users and news. In addition, these two views are the complementary driving forces to improve the experimental results in different aspects, and improve the performance of contrastive learning.

Table 3. Performance of HGCL on MIND dataset without hypergraph structure and intent interaction learning.

	AUC	MRR	nDCG@5	nDCG@10
HGCL w/o I&H	67.91	33.41	36.46	42.14
HGCL w/o I	67.97	34.68	37.96	44.63
HGCL	69.12	69.89	55.7	55.13

4.4   Parameter Analysis

In our hypergraph framework, the effect of temperature is τ. In order to analyze the influence of temperature τ on HGCL, we control it within the range of 0.05 to 0.15. As shown in Fig. 3, we can observe that too large or too small value τ will lead to poor performance. The deeper layer L graph encoder is sufficient to provide better performance, because our hypergraph enhanced contrast learning explores information that ordinary graphs cannot model. While intent interaction learning enriches user modeling through more fine-grained representation, it alleviates the over-smoothing problem brought by traditional graph neural network via hypergraph structure contrastive learning.

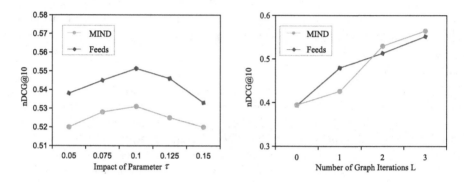

Fig. 3. Performance comparison w.r.t. different parameter τ and numbers of graph iterations L.

5   Conclusion

This paper considers the informative intent interaction learning and distinguishable hypergraph structure learning of user-news interaction, and proposes a new hypergraph enhanced contrastive learning news recommendation model HGCL. The model adds attention intent to the bipartite graph of interaction between users and news, and encodes the interactions between users and news through graph and hypergraph convolution neural network. (1) Through the attention mechanism, the learned weighed intent representation is separated, and the expressiveness and interpretability are enhanced. The hybrid normalization is also designed to make the node representation more reliable in the domain. (2) The quality of user and news embedding is further improved by contrastive learning in the two views. The experimental experiments on real-world news datasets show that our model has achieved significant performance improvement compared to state-of-the-art methods, supporting the importance of development intent modeling and hypergraph contrastive learning in users and news representation.

References

1. Wu, C., Wu, F., An, M., Huang, J., Huang, Y., Xie, X.: NPA: neural news recommendation with personalized attention. In: KDD, pp. 2576–2584 (2019)
2. Okura, S., Tagami, Y., Ono, S., Tajima, A.: Embedding-based news recommendation for millions of users. In: KDD, pp. 1933–1942 (2017)
3. Kipf, T.N., Welling, M.: Semi-supervised classification with graph convolutional networks. In: ICLR (2017)
4. Wang, H., Wu, F., Liu, Z., Xie, X.: Fine-grained interest matching for neural news recommendation. In: ACL, pp. 836–845 (2020)
5. An, M., Wu, F., Wu, C., Zhang, K., Liu, Z., Xie, X.: Neural news recommendation with long-and short-term user representations. In: ACL, pp. 336–345 (2019)
6. Liu, D., Xie, X.: KRED: knowledge-aware document representation for news recommendations. In: RecSys, pp. 200–209 (2020)
7. Hu, L., Li, C., Shi, C., Yang, C., Shao, C.: Graph neural news recommendation with long-term and short-term interest modeling. Inf. Process. Manag. **57**(2), 102142 (2020)
8. He, X., Deng, K., Wang, X., Li, Y., Zhang, Y., Wang, M.: LightGCN: simplifying and powering graph convolution network for recommendation. In: SIGIR, pp. 639–648 (2020)
9. Feng, Y., You, H., Zhang, Z., Ji, R., Gao, Y.: Hypergraph neural networks. In: AAAI, pp. 3558–3565 (2019)
10. Wu, J., et al.: Self-supervised graph learning for recommendation. In: SIGIR, pp. 726–735 (2021)
11. Yu, J., Yin, H., Xia, X., Chen, T., Cui, L., Nguyen, Q.V.H.: Are graph augmentations necessary? Simple graph contrastive learning for recommendation. In: SIGIR, pp. 1294–1303 (2022)
12. Lin, Z., Tian, C., Hou, Y., Zhao, W.X.: Improving graph collaborative filtering with neighborhood-enriched contrastive learning. In: WWW, pp. 2320–2329 (2022)
13. Wu, C., Wu, F., Huang, Y., Xie, X.: Personalized news recommendation: a survey. arXiv preprint arXiv:2106.08934 (2021)
14. Wu, F., et al.: MIND: a large-scale dataset for news recommendation. In: ACL, pp. 3597–3606 (2020)
15. Wang, H., Zhang, F., Xie, X., Guo, M.: DKN: deep knowledge-aware network for news recommendation. In: WWW, pp. 1835–1844 (2018)
16. Zhu, Q., Zhou, X., Song, Z., Tan, J., Guo, L.: DAN: deep attention neural network for news recommendation. In: AAAI, vol. 33, pp. 5973–5980 (2019)
17. Wu, C., Wu, F., Huang, Y., Xie, X.: Neural news recommendation with attentive multi-view learning. In: IJCAI, pp. 3863–3869 (2019)
18. Wu, C., Wu, F., Ge, S., Qi, T., Huang, Y., Xie, X.: Neural news recommendation with multi-head self-attention. In: EMNLP-IJCNLP, pp. 6389–6394 (2019)
19. Qi, T., et al.: HieRec: hierarchical user interest modeling for personalized news recommendation. In: ACL/IJCNLP, pp. 5446–5456 (2021)
20. Wu, C., Wu, F., Huang, Y., Xie, X.: User-as-graph: user modeling with heterogeneous graph pooling for news recommendation. In: IJCAI, pp. 1624–1630 (2021)

Reinforcement Learning-Based Recommendation with User Reviews on Knowledge Graphs

Siyuan Zhang[1], Yuanxin Ouyang[1(✉)], Zhuang Liu[2], Weijie He[2], Wenge Rong[2], and Zhang Xiong[2]

[1] State Key Laboratory of Software Development Environment, Beihang University, Beijing, China
{zhangsiyuan,oyyx}@buaa.edu.cn
[2] Engineering Research Center of Advanced Computer Application Technology, Ministry of Education, Beihang University, Beijing, China
{liuzhuang,weijiehe,w.rong,xiongz}@buaa.edu.cn

Abstract. Introducing knowledge graphs (KGs) into recommendation systems can improve their performance, while reinforcement learning (RL) methods can help utilize graph data for recommendation. We investigate existing RL-based methods for recommendation on KGs, and find that such approaches do not make full use of information from user reviews. Introducing user reviews into a recommendation system can reveal user preferences more deeply and equip a RL agent with a stronger ability to distinguish users' preferences for an item or not, which in turn improves the accuracy of recommendation results. We propose *Reinforced Knowledge Graph Reasoning with User Reviews* (RKGR-UR) by introducing user reviews into a RL-based recommendation model, which combines a rating prediction task to transform predicted ratings into rewards feedback for the RL agent. Experiments on three real datasets demonstrate the effectiveness of our method.

Keywords: Recommendation system · Knowledge graph · Reinforcement learning · User reviews

1 Introduction

With the rapid development of e-commerce and social media platforms, recommendation systems are widely used in many fields. Users can rely on recommendation systems to filter out masses of useless information, greatly improving the efficiency of obtaining information in the era of information overload.

To improve the performance of recommendation systems, researchers introduce additional side information, such as knowledge graphs (KGs), into recommendation systems. KG is a heterogeneous graph containing multiple types of nodes and relations, usually using triples (h, r, t) to represent knowledge content.

Reinforcement learning (RL) is helpful in utilizing graph data for recommendation. The agent in RL recommends items to users by exploring paths on

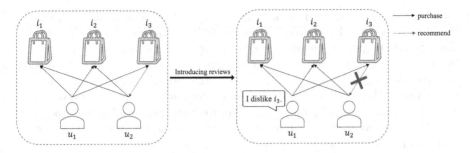

Fig. 1. Recommendation with user reviews.

the graph. Xian *et al.* [1] first apply RL to KGs for recommendation, proposing PGPR which uses a soft reward strategy. Park *et al.* [2] take sentiment information into consideration and propose SAPL. Wang *et al.* [3] propose ReMR which introduces high-level concepts into PGPR. However, these methods tend to assume that user purchases indicate their preferences. In reality, a user's purchase does not always reflect their interests, and user reviews and ratings can provide more accurate information. If the user expresses negative emotions towards a product in a review or gives it a low rating, it actually implies that the user is not interested in the product. In CF-based recommendation models, common interests among users are often considered for recommendation. As shown in Fig. 1, both user u_1 and user u_2 have purchased item i_1 and i_2, so it can be inferred that the two users have similar preferences. Based on the idea of CF, if user u_1 purchases item i_3, item i_3 will also be recommended to user u_2. However, if user u_1 expresses dissatisfaction with item i_3 in the review, then instead, item i_3 should not be recommended to user u_2. Therefore, considering user reviews and ratings on items in the recommendation process can help to more accurately identify the user's true interests.

We propose a RL-based model for recommendation, *Reinforced Knowledge Graph Reasoning with User Reviews* (RKGR-UR), which introduces user reviews in the RL-based recommendation model to improve the final recommendation performance. In our model, we combine the recommendation task with the rating prediction task and convert the rating prediction scores into RL environment rewards to be fed back to the agent for the learning of the agent's policy network. We evaluate the effectiveness of our model on three Amazon e-commerce datasets, and the results show that our model gets better results than the state-of-the-art baseline.

2   Related Work

2.1   Reinforcement Learning for Recommendation

RL is a field of machine learning that studies problems and their solutions where agents learn to maximize a cumulative discounted reward by interacting with their environment. The environment in RL is typically formulated in the form of the Markov Decision Process (MDP) [4]. A MDP is defined by $M = \{\mathcal{S}, \mathcal{A}, \mathcal{P}, \mathcal{R}\}$. Here, $\mathcal{S}$ and $\mathcal{A}$ represent the state and action space, respectively. $\mathcal{R}$ is the reward function that maps a state-action pair to a value, and $\mathcal{P}$ is the transition function that calculates the probability that a state transitioning to the next state. In recent years, RL has been increasingly used in recommendation systems to enable them to search for meaningful paths rather than enumerate all possible paths in KGs [5]. Some RL-based recommendation models, such as [6–8], have achieved outstanding performance in recommendation.

2.2 User Reviews for Recommendation

With the development of the internet, users increasingly prefer to use text reviews on electronic platforms to express personal opinions and share their views on items. Typically, users provide a numeric rating (usually ranging from 1 to 5) for the product and explain the reasons behind the rating with text reviews. In recent years, many studies have focused on extracting user interest information from comment texts for rating prediction. These works can be divided into three main categories: words-based methods, topics-based methods, and sentiments-based methods [9]. Words-based methods [10] use the review words by factorizing them into CF. Topics-based methods [11] extract aspects from reviews and combines them with ratings for generating recommendations. Sentiments-based methods [12] use the user's expressed sentiment on the item itself or on its different aspects in reviews, to boost the rating prediction task.

3   Methodology

In this section, we introduce our RKGR-UR in detail. Figure 2 shows the framework of RKGR-UR, which consists of three components: explorer, KG environment, and rating prediction model. In order to complete the task of recommendation, the model needs to learn the parameter Θ_R of the rating prediction model and the policy network π_e of explorer. We first introduce the rating prediction model in Sect. 3.1, then the explorer in Sect. 3.2, followed by the policy path reasoning method for recommendations in Sect. 3.3, finally the comparative model for in-depth study in Sect. 3.4.

For the convenience of description, the user-item interactions set $\mathcal{O}$ with user set $\mathcal{U}$ and item set $\mathcal{I}$ is defined as $\mathcal{O} = \{(u, i)|u \in \mathcal{U}, i \in \mathcal{I}\}$. The KG combined user-item interactions $\mathcal{G}$ with entity set $\mathcal{E}$ and relation set $\mathcal{R}$ is defined as $\mathcal{G} = \{(e_1, r, e_2)|e_1, e_2 \in \mathcal{E}, r \in \mathcal{R}\}$, where $\mathcal{U}, \mathcal{I} \subseteq \mathcal{E}$.

3.1   Rating Prediction Model

One of the drawbacks of most current CF techniques used for the rating prediction task is that they model users and items based solely on numerical ratings provided by users, ignoring the rich information present in the accompanying

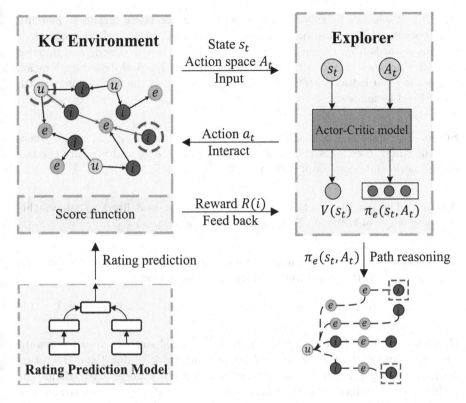

Fig. 2. Framework of RKGR-UR. The explorer is a RL agent for recommendation. The KG environment interacts with the agent. The rating prediction model is used to predict user ratings for products as reward feedback to the agent.

review text. In this section, we aim to fully utilize the information from users' reviews of items and therefore employ DeepCoNN [10], a convolutional neural network-based model, to jointly model users and items using review texts and fulfil the rating prediction task. The model uses two parallel convolutional neural networks (CNNs) to learn the latent representations of users and items through the words in the reviews. When predicting the rating score, the user and item representations are first concatenated and then jointly passed to a regression layer that uses factorization machine (FM) for prediction. Since the rating prediction model is not the focus of this paper, it is not presented in detail here. If you want to learn more about this model, you can read paper [10] for more information.

3.2 Explorer

The explorer starts from a user node and obtains the probability distribution of actions (i.e., next-hop neighbors) in the action space based on its policy network

π_e. Then it selects a neighboring node as the next hop based on this probability distribution, and reaches an item node after several hops. In this progress, it obtains rewards from the environment based on the explored node and updates its policy network π_e according to these rewards. Such a path-based exploration process is regarded as a MDP, and the key elements of the environment in RL are defined as follows:

State. The state $s_t \in \mathcal{S}$ at time t is defined as a tuple $(u, e_t, e_{t-1}, r_{t-1})$, where u is the target user, e_t is the node currently visited, e_{t-1} and r_{t-1} are the last visited node and edge (empty when $t = 0$), respectively.

Action. The complete action space $\mathcal{A}_t$ of state s_t is defined as all possible outgoing edges of entity e_t. Formally, $\mathcal{A}_t = \{(r, e) | (e_t, r, e) \in \mathcal{G}\}$.

Transition. Due to the graph properties, a state is determined by the position of the entity and the transition for state s_t to the next state s_{t+1} is:

$$\mathbb{P}(s_{t+1} = (u, e_{t+1}, e_t, r_t) | s_t = (u, e_t, e_{t-1}, r_{t-1}), a_t = (r_{t+1}, e_{t+1})) = 1. \quad (1)$$

Reward. We only feed back rewards in the terminal state s_T, and the reward consists of two parts: the soft reward (as previous work [1] does) and the rating prediction reward. For the rating prediction reward, it is necessary to divide the rating scores obtained by DeepCoNN into positive and negative rewards, but it is not appropriate to select a fixed score as the threshold for division. Therefore, the normalized quantile ρ is introduced. The predicted rating scores are sorted in descending order, and the scores that account for the top ρ proportion are normalized as positive rewards, while the remaining scores are normalized as negative rewards. Finally, We define the reward function as follows:

$$R(e_T) = \begin{cases} \max\left(0, \frac{g(u, e_T)}{\max_{i \in \mathcal{J}} g(u, i)}\right) + \mu \cdot f_r(u, e_T), & \text{if } e_T \in \mathcal{J} \\ 0, & \text{otherwise,} \end{cases} \quad (2)$$

where $g(u, i) = (\mathbf{r}_u + \mathbf{r}_p)^\top \mathbf{r}_i$ is the soft reward function, $\mathbf{r}_u$, $\mathbf{r}_p$ and $\mathbf{r}_i$ are the embeddings of user u, purchase relation p and item e_t, respectively; μ is the rating prediction reward ratio; $f(u, i)$ is the rating prediction reward normalization function, which is defined as follows:

$$f_r(u, i) = \begin{cases} \frac{\hat{p}_{\max} - \hat{p}_{u,i}}{\hat{p}_{\max} - \hat{p}_\rho}, & \text{if } \hat{p}_{u,i} \geq \hat{p}_\rho \\ -\frac{\hat{p}_{u,i} - \hat{p}_{\min}}{\hat{p}_\rho - \hat{p}_{\min}}, & \text{otherwise ,} \end{cases} \quad (3)$$

where $\hat{p}_{\max}$, $\hat{p}_{\min}$ are the maximum and minimum prediction scores among all rating prediction scores, respectively; $\hat{p}_{u,i}$ is the rating prediction score of user u for item i, and $\hat{p}_\rho$ is the predicted score that ranks at position ρ among all rating prediction scores sorted in descending order, where ρ represents the proportion of the total number of ratings.

Optimization. The goal of the policy π_e is to maximize the expected cumulative discounted reward as follows:

$$\max_{\Theta_E} \sum_{u \in \mathcal{U}} \mathbb{E}_{\pi_e} \left[\sum_{t=1}^{T} \gamma^{t-1} R(e_t) \right], \tag{4}$$

where γ is the decay factor. We solve the problem using an actor-critic model [13] which is consist of a policy network $\pi_e(s_t, \mathcal{A}_t)$ and a value network $\mathcal{V}(s_t)$. The policy network takes the state s_t and corresponding action space $\mathcal{A}_t$ as input and emits the probability of each action. The value network maps the state s_t to a value. These two networks are defined as follows:

$$\mathbf{x} = dropout \left(ELU \left(dropout \left(ELU \left(\mathbf{s}_t \mathbf{W}_1 \right) \right) \mathbf{W}_2 \right) \right), \tag{5}$$

$$\pi_e(s_t, \mathcal{A}_t) = softmax \left(\mathbf{A}_t \odot (\mathbf{x} \mathbf{W}_a) \right), \tag{6}$$

$$\mathcal{V}(s_t) = \mathbf{x} \mathbf{W}_v, \tag{7}$$

where ELU is an activation function; $\mathbf{s}_t \in \mathbb{R}^{1 \times d_s}$ is the vector of s_t; $\mathbf{A}_t \in \mathbb{R}^{1 \times d_a}$ is the binary vector of $\mathcal{A}_t$; $\mathbf{W}_1 \in \mathbb{R}^{d_s \times d_1}$, $\mathbf{W}_2 \in \mathbb{R}^{d_1 \times d_2}$, $\mathbf{W}_a \in \mathbb{R}^{d_2 \times d_a}$ and $\mathbf{W}_v \in \mathbb{R}^{d_2 \times 1}$ are parameters to be learned.

For the policy network, we updated its parameter Θ_E by the policy gradient [14] based on RL method, such that the gradient $\mathcal{L}_E$ is calculated as:

$$\nabla_{\Theta_E} \mathcal{L}_E = \sum_{u \in \mathcal{U}} \frac{1}{T} \sum_{t=1}^{T} \left[\left(G_t - \mathcal{V}(s_t) \right) \nabla_{\Theta_E} \log \pi_e(s_t, \mathcal{A}_t) \right], \tag{8}$$

where G is the discounted cumulative reward from state s_t to terminal state s_T and is defined as:

$$G_t = \sum_{k=t+1}^{T} \gamma^{k-t-1} R(e_k). \tag{9}$$

For the value network, its loss function is defined as:

$$\mathcal{L}_C = \sum_{u \in \mathcal{U}} \frac{1}{T} \sum_{t=1}^{T} \left(G_t - \mathcal{V}(s_t) \right)^2. \tag{10}$$

3.3   Knowledge Graph Reasoning

At last, we can apply our model for recommendation. The explorer recommends items to users through path exploration on KGs, which is called *Knowledge Graph Reasoning* (KGR). Considering both the diversity and accuracy of recommendation, we take a three-hop path sampling method with parameters $N_1 \times N_2 \times N_3$. When recommending items for user u, the explorer starts from the user node and selects the top N_1 nodes with the highest probability as the next nodes to visit according to the policy network π_e. Then, for each node selected through the first hop, top N_2 nodes with the highest probability are selected as the next nodes to visit. In this way, the explorer reaches some nodes after three hops. If the node is an item node, this item i is recommended to user u, and the reasoning path $(u \xrightarrow{r_1} e_1 \xrightarrow{r_2} e_2 \xrightarrow{r_3} i)$ is taken as the recommended explanation. If the same item has multiple reasoning paths to reach from user u, calculate the cumulative probability of three hops $P_{a_1} \times P_{a_2} \times P_{a_3}$ where P_{a_i} is obtained from the policy network π_e. The path with the highest cumulative probability is regarded as the recommended explanation. For all items of user u obtained through KGR, we calculate the inner product between the embedding of user u and the embedding of each items as a score, and the top N items with the highest scores are taken as the final recommendation.

3.4   Comparative Model

To investigate in depth the influence of user reviews in RL-based recommendation models on the policy learning of the agent, the following two comparative models are constructed: (1) The recommendation model with randomly sampled scores from a normal distribution as the rating prediction scores (RKGR-ND). (2) The recommendation model that combines a rating prediction model that considers only user ratings but not user reviews (RKGR-MF).

RKGR-ND. RKGR-UR utilizes users' predicted rating scores for items obtained through the rating prediction model in Sect. 3.1. To compare with this type of score, RKGR-ND uses randomly sampled scores from a normal distribution as the rating prediction scores. The rating equation for RKGR-ND is as follows:

$$\hat{p}_{u,i} = X \sim N(3,1), \tag{11}$$

where X is a random variable following a normal distribution with mathematical expectation of 3 and standard variance of 1. The reward function for RKGR-ND is also Eq. 2, where the rating prediction function in Eq. 3 is replaced with Eq. 11, and ρ is taken as 0.5.

RKGR-MF. The rating prediction model in Sect. 3.1 utilizes users' reviews and ratings of items to accomplish the rating prediction task. Some early methods for rating prediction, such as matrix factorization (MF) [15], only utilized user ratings without utilizing user reviews to accomplish this task. In order to explore the impact of user reviews on the performance of recommendation model, RKGR-MF utilizes rating prediction scores obtained through MF, which predicts ratings by separately learning the latent features γ_u and γ_i of user u and item i, respectively, and the prediction function is defined as:

$$\hat{p}_{u,i} = \alpha + \beta_u + \beta_i + (\gamma_u \cdot \gamma_i), \tag{12}$$

where α is the global bias, β_u and β_i are the bias of user u and item i, respectively.

Then, similar to RKGR-ND, Eq. 2 is used as the reward function and the rating prediction function in Eq. 3 is replaced with Eq. 12.

Table 1. Statistics of datasets.

Datasets	Beauty	Clothing	Cell Phones
Users	22,363	39,384	27,879
Items	12,101	23,033	10,429
Interactions	198,502	278,677	194,439
Entities	224,074	425,528	163,249
Triplets	7,832,720	10,671,090	6,299,494

4 Experiments

4.1 Experimental Setup

Datasets. We use three Amazon e-commerce datasets to conduct experiments. The datasets include *Beauty, Clothing and Cell Phones* which constitute KGs containing 6 types of entities and 8 types of relations. The 6 types of entities are *user, item, category, brand, related item,* and *feature.* The 8 types of relationships are (*user, purchase, item*), (*user, mention, feature*), (*item, described by, feature*), (*item, belongs to, category*), (*item, produced by, brand*), (*item, co-purchased with, related item*), (*item, also purchased, related item*), and (*item, also viewed, related item*). Table 1 gives the statistics of the datasets. We randomly select 70% of the user interaction history as the training data and consider the remaining 30% as the test data.

Baselines. We compare our method with 5 recommendation models. **BPR** [16] is a Bayesian personalized ranking model that assumes users have a total order relationship with items, meaning users can rank items according to their own level of interest. It learns the embeddings of users and items by maximizing the probability of user preferences for item rankings. **CKE** [17] is a modern neural recommendation system based on a joint model that integrates MF and heterogeneous format data, including textual content, visual information, and structural knowledge base. **KGAT** [18] is a recommendation model based on knowledge graph that maps users, items, and entities in the knowledge graph to the same embedding space. It leverages graph attention mechanisms to model the relationships between entities. **PGPR** [1] is the first model to use RL-based method for recommendation over KGs. **ReMR** [3] is the state-of-the-art model that uses RL-based method for recommendation.

Metrics and Settings. We adopt two representative top-N recommendation metrics: **Normalized Discounted Cumulative Gain (NDCG)** and **Recall**. These ranking metrics are computed based on the top-10 predictions for each user. The size of entity and relationship embeddings in KG is set to 100. The parameters in the policy network and value network are set to $\mathbf{W}_1 \in \mathbb{R}^{400 \times 512}, \mathbf{W}_2 \in \mathbb{R}^{512 \times 256}, \mathbf{W}_a \in \mathbb{R}^{256 \times 250}, \mathbf{W}_v \in \mathbb{R}^{256 \times 1}$. The decay

Table 2. Comparison of recommendation metrics. The results are reported in percentages and calculated based on the top-10 predictions in the test set. The best results are highlighted in bold.

Datasets	Beauty		Clothing		Cell Phones	
Metrics	NDCG	Recall	NDCG	Recall	NDCG	Recall
BPR	2.753	4.241	0.601	1.046	1.998	3.258
CKE	3.717	5.938	1.502	2.509	3.995	7.005
KGAT	5.020	7.794	2.824	4.674	4.803	7.982
PGPR	5.449	8.324	2.858	4.834	5.042	8.416
ReMR	5.878	8.982	2.977	5.110	5.294	8.724
RKGR-UR (ours)	**6.010**	**9.331**	**3.086**	**5.237**	**5.338**	**9.087**
Improvement (%)	+2.20	+3.74	+3.53	+2.43	+0.82	+3.99

factor in Eq. 4 is set to 0.99. The parameters in the three-hop path sampling method are set to $25 \times 5 \times 1$. The explorer is trained using the Adam optimizer with the learning rate set to 0.001. The number of training epochs for Deep-CoNN and MF is 3. The number of training epochs for RKGR-UR, RKGR-ND and RKGR-MF is 50.

Table 3. Effectiveness of recommendation models combining rating prediction results in different ways. RKGR does not use rating scores. RKGR-ND uses rating scores sampled from a normal distribution. RKGR-MF uses the rating scores predicted by MF. RKGR-UR uses the rating scores predicted by DeepCoNN.

Datasets	Beauty		Clothing		Cell Phones	
Mertics	NDCG	Recall	NDCG	Recall	NDCG	Recall
RKGR	5.653	8.691	2.894	4.910	5.014	8.417
RKGR-ND	5.678	8.730	2.899	4.905	5.073	8.580
RKGR-MF	5.873	9.135	2.982	5.063	5.308	8.899
RKGR-UR	**6.010**	**9.331**	**3.086**	**5.237**	**5.338**	**9.087**

4.2   Overall Performance

Table 2 demonstrates that our method consistently outperforms all baselines in terms of all the considered metrics. On average, our model boosts NDCG and Recall by 2.18% and 3.39%, respectively. To understand the reasons behind this improvement, we leverage user reviews to reveal deeper relationships between users and items in our modeling approach. Prior RL-based recommendation models (e.g., PGPR, ReMR) often reward the agent with a positive signal when it explores an item that a user has interacted with, assuming that this item

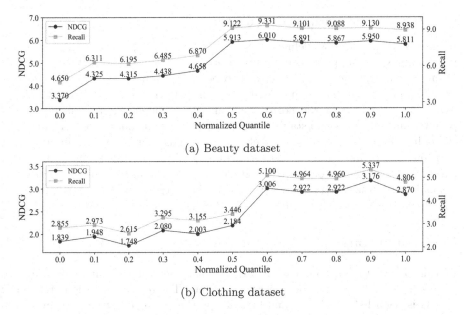

(a) Beauty dataset

(b) Clothing dataset

Fig. 3. Recommendation effectiveness of our model under different normalized quantile on the Beauty dataset and the Clothing dataset.

aligns with the user's preferences. However, if the agent mistakenly assumes that users like all items they interact with, it can be misled during the policy learning process. By integrating user reviews into our recommendation model, the agent is able to more accurately capture users' preferences for items, leading to stronger discrimination ability and improved recommendation performance.

4.3 Influence of Different Rating Prediction Scores

Table 3 presents the effect of the recommendation model using different methods to combine the rating prediction scores. Analysis of the data in the table reveals the following findings: (1) The RKGR-ND model and the RKGR model exhibit comparable performance, suggesting that the rating prediction scores obtained from random sampling do not contain useful information. As a result, the recommendation performance has not significantly improved or decreased. (2) The RKGR-MF and RKGR-UR models demonstrate improved recommendation performance compared to the RKGR and RKGR-ND models, indicating that user ratings for items reflect to some extent the user's preferences for the items. Incorporating this aspect can enhance the recommendation performance of the model. (3) The recommendation performance of the RKGR-UR model surpasses that of the RKGR-MF model, implying that considering users' reviews of items and merging them with users' ratings of items better models users' preferences for items than considering only users' ratings of items. Therefore, it is more conducive to improving the performance of the recommendation model.

4.4   Influence of Normalized Quantile

In our reward function, we define the normalized quantile ρ, where setting $\rho = 1.0$ normalizes all rating prediction scores to negative rewards, and setting $\rho = 0.0$ normalizes all rating prediction scores to positive rewards. Figure 3 illustrates the effect of this parameter on recommendation performance. The data from the figure indicates that as the normalized quantile ρ increases, recommendation performance improves and stabilizes. Our experiments demonstrate that during the policy learning process, the agent explores items that users have interacted with but do not like. In such cases, providing positive rewards to the agent for exploring these items would mislead its learning of the user's true preferences. Instead, appropriate negative rewards should be given to these low-rated items, which can help the agent learn a better policy network.

5   Conclusions

In this paper, we propose RKGR-UR, a novel method that introduces user reviews into a RL-based recommendation system. The recommendation problem on KG is regarded as a MDP, and by utilizing the user's reviews and ratings to complete the rating prediction task, the predicted rating scores are transformed into reward feedback in RL environment to enhance the agent's ability to discern user preferences. Additionally, we design two comparative models to explore the impact of different types of rewards on the learning of the policy network of the agent. Finally, we conduct several experiments. Experiments on recommendation performance demonstrate that our method outperforms the existing state-of-the-art. Experimental results using rating prediction scores obtained in different ways demonstrate the effectiveness of incorporating user reviews in improving recommendation performance. Experiments on the impact of normalized quantile demonstrate that providing negative rewards to low-rated items during the agent's learning process contributes to obtaining a better policy network.

Acknowledgments. This work was partially supported by the National Natural Science Foundation of China (No. 61977002) and the State Key Laboratory of Software Development Environment of China (No. SKLSDE-2022ZX-14). The authors of this work take full responsibilities for its content. We thank the anonymous reviewers for their insightful comments and suggestions on this paper.

References

1. Xian, Y., Fu, Z., Muthukrishnan, S., De Melo, G., Zhang, Y.: Reinforcement knowledge graph reasoning for explainable recommendation. In: Proceedings of the 42nd International ACM SIGIR Conference on Research and Development in Information Retrieval, pp. 285–294 (2019)
2. Park, S.J., Chae, D.K., Bae, H.K., Park, S., Kim, S.W.: Reinforcement learning over sentiment-augmented knowledge graphs towards accurate and explainable recommendation. In: Proceedings of the Fifteenth ACM International Conference on Web Search and Data Mining, pp. 784–793 (2022)

3. Wang, X., Liu, K., Wang, D., Wu, L., Fu, Y., Xie, X.: Multi-level recommendation reasoning over knowledge graphs with reinforcement learning. In: Proceedings of the ACM Web Conference 2022, pp. 2098–2108 (2022)
4. Shani, G., Heckerman, D., Brafman, R.I., Boutilier, C.: An MDP-based recommender system. J. Mach. Learn. Res. **6**(9) (2005)
5. Cui, Z., et al.: Reinforced KGs reasoning for explainable sequential recommendation. World Wide Web **25**(2), 631–654 (2022)
6. Chen, X., Huang, C., Yao, L., Wang, X., Zhang, W., et al.: Knowledge-guided deep reinforcement learning for interactive recommendation. In: 2020 International Joint Conference on Neural Networks (IJCNN), pp. 1–8. IEEE (2020)
7. He, X., et al.: Learning to collaborate in multi-module recommendation via multi-agent reinforcement learning without communication. In: Fourteenth ACM Conference on Recommender Systems, pp. 210–219 (2020)
8. Song, W., Duan, Z., Yang, Z., Zhu, H., Zhang, M., Tang, J.: Explainable knowledge graph-based recommendation via deep reinforcement learning. arXiv preprint arXiv:1906.09506 (2019)
9. Srifi, M., Oussous, A., Ait Lahcen, A., Mouline, S.: Recommender systems based on collaborative filtering using review texts-a survey. Information **11**(6), 317 (2020)
10. Zheng, L., Noroozi, V., Yu, P.S.: Joint deep modeling of users and items using reviews for recommendation. In: Proceedings of the Tenth ACM International Conference on Web Search and Data Mining, pp. 425–434 (2017)
11. Tan, Y., Zhang, M., Liu, Y., Ma, S.: Rating-boosted latent topics: understanding users and items with ratings and reviews. IJCAI **16**, 2640–2646 (2016)
12. Zhang, Y., Lai, G., Zhang, M., Zhang, Y., Liu, Y., Ma, S.: Explicit factor models for explainable recommendation based on phrase-level sentiment analysis. In: Proceedings of the 37th International ACM SIGIR Conference on Research & Development in Information Retrieval, pp. 83–92 (2014)
13. Konda, V., Tsitsiklis, J.: Actor-critic algorithms. In: Advances in Neural Information Processing Systems 12 (1999)
14. Sutton, R.S., McAllester, D., Singh, S., Mansour, Y.: Policy gradient methods for reinforcement learning with function approximation. In: Advances in Neural Information Processing Systems 12 (1999)
15. Koren, Y., Bell, R., Volinsky, C.: Matrix factorization techniques for recommender systems. Computer **42**(8), 30–37 (2009)
16. Rendle, S., Freudenthaler, C., Gantner, Z., Schmidt-Thieme, L.: BPR: Bayesian personalized ranking from implicit feedback. arXiv preprint arXiv:1205.2618 (2012)
17. Zhang, W., Yuan, Q., Han, J., Wang, J.: Collaborative multi-level embedding learning from reviews for rating prediction. IJCAI **16**, 2986–2992 (2016)
18. Wang, X., He, X., Cao, Y., Liu, M., Chua, T.S.: KGAT: knowledge graph attention network for recommendation. In: Proceedings of the 25th ACM SIGKDD International Conference on Knowledge Discovery & Data Mining, pp. 950–958 (2019)

A Session Recommendation Model Based on Heterogeneous Graph Neural Network

Zhiwei An[1], Yirui Tan[1], Jinli Zhang[1(✉)], Zongli Jiang[1], and Chen Li[2]

[1] Beijing University of Technology, Beijing, China
lz73798@gmail.com
[2] Nagoya University, Nagoya 464-8602, Japan

Abstract. In recent years, the amount of data generated by online platforms has grown exponentially, making it challenging for users to process large amounts of information. As a result, recommendation systems greatly improve user experience and retention by efficiently matching the content or products that users are interested in. However, most existing models only consider long-term preferences, ignoring the dynamic users' preferences. To address this issue, this paper proposes a novel recommendation method that leverages heterogeneous information networks to capture both long-term and short-term preferences. Our model involves two components: a heterogeneous graph neural network that captures the long-term preferences of users and an attention mechanism that focuses on short-term preferences. The heterogeneous graph neural network extracts relevant information from the input sessions to learn feature representations, and the attention mechanism weights the features according to each user's current interests. We evaluate our method on two public datasets, and our results show that our model outperforms existing approaches in terms of accuracy and robustness. In conclusion, our proposed method provides a useful framework for developing more efficient and proactive recommendation systems that can adapt to users' ever-changing preferences. The incorporation of both long-term and short-term preferences allows our model to provide more accurate and personalized recommendations, improving the user experience.

Keywords: Data Mining · Recommendation System · Graph Neural Network · Heterogeneous Graph · Session Embedding

1 Introduction

Recommender systems assist users in making informed choices and learn users' preferences based on their historical information [1]. However, traditional algorithms focus only on items that users have shown interest in over a long time period, and may not detect recent changes in user interests [2]. For instance, a user who frequently purchased jeans for a long time, but now he prefers sweatpants in some cases in Fig. 1. If traditional recommendation systems may still suggest jeans to this user, the merchant is likely to lose this user. To overcome this issue, analyzing user behavior at a session level can be

© The Author(s), under exclusive license to Springer Nature Switzerland AG 2023
Z. Jin et al. (Eds.): KSEM 2023, LNAI 14119, pp. 160–171, 2023.
https://doi.org/10.1007/978-3-031-40289-0_13

more useful in retaining information about user preferences [3]. Session-based recommendation is based on the observation that dependencies between items within a session have a stronger influence on predicting the next item compared to dependency between items across sessions. In other words, items that occur within the same session tend to have a higher relevance and co-occurrence than those across different sessions.

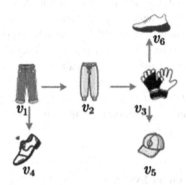

Fig. 1. The transitions between items in the traditional recommendation system

In the e-commerce platform, as shown in Fig. 2, users' behaviors in Fig. 1 are divided into smaller granularities, and session sequences s_1, s_2, s_3 are generated. Since the session-based recommendation system focuses more on the user's short-term transaction behavior, it is more conducive to extract the transaction network decomposed into multiple sessions. The recommendation system can focus on the preference transfer among users [4].

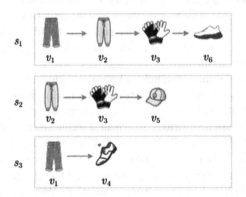

Fig. 2. The session sequence in session-based recommendation system

To avoid ignoring short-term preference shifts [5] and long-term user shopping habits [6], we consider the dependencies between sessions. This paper introduces a heterogeneous graph to construct users, items, and sessions. The heterogeneous graph that contains multiple types of nodes and edges, representing transitions between users, items, and sessions to extract more rich information. To address this issue, a heterogeneous graph neural network is designed to learn latent representations by aggregating heterogeneous neighbor information. This approach captures the heterogeneity of structure and content efficiently and considers transformation relationships of items.

The main work of this pater includes the following aspects:

- To fully consider the complex dependency relationships in different sessions, we propose constructing a heterogeneous graph from the session sequences.
- The proposed recommendation algorithm utilities a heterogeneous graph neural network to capture the latent information of users. It achieves accurate recommendations by analyzing the items in anonymous sessions and using this information to build a graph.
- We conducted experiments on real datasets, and the experimental results show that this method is better than other comparative models.

2 Related Work

2.1 Traditional Recommender Systems

Recommender systems usually adopt collaborative filtering techniques, which leverages users' historical interactions with items to provide recommendations. One commonly used method for modeling user preferences and item attributes in recommender systems is matrix factorization [7].

Due to its scalability and effectiveness in handling massive datasets (e.g., Amazon and eBay), matrix factorization has gained widespread adoption in various engineering applications [8]. The item-KNN approach [9] is based on the concept of calculating the similarity between items using historical preference data from all users. Once the similarity between items is calculated, the algorithm recommends items that are similar to the ones that the user has shown preference for in the past. Unfortunately, when faced with new users or previously unseen items, the problem of cold start arises, which means that it is difficult to learn accurate embeddings for these new entities since there is no prior interaction history available.

To alleviate this issue, some researchers have started to incorporate additional contextual information, also known as auxiliary data or auxiliary information, into the recommendation model. Recently, the emergence of deep learning has revolutionized the field of recommender systems. Various deep neural architectures, such as convolutional neural networks [10], graph neural networks [11], variational auto-encoders [12], and reinforcement learning [13], have been proposed to address recommendation tasks and have demonstrated impressive performance. However, traditional recommender systems are limited in their ability to handle heterogeneous information and cannot fully capture the complexity of real-world objects with diverse characteristics [14].

2.2 Recommendation Based on Graph Neural Networks

The rise of graph neural networks has been a recent topic of interest in the research community [15]. Graph neural networks aggregate information from neighboring nodes using neural networks. This method is advantageous over traditional graph embedding models because it explicitly incorporates high-order connectivity information in a comprehensive and end-to-end approach, making it useful for downstream tasks [16]. However, traditional network analysis methods are inadequate for managing and utilizing the heterogeneous and intricate information contained in such data. Heterogeneous Information Network (HIN) [17] propagates user preference data through meta-paths, and improved the model by considering personalization.

Recommendation models based on heterogeneous information networks rely mainly on similarity, and present high computational complexity [18]. In recent years, researchers have attempted to use heterogeneous network embedding to effectively mine user and item features based on heterogeneous networks [19]. Chen [20] et al. extract features from meta-paths by calculating PathCount for each meta-path, and learn user and item feature representations using multilayer perceptron. Hu [21] et al. consider the feature embeddings of different meta-paths in recommendation based on heterogeneous information networks.

2.3 Recommendation System with Sessions

With the growing popularity of graph neural networks (GNNs), research efforts have been made to extend their application to session-based recommendation, where these models aim to achieve state-of-the-art performance [22]. A common approach employed by numerous sequential recommender systems is to utilize item-item transition matrices to capture sequential patterns between adjacent items. GRU4Rec [23] is a session-based recommendation approach that employs a recurrent neural network framework. The framework operates by using the current item in the session as input, updating the hidden state recursively through time, and outputting the predicted next item based on the updated hidden state.

Recently, attention mechanisms have been considered effective in multiple recommendation tasks, such as text-aware recommendations [24], and point-of-interest [25]. SASRec [26] is a sequence recommendation model based on self-attention, which models the entire user sequence and makes recommendations adaptively based on the interaction history. GCE-GNN [14] utilizes a session-aware attention mechanism to extract relevant information from a global graph for the target session sequence. And, SR-GNN [27] treats session sequences as graphs and employs graph neural networks to learn embeddings for each individual item. The model then uses an attention network to combine global preferences with current interests, resulting in personalized recommendations for each user. These methods can provide more targeted recommendations by modeling a user's long-term and continually evolving interests, but they cannot capture the transfer of a user's own interests in a social network.

3 The Proposed Method

This section provides a detailed introduction to our session recommendation model based on heterogeneous graph neural networks. The model consists of three main components, as illustrated in Fig. 3. To optimize item transitions in user sessions and capture global information, we construct a heterogeneous graph using session sequences that accounts for the complex interdependencies among items, sessions, and users. Additionally, we design a session heterogeneous graph to learn session representations and user long-term preferences with semantic information. Finally, we use a session encoder to combine users' general preferences with the items to generate session representations. The following sections provide a detailed introduction to each of these modules.

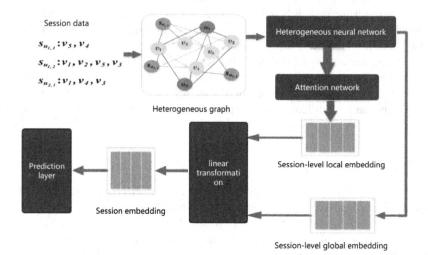

Fig. 3. An overview of the proposed framework

3.1 Build the Heterogeneous Graph

In this section, we discuss how to construct a heterogeneous information network with session sequence S as input. We create a heterogeneous graph G_n with item nodes V, session nodes S and user nodes U.

The initial feature representations of the nodes lack expressive power and cannot capture the complex transformations between items. Therefore, we designed a novel heterogeneous graph neural network to learn embedding representations of the nodes in the graph. To compute the embedding representations, we aggregate the information of all its neighboring nodes $N_{r_x}(v_j)$ for each type of edge r_x. The aggregation process is shown in formula 1 below:

$$P_{N_{r_x},(v_i)}^{k+1} = \frac{1}{|N_{rx}(v_i)|} \sum_{n \in N_{rx}(vi)} e_n^{(k)}$$

$$p_{v_i,r_x}^{(k+1)} = f\left(W_{(r_x)}^{(k+1)} \left[p_{N_{r_x}(v_i)}^{(k+1)} \Big\| p_{v_i}^{(k)} \right] + b_{r_x}^{(k+1)} \right)$$

(1)

where $N_{r_x}(v_i)$ represents the set of neighbor nodes connected to node v_i through edge type r_x. $W_{(r_x)}^{(k+1)}$ is a $d \times d$ dimensional matrix, $b_{r_x}^{(k+1)}$ is a specific parameter of dimension $d \times d$.

We accumulate the information propagated through various types of edges. Subsequently, we update the feature representation of the node using the Eq. 2 as shown below.

$$p_{v_i}^{(k+1)} = accum\left(p_{v_i,r_{interact}}^{(k+1)}, p_{v_i,r_{in}}^{(k+1)}, p_{v_i,r_{out}}^{(k+1)}, p_{v_i,r_{contain}}^{(k+1)}\right) \quad (2)$$

where $accum(\cdot)$ represents the additive operation.

The aggregation of user nodes is similar to that of project nodes. The updated representation of the user node is as follows:

$$q_{u_i}^{(k+1)} = accum\left(q_{u_i,r_{interact}}^{(k+1)}, p_{v_i,r_{contain}}^{(k+1)}\right) \quad (3)$$

After updating through K layer propagation, the embeddings obtained by each layer are combined, resulting in the final feature representation of users and items.

$$q_{u_i} = \sum_{k=0}^{K} \alpha_k q_{u_i}^{(k)}$$

$$q_{v_i} = \sum_{k=0}^{K} \alpha_k q_{v_i}^{(k)} \quad (4)$$

where α_k represents the importance of the k-th layer output. By using heterogeneous graph neural network, we can learn long-term preferences and obtain globally rich semantic embeddings of items.

3.2 Session Embedding

By learning the feature representations of projects through heterogeneous graph neural networks, session embeddings are then generated using the feature representations of projects. For a given session $s = \{v_{(s,1)}, v_{(s,2)}, v_{(s,3)}, ..., v_{(s,i)}\}$, the initial feature representation is calculated using the following formula:

$$s = v_{s,1} \oplus v_{s,2} \oplus ... \oplus v_{s,i} \oplus v_0 \quad (5)$$

where $v_{s,i}$ is the embedding of node $v_{s,i}$, v_0 is the zero vector with variable dimensions, and $\oplus$ denotes concatenation.

We incorporated an attention mechanism into the model to account for the varying influence of long-term and short-term user preferences on recommendation results, resulting in a mixed session embedding that captures both aspects. We consider the local embedding s_g of the session with the following equation.

$$s_l = v_{s,n} \quad (6)$$

where $v_{s,n}$ is the embedded representation of the last item of the current session.

To incorporate the long-term user preferences, we need to take into account the relationships between all the items. This requires utilizing a soft attention mechanism to learn the global embedding s_g of the session as follows.

$$\partial_i = W^T \sigma \left(W_1 v_{s,n} + W_2 v_{s,i} + c \right)$$
$$S_g = \sum_{i=1}^{n} \partial_i v_{s,i} \tag{7}$$

The dimension of W^T is d, and both W_1 and W_2 are $d \times 2d$ matrices used as weights. Once both the global and local embeddings of a session have been calculated, the mixed session embedding can be represented as follows:

$$s_h = W_3 \left[s_l; s_g \right] \tag{8}$$

where the matrix $W_3 \in R^{d \times 2d}$ was used to fuse s_l and s_g into the mixed session embedding.

3.3 Rating Prediction and Optimization

After generating session embeddings, the initial embeddings of candidate items $q_{v_i}^{(0)}$ are calculated based on the session embeddings s, and the score $\hat{y}$ of each candidate item is computed by a softmax layer.

$$\hat{y}_i = soft \max \left(s^T q_{v_i}^{(0)} \right) \tag{9}$$

The cross-entropy loss represents the objective function:

$$\mathcal{L}(\hat{y}) = \sum_{i=0}^{|v|} y_i \log(\hat{y}_i) + (1 - y_i) \log(1 - \hat{y}_i) \tag{10}$$

where $y \in \mathbb{R}^{|v|}$ is the one-heat vector of the true value.

4 Experiments and Results

4.1 Datasets

We test our model on two real-world datasets that are widely employed in research on session recommendation system.

The Reddit dataset consists of posts from the Reddit forum, containing comments and titles from 25,000 Reddit usernames on different articles. The data includes Reddit usernames, evaluated article names, and evaluation times. To prepare the data, we specified an idle time threshold and used timestamps to group continuous interactions that occurred within the time threshold into the same session. We set the idle threshold of this dataset to 60 min to divide the Reddit data into sessions.

The Xing dataset collects recruitment information from social networking platforms, including interactions between 770,000 users and recruitment information within 80 days. According to the preprocessing program, we set a 30-min idle threshold to divide the Xing data into sessions and discard the "deletion" interaction.

4.2 Comparison Models

To evaluate the performance of our method in session recommendation, we compared it with several existing models: traditional item-KNN-based session recommendation method, GRU-based method, and homogeneous graph neural network-based method.

Item-KNN [9]: This approach draws inspiration from conventional content-based filtering approaches and is utilized for session recommendation. It suggests items similar to the currently viewed item, judging their similarity on the basis of their co-occurrence in the session. The top k items with the greatest similarity to the current item are suggested.

GRU4Rec [23]: Based on a recurrent neural network, GRU4Rec inputs the embedding representations of the items extracted from the session history into one or more GRU layers and a feedforward layer, and predicts the similarity between each item and the next item in the session.

SR-GNN [27]: The SR-GNN model converts the session sequence into a homogeneous graph and utilizes a graph neural network to obtain embeddings for each item. This is achieved by using the session sequence and a graph neural network to learn the feature representations of each item.

4.3 Evaluation Metrics

To evaluate the recommendation performance of our model, we used two widely used evaluation metrics in recommendation: recall rate (Recall@k) and mean reciprocal rank (MRR@k).

In the test set, the evaluation metrics measure whether the items relevant to the user actually appeared in the recommendation list, regardless of their position in the list. The calculation formula for recall rate is as follows:

$$Recall@k = \frac{\text{Number of related items in the recommended k items}}{\text{Number of all items related to the user}} \quad (11)$$

We also measured the performance of recommendations using the mean reciprocal rank, which takes into account the position of relevant items in the recommended item list. The calculation formula is as follows:

$$MRR@k = \frac{1}{K} \sum_{i=1}^{K} \frac{1}{rank_i} \quad (12)$$

4.4 Experimental Results and Analysis

To demonstrate the performance of our proposed model, we compared it with other commonly used recommendation methods. We analyzed the experimental results and presented them in Table 1.

Compared with other methods, the performance of Item-KNN is the worst, indicating that both the RNN-based session-based recommendation model that considers the order of interaction and the GNN-based session-based recommendation model that considers the historical interaction information have certain performance improvement effects.

Table 1. Experimental results of different models on two datasets

Model	Reddit		Xing	
	Recall@10	MRR@10	Recall@10	MRR@10
Item-KNN	0.3032	0.1289	0.1185	0.0542
GRU4Rec	0.4173	0.2436	0.1315	0.0636
SR-GNN	0.4238	0.2590	0.1617	0.0939
Our Model	**0.5832**	**0.3016**	**0.1705**	**0.1169**

Based on session recommendation model, GRU4Rec constructs the session sequence as a graph achieved more significant improvement. While GRU4Rec, which constructs the session sequence as a graph, achieved more significant improvements, it does not consider the correlation between distant items and overlooks certain details in the session sequence. In contrast, SR-GNN generates an embedding representation of the items and works with a homogeneous graph, representing session sequences as a graph of items. It captures the relationships between different items in different sessions, making the learned feature embeddings of items more expressive. However, it only considers transitions between items and neglects other data in the session sequence. Constructing the session sequence as a heterogeneous graph could provide more information.

Hyperparameters play a crucial role in model training and can significantly impact the quality of the training results. In addition, we investigated the influence of the learning rate on model outcomes. The learning rate determines how and when the objective function reaches the minimum value. We trained the model with various learning rates and display the final experiment results in Fig. 4. The figure shows that when the learning rate is set to 0.0002, the model outperforms the others on both datasets. Therefore, the optimal learning rate for this model is 0.0002.

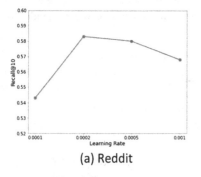
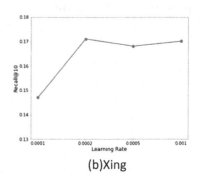

(a) Reddit   (b)Xing

Fig. 4. Experimental results with different learning rates on two datasets

We also examined the impact of node embedding dimensions on the model's performance. Node embedding dimensions were set to {32, 64, 96, 128, 256}, and the experimental results are presented in Fig. 5. The results show that the model performs best when the node dimension is 128. Performance improves consistently as the node dimension increases from 32 to 128. However, when the node dimension is larger than 128, the performance no longer improves with longer dimension information.

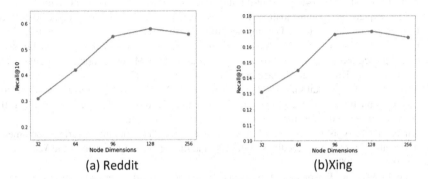

(a) Reddit   (b)Xing

Fig. 5. Experimental results with different node dimensions on two datasets

5   Conclusion

In this paper, we proposed a heterogeneous graph neural network for session-based recommendation to address the problem of neglecting users' short-term preferences in the previous model. Our method aims to alleviate the issue of previous models neglecting users' short-term preferences. Unlike previous recommendation techniques, we consider the impact of users' historical interactions and establish a heterogeneous graph incorporating session, item, and user nodes. Additionally, we utilize attention mechanisms to generate session representations that capture users' long-term and short-term preferences. Our experiments on two public datasets demonstrate that our model outperforms other session-based recommendation models. In future research, we plan to work with real-world datasets that feature multiple types of nodes. Therefore, our future work will focus on optimize the heterogeneous graph neural network model, leading to further improved performance results.

References

1. Wang, Y., Zhao, Y., Zhang, Y., Derr, T.: Collaboration-aware graph convolutional network for recommender systems. In: Proceedings of the ACM Web Conference 2023, pp. 91–101 (2023)
2. Vančura, V., Alves, R., Kasalick'y, P., Kordík, P.: Scalable linear shallow autoencoder for collaborative filtering. In: Proceedings of the 16th ACM Conference onRecommender Systems, pp. 604–609 (2022)
3. Su, J., Chen, C., Liu, W., Wu, F., Zheng, X., Lyu, H.: Enhancing hierarchy-aware graph networks with deep dual clustering for session-based recommendation. In: Proceedings of the ACM Web Conference 2023, pp. 165–176 (2023)

4. He, B., He, X., Zhang, Y., Tang, R., Ma, C.: Dynamically expandable graph convolution for streaming recommendation. arXiv preprint arXiv:2303.11700 (2023)
5. Chen, Y., Liu, Z., Li, J., McAuley, J., Xiong, C.: Intent contrastive learning forsequential recommendation. In: Proceedings of the ACM Web Conference 2022, pp. 2172–2182 (2022)
6. Zhao, Q.: RESETBERT4REC: a pre-training model integrating time and user historical behavior for sequential recommendation. In: Proceedings of the 45th International ACM SIGIR Conference on Research and Development in Information Retrieval, pp. 1812–1816 (2022)
7. Ouyang, Y., Wu, P., Pan, L.: Asymmetrical context-aware modulation for collaborative filtering recommendation. In: Proceedings of the 31st ACM International Conference on Information & Knowledge Management, pp. 1595–1604 (2022)
8. Melchiorre, A.B., Rekabsaz, N., Ganhör, C., Schedl, M.: Protomf: Prototype-based matrix factorization for effective and explainable recommendations. In: Proceedings of the 16th ACM Conference on Recommender Systems, pp. 246–256 (2022)
9. Sarwar, B., Karypis, G., Konstan, J., Riedl, J.: Item-based collaborative filtering recommendation algorithms. In: Proceedings of the 10th international conference on World Wide Web, pp. 285–295 (2001)
10. Tang, J., Wang, K.: Personalized top-n sequential recommendation via convolutional sequence embedding. In: Proceedings of the eleventh ACM International Conference on Web Search and Data Mining, pp. 565–573 (2018)
11. Hsu, C., Li, C.T.: Retagnn: relational temporal attentive graph neural networks for holistic sequential recommendation. In: Proceedings of the Web Conference 2021, pp. 2968–2979 (2021)
12. Xie, Z., Liu, C., Zhang, Y., Lu, H., Wang, D., Ding, Y.: Adversarial and contrastive variational autoencoder for sequential recommendation. In: Proceedings of the Web Conference 2021, pp. 449–459 (2021)
13. Zhao, K., et al.: Leveraging demonstrations for reinforcement recommendation reasoning over knowledge graphs. In: Proceedings of the 43rd International ACM SIGIR Conference on Research and Development in Information Retrieval, pp. 239–248 (2020)
14. Wang, Z., Wei, W., Cong, G., Li, X.L., Mao, X.L., Qiu, M.: Global context enhanced graph neural networks for session-based recommendation. In: Proceedings of the 43rd International ACM SIGIR Conference on Research and Development in Information Retrieval, pp. 169–178 (2020)
15. Shi, C., Zhang, Z., Ji, Y., Wang, W., Yu, P.S., Shi, Z.: Semrec: a personalized semantic recommendation method based on weighted heterogeneous information networks. World Wide Web 22, 153–184 (2019)
16. Feng, W., Wang, J.: Incorporating heterogeneous information for personalized tag recommendation in social tagging systems. In: Proceedings of the 18th ACM SIGKDD International Conference on Knowledge Discovery and Data Mining. New York: ACM, pp. 1276–1284 (2012)
17. Yu, X., Ren, X., Sun, Y., et al.: Recommendation in heterogeneous information networks with implicit user feedback. In: Proceedings of the 7th ACM Conference on Recommender Systems. New York: ACM, pp. 347–350 (2013)
18. Zhang, J., Jiang, Z., Li, T.: Chin: classification with meta-path in heterogeneou information networks. In: Florez, H., Diaz, C., Chavarriaga, J. (eds.) Applied Informatics, pp. 63–74. Springer International Publishing, Cham (2018)
19. Zhang, J., Jiang, Z., Du, Y., Li, T., Wang, Y., Hu, X.: Hierarchy construction and classification of heterogeneous information networks based on rsdaef. Data Knowl. Eng. 127, 101790 (2020)
20. Chan, L., Liu, Y., Zheng, Z., et al.: Heterogeneous neural attentive factorization ma-chine for rating prediction. In: Proceedings of the 27th ACM International Conference on Information and Knowledge Management. New York: ACM, pp. 833–842 (2018)

21. Hu, B., Shi, C., Zhao, W.X., et al.: Leveraging meta-path based context for top-n recommendation with a neural co-attention model. In: Proceedings of the 24th ACM SIGKDD International Conference on Knowledge Discovery & Data Mining. New York: ACM, pp. 1531–1540 (2018)
22. Chen, T., Wong, R.C.W.: Handling information loss of graph neural networks for session-based recommendation. In: Proceedings of the 26th ACM SIGKDD International Conference on Knowledge Discovery & Data Mining, pp. 1172–1180 (2020)
23. Hidasi, B.A.Z., Alexandros, K., Linas, B., et al.: Session-based recommendations with recurrent neural networks. arXiv preprint arXiv:1511.06939 (2015)
24. Zhou, J.P., Cheng, Z., Pérez, F., Volkovs, M.: TAFA: two-headed attention fused autoencoder for context-aware recommendations. In: Proceedings of the 14th ACM Conference on Recommender Systems, pp. 338–347 (2020)
25. Luo, Y., Liu, Q., Liu, Z.: STAN: spatio-temporal attention network for next location recommendation. In: Proceedings of the Web Conference 2021, pp. 2177–2185 (2021)
26. Kang, W.C., McAuley, J.: Self-attentive sequential recommendation. In: 2018 IEEE International Conference on Data Mining (ICDM), pp. 197–206. IEEE (2018)
27. Wu, S., Tang, Y., Zhu, Y., Wang, L., Xie, X., Tan, T.: Session-based recommendation with graph neural networks. In: Proceedings of the AAAI Conference on Artificial Intelligence. vol. 33, pp. 346–353 (2019)

Dialogue State Tracking with a Dialogue-Aware Slot-Level Schema Graph Approach

Jie Yang, Hui Song$^{(\boxtimes)}$, Bo Xu, and Haoran Zhou

School of Computer Science and Technology, Donghua University, Shanghai, China
{2212525,2202423}@mail.dhu.edu.cn, {songhui,xubo}@dhu.edu.cn

Abstract. Dialogue State Tracking (DST) aims to keep dialogue states updated over the whole dialogue. Recently, slot self-attention mechanism and token-level schema graph are both proposed to capture slot relations based on prior knowledge or human experience, avoiding the independent prediction of slot values. However, they fall short in modeling the correlations among slots across domain, and the dialogue history encoding method injects noises into the slot representations. To address these issues, we propose a novel slot-level schema graph to involve high cooccurrence slot relations across domain. A two layers network is then adopted to force slots to pay attention only on the relevant dialogue context and related slots successively. We make a further comparison study in modeling slot relation to quantify that the improvement of our schema graph is superior to slot self-attention. Empirical results on benchmark datasets (i.e., MultiWOZ 2.0, MultiWOZ 2.1, and MultiWOZ 2.4) show that our approach outperforms strong baselines in both predefined ontology-based DST and open vocabulary-based DST methods.

Keywords: Dialogue State Tracking · Schema Graph · Slot Self-Attention

1 Introduction

Task-oriented dialogue system helps users complete numerous daily tasks through conversation, such as restaurant reservation, weather query and travel arrangements. The system action and response directly dependent on detecting the intentions and goals of users. Dialogue State Tracking (DST) tracks the intentions and goals by representing them as a dialogue state, i.e. a set of predefined domain-slots (simply referred as slots for convenience) and their corresponding values, which is absolutely essential and vital.

DST methods generally fall into two categories: predefined ontology-based DST [1] and open vocabulary-based DST [2,3]. [4] employs a triple-copy strategy to fill the slots and achieve a better performance, called TripPy. But, the ellipsis and reference phenomena, usually occurring in the multi-domain dialogue utterances, makes it difficult to generate the right dialogue state either way. To tackle this issue, a slot self-attention mechanism in a fully data-driven way [5–7] and a schema graph based on prior knowledge [8–10] have been separately proposed to capture slot correlations. [5] uses slot self-attentive attention to extract slot-specific information for each slot to model different slot relations, named as STAR.

© The Author(s), under exclusive license to Springer Nature Switzerland AG 2023
Z. Jin et al. (Eds.): KSEM 2023, LNAI 14119, pp. 172–183, 2023.
https://doi.org/10.1007/978-3-031-40289-0_14

However, the DST models mentioned above may suffer from three major drawbacks, some examples are shown in Fig. 1. First, statistics show that not all slots are related to each other. For example, *train-book_people* and *taxi-leaveat* are hardly uttered in one dialogue. That is to say, such relationships may be overestimated. Second, they simply leverage the semantic relevance of slot name when constructing the schema graph, yet ignore the implicit slot relationship hidden in the dataset. In *Situation 3*, *train-day* and *hotel-name* slot pairs have a high frequency of cooccurrence. Last, they encode schema graph and dialogue context encoding simultaneously at the token-level by internal attention mechanism. The irrelevant context tokens bring noises to the information flow of graph nodes.

Situation 1: *The destination of a taxi has the probability to be a hotel.*
Sys: Where are you departing from? What is your destination?
Usr: I'm going to be headed from the Cambridge punter back to the hotel.

Situation 2: *Hotels with higher stars are usually more expensive.*
Sys: I can definitely help with that. Do you prefer a hotel or guesthouse?
Usr: I'd like it to be expensive. 4 star rated.

Situation 3: *The high co-occurrence rate of slots in different domain.*
Sys: What day will you be traveling?
Usr: This will be for Wednesday.
...
Sys: Anything else I can do for you?
Usr: I also need to find a place to stay.

Fig. 1. Examples of dialogue in multi-domain.

In this paper, we propose a novel dialogue state tracking method with a **DialO**gue-aware s**L**ot-**L**evel schem**A** g**R**aph (**DOLLAR**). Firstly, we make a profound study to verify the following assumption: removing interference information directly between irrelevant slot pairs will be more conducive to value prediction. Then, to capture slot pairs correlation more accurately and effectively, we construct a slot-level schema graph and add three edge types: pairs with *same domain*, pairs with *same domain-specific slots* and pairs with *high cooccurrence probability across domain*. Next, a two layers network is adopted to conduce the associated dialogue understanding and slot dependency for each slot step by step, instead of modeling the relationships between different slots, slots and dialogue tokens synchronously in one module. It consists of a slot-token attention module and a slot-level schema graph. DOLLAR is applicable to both two types of DST value prediction approaches. Experimental results show that DOLLAR achieves a new state-of-the-art performance of on three benchmark datasets (i.e., MultiWOZ 2.0, MultiWOZ 2.1, and MultiWOZ 2.4). Compared with the previous SOTA model, both two kinds of DST models have been further improved, which proves the effectiveness of DOLLAR. The contributions of this paper can be summarized as follows:

1. We conduct an experiment to demonstrate the superiority of modeling partial high-related slot connections than all connections in joint goal accuracy performance. And slots interacting with a few reliant slots significantly reduces the model parameters.

2. To avoid the interference of redundant information and alleviate the data sparsity problem, we exploit high-related slots correlation within the schema graph at the slot-level based on prior knowledge and statistical information.

3. To sufficiently encode the slot-level schema graph, we adopt a two layers network to integrate the dialogue information associated with each slot, offering the opportunity to the information sharing and interchange among various slots exactly.

2   Related Work

The early rule-based DST models [11,12] and neural network-based methods [13–16] have poor scalability. As the pretraining language models such as BERT and GPT-2 have achieved superior performance in many natural language processing tasks, [1,17] use BERT to learn the representation of slots and dialogue history, and then exploit attention mechanism to further enrich slot representations. [18] collects multiple task-oriented dialogue datasets to deeply train BERT. [10,19,20] utilize GPT-2 as the dialogue context encoder, and describe DST as the language generation task. Recent works seemed to reveal the significance of slot relations that previous works may overlook. [21] controls the information flow between correlated slots by constructing slot similarity matrix. [5–7] apply slot self-attentive attention to model different slot relations. However, not all slots are related. Excessive connections will bring about irrelevant redundant information and affect the information flow between slots. [22] proposes a top-k slot self-attention to force each slot to involve information from other k prominent slots and mask the rest out. This fine-grained slot correlation further improves performance. Recent popular researches attempt to apply predefined schema graphs to incorporate the slot relations defined on human experience. [8–10,23] define a token-level or slot-level schema graph using GCNs or GATs that involves dependency among domain nodes, slot nodes and value nodes. But these models fail to build the relation between dialogue context and slots at the slot-level in a dialogue-aware way.

3   Methodology

In this section, we describe our proposed model in detail. The overall architecture of DOLLAR is depicted in Fig. 2. DOLLAR consists of three components: (1) a context and schema encoder learns the dialogue and slots representation; (2) a two layers network includes a slot-token attention module to fuse the associated dialogue-aware information into slots first and then a schema graph to capture the relevant slot relations in the slot-level way; (3) with rich knowledge of slot representations, two different value prediction modules are both suitable for DOLLAR.

3.1   Context and Schema Encoder

DOLLAR exploits BERT to encode the context and schema. For turn t, R_t and U_t is the system response and user utterance. A dialogue utterance can be represented as $Z_t = R_t \oplus U_t$ and the dialogue history is denoted as $D_t = Z_1 \oplus Z_2 \oplus \cdots \oplus Z_{t-1}$, where $\oplus$ is the sequence concatenation operator. The schema consists of each slot S_p in the set $S = \{S_1, \cdots, S_P\}$ and its candidate value $V_p^t \in \mathcal{V}_p$. A fine-tuned and parameter-fixed BERT is individually applied to obtain the context and schema representations:

$$H_t = BERT_{finetune}([CLS] \oplus U_t \oplus [SEP] \oplus D_t \oplus [SEP]) \in \mathbb{R}^{L \times d} \quad (1)$$

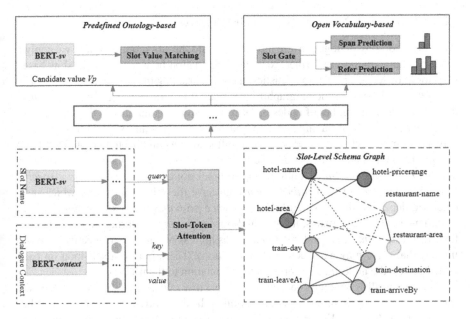

Fig. 2. The architecture of DOLLAR.

$$h_{[CLS]}^{S_p} = BERT_{fixed} \left([CLS] \oplus S_p \oplus [SEP] \right) \in \mathbb{R}^d \tag{2}$$

$$h_{[CLS]}^{V_p^t} = BERT_{fixed} \left([CLS] \oplus V_p^t \oplus [SEP] \right) \in \mathbb{R}^d \tag{3}$$

where $[CLS]$ and $[SEP]$ are two special tokens of BERT. L is the length of input sequence and d is the hidden dimension of BERT. Note that $BERT_{finetune}$ means its parameters will be fine-tuned during the training stage, with the aim of making BERT more adaptive to the dialogue representations in DST task. Meanwhile, $BERT_{fixed}$ facilitates DOLLAR to compute the representations of slot and value off-line, reducing model size and slot-value matching difficulty.

3.2 A Two Layers Network: Slot-Token Attention Layer

The dialogue history in multi-domain usually includes complex and diverse information and how to effectively utilize this rich information is a critical problem in value prediction. It is necessary to retrieve the most relevant and useful dialogue information corresponding to each slot separately. Specifically, we first employ a multi-head attention module [24] to acquire high related contextual information in token-level for each slot, using the representation $h_{[CLS]}^{S_p}$ of slot S_p as the query matrix and the dialogue context representation H_t as both the key and value matrix. Then the slot-specific information, also called the dialogue-aware slot vector $c_t^{S_p}$, is represented as:

$$c_t^{S_p} = MultiHead \left(h_{[CLS]}^{S_p}, H_t, H_t \right) \in \mathbb{R}^d \tag{4}$$

3.3   A Two Layers Network: Schema Graph Layer

After incorporating dialogue-aware information into the slot representation, we apply a schema graph structure to further exchange information between different slots based on prior knowledge and dataset statistics, thereby enriching the slot representation. The nodes of the slot-level schema graph G are made up of all slot, e.g. *attraction-name*, *hotel-internet*. The number of nodes is consistent with slots number in the schema. We do not take the step of having separate nodes for domains and slots in a token-level way, i.e. domain nodes, slot nodes, since it will lead to a complicated graph. DOLLAR defines three types edge of slot pair relations in multi-domain: (1) *Same Domain (SD)*, *hotel-parking* and *hotel-area* both belong to hotel domain. (2) *Same domain-specific Slots (SS)*, *taxi-leaveat* and *train-leaveat* both have the same value type, which indicates the departure time. (3) *High Cooccurrence probability across domain (HC)*. In accordance with our statistics, the probability of *train-day* appearing in the same context with *restaurant-name* and *hotel-name* is as high as 6% and 7% respectively, which implies that there may exist potential connections. There is also a self-loop on each node because the nodes need to propagate information to themselves.

We statistically count the cooccurrence probability of each possible slot pairs on the training dataset, Fig. 3 shows the visualization of the cooccurrence probability distribution on MultiWOZ 2.1. We only visualize slot pairs with probability of more than 6%, and the rest will not be considered and displayed anymore. In addition to those slot pairs in the same domain, there are still several pairs across domains that appear in a dialogue with a high frequency which are usually neglected. We focus on such relationships.

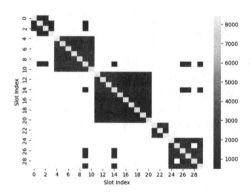

Fig. 3. Visualization of cooccurrence probability among different slot pairs. For simplicity, we use slot index to represent slot name.

To fuse the dialogue context information into the graph and get rid of the interference of redundant token information in dialogue history, the input feature of each node in G is no longer $h_{[CLS]}^{S_i}$, but will be initialized with the dialogue-aware slot representation $c_t^{S_i}$, obtained in the first layer of the two layer networks in DOLLAR. Thus, the node set can be denoted as $N = \left\{ n_i = c_t^{S_i} \epsilon \mathbb{R}^d \middle| 1 \leq i \leq P \right\}$. Our goal is to learn the relevant information of slot properly and generate more rich node representations through GATs, thus we are able to acquire the updated node set $\widetilde{N} = \{\widetilde{n}_i \epsilon \mathbb{R}^d | 1 \le i \le P\}$. The graph adjacency matrix $A \in \mathbb{R}^{P \times P}$ is involved to mask nodes unrelated, where $A_{ij} = 1$ represents there exists a correlation between node i and node j, conversely, $A_{ij} = 0$ indicates the uncorrelated node pairs. The whole process can be expressed briefly as:

$$\widetilde{N} = GAT\,(N, A) \tag{5}$$

More concretely, for each node in G, we calculate the attention scores of its neighbors to measure the contribution of each neighbor node with LeakyReLU function:

$$attn\,(n_i, n_j) = LeakyReLU\left(a^T\,[Wn_i || Wn_j]\right) \tag{6}$$

$$\alpha_{ij} = \frac{\exp\left(attn\,(n_i, n_j)\right)}{\sum\limits_{k \in \mathcal{N}_i} \exp\left(attn\,(n_i, n_k)\right)} \tag{7}$$

where $\mathcal{N}_i$ denotes the neighbor set (including node i itself) of the i-th node, $a\epsilon\mathbb{R}^{2d}$ and $W\epsilon\mathbb{R}^{d \times d}$ are both trainable parameter matrix. The attention coefficient α_{ij} signifies the relevance of each neighboring node j to node i. Once obtained, the normalized attention coefficients are used to compute a linear combination, to serve as the output features for every node. σ is a non-linear activate function:

$$\widetilde{n}_i = \sigma\left(\sum_{j \in \mathcal{N}_i} \alpha_{ij} Wn_i\right) \tag{8}$$

Multi-head attention mechanism is also used in our GATs and the nodes with different heads are represented by taking the average after concatenation as the final representation. As a result, $\widetilde{n}_i$ contains knowledge about the most relevant slots and non-redundant global dialogue context.

3.4 Value Prediction

DST models typically have two types of slot value prediction methods. With knowledgable slot representations, DOLLAR is capable of being applicable on both approaches.

Open Vocabulary-Based. DOLLAR attempt to employ a triple-copy mechanism to complete the value prediction following TripPy [4], thus transforming value prediction into a multi-classification task. A slot gate is firstly equipped to decide the class labels $C = \{none, dontcare, true, false, span, inform, refer\}$ of each slot. If the output label is *span* or *refer*, two different classification layers will be applied to accomplish prediction respectively. The only difference between TripPy and DOLLAR is that there is only one slot gate for all slots, which reduces the model size by a large margin compared to TripPy. The joint cross-entropy loss $\mathcal{L}_t$ at each turn t is the weighted sum of the three classification layers.

Predefined Ontology-Based. Followed by STAR [5], DOLLAR predicts the value of each slot S_p via the Euclidean distance between $\tilde{n}_p$ and a candidate value V_p^t. Then the value with the smallest distance is selected as the final prediction:

$$p\left(V_p^t \middle| X_t, S_p\right) = \frac{e^{\left(-\left\|\tilde{n}_p - h_{[CLS]}^{V_p^t}\right\|_2\right)}}{\sum\limits_{V_p' \in \mathcal{V}_p} e^{\left(-\left\|\tilde{n}_p - h_{[CLS]}^{V_p'}\right\|_2\right)}} \tag{9}$$

DOLLAR is trained to maximize the joint probability of all slots with the sum of the negative log-likelihood.

$$\mathcal{L}_t = \sum_{p=1}^{P} -\log\left(p\left(V_p^t \middle| X_t, S_p\right)\right) \tag{10}$$

4   Experiment

4.1   Data and Experimental Setup

We evaluate our approach on three task-oriented dialogue datasets: MultiWOZ 2.0, MultiWOZ 2.1, and the latest MultiWOZ 2.4, containing over 10,000 multi-turn dialogues, covering 7 different domains: taxi, train, hotel, restaurant, attraction, hospital and police. MultiWOZ 2.1 modifies about 32% of the state anotations in MultiWOZ 2.0. MultiWOZ 2.4 mainly corrects the annotation errors in the test set in MultiWOZ 2.1. Since hospital domain and police domain are not included in the validation set and test set, we use only the remaining 5 domains in the experiments in consistent with previous studies. We compute the Joint Goal Accuracy (JGA) on the test set, which defined over a dataset is the ratio of dialogue turns where all slots have been filled with the correct values according to the ground truth.

We utilize the pre-trained BERT-base-uncased[1] model as the dialogue context encoder and schema encoder. For slot-token attention module, we set the number of attention heads to 4. The schema graph is implemented with 1-layer GAT[2], which includes 8-head attention component. We first rerun TripPy and STAR model several times with different seeds in our machine respectively, then run DOLLAR in the same way. Finally, the average performance is presented.

4.2   Result

Main Result. Table 1 shows the JGA of DOLLAR in comparison to various predefined ontology-based DST and open vocabulary-based DST models in the test set of MultiWOZ 2.0, 2.1, and 2.4. As can be seen, our approach outperforms all the baseline models and achieves the best performance on these datasets with joint goal accuracy of 54.97%, 56.27%, and 74.90%.

---

[1] https://huggingface.co/transformers/model_doc/bert.html.
[2] https://github.com/Diego999/pyGAT.

Table 1. The JGA of various methods on the test set of MultiWOZ 2.0, 2.1 and 2.4. † indicates the results reproduced by us using the source codes and remaining results reported in the literature. ‡ means that the result comes from its ablation study for comparative comparison. § means the results are all from literature of CSFN-DST.

Model	Slot Correlations	Dialogue Information	JGA(%)		
			MultiWOZ 2.0	MultiWOZ 2.1	MultiWOZ 2.4
Predefined ontology-based DST					
CHAN	–	✗	53.06	53.38	68.23
STAR†	Slot Attention	✓	52.50	55.10	67.84
LUNA‡	Slot Attention	✓	–	55.29	–
SST	Schema Graph	✗	50.26	53.85	–
SST	Schema Graph	✓	51.17	55.23	–
DOLLAR	Schema Graph	✗	53.49	54.37	74.50
DOLLAR	Schema Graph	✓	**54.97**	**55.76**	**74.90**
Open vocabulary-based DST					
TripPy†	–	✗	50.31	54.39	63.66
SAVN	–	✗	**54.52**	54.86	60.55
GCDST	Schema Graph	✗	50.68	46.09	–
CSFN – DST§	Schema Graph	✓	51.57	52.88	–
SOM – DST§	Schema Graph	✓	52.23	53.19	–
DOLLAR	Schema Graph	✗	50.50	55.21	67.09
DOLLAR	Schema Graph	✓	51.04	**56.27**	**68.83**

The Importance of Slot Relation. Compared with those models that do not have taken slot relations into consideration (TripPy, SAVN and CHAN), DOLLAR has a measurable improvement on three benchmarks respectively expect for SAVN on MultiWOZ 2.0 dataset. It directly illustrates that building the relationship among the relevant slots is effective when DST models makes the slot value prediction whether based on open vocabulary or predefined ontology, which provides mutual guidance among slots and enhances the model's ability to deduce appropriate slot values from dependent slots.

The Effective Schema Graph in DOLLAR. We also observe that our approach achieves higher joint goal accuracy than the graph-based DST models such as GCDST, CSFN-DST, SOM-DST and SST, with the performance promotion of 10.18%, 3.39%, 3.08% and 0.53% separately on MultiWOZ 2.1 test set. Based on the slot-level graph, DOLLAR not only captures the relationship between different domains and different slots, but also takes the potential cooccurrence slot connection across domain into consideration. Therefore, DOLLAR is capable of catching the referential phenomenon in the multi-domain dialogue utterances.

The Useful two Layers Network in DOLLAR. Besides, GCDST only utilize prior ontology knowledge and the name properties of the slot when constructing the graph, ignoring the information of the dialogue context. CSFN-DST, SOM-DST and SST augment the dialogue information at the token-level in a fusion network with an internal attention module, failing to capture the more important slot-level feature and still showing a deficiency in utilizing the dialogue history. Additionally, useless context token will interfere with nodes interaction, thus these models cannot describe the slot relations absolutely. Our two layers network, which learns slot-specific feature from the dialogue history first and then constructs the schema graph, provides the mutual guidance among slots at the slot-level and enhances the model's ability to generate appropriate slot values. To further investigate the effectiveness of the dialogue context on node information interaction in our slot-level schema graph, we initialize the node with slot name vector instead of dialogue-aware slot embedding. DOLLAR (without dialogue information) gains only 55.21% and 54.37% JGA on MultiWOZ 2.1 in two DST methods respectively, and there is nearly 1.06% and 1.39% drop of performance. Similar JGA drop can also be verified in the other two datasets.

Do we Need more Slot Interaction? We conduct a further comparison experiment to quantify whether it is more efficient to model the correlation among all slots on MultiWOZ 2.1 dataset. To reveal that modeling partial slot relationships is more suitable for exploiting the slots dependencies than all slot associations and gains better from those highly relevant slots, we first introduce a stacked slot self-attention module into TripPy, the open vocabulary-based DST model. As shown in Table 2, JGA gains 0.83% improvement. Most notably, when we replace the stacked slot self-attention module with our schema graph in DOLLAR, the performance continues to increase 1.05%. Similarly, STAR drops 0.66% accuracy compared with DOLLAR as we can see from Table 1, which also demonstrates our conjecture in predefined ontology-based DST method. Therefore, we can infer that not all slots play a positive role in predicting the current slot value and it is worth mentioning that urging slots learn from those highly-related slots seem to more useful. What is more, DOLLAR is more elegant with fewer parameters, for the reason that there is nearly 10 million fewer parameters in 1-layer GAT module compared to the slot self-attention module. It means that we are able to achieve better performance in a simpler and more convenient way.

Table 2. The comparison between Slot Attention and Schema Graph on MultiWOZ 2.1.

Model	JGA(%)
TripPy	54.39
TripPy + Slot Attention	55.22
DOLLAR	56.27

Ablation Study. To explore the effectiveness of each relation in DOLLAR, we conduct an ablation study on the test set of MultiWOZ 2.1 and MultiWOZ 2.4 based on open vocabulary-based DST model, as shown in Table 3. We have counted the number of slot pairs for each type. One can see that the performance of DOLLAR with each type of slot relation surpasses that without any relations considerably. We find a 1.09% and 1.40% drop when *SS* is removed. We conjecture that it is due to the fact that slot pairs with such relationship have highly coincident values. Notably, the relatively sharp decrease of *HC* reveals that augmenting these edges into the graph has a desirable effect on DST models despite there is only 8 slot pairs. Interestingly, we also do an investigation to further prove that all slot connections are not acceptable. We replace the three kinds of slot relations with a *Fully-Connected (FC)* graph and the performance in terms of JGA degrades dramatically compared to DOLLAR. We believe that the noise introduced by the redundancy captured by the relations between all pairs of slots is the main reason.

Table 3. Ablation study on MultiWOZ 2.1 and MultiWOZ 2.4.

Model	Pair Number	JGA(%)	
		MultiWOZ 2.1	MultiWOZ 2.4
DOLLAR	114	56.27	68.83
– SD	90	55.45 (–0.82)	67.11(–1.72)
– SS	16	55.18 (–1.09)	67.43(–1.40)
– HC	8	55.49 (–0.78)	67.76(–1.07)
+ FC	400	55.06 (–1.11)	66.88(–1.95)

Case Study. Table 4 displays two examples of predicted dialogue state in MultiWOZ 2.1 test set, which demonstrates that DOLLAR captures the correlation of different slots in multi-domain while TripPy fails. In *Example 1*, user want to find a taxi from the attraction to the restaurant, which indicates that the value of *taxi-destination* should be same as *attraction-name* and the value of *taxi-departure* should copy from *restaurant-name*. Although such information is provided by user indirectly, DOLLAR can accurately classify and deduce their values by finding the relationship of these relevant slots. In *Example 2*, DOLLAR makes the accurate reference of the phrase *for the same group of people* through the context despite *train-book_people* and *hotel-book_people* are separated by several turns. However, it is too complicated for TripPy to find the reference, especially after a few dialogue turns.

Table 4. Case Study of DOLLAR and TripPy on MultiWOZ 2.1.

Example 1

Usr: Hey, are there any interesting attractions in town centre today?

Sys: Great saint mary's church is an architecture location in the centre of town

Usr: Great, are there in Korean restaurants in the centre area?

Sys: There is Little Seoul located at 108 Regent Street City Centre. Would you like to book a table there?

Usr: Yes! Thanks. I also need a taxi to get from the church attraction to the restaurant, please

TripPy: taxi-destination = none (class = *none*), taxi-departure = none (class = *none*)

DOLLAR: taxi-destination = Little Seoul (class = *refer*), taxi-departure = great saint mary's church (class = *refer*)

Example 2

Usr: I would like to book it for 5 nights for two people starting on Monday

Sys: I have booked the cityroomz for you. Is there anything else I can help you with today?

Usr: Thank you. I am going to birmingham new street on Saturday and arrive by 12:45

Sys: They leave every hour starting at 5:01 to 10:01, and then one more at 23:01

Usr: Please book one for the same group of people, just choose one and remember it must arrive by 12:45

TripPy: train-book_people = none (class = *none*)

DOLLAR: train-book_people = 2 (class = *refer*)

5 Conclusion

In this paper, we have presented a multi-domain dialogue state tracker with a dialogue-aware slot level schema graph, referred to as DOLLAR, which addresses the correlation among high cooccurrence slot pairs across domain and fuses slot-specific dialogue information into the slot-level schema graph. DOLLAR outperforms two categories of DST baselines on MultiWOZ 2.0, 2.1 and 2.4 benchmarks. We further conduct various experiments to prove the superiority of establishing connections between related slot pairs than full connections. Ablation studies also show that the effectiveness of the three kinds of slot relationships. In this paper, our schema graph is static in the sense that it is constructed according to predefined schema and dataset characteristics. For future work, we intend to investigate more complex schema and explore dynamic slot relationships across domains to facilitate knowledge transfer to new domains.

References

1. Lee, H., Lee, J., Kim, T.: SUMBT: slot-utterance matching for universal and scalable belief tracking. In: Proceedings of the 57th Annual Meeting of the Association for Computational Linguistics, pp. 5478–5483. Association for Computational Linguistics, Florence, Italy (2019)
2. Wu, C.S., Madotto, A., Hosseini-Asl, E., Xiong, C., Socher, R., Fung, P.: Transferable multi-domain state generator for task-oriented dialogue systems. In: Proceedings of the 57th Annual Meeting of the Association for Computational Linguistics, pp. 808–819. Association for Computational Linguistics, Florence, Italy (2019)
3. Kim, S., Yang, S., Kim, G., Lee, S.: Efficient dialogue state tracking by selectively overwriting memory. In: Proceedings of the 58th Annual Meeting of the Association for Computational Linguistics, pp. 567–582. Association for Computational Linguistics, Online (2020)
4. Heck, M., et al.: TripPy: a triple copy strategy for value independent neural dialog state tracking. In: Proceedings of the 21st Annual Meeting of the Special Interest Group on Discourse and Dialogue, pp. 35–44. Association for Computational Linguistics, 1st virtual meeting (2020)
5. Ye, F., Manotumruksa, J., Zhang, Q., Li, S., Yilmaz, E.: Slot self-attentive dialogue state tracking. In: The Web Conference (WWW), pp. 1598–1608. New York, USA (2021)
6. Wang, Y., Zhao, J., Bao, J., Duan, C., Wu, Y., He, X.: LUNA: learning slot-turn alignment for dialogue state tracking. In: Proceedings of the 2022 Conference of the North American Chapter of the Association for Computational Linguistics: Human Language Technologies, pp. 3319–3328. Association for Computational Linguistics, Seattle, United States (2022)
7. Zhou, Y., Zhao, G., Qian, X.: Dialogue state tracking based on hierarchical slot attention and contrastive learning. In: Proceedings of the 31st ACM International Conference on Information & Knowledge Management, pp. 4737–4741 (2022)
8. Zhu, S., Li, J., Chen, L., Yu, K.: Efficient context and schema fusion networks for multi-domain dialogue state tracking. In: Findings of the Association for Computational Linguistics: EMNLP 2020, pp. 766–781. Association for Computational Linguistics, Online (2020)
9. Chen, L., Lv, B., Wang, C., Zhu, S., Tan, B., Yu, K.: Schema-guided multi-domain dialogue state tracking with graph attention neural networks. In: The Thirty-Fourth AAAI Conference on Artificial Intelligence, pp. 7521–7528. AAAI Press (2020)

10. Lin, W., Tseng, B.H., Byrne, B.: Knowledge-aware graph-enhanced GPT-2 for dialogue state tracking. In: Proceedings of the 2021 Conference on Empirical Methods in Natural Language Processing, pp. 7871–7881. Association for Computational Linguistics, Online and Punta Cana, Dominican Republic (2021)
11. Wang, Z., Lemon, O.: A simple and generic belief tracking mechanism for the dialog state tracking challenge: On the believability of observed information. In: Proceedings of the SIGDIAL 2013 Conference, pp. 423–432. Association for Computational Linguistics, Metz, France (2013)
12. Henderson, M., Thomson, B., Young, S.: Word-based dialog state tracking with recurrent neural networks. In: Proceedings of the 15th Annual Meeting of the Special Interest Group on Discourse and Dialogue (SIGDIAL), pp. 292–299. Association for Computational Linguistics, Philadelphia, PA, U.S.A. (2014)
13. Mrkšić, N., Ó Séaghdha, D., Wen, T.H., Thomson, B., Young, S.: Neural belief tracker: data-driven dialogue state tracking. In: Proceedings of the 55th Annual Meeting of the Association for Computational Linguistics (Volume 1: Long Papers), pp. 1777–1788. Association for Computational Linguistics, Vancouver, Canada (2017)
14. Nouri, E., Hosseini-Asl, E.: Toward scalable neural dialogue state tracking. In: NeurIPS 2018, 2nd Conversational AI workshop (2018)
15. Ouyang, Y., Chen, M., Dai, X., Zhao, Y., Huang, S., Chen, J.: Dialogue state tracking with explicit slot connection modeling. In: Proceedings of the 58th Annual Meeting of the Association for Computational Linguistics, pp. 34–40. Association for Computational Linguistics, Online (2020)
16. Ren, L., Xie, K., Chen, L., Yu, K.: Towards universal dialogue state tracking. In: Proceedings of the 2018 Conference on Empirical Methods in Natural Language Processing, pp. 2780–2786. Association for Computational Linguistics, Brussels, Belgium (2018)
17. Shan, Y., et al.: A contextual hierarchical attention network with adaptive objective for dialogue state tracking. In: Proceedings of the 58th Annual Meeting of the Association for Computational Linguistics, pp. 6322–6333. Association for Computational Linguistics, Online (2020)
18. Wu, C.S., Hoi, S.C., Socher, R., Xiong, C.: TOD-BERT: pre-trained natural language understanding for task-oriented dialogue. In: Proceedings of the 2020 Conference on Empirical Methods in Natural Language Processing (EMNLP), pp. 917–929. Association for Computational Linguistics, Online (2020)
19. Ham, D., Lee, J.G., Jang, Y., Kim, K.E.: End-to-end neural pipeline for goal-oriented dialogue systems using GPT-2. In: Proceedings of the 58th Annual Meeting of the Association for Computational Linguistics. Association for Computational Linguistics, Online (2020)
20. Hosseini-Asl, E., McCann, B., Wu, C.S., Yavuz, S., Socher, R.: A simple language model for task-oriented dialogue. Adv. Neural Inf. Process. Syst. **33**, 20179–20191 (2020)
21. Hu, J., Yang, Y., Chen, C., He, L., Yu, Z.: SAS: dialogue state tracking via slot attention and slot information sharing. In: Proceedings of the 58th Annual Meeting of the Association for Computational Linguistics, pp. 6366–6375. Association for Computational Linguistics, Online (2020)
22. Yang, L., Li, J., Li, S., Shinozaki, T.: Multi-domain dialogue state tracking with top-k slot self attention. In: Proceedings of the 23rd Annual Meeting of the Special Interest Group on Discourse and Dialogue, pp. 231–236 (2022)
23. Wu, P., Zou, B., Jiang, R., Aw, A.: GCDST: a graph-based and copy-augmented multi-domain dialogue state tracking. In: Findings of the Association for Computational Linguistics: EMNLP 2020, pp. 1063–1073. Association for Computational Linguistics, Online (2020)
24. Vaswani, A., et al.: Attention is all you need. In: Advances in Neural Information Processing Systems. vol. 30 (2017)

FedDroidADP: An Adaptive Privacy-Preserving Framework for Federated-Learning-Based Android Malware Classification System

Changnan Jiang[1], Chunhe Xia[1,2], Zhuodong Liu[1], and Tianbo Wang[3,4(✉)]

[1] Key Laboratory of Beijing Network Technology, Beihang University, Beijing 100191, China
[2] Guangxi Key Lab of Multi-source Information Mining and Security, Guangxi Normal University, 541004 Guilin, China
[3] Shanghai Key Laboratory of Computer Software Evaluating and Testing, Shanghai, China
[4] School of Cyber Science and Technology, Beihang University, Beijing 100191, China
wangtb@buaa.edu.cn

Abstract. Federated-Learning-based Android malware classification framework has attracted much attention due to its privacy-preserving and multi-party joint modeling. However, research shows indirect privacy inferences from curious central servers threaten this framework. Adding noise to the model parameters to limit the adversary's inference to sensitive knowledge is widely used to prevent this threat. Still, it dramatically reduces the classification performance of the model. In response to this challenge, we propose a privacy-preserving framework Fed-DroidADP, which can adapt to the law of privacy risk distribution to protect the privacy of FL-based Android malware classifier users while maintaining model utility. First, we estimate the privacy risk of Android users in the classification system by calculating the mutual information between the sharing gradient and the user's sensitive information (Such as the category of the user's app and malware). Then, we designed an adaptive differential privacy protection mechanism ADP according to the distribution law of the privacy risk in time and space dimensions. The mechanism calculates the added lightweight noise required to protect the user's sensitive information (to a certain extent) in a fine-grained manner to trade off model privacy and utility during the training of Android malware classification models. Extensive experiments on the Androzoo dataset show that FedDroidADP's ability to protect user's sensitive information is superior to the baseline differential privacy methods and achieves better model utility (about 8% higher classification accuracy) in the same privacy budget.

Keywords: Federated learning · Privacy-preserving · Sensitive knowledge · Android malware classification

1 Introduction

Due to the open-source nature and widespread usage of the Android system, users are susceptible to various malware attacks. To do this, the scientists used machine learning methods to train malware classifiers to identify malware by centrally collecting users'

Z. Jin et al. (Eds.): KSEM 2023, LNAI 14119, pp. 184–199, 2023.
https://doi.org/10.1007/978-3-031-40289-0_15

app samples. However, the app training sample set uploaded by users contains much personal information, such as user identity, preferences, and device security status [1]. If the curious server directly analyzes the user's app sample, it will gain sensitive knowledge about the user and violate the user's privacy [2]. Recent scandals over the misuse of user data by some service providers and the introduction of privacy laws have limited traditional malware classifiers based on a centralized ML approach. In order to solve the privacy concerns of users, the malware classification framework with a privacy protection function based on federated learning comes into being. In the FL framework, each participant uses a global training model, sharing only the model parameters of the classifier, and does not upload their private app samples to a third-party server, avoiding direct privacy violations. However, some privacy inference attack methods targeting FL have emerged in recent years, such as member inference attacks [3], model inversion attacks [4], attribute inference attacks [5], and model extraction attack [6]. These attacks can infer the user's original data from the shared model parameters, leading to indirect privacy disclosure. The vulnerability of joint training to privacy attacks was demonstrated in FL-based CV and NLP scenarios. However, the existing FL-based malware classification framework does not consider the impact of privacy inference attacks nor proposes mitigation plans, which are inconsistent with existing privacy protection laws. At the same time, with the advent and popularity of the ChatGPT, users have raised privacy concerns about central servers with increasingly powerful model reasoning capabilities. These factors hinder its development and application.

In order to solve the problem of user privacy disclosure in the FL framework, the current work introduces a series of privacy protection methods such as homomorphic encryption [7, 8], secure multi-party computing [9], trusted computing [10], secret sharing [11] and so on. However, these solutions consume significant communication and computing costs or require complex hardware equipment or mechanisms. In contrast, differential privacy has attracted much attention from researchers because of its simplicity and solid theoretical guarantee. The method based on differential privacy [12, 13] is to blur sensitive information in shared data by adding noise so that sensitive information cannot be mined and identified. However, due to the addition of noise, the accuracy of the classification model will be significantly lost. In the existing privacy protection schemes, how to trade-off between model privacy and utility is still a challenge.

Therefore, in the existing FL-based Android malware classification framework, a privacy protection mechanism is urgently needed to meet the privacy needs of Android users and maintain a good classification accuracy of the model. Therefore, in this work, we designed an adaptive privacy protection mechanism FedDroidADP according to the distribution law of users' privacy risks in the FL-based Android malware classification framework. This mechanism optimizes the balance between privacy and utility by providing an adaptive defense against privacy risks Android users suffer in a fine-grained manner.

The contributions of this paper are summarized below:

(1) Aiming at the privacy needs of users in the FL-based Android malware classification framework, we propose an adaptive privacy-preserve framework FedDroidADP, which can effectively protect the sensitive information of Android users. It is the

first effort to implement adaptive differential privacy protection for Android users' sensitive information in the federal Android malware classification framework.

(2) We capture the spatial and temporal distribution rules of users' privacy risks through mutual information between users' sensitive information and gradient; In terms of space dimension, we design a hierarchical privacy budget setting method. In the time dimension, we design a gradient real-time clipping method. Finally, based on the adaptive method of risk in time and space, the lightweight noise needed to achieve sufficient privacy protection is added to optimize the trade-off between model utility and privacy in privacy protection.

(3) Using the Androzoo dataset, we evaluate the proposed FedDroidADP for privacy protection and model utility retention capabilities against privacy inference attacks in FL-based malware classifiers. The experimental results show that compared with the baseline differential privacy methods, the inferred success rate of the attack can be reduced by more than 7% in our protection mechanism. In addition, the results also verify that FedDroidADP can achieve an accuracy loss of less than 8% in the same privacy budget. FedDroidADP achieves a better trade-off between model utility and privacy.

The remainder of this paper is organized as follows. In Sect. 2, we briefly review some work related to this article. In the Sect. 3, we briefly introduce the application scenario, threat model, and relevant principles of differential privacy. Section 4 illutrates our proposed model. In Sect. 5, our method is experimented and analyzed. Finally, we conclude the paper in Sect. 6.

2 Related Work

In this section, we review recent work in the areas of FL-based malware classification and differential privacy.

2.1 FL-Based Malware Classification

In the traditional centralized malware classifier, the central server directly analyzes app training samples with sensitive user information, and the user's privacy is compromised. To solve this problem, there has been a recent upsurge of research on malware classification frameworks based on federated learning.

Taheri [14] proposed a robust FL-based classification scheme, Fed-IIoT, for detecting Android malware in the IOT. It realizes a robust cooperative training mechanism by adjusting two GAN-based antagonistic mechanisms. Narendra [15] proposed a lightweight model based on CNN to generate hidden data for training through an auxiliary GAN. Shukla [16] introduced a performance-aware FL framework to reduce client communication overhead. The existing FL-based Android malware classification framework focuses on the classification performance of the model, the efficiency of calculation and communication, and the robustness of the aggregation method.

However, recent studies have shown that the FL training model alone does not ensure the privacy of user training data. The curious server in the FL framework can infer the user's privacy information by the gradient uploaded during training. The training gradient will remember the attribute and label information in the user sample. However, the existing FL-based malware classification framework does not consider the harm of privacy inference attacks, or there are no effective privacy protection methods.

2.2 Privacy Protection Methods in Federated Learning

With the application of federated learning in privacy-sensitive scenarios, such as face recognition and medical services, its privacy vulnerabilities have attracted the attention of researchers. Some researchers have proposed some defense mechanisms to protect privacy, which can be divided into three types: differential privacy (DP) based [17], secure multi-party computing based [18], and homomorphic encryption based [19].

MPC-based techniques primarily utilize garbled circuitry or secret sharing, allowing multiple parties to collaborate to compute a function in a protocol where each party only knows the inputs and outputs, satisfies the zero-knowledge definition. However, the technology's high communication costs limit its scope. Homomorphic encryption is based on specific algebraic calculation without decrypting the ciphertext to prevent the calculation data from being exposed to any external party, including the server. However, the privacy of homomorphic encryption depends on the size of encrypted data, and more robust privacy protection will reduce computing efficiency. DP is to make the training sample of the client satisfy the DP by injecting noise into the client to ensure that the opponent is difficult to identify any individual in the user's sample set. However, DP's strict privacy protection effect will sacrifice the model's classification accuracy. Therefore, the DP protection mechanism applied in the federal malware classification system must be further improved to meet users' privacy requirements while maintaining the model's utility.

3 Preliminaries

3.1 FL-Based System Model

We consider an FL-based Android malware classification system that includes an FL server for model aggregation and updating and N Android clients with multiple app training samples.

In the initialization phase, FL server [30] assigns an initialized global model w_t to each Android client. Then, each client trains and updates the current global model w_t by using the local dataset $\mathcal{D}_k$ of D_k size in round t. In the aggregation phase, FL server receives local gradients of client uploads. The global loss function $F(w)$ and local loss function $F_k(w)$ to be optimized in FL are shown in Eq. (1 and 2):

$$\min_{w \in R^d} F(w) = \frac{\varphi_k}{N} \sum\nolimits_{k=1}^{N} F_k(w) \tag{1}$$

$$F_k(w) = \frac{1}{\varphi_k} \sum\nolimits_{z_i \in D_k} f(w; z_i) \tag{2}$$

where $f(\cdot)$ is the local loss function of Android client $k, k \in [1, N]$, $z_i = (x_i, y_i, fun_i), \forall i \in [1, \ldots, \varphi_k]$ is sampled from the local dataset D_k of k clients; N

is the total number of global samples, φ_k is the number of samples of client k; $x_i \in \mathcal{X}$ is the feature of Android malware, and $y_i \in \mathcal{Y}$ is the category label of Android malware. In addition, $fun_i \in Fun$ is the category of application functions of app sample z_i.

$$w^{t+1} \leftarrow w^t + \frac{\varphi_k}{N} \sum\nolimits_{k=1}^{N} \nabla_{w^t} F_k^t \qquad (3)$$

In the update phase, FL server uses the Federated average algorithm (Fedavg) [20] to generate a new global model w_{t+1} for the next round, as shown in Eq. (3).

During training, the FL server does not have access to the user's app training sample but does have access to the local gradient that the user participates in sharing.

3.2 Threat Model

The adversary considered in this article is a curious and honest server that is jointly trained according to the proper FL-based malware classifier training protocols but is curious about sensitive information in user data on the client side. Poisoning and active attacks are not considered. In addition, the communication between the server and the client is confidential and protected from external adversaries. We consider the worst case to ensure the protection of user privacy information: (1) The adversary server knows all the parameters about the user model. (2) The adversary has sufficient auxiliary data sets with the same distribution as the client. In addition, adversary can use member inference attacks [3], model inversion attacks [4], attribute inference attacks [5], and other privacy inference attack methods are used to infer sensitive information in users' training data.

3.3 Local Differential Privacy

Local differential privacy [21] ensures users' privacy during information sharing. Specifically, a certain amount of Gaussian noise is added to the shared data before the user uploads it to an untrusted third party.

Definition 1 ((ϵ, δ)-Local differential privacy). *For any two adjacent data sets* D *and* D$'$, *if there is an arbitrary algorithm* M, *then any output* ψ *of the* M *satisfies:*

$$Pr[M(D) \in \psi] \leq e^{\epsilon} Pr[M(D\prime) \in \psi] + \delta \qquad (4)$$

Then the algorithm M satisfies (ϵ, δ)-*LDP*, where δ is the privacy deviation, and ϵ is the privacy budget. The smaller it is, the stronger the privacy protection level is.

Definition 2 (Global sensitivity). *Given function* f : D $\rightarrow$ R^d, *for any two adjacent data sets* D *and* D', *define the global sensitivity of* $\Delta_2 f$ *as follows:*

$$\Delta_2 f = \max_{D,D\prime} \|f(D) - f(D\prime)\|_2 \qquad (5)$$

Among them, R^d represents a d dimensional real vector, $\|f(D) - f(D')\|_2$ is $f(D)$ and $f(D')$ between the $L2$ distance.

Definition 3 (Gaussian mechanism). *The Gaussian mechanism with parameter* δ *is to add independent and identically distributed Gaussian noise to the output of the function* f. *The definition is as follows:*

$$M(D) = f(D) + Noise \qquad (6)$$

where $Noise \sim N(0, \sigma^2 I)$ satisfies the Gaussian distribution.

3.4 Statement of Problems

Existing local differential privacy schemes, such as DP-SGD, provide the strictest privacy protection for all information of each user sample. However, this coarse-grained excessive privacy policy leads to a significant loss of model accuracy; At the same time, they adopt a fixed privacy policy based on expert experience, which requires many labor costs and cannot adapt to the complex and time-varying training process of Android malware classification model. Therefore, applying it directly to an FL-based Android malware classification framework has the following problems and limitations:

(1) Users only care about whether their sensitive information is effectively protected rather than all the information carried in the gradient;
(2) In the malware classification model, the distribution of sensitive user information across different layers of the gradient is uneven, rendering it inefficient to utilize a uniform privacy budget;
(3) The risk of sensitive information leakage in the gradient is not fixed in real time and is related to the real-time state of the model.

4 Proposed Model

In view of the problem existing in the existing methods, this paper proposes an adaptive privacy protection framework to effectively prevent the privacy risks of Android users and maintain the classification ability of the model.

4.1 Overview

The overall framework of FedDroidADP is shown in Fig. 1. It includes RiskMeter, a user privacy risk estimator, and ADP, an adaptive differential privacy protector. The detailed workflow can be described as follows:

Step 1: The user accepts the model w^t from the server for local training. Then, the gradient g_t^k of this round of training is sent to RiskMeter for privacy risk estimation.

Step 2: ADP calculates the hierarchical privacy budget and gradient clipping norm of the level of the epoch, respectively, according to the time and space distribution law of privacy risk score. Then, the corresponding Gaussian noise is calculated, added to shared gradient g_t^k, and the gradient $g_{t,noise}^k$ with noise is uploaded to the server.

Step 3: The server receives the $g_{t,noise}^k$, summarizes it, and updates the global model w^{t+1}. Then proceed to the first step, loop until the model converges.

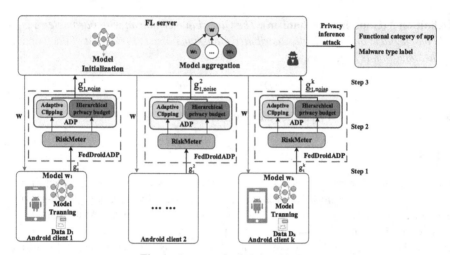

Fig. 1. Framework of FedDroidADP.

4.2   Privacy Risk Estimation of Android Users' Sensitive Information

Analysis of User's Sensitive Information in FL-Based Malware Classifier. In order to capture the privacy risk in the training process, namely the risk of sensitive information disclosure, we first analyzed and defined the sensitive information involving user privacy in the framework of Android malware classification. Sensitive information is the information in app training samples that the enemy is interested in, violates the user's privacy, and may be inferred by the enemy. User privacy is divided into two categories: identity privacy and attribute privacy. In this article, we consider the attribute privacy of the user because, in the FL system, the user's ID number (identity) is a known variable. Attribute privacy is the ability of individuals or groups whose identities are known to hide their sensitive information(such as user preferences and security status).In the FL-based malware classification framework, what an attacker is interested in and can infer is the functional category (fun) and malware label (y) of the app sample in the data in the training batch, which helps to infer further the security status and identity information of the user [2]. Therefore, the sensitive information is $S = \{y, fun\}$.

Calculation of User's Privacy Risk Score. According to the above enemy threat analysis and the FL-based Android malware classification system characteristics, the enemy's methods to steal sensitive user information are attribute inference attack and label inference attack. In essence, these two attack methods use the gradient change rule to distinguish the existence of attribute and label. In information theory, mutual information measures standard information between two random variables, reflecting the dependence between variables. If the mutual information between the gradient and sensitive information is more significant, it is easier for opponents to infer the sensitive information from the shared gradient. Therefore, we use the mutual information MI between sensitive information (There are $m + n$ categories) and gradient as the privacy risk estimate, namely privacy risk score. The calculation formula is as follows:

$$Risk_{\mathbb{C},S}^{t,k} = \frac{\sum_{u=1}^{u=n} M I\big(fun_u; g_t^k\big) + \sum_{j=1}^{j=m} M I\big(Y_j; g_t^k\big)}{m+n}$$ (7)

where $Risk_{\mathbb{C},S}^{t,k}$ represents the privacy disclosure risk of sensitive information S in the dataset of client k in the Android malware classification framework $\mathbb{C}$ at time t. The overall privacy disclosure risk in the classification framework $\mathbb{C}$ is described through the mutual information between all the sensitive information S and the shared gradient g_t^k. Due to the complex nonlinear relationship between sensitive information and gradient, we adopt the parameterized MI estimation method proposed in the article [22]. This method estimates the approximate value of their MI by iteratively sampling the samples in the joint distribution $\mathbb{P}_{S,g}$ and edge distribution $\mathbb{P}_S$ and $\widehat{\mathbb{P}}_g$ of S and g. The estimated formula is as follows:

$$M\widehat{I(S; g)}_l = \sup_{\theta \subset \Theta} \mathbb{E}_{\mathbb{P}_{S,g}^{(l)}} [\mathcal{G}_\theta] - \log\bigg(\mathbb{E}_{\mathbb{P}_S^{(l)} \otimes \widehat{\mathbb{P}}_g^{(l)}} e^{[\mathcal{G}_\theta]}\bigg)$$ (8)

$\mathcal{G}_\theta : S \times g \rightarrow R$ was based on a NN network (this paper adopted a three-layer MLP) with parameter θ to assess MI. $\mathbb{G} = \{\mathcal{G}_\theta\}_{\theta \subset \Theta}$ is a family of functions that maps two random variables to a constant. θ is optimized from l samples sampled iteratively to get an approximate estimation of MI. For details, please refer to the article [22].

4.3 Privacy Risk-Based Adaptive Differential Privacy Protector ADP

The adaptive differential privacy protector ADP workflow consists of hierarchical differential privacy budget and real-time gradient clipping.

Hierarchical Privacy Budget Settings in Spatial Dimensions. It is well known that at different layer of the malware classification model (DNN), the characteristics of Android malware extracted are different [31]. Therefore, the distribution of sensitive information represented by the combination of Android APIs or Permissions are different in each layer of gradient. In order to protect sensitive information efficiently, we need to design corresponding adaptive protection strategies based on the spatial differences of privacy risks. Therefore, we used the values of privacy risk scores at different layers to capture this distribution difference and allocated the corresponding ratio of the privacy budget to achieve fine-grained lightweight defense. Specifically, we allocate a smaller privacy budget (higher privacy level) to the gradient layer with higher risk and a larger share (lower privacy level) to the gradient layer with lower risk. We set the entire shared gradient to meet $(\epsilon_k, \delta) - \text{LDP}$ and the gradient of each layer q to meet $(\epsilon_t^{k,q}, \delta\prime) - \text{LDP}$. In order to meet the set of the ratio of privacy risks, and according to the advanced composition theorem in the literature [17], our hierarchical (The total number of layers is τ) privacy budget $\epsilon_t^{k,q}$ calculation formula is as follows:

$$\epsilon_{t,k}^q = ratio_q \cdot \epsilon_k \cdot \sqrt{\tau}$$ (9)

$$ratio_q = \frac{\frac{1}{Risk_{C,S}^{t,k,q}}}{\sum_{h=1}^{h=\tau} \frac{1}{Risk_{C,S}^{t,k,h}}} \tag{10}$$

Adaptive Clipping of Gradients in Time Dimensions. In the Android malware classification model's training process, the norm value of the gradient changes significantly with the real-time state of model training. The exposure risk of sensitive information also changes at any time. Therefore, our defensive instinct is to follow the law of risk change to some extent and configure the appropriate gradient clipping norm. For example, under the trend of increasing risk, the average norm of gradient tends to increase to some extent, so we appropriately increase the clipping norm of gradient to avoid performance degradation caused by excessive clipping. At the same time, higher Gaussian noise is allocated according to the privacy budget to protect users' sensitive information. Therefore, according to the time variation rule of privacy risk score, the adaptive clipping mechanism of gradient is as follows:

$$v_t^{k,q} = \alpha v_{t-1}^{k,q} + \frac{Risk_t^{k,q}}{Risk_{t-1}^{k,q}} \tag{11}$$

$$C_t^{k,q} = \gamma \cdot v_t^{k,q} \cdot C_{t-1}^{k,q} \tag{12}$$

$$\overline{g}_t^{k,q}(x_i) = g_t^{k,q}(x_i)/max(1, \frac{\|g_t^{k,q}(x_i)\|_2}{C_t^{k,q}}) \tag{13}$$

where α is the momentum factor of privacy risk change, v_t is the rate of risk change, $C_t^{k,q}$ is the clipping norm of q layer of gradient, and γ is the damping coefficient.

Calculation of Noise. To ensure that client k meets $(\epsilon_k, \delta) - LDP$ in each round, each layer of the shared gradient to add Gaussian noise standard deviation $\sigma_t^{k,q}$ shall meet is as follows:

$$\sigma_t^{k,q} \geq \frac{\alpha \cdot \Delta_2 f^{k,q}}{\epsilon_t^{k,q}} = \frac{\alpha \cdot 2C_t^{k,q}}{|D^s| \cdot \epsilon_t^{k,q}} \tag{14}$$

$$\alpha^2 > 2\ln(1.25/\delta) \tag{15}$$

where $\Delta_2 f^{k,q}$ is the sensitivity of the layer q.| D^s | is the size of the local training data. Then we add Gaussian noise to the clipping gradient to obtain $g_{t,noise}^k$ as follows:

$$g_{t,noise}^{k,q} \leftarrow \frac{1}{|D^s|} \sum_{x_i \in D^s} \overline{g}_t^{k,q}(x_i) + \mathcal{N}(0, (\sigma_t^{k,q})^2 I) \tag{16}$$

$$g_{t,noise}^k = [g_{t,noise}^{k,q_1}, g_{t,noise}^{k,q_2} \cdots g_{t,noise}^{k,q_\tau}] \tag{17}$$

The total value of privacy loss in the whole training cycle T is calculated as follows:

$$\epsilon_{k,T} = \mu \sqrt{T} \epsilon_k \tag{18}$$

where μ for sampling ratio (No putback sampling).

Algorithm 1. FedDroidADP

Input: Gradient of client k in round t is g_k^t, the LDP parameter (ϵ_k, δ), D^s, τ.

Output: $g_{t,noise}^k$

1:    Calculate $Risk_{C,S}^{t,k}$ by Equation (7)

2:    Calculate $\epsilon_t^{k,q}$ by Equation (9)

3:    Calculate $C_t^{k,q}$ by Equation (11-12)

4:    $$\sigma_t^{k,q} = \frac{\sqrt{2ln(1.25/\delta)} \cdot 2C_t^{k,q}}{|D^s| \cdot \epsilon_t^{k,q}}$$

5:    $$\bar{g}_t^{k,q}(x_i) = g_t^{k,q}(x_i)/max(1, \frac{\| g_t^{k,q}(x_i) \|_2}{C_t^{k,q}})$$

6:    $$g_{t,noise}^{k,q} \leftarrow \frac{1}{| D^s |} \sum_i \bar{g}_t^{k,q}(x_i) + \mathcal{N}(0, (\sigma_t^{k,q})^2 I)$$

7:    return $g_{t,noise}^k = [g_{t,noise}^{k,q_1}, g_{t,noise}^{k,q_2}, \cdots g_{t,noise}^{k,q_\tau}]$

8:    **end**

4.4 Privacy Analysis

As described in Sect. 4.3, in the FedDroidADP (Algorithm **1**), the sharing gradient of each round of user uploads adds Gaussian noise satisfying $(\epsilon_k, \delta) - LDP$, which can defend against the attacks mentioned in the threat model in Sect. 3. It should be emphasized that the privacy risk score used to calculate the gradient's clipping norm reflects the model's exposure to sensitive information and is generated by sampling the auxiliary dataset (about four thousand publicly available samples). It introduces no additional loss of privacy. Therefore, according to the advanced combination theorem, the protection mechanism in this paper provides a theoretical guarantee for the client to meet the $(\mu\sqrt{T}\epsilon_k, \delta\prime) - LDP$ in the training process.

5 Experiments

5.1 Data and Data Settings

To verify the FedDroidADP's validity, we built a dataset from the open-source project AndroZoo [23], which has about 50,000 apps(9 categories) for the Android malware classification task. At the same time, we extract app functional categories (10 categories) from the metadata of APK files for attribute labeling, as shown in Table 1. We use 10-fold cross-validation, randomly generating the test set from 1/10 of the users. The reported results correspond to an average of 20 replicates per experiment (inferred attack and malware classification). The inference model uses training data from whole datasets as background knowledge.

Table 1. Dataset

Malware Label	Quantity	App Category	Quantity
Benign	29977	Game	4874
Malicious	29932	Books	4861
Adware	3865	Weather	4632
Trojan	3338	Travel and maps	4793
Riskware	4894	Health And Fitness	4842
Ransom	4322	Photography	4665
Exploit	3225	Finance	4745
Spyware	2489	Music and Audio	4443
Downloader	4023	Shopping	4174
Fraudware	3776	Communication	4656

5.2 Model and Training Setup

The Setup of FL-based Malware Classification System. To verify the performance of the proposed privacy protection system, we selected two baselines federated Android malware classification frameworks, FedIIoT [14] and FedRAPID [16], as protected systems. FedIIoT uses a classifier structure of seven FC layers, using APIs, Permissions, and Intents as input characteristics; FedRAPID uses a classifier structure of five Conv layers and four FC layers, with the grayscale image converted by the app binary as the input feature. For FL training, we set up ten clients with a batch size of 64 and a learning rate of 0.02. We evaluated the experiment on an Intel Golden 6240CPU and an NVIDIA A100 GPU. Different privacy protection methods and FL-based malware classifiers are implemented in PyTorch.

Attack Model and Defense Baseline. For the inference of user's sensitive information in FL-based malware classification framework, we choose the attribute inference attack model proposed in [24] and [5], and use the shared gradient to infer the functional types of apps in the training sample; We choose the tag inference attack model proposed in [25] and [26], and use the shared gradient to infer the types of malware tags in the training samples. Baseline differential privacy methods for comparison include DP-SGD [17], a fixed privacy policy widely used in privacy protection methods, and two other state-of-the-art adaptive differential privacy methods, FedAdaptClip [27] and Adap DP-FL [28]. We compare the proposed FedDroidADP with their privacy protection effects and model utility retention performance.

Evaluation Methods and Metrics. We compare our defense approach FedDroidADP to other baseline defense approaches with reasonable hyperparameter settings. We evaluate the effectiveness of our defense from two aspects: privacy protection, that is, the average accuracy of adversaries to infer sensitive information; The other is model utility, that is, the effect of different defense methods on the accuracy of model classification. The index of privacy protection effect is the average accuracy of a privacy inference attack. We perform twenty inference experiments on the inference attack model with reasonable hyperparameters. In a real scenario, the configuration of the attacker is unknowable. Therefore, to verify the effectiveness of various privacy protection algorithms, we choose the maximum attack accuracy among the test results of various attack methods as the measure of attack effect (Average the highest accuracy values of tag attacks and attribute attacks on all clients). The model utility evaluation index is the average accuracy of multiple classification tasks of Android malware [29]. The higher the classification accuracy, the better the model's utility.

5.3 Evaluation of the Effectiveness of Privacy Protection

In this section, we evaluate the ability of different privacy protection methods to protect users' sensitive information in the FL-based Android malware classification system. For the rationality of comparison, we obtained the globally optimal gradient clipping norm in the literature [27], obtained $[C_t^{\text{FedIIoT}} = 3.5, C_t^{\text{FedRAPID}} = 2.9]$ as the initial value of all protection methods, and set the overall privacy budget as 5. The experimental results are shown in Fig. 2. In addition, Fig. 3 shows the real-time gradient's clipping norm and the hierarchical risk ratio, calculated based on privacy risk scores during the training process (in two federal systems).

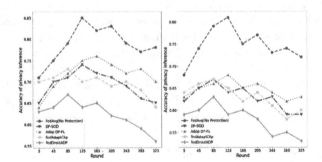

Fig. 2. Accuracy of opponent inference attack in FedIIoT(left) and FedRAPID(right).

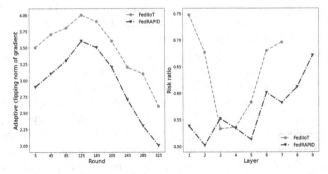

Fig. 3. Adaptive gradient clipping norm(left) and hierarchical risk ratio (right).

First, the results show that without any protection (FedAvg), the curious server poses a very high threat to privacy inferences on the sensitive information of participating users (the highest inferences accuracy for FedIIoT and FedRAPID are about 85% and 81%). It means that the sharing gradient uploaded by Android users carries a large amount of sensitive information about users, which adversaries can infer to increase sensitive knowledge about users. Secondly, in Fig. 3, we can preliminarily find the change rule of privacy risk distribution in time and space. In FedIIoT, the first and last layers near the FC layer have a higher risk ratio, and a lower privacy budget is allocated; In FedRAPID, privacy risks are higher near the pooling and output FC layers. We analyze that this is caused by the processing mechanism of the FC layer and Conv layer on the original feature. Due to the connection operation of all features in the FC layer, there is a relatively complete original feature view of sensitive information. In the Conv layer, the processing of the features of Android malware is segmented and only converged in the FC layer (after Pooling layer). In addition, in terms of time, the privacy risks in both systems have a similar law of first increasing and then decreasing. We analyze that changes in the degree of fit of the classification model cause this.

Finally, the results show that the overall inference accuracy of FedDroidADP is close to the random guess (50% ~ 60%) in the two federal classification systems, which successfully limits the opponents' inference of users' private information. FedDroidADP provides about 6% more privacy protection effect than fixed DP-SGD and other adaptive methods. The privacy protection effect of DP-SGD is second only to FedDroidADP. We analyze this because DP-SGD adopts the most prominent clipping norm and generally adds the most Gaussian noise. The AdapDP-FL and FedAdaptClip use the gradient norm or the privacy budget coarse-grained relaxation strategy, which leads to the privacy protection level being set too low in some cases with high privacy risk. Hence, their overall attack degree is high. Compared with DP-SGD, FedDroidADP sets fine-grained privacy budgets for different layers according to the spatial distribution of privacy risks. It gives FedDroidADP a better defense for the same privacy budget.

5.4 Evaluation of the Effectiveness of Maintaining the Models's Utility

In order to verify FedDroidADP keep the effect of model utility, we set different overall privacy budget $\epsilon = [28, 22, 16, 10, 5, 3, 1]$, and keep the rest of the parameters fixed for each protection method generate utility-privacy trade-off curve, as shown in Fig. 4. We then use these curves to compare the ability of different protection methods to maintain the model's classification accuracy with the same privacy budget.

First, the results show that the traditional fixed strategy DP-SD is challenging to balance the privacy and utility of the model. With the increase in privacy level, model performance decays rapidly. In the case of privacy (estimated accuracy close to 50%), the accuracy drops by about 20%. It illustrates the importance of adaptive strategies.

Secondly, two other adaptive schemes, obtain a better model privacy-utility trade-off than the fixed-policy DP-SGD by setting gradient clipping or privacy budget relaxed to some extent. However, their adjustment strategy is coarse-grained and does not have a targeted setting for the actual privacy risk. Therefore, they cannot effectively protect users' privacy information (adversary reasoning accuracy up to 70%) while maintaining reasonable model utility settings. In contrast, the FedDroidADP scheme has the closest accuracy to the unprotected model. This is because FedDroidADP only deploys strict privacy parameters in high-risk periods and spatial locations, avoiding excessive sacrifice of model usability. In the strictest privacy level, the loss of model accuracy is controlled within 9%. The accuracy of others decreased by more than 13%, which suggests that FedDroidADP achieves a better trade-off between model utility and privacy.

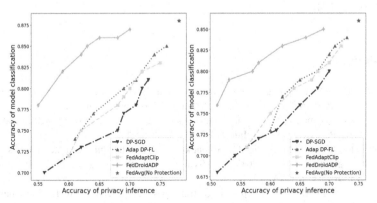

Fig. 4. Utility-privacy trade-off curve in FedIIoT (left) and FedRAPID (right).

5.5 Experimental Discussions

We found that the distribution of privacy risks in the FL-based Android malware classification system differs over time and space. Hence, a fixed privacy policy is difficult to strike a balance between privacy and model utility. On the other hand, in the system, the coarse-grained privacy parameter adjustment strategy cannot achieve the desired privacy protection effect because some high-risk gradient layers require a high level of protection. Therefore, only a targeted and adaptive privacy protection mechanism designed according to the actual privacy needs of users and the privacy risk distribution law of the classification system can achieve a practical and balanced defense effect.

6   Conclusion and Future Work

This paper proposes an adaptive differential privacy protection mechanism Fed-DroidADP, which is used to protect users' sensitive information of the FL-based Android malware classification system while maintaining good classification accuracy. Fed-DroidADP adopts a fine-grained adaptive DP mechanism according to the FL-based Android malware classification system's user-sensitive information exposure risk rule, thus improving the effectiveness of privacy protection and reducing the damage to the model's accuracy. Extensive experiments show that FedDroidADP is more effective in protecting the user's sensitive information (about 6% better against opponents) than existing baseline DP protection methods. At the same time, a better trade-off between model privacy and utility is obtained, and the model's classification accuracy is about

8% higher in the same privacy budget. In the future, we will further optimize the computational efficiency and communication efficiency of FedDroidADP and its robustness in non-IID and original traffic data scenarios to improve the application efficiency of FedDroidADP in the FL-based Android malware classification system.

Acknowledgement. This research was funded by the National Natural Science Foundation of China (No.62272024).

References

1. Tu, Z., et al.: Your apps give you away: distinguishing mobile users by their app usage fingerprints. Proc. ACM Interact. Mob. Wearable Ubiquitous Technol. **2**, 1–23 (2018)
2. Tu, Z., et al.: Demographics of mobile app usage: Long-term analysis of mobile app usage. CCF Trans. Pervasive Comput. Interact. **3**, 235–252 (2021)
3. Shokri, R., Stronati, M., Song, C., Shmatikov, V.: Membership inference attacks against machine learning models. In: 2017 IEEE Symposium on Security and Privacy (SP), pp. 3–18. IEEE, San Jose, CA, USA (2017)
4. Zhu, L., Liu, Z., Han, S.: Deep leakage from gradients. In: Wallach, H., Larochelle, H., Beygelzimer, A., Alché-Buc, F. d', Fox, E., Garnett, R. (eds.) Advances in Neural Information Processing Systems. Curran Associates, Inc. (2019)
5. Melis, L., Song, C., De Cristofaro, E., Shmatikov, V.: Exploiting unintended feature leakage in collaborative learning. In: 2019 IEEE Symposium on Security and Privacy (SP), pp. 691–706. IEEE, San Francisco, CA, USA (2019)
6. Orekondy, T., Schiele, B., Fritz, M.: Knockoff nets: Stealing functionality of black-box models. In: Proceedings of the IEEE/CVF Conference on Computer Vision and Pattern Recognition, pp. 4954–4963 (2019)
7. Qi, T., Wu, F., Wu, C., Huang, Y., Xie, X.: Privacy-preserving news recommendation model learning. In: Findings of the Association for Computational Linguistics: EMNLP 2020, pp. 1423–1432. Association for Computational Linguistics, Online (2020)
8. Rivest, R.L., Adleman, L., Dertouzos, M.L.: others: On data banks and privacy homomorphisms. Found. Sec. Comput. **4**, 169–180 (1978)
9. Zhang, X., Ji, S., Wang, H., Wang, T.: Private, yet practical, multiparty deep learning. In: 2017 IEEE 37th International Conference on Distributed Computing Systems (ICDCS), pp. 1442–1452. IEEE, Atlanta, GA, USA (2017)
10. Mo, F., Haddadi, H., Katevas, K., Marin, E., Perino, D., Kourtellis, N.: PPFL: privacy-preserving federated learning with trusted execution environments. In: Proceedings of the 19th Annual International Conference on Mobile Systems, Applications, and Services, pp. 94–108. ACM, Virtual Event Wisconsin (2021)
11. Bonawitz, K., Ivanov, V., Kreuter, B.: Practical secure aggregation for privacy-preserving machine learning. In: Proceedings of the 2017 ACM SIGSAC Conference on Computer and Communications Security, pp. 1175–1191. ACM, Dallas Texas USA (2017)
12. Wei, K., Li, J., Ding, M., Ma, C.: Federated learning with differential privacy: algorithms and performance analysis. IEEE Trans. Inform. Forensic. Secur. **15**, 3454–3469 (2020)
13. Triastcyn, A., Faltings, B.: Federated learning with bayesian differential privacy. In: 2019 IEEE International Conference on Big Data (Big Data), pp. 2587–2596. IEEE, Los Angeles, CA, USA (2019)
14. Taheri, R., Shojafar, M., Alazab, M.: Fed-IIoT: a robust federated malware detection architecture in industrial IoT. IEEE Trans. Ind. Inf. **17**, 8442–8452 (2021)

15. N Singh H Kasyap S Tripathy 2020 Collaborative learning based effective malware detection system I Koprinska Eds ECML PKDD 2020 Workshops ECML PKDD 2020 Workshops of the European Conference on Machine Learning and Knowledge Discovery in Databases (ECML PKDD 2020): SoGood 2020, PDFL 2020, MLCS 2020, NFMCP 2020, DINA 2020, EDML 2020, XKDD 2020 and INRA 2020, Ghent, Belgium, September 14–18, 2020, Proceedings Ghent Belgium 09 14 2020 09 18 Communications in Computer and Information Science CCIS 1323 Springer Cham 205 219https://doi.org/10.1007/978-3-030-65965-3_13

16. Shukla, S., Sai Manoj, P.D., Kolhe, G.: On-device malware detection using performance-aware and robust collaborative learning. In: 2021 58th ACM/IEEE Design Automation Conference (DAC), pp. 967–972. IEEE, San Francisco, CA, USA (2021)

17. Abadi, M., Chu, A., Goodfellow, I., McMahan, H.B., Mironov, I.: Deep learning with differential privacy. In: Proceedings of the 2016 ACM SIGSAC Conference on Computer and Communications Security, pp. 308–318. ACM, Vienna Austria (2016)

18. Lia, D., Togan, M.: Privacy-preserving machine learning using federated learning and secure aggregation. In: 2020 12th International Conference on Electronics, Computers and Artificial Intelligence (ECAI), pp. 1–6. IEEE, Bucharest, Romania (2020)

19. Zhang, C., et al.: Efficient homomorphic encryption for cross-silo federated learning. In: Gavrilovska, A. and Zadok, E. (eds.) 2020 USENIX Annual Technical Conference, USENIX ATC 2020, 15–17 July 2020, pp. 493–506. USENIX Association (2020)

20. Ang, Q., Liu, Y., Chen, T., Tong, Y.: Federated machine learning: concept and applications. ACM Trans. Intell. Syst. Technol. **10**, 12:1–12:19 (2019)

21. Wang, S., Huang, L., Nie, Y.: Local differential private data aggregation for discrete distribution estimation. IEEE Trans. Parallel Distrib. Syst. **30**, 2046–2059 (2019)

22. Belghazi, I., Rajeswar, S., Baratin, A., Hjelm, R.D., Courville, A.C.: MINE: Mutual Information Neural Estimation. arXiv preprint arxiv:1801.04062 (2018)

23. Allix, K., Bissyandé, T.F., Klein, J., Traon, Y.L.: AndroZoo: collecting millions of Android apps for the research community. In: Kim, M., Robbes, R., Bird, C. (eds.) Proceedings of the 13th International Conference on Mining Software Repositories, MSR 2016, Austin, TX, USA, 14–22 May 2016, pp. 468–471. ACM (2016)

24. Song, C., Shmatikov, V.: Overlearning reveals sensitive attributes. In: 8th International Conference on Learning Representations, ICLR 2020, Addis Ababa, Ethiopia, 26–30 April 2020. OpenReview.net (2020)

25. Zhao, B., Mopuri, K.R., Bilen, H.: iDLG: Improved Deep Leakage from Gradients. arXiv preprint arxiv:2001.02610 (2020)

26. Wainakh, A., Ventola, F., Müßig, T., Keim, J.: Cordero: User-Level Label Leakage from Gradients in Federated Learning. Proc. Priv. Enhancing Technol. **2022**, 227–244 (2022)

27. Andrew, G., Thakkar, O., McMahan, B.: Differentially private learning with adaptive clipping. In: NeurIPS 2021, 6–14 December 2021, virtual, pp. 17455–17466 (2021)

28. Fu, J., Chen, Z., Han, X.: Adap DP-FL: differentially private federated learning with adaptive noise. In: TrustCom2022, pp. 656–663. IEEE, Wuhan, China (2022)

29. Liu, C., Yan, A., Chen, Z., Zhang, H.: IEdroid: Detecting malicious android network behavior using incremental ensemble of ensembles. In: 2021 IEEE 27th International Conference on Parallel and Distributed Systems (ICPADS), pp. 788–795. IEEE, Beijing, China (2021)

30. Pang, Y., Zhang, H., Deng, J.D., Peng, L.: Rule-Based collaborative learning with heterogeneous local learning models. In: Gama, J., Li, T., Yu, Y., Chen, E., Zheng, Y., Teng, F. (eds.) Advances in Knowledge Discovery and Data Mining, pp. 639–651. Springer International Publishing, Cham (2022). https://doi.org/10.1007/978-3-031-05933-9_50

31. Yan, A., Chen, Z., Zhang, H., Peng, L.: Effective detection of mobile malware behavior based on explainable deep neural network. Neurocomputing **453**, 482–492 (2021)

Multi-level and Multi-interest User Interest Modeling for News Recommendation

Yun Hou[1], Yuanxin Ouyang[1]([✉]), Zhuang Liu[2], Fujing Han[2], Wenge Rong[2], and Zhang Xiong[2]

[1] State Key Laboratory of Software Development Environment,
Beihang University, Beijing, China
{houyun,oyyx}@buaa.edu.cn
[2] Engineering Research Center of Advanced Computer Application Technology,
Ministry of Education, Beihang University, Beijing, China
{liuzhuang,hfj99,w.rong,xiongz}@buaa.edu.cn

Abstract. User interest modeling is crucial for personalized news recommendation. Existing personalized news recommendation methods usually take the news data as the minimum interest modeling unit when modeling user's interests. They ignored the low-level and high-level signals from user's behaviors. In this paper, we propose a news recommendation method combined with multi-level and multi-interest user interest modeling, named MMRN. In contrast to existing methods, our MMRN model captures user interest at multiple levels, including word-level, news-level and higher-levels, then learns multiple user interests vectors in each level. Extensive experiments on a real-world dataset show our method can effectively improve the recommendation effect.

Keywords: Personalized news recommendation · Attention mechanism · Graph convolutional neural network

1 Introduction

With the development of internet technology, online news platforms have become a popular means for users to access news information [1]. However, the rapid growth of news items has made it difficult for users to choose their interested news. Thus, personalized news recommendation technology has become a core component for online news platforms to alleviate information overload and improve user reading experience.

Learning accurate user interest representations is essential for effective personalized news recommendation [2]. Existing personalized news recommendation methods usually take the news data as the minimum interest modeling unit and learn a single interest vector for each user [3–5]. However, user interests are

Supported by organization x.

Table 1. Click and non-click logs of a example user.

ID	Click	Category	Subcategory	Title
1	Y	Sports	Football	Ravens get CB Marcus Peters in a trade with Rams.
2	Y	Sports	Football	Ravens vs. Seahawks final: MVP, winners & losers.
3	N	Sports	Football	Should Chargers throw 2019 season away?
4	N	Sports	Baseball	The Nationals World Series parade will be Saturday.
5	Y	Finance	Taxes	President Trump's trillion-dollar hit to homeowners.
6	Y	Finance	Career	50 Great Jobs for Retirees.
7	Y	Movies	Gallery	Ranking the 25 best films with surprise endings.
8	N	health	Weightloss	Ways to Lose Weight: 36 Fast, Easy Tips.

diverse and multi-grained. As the example shown in Table 1, a user may have diverse interests, such as sport, movie, finance. Meanwhile, user interests are multi-grained. For instance, sports enthusiasts like the user in Fig. 1 may have a specific interest in a particular sport, such as the football. Moreover, within football, the users in Fig. 1 may prefer news related to the particular team "Ravens". Therefore, modeling user interests at multiple granularities is crucial.

In this paper, we propose a news recommendation method, MMRN, that combines multi-level and multi-interest user interest modeling to accurately capture diverse and multi-grained user interests. We use pre-trained BERT as the news encoder to capture news title semantics and introduce three user interest encoders at different levels. The first one is word-level user interest encoder, used to learn user interests in specific words or phrases. The second one is news-level user interest encoder, focused on the user overall interest. The last encoder is higher-level user interest encoder, in which we employ the graph convolutional network and the attention network to aggregate the user clicked news vectors multiple times, then we use the dynamic routing network to generate multiple interest vectors at each aggregation step, to capture diverse and multi-grained user interest representations. Finally, we use a target-aware attention network to calculate the matching score between user and candidate news vectors, and aggregate the final representation vector by the matching scores at each level. Extensive experiments on a real-world dataset show that MMRN can effectively improve the recommendation performance.

2   Related Works

Traditional personalized news recommendation techniques are mainly based on feature engineering [6–8]. These methods require extensive domain expertise and manual feature selection, which is time-consuming. Moreover, they do not consider the rich semantic information in news texts.

In recent years, several news recommendation methods based on deep learning have been proposed, which have achieved better recommendation performance [3–5,9]. However, these methods take the news data as the minimum interest modeling unit and only learn a single representation vector for each user, which is insufficient for modeling diverse user interests.

Different from these methods, our method proposes three user interest encoders, which enables us to learn user interest at multiple granularities, and more accurately represent diverse and multi-grained user interests.

3   Method

In this section, we will first present the problem formulation for personalized news recommendation. Next, we will introduce our proposed MMRN method in detail. The overall framework of MMRN is illustrated in Fig. 1, which consists of five components: the news encoder, word-level user interest encoder, news-level user interest encoder, higher-level user interest encoder, click predictor.

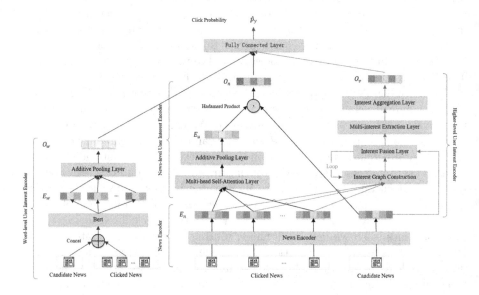

Fig. 1. The overall framework of MMRN model.

3.1   Problem Formulation

Given a candidate news n_c and a user u, the goal of the model is to calculate the interest score $\hat{p}_y$ of user u for that candidate news. Then sort all candidate news N_c by interest scores and recommend the top ones to user. We assume the user u has m historical news $N_u = [n_u^1, n_u^2, ..., n_u^m]$. Each news item n contains a title t, a category v and a subcategory v_sub. The news title consists of a sequence of words $t = [w_1, w_2, ..., w_n]$, where w_i denotes the i-th word in the title and n denotes the number of the words in the title.

3.2 News Encoder

The news encoder is used to learn the comprehensive news representation from news title t, category v and subcategory v_{sub}. As shown in Fig. 2, it is composed of two modules, i.e., a title encoder and a category encoder.

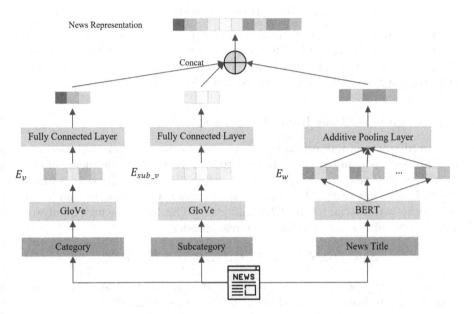

Fig. 2. The framework of the news encoder.

The first part is the title encoder, whose input is a news title $t = [w_1, w_2, ..., w_n]$. We use the pre-trained BERT [10] to learn the contextual word vectors E_h. We use an additive attention network [5] to aggregate the word vectors into news representation vector e_t.

$$E_h = BERT(t) \tag{1}$$

$$\alpha_t^i = softmax(q_t^T (W_t E_h + b_t)) \tag{2}$$

$$e_t = \alpha_t^i E_h \tag{3}$$

where α denotes the attention weight of the i-th word representation, q_t is the query vector, W_t and b_t denote the weight parameter and bias of the projection matrix. e_t denotes the news title representation.

The second part is the category encoder. Online news platforms usually provide news categories, subcategories to help user target news interested in. Thus, news categories and subcategories can provide effective information for news modeling. In order to accurately capture the potential relationships between different categories and subcategories, we use the pre-trained GloVe model to learn the representation vector of categories and subcategories.

$$e_v = W_c(GloVe(v)) + b_c \qquad (4)$$

$$e_{v\_sub} = W_{c\_sub}(GloVe(v\_sub)) + b_{c\_sub} \qquad (5)$$

where e_v and e_{v_sub} denote the final news category and subcategory representations, while W_t, W_{c_sub} and b_t, b_{c_sub} denote the weight parameter and bias of the projection matrix. The final news representation is the concatenation of the title, category, and sub-category representations, i.e., $e_n = [e_t, e_v, e_{v\_sub}]$.

3.3   Word-Level User Interest Encoder

The word-level user interest encoder is utilized to learn the low-level user interests. Give a user u and a candidate news title t_c, we denote the sequence of titles of user history news $T_u = [t_u^1, t_u^2, ..., t_u^m]$, where t_u^i denotes the word sequence of i-th history news title. We concatenate the candidate news titles and history news titles with special tokens [CLS] and [SEP]. This forms the final input word sequence S_w of the word-level user interest encoder.

$$S_w = [[CLS], t_c, [SEP], t_u^1, [SEP], t_u^2, ..., [SEP], t_u^n] \qquad (6)$$

Same as the news encoder, we use pre-trained BERT and the additive attention network to learn the word-level user interest representations O_w.

3.4   News-Level User Interest Encoder

News-level user interest Encoder is used to learn the overall user interest representation. Given a user u and a candidate news n, we define the user's historical reading news sequence $N_u = [n_u^1, n_u^2, ..., n_u^m]$, where n_u^i denotes the i-th news item in the user's history of reading news.

News-level user interest Encoder is composed of a stack of $L = 2$ identical encoder layers. Each layer contains two sub-layers. The first sub-layer is a multi-head self-attention network, used to learn the combination weights from user clicked news representations.

$$head_k = softmax(\frac{Q_k K_k^T}{\sqrt{d_n}})V_k \qquad (7)$$

$$Z_u = Concat(head_1, head_2, ..., head_K) \qquad (8)$$

where Q_k, K_k, and V_k denote the k-th $Query, Key, Value$ matrices. $\sqrt{d_n}$ denotes the dimension of the news representation. K denotes the number of attention head, and Z_u denotes the output of the historical news sequence obtained after the aggregation multi-head output.

The second sub-layer is a fully connected feed-forward network, which consists of two linear transformations with a LeakyRelu activation in between.

$$Z_u^{ffn} = W_2(LeakyRelu(W_1 Z_u + b_1)) + b_2 \qquad (9)$$

where W_1, W_2 and b_1, b_2 are the weight parameters and bias of the projection matrix. In addition, residual connections are applied in two sub-layer.

Finally, we use an additive attention network to aggregate the user clicked news representations proposed by L=2 encoder layers and get the news-layer user interest representation O_n.

3.5   Higher-Level User Interest Encoder

Recently, multi-interest recommendation and multi-level recommendation methods have achieved good results in the sequential recommendation field [11,12]. In particular, the SURGE model uses graph convolutional neural networks and attention network to aggregate user historical item representations at multiple levels, and uses the AU-GRU to learn the user interest representation. The MIND model uses the capsule network [13] to learn a variable number of user interest vectors for each user, in order to capture user interests more effectively.

Inspired by the above works, we propose a higher-level user interest encoder that combines the features of multi-level and multi-interest recommendation methods, propose a higher-level user interest encoder, to capture the diverse and multi-grained user interests.

The Higher-level user interest Encoder consists of a stack of $L = 2$ identical layers, each layer contains three sub-layers: interest graph construction layer, interest fusion layer, and multi-interest extraction layer.

Interest Graph Construction. The first layer is the interest graph construction layer, which takes the sequence of user clicked news N_u as input and constructs the adjacency matrix A of news items.

User interest can be divided into core interests and peripheral interests. In the graph representation, core interest nodes typically have higher degrees than peripheral interest nodes, resulting in a higher concentration of similar news around them and leading to the formation of a dense subgraph. Therefore, we use the weighted cosine similarity [12] to measure the relationship between news items.

$$M_{i,j}^{n_{heads}} = \cos\left(w^{n_{heads}} \odot n_u^i, w^{n_{heads}} \odot n_u^j\right) \qquad (10)$$

where $M_{i,j}$ denotes the weighted cosine similarity between i-th and j-th clicked news. $w^{n_{heads}}$ is a learnable parameter. To improve the model's ability to learn information at different positions, we extend the similarity learning to multiple subspaces, where $n_h eads$ representing the number of subspaces. The final similarity score is obtained by averaging the similarity results across all subspaces.

$$M_{i,j} = \frac{1}{n_{heads}} \sum_{k=1}^{n_{heads}} M_{i,j}^k \qquad (11)$$

To mitigate the effects of the noise introduced during similarity measurement and reduce the computational cost during the interest fusion, we utilize a rank truncation threshold $Rank_{\epsilon n^2}$ to truncate the similarity scores:

$$A_{ij} = \begin{cases} 1, & M_{ij} \geq Rank_{\epsilon m^2}(M) \\ 0, & otherwise \end{cases} \quad (12)$$

where ϵ (set to 0.5 in our experiments) is a hyper-parameter and m is the number of the clicked news representations.

Interest Fusion. In order to model user interests at multi levels, we use interest fusion layer that propagates information from peripheral interest nodes to core interest nodes to model multi-grained user interests.

When using the additive rule for node aggregation, the values of nodes with higher degrees will become larger, while those with lower degrees will become smaller, which may lead to the problem of gradient explosion or vanishing. So it is necessary to perform the GCN normalization [14] on the adjacency matrix A to generate weight matrix A'.

Secondly, we fuse the node representations of the $X = 2$ hop neighbor nodes to the central node to form different interest clusters:

$$N'_u = \left(\prod_{i=1}^{X} A' \right) N_u \quad (13)$$

where X controls the number of neighbor hops passed to the central node, forming the clusters N'_u. Then, we use the graph attention network to redistribute attention weights among peripheral interest nodes.

$$\alpha_i^{n_{heads}} = Attention_c \left(W_c^{n_{heads}} n_u^i || n_u^{i'} || W_c^{n_{heads}} n_u^i \odot n_u^{i'} \right) \quad (14)$$

where $W_c^{n_{heads}}$ is a learnable parameter, n_{heads} denotes the number of the subspaces. n_u^i represents the i-th node in the node representation sequence N_u. $n_u^{i'}$ represents the i-th central node in the cluster N'_u. $||$ denotes concatenation operator. The attention network $Attention_c$ consists of two feed-forward neural network layers with a LeakyReLU activation function in between, followed by a softmax normalization function. Meanwhile, in order to capture the evolution of user interests towards different target items, it is important to consider the correlation between the candidate news node n and the source node n_u^i:

$$\beta_i^{n_{heads}} = Attention_t \left(W_t^{n_{heads}} n_u^i || n || W_t^{n_{heads}} n_u^i \odot n \right) \quad (15)$$

where $W_t^{n_{heads}}$ is a learnable parameter, n denotes the node representation of candidate news, and $Attention_t$ has the same structure with $Attention_c$. Then we calculate the overall attention weight matrix a for each node. For a node a_{ij} in the matrix, its calculation is as follows:

$$a_{ij}^{n_{heads}} = LeakyRelu \left(\alpha_i^{n_{heads}} A'_{ij} + \beta_j^{n_{heads}} A'_{ij} \right) \quad (16)$$

We utilize the overall attention weight $a^{n_{heads}}$ to aggregate the clicked news representations and generate the higher-level multi-head node representations. The final higher-level user interest representation E_c is obtained by averaging the multi-head output results.

$$E_c = \frac{1}{n_{heads}} \sum_{i=1}^{n_{heads}} (a^{n_{heads}} N_u) \tag{17}$$

Multi-interest Extraction. In capsule network, the high-level capsule representation is learned from the low-level capsule networks, which is akin to learning user interests from historical behaviors. So we use capsule networks as a multi-interest extractor.

Suppose that we have two capsule layers: the user behavior capsules E_c and the user interest capsules U. The goal of dynamic routing is to compute the values of the user interest capsules from the given values of behavior capsules in an iterative way. In each iteration, we have the user behavior capsule $E_c = [e_c^1, e_c^2, ..., e_c^m]$, and the routing logit b_{ij} between the behavioral capsule and the interest capsule, the j-th interest capsule u_j is calculated by:

$$u_j = w_{ij} S e_c^i \tag{18}$$

where e_c^i denotes the i-th user behavior representation. S is a learnable parameter. w_{ij} denotes the weight parameter for connecting the behavior capsule e_c^i and the interest capsule u_j, which is calculated by performing softmax normalization on routing logits b_{ij}. Then, a non-linear activation function "squash function" is applied to obtain the final interest capsule representation.

$$u_j = squash(u_j) = \frac{||u_j||^2}{1 + ||u_j||^2} \frac{u_j}{||u_j||} \tag{19}$$

Next, we calculate the offset of the routing logits and update the values of the routing logits by adding the offset:

$$b_{ij} = u_j^T S e_c^i + b_{ij} \tag{20}$$

The routing logits b_{ij} is initialized to zero and the dynamic routing phase is repeated for a fixed number of iterations (typically three) to converge. At the end of the final iteration, the interest capsule representation u_j is taken as the final user interest representation.

Finally, we calculate the attention weights for each interest capsule using the target-aware attention network. The interest capsules are then aggregated by these attention weights to generate the final user interest representation.

$$w_j = softmax(u_j^T gelu(W_u n)) \tag{21}$$

$$u = \sum_{k=1}^{K} w_j u_j \tag{22}$$

where W_u is a learnable parameter, w_j is the attention weight score of interest capsule u_j, and the final scoring vector u is obtained by aggregating all the interest capsule vectors. After $L = 2$ iterations of interest graph construction, interest fusion, and multi-interest extraction operations, we obtain the user scoring vectors u at L higher granularities. These scoring vectors are concatenated to form the final higher-level user interest encoder output O_v.

3.6 Click Predictor

Through the three level user interest encoders, we obtain $L + 2 = 4$ user interest vectors at multiple granularities, which are concatenated to form a multi-grained user interest representation $O = [O_w, O_n, O_v]$. For the i-th user interest representation, we compute the interaction result $r_i = Concat(O_i||n||O_i \odot n)$. Then, we tile all the interaction results and feed them into a fully connected feed-forward network, and apply a sigmoid activation function to the result to obtain the final click prediction probability.

$$\hat{p}_y = sigmoid\,(WF + b) \tag{23}$$

where W and b are learnable parameters, F is the tiled interaction results, and $\hat{p}_y$ denotes the user's click probability for the candidate news n.

4   Experiments

4.1   Dataset and Experimental Settings

Dataset. We conduct experiments on a real-world news dataset MIND [15], which consists of two versions: MIND-small and MIND-large. The detailed dataset statistics are summarized in Table 2.

Table 2. Statistics of the MIND-small and MIND-large dataset.

	News	Categories	Impressions	Clicks
MIND-small	65,238	18	230,117	347,727
MIND-large	161,013	20	15,777,377	24,155,470

Experimental Settings. Based on previous work [9], we use the user's last 50 clicked news to learn the user representation. Besides, we use news titles, categories, and subcategories as model inputs, use the pre-trained model Bert-medium-uncased as the word contextual encoder, utilize the 300-dimensional GloVe model to generating the category and subcategory representations. The rank truncation threshold ϵ is set to 0.5. The interest count K of each user is set to 8, which we will analyze in the following section. In the training process, we use the Binary Cross-Entropy Loss function (BCELoss) and the AdamW [16] as the loss function and optimizer. We train the model for 5 epochs with a batch size of 64 and a learning rate of $2e^{-6}$. Follow the previous works [5], we use AUC, MRR, NDCG@5, NDVG@10 as the performance evaluation for the model.

4.2   Main Results

We first introduce the baseline method used in our experiments: (1) DKN [4]: using a target aware network to learn user representation. (2) NPA [17]: learning news and user representations by using personalized attention vectors generated from ID. (3) LSTUR [3]: using both long-term and short-term interest to represent user overall interest. (4) NRMS [5]: learning news and user representation by using multi-head self-attentive networks. (5) FIM [18]: using the dilated CNN network to learn the news representation and 3-D CNN network to learn the user interest. (6) HieRec [9]: modeling user interest at three granularities: sub-topic, topic, and overall user interest.

The overall performance of the baseline and MMRN models is presented in Table 3. The best results are shown in boldfaced. Firstly, MMRN signidicantly outperforms other baseline methods that learn a single user representation. This is because user interests are diverse and multi-grained, and learning a single user interest is insufficient to capture all of the user's interests. Secondly, our approach also outperforms the HieRec, which models user interest at the subtopic, topic, and news levels. However, the real user interest may not be limited to these three granularities, they may ignored some potential user interests. Unlike these methods, the MMRN model is able to model user interests at multiple granularities, effectively capturing low-level and high-level user interests, leading to the optimal performance.

Table 3. The overall performance of different methods on MIND.

Method	MIND-small				MIND-large			
	AUC	MRR	NDCG@5	NDCG@10	AUC	MRR	NDCG@5	NDCG@10
DKN	0.6137	0.2803	0.2954	0.3523	0.641	0.3025	0.3262	0.3821
NPA	0.6346	0.2978	0.3175	0.3895	0.6557	0.3285	0.3442	0.3997
LSTUR	0.6473	0.3006	0.3318	0.3922	0.6663	0.3296	0.3413	0.4052
NRMS	0.6419	0.3024	0.3382	0.3937	0.6645	0.3282	0.3479	0.4123
FIM	0.6485	0.3006	0.3167	0.3924	0.6681	0.3326	0.3613	0.4221
HieRec	0.6643	0.3147	0.3543	0.4121	0.6795	0.3376	0.3621	0.4237
MMRN	**0.6779**	**0.3293**	**0.369**	**0.425**	**0.6881**	**0.3425**	**0.3741**	**0.4306**

4.3   Ablation Study

To demonstrate the effectiveness of the word-level and higher-level user interest encoders used in our MMRN model, we conducted the ablation experiment.

Table 4. Effects of different level MMRN encoers.

Method	MIND-small			
	AUC	MRR	NDCG@5	NDCG@10
MMRN	**0.6779**	**0.3293**	**0.369**	**0.425**
-w/o Word-level	0.6623	0.3147	0.3501	0.4189
-w/o Higher-level	0.6464	0.2924	0.3307	0.3951
-w/o Both	0.6388	0.2879	0.3276	0.3904

As shown in Table 4, the complete MMRN model achieves the optimal results. The reasons are as follows: Firstly, users may prefer to select news containing specific words or phrases, and the word-level user interest encoder can learn the lexical association between candidate news and historical news, enabling the model to effectively capture low-level user interests. Secondly, users may have clear tendencies in news selection, but these tendencies are distributed at different granularities. MMRN model can control the granularity of the user interest learning through interest fusion operation. Also, the multi-interest extraction operation allows the model to capture multiple interest tendencies at the same granularity. Thus, the MMRN model can effectively capture the diverse and multi-grained user interests, leading to better recommendation results.

4.4 Number of Interest Vectors

In order to explore the influence of hyper-parameter K, which represents the number of extracted user interest vectors. We evaluate the model's performance on the MIND-small dataset using AUC and NDCG@10 as evaluation metrics for different values of K. The results of the experiment are presented in Fig. 3.

As shown in Fig. 3, the performance of the MMRN model first increases and then decreases as the hyper-parameter K increases. When $K = 8$, the model achieves the best performance. The reasons are as follows: In the early stage, with the increases of K, the MMRN model is able to learn more information about user interests, which improves the model's recommendation performance. However, as K continues to increase, the model introduces more redundant parameters, which may lead to overfitting and degrade the recommendation performance. Additionally, too many interest vectors may cause conflicts and make it difficult for the model to accurately capture the main interests of users.

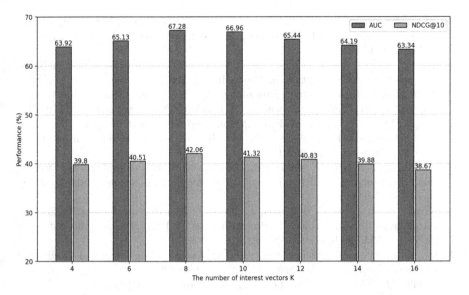

Fig. 3. Influence of the number of interest vectors K.

5 Conclusion

In this paper, we propose a news recommendation method combined with multi-level and multi-interest user interest modeling, named MMRN. Our MMRN model captures user interest at multiple levels, including word-level, news-level and higher-levels, and learn multiple user interest vectors for each level. Our experimental results on a real-world dataset demonstrate that our proposed method can effectively enhance the recommendation performance.

There are also some future works to consider. For instance, utilizing more complex pre-trained language models, such as BERT-based model or optimized models based on BERT, could help in learning word representations with richer semantic information. This could ultimately improve the recommendation performance of the model.

References

1. Das, A.S., Datar, M., Garg, A., Rajaram, S.: Google news personalization: scalable online collaborative filtering. In: Proceedings of the 16th International Conference on World Wide Web, pp. 271–280 (2007)
2. Okura, S., Tagami, Y., Ono, S., Tajima, A.: Embedding-based news recommendation for millions of users. In: Proceedings of the 23rd ACM SIGKDD International Conference on Knowledge Discovery and Data Mining, pp. 1933–1942 (2017)
3. An, M., Wu, F., Wu, C., Zhang, K., Liu, Z., Xie, X.: Neural news recommendation with long-and short-term user representations. In: Proceedings of the 57th Annual Meeting of the Association for Computational Linguistics, pp. 336–345 (2019)

4. Wang, H., Zhang, F., Xie, X., Guo, M.: DKN: deep knowledge-aware network for news recommendation. In: Proceedings of the 2018 World Wide Web Conference, pp. 1835–1844 (2018)
5. Wu, C., Wu, F., Ge, S., Qi, T., Huang, Y., Xie, X.: Neural news recommendation with multi-head self-attention. In: Proceedings of the 2019 Conference on Empirical Methods in Natural Language Processing and the 9th International Joint Conference on Natural Language Processing (EMNLP-IJCNLP). pp. 6389–6394 (2019)
6. Liu, J., Dolan, P., Pedersen, E.R.: Personalized news recommendation based on click behavior. In: Proceedings of the 15th International Conference on Intelligent User Interfaces, pp. 31–40 (2010)
7. Phelan, O., McCarthy, K., Smyth, B.: Using twitter to recommend real-time topical news. In: Proceedings of the Third ACM Conference on Recommender Systems, pp. 385–388 (2009)
8. Sarwar, B., Karypis, G., Konstan, J., Riedl, J.: Item-based collaborative filtering recommendation algorithms. In: Proceedings of the 10th International Conference on World Wide Web, pp. 285–295 (2001)
9. Qi, T., et al.: HieRec: hierarchical user interest modeling for personalized news recommendation. arXiv preprint arXiv:2106.04408 (2021)
10. Devlin, J., Chang, M.W., Lee, K., Toutanova, K.: BERT: pre-training of deep bidirectional transformers for language understanding. arXiv preprint arXiv:1810.04805 (2018)
11. Li, C., et al.: Multi-interest network with dynamic routing for recommendation at Tmall. In: Proceedings of the 28th ACM International Conference on Information and Knowledge Management, pp. 2615–2623 (2019)
12. Chang, J., et al.: Sequential recommendation with graph neural networks. In: Proceedings of the 44th International ACM SIGIR Conference on Research and Development in Information Retrieval, pp. 378–387 (2021)
13. Sabour, S., Frosst, N., Hinton, G.E.: Dynamic routing between capsules. In: Advances in Neural Information Processing Systems. vol. 30 (2017)
14. Kipf, T.N., Welling, M.: Semi-supervised classification with graph convolutional networks. arXiv preprint arXiv:1609.02907 (2016)
15. Wu, F., et al.: MIND: a large-scale dataset for news recommendation. In: Proceedings of the 58th Annual Meeting of the Association for Computational Linguistics, pp. 3597–3606 (2020)
16. Sarzynska-Wawer, J., et al.: Detecting formal thought disorder by deep contextualized word representations. Psychiatry Res. **304**, 114135 (2021)
17. Wu, C., Wu, F., An, M., Huang, J., Huang, Y., Xie, X.: NPA: neural news recommendation with personalized attention. In: Proceedings of the 25th ACM SIGKDD International Conference on Knowledge Discovery & Data Mining, pp. 2576–2584 (2019)
18. Wang, H., Wu, F., Liu, Z., Xie, X.: Fine-grained interest matching for neural news recommendation. In: Proceedings of the 58th Annual Meeting of the Association for Computational Linguistics, pp. 836–845 (2020)

CoMeta: Enhancing Meta Embeddings with Collaborative Information in Cold-Start Problem of Recommendation

Haonan Hu, Dazhong Rong, Jianhai Chen$^{(\boxtimes)}$, Qinming He,
and Zhenguang Liu

Zhejiang University, Hangzhou, China
{huhaonan,rdz98,chenjh919,hqm}@zju.edu.cn

Abstract. The cold-start problem is quite challenging for existing recommendation models. Specifically, for the new items with only a few interactions, their ID embeddings are trained inadequately, leading to poor recommendation performance. Some recent studies introduce meta learning to solve the cold-start problem by generating meta embeddings for new items as their initial ID embeddings. However, we argue that the capability of these methods is limited, because they mainly utilize item attribute features which only contain little information, but ignore the useful collaborative information contained in the ID embeddings of users and old items. To tackle this issue, we propose CoMeta to enhance the meta embeddings with the collaborative information. CoMeta consists of two submodules: B-EG and S-EG. Specifically, for a new item: B-EG calculates the similarity-based weighted sum of the ID embeddings of old items as its base embedding; S-EG generates its shift embedding not only with its attribute features but also with the average ID embedding of the users who interacted with it. The final meta embedding is obtained by adding up the base embedding and the shift embedding. We conduct extensive experiments on two public datasets. The experimental results demonstrate both the effectiveness and the compatibility of CoMeta.

Keywords: Recommendation system · Item cold-start problem · Meta-learning · Item ID embedding · Deep learning

1 Introduction

Fueled by the boom of internet, every day a large amount of information is produced. Nowadays, information overload has become a severe problem affecting people's daily life. Recommendation systems, which filter useful information for users, can effectively relieve the information overload problem. Therefore, recommendation systems have been deployed in various web services (*e.g.*, short videos [3], e-commerce [24] and news portals [23]). Collaborative filtering [14], which learns users' potential interests based on historical interactions, is one of the most widely used traditional recommendation methods. Beyond collaborative filtering, many recent studies (*e.g.*, Wide&Deep [2] and DeepFM [6])

Z. Jin et al. (Eds.): KSEM 2023, LNAI 14119, pp. 213–225, 2023.
https://doi.org/10.1007/978-3-031-40289-0_17

utilize user's features and items' features additionally and apply deep neural networks (DNNs) to achieve better recommendation performance. These deep recommendation models typically consist of two parts: an embedding layer and a multi-layer perceptron (MLP). The embedding layer transforms the raw features into dense vectors, and the MLP captures more complicated semantics.

Despite the remarkable success of these models, they still suffer from the cold-start problem [17]. In these models, sufficient interaction data are required to train a reasonable ID embedding for each item. However, in real scenarios many new items only have limited number of interactions, and hence their ID embeddings are insufficiently trained, which leads to a decrease in recommendation accuracy. The cold-start problem is one of the major challenges for recommendation systems.

Lately, some methods have been proposed to address the cold-start problem. DropoutNet [19] and MTPR [4] dropout ID embeddings to improve the robustness of the recommendation model. MetaEmb [11] trains an embedding generator to generate a good initial ID embedding for each new item. GME [10] aims to build an item graph and learn a desirable initial ID embedding for each new item by utilizing its attribute features and other related old items' attribute features. MWUF [28] proposes two meta networks to transform cold item ID embeddings into warm feature space.

The ID embeddings of users and old items are well-trained with sufficient interactions, and hence contain highly useful collaborative information. However, all of the above methods do not take into account the collaborative information. We argue the capability of these methods is still limited. In this paper, we propose CoMeta to enhance the meta embeddings of new items with the collaborative information. CoMeta consists of two components: Base Embedding Generator (B-EG) and Shift Embedding Generator (S-EG). Under the common research settings, the cold-start problem is divided into two phases: cold-start phase (new items do not have any interactions in the training dataset) and warm-up phase (new items have a few interactions in the training dataset). The calculation of both the base embeddings in B-EG and the average interacted user ID embeddings in S-EG relies on the interactions of new items. Hence, our proposed CoMeta mainly aims to learn desirable initial ID embeddings for new items in the warm-up phase. Moreover, since CoMeta is an extra module that generates initial ID embeddings for new items and has no influence on old items, CoMeta can be applied upon various recommendation models.

We summarize the main contributions of this paper as follows:

- We propose a meta learning based method named CoMeta to solve the item cold-start problem by learning good initial ID embeddings for new items. CoMeta can be easily applied upon various recommendation models.
- In CoMeta, we propose two submodules, which are termed as B-EG and S-EG, to enhance the generated meta embeddings by utilizing the collaborative information. More Specifically, B-EG utilizes the collaborative information through the ID embeddings of old items. S-EG utilizes the collaborative information through the ID embeddings of the interacted users.

– We conduct extensive experiments on two large-scale public datasets. The experimental results show that CoMeta outperforms existing cold-start methods and can significantly improve the recommendation performance in addressing the cold-start problem.

2 Related Work

Recommendation systems are designed to recommend personalized items to users. In early works, many researchers attempt to use traditional machine learning methods to make recommendations. FM [13], which models low-order feature interactions, is one of the most widely used traditional machine learning recommendation methods. For its simplicity and effectiveness, many methods based on it are proposed, However, the above methods can not capture high-order interactions. Recently, various deep learning models are proposed to solve this issue. Wide&Deep [2], DeepFM [6], PNN [12] and DCN [21] automatically cross high-order features to learn more information. DIN [27] and DIEN [26] utilize attention mechanism to capture users' interest based on users' historical interactions. It is worth mentioning that some works also focus on the recommendation security [15,16].

Despite the remarkable success of these models, they still suffer from the cold-start problem. It is challenging to make reasonable recommendations for new users or new items with limited interaction data in recommendation systems. To address the cold-start problem, some methods aim to learn a more robust model. DropoutNet [19] and MTPR [4] dropout ID embeddings to reduce the model's dependency on them. CC-CC [18] replaces ID embeddings with random vectors. Another way to solve this problem is to use variational autoencoder [7]. CVAR [25] uses variational autoencoder to model the relationship between item ID and item features in the latent space.

Besides, many recent works introduce meta learning to tackle the cold-start problem. Meta learning, also known as learning to learn, enables models to quickly adapt to new tasks with only few samples by utilizing prior knowledge from several related tasks. MeLU [8] generates the initial parameter of the model for all users based on Model-Agnostic Meta-Learning (MAML) [5] framework. PAML [20] introduces the social network to MeLU. MetaEmb [11] generates good initial ID embeddings for new items with their attribute features. GME [10] learns how to generate desirable initial ID embeddings for new items by considering both the new item attribute features and other related old items' attribute features. MWUF [28] aims to train meta scaling and meta shifting networks to warm up cold ID embeddings.

3 Method

In this section, we propose CoMeta to generate desirable meta embeddings with collaborative information for new item IDs.

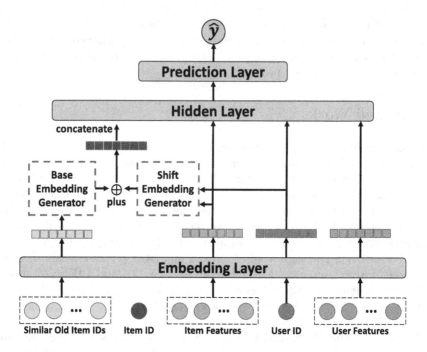

Fig. 1. The framework of CoMeta.

3.1 Overview

In this paper, only the new item ID embeddings are generated by the proposed CoMeta, and the old item ID embeddings can be used directly. As shown in Fig. 1, our proposed CoMeta includes two components:

1) Base Embedding Generator (B-EG). In B-EG, for each new item, we first compute the similarity scores between it and old items. Then we calculate the weighted sum of the ID embeddings of old items according to the similarity scores, and take the result as the generated base embedding.
2) Shift Embedding Generator (S-EG). In S-EG, for each new item, we first calculate the average ID embeddings of the users who have interactions with it. And then we use deep neural networks to generate its shift embedding with its attribute features and the average interacted user ID embedding as the input.

The final generated new item ID embedding can be denoted as:

$$\mathbf{v}_{new} = \mathbf{v}_{BEG} + \mathbf{v}_{SEG}, \tag{1}$$

where $\mathbf{v}_{BEG}$ is the base embedding, and $\mathbf{v}_{SEG}$ is the shift embedding.

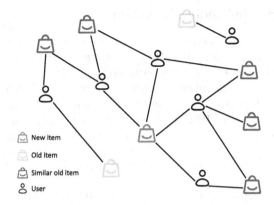

Fig. 2. Illustration of finding similar old items for a new item.

3.2 B-EG: Base Embedding Generator

As the ID embeddings of new items are learned with only a few interactions, they lack the collaborative information to fit the recommendation model well. However, the old item ID embeddings, which are trained with sufficient interactions, contain useful collaborative information. Thus, we propose B-EG to capture the collaborative information in the old item ID embeddings to improve the ID embeddings of new items.

Inspired by ItemCF [9], we consider that two items may be similar if they interact with a same user. Moreover, [1] indicates that the more interactions a user has, the less he/she contributes to item similarity. Hence, we design the item similarity score between item i and item j as following:

$$Sim\,(i,j) = \frac{\sum_{a \in (U(i) \cap U(j))} \frac{1}{\log(1+|I(a)|)}}{\sqrt{|U(i)|\,|U(j)|}}, \tag{2}$$

where $U(i)$ is the set of the users who interacted with item i; $|U(i)|$ is the number of users in $U(i)$; $|I(a)|$ is the number of the items which were interacted with by user a. We keep the top-K similar old items as set $T(i)$ for item i, and the similar old items' weight can be expressed as:

$$\alpha_{ij} = \frac{Sim\,(i,j)}{\sum_{k \in T(i)} Sim\,(i,k)}. \tag{3}$$

Figure 2 illustrates finding similar old items for a new item in B-EG.

Finally, B-EG generates the base embeddings for new items based on the ID embeddings of similar old items. More specifically, for a new item i we obtain its base embedding $\mathbf{v}_{BEG[i]}$ by computing the weighted sum of the ID embeddings of old items:

$$\mathbf{v}_{BEG[i]} = \sum_{k \in T(i)} \alpha_{ik} \mathbf{v}_k. \tag{4}$$

3.3 S-EG: Shift Embedding Generator

Existing models such as MetaEmb [11] use item attribute features to generate meta embeddings for new item IDs. However, these models do not pay attention to the collaborative information. As with old items' ID embeddings, users' ID embeddings also contain useful collaborative information. Therefore, in S-EG we generate a shift embedding for each new item by using its attribute features and the average interacted user ID embedding of the new item. More specifically, as for new item i, we first compute its refined interacted users representation as:

$$\mathbf{h}_i^u = \mathbf{W}_u Mean\left(\{\mathbf{u}_j, j \in U\left(i\right)\}\right), \tag{5}$$

where $\mathbf{W}_u$ is a learnable parameter; $Mean\left(\cdot\right)$ is mean pooling.
Then, we compute its refined attribute features representation as:

$$\mathbf{h}_i^f = \mathbf{W}_f \mathbf{Z}_i, \tag{6}$$

where $\mathbf{W}_f$ is a learnable parameter.

Finally, given its refined interacted users representation and attribute features representation, we obtain its shift embedding as:

$$\mathbf{v}_{SEG[i]} = g_\omega\left(\mathbf{h}_i^u, \mathbf{h}_i^f\right), \tag{7}$$

where $g_\omega\left(\cdot\right)$ is a MLP with parameters ω.

The Training Process of S-EG. Following the cold-start work [11], we view learning a shift embedding for each item as a task. To achieve fast adaptation with limited interaction data, we use a gradient-based meta learning method, which generalizes MAML [5]. When training S-EG, we only update the parameters $\{\mathbf{W}_u, \mathbf{W}_f, \omega\}$ and freeze other parameters. We use old items' interaction data to train S-EG. Given an item i, we randomly select two disjoint minibatches of labeled data $\mathcal{D}_i^a$ and $\mathcal{D}_i^b$, each with M samples.

We first make predictions on the first minibatch $\mathcal{D}_i^a$ as:

$$\hat{y}_{aj} = f_\theta\left(\mathbf{u}_{aj}, \mathbf{Z}_{aj}, \mathbf{v}_{BEG[i]} + \mathbf{v}_{SEG[i]}, \mathbf{Z}_i\right), \tag{8}$$

where the subscript aj denotes the j-th sample from $\mathcal{D}_i^a$; $f_\theta\left(\cdot\right)$ is the recommendation model. Then, the average loss over these samples is calculated as following:

$$loss_a = -\frac{1}{M}\sum_{j=1}^{M} y_{aj}\log\hat{y}_{aj} + (1-y_{aj})\log(1-\hat{y}_{aj}). \tag{9}$$

We get a new embedding by computing the gradient of $loss_a$ w.r.t. the initial shift embedding and taking a step of gradient descent:

$$\mathbf{v}'_{SEG[i]} = \mathbf{v}_{SEG[i]} - \eta\frac{\partial loss_a}{\partial \mathbf{v}_{SEG[i]}}, \tag{10}$$

where η is the step size of gradient descent.

Next, we use the new embedding and make predictions on minibatch $\mathcal{D}_i^b$ as:

$$\hat{y}_{bj} = f_\theta \left(\mathbf{u}_{bj}, \mathbf{Z}_{bj}, \mathbf{v}_{BEG[i]} + \mathbf{v}'_{SEG[i]}, \mathbf{Z}_i \right). \tag{11}$$

Then we calculate the average loss:

$$loss_b = -\frac{1}{M} \sum_{j=1}^{M} y_{bj} \log \hat{y}_{bj} + (1 - y_{bj}) \log(1 - \hat{y}_{bj}). \tag{12}$$

The final loss function of the S-EG is:

$$loss_{SEG} = \beta loss_a + (1 - \beta) loss_b, \tag{13}$$

where $\beta \in [0, 1]$ is a hyperparameter to balance the two losses. The loss function considers two aspects: 1) The error of recommendation for the new items should be small. 2) The generated embeddings should adapt fast with limited interaction data.

4   Experiments

4.1   Datasets

We evaluate CoMeta on two public datasets MovieLens-1M and Taobao Ad.

MovieLens-1M Dataset[1]. It is one of the most well-known benchmark datasets, which contains 1 million movie rating records over thousands of movies and users. Each movie can be seen as an item and has 4 features: ID, title, genre and year of release. The associated features of each user include ID, age, gender and occupation. We transform the ratings that are at least 4 to 1 and the others to 0.

Taobao Ad Dataset[2]. It is collected from the ad display logs in Taobao[3] and contains 26 million click records from 1.14 million users in 8 days. Each ad can be seen as an item, with features including its ad ID, category ID, campaign ID, brand ID and price. Each user has 9 features: user ID, micro group ID, cms group ID, gender, age, consumption grade, shopping depth, occupation and city level.

4.2   Backbones and Baselines

Backbones. The proposed CoMeta is model-agnostic and it can be applied upon various recommendation models. Thus, we conduct experiments on the following backbones:

---

[1] http://www.grouplens.org/datasets/movielens/.
[2] https://tianchi.aliyun.com/dataset/dataDetail?dataId=56.
[3] https://www.taobao.com/.

- **Wide&Deep** [2]. Wide&Deep consists of logistic regression (LR) and DNNs which capture both low-order and high-order interactions.
- **DeepFM** [6]. DeepFM combines factorization machine (FM) and DNNs. FM models first-order and second-order feature interactions, and DNNs model high-order feature interactions.
- **PNN** [12]. Product-Based Neural Network introduces a product layer into DNNs. We use two variants of PNN in the experiments: IPNN (PNN with an inner product layer) and OPNN (PNN with an outer product layer).
- **AFM** [22]. Attentional Factorization Machine introduces the attention mechanism into FM, which can distinguish the importance of different feature interactions.

Baselines. We choose some state-of-the-art (SOTA) meta-learning methods for the cold-start problem as baselines:

- **MetaEmb** [11]. Using a meta-learning approach, Meta-Embedding trains an embedding generator to generate good initial embeddings for new item IDs by using the attribute features of the new items.
- **GME** [10]. Graph Meta Embedding generates desirable initial embeddings for new item IDs based on meta learning and graph neural networks. We use GME-A, which has the best performance among all GME models, as a baseline.
- **MWUF** [28]. Meta Warm Up Framework trains meta scaling and meta shifting networks to transform cold item ID embeddings into warm feature space. The scaling function transforms the cold ID embedding into the warm feature space, and the shifting function is able to produce more stable embeddings.

Table 1. Statistics of the datasets.

Dataset	old items			new items		
	# item IDs	# samples for pre-training the recommendation model	# samples for training the cold-start model	# item IDs	# samples for warm-up training	# samples for testing
MovieLens-1M	1,058	765,669	84,640	1,127	67,620	123,787
Taobao Ad	892	3,592,047	1,784,000	540	810,000	109,712

4.3   Experimental Settings

Dataset Splits. We group the items by their sizes following [11] and [28]:

- **Old items:** We regard the items whose number of samples is larger than a threshold N_{old} as old items. For MovieLens-1M and Taobao Ad datasets, we use N_{old} of 200 and 2000, respectively.

– **New items:** We regard the items whose number of samples is less than N_{old} but larger than N_{new} as new items. We sort the samples of each new item by timestamp and divide them into 4 groups. Subsequently, we use the first $3 \times K_{fold}$ samples as warm-a, warm-b and warm-c sets while the rest as test set. N_{new} is set as $\{80, 1500\}$ and K_{fold} is set as $\{20, 500\}$ for the two datasets, respectively.

Table 1 shows the details of the datasets.

Implementation Details. We set the embedding size for each feature as 16 and the balance hyperparameter β as 0.1. The MLP in recommendation models uses the same structure with three hidden layers (64-64-64). In addition, we set learning rate of 0.001 and optimize the parameters of the models with the Adam algorithm. Following [11], the experiments are done with the following steps:

1) Pre-train the base recommendation model with old item interaction data.
2) Train extra modules (*e.g.*, embedding generators, meta networks).
3) Initialize the new item ID embeddings with the extra modules and calculate evaluation metrics on the test set. In this step, the new items do not have any interactions.
4) Generate the better meta embeddings for new item IDs. In this step, the new items have a few interactions. **Note that only CoMeta needs this step.**
5) Update the new item ID embeddings with warm-a set and calculate evaluation metrics on the test set.
6) Update the new item ID embeddings with warm-b set and calculate evaluation metrics on the test set.
7) Update the new item ID embeddings with warm-c set and calculate evaluation metrics on the test set.

We denote the step 3 as cold phase, and the steps 5–7 as warm-a, warm-b and warm-c phases. In the cold phase, as new items do not have any interactions, we can not calculate the base embeddings in B-EG and the average interacted user ID embeddings in S-EG. To address this challenge, we take the average ID embeddings of global items and global users as the base embeddings and the average interacted user ID embeddings, respectively. In the warm phase, unlike other methods that use the embeddings generated in the cold phase as the initial ID embeddings of new items, CoMeta regenerates the meta embeddings according to the interaction data in the warm phase. Following [11], for each training step, we only update the model parameters for 1 epoch.

Evaluation Metrics. We adopt two widely used evaluation metrics to evaluate the performance: 1) **AUC.** Area under the ROC curve. The larger the better. 2) **Logloss.** Binary cross-entropy loss. The smaller the better.

Table 2. Experimental results on two public datasets. The best result is bolded.

Dataset	Backbone	Method	Cold phase		Warm-a phase		Warm-b phase		Warm-c phase	
			AUC	Logloss	AUC	Logloss	AUC	Logloss	AUC	Logloss
MovieLens-1M	DeepFM	DeepFM	0.7043	0.6660	0.7311	0.6370	0.7520	0.6126	0.7679	0.5920
		MetaEmb	0.7120	0.6508	0.7380	0.6235	0.7577	0.6011	0.7724	0.5826
		GME	**0.7168**	0.6443	0.7405	0.6188	0.7588	0.5978	0.7727	0.5804
		MWUF	0.7099	0.6598	0.7471	0.6220	0.7686	0.5918	0.7821	0.5702
		CoMeta	0.7106	**0.6381**	**0.7789**	**0.5706**	**0.7861**	**0.5607**	**0.7917**	**0.5526**
	Wide&Deep	Wide&Deep	0.7026	0.6686	0.7308	0.6386	0.7522	0.6139	0.7678	0.5936
		MetaEmb	0.7108	0.6524	0.7376	0.6247	0.7574	0.6025	0.7718	0.5845
		GME	**0.7158**	0.6435	0.7397	0.6182	0.7580	0.5978	0.7716	0.5812
		MWUF	0.7067	0.6636	0.7441	0.6254	0.7664	0.5947	0.7797	0.5735
		CoMeta	0.7081	**0.6375**	**0.7789**	**0.5695**	**0.7854**	**0.5609**	**0.7903**	**0.5538**
Taobao Ad	DeepFM	DeepFM	0.5740	0.2270	0.5910	0.2244	0.6025	0.2229	0.6124	0.2218
		MetaEmb	0.5770	0.2263	0.5934	0.2239	0.6042	0.2226	0.6138	0.2216
		GME	**0.5787**	0.2260	0.5935	0.2238	0.6034	0.2226	0.6125	0.2216
		MWUF	0.5779	0.2259	0.5932	0.2247	0.6020	0.2234	0.6107	0.2223
		CoMeta	0.5781	**0.2258**	**0.5982**	**0.2234**	**0.6078**	**0.2223**	**0.6165**	**0.2213**
	Wide&Deep	Wide&Deep	0.5952	0.2257	0.6098	0.2234	0.6195	0.2220	0.6281	0.2208
		MetaEmb	0.5970	0.2246	0.6111	0.2227	0.6204	0.2215	0.6287	0.2205
		GME	**0.6001**	0.2240	0.6134	0.2223	0.6220	0.2212	0.6297	0.2203
		MWUF	0.5974	0.2236	0.6102	0.2223	0.6188	0.2213	0.6271	0.2204
		CoMeta	0.5974	**0.2235**	**0.6153**	**0.2219**	**0.6231**	**0.2210**	**0.6304**	**0.2201**

4.4   Experimental Results

Overall Performance. We conduct experiments on two public datasets and choose Wide&Deep, DeepFM as backbones. Meanwhile, we compare CoMeta with three SOTA cold-start methods: MetaEmb, GME, MWUF. For each method, we run it five times and report the average result in Table 2.

The Cold-Start Phase. MetaEmb and GME have better performance than the backbones, which indicates the attribute features can contribute useful information to item IDs. In addition, GME performs much better than MetaEmb because the neighbor items contain more information. MWUF takes the average embeddings of global items to initialize the new item ID embeddings, which is also helpful. Although we focus on the warm-up phase, the proposed CoMeta can improve the new item ID embeddings in the cold-start phase as well.

The Warm-Up Phase. Since MetaEmb and GME both learn desirable initial embeddings for new item IDs in the cold-start phase, they still perform better than the backbones in the warm-up phase. MWUF performs well on MovieLens-1M, but has poor prediction on Taobao Ad. We guess the reason is that the attribute features of new items are not well-trained on Taobao Ad, which leads to MWUF can not correctly transform cold item ID embeddings into warm feature space. It is observed that our CoMeta achieves the best performance among all methods on the two datasets. Because we generate better meta embeddings, which contain much useful collaborative information.

Table 3. The results of ablation study.

Dataset	Method	Cold phase		Warm-a phase		Warm-b phase		Warm-c phase	
		AUC	Logloss	AUC	Logloss	AUC	Logloss	AUC	Logloss
MovieLens-1M	DeepFM	0.7043	0.6660	0.7311	0.6370	0.7520	0.6126	0.7679	0.5920
	CoMeta (without B-EG)	**0.7118**	0.6475	0.7378	0.6227	0.7576	0.6007	0.7723	0.5824
	CoMeta (without S-EG)	0.7045	0.6636	0.7743	0.5884	0.7823	0.5747	0.7887	0.5631
	CoMeta	0.7106	**0.6381**	**0.7789**	**0.5706**	**0.7861**	**0.5607**	**0.7917**	**0.5526**
Taobao Ad	DeepFM	0.5740	0.2270	0.5910	0.2244	0.6025	0.2229	0.6124	0.2218
	CoMeta (without B-EG)	**0.5781**	0.2261	0.5945	0.2238	0.6051	0.2225	0.6145	0.2215
	CoMeta (without S-EG)	0.5779	0.2259	0.5948	0.2239	0.6049	0.2226	0.6140	0.2216
	CoMeta	**0.5781**	**0.2258**	**0.5982**	**0.2234**	**0.6078**	**0.2223**	**0.6165**	**0.2213**

Ablation Study. To explore the impact of different components in CoMeta, we conduct an ablation study on the two datasets with DeepFM: 1) DeepFM: the backbone. 2) CoMeta (without B-EG): CoMeta without the B-EG. 3) CoMeta (without S-EG): CoMeta without the S-EG. 4) CoMeta: the overall framework. As shown in Table 3, an interesting finding is that the B-EG contributes more than the S-EG on MovieLens-1M, but they contribute similarly on Taobao Ad. Generally, for a new item, its old similar items contain more useful information than its attribute features and interacted users. But Taobao Ad has more noisy interactions than MovieLens-1M, and we can not exactly calculate the base embeddings for new items on Taobao Ad. The overall CoMeta achieves the best performance, which shows each component is important for CoMeta.

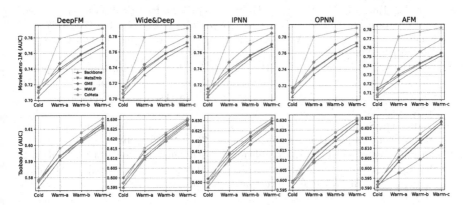

Fig. 3. AUC on two datasets, over five popular backbones.

Method Compatibility. Since CoMeta is model-agnostic, we conduct experiments upon more backbones. Figure 3 shows the results on five representative backbones (DeepFM, Wide&Deep, IPNN, OPNN, AFM) and two datasets. We observe that our CoMeta can significantly improve the recommendation performance on new items with different backbones. In general, the performance of AFM is worse than other backbones, because AFM can not capture high-order interactions.

5 Conclusion

In this paper, we focus on addressing the item cold-start problem. We propose CoMeta that generates desirable meta embeddings with collaborative information for new item IDs. The experimental results on two datasets demonstrate that our proposed CoMeta outperforms SOTA cold-start methods and has good compatibility. In the future, we would like to extend our work to more scenarios (*e.g.*, user cold-start problem).

References

1. Breese, J.S., Heckerman, D., Kadie, C.: Empirical analysis of predictive algorithms for collaborative filtering. arXiv preprint arXiv:1301.7363 (2013)
2. Cheng, H.T., et al.: Wide & deep learning for recommender systems. In: Proceedings of the 1st Workshop on Deep Learning for Recommender Systems, pp. 7–10 (2016)
3. Dai, S., et al.: POSO: personalized cold start modules for large-scale recommender systems. arXiv preprint arXiv:2108.04690 (2021)
4. Du, X., Wang, X., He, X., Li, Z., Tang, J., Chua, T.S.: How to learn item representation for cold-start multimedia recommendation? In: Proceedings of the 28th ACM International Conference on Multimedia, pp. 3469–3477 (2020)
5. Finn, C., Abbeel, P., Levine, S.: Model-agnostic meta-learning for fast adaptation of deep networks. In: International Conference on Machine Learning, pp. 1126–1135. PMLR (2017)
6. Guo, H., Tang, R., Ye, Y., Li, Z., He, X.: DeepFM: a factorization-machine based neural network for CTR prediction. arXiv preprint arXiv:1703.04247 (2017)
7. Kingma, D.P., Welling, M.: Auto-encoding variational bayes. arXiv preprint arXiv:1312.6114 (2013)
8. Lee, H., Im, J., Jang, S., Cho, H., Chung, S.: MeLU: meta-learned user preference estimator for cold-start recommendation. In: Proceedings of the 25th ACM SIGKDD International Conference on Knowledge Discovery & Data Mining, pp. 1073–1082 (2019)
9. Linden, G., Smith, B., York, J.: Amazon.com recommendations: item-to-item collaborative filtering. IEEE Internet Comput. **7**(1), 76–80 (2003)
10. Ouyang, W., et al.: Learning graph meta embeddings for cold-start ads in click-through rate prediction. In: Proceedings of the 44th International ACM SIGIR Conference on Research and Development in Information Retrieval, pp. 1157–1166 (2021)
11. Pan, F., Li, S., Ao, X., Tang, P., He, Q.: Warm up cold-start advertisements: improving CTR predictions via learning to learn ID embeddings. In: Proceedings of the 42nd International ACM SIGIR Conference on Research and Development in Information Retrieval, pp. 695–704 (2019)
12. Qu, Y., et al.: Product-based neural networks for user response prediction. In: 2016 IEEE 16th International Conference on Data Mining (ICDM), pp. 1149–1154. IEEE (2016)
13. Rendle, S.: Factorization machines. In: 2010 IEEE International Conference on Data Mining, pp. 995–1000. IEEE (2010)
14. Rendle, S., Freudenthaler, C., Gantner, Z., Schmidt-Thieme, L.: BPR: Bayesian personalized ranking from implicit feedback. arXiv preprint arXiv:1205.2618 (2012)

15. Rong, D., He, Q., Chen, J.: Poisoning deep learning based recommender model in federated learning scenarios. In: Raedt, L.D. (ed.) Proceedings of the Thirty-First International Joint Conference on Artificial Intelligence, IJCAI 2022, Vienna, Austria, 23–29 July 2022, pp. 2204–2210. ijcai.org (2022). https://doi.org/10.24963/ijcai.2022/306

16. Rong, D., Ye, S., Zhao, R., Yuen, H.N., Chen, J., He, Q.: FedRecAttack: model poisoning attack to federated recommendation. In: 2022 IEEE 38th International Conference on Data Engineering (ICDE), pp. 2643–2655. IEEE (2022)

17. Schein, A.I., Popescul, A., Ungar, L.H., Pennock, D.M.: Methods and metrics for cold-start recommendations. In: Proceedings of the 25th Annual International ACM SIGIR Conference on Research and Development in Information Retrieval, pp. 253–260 (2002)

18. Shi, S., et al.: Adaptive feature sampling for recommendation with missing content feature values. In: Proceedings of the 28th ACM International Conference on Information and Knowledge Management, pp. 1451–1460 (2019)

19. Volkovs, M., Yu, G., Poutanen, T.: DropoutNet: addressing cold start in recommender systems. In: Advances in Neural Information Processing Systems, vol. 30 (2017)

20. Wang, L., et al.: Preference-adaptive meta-learning for cold-start recommendation. In: IJCAI, pp. 1607–1614 (2021)

21. Wang, R., Fu, B., Fu, G., Wang, M.: Deep & cross network for ad click predictions. In: Proceedings of the ADKDD 2017, pp. 1–7 (2017)

22. Xiao, J., Ye, H., He, X., Zhang, H., Wu, F., Chua, T.S.: Attentional factorization machines: learning the weight of feature interactions via attention networks. arXiv preprint arXiv:1708.04617 (2017)

23. Zhang, Q., et al.: UNBERT: user-news matching BERT for news recommendation. In: IJCAI, pp. 3356–3362 (2021)

24. Zhao, K., Zheng, Y., Zhuang, T., Li, X., Zeng, X.: Joint learning of e-commerce search and recommendation with a unified graph neural network. In: Proceedings of the Fifteenth ACM International Conference on Web Search and Data Mining, pp. 1461–1469 (2022)

25. Zhao, X., Ren, Y., Du, Y., Zhang, S., Wang, N.: Improving item cold-start recommendation via model-agnostic conditional variational autoencoder. arXiv preprint arXiv:2205.13795 (2022)

26. Zhou, G., et al.: Deep interest evolution network for click-through rate prediction. In: Proceedings of the AAAI Conference on Artificial Intelligence, vol. 33, pp. 5941–5948 (2019)

27. Zhou, G., et al.: Deep interest network for click-through rate prediction. In: Proceedings of the 24th ACM SIGKDD International Conference on Knowledge Discovery & Data Mining, pp. 1059–1068 (2018)

28. Zhu, Y., et al.: Learning to warm up cold item embeddings for cold-start recommendation with meta scaling and shifting networks. In: Proceedings of the 44th International ACM SIGIR Conference on Research and Development in Information Retrieval, pp. 1167–1176 (2021)

A Graph Neural Network for Cross-domain Recommendation Based on Transfer and Inter-domain Contrastive Learning

Caihong Mu[1] (ORCID), Jiahui Ying[1], Yunfei Fang[1(✉)], and Yi Liu[2]

[1] Key Laboratory of Intelligent Perception and Image Understanding of Ministry of Education, Collaborative Innovation Center of Quantum Information of Shaanxi Province, School of Artificial Intelligence, Xidian University, Xi'an, China
caihongm@mail.xidian.edu.cn, {jhying, fangyunfeixd}@stu.xidian.edu.cn
[2] School of Electronic Engineering, Xidian University, Xi'an, China
yiliu@xidian.edu.cn

Abstract. Cross-domain recommendation (CDR) is an effective method to deal with the problem of data sparsity in recommender systems. However, most of the existing CDR methods belong to single-target CDR, which only improve the recommendation effect of the target domain without considering the effect of the source domain. Meanwhile, the existing dual-target or multi-target CDR methods do not consider the differences between domains during the feature transfer. To address these problems, this paper proposes a graph neural network for CDR based on transfer and inter-domain contrastive learning (TCLCDR). Firstly, user-item graphs of two domains are constructed, and data from both domains are used to alleviate the problem of data sparsity. Secondly, a graph convolutional transfer layer is introduced to make the information of the two domains transfer bidirectionally and alleviate the problem of negative transfer. Finally, contrastive learning is performed on the overlapping users or items in the two domains, and the self-supervised contrastive learning task and supervised learning task are jointly trained to alleviate the differences between the two domain.

Keywords: Cross-domain recommendation · User-item graphs · Transfer · Contrastive learning

1 Introduction

Recommendation algorithms are usually divided into three categories: content-based [1], collaborative filtering-based [2] and hybrid ones [3]. Cross-domain recommendation (CDR) algorithm is a kind of model-based collaborative filtering recommendation algorithm, which is a challenge in recommender systems.

To further improve the model's ability to extract representation vectors and the recommendation performance of the model in two domains, this paper proposes a graph neural

Z. Jin et al. (Eds.): KSEM 2023, LNAI 14119, pp. 226–234, 2023.
https://doi.org/10.1007/978-3-031-40289-0_18

network for CDR based on transfer and inter-domain contrastive learning (TCLCDR). The main contributions of this paper are as follows:

- The information of two domains is used to alleviate the problem of data sparsity.
- A graph convolutional transfer layer (GCTL) is designed to make full use of the information of its own domain and the other domain, which improves the ability of the model to extract representation vectors and alleviates the problem of negative transfer.
- Considering that the similarity of overlapping users or items in the two domains is greater than that of non-overlapping users or items, a contrastive learning loss function (CLLF) is proposed to alleviate the difference between the two domains during information transfer.

2 Related Work

Single-domain Recommendation. In 2018, Berg et al. [4] proposed the Graph convolutional matrix completion for bipartite edge prediction (GCMC),which effectively combined user interaction data and side information to predict the score. In 2019, Wang et al. [5] proposed Neural Graph Collaborative Filtering (NGCF). In 2020, He et al. [6] proposed a Simplifying and Powering Graph Convolution Network for Recommendation (LightGCN). Compared with NGCF, LightGCN simplified feature transformation and nonlinear activation, which improved the recommendation effect while reducing model training time.

Single-target CDR. The task goal of the single-target CDR is to use the data-rich source domain for modeling to improve the recommendation accuracy of the model for the data-sparse target domain.

Dual-target CDR. In 2018, Hu et al. [7] proposed Collaborative Cross Networks for CDR (CoNet). The algorithm cross-mapped and connected the hidden layers of the two domains to form a collaborative cross network. In 2019, Zhao et al. [8] proposed a CDR via Preference Propagation GraphNet (PPGN). The algorithm put the users and items of the two domains into a graph, and then aggregated the information of the two domains through graph convolution. In 2020, Liu et al. [9] proposed a CDR via Bi-directional Transfer Graph Collaborative Filtering Networks (BiTGCF). The bidirectional transfer learning method was used to realize the mutual transfer of knowledge between the two domains.

Multi-target CDR. The task goal of the multi-target CDR is to improve the recommendation accuracy of all domains by using data from multiple domains.

3 Method

This section will describe the TCLCDR's framework (see Fig, 1). Firstly, the model uses the user-item rating matrixes of the two domains to construct the source and the target domain user-item graph respectively, and aggregates the information of the two domains through the GCTL. Specifically, taking the update of the source-domain user representation vector (URV) as an example, it can be implemented in three steps: (1) the user-item graphs of the two domains are input into the graph convolutional layer (GCL) to obtain the user graph convolutional representation vectors (GCRVs); (2) The user GCRV in the source domain and that in the target domain are transmitted to the transfer layer to obtain the user transfer representation vector (TRV). (3) Then, the source-domain user GCRV and the user TRV are aggregated to obtain a new source-domain URV. The other representation vectors are updated in the same way. Finally, the representation vector is transmitted to the prediction layer to output the recommendation list. Considering that the representation vectors of overlapping users or items should be more similar than those of non-overlapping users or items, the model performs contrastive learning in the source and target domain, and jointly trains the self-supervised contrastive learning task and the supervised learning task.

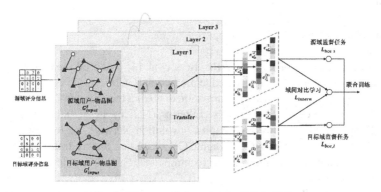

Fig. 1. The overall framework of TCLCDR

3.1   Construction of Graphs

Taking M^s users $u^s = u_1^s, u_2^s, \ldots, u_{M^s}^s$ and N^s items $i^s = i_1^s, i_2^s, \ldots, i_{N^s}^s$ in the source domain as nodes and all interaction information L^s as edges, a user-item graph in the source domain is constructed in the form of a matrix as shown in Eq. (1):

$$G_{input}^s = \begin{bmatrix} 0^{M^s \times M^s} & R^s \\ R^{s^T} & 0^{N^s \times N^s} \end{bmatrix} \tag{1}$$

where R^s denotes the matrix of size $M^s \times N^s$, the m-th row and n-th column array element is $R_{m,n}^s$, and R^{s^T} denotes the transpose result of R^s. if iteraction exists between u_m^s and i_n^s, $R_{m,n}^s = 1$; otherwise, $R_{m,n}^s = 0$. The target-domain user-item graph is constructed in the same way.

3.2   Graph Convolutional Transfer Layer

The representation vector $\{e_{u^s}^{(0)}, e_{i^s}^{(0)}\}$ of users and items in the source domain and the representation vector $\{e_{u^t}^{(0)}, e_{i^t}^{(0)}\}$ of users and items in the target domain are initialized.

Extraction of the Graph Convolutional Representation Vector. The source-domain user-item graph is input into the GCL to obtain the source-domain user and item GCRV $\{\left(e_{u_m^s}^{gcf}\right)^{(k)}, \left(e_{i_n^s}^{gcf}\right)^{(k)}\}$, and the target-domain user-item graph is input into the GCL to obtain the target-domain user and item GCRV $\{\left(e_{u_m^t}^{gcf}\right)^{(k)}, \left(e_{i_n^t}^{gcf}\right)^{(k)}\}$. The source-domain user GCRV is extracted as shown in Eq. (2):

$$\left(e_{u_m^s}^{gcf}\right)^{(k)} = \left(e_{u_m^s}^{gcf}\right)^{(k-1)} + \frac{\sum_{n\in G_m^s} G_{m,n}^s \left(e_{i_n^s}^{gcf}\right)^{(k-1)}}{\sum_{n=0}^{M^s+N^s-1} G_{m,n}^s} \tag{2}$$

where k is the number of GCL, $\left(e_{u_m^s}^{gcf}\right)^{(k)} \left(e_{i_n^s}^{gcf}\right)^{(k)}$ is the k-th GCRV, $G_m^s = \{n|G_{m,n}^s > 0\}$ is the collection of items that u_m^s interacts with in the source-domain. The other GCRV are calculated in the same way.

Extraction of the Transfer Representation Vector. The transfer layer is an important part of the TCLCDR. By extracting the TRV, the model uses the information of its own domain and other domains, and realizes the information transfer between the two domains. Specifically, the TRV can be obtained by transferring the source-domain GCRV and the target-domain GCRV to the transfer layer, as shown in Eq. (3) and (4):

$$(e_{u_m}^{tr})^{(k)} = W_u(l_{u_m^s}(e_{u_m^s}^{gcf})^{(k)} + l_{u_m^t}(e_{u_m^t}^{gcf})^{(k)}) \tag{3}$$

$$(e_{i_n}^{tr})^{(k)} = W_i(l_{i_n^s}(e_{i_n^s}^{gcf})^{(k)} + l_{i_n^t}(e_{i_n^t}^{gcf})^{(k)}) \tag{4}$$

where W_u, W_i represent the mapping matrix, and $l_{u_m^s}$ is calculated as shown in Eq. (5):

$$l_{u_m^s} = \frac{N_{u_m^s}}{N_{u_m^s} + N_{u_m^t}} \tag{5}$$

where $N_{u_m^s}$ and $N_{u_m^t}$ represents the number of interactions of user u_m in the source and target domain, respectively. $l_{u_m^t}$, $l_{i_n^s}$ and $l_{i_n^t}$ are calculated in the same way.

Aggregataion of the Representation Vectors. Finally, the TRV and the GCRV are aggregated to update the representation vectors of the source and target domain. The aggregation of the URVs is shown in Eq. (6) and (7):

$$e_{u_m^s}^{(k)} = (e_{u_m}^{tr})^{(k)} + \lambda^s (e_{u_m^s}^{gcf})^{(k)} + (1-\lambda^s)(e_{u_m^t}^{gcf})^{(k)} \tag{6}$$

$$e_{u_m^t}^{(k)} = (e_{u_m}^{tr})^{(k)} + \lambda^t (e_{u_m^t}^{gcf})^{(k)} + (1-\lambda^t)(e_{u_m^s}^{gcf})^{(k)} \tag{7}$$

where λ^s, λ^t represent hyperparameters ranging from 0 to 1 that control the weights of the graph convolutional vectors for the source and target domain. The same goes for item representation vectors (IRVs).

After obtaining the representation vector of each GCTL, the final URV and IRV are obtained by concatenation. When the number of layers is 3, the user representations in the source domain are obtained as shown in Eq. (8):

$$e_{u_m^s} = \text{concat}\left(e_{u_m^s}^{(1)}, e_{u_m^s}^{(2)}, e_{u_m^s}^{(3)}\right) \tag{8}$$

3.3 Construction of the Contrastive Learning Loss Function

From the user's perspective, each user u_m has two different representation vectors $e_{u_m^s}$, $e_{u_m^t}$ in the source and target domains after passing through the GCTL. Although the same user may have different preferences and interaction histories in the two domains, the vectors of its source domain and its target domain should be more similar than the representation vectors of other users in the target domain, so the loss function of user-based inter-domain contrastive learning is constructed as shown in Eq. (9):

$$L_{inter}^u = \sum_{u_m^s \in u^s} -\log \frac{\exp\left(s\left(e_{u_m^s}, e_{u_m^t}\right)/\tau\right)}{\sum_{u_{m'} \in u^t} \exp\left(s\left(e_{u_m^s}, e_{u_{m'}^t}\right)/\tau\right)} \tag{9}$$

where $s\,(\cdot)$ is the similarity function (cosine similarity is used in this paper), and τ is the temperature parameter. The loss function of item-based inter-domain contrastive learning (L_{inter}^i) is calculated in the same way.

3.4 Rating Prediction and Model Training

After obtaining the URV and IRV, the user's rating of the item is calculated through the prediction layer, and the calculation method is shown in Eq. (10):

$$\hat{y}_{u_m i_n}^s = < e_{u_m}^s, e_{i_n}^s > \tag{10}$$

The loss function of the supervised learning task uses the cross-entropy loss function. Because the effect of the two domains needs to be improved simultaneously, the loss function of the two domains needs to be calculated, as shown in Eq. (11) and (12):

$$L_{bce_s} = -\sum_{(u_m^s, i_n^s \in O^s)} y_{u_m i_n}^s \log\left(\hat{y}_{u_m i_n}^s\right) + \left(1 - y_{u_m i_n}^s\right)\log\left(1 - \hat{y}_{u_m i_n}^s\right) \tag{11}$$

$$L_{bce_t} = -\sum_{(u_m^t, i_n^t \in O^t)} y_{u_m i_n}^t \log(\hat{y}_{u_m i_n}^t) + (1 - y_{u_m i_n}^t)\log(1 - \hat{y}_{u_m i_n}^t) \tag{12}$$

where O^s represents the training sample set composed of source-domain users and items, $y_{u_m i_n}^s$ represents the real label of the source-domain training set. When u_m^s interacts with i_n^s, $y_{u_m i_n}^s = 1$; otherwise, $y_{u_m i_n}^s = 0$. The same goes for the target domain.

Finally, contrastive learning loss functions and cross-entropy loss functions are combined to jointly train the TCLCDR, and the final loss function is shown in Eq. (13):

$$L = L_{bce_s} + L_{bce_t} + \lambda_1(L_{inter}^u + L_{inter}^i) \tag{13}$$

where λ_1 and λ_2 represent hyperparameters ranging from 0 to 1.

4 Experiments and Results

4.1 Datasets

In this paper, we conduct experiments on the Amazon dataset including: *"Electronics (Elec)"*, *"Cell Phones (Cell)"*, *"Sports and Outdoors (Sport)"*, *"Clothing Shoes and Jewelry (Cloth)"*, *"Grocery and Gourmet Food (Groc)"*, *"Tools and Home (Tool)"*. For each dataset, We filter the data to include users who have at least 5 interactions and items that have at least 10 interactions [5]. These six datasets are then used to form three groups of datasets for experiments. Finally, we keep the overlapping users and all items. The statistics of datasets are shown in Table 1.

Table 1. The Statistics of Datasets

dataset	users	items	interactions	Sparsity (%)
Elec & Cell	3325&3325	39463&18462	118879&53732	99.90&99.91
Sport & Cloth	9928&9928	32310&41303	102540&97757	99.96&99.97
Groc & Tool	22746&22746	49217&66961	340857&333588	99.97&99.98

We use the leave-one-out to build the training and test sets. The leave-one-out is different from K-fold verification. The leave-one-out takes the last interaction item of the user as the test set of the user, and the remaining interaction items as the training set.

4.2 Baseline Model Comparison

In this section, we compare TCLCDR with three single-domain models and three CDR models on three datasets (*Elec & Cell, Sport & Cloth* and *Groc & Tool*) by using two metrics including Hit Rate (HR) and Normalized Discounted Cumulative Gain (NDCG). The larger the values of these two metrics, the better the performance of the model. The results are shown in Table 2, where the best results are in bold.

It can be seen from Table 2 that two metrics values obtained by TCLCDR on all the datasets are the best, which illustrates the effectiveness of TCLCDR. For the single-domain model, the indicators of the LightGCN are always higher than those of NGCF and GCMC, indicating that the simplified feature transformation of LightGCNF can improve the recommendation effect. For the cross-domain model BiTGCF, the performance of which is greatly improved compared with other baseline models, indicating that the bidirectional transfer effect in BiTGCF is significant. On the whole, the proposed TCLCDR outperforms other baseline models significantly.

4.3 Model Ablation Experiments

The Effect of Transfer Layers. Three models are compared, which are (1) TCLCDR, (2) TCLCDR-notrans without using GCTL, and (3) TCLCDR-noW without the mapping matrix in the GCTL. Figure 2 shows the experimental results.

Table 2. Baseline Model Comparison

dataset	metrics	Single-Domain Model			Cross-Domain Model			
		GCMC	NGCF	LightGCN	CoNet	PPGN	BiTGCF	TCLCDR
Elec	HR	0.3883	0.4096	0.4087	0.4484	0.4600	0.5657	**0.6364**
	NDCG	0.2238	0.2548	0.2560	0.2861	0.2644	0.3535	**0.3793**
Cell	HR	0.4063	0.4334	0.4499	0.4643	0.5126	0.5621	**0.6496**
	NDCG	0.2364	0.2749	0.2847	0.3004	0.2504	0.3542	**0.4044**
Sport	HR	0.3405	0.3360	0.3917	0.3667	0.3659	0.4473	**0.5295**
	NDCG	0.1874	0.1953	0.2470	0.2244	0.1512	0.2768	**0.3280**
Cloth	HR	0.2878	0.2953	0.3219	0.3235	0.3380	0.4191	**0.5038**
	NDCG	0.1581	0.1633	0.1931	0.2127	0.1445	0.2474	**0.2961**
Groc	HR	0.4808	0.4859	0.5528	0.5099	0.5555	0.5683	**0.6418**
	NDCG	0.3011	0.3050	0.3584	0.3173	0.2867	0.3935	**0.4527**
Tool	HR	0.4268	0.4334	0.4836	0.5626	0.5079	0.4956	**0.5720**
	NDCG	0.2438	0.2506	0.2872	0.3696	0.2837	0.3203	**0.3812**

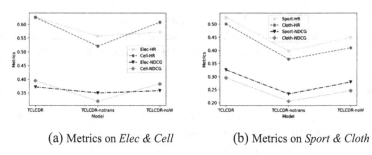

(a) Metrics on *Elec & Cell*   (b) Metrics on *Sport & Cloth*

Fig. 2. Experimental results for different transfer layers

From Fig. 2, it can be seen that on the two datasets, when the model uses GCTL, the values of two metrics in the two domains are higher than those when GCTL is not used or the mapping matrix is not used.

The Effect of Contrastive Learning Loss Function. We design four variant models based on TCLCDR to test the effect of CLLF as shown in Table 3, where 'nossl' denotes the model not using self-supervised contrastive learning. Figure 3 shows the results.

From Fig. 3, it can be seen that on the dataset *Elec & Cell*, when the model uses L_{inter}^u, the values of two metrics in the two domains are higher than those when L_{inter}^u is not used. On the dataset *Sport & Cloth*, in most cases, the values of metrics obtained by the the model using CLLF are higher than those obtained by the one without using CLLF.

Table 3. Models Using Different Contrastive Learning Loss Functions

dataset	Elec & Cell		Sport & Cloth			
Models	user	nossl	user	item	both	nossl
L_{inter}^{u}	√		√		√	
L_{inter}^{i}				√	√	

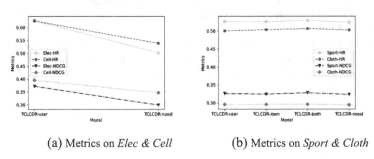

(a) Metrics on *Elec & Cell*   (b) Metrics on *Sport & Cloth*

Fig. 3. Experimental results for different contrastive learning loss functions

5 Conclusion

A graph neural network for cross-domain recommendation based on transfer and inter-domain contrastive learning (TCLCDR) is proposed to recommend a list of favorite items to users in two domains. Compared with the baseline models, the extensive experimental results show that the proposed TCLCDR performs better in the hit rate and normalized discounted cumulative gain. The results of ablation experiments show that the graph convolutional transfer layer and contrastive learning can improve the model's ability to extract representation vectors and help the model generate more accurate item recommendation lists in both domains.

Acknowledgement. This work was supported by the National Natural Science Foundation of China (Nos. 62077038, 61672405, 62176196 and 62271374).

References

1. Balabanovi, M., Shoham, Y.: Fab: content-based, collaborative recommendation. Commun. ACM **40**(3), 66–72 (1997)
2. Herlocker, J.L., Konstan, J.A., Riedl, J.: Explaining collaborative filtering recommendations. In: Conference on Computer Supported Cooperative Work, pp. 241–250 (2000)
3. Chen, W., Niu, Z., Zhao, X., Li, Y.: A hybrid recommendation algorithm adapted in e-learning environments. World Wide Web **17**(2), 271–284 (2012). https://doi.org/10.1007/s11280-012-0187-z
4. Wu, Y., Liu, H., Yang, Y.: Graph convolutional matrix completion for bipartite edge prediction. In: International Conference on Knowledge Discovery and Information Retrieval, pp. 49–58 (2018)

5. Wang, X., He, X., Wang, M., Feng, F., Chua, T.S.: Neural graph collaborative filtering. In: 42nd International ACM SIGIR Conference, pp. 165–174 (2019)
6. He, X., Deng, K., Wang, X., Li, Y., Zhang, Y., Wang, M: Lightgcn: simplifying and powering graph convolution network for recommendation. In: 43rd International ACM SIGIR Conference, pp. 639–648 (2020)
7. Hu, G., Zhang, Y., Yang, Q.: Conet: collaborative cross networks for cross-domain recommendation. In: 27th ACM International Conference on Information and Knowledge Management, pp. 667–676 (2014)
8. Zhao, C., Li, C., Fu, C.: Cross-domain recommendation via preference propagation graphnet. In: 28th ACM International Conference on Information and Knowledge Management, pp. 2165–2168 (2019)
9. Liu, M., Li, J., Li, G., Pan, P.: Cross domain recommendation via bi-directional transfer graph collaborative filtering networks. In: 29th ACM International Conference on Information & Knowledge Management, pp. 885–894 (2020)

A Hypergraph Augmented and Information Supplementary Network for Session-Based Recommendation

Jiahuan Chen[1]([✉]), Caihong Mu[1] [iD], Mohammed Alloaa[1], and Yi Liu[2]

[1] Key Laboratory of Intelligent Perception and Image Understanding of Ministry of Education, Collaborative Innovation Center of Quantum Information of Shaanxi Province, School of Artificial Intelligence, Xidian University, Xi'an 710071, China
`jiahuan_chen@stu.xidian.edu.cn, caihongm@mail.xidian.edu.cn`
[2] School of Electronic Engineering, Xidian University, Xi'an 710071, China
`yiliu@xidian.edu.cn`

Abstract. Predicting the next interaction from a session without long-term historical data is challenging in session-based recommendation. Traditional approaches based on hypergraph modeling treat all items in sessions as interactions at the same time, producing hypergraphs that lose sequential information, which are susceptible to the interference of noise in long sessions. Besides, the way in which the information interacts through hyperedges in hypergraph convolution will lead to item embeddings lacking of global information. To address these issues, we propose a Hypergraph Augmented and Information Supplementary Network (HAISN), where the global graph self-supervised learning (GGSL) channel is designed to provide global and sequential information to the hypergraph. The Hypergraph augmented learning (HAL) channel is devised to supplement the hypergraph with filtered session information. Self-supervised learning is used to provide the information of the GGSL and HAL channels for the hypergraph convolution channel, improving the model effectively. Extensive experiments validate the effectiveness of HAISN.

Keywords: Hypergraph augmentation · Session-based recommendation · Global graph

1 Introduction

Due to the protection of users' privacy and the occurrence of non-login behaviors, the information of users is difficult to collect. Therefore, session-based recommendation (SBR) has attracted great attention. Recently, hypergraphs were found to be good at capturing the high-order correlations between items [1]. However, hypergraphs still suffer from several problems. Firstly, it is difficult for hypergraphs to capture the chronological interaction order of different items in sessions. For example, a user will buy a phone case only after purchasing a phone. In hypergraph, the purchase time of all items in all sessions is considered to be the same. This will make the model unable to utilize the items' position in the session to extrapolate the results. Secondly, items in hypergraph convolutions need to pass information through hyperedges (i.e., sessions). This will lead to difficulties in passing information between items. As a result, the hypergraph structures lead to item embeddings lacking global information. Finally, much literature indicates that noise exists in long sessions in SBR [2]. Noise in long sessions can interfere with other nodes as message passing in graph neural networks (GNNs).

To solve these problems, we propose a Hypergraph Augmented and Information Supplementary Network (HAISN) for SBR. The contributions are as follows:

- We design a global graph self-supervised learning (GGSL) channel. It provides both sequential and global information to the hypergraph through global graph convolution (GGC) and self-supervised learning.
- We design a hypergraph augmented learning (HAL) channel. It prunes the hyperedges to provide filtered session information for the hypergraph. This channel reduces the impact of noisy data on the model.
- We propose the HAISN combining the above two channels with the hypergraph convolution channel (HCC), in which the self-supervised learning method provides the information of the GGSL and HAL channels for the HCC. Extensive experiments show that HAISN performs better than the state-of-the-art (SOTA) methods.

2 Related Works

2.1 Graph Augmentation

Graph augmentation methods are often used to solve various problems in the fields of graph classification and complex networks. In the field of recommender systems, Niu et al. [3] used multi-view graph attention networks to denoise and augment users' representations. However, as far as we know, no researcher has tried to introduce hypergraph augmentation into SBR. In this paper, we propose to apply hypergraph augmentation to SBR and find it efficient in improving the performance of algorithms for SBR.

2.2 Graph-Based Methods for Session-Based Recommendation

"Session-based recommendation with GNNs" (SR-GNN) [4] firstly used GNNs for SBR with a directed graph. However, this method cannot capture the higher-order correlations between different items. To solve this problem, Dual Channel Hypergraph Convolutional Networks (DHCN) [1] used a hypergraph to model sessions. Nevertheless, hypergraphs ignore the order in sessions, message propagation mechanisms slow down the transmission of information, and noise degrades the performance of GNNs. Therefore, we remove the line graph channel with severe information compression and only retain the HCC. On this basis, we propose GGSL and HAL to supplement the lost information for the HCC.

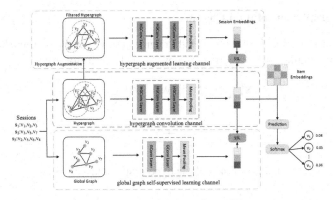

Fig. 1. The overview of HAISN

3 Preliminaries

3.1 Notations and Definitions

Let $I = \{i_1, i_2, \ldots, i_N\}$ denotes the set of items and N is the number of items. Each session is denoted as $s = [i_{s,1}, i_{s,2}, \ldots, i_{s,m}]$, where m is the length of the session. $i_{s,k}$ denotes the kth item belonging to the session S, and $k \in [1, m]$. Item i in layer l is denoted as $x_i^{(l)} \in \mathbb{R}^d$, d is the dimension of item embeddings. The set of embeddings of all items is $X^{(l)} \in \mathbb{R}^{N \times d}$.

3.2 Definition of the Global Graph and the Hypergraph

Global Graph. As shown in Fig. 1, a global graph can be regarded as a connected graph of items in all sessions. Let the global graph $G_{global} = (V, E_{global})$, where V is the set of items and E_{global} is the set of edges. The global graph can be represented by the adjacency matrix A. If $i_{s,k-1} \rightarrow i_{s,k}$ exists in sessions, then $e_{k-1,k} = 1$, $e_{k-1,k} \in E_{global}$ and the adjacency matrix $A_{k-1,k} = A_{k,k-1} = 1$. We add self-loops to the adjacency matrix (i.e., $\hat{A} = A + E$, where E is the unit matrix). The degree matrix of $\hat{A}$ is $\hat{D}_{i,i} = \sum_{j=1}^{N} \hat{A}_{i,j}$.

Hypergraph. Based on the construction rules of the hypergraph in the literature [5], we also construct a hypergraph $G_{hyper} = (V, E_{hyper})$ to represent sessions. Let $\varepsilon \in E_{hyper}$ and the number of E_{hyper} is M. Each hyperedge is assigned a positive weight $W_{\varepsilon\varepsilon}$. The hypergraph can be represented by the incidence matrix $H \in \mathbb{R}^{N \times M}$ where $H_{i\varepsilon} = 1$ if the hyperedge $\varepsilon \in E_{hyper}$ contains the vertex $v_i \in V$, otherwise 0. For each vertex and hyperedge, their degree can be represented as:

$$D_{ii} = \sum_{\varepsilon=1}^{M} W_{\varepsilon\varepsilon} H_{i\varepsilon} \qquad (1)$$

$$B_{\varepsilon\varepsilon} = \sum_{i=1}^{N} H_{i\varepsilon} \qquad (2)$$

3.3 Hypergraph Convolution Channel

We first construct the incidence matrix H, the degree matrix of vertices D, and hyperedges B based on the training set. Hypergraph convolution [1] is as follows:

$$X_{hyper}^{(l+1)} = D^{-1}HWB^{-1}H^T X_{hyper}^{(l)} \tag{3}$$

$$X_{hyper} = \frac{1}{L+1} \sum_{l=0}^{L} X_{hyper}^{(l)} \tag{4}$$

$X_{hyper}^{(l)}$ denotes item embeddings of the hypergraph at layer l. X_{hyper} is the output of the HCC.

4 The Proposed Approach

To alleviate the disadvantage of hypergraphs, we design the GGSL channel and the HAL channel, respectively. The Hypergraph Augmented Network makes the results of SBR more accurate. The Information Supplementary Network can improve the order of recommended results in SBR. Next, we will introduce the proposed HAISN in detail.

4.1 Global Graph Self-supervised Learning Channel

We first construct the adjacency matrix $\hat{A}$, degree matrix $\hat{D}$ and initialize item embeddings $X_{global}^{(0)}$ based on the training set. We design a GGC to capture the sequential and global information of items. It can be expressed as follows:

$$X_{global}^{(l+1)} = \hat{D}^{-\frac{1}{2}} \hat{A} \hat{D}^{-\frac{1}{2}} X_{global}^{(l)} \tag{5}$$

$$X_{global}^{out} = \frac{1}{L+1} \sum_{l=0}^{L} X_{global}^{(l)} \tag{6}$$

$X_{global}^{(l)}$ denotes the item embeddings at layer l. X_{global}^{out} is the output of the GGC.

4.2 Hypergraph Augmented Learning Channel

Hypergraph Augmentation. To remove the noise in long sessions, we perform augmentation on the hypergraph. We use the hyperedges degree of centrality (HDC) to estimate the probability that noise exists in sessions, denoted as:

$$C_D(\varepsilon) = \log(\sum_{i=1}^{N} H_{i\varepsilon}) \tag{7}$$

Longer sessions have higher HDC. Next, the probability that the session ε will drop items is defined as:

$$P_\varepsilon = \frac{C_D(\varepsilon) - C_D(\varepsilon)_{\min}}{C_D(\varepsilon)_{\max} - C_D(\varepsilon)_{\min}} \cdot P_e \tag{8}$$

where ε denotes the hyperedge, P_e is the global filter probability. $C_D(\varepsilon)_{\min}$ and $C_D(\varepsilon)_{\max}$ denote the minimum and maximum values of all HDC, respectively. Based on the probability formula above, we filter the hyperedges to obtain a filtered hypergraph. For the filtered hypergraph, we also construct the incidence matrix $H_{f-hyper}$, the degree matrix of vertices $D_{f-hyper}$ and hyperedges $B_{f-hyper}$ as in Sect. 3.2. The item embeddings of the filtered hypergraph are initialized as $X_{f-hyper}^{(0)}$.

Hypergraph Convolution in the HAL Channel. We pass $X_{f-hyper}^{(0)}$ through the hypergraph convolutional layers and a mean-pooling layer to output item embeddings $X_{f-hyper}$.

$$X_{f-hyper}^{(l+1)} = D_{f-hyper}^{-1} H_{f-hyper} W B_{f-hyper}^{-1} H_{f-hyper}^T X_{f-hyper}^{(l)} \tag{9}$$

$$X_{f-hyper} = \frac{1}{L+1} \sum_{l=0}^{L} X_{f-hyper}^{(l)} \tag{10}$$

4.3 Readout Function

The role of the readout function is to convert item embeddings into session embeddings. We combine the position matrix $P = [p_1, p_2, ..., p_m]$ and the embedding of tth item x_t as:

$$x_t^* = \sigma(x_t W_1 + [x_t || p_{m-t+1}] W_2 + b) \tag{11}$$

where $W_1 \in \mathbb{R}^{d \times d}$, $W_2 \in \mathbb{R}^{2d \times d}$ and $b \in \mathbb{R}^d$ are trainable parameters, x_t^* is the item embeddings with position information added, and $||$ denotes the connection operation. σ is the sigmoid function. We use the soft attention mechanism to aggregate items into the session as follows:

$$u_t = \sigma(W_3(\frac{1}{m}\sum_{t=1}^{m} x_t) + W_4 x_t^*)q^T, \theta = \sum_{t=1}^{m} u_t x_t^* \tag{12}$$

where $q \in \mathbb{R}^d$, $W_3, W_4 \in \mathbb{R}^{d \times d}$ are trainable parameters. θ denotes the session embeddings. After passing through this function, we can also obtain the session embeddings of the hypergraph θ^{hyper}, the filtered hypergraph $\theta^{f-hyper}$ and the global graph θ^{global}.

4.4 Metric Function

To get the score r_i of sessions on the items $i \in I$, we calculate the inner product of the embeddings of sessions and all the candidate items as follows.

$$r_i = x_i^T \theta^{hyper} \tag{13}$$

where x_i is taken from X_{hyper}. Then, we use the softmax function to predict the probability that the candidate items will be chosen as the next interaction item of the session.

$$\hat{y} = \text{soft max}(r) \tag{14}$$

Finally, we use the cross-entropy loss function as the main loss function.

$$\mathcal{L}_{main} = -\sum_{i=1}^{N} y_i \log(\hat{y}_i) + (1 - y_i) \log(1 - \hat{y}_i) \tag{15}$$

where $y \in \mathbb{R}^{|V|}$ is a one-hot vector of ground truth.

4.5 Self-supervised Learning

We adopt Information Noise Contrastive Estimation (InfoNCE) with a cross-entropy loss [1]. Specifically, the two auxiliary loss functions are expressed as follows:

$$\mathcal{L}_{s1} = -\log \sigma(\theta_i^{hyper} \cdot \theta_i^{global}) - \log \sigma(1 - (\theta_i^{hyper} \cdot \tilde{\theta}_i^{global})) \tag{16}$$

$$\mathcal{L}_{s2} = -\log \sigma(\theta_i^{hyper} \cdot \theta_i^{f-hyper}) - \log \sigma(1 - (\theta_i^{hyper} \cdot \tilde{\theta}_i^{f-hyper})) \tag{17}$$

where $\cdot$ denotes the inner product. $\tilde{\theta}_i^{global}$ denotes the negative samples of the global graph, which are obtained by disrupting the rows of the positive sample matrix θ^{global}. $\tilde{\theta}_i^{f-hyper}$ can be obtained in the same way. Using $\mathcal{L}_{s1}$ and $\mathcal{L}_{s2}$ as auxiliary loss functions, the objective function for joint learning is defined as:

$$\mathcal{L} = \mathcal{L}_{main} + \alpha\mathcal{L}_{s1} + \beta\mathcal{L}_{s2} \tag{18}$$

α and β are used to adjust the weights of the auxiliary loss functions.

5 Experiments

To evaluate the performance of HAISN, we design several sets of experiments to answer the following questions. (1) RQ1: How does our model perform compared with other SOTA SBR methods? (2) RQ2: How do different self-supervised learning channels influence the performance of the HCC?

5.1 Experimental Setup

Datasets. We conducted experiments on three datasets: Diginetica, Tmall and Nowplaying [1]. The Diginetica dataset contains sessions extracted from search engine logs for e-commerce. The Tmall dataset contains shopping logs of anonymous users on the Tmall online shopping platform. The Nowplaying dataset is a publicly available music recommendation dataset consisting of real-time music playback histories of Twitter users. We follow the same dataset processing method as in [6].

Baseline Models and Evaluation Metrics. To evaluate our approach, we use several classes of methods to compare them with our model: (1) Item-KNN [7]: recommendations are made by using the cosine similarity of different vectors of sessions. (2) NARM [8]: It is an algorithm based on RNN models that models sequential behavior to generate recommendations. (3) DHCN [1]: It captures the higher-order relationships of different items using a hypergraph and a line graph. (4) AutoGSR [9]: It uses neural architecture search to find the optimal GNNs-based model automatically. To verify the performance of the proposed model, we use two commonly used evaluation metrics: P@K (Precision, Prec) and MRR@K (Mean Reciprocal Rank, MRR) [9], where K = 10.

Implementation Details. We implement our algorithm via Pytorch. We use the Adam optimizer to tune the learning rate. The initial learning rate η is set to 0.05. For all models, we set the batch-size to 100. For the general settings, the L_2 regularization parameter is 10^{-5}, and the dimension of embeddings is set to 100. For HAISN, P_e is 0.1, α and β are both 0.01 on Diginetica and Nowplaying datasets. P_e, α, and β are 0.15, 0.02 and 0.002 on Tmall dataset, respectively.

5.2 Model Comparison (RQ1)

We compare our model with other excellent methods, and the experimental results are shown in Table 1. For methods using the same dataset as ours, we refer to the data reported in their paper. Otherwise, we use the experimental results obtained by implementing the algorithms. The experimental results are analyzed as follows:

Table 1. Results (%) of different models. The * means the best results in baseline models. *Improv.* Means improvement over the results with *. Best values are in bold.

Method	Diginetica		Tmall		Nowplaying	
	P@10	M@10	P@10	M@10	P@10	M@10
Item-KNN	25.07	10.77	6.65	3.11	10.96	4.55
NARM	35.44	15.13	19.17	10.42	13.6	6.62
DHCN	40.21	17.59*	26.22	14.60	17.35*	7.87*
AutoGSR	40.36*	17.52	26.87*	15.19*	16.92	7.66
HAISN	**40.83**	**18.04**	**27.71**	**15.46**	**17.64**	**7.97**
Improv. (%)	1.16	2.56	3.13	1.78	1.67	1.27

Compared to rule-based methods (e.g., Item-KNN) and RNN models (e.g., NARM), graph-based algorithms (e.g., DHCN) are more effective because graph structures can represent the relationships between sessions better; HAISN outperforms all graph-based models, showing it can better capture global and sequential information and recognize the underlying semantic information; Our model performs better than the SOTA SBR models such as AutoGSR. This shows that our model is more robust and can extract session information more efficiently.

5.3 Ablation and Effectiveness Analyses (RQ2)

This section discusses the impact of two self-supervised learning channels on our hypergraph model. As shown in Table 2, we developed three variants of HAISN. They are compared with HAISN on Nowplaying. Prec@20 and MRR@20 are collected.

The experimental results are displayed in Fig. 2, showing that HAISN achieves the best results in both Prec and MRR. This means both proposed channels have a positive impact on the HCC. The missing information in the hypergraph is supplemented.

Table 2. The variants of HAISN.

	HAISN	HAISN-NA	HAISN-NG	HAISN-NAG
HCC	✓	✓	✓	✓
GGSL channel	✓	✓		
HAL channel	✓		✓	

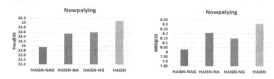

Fig. 2. Contribution of each component.

6 Conclusion

In this paper, we propose a hypergraph augmented and information supplementary network to perform information supplementation for the hypergraph convolution channel (HCC). The global graph self-supervised learning channel provide sequential and global information to the HCC. The hypergraph augmented learning channel provide filtered session information to the HCC. Extensive experiments demonstrate that our model outperforms other baseline algorithms. In the future, we will design hypergraph algorithms with lower time complexity.

Acknowledgement. This work was supported by the National Natural Science Foundation of China (Nos. 62077038, 61672405, 62176196 and 62271374).

References

1. Xia, X., Yin, H., Yu, J., et al.: Self-supervised hypergraph convolutional networks for session-based recommendation. In: Proceedings of the AAAI Conference on Artificial Intelligence, vol. 35, no. 5, pp. 4503–4511 (2021)
2. Feng, L., Cai, Y., Wei, E., et al. Graph neural networks with global noise filtering for session-based recommendation. Neurocomputing **472**, 113–123 (2022)
3. Niu, X., Li, B., Li, C., et al. Heterogeneous graph augmented multi-scenario sharing recommendation with tree-guided expert networks. In: Proceedings of the 14th ACM International Conference on Web Search and Data Mining, pp. 1038–1046 (2021)
4. Wu, S., Tang, Y., Zhu, Y., et al.: Session-based recommendation with graph neural networks. In: Proceedings of the AAAI Conference on Artificial Intelligence, vol. 33, no. 01, pp. 346–353 (2019)
5. Whitney, H.: Congruent graphs and the connectivity of graphs. In: Hassler Whitney Collected Papers, pp. 61–79 (1992)
6. Velickovic, P., Fedus, W., Hamilton, W.L., et al.: Deep graph infomax. In: ICLR (Poster), vol. 2, no. 3, p. 4 (2019)

7. Sarwar, B., Karypis, G., Konstan, J., et al.: Item-based collaborative filtering recommendation algorithms. In: Proceedings of the 10th International Conference on World Wide Web, pp. 285–295 (2001)

8. Li, J., Ren, P., Chen, Z., et al.: Neural attentive session-based recommendation. In: Proceedings of the 2017 ACM on Conference on Information and Knowledge Management, pp. 1419–1428 (2017)

9. Chen, J., Zhu, G., Hou, H., et al.: AutoGSR: Neural architecture search for graph-based session recommendation. In: Proceedings of the 45th International ACM SIGIR Conference on Research and Development in Information Retrieval, pp. 1694–1704 (2022)

Candidate-Aware Attention Enhanced Graph Neural Network for News Recommendation

Xiaohong Li$^{(\boxtimes)}$, Ruihong Li, Qixuan Peng, and Huifang Ma

College of Computer Science and Engineering, Northwest Normal University,
Lanzhou 730070, China
{xiaohongli,2021212111}@nwnu.edu.cn

Abstract. Facing the daily explosive growth of the news quantity, personalized news recommendation for users becomes an increasingly challenging problem. Modeling user interests is critical for accurate news recommendation. Most of existing methods are often lack of comprehensiveness because they do not fully consider the higher-order structure between user interaction and the news, the variation of sequences, and the importance of candidate news to user modeling. In this paper, we propose Candidate-aware Attention Enhanced Graph Neural Network for News Recommendation (GNNR), which encodes high-order connections into the representation of news through information propagation along the graph. And then combine obtained representations with representations from news content. For news representations, we learn click news and candidate news content information embedding. Then we combine it with the information from high-order structure in the graph via a graph neural network. This allows node information and topology to be integrated naturally, and dependencies between nodes can be effectively modeled. In addition, to address users' diverse interests, we also design an attention module to dynamically aggregate a user's history with respect to current candidate news. Extensive experiments on benchmark datasets show that our approach can effectively improve performance in news recommendation.

Keywords: Graph neural network · Candidate-aware attention network · Gated recurrent unit · News recommendation

1 Introduction

News APP website have attracted a large number of users to read the news they are interested in online [1,2]. Due to the convenience and timeliness of online news services, many users have shifted their news reading habits from traditional newspapers to digital news content. However, with a large number of news articles being created and published every day, it is impossible for users to browse through all the available news to find news information that interests them. Therefore, the news recommendation system is essential for news platforms to help reduce the user's information overload. Personalized news recommendations

Z. Jin et al. (Eds.): KSEM 2023, LNAI 14119, pp. 244–255, 2023.
https://doi.org/10.1007/978-3-031-40289-0_20

has attracted great attention from industry and academia [3,4]. Traditional news recommendation methods can be divided into content-based, collaborative filtering, and hybrid. Content-based methods recommend news solely based on content similarity [5]. Collaborative filtering methods utilize users' feedback to news articles to make recommendation [6], suffering from serious cold-start problems. Xue et al. [7] proposed DMF, which uses a nonlinear layer to process display ratings and implicit feedback from users and news. Wang et al. [8] proposed graph neural collaborative filter framework to spread the embedding on the graph to learn the graph structure. However, the recommendation algorithm of collaborative filtering faces the problem of cold start. In order to solve this problem, researchers propose content-based recommendation algorithms and hybrid recommendation algorithms. Bansal et al. [9] integrate topic modeling, collaborative filtering, and Bayesian personal sorting into a single framework. Cheng et al. [10] fused linear models and feed forward neural networks for feature interaction modeling. There are also several ways to learn news representations from graph networks. For example, GNewsRec [11] is a hybrid approach that takes into account graphical information about users and news, as well as news topic categories. GERL [12] learns news headline representation by combining the multi-head self-attention mechanism with the additional attention network, and combines the headline representation with the embedding of news categories. MVL [13] uses the content view to merge news titles, body text, and categories, and uses the chart view to enhance the news representation with neighbors on the user's news graph. GNUD [14] also uses the same news encoder as DAN to learn text-based news representations and graph conventional networks to learn news representations on user news graphs.

Although these methods achieve good performance, there are still shortcomings in the representation of user interest and news embedding. In this paper, We explore better modeling of the correlation between candidate news and user interests to achieve accurate interest matching. Our main contributions can be summarized as follows.

- We propose a graph neural news recommendation model GNNR with high-order information encoded by propagating embedding over the graph.
- We construct a heterogeneous user-news graph to model user-item interactions, which alleviates the sparsity of user-item interactions. Then it applies graph neural networks to learn user and news embeddings with high-order information encoded by propagating embeddings over the graph.
- Experimental results on real-world datasets demonstrate the effectiveness of our method.

2 Problem Formulation

The news recommendation problem in our paper is illustrated as follows. Given a target user u and a candidate news n_{candi}, our goal is to calculate the probability y of clicking to predict the user's preference for candidate news. User u historical clicks on the news sequence are represented as $[n_1, ..., n_i, n_M]$,M indicates the number of clicks on the news. This paper considers the title, body and entity.

Each news title contains a sequence of words $T = [w_1, w_2, w_3....., w_T]$, where w_i denote the i-th word in news title. The body is composed of a text sequence $B = [b_1, b_2, ..., b_B]$, where b_i denote the i-th word in news body. Body contains the entity sequence $E = [e_1, e_2, ..., e_E]$, where e_i denote the i-th entity. T, B and E respectively denote the number of words. This article abbreviates Content-based Representation as C and Graph Neural Network as G.

3   Proposed Method

3.1   News Representation

Content-Based Presentation. Tn this section, we introduce the details of news representation component. This article considers to learn news representation from various news attributes (i.e., title, body and entity). Since news titles directly determine the user's click behavior, we model them and learn the semantic representation of news. Each title can be represented as word embedding matrix $T = [w_1, w_2, w_3....., w_T] \in R^{T \times d}$, w_i denote the i-th word embedding in news title. Then use a Conventional neural network(CNN), which extracts more effective news features, incorporate the contextual features to word sequence. Specifically, the matrix T would be applied to a filter $H \in R^{T \times l}$, where $l(l \ll T)$ is the window size of the filter. Thus produce a new feature map m as follows:

$$m = f(T \odot H + b) \tag{1}$$

where f is a non-linear function, $\odot$ is the convolution operator, and $b \in R^{T \times l}$ is a bias. Then we use a max-over-time pooling operation on feature map m to identify the most significant feature b :

$$\tilde{t} = max(m) \tag{2}$$

Meanwhile we utilize multiple filters to obtain multiple features, and concatenate them together to obtain finally representation t of the news title. Next, we briefly introduce the learning process of entity and body representation. Representation of the body is randomly initialized, and each entity is associated with its embeddings pre-trained based on the knowledge graph. Motivated by Geet al. [15], We utilize transformer and an attention network to model entities representation e and body representation b. Finally, we concatenate three news attributes embeddings, and we send the concatenated vector representation to a Fully Connected Network (FNN). From this, vector representation $[n_1^C, n_2^C, ..., n_M^C]$ of each clicked news and candidate news n_{candi}^C can be obtained.

Graph Neural Networks. The collaborative signals contained in Users-News Bipartite Graph play a crucial role in optimizing the semantic representation of news. To enhance news representation learning, we propose to solve the mining of collaborative signals and the modeling of embedding based on high-order connectivity in user-item bipartite graph. First, we construct a heterogeneous

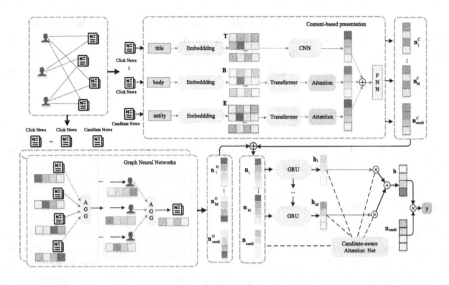

Fig. 1. The GNNR model.

user-news bipartite graph by taking advantage of the Users-News interaction matrix **M**. In our bipartite graph, users and news are both viewed as nodes, user click behaviors are viewed as edges. Expanding clicked news $[n_1, n_2, ..., n_M]$ and candidate news n_{candi}, their corresponding high-order structure graph can be obtained. Then we apply graph neural networks for learning embeddings of users and news, which encodes the high-order information between users and news through propagating embeddings over the graph.

Specifically, GNN iteratively aggregates two-hop neighborhood information to encode news nodes. Motivated by [16], Taking click news n_i as an example, the two-order structure aggregation process after expansion is as follows:

$$\mathbf{g}_{n_i}^k = \sigma(\mathbf{W}_{n_i}^k \cdot CONCAT(\mathbf{g}_{n_i}^{k-1}, \mathbf{g}_{N(n_i)}^{k-1})), \mathbf{g}_{n_i}^0 = \mathbf{e}_{n_i} \tag{3}$$

$$\mathbf{g}_{N(n_i)}^{k-1} = \sigma(MEAN(\left\{\mathbf{g}_{u_i}^{k-1} \cdot \mathbf{Q}_{n_i}^k, u_i \in N(n_i)\right\})) \tag{4}$$

$$\mathbf{g}_{u_i}^k = \sigma(\mathbf{W}_{u_i}^k \cdot CONCAT(\mathbf{g}_{u_i}^{k-1}, \mathbf{g}_{N(u_i)}^{k-1})), \mathbf{g}_{u_i}^0 = \mathbf{e}_{u_i} \tag{5}$$

$$\mathbf{g}_{N(u_i)}^{k-1} = \sigma(MEAN(\left\{\mathbf{g}_{n_i}^{k-1} \cdot \mathbf{Q}_{u_i}^k, n_i \in N(u_i)\right\})) \tag{6}$$

where $\mathbf{e}_{n_i}$ and $\mathbf{e}_{u_i}$ are separately the initial news embeddings and user embeddings, $CONCAT$ represents concatenation, $\sigma(\cdot)$ is the tanh activation function, $\mathbf{W}_{u_i}^k$, $\mathbf{W}_{n_i}^k$ is the layer-k transformation weight matrix shared across all user nodes and news nodes. $\mathbf{g}_N^{k-1}(n_i)$, $\mathbf{g}_N^{k-1}(u_i)$ is the learned neighborhood embedding. $MEAN$ donate mean aggregator. $\mathbf{Q}_{n_i}^k$, $\mathbf{Q}_{u_i}^k$ is the layer-k aggregator weight matrix, which is shared across all user nodes and news nodes at layer k. After the above calculation, you can get a two-hop aggregate information representation of click news $\mathbf{n}_i^G$ ($\mathbf{g}_{n_i}^k$), and the same reason can get the two-hop aggregate information representation of candidate news $\mathbf{n}_{candi}^G$ ($\mathbf{g}_c^k$). Finally, we concatenate the click news and candidate news representation correspond to the two-hop aggregate representation of click news and candidate news, which is expressed as follows:

$$\mathbf{n}_i = (\mathbf{n}_i^C ; \mathbf{n}_i^G) \tag{7}$$

$$\mathbf{n}_{candi} = (\mathbf{n}_{candi}^C ; \mathbf{n}_{candi}^G) \tag{8}$$

Thus the new click news representation sequence $[\mathbf{n}_1, \mathbf{n}_2, \mathbf{n}_3, \mathbf{n}_i, \mathbf{n}_M]$ and candidate news $\mathbf{n}_{candi}$ are obtained.

3.2   User Represents Learning

In order to process the time sequential characteristics brought by the user browsing time, extract correlations between historical click news and based on the candidate news, find out the key news that affects users. we build User Represents Learning. It consists of two component. i.e., Gated recurrent unit(GRU) for sequential feature extraction, canditate-aware attention for user modeling.

GRU for Sequential Feature Extraction. In order to model the sequence characteristics of user browsing records and the characteristics of browsing content at the same time, GRU is used to process the time sequential characteristics, learn a large amount of interest information hidden in the user's news click order, and capture the dynamic change of user interests. For historical news vectors after encoded representation $\mathbf{h}_i$, The calculation process is as follows:

$$\mathbf{r}_i = \sigma(\mathbf{W}_r \cdot [\mathbf{h}_{i-1}, \mathbf{n}_i]) \tag{9}$$

$$\mathbf{z}_i = \sigma(\mathbf{W}_z \cdot [\mathbf{h}_{i-1}, \mathbf{n}_i]) \tag{10}$$

$$\widetilde{\mathbf{h}}_i = \tanh(\mathbf{W}_{\widetilde{h}} \cdot [\mathbf{h}_{i-1}, \mathbf{n}_i]) \tag{11}$$

$$\mathbf{h}_i = \mathbf{z}_i \odot \mathbf{h}_i + (1 - \mathbf{z}_i) \odot \widetilde{\mathbf{h}}_i \tag{12}$$

i stands for moment, σ is a sigmoid function, $\mathbf{W}_r, \mathbf{W}_z, \mathbf{W}_{\widetilde{h}}$ are parameters of the GRU network, $\mathbf{r}_i$ is the reset gate, which represents whether the information before the i moment needs to be reset, $\mathbf{z}_i$ is the update gate, which represents whether the information before the i moment needs to be updated, $\widetilde{\mathbf{h}}_i$ is a candidate hidden state for moment i, $\mathbf{h}_i$ is the hidden state of moment i.

Candidate-Aware Attention for User Modeling. User interest in news topics may vary, and news clicked by the user is considered to have a different impact on candidate news. In order to characterize the different interests of users, We use candidate-aware attention to simulate the different effects of click news on candidate news. It automatically matches each clicked news to candidate news and aggregates the user's current interest with different weights. Specifically, according to user click news embedding representation sequence$[\mathbf{h}_1, \mathbf{h}_2 ... \mathbf{h}_M]$ and candidate news embedding representation $\mathbf{n}_c$, user's current interest feature representations $\mathbf{h}_c$ is calculated as follows:

$$\mathbf{v}_i = \tanh(\mathbf{P}_w \cdot \mathbf{h}_i + \mathbf{b}_w) \tag{13}$$

$$\mathbf{v}_{candi} = \tanh(\mathbf{P}_c \cdot \mathbf{n}_{candi} + \mathbf{b}_c) \tag{14}$$

$$\alpha_{i,candi} = \frac{exp(\mathbf{a}^\top(\mathbf{v}_i + \mathbf{v}_{candi}))}{\sum_i exp(\mathbf{a}^\top(\mathbf{v}_i + \mathbf{v}_{candi}))} \tag{15}$$

$$\mathbf{h} = \sum_i \alpha_{i,candi} \cdot \mathbf{h}_i \tag{16}$$

where $\mathbf{P}_w, \mathbf{b}_w, \mathbf{P}_c, \mathbf{b}_c$ represent the parameters in the attention mechanism, respectively; $\mathbf{a}$ represents a query vector; $\alpha_{i,candi}$ indicates the weight of the impact of a user's click on a news candidate news.

3.3   Click Predictor

For each candidate news n_{candi}, we calculate a matching score with the user representation h via inner product:

$$y = \mathbf{h}^\top \mathbf{n}_{candi} \tag{17}$$

Table 1. Statistics of datasets

Items	Datasets	
	MIND	Adressa
Language	English	Norwegian
#Users	1,000,000	3,083,438
#News	161,013	48,486
#Clicks	24,155,470	27,223,576
News Information	title, abstract, body, category	title, body, category

4   Experiment

4.1   Datasets and Experimental Settings

To assess the performance of the proposed method, we conduct experiments on a real-world online news dataset Adressa [17]. The second one is the public MIND [18] datasets. It is constructed by user behavior data collected from Microsoft News from October 12 to November 22, 2019 (six weeks). Table 1 summarizes the statistics of the above two datasets.

In our experiments, word embeddings were 300-dimensional, We used Glove to initialize the word embeddings. The attention networks had 16 heads, and each head was 16-dimensional. The attention query was 200-dimensional. The intensity of dropout was 20%. The batch size was set to 32. These hyper-parameters were tuned on the validation set. Each experiment was repeated 10 times to mitigate occasional.

Following previous works, we use average AUC, MRR, nDCG@5, and nDCG@10 to evaluate model performance.

Table 2. News recommendation performance of different methods on MIND.

model	AUC(%)	MRR(%)	nDCG@5(%)	nDCG@10(%)
DKN	64.08±0.12	29.06±0.16	31.82±0.11	38.52±0.14
NAML	64.28±0.27	29.77±0.21	32.10±0.28	39.75±0.24
NRMS	65.52±0.23	30.10±0.16	33.42±0.09	40.61±0.18
LSTUR	65.85±0.19	31.22±0.21	33.98±0.58	40.76±0.34
FIM	64.46±0.22	29.52±0.26	32.26±0.24	39.08±0.27
GnewsRec	66.38±0.09	32.46±0.22	34.44±0.23	41.15±0.20
GNNR	**67.21±0.04**	**33.25±0.11**	**35.34±0.13**	**41.99±0.20**

Table 3. News recommendation performance of different methods on Adressa.

model	AUC(%)	MRR(%)	nDCG@5(%)	nDCG@10(%)
DKN	62.91±0.26	28.08±0.20	32.20±0.24	37.75±0.22
NAML	64.24±0.38	28.81±0.21	33.06±0.28	38.52±0.29
NRMS	65.15±0.13	29.29±0.12	33.78±0.13	39.24±0.13
LSTUR	64.66±0.33	29.04±0.26	33.44±0.32	38.82±0.30
FIM	65.67±0.20	29.83±0.24	34.51±0.31	39.97±0.25
GnewsRec	66.32±0.12	30.21±0.32	34.64±0.13	40.75±0.10
GNNR	**67.12±0.01**	**31.18±0.11**	**35.64±0.12**	**40.99±0.09**

4.2 Performance Evaluation

We use the following state-of-the-art methods as baselines in our experiments.

- DKN [19] is a deep matrix factorization model which uses multiple nonlinear layers to process raw rating vectors of users and items.
- NAML [20] is a deep learning based model that combines the linear model and feed-forward neural network to model low-level and high-level feature interactions

- NRMS [21] is also a general deep model for recommendation, which combines a component of factorization machines and a component of deep attention network.
- LSTUR [22] is a deep content based recommendation framework, which fuses semantic-level and knowledge-level representations of news by a multichannel CNN.
- FIM [23] propose multi-level user and news representations and use hierarchical dilated convolutions to construct representations.
- GnewsRec [11] model graph neural news recommendation model with long-term and short-term interest modeling.

We repeat experiments of different methods 5 times and show average results and standard deviations in Table 2 and Table 3, and we have several observations. Firstly, the method of directly extracting information from news text to represent news performs better than feature based methods. However, due to the limited information in news content, most of these methods are affected by cold start issues and their performance is limited. The advantage of this method is that it not only comprehensively learns the content features of news, but also takes into account higher-order structural information, making more full use of interaction graphs to encode neighboring users and news information, and incorporating relevant information into node representations. Therefore, our proposed method GNNR can consistently outperform other baseline methods.

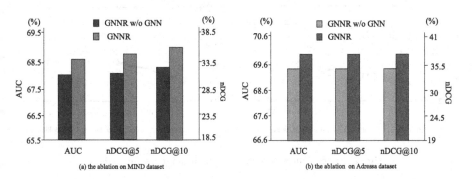

Fig. 2. Effectiveness of GNN.

4.3 Ablation Study

In this section, to investigate the effectiveness of different components in our GNNR framework, we conduct an ablation study. We assess the effectiveness of GNN (i.e. graph neural networks) in modeling news high-order structure information. We used three evaluation metrics NDCG, nDCG@5, and nDCG@10 to illustrate the experimental results. The experimental results are shown in Fig. 2, from which we have several observations. Removing high-order structure information (i.e. GNN) can seriously harm the performance of GNNR. This is because in the user news click network, the user information that clicks on different news is also very important for modeling news representation. Click relationships between user news often contain a wealth of information, which is essential for the understanding of the news. Removing high-order structure information causes the news representation to lose a lot of important information and make it impossible to accurately model the news representation.

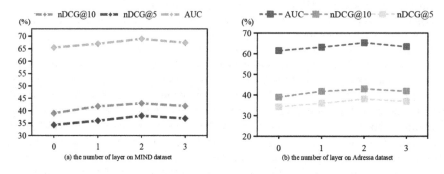

Fig. 3. Effectiveness of the number of layer.

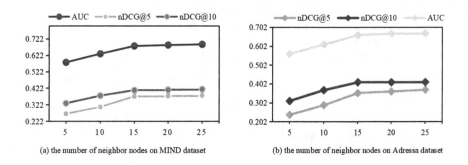

Fig. 4. Effectiveness of the number of neighboring nodes.

4.4   Influence of Hyper-parameters

The Number of Layer. We evaluate the influence of the number of layers of graph neural networks. The results is shown in Fig. 3. We have the following observations. First, the performance of the model first improves as the number of layers K of convolution increases. This is because there is an important potential relationship between the user's multiple click news, and the connection between these click news contains important knowledge that reflects the user's interests. Second, when K is too large, the performance of GNNR begins to degrade. This is because when K becomes too large, too many multi-hop neighbors are considered when modeling the higher-order connection structure of the user's news click relationship. This will accumulate a lot of useless information, which will harm the performance of the model. Thus, a moderate value of K, i.e., 2, is suitable for GNNR.

The Number of Neighbor Nodes. The number of neighbor nodes determines the amount of information aggregated by the target node, and has a significant impact on the quality of the vector representation of the target node. The experimental results are shown in Fig. 4, from which we can draw the conclusion that, in the initial period, as the number of neighbor nodes increases, the performance of the model improves on three evaluation metrics. However, when the number of neighbor nodes increases to a certain value, the performance improvement of the model becomes slow. This is because an appropriate number of neighbor nodes does enhance the vector representation of the target node, but when the number exceeds a certain value, noise data will be introduced, impairing the performance of the model.

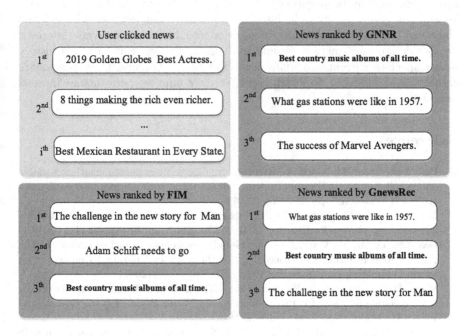

Fig. 5. case study. The blue news is the user clicked news. (Color figure online)

4.5   Case Study

To intuitively demonstrate the efficacy of our model, we conduct a case study to show the effectiveness of GNNR by comparing it with GnewsRec and FIM. We chose them because they achieve the better performance (Table 2 and Table 3) in the baseline method. The experimental results are shown in Fig. 5. We randomly pick a user and pull out the first few news items he clicked on. At the same time, we show the top news recommended by the three methods listed, and the top-ranked news is the candidate news that users click on, from which we have several observations. First, GNNR gets higher rankings for click-on news candidates than GnewsRec and FIM. This is because GNNR not only considers the text content information of the news, but also considers the high-level structure information, and integrates the potential information in the user's news click map into the news representation, improving the quality of the news representation.

5   Conclusion

We propose a Candidate-aware Attention Enhanced Graph Neural Network for News Recommendation (GNNR). Our model constructs a heterogeneous user-news graph to model user-item interactions. Then it applies graph conventional networks to learn user and news embeddings with high-order information encoded by propagating embeddings over the graph. This allows node information and topology to be integrated naturally, and dependencies between nodes can be effectively modeled. In addition, to address users' diverse interests, we also design an attention module to dynamically aggregate a user's history with respect to current candidate news. Extensive experiments on benchmark datasets show that our approach can effectively improve performance in news recommendation.

References

1. Das, A.S., Datar, M., Garg, A., Rajaram, S.: Google news personalization: scalable online collaborative fifiltering. In: Proceedings of the 16th international conference on World Wide Web, pp. 271–280 (2007)
2. Lavie, T., Sela, M., Oppenheim, I., Inbar, O., Meyer, J.: User attitudes towards news content personalization. Int. J. Hum Comput Stud. **68**(8), 483–495 (2010)
3. Das A.S., Datar, M., Garg, A., et al.: Google news personalization: scalable online collaborative filtering. In: Proceedings of the 16th International Conference on World Wide Web, New York, USA, pp. 271–280. ACM (2007)
4. Wang, H.W., Zhang, F.Z., Xie, X., et al.: DKN: deep knowledge-aware network for news recommendation. In: Proceedings of the World Wide Web Conference, pp. 1835–1844. ACM, New York, USA (2018)
5. Wu, C., Wu, F., An, M., Huang, Y., Xie, X.: Neural news recommendation with topic-aware news representation. In: ACL (2019)
6. Xue, H.J., Dai, X.Y., Zhang, J.B., et al.: Deep Matrix Factorization Models for Recommender Systems. In: Proceedings of the 26th International Joint Conference on Artificial Intelligence, San Francisco, USA, Morgan Kaufmann, pp. 203–3209 (2017)
7. Wang, X., He, X.N., Wang, M., et al.: Neural graph collaborative filtering. In: Proceedings of the 42nd International ACM SIGIR Conference on Research and Development in Information Retrieval, New York, USA, pp. 165–174. ACM (2019)

8. Bansal, T., Das, M., Bhattacharyya, C.: Content driven user profiling for comment-worthy recommendations of news and blog articles. In: Proceedings of the 9th ACM Conference on Recommender Systems, New York, USA, pp. 195–202 ACM (2015)
9. Cheng, H.T., Koc, L., Harmsen, J., et al.: Wide & deep learning for recommender systems. In: Proceedings of the 1st Workshop on Deep Learning for Recommender Systems, pp. 7–10. ACM, New York, USA (2016)
10. Wu, C.H., Wu, F.Z., Ge, S.Y., et al.: Neural news recommendation with multi-head self-attention. In: Proceedings of the Conference on Empirical Methods in Natural Language Processing and the 9th International Joint Conference on Natural Language Processing, Stroudsburg, USA, ACL, pp. 6389–6394 (2019)
11. Hu, L., Li, C., Shi, C., et al.: Graph neural news recommendation with long-term and short-term interest modeling. Inf. Process. Manage. **57**(2), 102142 (2020)
12. Ge, S., Wu, C., Wu, F., et al.: Graph enhanced representation learning for news recommendation. In: Proceedings of The Web Conference 2020, pp. 2863–2869 (2020)
13. Santosh, T., Saha, A., Ganguly, N.: MVL: multi-view learning for news recommendation. In: Proceedings of the 43rd International ACM SIGIR Conference on Research and Development in Information Retrieval, pp. 1873–1876 (2020)
14. Hu, L., Xu, S., Li, C., et al.: Graph neural news recommendation with unsupervised preference disentanglement. In: Proceedings of the 58th Annual Meeting of the Association for Computational Linguistics, pp. 4255–4264 (2020)
15. Vaswani, A., et al.: Attention is all you need. In: NIPS, pp. 6000–6010 (2017)
16. Sun, J., et al.: Multi-graph convolution collaborative filtering. In: 2019 IEEE International Conference on Data Mining (ICDM), Beijing, China, pp. 1306–1311 (2019). https://doi.org/10.1109/ICDM.2019.00165
17. Gulla, J.A., Zhang, L., Liu, P., et al.: The Adressa dataset for news recommendation. In: Proceedings of the International Conference on Web Intelligence (2017)
18. Wu, F., Qiao, Y., Chen, J., et al.: Mind: a large-scale dataset for news recommendation. In: Proceedings of the 58th Annual Meeting of the Association for Computational Linguistics (2020)
19. Wang, H., Zhang, F., Xie, X., et al.: DKN: Deep knowledge-aware network for news recommendation. In: Proceedings of the 2018 World Wide Web Conference (2018)
20. Wu, C., Wu, F., An, M., et al.: Neural news recommendation with attentive multi-view learning. arXiv preprint arXiv:1907.05576 (2019)
21. Wu, C.H., Wu, F.Z., Ge, S.Y., et al.: Neural news recommendation with multi-head self-attention. In: Proceedings of the Conference on Empirical Methods in Natural Language Processing and the 9th International Joint Conference on Natural Language Processing. Stroudsburg, USA, pp. 6389–6394. ACL (2019)
22. An, M., Wu, F., Wu, C., Zhang, K., Liu, Z., Xie, X.: Neural news recommendation with long-and short-term user representations. In: Proceedings of the 57th Annual Meeting of the Association for Computational Linguistics, pp. 336–345 (2019)
23. Cheng, H.T., Koc, L., Harmsen, J., et al.: Wide & deep learning for recommender systems. In: Proceedings of the 1st Workshop on Deep Learning for Recommender Systems, New York, USA, pp. 7–10. ACM (2016)

Heavy Weighting for Potential Important Clauses

Hanyi Yu[1], Menghua Jiang[1], and Yin Chen[1,2(✉)]

[1] School of Computer Science, South China Normal University, Guangzhou, China
jiangmenghua@m.scnu.edu.cn, ychen@scnu.edu.cn
[2] School of Artificial Intelligence, South China Normal University, Guangzhou, China

Abstract. The Partial Maximum Satisfiability Problem (PMS) is an optimization variant of the satisfiability problem. It involves separating constraints into hard and soft categories, making it useful for modeling complex problems such as scheduling, vehicle routing, and circuit design automation. Because PMS serves both verification and optimization functions, studying fast and efficient solving methods for it has significant theoretical and practical value. The Stochastic Local Search (SLS) algorithm is widely recognized as an effective method for solving PMS, providing high-quality solutions within reasonable timeframe. While recent research has focused on overcoming the challenge of getting stuck in local optima, this paper proposes a novel approach to improve the initial solution construction process in order to solve more PMS instances. Specifically, we adjust the initial weights of clauses based on contradictory information generated in building an initial solution. Experimental results on the MaxSAT Evaluation (MSE) benchmarks demonstrate that our resulting method, SATLC, outperforms the state-of-the-art PMS SLS, SATLike3.0, in terms of both solution quantity and quality. (The source code can be found at https://github.com/whyte-yhy/SATLC).

Keywords: Stochastic local search · Clause weighting · SATLike3.0 · Partial maximum satisfiability · Initial solution

1 Introduction

The Propositional Boolean Satisfiability (SAT) problem is a fundamental problem in computer science and artificial intelligence. The problem is to determine whether there is an assignment to all variables such that the entire formula evaluates to true. Partial Maximum Boolean Satisfiability (PMS) is an optimization version of SAT, which is more expressive than the standard SAT problem, as it introduces the concepts of hard constraints (which must be satisfied) and soft constraints (which are satisfied as much as possible) [11]. This allows PMS to

© The Author(s), under exclusive license to Springer Nature Switzerland AG 2023
Z. Jin et al. (Eds.): KSEM 2023, LNAI 14119, pp. 256–267, 2023.
https://doi.org/10.1007/978-3-031-40289-0_21

model a wide range of practical problems, including timetabling, vehicle routing, and various processes related to circuit design automation [7,18,19].

In the context of solving the PMS problem, two main categories of methods are commonly used: complete and incomplete methods. Complete methods exhaustively search through all possible solutions to identify the optimal one [12,15]. They are effective for small to medium-sized problem instances. However, for many modern applications in engineering and industrial domains that involve larger-scale problem instances, complete methods may not be able to deliver a solution within an acceptable timeframe. In these cases, incomplete methods can be a more suitable option as they can provide quick responses to real-world needs.

Stochastic local search solver (SLS) is an efficient and anytime implementation of incomplete method that can often return a set of high-quality solutions within a reasonable timeframe. Early SLS usually begins with a random assignment and greedily improves it by flipping values of variables [16,17]. However, this approach often suffers from several limitations, which can prevent these algorithms from achieving the same performance as complete solvers in a short cutoff time. Thanks to years of progress, SLS has successfully incorporated tabu and configuration checking (CC) strategies to mitigate variable cycle flipping issues [6]; by distinguishing between hard and soft clauses, SLS can be highly adaptable in optimizing soft constraints or satisfying hard constraints at different stages [4]; the dynamically adjusted weight mechanism allows SLS to strike a balance between easy-to-satisfy hard clauses and difficult-to-satisfy soft clauses [10]; unit propagation technique and the concept of entropy are used to guide the generation of high-quality initial solutions [5,21]; to further expand exploration of the solution space and escape local optima, SLS leverages Variable Neighborhood Search (VNS) and Variable Depth Neighborhood Search (VDS) to explore a larger neighborhood space [20,22].

SATLike is the first solver whose ability to solve industrial problem instances can be compared to that of complete solvers [10], which is also the most recently proposed algorithm in the MSE that does not rely on a SAT solver. In 2020, the author introduced an improved version of SATLike, known as SATLike3.0 [3]. However, research on utilizing information generated during the initial solution generation stage remains limited. As a result, despite incorporating a strategy that prioritizes feasible solutions, SATLike3.0 is still unable to solve more unweighted PMS instances (referred to as PMS for the rest of this paper). The reason may be that SATLike3.0 cannot effectively utilize the community structure [1] of specific problem instances solely through its weight mechanism, and exhibits blindness in its search direction. On the other hand, modern SAT solvers rely on heuristics such as VSIDS to identify variables that frequently lead to contradictions in order to find bridge variables, which can effectively solve problem instances with high modularity [8,13]. Therefore, we believe that by dynamically adjusting the initial weights of clauses based on the contradictory information during the algorithm's construction of initial solutions, SATLike3.0 can be endowed with greater capabilities to solve PMS instances and enhance its heuristic strategy for prioritizing feasible solutions.

Our Contributions. We develop an initial clause weight adjustment strategy based on statistical contradictions of hard clauses. We also make modifications to the implementation details of the algorithm, such as using local optimal solutions for assigning values when encountering conflicts during the propagation of hard clauses, and adding extra weights to satisfied clauses after completing a round of local search. We discuss the effectiveness and implementation details of the aforementioned strategy, resulting in the algorithm SATLC (SAT-Like3.0 based on contradictions). Compared to the state-of-the-art PMS SLS SATLike3.0, SATLC successfully solves significantly more problem instances in the incomplete track benchmarks of MSE from 2019 to 2021.

2 Preliminaries

Given a set of Boolean variables $V = \{v_1, v_2, \ldots, v_n\}$, a literal is either a Boolean variable itself (a positive literal) or its negation (a negative literal). A clause is a disjunction of literals, represented as $c_i = \{l_{i1}, l_{i2}, \ldots, l_{ij}\}$. In particular, a clause is called a unit clause when it contains exactly one literal. A clause is satisfied when at least one literal is true, and the formula F is satisfied when all clauses are satisfied. The above normal form for expressing a propositional formula is called conjunctive normal form (CNF).

If we use "1" and "0" to denote the positive and negative polarity of a variable, then a mapping $\alpha : V \rightarrow \{0, 1\}$ is an assignment of F. α is called a complete assignment when it maps all variables. In the context of finding solutions for PMS instances, we consider an assignment to be a feasible solution only if all hard clauses are satisfied.

Here we provide some definitions.

- **The hard variable** is a variable that appears in a hard clause.
- **The soft variable** represents a variable that is not a hard variable.
- **The make_score(v)** is defined as the number of the clauses that would become satisfied by flipping v.
- **The break_score(v)** is defined as the number of the clauses that would become unsatisfied by flipping v.
- **The score(v)** is the increment of the number of clauses that would become satisfied by flipping v, which can be calculated as $make\_score(v) - break\_score(v)$. $score(v)$ is used during the local search process in SAT-Like3.0.
- **A good_var** is a variable with positive $score$.
- **The h_true_score(v)** is the increment of the number of hard clauses that would become satisfied by assigning v with true.
- **The h_false_score(v)** is the increment of the number of hard clauses that would become satisfied by assigning v with false.
- **The hscore(v)** is the greater of $h\_true\_score(v)$ and $h\_false\_score(v)$, used during initial solutions in SATLike3.0.

- **The sscore(v)** is the greater of $s\_true\_score(v)$ and $s\_false\_score(v)$, used during initial solutions in SATLike3.0.
- **The cost** represents the number of unsatisfied soft clauses under current assignment α in PMS. If there are any unsatisfied hard clauses, the cost is considered as positive infinity.

The **Unit Propagation (UP)** is an iterative process that selects unit clauses for variable assignment and propagation. The core idea behind UP is that to satisfy a unit clause, we must assign the only literal in it with a true value. This enables us to delete any clauses containing the same literal, as they are now satisfied. We can also delete any literals in clauses with opposite polarity to the assigned literal, as they cannot contribute to satisfy their belonging clauses. UP is a powerful tool for simplifying the representation of a logical problem, which is used for constructing initial solutions in SATLike3.0.

The **UP-based Decimation (UPDeci)** is an approach for generating a complete assignment in SATLike3.0. It operates iteratively, assigning variables one by one until all variables are assigned. If there are any hard unit clauses, UPDeci propagates a hard unit clause. Otherwise, if there are any soft unit clauses, it propagates a soft unit clause. If no unit clauses are found, UPDeci propagates a random unassigned variable. Whenever a contradiction is encountered during the propagation process, UPDeci prioritizes the decision made by the hard propagation method over other methods, or it randomly chooses a value for the conflicting variable.

SATLike3.0 is currently the most advanced SLS in MSE that does not rely on a SAT solver [3], which mainly includes two processes: constructing initial solutions and local search. According to Fig 1, SATLike3.0 builds an initial solution using UPDeci. During the local search stage, SATLike3.0 prioritizes flipping a *good_var* with high *score*. If there are no such variables, it updates the clause weight and flips a variable in a falsified clause to explore other potential solutions. Moreover, SATLike3.0 integrates several effective strategies to handle various cases and reduce the computational overhead.

3   Implementation and Analysis of SATLC

Our idea aimed at helping SATLike3.0 solve more PMS instances by adjusting the initial weights of clauses is as follows.

Since the PMS problem requires the satisfaction of all hard clauses and the satisfaction of soft clauses is not guaranteed, it is often beneficial to prioritize the propagation process of the hard clauses to find a feasible solution. By focusing on the propagation of hard clauses, we can guide SATLike3.0 to narrow down the search space and increase the chances of finding a feasible solution. Furthermore, it is well-known that SAT solvers improve solving performance by bumping and decaying variable *activity* based on counting contradictions [1,2]. This strategy effectively utilizes the structural characteristics of the problem instances, which can be implemented in a subtle and concise way: whenever a contradiction is

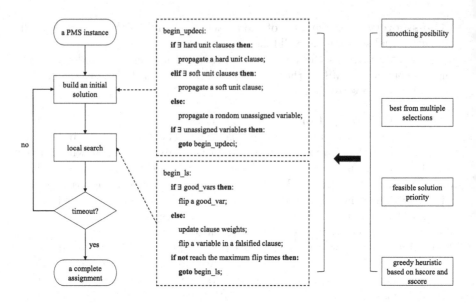

Fig. 1. The workflow of SATLike3.0.

detected while propagating a variable v in a hard unit clause, we assign extra weight to all clauses associated with the single variable v in that unit clause. We denote this set of clauses as $N(v)$. The increment of weight is set to 1.

The general idea is shown in Fig 2. Assuming that variable v_1 links three hard clauses and two soft clauses, it is noted that two of the hard clauses (huc_1 and huc_2) are unit clauses; there is a contradiction between the hard unit clauses huc_1 and huc_2 during the propagation of v_1, then extra weight is added to all clauses in $N(v_1)$. The extra weights are independent of the clause weights originally maintained by the algorithm. During the initialization stage of UPDeci-C, as well as during local search, extra weights are assigned to the initial weights determined by the original algorithm. These extra weights contribute to the calculation of the final initial weight of each clause, which, in turn, affects the calculation of variable scores. The resulting algorithm UPDeci-C (UPDeci based on contradictions) is shown in Algorithm 1. Before obtaining a complete assignment, UPDeci-C continually propagates an unassigned variable, which involves two actions: assigning a value to the variable and simplifying the current problem formula according to UP's rules. When there are unit clauses, UPDeci-C prioritizes propagating hard unit clauses (lines 2–16), followed by soft unit clauses (lines 17–23). Specifically, when there are conflicting hard unit clauses, the *sscore* of the conflicting variable is used for assignment (line 7), or a random assignment is made (line 9), and extra weights are added to all clauses containing this variable (lines 11–13). When there are conflicting soft unit clauses, a random assignment is made for the variable (line 20). When there are no unit clauses, an unassigned variable is randomly propagated (line 25).

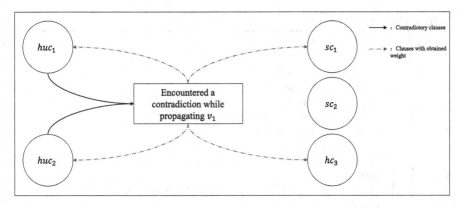

Fig. 2. Exploit conflicts between hard clauses.

3.1 Further Improvements

Extract Partial Possible "High-Quality" Clauses. There is a study (Loren & Wörz, 2020) [14] experimentally demonstrate that clauses with a fixed solution are beneficial to the runtime of SLS. A clause with a fixed solution is one in which the truth value of its literals never changes. Therefore, when a high-quality clause is a satisfying truth assignment, it must contain a set of always-true literals known as the backbone [9]. This type of high-quality clause is consistently satisfied, making it easily identifiable: add extra weights to all satisfied clauses in the current local solution after each round of local search, and the increment of weights is set to 1. This method will make this part of the clauses get more attention in the early stage of the next round of local search, thus affecting the subsequent search process.

Assigning Values by Referencing Local Optima of Global Scope. When propagating hard unit clauses, UPDeci detects contradictions that may arise. If a contradiction is encountered, the algorithm verifies whether $sscore(v)$ is non-positive. If this condition holds true, UPDeci randomly assigns values to variables. This approach may lose good decisions in the local optimal solution, it may be beneficial to develop a strategy that considers the local optimal solution. In particular, when a hard variable encounters a contradiction and its $sscore$ is non-positive, the algorithm should determine the variable's polarity by referring to the current local optimal assignment.

3.2 Implementation Details

Lazy Strategy. We consider the construction of the initial solution process and the local search process as two distinct steps that are cyclically executed. The information collected after each step is used in the subsequent step rather than directly affecting the ongoing execution of the current step. This approach aims to prevent real-time information from misleading the current process.

Algorithm 1: UPDeci-C

---

input : PMS instance F
output: A complete assignment of variables in F

```
1  while ∃ unassigned variables do
2  │   if ∃ hard unit clauses then
3  │   │   c := a hard unit clause;
4  │   │   if c has a contradictory hard unit clause then
5  │   │   │   x := the related variable;
6  │   │   │   if sscore(x) > 0 then
7  │   │   │   │   propagate x with the polarity achieves sscore(x);
8  │   │   │   else
9  │   │   │   │   propagate x with the polarity in the last best solution;
10 │   │   │   end
11 │   │   │   for clause xc ∈ N(x) do
12 │   │   │   │   add 1 extra weight to xc;
13 │   │   │   end
14 │   │   else
15 │   │   │   perform unit propagation using c;
16 │   │   end
17 │   else if ∃ soft unit clauses then
18 │   │   c := pick a soft unit clause with highest sscore using BMS startegy;
19 │   │   if c has a contradictory soft unit clause then
20 │   │   │   propagate c with a random value;
21 │   │   else
22 │   │   │   perform unit propagation using c;
23 │   │   end
24 │   else
25 │   │   randomly propagate an unassigned variable;
26 │   end
27 │   return the resulting assignment;
28 end
```

Limit the Scope of Extra Weights. During the initial solution construction process, the weight of each clause is utilized to compute both the $sscore(v)$ and $hscore(v)$. This calculation helps to determine the polarity of the variable. In the local search phase, the clause weight is used to compute $score(v)$, which ultimately determines which variable's polarity should be flipped. Hence, the weight assigned to each clause plays a pivotal role in guiding the algorithm's search direction. As a feasible solution necessarily satisfies all hard clauses, the weights of these clauses will consistently increase in each round of local search. Failure to impose restrictions on the extra weights of hard clauses can lead the algorithm to overly prioritize their satisfaction, ultimately resulting in a reduction of the solution space. As a result, we decide that no extra weights should be added to the hard clauses once the first feasible solution is found by the algorithm.

4   Experimental Evaluations

In this section, we begin by presenting our experimental setup. Following that, we compare the performance of SATLC and SATLike3.0. Finally, we analyze the results obtained from our experiments.

4.1   Experiment Preliminaries

Benchmarks: We evaluate SATLC and SATLike3.0 on PMS instances in the incomplete track of MSE[1] from 2019 to 2021. For convenient, benchmarks are referred to as pms2019, pms2020 and pms2021.
Implementation: SATLC is implemented in C++ and complied by g++ with "-O3" option, the same as SATLike3.0.
Experiment Set-up: all experiments are conducted on AMD Ryzen 7 4800U with Radeon Graphics 1.80 GHz, 16G RAM, running WSL2 (ubuntu 20.04) subsystem on windows 10. Each solver is executed once on each instance for 60s and 300s, which are the classical time limits applied in MSE. We present the results of each benchmark by showcasing the number of times each solver achieves a lower cost, represented by the notation "#win", along with the average time taken by the solver to find its best solution on each instance, denoted as "time". If a solver cannot find a feasible solution within time limit, we consider its solving time as twice as the time limit. The number of instances in according benchmark is denoted by "#inst". Moreover, we report average incomplete score (rule used in MSE 2019) on each benchmark, denoted by "score".

- $lowest\_score$ = cost of best solution for a instance found by any solver + 1.
- cur_score = cost of solution for a instance found by current solver + 1.
- $incomplete\,score = \sum_i (\dfrac{lowest\_score}{cur\_score})$, $i \in$ instances.
- For each instance we consider the best solution found by all incomplete solvers within 300 s.
- For an instance i, incomplete score is 0 if no solution was found by that solver.
- For each instance the incomplete score is a value in $[0, 1]$.

4.2   Experimental Results

Table 1 summarizes the results comparing SATLC and SATLike3.0 across all benchmarks, using a typical time limit of 300 s. The data indicates that SATLC significantly outperforms SATLike3.0 in both the number of problems solved and the quality of solutions found for PMS instances.

Table 2 display the detailed experimental results of PMS benchmarks from 2019 to 2021, the time limit is 300s. We report the frequency at which SATLC finds a solution with lower cost compared to SATLike3.0 grouped by instance families across all benchmarks, denoted by "#win". By treating each variable of

---

[1] The detailed description is available at https://maxsat-evaluations.github.io.

Table 1. Summary results on all benchmarks.

benchmark	#inst	SATLike3.0				SATLC			
		#solved	#win	time(s)	score	#solved	#win	time(s)	score
60s									
pms2019	299	211	59	187.32	0.69	**226**	**63**	**160.45**	**0.74**
pms2020	262	180	42	198.31	0.68	**195**	**62**	**166.10**	**0.73**
pms2021	155	94	**34**	245.08	0.60	**106**	29	**201.32**	**0.67**
300s									
pms2019	299	214	53	218.30	0.70	**244**	**80**	**176.82**	**0.81**
pms2020	262	184	36	226.04	0.69	**206**	**70**	**191.55**	**0.78**
pms2021	155	96	29	267.67	0.62	**116**	**40**	**210.85**	**0.74**

an instance as a node and connecting variables that appear in the same clause with edges, we can construct an undirected graph G [1]. We use the Louvain algorithm to calculate the average modularity of each instance family, each instance in 5 min. A higher modularity indicates a stronger structural organization of the instance, and is denoted as "mod" in the table. The results indicate that SATLC generally exhibits good performance in instances with high modularity (greater than 0.3). This demonstrates the efficacy of the method proposed in this paper, as structural information can effectively guide the search process to find a feasible solution. However, we also observe that SATLC does not perform well on certain instance families with high modularity (e.g. "extension-enforcement"). On one hand, clause contradictions are observed through conflict analysis when assigning values to variables, but our method cannot reason and backtrack to the root cause of the contradictions, which may result in increasing the weight of clauses that are not strongly associated with the contradictions. On the other hand, it is not only the clauses prone to contradiction that are effective for solving PMS, we enhance the importance of clauses that we consider to be helpful. Overall, it can still be conservatively assumed that variables that cannot be determined by simple decisions of polarity, as well as the clauses they belong to, are worth paying more attention to. Note that some instance families do not contain hard clauses, which means our main improvement strategy cannot be applied on these instance families. These families majorly include "SeanSafarpour", "maxclique", "maxcut", "ramsey", and "set-covering". In particular, we observe poor performance of SATLC on "maxcut" instances, while demonstrating good results on "SeanSafarpour" instances. There is a significant difference in the modularity values between these two problem families, indicating that the structure of the "maxcut" instance is notably weak, while that of "SeanSafarpour" is considerably strong. One potential reason is that our strategy of adding extra weights to satisfied clauses could reduce the search space, making it difficult for SATLC to escape from local optima.

Table 2. #win grouped by instance families on all benchmarks.

instance family	pms2019			pms2020			pms2021		
	#inst	#win	mod	#inst	#win	mod	#inst	#win	mod
MaxSATQueries	15	4	0.38	19	0	0.37	1	−1	0.25
MaximumCommonSub	15	0	0.67	11	2	0.64	1	0	0.63
SeanSafarpour	13	7	0.95	10	6	0.95	–	–	
aes	5	2	-^{a}	5	2	N/A^b	6	2	0.22
aes-key-recovery	5	0	0.96	3	0	0.96	–	–	–
atcoss	14	1	0.84	14	1	0.84	7	1	0.83
decision-tree	–	–	–	–	–	–	23	14	0.43
bcp	8	−1	0.73	14	-2	0.73	–	–	–
causal-discovery	8	−1	0.73	–	–	–	–	–	–
close_solutions	14	1	0.86	4	1	0.86	–	–	–
des	12	0	0.92	3	0	0.92	–	–	–
exploits-synthesis	–	–	–	2	0	N/A	2	0	N/A
extension-enforcement	15	−2	0.97	12	−2	0.97	2	−1	0.97
fault-diagnosis	8	8	0.85	4	4	N/A	–	–	–
gen-hyper-tw	18	−2	0.69	8	−2	0.7	8	-1	0.72
hs-timetabling	1	1	0.95	1	1	0.95	1	1	0.95
large-graph-commmunity	–	–	–	3	−1	0.96	3	−1	0.96
logic-synthesis	1	1	0.29	1	1	0.28	1	1	0.28
maxclique	17	−4	0.13	11	−1	0.1	3	0	0.1
maxcut	12	−8	0.12	9	−4	0.06	11	−11	0.27
mbd	6	1	0.78	5	0	0.79	–	–	–
min-fill	15	5	0.47	12	6	0.47	7	4	0.48
optic	16	6	0.26	15	7	0.26	1	-1	0.39
phylogenetic-trees berg	–	–	–	–	–	–	8	0	N/A
planning-bnn	–	–	–	–	–	–	8	0	N/A
phylogenetic-trees	–	–	–	5	0	N/A	–	–	–
program disambiguation	–	–	–	2	0	N/A	1	0	N/A
pseudoBoolean	6	1	0.82	6	1	0.82	–	–	–
railroad scheduling	–	–	–	4	4	0.64	–	–	–
railroad reisch	–	–	–	–	–	–	8	4	0.64
railway-transport	4	−1	0.77	4	−1	0.78	4	−1	0.78
ramsey	14	0	0	11	0	0	11	0	0
reversi	11	0	0.87	11	0	0.87	7	0	0.87
scheduling	5	−1	0.79	3	0	0.79	3	0	0.79
scheduling xiaojuan	–	–	–	–	–	–	8	−3	0.68
set-covering	9	2	0.29	9	2	0.3	9	2	0.29
setcover-rail zhendong	–	–	–	–	–	–	4	0	0
treewidth-computation	8	1	0.51	8	2	0.51	3	0	0.51
uaq	15	0	0.19	18	0	0.18	1	0	0.14
uaq gazzarata	–	–	–	–	–	–	1	1	0.14
xai-mindset2	14	5	0.83	15	7	0.85	2	1	0.89

^{a} "-" indicates that the dataset does not contain the problem family.
^{b} "N/A" refers to the failure to calculate "mod" within 300s.

5   Conclusions

Building upon the current state-of-the-art PMS SLS SATLike3.0, this paper presents a lightweight method for contributing clause contradictions to initial clause weights. The resulting algorithm, SATLC, achieves significant advantages in solving PMS instances. The effectiveness of this method stems from related research on SAT solvers, which shows that frequently contradictory variables and clauses imply structural information regarding the current instance. Additionally, we further improved the solution details by incorporating extra weights to partially satisfied clauses, referencing local optimal solutions when encountering contradictions while propagating hard unit clauses, and delaying extra weights. However, one limitation of this work is the absence of exploration into adaptive weight adjustment values, which results in unstable performance when dealing with weighted version problems.

In future work, we will explore strategies for configuring inital clause weights. The weight mechanism proposed in NUWLS-c, which participated in MSE 2022, indicates a promising direction for improvement.

References

1. Ansótegui, C., Bonet, M.L., Giráldez-Cru, J., Levy, J., Simon, L.: Community structure in industrial SAT instances. J. Artif. Intell. Res. **66**, 443–472 (2019)
2. Ansótegui, C., Giráldez-Cru, J., Levy, J., Simon, L.: Using community structure to detect relevant learnt clauses. In: Heule, M., Weaver, S. (eds.) SAT 2015. LNCS, vol. 9340, pp. 238–254. Springer, Cham (2015). https://doi.org/10.1007/978-3-319-24318-4_18
3. Cai, S., Lei, Z.: Old techniques in new ways: clause weighting, unit propagation and hybridization for maximum satisfiability. Artif. Intell. **287**, 103354 (2020)
4. Cai, S., Luo, C., Thornton, J., Su, K.: Tailoring local search for partial maxsat. In: Proceedings of the 28th AAAI Conference on Artificial Intelligence, Québec City, Canada. pp. 2623–2629 (2014)
5. Cai, S., Luo, C., Zhang, H.: From decimation to local search and back: a new approach to maxsat. In: Proceedings of the Twenty-Sixth International Joint Conference on Artificial Intelligence, IJCAI 2017, Melbourne, Australia, pp. 571–577 (2017)
6. Cai, S., Su, K.: Local search for boolean satisfiability with configuration checking and subscore. Artif. Intell. **204**, 75–98 (2013)
7. Coster, A.D., Musliu, N., Schaerf, A., Schoisswohl, J., Smith-Miles, K.: Algorithm selection and instance space analysis for curriculum-based course timetabling. J. Sched. **25**(1), 35–58 (2022)
8. Eén, N., Sörensson, N.: An extensible SAT-solver. In: Giunchiglia, E., Tacchella, A. (eds.) SAT 2003. LNCS, vol. 2919, pp. 502–518. Springer, Heidelberg (2004). https://doi.org/10.1007/978-3-540-24605-3_37
9. Kilby, P., Slaney, J.K., Thiébaux, S., Walsh, T.: Backbones and backdoors in satisfiability. In: Proceedings, The 20th National Conference on Artificial Intelligence and the 17th Innovative Applications of Artificial Intelligence Conference, Pittsburgh, USA, pp. 1368–1373 (2005)

10. Lei, Z., Cai, S.: Solving (weighted) partial maxsat by dynamic local search for SAT. In: Proceedings of the 27th International Joint Conference on Artificial Intelligence, Stockholm, Sweden, pp. 1346–1352 (2018)
11. Li, C.M., Manyà, F.: Maxsat, hard and soft constraints. In: Handbook of Satisfiability - Second Edition, Frontiers in Artificial Intelligence and Applications, vol. 336, pp. 903–927. IOS Press (2021)
12. Li, C., Xu, Z., Coll, J., Manyà, F., Habet, D., He, K.: Combining clause learning and branch and bound for maxsat. In: Proceedings of the 27th International Conference on Principles and Practice of Constraint Programming, Montpellier, France (Virtual Conference), LIPIcs, vol. 210, pp. 38:1–38:18 (2021)
13. Liang, J.H., Ganesh, V., Zulkoski, E., Zaman, A., Czarnecki, K.: Understanding VSIDS branching heuristics in conflict-driven clause-learning SAT solvers. In: Piterman, N. (ed.) HVC 2015. LNCS, vol. 9434, pp. 225–241. Springer, Cham (2015). https://doi.org/10.1007/978-3-319-26287-1_14
14. Lorenz, J.-H., Wörz, F.: On the effect of learned clauses on stochastic local search. In: Pulina, L., Seidl, M. (eds.) SAT 2020. LNCS, vol. 12178, pp. 89–106. Springer, Cham (2020). https://doi.org/10.1007/978-3-030-51825-7_7
15. Narodytska, N., Bacchus, F.: Maximum satisfiability using core-guided maxsat resolution. In: Proceedings of the 28th AAAI Conference on Artificial Intelligence, Québec City, Canada, pp. 2717–2723. AAAI Press (2014)
16. Selman, B., Kautz, H.A., Cohen, B.: Noise strategies for improving local search. In: Proceedings of the 12th National Conference on Artificial Intelligence, Seattle, USA, vol. 1, pp. 337–343 (1994)
17. Selman, B., Levesque, H.J., Mitchell, D.G.: A new method for solving hard satisfiability problems. In: Proceedings of the 10th National Conference on Artificial Intelligence, San Jose, USA, pp. 440–446 (1992)
18. Shaw, P.: Using constraint programming and local search methods to solve vehicle routing problems. In: Maher, M., Puget, J.-F. (eds.) CP 1998. LNCS, vol. 1520, pp. 417–431. Springer, Heidelberg (1998). https://doi.org/10.1007/3-540-49481-2_30
19. Silva, J.P.M., Sakallah, K.A.: Boolean satisfiability in electronic design automation. In: Proceedings of the 37th Conference on Design Automation, Los Angeles, USA, pp. 675–680. ACM (2000)
20. Wu, Q., Hao, J., Glover, F.W.: Multi-neighborhood tabu search for the maximum weight clique problem. Ann. Oper. Res. **196**(1), 611–634 (2012)
21. Zhang, Z., Zhou, J., Wang, X., Yang, H., Fan, Y.: Initial solution generation and diversified variable picking in local search for (weighted) partial maxsat. Entropy **24**(12), 1846 (2022)
22. Zheng, J., Zhou, J., He, K.: Farsighted probabilistic sampling based local search for (weighted) partial maxsat. CoRR abs/2108.09988 (2021)

Knowledge-Aware Two-Stream Decoding for Outline-Conditioned Chinese Story Generation

Huahai Lin[1], Yong Wen[1(✉)], Ping Jiang[2], Wu Wen[3], and Xianye Liang[1]

[1] School of Artificial Intelligence, Guangxi Minzu University, Nanning 530006, China
hethree@stu.gxmzu.edu.cn, {wenyong,20210037}@gxmzu.edu.cn
[2] School of Computer and Information Technology, Guangxi Police College,
Nanning 530028, China
j_pingzi@163.com
[3] Weibin Zhongye Information Technology Ltd. Co, Nanning, China
wenwu_gx@163.com

Abstract. Generating a coherent and reasonable story for a given story outline, i.e., outline-conditioned story generation, is an important and challenging task. The key challenges of the task lie in how to ensure that the majority of the story outline points appear in the generated story sufficiently and expand the source of information for the story outline effectively, these challenges are still under-explored by prior works, especially for outline-conditioned Chinese story generation. In this paper, we propose a novel outline-conditioned Chinese story generation framework that utilizes a two-stream decoding mechanism to make sure most of the points listed in the outlines of the stories are included in the generated stories by training the generative model and generating the stories twice. Moreover, we enlarge the outline points by incorporating external knowledge from a Chinese commonsense knowledge base to generate various Chinese stories. Extensive experiments show that our framework outperforms the state-of-the-art Chinese generation models on several evaluation metrics, demonstrating the importance of the two-stream decoding mechanism and the necessity of incorporating extra Chinese knowledge into the story outline for generating more diverse Chinese stories.

Keywords: Story Outline · Chinese Story Generation · Commonsense Knowledge · Two-Stream Decoding

1 Introduction

Storytelling nowadays plays an important role in natural language generation, and outline-conditioned story generation is a specialized task within this domain. Given a story outline, i.e., a sequence of key phrases containing key characters and events, outline-conditioned story generation aims to generate a coherent story that is highly conditioned on and accorded with the outline [3]. Significant advances have been made in outline-conditioned story generation using pre-trained language models. Rashkin et al. [21] employed GPT [18] that learns

© The Author(s), under exclusive license to Springer Nature Switzerland AG 2023
Z. Jin et al. (Eds.): KSEM 2023, LNAI 14119, pp. 268–281, 2023.
https://doi.org/10.1007/978-3-031-40289-0_22

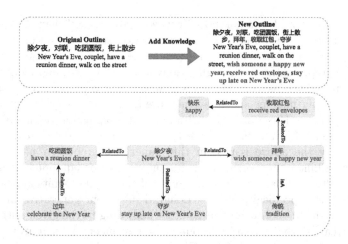

Fig. 1. The top graph exemplifies how to integrate Chinese commonsense knowledge into the original story outline, with entities and events highlighted in blue to indicate supplementary knowledge. The bottom graph manifests the implicit knowledge behind the Chinese story. (Color figure online)

to convert outlines into full stories with dynamic plot state tracking. Besides, Guan et al. [6] released a new Chinese pre-trained model named LongLM that presents a great performance in outline-conditioned Chinese story generation. While these models have demonstrated the capability to generate coherent stories that adhere to the given outlines, there are still some missing outline points in the generated stories, which comes from the fact that the models need to figure out how these outline points will interact with each other throughout the stories and therefore it may cause the missing outline points in the generated stories during the process of long text modeling.

In general, a story context consists of a series of entities and events that can have strong logical connections with one another, resulting in complex interactive relationships throughout the context. For outline-conditioned Chinese story generation, humans can rely on their own commonsense knowledge to understand the story events and entities and incorporate knowledge related to these events and entities into the original outline, and then create the story content based on the new outline. As exemplified in Fig. 1, the new outline point "拜年" (wish someone a happy new year) can be perceived as commonsense knowledge about "除夕夜" (New Year's Eve). Such knowledge can be important for outline-conditioned Chinese story generation. Figure 1 shows an example of adding Chinese commonsense knowledge to the original story outline. The connections between these concepts, such as "除夕夜" (New Year's Eve), "拜年" (wish someone a happy new year), "守岁" (stay up late on New Year's Eve), and "收取红包" (receive red envelopes), can be represented as a graph. Instead of focusing on just one concept, the story outline in outline-conditioned story generation should take into account most of the concepts that are connected. However, for prior works in outline-conditioned story generation, the explorations of introducing external commonsense knowledge are not sufficient. For example, Huang et al. [9] made use of a data augmentation story generation framework that informs the generative model of dependencies between words and augments the semantic representation through synonym denoising training. Fang et al. [3] leveraged special tokens as delimiters to connect outline events with paragraphs in an interleaving manner and fine-tuned pre-trained language models on augmented sequences. These methods all adopt data augmentation strategies but ignore the usage of commonsense knowledge behind the story context.

To remedy the above issues, in this paper, we propose a novel outline-conditioned Chinese story generation framework that is equipped with a two-stream decoding mechanism to ensure most of the outline points appear in the generated story. Specifically, we use LongLM [6] as our generative model and we first train this model to generate a story according to the given outline (i.e., the first stream decoding) and find out missing elements of the outline that do not appear in the generated story. We form these missing outline points as a sentence and add this sentence to the end of the generated story correspondingly, and this story is referred to as the pseudo story. Given the outline and the pseudo story, we train the generative model once more. After finishing the training process, eventually, the generative model can generate a whole story containing more outline points than the first generated story (i.e., the second stream decoding), resulting in most of the outline points being included in the generated story. Moreover, the framework also applies commonsense knowledge retrieved from Chinese ConceptNet [1] which is refined from multilingual ConceptNet [22] to the story outline to enhance the diversity of the generated story. In detail, we conduct Chinese word tokenization on the original story and we utilize HanLP [8] as our tool for calculating the similarity scores between the segmentary words from the story and the commonsense knowledge in Chinese ConceptNet. Then we choose at most seven words or phrases with the highest similarity scores in Chinese ConceptNet as our additional outline points.

The main contributions of this paper are summarized as follows:

- We propose a novel outline-conditioned Chinese story generation framework that leverages the two-stream decoding mechanism to ensure most of the outline points appear in the generated story.
- To facilitate story comprehension, we enlarge story outline points by incorporating external commonsense knowledge extracted from the Chinese ConceptNet knowledge base. The enlarged outline used for training the framework leads to a notable improvement in the diversity of the generated stories.
- Empirical results show that our framework can achieve new state-of-the-art performances on several evaluation metrics and generate more diverse and comprehensive stories that cover most of the outline points.

2 Related Work

Controllable Story Generation. Controllable story generation aims to generate stories with the help of specified attributes (e.g., premises, knowledge). For instance, Fan et al. [2] enabled their model to first generate a premise and then transformed it into a passage of a story. Tambwekar et al. [24] used large-scale language models and added control to story generation by incorporating external knowledge. Besides, there are some similar works in the creative generation that have been conditioned on topics for essay generation [4,28]. Similar to our work, recently, Rashkin et al. [21] proposed a neural narrative model that learns to transform an outline into a coherent story by tracking the dynamic plot states. Moreover, Fang et al. [3] fine-tuned pre-trained language models on augmented sequences of outline-story pairs with simple language modeling objective to generate stories. However, these recent works still suffer from some missing outline points in the generated stories. In this work, we make use of a two-stream decoding mechanism to make sure most of the outline points appear in the generated stories. Inspired by the recent similar works, we leverage LongLM [6] based on transformer architecture as our generative model.

Commonsense Knowledge. Commonsense knowledge has been proven to play a vital role in some generation tasks such as story ending generation [26] and conversation generation [31]. Recently, several works have attempted to explore how pre-trained language models such as GPT-2 [19] and BART [12] leverage commonsense knowledge to enhance language representation for neural argument generation [11] and generative commonsense reasoning [15]. Furthermore, Guan et al. [7] enhanced GPT-2 with knowledge for commonsense story generation by post-training the model on the knowledge examples constructed from external commonsense knowledge bases such as ConceptNet [23] containing abundant semantic knowledge of concepts and inferential knowledge for commonsense reasoning. Moreover, Ji et al. [10] enabled pre-trained models with dynamic multi-hop reasoning on multi-relational paths extracted from the external commonsense knowledge graph to facilitate explicit commonsense reasoning in text generation. These works suggest that the use of commonsense knowledge is beneficial and important for downstream applications so we consider integrating external commonsense knowledge into the story outline in outline-conditioned Chinese story generation to generate more coherent and diverse Chinese stories.

3 Methodology

3.1 Problem Formulation

Outline-conditioned Chinese story generation task aims to generate a Chinese story that is highly conditioned on and consistent with the corresponding Chinese outline. We use $X = \{x_1, x_2, ..., x_m\}$ to represent the Chinese story outline, where x_i represents the i-th outline point pertaining to certain characters or events, and m indicates the total number of outline points. Meanwhile, the generated story is represented as $S = \{t_1, t_2, ..., t_n\}$, where t_j denotes the j-th token in the story. We define $K = \{k_1, k_2, ..., k_l\}$ as the knowledge associated with the corresponding story S, where k_z denotes the z-th knowledge phrase or sentence.

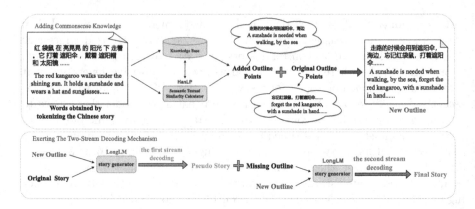

Fig. 2. Overview of our framework and generation process. We resort to a semantic textual similarity calculator provided by HanLP to find the relevant knowledge from an external knowledge base to get knowledge outline points. A two-stream decoding mechanism is introduced to improve the coverage of story outline points in the generated story.

Note that the number of knowledge phrases or sentences per story can vary and may even be zero. Given this notation, we define the new outline as $N = \{[X, K]\}$. The goal of this work is to generate a story S related to the given new outline N.

3.2   Overview

Figure 2 shows the overview of our proposed framework and our generation process. Firstly, in order to increase the variety of the generated story, we leverage the semantic textual similarity calculator[1] from HanLP [8] to find the appropriate knowledge and incorporate the knowledge from the Chinese ConceptNet [1] knowledge base[2] into the framework. Furthermore, we introduce a two-stream decoding mechanism utilizing LongLM [6] as the story generator into the framework to improve the coverage of the story outline points in the generated story.

3.3   Adding Commonsense Knowledge

There is a lot of commonsense knowledge in the Chinese ConceptNet knowledge base which means we have to extract the knowledge we need in a suitable way. For each story in the train set, we first conduct word tokenization as much as possible by using jieba tokenizer[3] and get rid of the redundant space characters. We keep those words that are at least three characters and ignore words that are less than three characters since the Chinese ConceptNet knowledge base

---

[1] https://hanlp.hankcs.com/docs/api/hanlp/pretrained/sts.html.
[2] https://github.com/play0137/Chinese_ConceptNet.
[3] https://github.com/fxsjy/jieba.

contains many texts about commonsense knowledge, matching each word in the story with every knowledge word or sentence in the knowledge base will require a lot of time and computational resources, which is beyond our capacity. After preprocessing the words in the story, we convert the Chinese text in the knowledge base from traditional Chinese to simplified Chinese for aligning the text in the knowledge base with our simplified Chinese dataset. We construct a corresponding knowledge dictionary that can relate one Chinese phrase to another corresponding Chinese phrase or even sentence. Subsequently, we employ HanLP [8] to calculate the semantic textual similarity of the retained words with the knowledge corresponding to these words in the knowledge dictionary. HanLP provides some Chinese pre-trained semantic textual similarity models which can be used to calculate the semantic textual similarity between two Chinese phrases or even Chinese sentences. For example, given the input "樱花树开满樱花" (the cherry blossom tree is in full bloom with cherry blossoms) and "樱花树的樱花开了" (the cherry blossoms on the cherry blossom tree have bloomed), the HanLP pre-trained semantic textual similarity model can calculate a semantic similarity score of approximately 0.706 between them. The calculation process can be depicted below:

$$V = STS[(C_1, C_2)] \tag{1}$$

where STS is the semantic textual similarity calculator provided by HanLP, C_1 and C_2 are Chinese phrases or sentences, and V is the score of semantic textual similarity between C_1 and C_2 which ranges from 0 (bad) to 1 (good). We then sort the matching results by similarity scores in descending order, take the first seven elements at most as the knowledge outline points, and add them to the original outline points, eventually resulting in a new outline:

$$N = [x_1, x_2, \ldots, x_m, k_1, k_2, \ldots, k_l] \tag{2}$$

where N denotes the new outline, x_i represents the i-th original outline point, k_z refers to the z-th additional knowledge outline point, and l is the total number of the knowledge outline points which ranges from 0 to 7.

3.4   Neural Story Generator

We leverage LongLM [6] as the story generator of our framework. LongLM is a Chinese long text pre-trained language model based on the encoder-decoder architecture of Transformer [25]. The maximum sequence length of LongLM is set to 512 for both the encoder and decoder. LongLM comes in three different versions, with parameter counts ranging from a low of 60 million to a high of 1 billion, and we utilize the version of $LongLM_{base}$ which has 223M parameters.

Given a new outline N and its corresponding story S, the LongLM first converts N into a vector representation through an embedding layer composed of word embedding and positional embedding, then passes it to the encoder of LongLM to produce the hidden states:

$$h_0^N = \text{Embedding}(N) \tag{3}$$

$$h_r^N = \text{EncoderBlock}(h_{r-1}^N), \quad r \in \{1, \ldots, u\} \tag{4}$$

where h_0^N denotes the initial hidden state of the encoder, the EncoderBlock will perform multi-head attention and feedforward operations, generating a set of representations of the hidden states $H_N = \{h_0^N, h_1^N, \ldots, h_u^N\}$.

The decoder of LongLM takes the embedding of the story S and the hidden representations H_N as input and produces a set of hidden representations $H_S = \{h_0^S, h_1^S, \ldots, h_v^S\}$. The hidden states of the decoder are then used to compute the probability distribution over the target vocabulary for the next token using a softmax function:

$$h_0^S = \text{Embedding}(S) \tag{5}$$

$$h_d^S = \text{DecoderBlock}(h_{d-1}^S, H_N), \quad d \in \{1, \ldots, v\} \tag{6}$$

$$P(t) = \text{Softmax}(h_v^S W_e^T) \tag{7}$$

where h_0^S represents the initial hidden state of the decoder, v indicates the number of the decoder blocks, and W_e^T signifies the transpose embedding matrix of the story S.

The training phase commences with the initialization of our framework using LongLM$_{base}$ parameters. We then fine-tune it by minimizing the cross-entropy loss:

$$\mathcal{L} = -\sum_{n=1}^{G} \log P(t_n | t_{<n}, N) \tag{8}$$

where G is the number of tokens in the story S, t_n is the n-th token, and $P(t_n|t_{<n}, N)$ is the probability of generating t_n given the previous tokens $t_{<n}$ and the new outline N.

3.5   Exerting the Two-Stream Decoding Mechanism

In order to improve the coverage of story outline points in the generated story, we incorporate a two-stream decoding mechanism into our framework. As shown in Fig. 2, LongLM first receives the new outline, which is created by combining commonsense knowledge outline points and the original outline points, and the corresponding original story from the train set as input. We train the LongLM for the first time, and once the training is complete, we utilize it to generate a story given the new outline and call this generated story the pseudo story because the coverage of story outline points in this story is not yet sufficient. We refer to this generation process as the first stream decoding. Upon obtaining the pseudo story, we use it to find the missing outline points that do not appear in this pseudo story. We match the words in the pseudo story with the new outline points used for inference and only consider those outline points with coverage less than or equal to 0.5 as the missing outline points. Once all the missing outline points are acquired, we form the corresponding sentence using these missing outline points of the corresponding story and append this sentence to the end of the corresponding story. With these altered stories and the corresponding new outlines, we train the LongLM once more from the scratch. Following completion of training, the model is able to generate a story with increased coverage of outline points by inputting a new outline, and we refer to this generation process as the second stream decoding. Algorithm 1 describes the process of two-stream decoding. With the help of the two-stream decoding mechanism, the model can be ensured that most of the outline points appear in the generated story.

Algorithm 1. The Process of Two-Stream Decoding

Input: New outline N and its corresponding original story S
Output: Final generated story S^F
 1: Train LongLM with the new outline N and its corresponding original story S
 2: Finish the first training
 3: Use LongLM to generate a pseudo story S^P given the new outline N (i.e., the first stream decoding)
 4: Find out the missing outline points from the pseudo story S^P
 5: Form a sentence using the found missing outline points
 6: Append the formed sentence to the end of the corresponding pseudo story S^P (i.e., obtain an altered story)
 7: Train LongLM from the scratch with the new outline N and its corresponding altered story
 8: Finish the second training
 9: Use LongLM to generate the final story S^F given the new outline N (i.e., the second stream decoding)
10: **return** final generated story S^F with more outline points

---

4 Experiments

4.1 Dataset

Our proposed framework is evaluated on the OutGen task dataset of LOT [6], a Chinese story benchmark for evaluating long text understanding and generation that contains 2427 high-quality stories within the OutGen task, each of which corresponds to an outline and a title. Each outline in the dataset consists of a set of 8 out-of-order phrases, the order of them does not necessarily correspond to their order within a story. We use the 60/10/30 data split for training/validation/testing, respectively, as specified in the LOT benchmark. Table 1 shows the dataset statistics.

Table 1. The statistics of the dataset of the OutGen task in LOT. The abbreviations char/sent denote character/sentence, respectively.

Dataset	Train	Val	Test
# Examples	1,456	242	729
Vocabulary Size	19k	6k	12k
Avg. # Word in Input Title	4.64	4.89	4.64
Avg. # Word in Input Outline	19.20	19.05	19.47
Avg. # Phrase in Input Outline	8.00	8.00	8.00
Avg. # Char in Output Text	169.94	169.80	170.49
Avg. # Word in Output Text	108.91	108.68	109.04
Avg. # Sent in Output Text	7.20	7.11	7.15

Table 2. Experimental results of automatic evaluation of the generated stories on the validation set and test set. We show the best score on each metric in bold and the second best score is underlined. The higher the score on the metric, the better the performance.

Models	Validation Set						Test Set					
	B-1	B-2	D-1	D-2	cover	order	B-1	B-2	D-1	D-2	cover	order
ConvS2S	29.23	10.38	3.45	21.79	14.81	25.34	29.00	10.14	1.60	13.95	15.45	25.77
Fusion	29.22	10.34	3.39	22.67	17.41	26.55	28.77	10.22	1.47	14.12	17.10	26.36
$GPT2_{base}$	30.43	14.87	10.95	44.38	60.90	55.52	30.17	14.91	7.62	36.87	60.87	55.90
$GPT2_{base}^{\dagger}$	35.29	18.31	13.89	51.36	64.01	57.64	35.79	18.68	9.89	43.52	64.43	56.96
PM	31.81	14.94	12.99	50.56	62.98	56.75	31.85	15.24	8.62	41.32	63.15	57.21
PW	35.84	18.47	11.86	47.62	64.93	57.30	35.12	17.96	8.68	40.17	63.70	55.17
$mT5_{base}$	36.71	22.25	14.52	50.01	77.98	<u>63.15</u>	36.33	22.07	<u>10.90</u>	43.65	78.66	<u>63.79</u>
$LongLM_{base}$	**40.33**	**24.29**	<u>14.66</u>	<u>51.82</u>	<u>79.60</u>	62.78	**40.25**	<u>24.15</u>	10.75	<u>44.40</u>	<u>79.88</u>	63.67
Ours	<u>37.53</u>	<u>22.71</u>	**15.50**	**56.82**	**91.52**	**66.33**	<u>39.24</u>	**24.17**	11.73	**49.48**	**92.17**	**67.33**

4.2 Baselines

We compare our generative framework with the following competitive baselines from Huggingface[4]: (1) **ConvS2S** [5]: It is a seq2seq model that uses convolutional layers in the encoder and decoder, and an attention mechanism in the decoder, to process the input and generate the output sequences. (2) **Fusion** [2]: It generates a story by first training a convolutional seq2seq model, which is then fixed and the second clone model is initialized. These two models are subsequently trained jointly via a fusion mechanism. (3) $\mathbf{GPT2}_{base}$ [30]: This version of GPT-2 [19] is based on the uer/gpt2chinese-cluecorpussmall model. (4) $\mathbf{GPT2}_{base}^{\dagger}$ [6]: It has the same model architecture as the $GPT2_{base}$ and is pretrained on the corpus of LOT benchmark. (5) **PlotMachines (PM)** [21]: This model generates paragraphs by taking an outline as input and updating a memory matrix that tracks plot elements from the outline. We use $GPT2_{base}$ as the backbone of this model. (6) **Plan&Write (PW)** [29]: It generates a story by first planning a storyline and using that storyline as a guide. We also use

---

[4] https://huggingface.co/models.

GPT2$_{base}$ as the backbone of this model. (7) **mT5**$_{base}$ [27]: It is a multilingual variant of T5 [20] and is based on the google/mt5-base model.

4.3 Evaluation Metrics

We conduct both automatic evaluation and human evaluation in our experiments.

Automatic Evaluation Metrics. In line with the LOT benchmark [6], we utilize the metrics of BLEU-n (B-n) [17], Distinct-n (D-n) [13], Coverage (cover), and Order (order) for automatic evaluation, setting n = 1, 2 for both BLEU-n (B-n) and Distinct-n (D-n). The quality of the generated texts is measured by the BLEU-n, which compares the degree of n-gram overlap with the ground-truth texts. The textual diversity of the generated texts is evaluated by the Distinct-N, which calculates the number of distinct n-grams. The Coverage score, which is calculated as the recall rate [14] between the generated texts and input outline phrases, is used to evaluate the controllability of the generated texts. The Order score is computed as the average of the ratio between the number of inversions in the generated story and the total number of possible pairs of positions for any two phrases [6].

Human Evaluation Metrics. The automatic evaluation may have limitations in evaluating the generated texts, therefore we perform the human evaluation to gain a better understanding of the capability of our framework in generating stories. We randomly select 100 examples from the test set and employ three proficient Chinese annotators to evaluate 500 stories generated by our proposed framework and four typical models including ConvS2S, GPT2$_{base}$, mT5$_{base}$, and LongLM$_{base}$. The annotators are asked to score each generated story from 1 (bad) to 5 (good) in terms of the following three human evaluation metrics: (1) grammaticality (Gram): whether the generated story is grammatically correct and fluent; (2) coherence (Cohe): whether the generated story adheres to causal and temporal dependencies; and (3) relatedness (Relat): whether the generated story contains those input outline points that are used reasonably.

4.4 Implementation Details

Our proposed framework employs LongLM$_{base}$ restored from the available checkpoint[5] in Huggingface as the generative model, which is implemented in pytorch. The total number of parameters in LongLM$_{base}$ is 223M, with 12 attention heads and 12 hidden layers in each encoder and decoder. We fine-tune LongLM$_{base}$ with the cross-entropy loss on 2 T T4 GPUs. We use AdamW optimizer [16] with an initial learning rate of 1e-4. We set the batch size to 5, the maximum sequence length to 512, and the number of steps for linear warmup to 100. We leverage top-k sampling [2] with k=40 to generate outputs. All the baseline models are set to the base version due to our limited computational resources.

---

[5] https://huggingface.co/thu-coai/LongLM-base.

4.5   Results and Analysis

Automatic Evaluation. Table 2 presents the experimental results of the automatic evaluation of the generated stories on the validation set and the test set. The results show that our framework performs well among all the baseline models. Specifically, our framework outperforms the second best model LongLM$_{base}$ on the D-1, D-2, cover, and order metrics on the validation set, achieving scores that are 5.73%/9.65%/14.98%/5.66% higher, respectively. On the test set, our framework also achieves significantly better results than the LongLM$_{base}$ on the D-1, D-2, cover, and order metrics, with improvements of 9.12%/11.44%/15.39%/5.75%, respectively. The performance on D-n indicates that the stories generated by our framework exhibit diversity, which is largely attributed to the incorporation of Chinese commonsense knowledge into the story outlines in the train set. In addition, the high score obtained by our framework on the cover metric further demonstrates the high coverage of outline points in the generated stories, indicating the importance of the two-stream decoding mechanism. Meanwhile, the score on the order metric is relatively high, and we attribute this to the two-stream decoding mechanism. We have also noticed that our score on the B-n metric is nearly or even lower than that of LongLM$_{base}$, which might be caused by incorporating knowledge with low relevance to the story outlines when we add commonsense knowledge to them and then appending the sentences formed by the missing outlines with such knowledge to the pseudo stories during the two-stream decoding process. We leave the further study of solving this problem to future work.

Human Evaluation. The human evaluation results are shown in Table 3. The results demonstrate that our proposed framework exhibits superior performance compared to the baselines in all three metrics. The metrics Gram has been enhanced over the two strong baselines LongLM$_{base}$ and mT5$_{base}$ by 7.40%/25.64%, respectively, which shows the benefit of the incorporation of commonsense knowledge. Furthermore, our framework outperforms the model LongLM$_{base}$ by 5.60% on the metric Relat, and only 0.93% on the metric Cohe, indicating that although the two-stream decoding mechanism can make outline points appear more reasonably in the generated stories, it may not effectively ensure that the generated stories adhere to causal and temporal dependencies, potentially due to the incorporation of low-relevance knowledge during the two-stream decoding process. The human evaluation results support the intuition that our proposed framework could generate stories with diversity and increased outline points coverage, thereby further validating the effectiveness of our proposed framework.

Ablation Study. In order to evaluate the individual contributions of each component of our framework, we conduct ablation tests by removing the proposed components respectively. We present the results of our ablation tests in Table 4. As shown in Table 4, when we remove the commonsense knowledge component

Table 3. Human evaluation results on generated stories for four typical models and our proposed framework. We highlight the best performance in bold.

Models	Gram	Cohe	Relat
ConvS2S	2.23	1.03	1.27
GPT2$_{base}$	2.74	1.87	1.73
mT5$_{base}$	3.12	1.65	2.36
LongLM$_{base}$	3.65	2.15	2.68
Ours	**3.92**	**2.17**	**2.83**

Table 4. Ablation study of our proposed framework. The abbreviation w/o means without. Knowledge indicates the commonsense knowledge component and Two-Stream Decoding indicates the component of the two-stream decoding mechanism.

Models	Validation Set						Test Set					
	B-1	B-2	D-1	D-2	cover	order	B-1	B-2	D-1	D-2	cover	order
Ours	37.53	**22.71**	**15.50**	56.82	**91.52**	66.33	39.24	**24.17**	**11.73**	**49.48**	92.17	**67.33**
w/o Knowledge	38.15	22.36	14.76	52.23	91.05	65.79	38.94	23.87	11.64	46.16	91.39	66.85
w/o Two-Stream Decoding	**38.70**	22.53	15.28	**57.36**	86.12	64.45	**39.25**	23.51	11.51	48.87	87.95	65.04

and only assemble the component of the two-stream decoding mechanism, our framework achieves the highest score on the cover metric, indicating the effectiveness of the component of the two-stream decoding mechanism in ensuring greater coverage of outline points in the generated story. Removing the component of the two-stream decoding mechanism and only using the commonsense knowledge component in our framework decreases the cover metric score and substantially increases the D-n metric score, demonstrating the ability of the commonsense knowledge component to enhance the diversity of the generated story. However, the B1 and D-2 metrics performance of an individual commonsense knowledge component remains similar to, or even somewhat exceeds, that of the combined components. We hypothesize that some irrelevant knowledge is introduced during the period of two-stream decoding, which might impact the quality of the generated stories to some degree. In conclusion, our framework can generate stories that are both diverse and cover a majority of outline points by integrating Chinese commonsense knowledge and the two-stream decoding mechanism components.

5 Conclusion and Future Work

In this paper, we present a novel outline-conditioned Chinese story generation framework that combines a two-stream decoding mechanism and Chinese commonsense knowledge integration. By integrating Chinese commonsense knowledge into the story outlines, our framework can further increase the diversity of the generated stories. To enhance the coverage of story outline points in the generated stories, we introduce the two-stream decoding mechanism to our framework. Experimental results demonstrate that the stories generated by our framework exhibit improved diversity and cover most of the outline points in the generated stories. In the future, we would like to investigate a suitable method to better control the appropriate appearance of outline points in the generated stories for enhancing the overall quality of these stories. Also, we will further consider designing a mechanism to better integrate external Chinese knowledge into the generated stories, making them more logical and diverse.

Acknowledgements. This work is supported in part by the Guangxi Key Technologies Research and Development Program Project (Grant No.AB22035034) and in part by the Guangxi Science and Technology Base and Talent Project (2021AC19285).

References

1. Chen, Y.R.: Generate coherent text using semantic embedding, common sense templates and Monte-Carlo tree search methods. Master's thesis, National Tsing Hua University (2021)
2. Fan, A., Lewis, M., Dauphin, Y.: Hierarchical neural story generation. In: ACL, pp. 889–898 (2018)
3. Fang, L., Zeng, T., Liu, C., Bo, L., Dong, W., Chen, C.: Outline to story: fine-grained controllable story generation from cascaded events. arXiv preprint arXiv:2101.00822 (2021)
4. Feng, X., Liu, M., Liu, J., Qin, B., Sun, Y., Liu, T.: Topic-to-essay generation with neural networks. In: IJCAI, pp. 4078–4084 (2018)
5. Gehring, J., Auli, M., Grangier, D., Yarats, D., Dauphin, Y.N.: Convolutional sequence to sequence learning. In: ICML, vol. 70, pp. 1243–1252 (2017)
6. Guan, J., et a;.: Lot: a story-centric benchmark for evaluating Chinese long text understanding and generation. In: TACL, vol. 10, pp. 434–451 (2022)
7. Guan, J., Huang, F., Zhao, Z., Zhu, X., Huang, M.: A knowledge-enhanced pre-training model for commonsense story generation. In: TACL, vol. 8, pp. 93–108 (2020)
8. He, H., Choi, J.D.: The stem cell hypothesis: dilemma behind multi-task learning with transformer encoders. In: EMNLP, pp. 5555–5577 (2021)
9. Huang, H., Tang, C., Loakman, T., Guerin, F., Lin, C.: Improving Chinese story generation via awareness of syntactic dependencies and semantics. In: AACL-IJCNLP, pp. 178–185 (2022)
10. Ji, H., Ke, P., Huang, S., Wei, F., Zhu, X., Huang, M.: Language generation with multi-hop reasoning on commonsense knowledge graph. In: EMNLP, pp. 725–736 (2020)
11. Khatib, K.A., Trautner, L., Wachsmuth, H., Hou, Y., Stein, B.: Employing argumentation knowledge graphs for neural argument generation. In: ACL-IJCNLP, pp. 4744–4754 (2021)
12. Lewis, M., et al.: BART: denoising sequence-to-sequence pre-training for natural language generation, translation, and comprehension. In: ACL, pp. 7871–7880 (2020)
13. Li, J., Galley, M., Brockett, C., Gao, J., Dolan, B.: A diversity-promoting objective function for neural conversation models. In: NAACL, pp. 110–119 (2016)
14. Lin, C.Y.: Rouge: a package for automatic evaluation of summaries. In: ACL, pp. 74–81 (2004)
15. Liu, Y., Wan, Y., He, L., Peng, H., Philip, S.Y.: KG-BART: knowledge graph-augmented BART for generative commonsense reasoning. In: AAAI, pp. 6418–6425 (2021)

16. Loshchilov, I., Hutter, F.: Decoupled weight decay regularization. arXiv preprint arXiv:1711.05101 (2017)
17. Papineni, K., Roukos, S., Ward, T., Zhu, W.J.: Bleu: a method for automatic evaluation of machine translation. In: ACL, pp. 311–318 (2002)
18. Radford, A., Narasimhan, K., Salimans, T., Sutskever, I.: Improving language understanding by generative pre-training (2018)
19. Radford, A., Wu, J., Child, R., Luan, D., Amodei, D., Sutskever, I., et al.: Language models are unsupervised multitask learners. OpenAI blog 1(8), 9 (2019)
20. Raffel, C., et al.: Exploring the limits of transfer learning with a unified text-to-text transformer. arXiv preprint arXiv:1910.10683 (2019)
21. Rashkin, H., Celikyilmaz, A., Choi, Y., Gao, J.: PlotMachines: outline-conditioned generation with dynamic plot state tracking. In: EMNLP, pp. 4274–4295 (2020)
22. Speer, R., Chin, J., Havasi, C.: Conceptnet 5.5: an open multilingual graph of general knowledge. In: AAAI, pp. 4444–4451 (2017)
23. Speer, R., Havasi, C., et al.: Representing general relational knowledge in conceptnet 5. In: LREC, pp. 3679–3686 (2012)
24. Tambwekar, P., Dhuliawala, M., Martin, L.J., Mehta, A., Harrison, B., Riedl, M.O.: Controllable neural story plot generation via reward shaping. In: IJCAI, pp. 5982–5988 (2019)
25. Vaswani, A., et al.: Attention is all you need. In: NIPS, pp. 5998–6008 (2017)
26. Wang, J., et al.: Incorporating commonsense knowledge into story ending generation via heterogeneous graph networks. In: DASFAA, pp. 85–100 (2022)
27. Xue, L., et al.: mT5: a massively multilingual pre-trained text-to-text transformer. In: NAACL, pp. 483–498 (2021)
28. Yang, P., Li, L., Luo, F., Liu, T., Sun, X.: Enhancing topic-to-essay generation with external commonsense knowledge. In: ACL, pp. 2002–2012 (2019)
29. Yao, L., Peng, N., Weischedel, R., Knight, K., Zhao, D., Yan, R.: Plan-and-write: towards better automatic storytelling. In: AAAI, pp. 7378–7385 (2019)
30. Zhao, Z., et al.: Uer: an open-source toolkit for pre-training models. arXiv preprint arXiv:1909.05658 (2019)
31. Zhou, H., Young, T., Huang, M., Zhao, H., Xu, J., Zhu, X.: Commonsense knowledge aware conversation generation with graph attention. In: IJCAI, pp. 4623–4629 (2018)

Multi-path Based Self-adaptive Cross-lingual Summarization

Zhongtian Bao[1,2]🔟, Jun Wang[3]🔟, and Zhenglu Yang[1,2(✉)]🔟

[1] TKLNDST, CS, Nankai University, Tianjin, China
1120200192@mail.nankai.edu.cn, yangzl@nankai.edu.cn
[2] Key Laboratory of Data and Intelligent System Security (DISSec),
Ministry of Education, Beijing, China
[3] Ludong University, Shandong, China
junwang@mail.nankai.edu.cn

Abstract. Cross-lingual summarization aims to generate a summary in one language from a document in another language. This research has garnered significant attention in recent studies, addressing the need for integrating diverse language sources. However, there is still room for improvement in fully fusing these sources, particularly in the context of readily available multi-parallel language samples. In this paper, we propose a novel model that employs a multi-path approach to adjust the model structure according to the specific information of the sample while facilitating cooperation between different languages and generation tasks. We utilize a language fusion module to integrate the information from various languages, followed by a generation fusion module that enables specific decoders to share this information. Specifically, we introduce a self-adaptive method for selecting and combining different paths between decoder layers based on the sample's context. Experimental results on English, French, and Spanish cross-lingual summarization tasks demonstrate that our proposed method outperforms established baselines.

Keywords: Cross-Lingual Summarization · Multi-Path Selection · Self-adaptive Network · Language Fusion · Generate Fusion

1 Introduction

The objective of Cross-Lingual Summarization (CLS) is to generate a summary in one language (e.g., English) by reading a document in another language (e.g., French). This research helps to efficiently comprehend the central concept of a foreign language document, which is increasingly important in highly interconnected global communities nowadays.

Due to its tight connection with the tasks of Machine Translation (MT) and Monolingual Summarization (MS), CLS models typically make use of the sufficiently large MT and MS corpora [3,5,20,21]. To further take advantage of the mature MT and MS techniques for CLS, researchers have recently turned to

Z. Jin et al. (Eds.): KSEM 2023, LNAI 14119, pp. 282–294, 2023.
https://doi.org/10.1007/978-3-031-40289-0_23

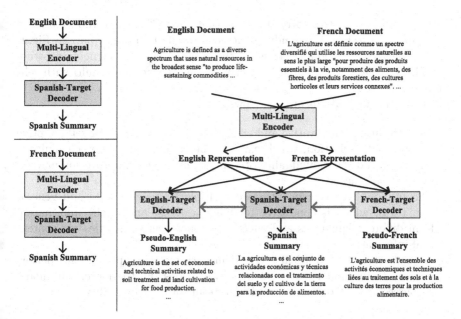

Fig. 1. An illustration of CLS procedures: The two sub-figures on the left show the traditional End2End mode w.r.t. English2Spanish and French2Spanish; In contrast, our model simultaneously reads multi-lingual documents and excavates the shared information across different languages. The red double-headed arrows between different language-target decoders indicate cooperation during summary generation. (Color figure online)

knowledge distillation methods such as Variational Auto-Encoder (VAE), compression rate, and other related approaches [11]. Conversely, the pre-trained technique shows promising potential in enhancing CLS performance, representing mT5 and mBart [8,19]. To accommodate the complex CLS scenarios, CLS-specific pre-trained models have been developed in recent years [6,11,12].

In addition to the above methodological contributions, enriching the CLS corpus is also deemed a promising way to improve performance. For instance, Wikipedia websites offer a rich source of multi-lingual data, which has benefited several CLS corpora with valuable information [10,12,14]. Other natural language processing datasets have also garnered interest from CLS research, including the datasets in dialogue summarization, query-based situations, and the legal domain [2,7,17].

Despite the success in enhancing CLS performance and enriching CLS corpus, most of the existing approaches resort to an End2End strategy, that is, compressing a document in language A to generate its summary in language B, as shown in the left part in Fig. 1. This strategy overlooks the possibility of concurrently reading multiple language documents. Moreover, the linguistic correlations across these documents are rarely attended by existing approaches.

To capture and model this correlation information in CLS, we introduce a novel multi-path approach in this study, as demonstrated at the right part in Fig. 1. This approach can self-adaptively select the optimal paths in the network structure. The existing CLS research has yet to be approached in a multi-path self-adaptive context.

Our main contributions are as follows:

(1) We introduce an innovative and efficient multi-path model for self-adaptive network path selection, which exploits the commonality between multiple languages and the individuality of a single language to improve summarization performance.

(2) The proposed model can integrate multiple language inputs and generation tasks, which is conducive to dynamically balancing the information from different languages and effectively generating summaries via contextual information.

(3) A comprehensive empirical study demonstrates the superior CLS performance of our model across various evaluations. Furthermore, our model surpasses the compared approaches in terms of interpretability.

2   Related Work

Intuitively, CLS encompasses two sub-tasks, MT and MS, as mentioned before [18]. Accordingly, traditional CLS methods are pipeline-based and typically assemble MT and MS as independent learning processes. These methods can be roughly classified as summarization-then-translation and translation-then-summarization ones [16]. While the two methods have distinctive advantages, this straightforward pipeline mode could hardly beat the best performance due to the error accumulation in translation and summarization steps. Moreover, the learning loss at one step cannot be propagated to the other step in this situation.

Researchers are working to address the error accumulation issue in translation and summarization processes by focusing on End-to-End (End2End) methods, aided by the Sequence-to-Sequence (Seq2Seq) architecture [5,18,20]. End2End methods can minimize error accumulation by directly employing a single model to generate the target cross-lingual summarization prediction without relying on the intermediate translation or summarization results. Due to the high performance of End2End models, this approach has become the primary trend in cross-lingual summarization [18]. Researchers are further integrating multi-task methods with the End2End model to enhance CLS performance, using translation or summarization sub-tasks to instruct the cross-lingual summarization model. In this process, the knowledge gained from MS and MT tasks can guide CLS learning. CLS research incorporates the Variational Auto-Encoder (VAE) [11], compression rate, and knowledge distillation techniques to create improved summaries with the help of this knowledge guidance.

CLS can also benefit from pre-trained models such as mBart and mT5 [8,19]. These transformer-based models are fine-tuned on extensive language corpora and learn statistical rules through large-scale data. The pre-trained models can achieve high performance in downstream tasks with few-shot learning. However, due to diverse CLS downstream scenarios, existing pre-trained models need to be improved in handling complex situations. Researchers have explored various cross-lingual tasks to address this gap to develop cross-lingual pre-trained models [6,13,17].

On the other hand, CLS requires sample improvements in both quality and scale. Researchers are addressing this issue by developing a range of CLS datasets and expanding them to cover different sub-tasks [1,6,10,12]. Initially, due to data source limitations, these datasets accumulated samples using back-translation methods [1,6,20]. However, researchers later discovered high-quality parallel language corpora in Wikipedia and began collecting samples from this platform [10,12,14]. Some CLS datasets also gathered instances from human-written scientific articles available in multiple languages [13]. In recent years, there has been a growing focus on assembling cross-lingual summarization datasets, which cover various aspects such as dialogue summarization, query-based situations, and the legal domain [2,7,17].

3   Our Framework

3.1   Preliminary

CLS. A typical CLS method reads a source document in language A, denoted as $D^A = \{x_1^A, x_2^A, ..., x_m^A\}$, to generate a summary in the target language B, represented as $S^B = \{y_1^B, y_2^B, ..., y_n^B\}$, where n is the length of label summary S^B. Given a source sequence $y_{<t}$, a CLS model will be trained to optimize the conditional probability of the target sequence y_t as follows:

$$Loss_{CLS} = \sum_{t=1}^{n} \log(S_t^B | S_{<t}^B, D^A), \tag{1}$$

Improving CLS Through Extra Language Information. This paper presents a novel method called Multi-document Cross-Lingual Summarization (MCLS), which utilizes information from other languages to enhance CLS performance. Given a document with similar semantics in other languages as inputs, represented as $D^A = \{D_1^A, D_2^A, ..., D_{m_A}^A\}$ in language A and $D^C = \{D_1^C, D_2^C, ..., D_{m_C}^C\}$ in language C, MCLS aims to generate a summary in the target language B, denoted as $S^B = \{S_1^B, S_2^B, ..., S_{n'}^B\}$, which compresses the semantic information of D^A and D^C.

MCLS leverages the monolingual summarization information in both languages A and C for CLS, as suggested in Fig. 1. The model's parameters are trained by optimizing the conditional probability, as expressed in the following equation:

$$Loss_{MCLS} = \sum_{t=1}^{n} \log(S_t^B | S_{<t}^A, S_{<t}^B, S_{<t}^C, D^A, D^C). \tag{2}$$

Based on the above theory, there exists a phenomenon that the documents and summaries will have different lengths under different language situations, which cause hard to align these inputs and outputs sequences. To better solve this situation, we first fine-tune the multi-lingual pre-trained model to capture this alignment information while focusing on the interaction between different languages in the second step. This fine-tuning progress can capture the entity's relationship in different language situations.

Transformer. Our method is based on the Transformer encoder-decoder framework [15], consisting of the stacked encoder and decoder layers. The encoder layers utilize a self-attention block to process the information generated by a position-wise feed-forward block. Meanwhile, the decoder layers incorporate encoder-decoder attention to extracting the relationship between encoders and decoders. Multi-head attention captures the subspace information within the encoder and decoder layers from different perspectives. Each head corresponds to a scaled dot-product attention mechanism that operates on the query Q, key K, and value V as follows:

$$\text{Attention}(Q, K, V) = \text{softmax}(\frac{QK^T}{\sqrt{d_k}})V, \tag{3}$$

where d_k represents the dimension of K.

The output values are combined with the outputs from multiple heads, and W^O is learned to project them to the desired dimension as follows:

$$\text{head}_i = \text{Attention}(QW_i^Q, KW_i^K, VW_i^V), \tag{4}$$

$$\text{MultiHead}(Q, K, V) = \text{Concat}(\text{head}_1, ..., \text{head}_h)W^O. \tag{5}$$

3.2   The Proposed Method

A visual depiction of the proposed method MCLS can be found in Fig. 2.

Language Fusion Module. In the transformer-based model, decoder layers employ self-attention to process predicted sequences and encoder-decoder-attention to capture the relationships within the encoder representation. In the scenario under consideration, the encoder shares the parameters to treat different language inputs while the decoder handles multiple language information based on the generation progress; Accordingly, we propose a language fusion module that combines different language information effectively.

The language fusion module employs an attention mechanism in each sub-word to dynamically estimate the weights of various languages' inputs based on the current generated context. This mechanism is formulated as follows:

$$\text{MultiHead}_i^{LF} = \Sigma_{l \in \mathbb{L}} \left(\alpha_l^{LF} \cdot \text{MultiHead}_i(v_l) \right), \tag{6}$$

$$\alpha_l^{LF} = \frac{\exp\left(w_{LF} \cdot \mathrm{MultiHead}_i(v_l)\right)}{\Sigma_{m\in\mathbb{L}} \exp\left(w_{LF} \cdot \mathrm{MultiHead}_i(v_m)\right)}, \tag{7}$$

where LF is the abbreviation of the Language Fusion, $\mathbb{L}$ is the set of different input languages, α_l^{LF}, is the actual weight of language l, and w_{LF} is the trainable weight to evaluate the importance of different languages.

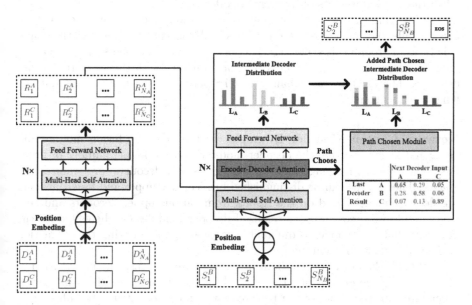

Fig. 2. Overview of MCLS. Initially, language documents (D^A, D^C) are fed into the encoder, generating representations (R^A, R^C). These representations are combined using the Encoder-Decoder Attention in the Language Fusion Module. Multiple Encoder-Decoder-Attention modules and Feed Forward Networks compute the intermediate distributions (S^A, S^B, S^C). The Path Chosen Module determines the relationship between the outcomes of different decoders and the inputs for the subsequent decoders. Based on the sample's context, our self-adaptive method selects the appropriate path through this relationship.

Generated Fusion Module. Decoders fine-tuned for specific tasks typically perform better than those designed for general tasks. This phenomenon is because the specialized decoders are fine-tuned from the same general decoder, resulting in high similarities among them. By visualizing the neural weights in various decoders, we observe that the most significant changes are concentrated in the Query portion of the self-attention layer and the encoder-decoder attention layer. Based on this finding, we propose a generative fusion module to facilitate collaboration between different generative tasks. During the target language (e.g., French) generation process, the decoder utilizes intermediate information generated from decoders of other languages (e.g., English and Spanish). The output can be represented as follows:

$$\text{MultiHead}_i^{GF} = \Sigma_{l \in \mathbb{L}} \left(\alpha_l^{GF} \cdot \text{MultiHead}_i^{LF}(\text{Parameter} = l) \right), \tag{8}$$

where GF is the abbreviation of the Generated Fusion, and α_l^{GF} is the weight calculated by different decoders' intermediate results. Given the fusion module incorporating multiple decoders' parameters, we utilize Parameter $= l$ to distinguish the varying weights of different decoders.

During this process, the outputs of the lower decoder modules will be fused, while the higher decoder modules will concentrate more on their specific tasks. Through this synergistic cooperation among decoders, the target language decoder can generate a cross-lingual summary with the support of other decoders. This strategy can enhance the CLS performance when reading multiple language documents.

Network Chosen Module. By employing the language fusion module and generated fusion module, the decoder model boasts an ample number of paths based on different language information inputs and decoders' pre-trained languages. These paths can be distinguished between the upper and lower layers of the decoder model based on the results from various upper decoders and specific modules. Moreover, the specialized decoder modules can benefit from the decoders that correspond to different language inputs, allowing the extraction of diverse semantic information.

Although the attention mechanism can dynamically fuse the information of different language documents, the position of the attention mechanism plays a crucial role due to the non-linear feature in neural network structures, illustrated as follows:

$$\text{Attention}\big(\text{Decoder}(l_x), \text{Decoder}(l_y)\big) \neq \text{Decoder}\big(\text{Attention}(l_x, l_y)\big). \tag{9}$$

The former term of Eq. 9 concentrates on the decoders' outcomes while disregarding the correlation between l_x and l_y. The latter term can capture the correlation without utilizing the entire decoder for information analysis. In contrast, our MCLS can integrate more critical information from various perspectives through self-adaptive multi-path selection. The attention mechanism of language numbers is employed to evaluate the connection across decoders, which enables MCLS to choose the paths considered in the attention mechanism self-adaptively.

The path-chosen method also plays a crucial role in our MCLS. We test the top-p and top-k paths to decide the connecting path between the upper and downer modules. The top-p method accumulates the path's weight until it exceeds the threshold p. The top-k method is to select the weightiest k path as the connection.

4 Experiments

4.1 Datasets

We conduct experiments on the WikiMulti dataset [14] and CrossSum dataset [4]. The WikiMulti dataset is a multi-lingual summarization dataset comprising 15 languages. We use these three subsets for the self-adaptive multi-path evaluation. The CrossSum dataset is a comprehensive cross-lingual abstractive summarization dataset derived from the XL-Sum dataset [9]. The following experiments extract English, Spanish, and Indonesian sections of CrossSum for testing.

Table 1. CLS performance under the F1 score of ROUGE on the English-Targeted, French-Targeted, and Spanish-Targeted WikiMulti Datasets: ROUGE-1, ROUGE-2, and ROUGE-L are represented by R-1, R-2, and R-L, respectively.

Model	English-Targeted			French-Targeted			Spanish-Targeted		
	R-1	R-2	R-L	R-1	R-2	R-L	R-1	R-2	R-L
pipeline-ST	28.38	8.57	17.01	29.93	9.92	17.39	32.85	10.75	19.66
pipeline-TS	29.41	9.97	18.14	32.16	12.51	20.12	33.18	12.71	20.52
mT5-m2m-CrossSum	38.41	12.99	21.21	40.23	17.29	26.32	40.89	16.83	26.12
VHM [11]	38.45	13.05	21.05	40.85	17.52	26.51	41.52	17.84	25.98
VHM + mBart [11]	39.41	13.51	21.05	41.55	18.64	27.54	43.02	18.45	27.58
mT5-General	36.23	12.10	20.34	39.75	16.77	26.16	40.57	16.12	25.71
mT5-Specific	38.10	12.53	20.70	40.10	17.10	26.36	40.85	16.85	26.09
Multi-Input Fusion	39.27	13.60	**21.37**	41.16	17.92	27.00	42.80	18.53	27.53
MP Global Pruning	39.22	13.55	21.15	41.61	18.62	**27.69**	43.03	**18.50**	27.60
MP Chosen	**39.54**	**13.61**	21.19	**41.97**	**18.79**	27.52	**43.21**	18.48	**27.64**

4.2 Experimental Setting

We train our models using the mT5-base configuration, which comprises a 12-layer encoder and a 12-layer decoder with 512-dimensional hidden representations. Following the setup of the mT5-m2m-CrossSum model [4], we employ the target language name as the decoder's starting token. Due to the extensive document length and limited GPU computational capacity, we constrain the mini-batch to one sample. To ease the oscillation of the loss function due to the one sample batch, we average the loss with every eight samples. We utilize the Adam Optimizer to adjust the entire model structure with parameters $\beta_1 = 0.9, \beta_2 = 0.998$, and $\varepsilon = 10^{-9}$. We implement a beam search with a beam size of four and a repetition penalty of 5.0 for evaluations.

Comparative Methods. We compare our method with (1) **Pipeline-TS**: a Transformer-based monolingual summarization model; (2) **Pipeline-ST**: utilizing Transformer-based monolingual summarization and Google Translator to generate summaries; (3) **mT5-m2m-CrossSum**: leveraging an extensive cross-lingual summarization dataset and fine-tuning the mT5 model using the LaSE (Language-agnostic Summary Evaluation) metric; and (4) **VHM**: using conditional VAE (Variational Auto-Encoder) to hybrid information taught by machine translation and monolingual summarization tasks.

4.3 Experimental Results

We evaluate the performance of all models using the standard ROUGE metric and report F1 scores for ROUGE-1, ROUGE-2, and ROUGE-L. Table 1 displays the results of various models on the English, French, and Spanish segments of the WikiMulti dataset. Table 2 displays model performance results on the English, Spanish, and Indonesian segments of the CrossSum dataset. The data shows that the Multi-Path Chosen method significantly surpasses the baseline mT5-Specific in all scenarios. Moreover, incorporating language fusion and generated fusion modules improves cross-lingual summarization performance through collaboration across different languages and generated tasks, particularly in Spanish, which has fewer samples in the training set. Furthermore, the Multi-Path Chosen method, featuring self-adaptive path selection, can dynamically modify the decoders' paths, outperforming the Multi-Path Global Pruning method.

Table 2. CLS performance under the F1 score of ROUGE on the English-Targeted, Spanish-Targeted, and Indonesian-Targeted CrossSum Datasets.

Model	English-Targeted			Spanish-Targeted			Indonesian-Targeted		
	R-1	R-2	R-L	R-1	R-2	R-L	R-1	R-2	R-L
mT5-m2m-CrossSum	34.66	12.50	26.87	34.02	12.68	25.69	28.92	10.46	24.03
VHM [11]	35.12	12.49	27.05	34.59	12.24	25.12	28.64	10.50	24.12
VHM + mBart [11]	35.44	12.65	27.11	34.85	12.61	25.98	28.75	10.51	24.23
mT5-General	32.54	10.48	22.54	31.23	10.57	22.48	26.41	9.78	20.21
mT5-Specific	33.98	12.05	26.41	33.85	12.24	24.89	28.76	10.51	24.11
Multi-Input Fusion	35.27	12.76	27.24	34.98	12.54	26.01	28.95	10.41	24.11
MR Global Pruning	35.42	12.81	**27.30**	**35.11**	12.71	**26.08**	29.05	10.58	**24.58**
MR Chosen	**35.61**	**12.88**	27.05	35.08	**12.80**	26.05	**29.21**	**10.62**	24.35

Table 3. CLS performance of adopting different path selection techniques on the French-targeted WikiMulti dataset.

Model	French R-1	French R-2	French R-L
top-k=3	41.15	17.93	27.05
top-k=5	41.93	18.58	27.64
top-k=7	41.67	18.45	27.49
top-p=0.6	41.45	18.20	27.10
top-p=0.7	**41.97**	**18.79**	**27.52**
top-p=0.8	41.76	18.65	27.38

The Impact of Path Selection Threshold. We employ various selection methods to investigate the impact of path selection and compare their experimental results. Table 3 displays the performance of different top-p and top-k selection methods in the French-Target cross-lingual summarization using the WikiMulti dataset. The model chooses the English2English, French2French, and Spanish2Spanish paths when top-k = 3, resulting in high similarity performance comparable to Multi-Input Fusion. The model selects most paths between the previous and subsequent modules when top-k=7 or top-p=0.8, which leads to information disturbance and reduced performance.

Ablation Study. We evaluate several model variants to examine the significance of various components in our model, whose performance is shown in Table 4. The model's performance could be enhanced by collaborating with various languages and incorporating diverse generated information. Our ablation experiment revealed that the number of languages and generated fusion modules did not significantly impact the cross-lingual summarization performance. An internal analysis of attention weight demonstrated that attention mechanisms in different decoder layers tend to produce similar results. Consequently, our extensive data experiments employ a shared attention mechanism, aiming to decrease the computational capacity required.

Table 4. The ablation study of the proposed model

Model	English R-1	English R-2	English R-L
baseline	36.23	12.10	20.34
w/ Language Fusion	38.42	13.25	20.89
w/ Language Fusion Individual	38.29	13.41	20.93
w/ Generated Fusion	36.63	12.38	20.14
w/ Generated Fusion Individual	36.58	12.42	20.15
w/ Language Fusion and Generated Fusion	**39.27**	**13.64**	**21.37**

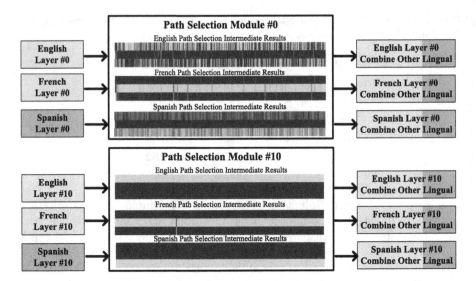

Fig. 3. Our proposed Path Selection Module features a neuron view in both Module #0 and #10. It consists of three rows, each representing a different decoder that calculates the relationship with English, French, and Spanish. The yellow section signifies a high weight, whereas the dark blue indicates a low weight. (Color figure online)

Path Selection Module Visualization. In order to analyze the internal correlations between inputs from different language documents, we visualize the intermediate results of the path selection module, as demonstrated in Fig. 3. We can observe the intricate path selection process between various layers. In the given sample, the model estimates a high correlation between the English-generated and Spanish-generated results, while the French-generated results exhibit a low relationship with the others. This sample's French summaries contain much more detailed information, which causes its path-chosen model to assess and reduce the correlation between French, English, and Spanish. Its French decoders focus on extract detail information to satisfy its French summary while ignoring information in English and Spanish.

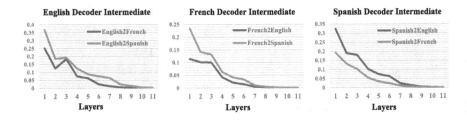

Fig. 4. The intermediate attention results w.r.t. connecting English, French, and Spanish in pairs.

Based on these intermediate estimates, the path selection module can combine information based on the sample's complicated situation. Our model's interpretability will significantly enhance with the assistance of this path selection module. Furthermore, by examining the inner visualizations of numerous samples, we can discern that the decoders concentrate on general information in the lower layer while focusing on specific information in the upper layer.

Language Interactive Visualization. In order to further examine the correlation among English, French, and Spanish languages, we compute the average attention weights within the language fusion modules. These attention results were derived from 11 layers of decoder modules using 1,000 training samples. The visualization of the intermediate attention results is depicted in Fig. 4. A detailed analysis reveals some samples extract more general information in the third layer than the second one, particularly in English-French scenarios. This phenomenon demonstrates our method can dynamically adjust the path selection between two layers to accommodate specific sample's information requirements. By employing this self-adaptive multi-path selection, our model outperforms baseline methods regarding cross-lingual summarization performance.

5 Conclusion

This paper presents a novel model that employs a multi-path approach to adapt the model structure based on individual sample information while allowing for cooperation between different languages and generation tasks. Our model integrates diverse language inputs to enable mutual complementation of information, subsequently fostering collaboration among various generation tasks. Experimental results have demonstrated that our method surpasses the baseline and achieves superior performance compared to the state-of-the-art approaches.

Acknowledgements. This work was supported in part by the National Natural Science Foundation of China under Grant No. 62106091 and Shandong Provincial Natural Science Foundation under Grant No. ZR2021MF054.

References

1. Shree Akshaya, A.T., Shankaran, S., Thrupthi, H., Mamatha, H.: Natural language processing based cross lingual summarization. In: Proceedings of 6th ICOEI, pp. 1825–1829 (2022)
2. Aumiller, D., Chouhan, A., Gertz, M.: EUR-Lex-Sum: a multi-and cross-lingual dataset for long-form summarization in the legal domain. In: Proceedings of 2022 EMNLP, pp. 7626–7639 (2022)
3. Bai, Y., et al.: Unifying cross-lingual summarization and machine translation with compression rate. In: Proceedings of 45th SIGIR, pp. 1087–1097 (2022)

4. Bhattacharjee, A., Hasan, T., Ahmad, W.U., Li, Y.F., bin Kang, Y., Shahriyar, R.: CrossSum: beyond English-centric cross-lingual abstractive text summarization for 1500+ language pairs. CoRR (2021)

5. Cao, Y., Liu, H., Wan, X.: Jointly learning to align and summarize for neural cross-lingual summarization. In: Proceedings of 58th ACL, pp. 6220–6231 (2020)

6. Cao, Y., Wan, X., Yao, J., Yu, D.: Multisumm: Towards a unified model for multi-lingual abstractive summarization. In: Proceedings of 34th AAAI, pp. 11–18 (2020)

7. Chen, Z., Lin, H.: Catamaran: a cross-lingual long text abstractive summarization dataset. In: Proceedings of 13th LREC, pp. 6932–6937 (2022)

8. Chipman, H.A., George, E.I., McCulloch, R.E., Shively, T.S.: mBART: multidi-mensional monotone BART. Bayesian Anal. **17**(2), 515–544 (2022)

9. Hasan, T., et al.: XL-sum: Large-scale multilingual abstractive summarization for 44 languages. In: Proceedings of 59th ACL-IJCNLP, pp. 4693–4703 (2021)

10. Ladhak, F., Durmus, E., Cardie, C., McKeown, K.: Wikilingua: a new bench-mark dataset for cross-lingual abstractive summarization. In: Proceedings of 2020 EMNLP, pp. 4034–4048 (2020)

11. Liang, Y., et al.: A variational hierarchical model for neural cross-lingual summa-rization. In: Proceedings of 60th ACL, pp. 2088–2099 (2022)

12. Perez-Beltrachini, L., Lapata, M.: Models and datasets for cross-lingual summari-sation. In: Proceedings of 2022 EMNLP, pp. 9408–9423 (2022)

13. Takeshita, S., Green, T., Friedrich, N., Eckert, K., Ponzetto, S.P.: X-SCITLDR cross-lingual extreme summarization of scholarly documents. In: Proceedings of 2022 JCDL. pp. 1–12 (2022)

14. Tikhonov, P., Malykh, V.: Wikimulti: a corpus for cross-lingual summarization. In: Proceedings of. 2022 AINL, pp. 60–69 (2022)

15. Vaswani, A., et al.: Attention is all you need. In: Proceedings of NIPS, pp. 5998–6008 (2017)

16. Wan, X., Luo, F., Sun, X., Huang, S., Yao, J.g.: Cross-language document summa-rization via extraction and ranking of multiple summaries. Knowl. Inf. Syst. **58**(2), 481–499 (2019)

17. Wang, J., et al..: Clidsum: a benchmark dataset for cross-lingual dialogue summa-rization. In: Proceedings of 2022 EMNLP, pp. 7716–7729 (2022)

18. Wang, J., et al..: A survey on cross-lingual summarization. Trans. Assn. Comput. Linguist. pp. 1309–1321 (2022)

19. Xue, L., et al.: A massively multilingual pre-trained text-to-text transformer. In: Proceedings of 2021 NAACL, pp. 483–498 (2021)

20. Zhu, J., et al.: Ncls: neural cross-lingual summarization. In: Proceedings of 2019 EMNLP-IJCNLP, pp. 3054–3064 (2019)

21. Zhu, J., Zhou, Y., Zhang, J., Zong, C.: Attend, translate and summarize: an efficient method for neural cross-lingual summarization. In: Proceedings of 58th ACL, pp. 1309–1321 (2020)

Temporal Repetition Counting Based on Multi-stride Collaboration

Guoxi Gan, Jia Su$^{(\boxtimes)}$, Zonghui Wen, and Shenmeng Zhang

Capital Normal University, Beijing, China
{ganguoxi,sujia,wenzonghui,zhangshenmeng}@cnu.edu.cn

Abstract. Visual repetition occurs in various forms in our world, such as human activities, animal behaviors, and even natural phenomena. Visual repetition counting remains a challenging task, especially in long videos, where repetitions exhibit certain characteristics such as discontinuous actions and inconsistent cycles. The existing methods that focus on counting repetitive actions in short videos face challenges in accurately counting repetitions in long videos due to these characteristics. To tackle this challenge, we propose a multi-stride collaborative counting framework based on adaptive temporal correlation to estimate repetitions in short and long videos. Our framework predicts the final counting result based on the counting results of the same video sampled with different strides. Additionally, since existing repetition counting datasets do not adequately cover all the challenging scenarios considered in our work, we have collected and labeled a new dataset called ActCount, which includes 172 videos with approximately 1,870 annotated repetitive actions. Our dataset includes repetitions that are non-human-centric, making it more realistic and challenging. Specifically, our model outperforms all previous models on the RepCount dataset, achieving an MAE of **0.3053** and an OBO of **0.3708**, setting a new state-of-the-art benchmark.

Keywords: Temporal repetition counting · Self-attention · Adaptive temporal correlation

1 Introduction

Repetitive actions are common in various real-world scenarios, such as physical exercise [1], stringed instrument performances, and even medical diagnosis [2]. Temporal repetition counting involves the task of counting repetitive actions in videos, offering valuable insights into our bodies and the world around us. In the field of computer vision, temporal repetition counting in videos plays a vital role as an auxiliary tool, supporting various tasks such as action classification and segmentation [3], medical assessment [4], action localization [5], 3D reconstruction [6], and camera calibration [7].

Computer vision solutions have a long tradition of addressing this challenging problem. Early research has emphasized the estimation of repetitive motion using the Fourier analysis [8] and continuous wavelet transform [9]. Current

Z. Jin et al. (Eds.): KSEM 2023, LNAI 14119, pp. 295–306, 2023.
https://doi.org/10.1007/978-3-031-40289-0_24

state-of-the-art solutions [10–13] for counting repetitions in videos rely on convolutional neural networks and large-scale datasets [12] annotated with counts. While existing works have achieved success, they primarily focus on short videos (*i.e.* with an average length of around 10 s) and may not be as effective for longer videos that feature repetitions with discontinuous actions or inconsistent cycles. A recent transformer-based counting method [14] has demonstrated efficacy for both long and short videos. However, further exploration is still necessary to enhance the performance of counting methods for videos of varying lengths.

In previous methods of repetitive action counting [12,14], a uniform approach was employed, where a fixed number of frames were extracted from each video, regardless of their length. This approach proves to be effective for short videos, as it allows for the extraction of sufficient information. However, for longer videos, this method is considered inadequate, as a limited number of frames cannot capture the comprehensive information present in the video. An alternative approach is to sample every video with an appropriate stride (*i.e.* frame rate). In general, small-stride sampling is appropriate for high-frequency actions (*e.g.*, battle rope) to prevent omissions, while large-stride sampling is suitable for low-frequency actions (*e.g.*, squatting) to avoid missing repetitions. However, in realistic scenarios involving long videos, actions usually display discontinuities or inconsistent cycles, makes it challenging to determine the most suitable stride. To balance performance and efficiency, we propose a multi-stride collaborative counting framework based on adaptive temporal correlation which can take into account videos of various lengths, as shown in Fig. 1. This method enables the collection of counting proposals from different temporal strides and synthesizes them to generate a final prediction.

Additionally, we observe that previous repetitive action datasets [11,12,14] are predominantly focus on human-centric actions or limited to short videos. These limitations hinder the effective validation of the model's generalization ability. Therefore, we introduce a new and challenging dataset named ActCount, which comprises not only repetitive movements in humans but also in other animals. Furthermore, our dataset exhibits competitive performance on various metrics, and additional details can be found in Sect. 4. This dataset offers a more comprehensive evaluation of the effectiveness and robustness of counting methods.

Our main contributions are summarized as follows:

- We present a new multi-stride collaborative counting framework based on adaptive temporal correlation, which can take care of not only high and low frequency actions, but also long and short videos, to count repetitive actions.
- We introduce a new dataset named ActCount, which contains not only various human repetitive actions, but also some other nonhuman repetitive actions in nature.
- We demonstrate state-of-the-art performance on a new benchmark, RepCount. Moreover, we achieve better performance on our proposed dataset, as well as on an unseen dataset called UCFRep, without fine-tuning.

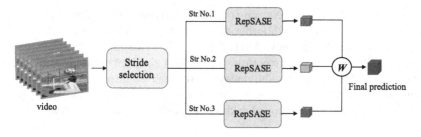

Fig. 1. Our counting framework consists of two parts, namely the stride selection module and the counting module(*i.e.* RepSASE). The RepSASE separately calculates the sampled videos obtained from the top three ranked strides, and weights the counting results based on the stride score to obtain the final prediction.

2 Related Work

2.1 Repetitive Activity Counting

In recent years, the task of counting repetitive actions from video has gained increasing attention from computer vision researchers. Levy and Wolf [10] introduced a classification network that was trained on synthetic data for real-time repetition estimation. However, the synthetic data are generated based on the assumption of continuous, uninterrupted, uniformly distributed motion with similar periods. Consequently, their network is incapable of handling repetitions with varying periods. To address non-static and non-stationary video dynamics, Runia et al. [9] utilized wavelet transform to handle the diverse range of repetitive appearances. However, their approach detects repetition solely based on the motion field, which conflicts with scenarios like summing, where repetitions cannot be distinguished by the motion field alone. Zhang et al. [11] proposed an effective context-aware framework based on a 3D convolution network. However, the approach predicts the temporal length of every two repetitions through iterative refinement, which can make it less appealing from a computational perspective. Dwibedi et al. [12] proposed a method that estimates repetitions using temporal self-similarity between video frames. While this approach seems promising, the rate selection scheme it employs is not optimal for accurate counting, as it tends to choose high frame rates that may lead to omissions. To leverage the available information in a video fully, Zhang et al. [13] pioneered the combination of both audio and visual information to address the challenge of counting repetitions. However, the applicability of this method is significantly limited since not all videos include audio data. All of the above works focus only on short videos, while our work covers both short and long videos simultaneously.

2.2 Video Feature Extraction

Convolution neural networks (CNNs) and vision transformers (ViTs) [15] have been two dominant frameworks for video spatiotemporal feature extraction in the past few years. Though CNNs can efficiently decrease local redundancy by convolution within a small neighborhood, the limited receptive field makes it hard to capture global dependency. Alternatively, ViTs can effectively capture long-range dependency via self-attention, while blind similarity comparisons among all the tokens lead to high redundancy. UniFormer architecture [16], which can seamlessly integrate the merits of convolution and self-attention in a concise transformer format, is a proper backbone for video feature extraction.

2.3 Adaptive Temporal Auto-Correlation

The temporal auto-correlation analysis can reveal potential connections between video sequences [17]. In the field of repetition counting, auto-correlation analysis in the time dimension helps us to extract periodic information. One approach to characterize temporal auto-correlation is through the implementation of a temporal self-similarity matrix [18] using Euclidean distance of frame deep features. Another approach to represent auto-correlation is through vector inner product. During the implementation of the attention mechanism, Vaswani et al. [19] construct two matrices (query and key), and then multiply these two matrices to obtain the auto-correlation matrix. Hu et al. [14] utilized the multi-head self-attention mechanism to compute the similarity matrix, enabling the acquisition of auto-correlation matrices for video embeddings. But their method treats these matrices as independent feature channels, ignoring the interdependence between the matrices, resulting in sub-optimal results. At this point, our proposed adaptive temporal auto-correlation encoding network, which can adaptively re-calibrates matrix-wise feature responses by explicitly modeling interdependencies between temporal correlation matrices, presents a superior option. With adaptive auto-correlation matrices, the periodicity information in complex and diverse situations can be effectively mined.

2.4 Temporal Stride Selection

Selecting the most appropriate temporal stride is crucial for video repetition counting task since clips with small strides may miss at least two repetitions, while excessively large strides may cause the network to overlook some repetitions. Dwibedi et al. [12] employed a multi-stride scoring strategy to determine the optimal stride for each video. Specifically, they needed to calculate the score of counting results at each stride, and then select the stride with the highest score as the optimal stride. While appealing, such a stride selection scheme is not optimal for accurate counting, as it is prone to select high frame rates leading to omissions. Hu et al. [13] have developed a time-efficient stride decision module for video action classification, although its improvements are somewhat limited. The possible reason is that the stride selection strategy under coarse-grained tasks (*e.g.*, video action classification) may not be suitable for fine-grained tasks (*e.g.*, repetition counting). Compared to their works, the stride selection model we proposed based on counting result can make a trade off between performance and efficiency.

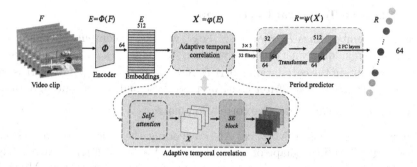

Fig. 2. RepSASE architecture. We use sliding windows with step size 1 to generate the video sub-clip with an overlap. Then extract features from video sub-clip by the encoder. Calculate the correlation matrix and assign them different weights by SE block. Then make adaptive temporal correlation matrices throughout the remaining network and output the final counts.

3   Method

Our proposed base model, RepSASE, consists of three components: the encoder, the adaptive temporal correlation and the period predictor. Figure 2 shows the overall architecture of RepSASE. Overall, given a sequence of N frames $F = [f_1, f_2, \ldots, f_N]$, we obtain the final output with the following steps. Firstly, we feed F to the encoder ϕ as $E = \phi(F)$ to produce double-frame embeddings $E = [e_1, e_2, \ldots, e_N]$, which $e_i = \phi(f_i, f_{i+1})$. Then, we use the embeddings E to obtain the adaptive temporal correlation matrices $X' = \left[x'_1, x'_2, \cdots, x'_n\right]$ by self-attention mechanism and SE block. Finally, X' is fed to the period predictor module which outputs the final prediction.

3.1   Encoder

We use the Uniformer [16] as the backbone to extract 3d features from video clip. It flexibly unifies convolution and self-attention in a concise transformer format, which can tackle both local redundancy and global dependency for effective and efficient visual recognition [16]. Let frame sequence F pass through the feature extraction block to extract the features. The resulting features are of size $7 \times 7 \times t \times 512$, where the t is equal to N in the temporal dimension. Building upon previous works [12], we pass these spatiotemporal features through a layer of 3D convolutions to add more local temporal context. 512 filters of size $3 \times 3 \times 3$ are used with ReLU activation. And then, for reducing the dimensionality of extracted spatiotemporal features, we use a Global 3D Max-pooling layer over the spatial dimensions to reduce model parameters. Finally, we can obtain the final result E of encoder ϕ as the embeddings in Fig. 2.

3.2   Adaptive Temporal Correlation

Once we get embeddings $E = [e_1, e_2, \ldots, e_N]$, we need to compute correlation x_i between e_i embedding with other e_j, where $i, j \in \{1, 2, \cdots, N\}$ and $j \neq i$, such that we can obtain the correlation matrices $X = [x_1, \quad x_2, \cdots, x_H]^T$, and H is the number of attention-head. After that, we pass these matrices X through an SE block to obtain the final adaptive correlation matrices $X' = \left[x_1', \quad x_2', \cdots, x_H'\right]^T$.

Adaptive Correlation Matrix. After encoding the video clip, we can get embeddings E. And the shape of embeddings is 64×512 as Fig. 2. Then we use the self-attention mechanism [19] to calculate the correlation matrix. Multiply two initialized weight matrices with embeddings E, matrix query(Q) and matrix key(K) will be obtained. Dot-product attention is used to calculate the attention scores. And we could get the attention scores matrix as correlation matrix. After that, we use a learnable component SE block [20] to assign weights to attention scores. Specifically, let attention scores matrix as input x, make it perform squeezing operation and excitation operation, and the final output of the block $\tilde{x}$, which called adaptive correlation matrix in this paper, is obtained by rescaling the output x with the activations.

Self-attention. In detail, given Q and K, we compute the dot product of the Q with K, divide each by $\sqrt{d_k}$, where d_k is dimension of K. Then the correlation matrix $C = [c_1, \quad c_2, \cdots, c_H]^T$ been constructed. As shown in Fig. 2, we use 4 heads with 512 dimensions and each head being 128 dimensions in size. Therefore, after the self-attention layer, the shape of output is $[N, N, H]$.

Squeeze-and-Excitation (SE) Block. The SE block we used in this paper comes from [20]. The squeeze operation is achieved by using global 2D average pooling to generate channel-wise statistics. For excitation operation, two fully connected layers are used, and the ReLU activation function is between them. After obtaining the correlation matrices computed by the multi-head self-attention mechanism, we feed these matrices $X = [x_1, \quad x_2, \cdots, x_H]^T$ into the SE block to adaptively capture attentions to different matrices. Then we obtain the final adaptive temporal correlation matrix $X' = \left[x_1', \quad x_2', \cdots, x_H'\right]^T$, which is used as the input of the predictor.

3.3   Period Predictor

The architecture of the period predictor module can be viewed in Fig. 2. Our predictor generates one output: the radio estimation after standardization $R = \psi(X')$ of d to L_{half}, where d means the distance of per frame to the nearest period boundary frame and L_{half} means the half of period length. The processing pipeline starts with 32 2D convolutional filters of size 3×3, followed by a transformer [19] layer which uses a multi-headed attention. Then two fully connected layers of size 512 are used to output $R = [r_1, r_2, \cdots, r_n]$, and we also refer to r as the relative distance from per frame to the nearest boundary frame (DNB).

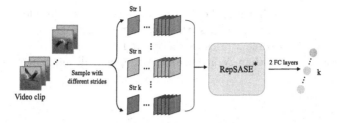

Fig. 3. Stride selection module. We send k clips from the same video with k different strides into the network, and the network outputs the score of each stride. We select the stride with highest score.

3.4 Temporal Stride Selection

We incorporate an extra module for regressing the score of different strides for each video, as shown in Fig. 3. We replace the output layer of RepSASE with a new layer of size k. For training this module, we define the loss function as follows:

$$L_{str} = \frac{1}{N} \sum_{i=1}^{N} L(s_i, \bar{s}_i),$$

where L is the smooth L1 loss [21], $\bar{s}$ is the score ground truth. During inference, we send a series of clips from the same video with different strides into the network, and select three strides with the highest score.

Training Details. For each training video, the trained RepSASE model predicts the counting result with a series of temporal strides, *i.e.* $str = 2, ..., n, ..., k$, where k is the maximum stride we use (k is set to 8 in this paper). Then we can obtain corresponding predictions $C_i^1, ..., C_i^k$. We choose the smallest stride that is enough to contain at least two repetitions as stride ground truth C_i^{gt}. For all strides, we compute their stride score ground truth by:

$$\bar{s}_i^k = \ln\left(\frac{min(C_i^k, C_i^{gt})}{max(C_i^k, C_i^{gt})}\right),$$

where $\bar{s}_i^k$ is the kth stride score ground truth with the parameterizations of scale-invariant center translation and the log-space counting result shifting [22].

3.5 Inference

To robustly output the number of repetitions in a given video, two primary operations are necessary:

Count From Period Predictor. Once we get $R = [r_1, r_2, \cdots, r_n]$, a linear sum is applied to R for obtaining the repetition counts c. Then three counts c_1, c_2 and c_3 were obtained duo to three branches. Finally, we use an equally weighted linear average to obtain the final result $C = avg(c_1, c_2, c_3)$.

Temporal Stride Selection. For an input video, the stride selection module outputs the scores of seven strides, then we sample three group N consecutive frames with the top three strides as the input for RepSASE. If the number of sampled frames is less than N at current stride, we will implement padding in the temporal domain.

4 Datasets

Existing datasets for repetition counting [11,14] focus only on human repetitive action counting. These datasets can only unilaterally test the ability of existing methods to count repetitions. As we focus on verifying method with a more comprehensive perspective, we collect a new hybrid dataset, containing both human and non-human repetitive actions, which named ActCount.

Data Collection and Labeling. We collected 172 video clips from *Douyin* and *Keep*. Some videos contain common human repetitive actions *e.g.*, jack jumping, pulling-up, squatting, etc. and others contain non-human repetitive actions *e.g.*, geese flying, woodpecker peaking, dog drinking, etc. The summary of our dataset is shown in Table 1. Our dataset is also challenging because it incorporates some repetitive action scenes in nature, which are more realistic.

Table 1. Dataset statistic of UCFRep [11] and the proposed ActCount. Our dataset is feature with containing non-human repetitive motion in videos, which not found in other datasets.

	UCFRep	ActCount
Num. of videos	526	172
Dur Avg. ± Std.	8.15 ± 4.29	**18.08±11.55**
Dur Min./Max	2.08/33.84	**2/59**
Count Avg. ± Std.	6.66	**10.99±8.24**
Count Min./Max	3/54	**2/57**
Hum/Non-hum	526/0	**142/30**

5 Experiment

5.1 Implementation Details

For training RepSASE, we use smooth L_1 [21] as loss function. All input video frames of the network are resized to 224×224. We initialize the encoder, uniformer-small-k400-16×4 [16], with weights from a *Kinetics*400 [23] pre-trained checkpoint. Due to GPU memory limitations, the parameters of the pre-trained encoder were frozen during the training process. For remaining model layers, we train them for 5K steps with a declining learning rate of 1×10^{-6}. Model optimized by the Adam optimizer [24] using a batch size of 8.

5.2   Benchmarks and Evaluation Metric

We evaluate our method on three datasets: UCFRep [11], RepCount (part-A) [14] and our ActCount. Due to privacy restrictions, RepCount (part-B) is not publicly available. Following the previous works [12, 14], two metrics are used in our work.

Off-By-One (OBO) Count Accuracy. If the error between the prediction and the ground truth is within one, we will consider this video counted correctly. Otherwise, it counts wrongly. The metric represents the accuracy rate of repetition count over the entire dataset.

Mean Absolute Error (MAE) of the Count. MAE means normalized absolute error between the ground truth count and the predicted count.

5.3   Evaluation and Comparison

We compare our method with four recent SOTA repetition counting methods [11–14]. Note that for method [13], we only use the sight stream due to the original sound track of some videos are unavailable. Additionally, we also compare two SOTA action recognition methods [25, 26] and change output layers accordingly to adapt to our task. All the networks are trained on RepCount, obtaining the results shown in Table 2. It can be observed that our model outperforms the others by a significant margin. In detail, we can see that RepNet achieves the weakest performance. A possible reason is that for long videos in the real scenario, extracting fixed frames lead to a significant loss of periodic information. For these methods [11, 13], their performance are also not well. This is because anomalies in long videos violate the strong assumption of action continuity, resulting in significant challenges in training these models. Compared with TransRAC, our model takes into account not only the interdependencies between temporal correlation matrices but also the collaborative effect of multi-strides, thereby achieving better performance.

Table 2. Comparison with state-of-the-art. Our model outperforms action recognition methods and recent counting methods by a large margin.

Method	RepCountA		UCFRep		ActCount	
	MAE↓	OBO↑	MAE↓	OBO↑	MAE↓	OBO↑
TANet [26]	0.6624	0.0993	-	-	-	-
Video SwinT [25]	0.5756	0.1324	-	-	-	-
Zhang et al. [11]	0.8786	0.1554	0.7492	0.3802	0.8377	0.1627
RepNet [12]	0.995	0.0134	0.9985	0.009	-	-
Zhang et al. [13]	0.5268	0.2039	0.6233	0.2909	0.6057	0.1454
TransRAC [14]	0.4431	0.2913	0.6401	0.324	0.5512	0.1973
Ours	**0.3053**	**0.3708**	**0.3204**	**0.535**	**0.2549**	**0.4476**

5.4   Ablation Studies

We conduct three ablation experiments to validate the design decisions made in our counting framework. Our model is trained on the RepCountA training set.

Correlation Matrix. We compare the performance of different correlation matrix applied to our model. As shown in Table 3, results show that our proposed adaptive temporal correlation matrix achieves SOTA performance. In detail, the temporal self-similarity matrix (TSM) [12] achieves the weakest performance. The possible reason is that it has only one channel result in failing to represent the correlation in complex and diverse realistic scenes. Compared with the self-attention (S-att) mechanism, our adaptive correlation matrix (ACM) which takes into account the interdependence between the matrices achieves better performance.

Period Regressor. Compared with density map regressor (DM), our DNB regressor performs better. Because the density map generated by the Gaussian kernel function tends to focus on the middle segments of repetitive actions, our DNB takes into account the entirety of the repetitive action.

Table 3. Results of our model applying different components when trained on RepCountA training set.

					RepCountA		ActCount	
DM	DNB	TSM	S-att	ACM	MAE↓	OBO↑	MAE↓	OBO↑
	✓	✓			0.5053	0.2317	0.5518	0.2151
	✓		✓		0.4722	0.2649	0.4696	0.2616
✓				✓	0.3959	0.3377	0.381	0.3139
	✓			✓	**0.3035**	**0.3708**	**0.2549**	**0.4476**

Effect of Stride Selection. We conduct a study on the optimal number of strides to be fused. As shown in Fig. 4, the "random" means that we randomly

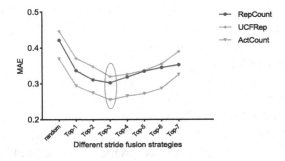

Fig. 4. The multi-stride collaborative counting method has significant advantages, especially when fusing the top three optimal strides.

select one stride from the candidate strides for testing. Regarding top-n, n means that we select the top n strides with the highest scores for testing. We observe that for long videos in realistic scenarios, randomly selecting strides results in significantly lower performance compared to the approach of strides collaboration. In particular, our model obtains the best result at $n = 3$, which is the value we use for all other experiments.

6   Conclusion

In this paper, we first propose the RepSASE, a new network designed to count repetitive actions. Based on RepSASE, we design the stride selection module and the final counting framework. Extensive experiments demonstrate the effectiveness of our framework which achieves state-of-the-art performance on multiple datasets. In addition, to comprehensively and objectively validate our proposed method, we introduce a new challenging counting dataset which contains both human and non-human repetitive actions. While our framework performs well on the majority of data, there are still some failure cases. For example, multiple individuals perform repetitive actions in one video. Our future work will focus on such hard cases.

References

1. Soro, A., Brunner, G., Tanner, S.: Recognition and repetition counting for complex physical exercises with deep learning. Sensors 19(3), 714 (2019)
2. Xie, W., Noble, J.A., Zisserman, A.: Microscopy cell counting and detection with fully convolutional regression networks. Comput. Methods Biomech. Biomed. Eng. Imaging Vis. 6(3), 283–292 (2018)
3. Lu, C., Ferrier, N.J.: Repetitive motion analysis: segmentation and event classification. IEEE Trans. Pattern Anal. Mach. Intell. 26(2), 258–263 (2004)
4. Li, X., Singh, V., Wu, Y., Kirchberg, K., Duncan, J., Kapoor, A.: Repetitive motion estimation network: recover cardiac and respiratory signal from thoracic imaging. arXiv preprint arXiv:1811.03343 (2018)
5. Laptev, I., Belongie, S.J., Pérez, P., Wills, J.: Periodic motion detection and segmentation via approximate sequence alignment. In: Proceedings of the IEEE International Conference on Computer Vision (ICCV), pp. 816–823 (2005)
6. Belongie, S.J., Wills, J.: Structure from periodic motion. In: Spatial Coherence for Visual Motion Analysis, pp. 16–24 (2006)
7. Huang, S., Ying, X., Rong, J., Shang, Z., Zha., H.: Camera calibration from periodic motion of a pedestrian. In: Proceedings of the IEEE Conference on Computer Vision and Pattern Recognition (CVPR), pp. 3025–3033 (2016)
8. Pogalin, E., Smeulders, A.W., Thean, A.H.: Visual quasi-periodicity. In: Proceedings of IEEE Conference on Computer Vision and Pattern Recognition (CVPR), pp. 1–8 (2008)
9. Runia, T.F., Snoek, C.G., Smeulders, A.W.: Real-world repetition estimation by div, grad and curl. In: Proceedings of the IEEE Conference on Computer Vision and Pattern Recognition (CVPR), pp. 9009–9017 (2018)

10. Levy, O., Wolf, L.: Live repetition counting. In: Proceedings of the IEEE International Conference on Computer Vision (ICCV), pp. 3020–3028 (2015)
11. Zhang, H., Xu, X., Han, G., He, S.: Context-aware and scale-insensitive temporal repetition counting. In: Proceedings of the IEEE Conference on Computer Vision and Pattern Recognition (CVPR), pp. 670–678 (2020)
12. Dwibedi, D., Aytar, Y., Tompson, J., Sermanet, P., Zisserman, A.: Counting out time: class agnostic video repetition counting in the wild. In: Proceedings of the IEEE Conference on Computer Vision and Pattern Recognition (CVPR), pp. 10387–10396 (2020)
13. Zhang, Y., Shao, L., Snoek, C.G.: Repetitive activity counting by sight and sound. In: Proceedings of the IEEE Conference on Computer Vision and Pattern Recognition (CVPR), pp. 14070–14079 (2021)
14. Hu, H., Dong, S., Zhao, Y., Lian, D., Li, Z., Gao, S.: Transrac: encoding multi-scale temporal correlation with transformers for repetitive action counting. In: Proceedings of the IEEE Conference on Computer Vision and Pattern Recognition (CVPR), pp. 19013–19022 (2022)
15. Dosovitskiy, A., et al.: An image is worth 16x16 words: Transformers for image recognition at scale. arXiv preprint arXiv:2010.11929 (2020)
16. Li, K., et al.: Uniformer: Unifying convolution and self-attention for visual recognition. arXiv preprint arXiv:2201.09450 (2022)
17. Kobayashi, T., Otsu, N.: Motion recognition using local auto-correlation of space-time gradients. Pattern Recogn. Lett. 33(9), 1188–1195 (2012)
18. Junejo, I.N., Dexter, E., Laptev, I., Perez, P.: View-independent action recognition from temporal self-similarities. IEEE Trans. Pattern Anal. Mach. Intell. 33(1), 172–185 (2010)
19. Vaswani, A., et al.: Attention is all you need. Adv. Neural. Inf. Process. Syst. 30, 5998–6008 (2017)
20. Hu, J., Shen, L., Sun, G.: Squeeze-and-excitation networks. In: Proceedings of the IEEE Conference on Computer Vision and Pattern Recognition (CVPR), pp. 7132–7141 (2018)
21. Girshick, R.: Fast r-CNN. In: Proceedings of the IEEE International Conference on Computer Vision (ICCV), pp. 1440–1448 (2015)
22. Girshick, R., Donahue, J., Darrell, T.: Rich feature hierarchies for accurate object detection and semantic segmentation. In: Proceedings of the IEEE Conference on Computer Vision and Pattern Recognition (CVPR), pp. 580–587 (2014)
23. Kay, W., et al.: The kinetics human action video dataset. arXiv preprint arXiv:1705.06950 (2017)
24. Kingma, D.P., Ba, J.: Adam: A method for stochastic optimization. arXiv preprint arXiv:1412.6980 (2014)
25. Liu, Z., et al.: Video swin transformer. In: Proceedings of the IEEE Conference on Computer Vision and Pattern Recognition (CVPR). pp. 3202–3211 (2022)
26. Liu, Z., Wang, L., Wu, W., Qian, C., Lu, T.: Tam: Temporal adaptive module for video recognition. In: Proceedings of the IEEE International Conference on Computer Vision (ICCV), pp. 13708–13718 (2021)

Multi-layer Attention Social Recommendation System Based on Deep Reinforcement Learning

Yinggang Li and Xiangrong Tong$^{(\boxtimes)}$

School of Computer and Control Engineering, Yantai University, 30 Qingquan Road,
Laishan District, YanTai 264000, ShanDong, China
txr@ytu.edu.cn

Abstract. The recommendation system based on deep reinforcement learning recommends interesting content to users through the interaction of recommendation agents and usersThis is to inform you that corresponding author has been identified as per the information available in the Copyright form.. However, most recommender systems based on deep reinforcement learning often face two limitations: **(1)** sparse user feedback data that makes the recommendation agent unable to accurately capture the user's dynamic preferences; and **(2)** users and items are isolated from each other due to the limitation of unstructured representation. To address this situation, this paper proposes a multi-layer attention social recommendation method based on deep reinforcement learning by fusing social network and user-item bipartite graph to form a heterogeneous information network. This method uses subgraphs in the heterogeneous information network to structurally represent users and items through a variant of the graph attention network. By doing so, users and items can perceive neighborhood information in the heterogeneous information network and enhance the correlation between nodes. At the same time, it can also avoid the repeated transmission of irrelevant nodes. Additionally, the attention mechanism is adopted in the graph attention network to reduce the influence of noisy nodes in the heterogeneous information network. Corresponding weights are given to the neighborhood information, and nodes with noise are given smaller weights. Then, the external attention mechanism is used to adjust the weight of historical items in the state information, which realizes the selective attention of different users to different items and generates the user's preference representation. Finally, the deep reinforcement learning method is used to simulate the interaction between the recommendation system and the user. This method adapts to the dynamic changes of user preferences and considers the long-term rewards brought by the recommended items. Experimental results show that this method can alleviate the above two problems and provide users with more accurate recommended items.

Keywords: deep reinforcement learning · attention mechanism · Recommendation System · social networks · graph neural network

1 Introduction

In the DRL approach, the agent learns the optimal strategy for maximizing long-term returns through trial-and-error and delayed rewards by interacting with the environment. However, in recommendation systems, it is not feasible to interact with users directly by deploying them on the platform because frequent trial and error may make users lose patience. As a result, a reasonable solution is to learn the offline recommendation strategy from the user-item bipartite graph [1]. Nevertheless, there are still two problems that need to be addressed in this approach.

(1) One of the key challenges in recommendation systems based on DRL is the sparse user interaction data problem. (2) Previous work in recommender systems based on DRL faced the challenge of isolating users and items due to unstructured representation.

An effective solution to address the data sparsity problem in recommendation systems is to integrate social networks. However, integrating social networks may introduce noise to the recommendation system, particularly from socially trusted neighbors who may not share similar preferences. To address this issue, MAS-DRLRC employs a multi-layer attention mechanism. Within the heterogeneous information network, the attention mechanism selectively focuses on neighboring nodes. When constructing the continuous state representation of users, an external attention mechanism assigns corresponding weights to users' historical interaction items based on different user characteristics, with greater weights given to key item information. This approach can help mitigate the noise introduced by socially trusted neighbors who do not share similar preferences.

Traditional deep learning methods have addressed the problem of isolated users and items by using Graph Convolution Networks (GCN) to aggregate node information in the entire graph and generate feature vectors for users and items. In summary, the main contributions of this paper are as follows:

(1) A multi-layer attentional social recommendation framework (MAS-DRLRC) based on deep reinforcement learning is proposed to explore items with long-term value by learning the dynamic preferences of users through deep reinforcement learning methods and end-to-end approaches.
(2) This method is designed to construct structured representations of users and items using sub-graphs.
(3) A two-layer attention mechanism has been designed to construct a state representation model.

2 Related Work

The interaction history between a user and a sequential recommendation system can be represented as a sequence, and the problem of sequential recommendation can be formulated as a Markov decision process and optimized through deep reinforcement learning. DRL-based recommendation systems aim to improve user state representations, design reward functions, and add additional neural networks to aid in DRL training. For example, Yu et al. [2] utilized a graph convolutional neural network to represent user states and actions as structured features in DQN to enhance connections between different users. Liu et al. [3] proposed four state representations based on deep deterministic policy gradient to improve product sequence perception in recommendation systems. Xin et al. [4] combined self-attention and convolutional neural networks to improve the user representation, and He et al.

3 Preliminaries

Define the heterogeneous information network $G = (U, I, E_{\text{trust}}, E_{\text{like}})$, where $U = \{u_1, u_2, \ldots, u_{m-1}, u_m\}$ is the set of users, $I = \{i_1, i_2, \ldots, i_{n-1}, i_n\}$ is the set of items. E_{trust} is the set of trust edges, which represents the trust relationship between user and user, if user u_c trusts user u_j, then the two are connected by directed edges $< u_c, u_j >$. E_{like} is the set of interaction edges indicating whether there is an interaction between the user and the item if the user u_c clicks or buys the item i_j, then the two are connected via directed edges $< u_c, i_j >$ and $< i_j, u_c >$ are connected. In addition, the sub-graph $G_f()$ denotes the node in parentheses and the nodes of order 1 to f neighbors to which the node directly points. As shown in Fig. 1, $G_1(u_1)$ denotes the first-order neighbor sub-graph of the target user u_1 and $G_2(i_5)$ denotes the second-order neighbor sub-graph of the target item i_5.

By common sense, there is the interaction between the user and the item, the item is not containing emotional color, and the relationship between the user and the item is mutual, we set the two-way edge is conducive to the transfer of information between the user and the item, beneficial to capture the potential connection between the user and the item.

Given a heterogeneous information network G, define a trust matrix $X \in \mathbb{R}^{m \times m}$. If user u_c trusts user u_j and there exists a directed edge between the two $< \mu_c, u_j >$, then $\chi_{cj} = 1$, otherwise $\chi_{cj} = 0$. Define the user-item interaction matrix $Y \in \mathbb{R}^{m \times n}$. If the user u_c clicks or purchases item i_j and both are connected by directed edges $< u_c, i_j >$, then $y_{cj} = 1$, otherwise $y_{cj} = 0$.

3.1 Problem Description

Given a heterogeneous information network G, a user $u_c \in U$ and an integer T, train a recommendation agent to be able to, at each time step $t(0 <= t <= T)$, from the set of items I in which u_c is most likely to click or buy the item. The recommendation process satisfies the sequential decision process and can be modeled as Markov Decision Process (MDP), where the recommendation system (agent) can sequentially recommend items to the user (environment) to maximize the long-term cumulative reward.

Usually, the MDP is represented by the quintet $\langle S, A, P, R, \gamma \rangle$.

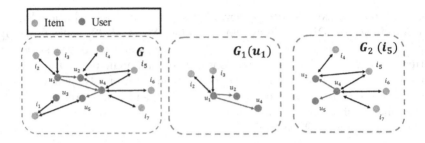

Fig. 1. Heterogeneous information network G and sub-graph $G_f()$

- S. S denotes the set of states, where at each time step t, the state $s_t \in S$ consists of a tuple (u, h_t), where $u \in U$ is the recommended user entity. $h_t = \{i_{t-k}, i_{t-k+1}, \ldots, i_{t-1}\}$ denotes the history of user u clicks or purchases before time step t.
- A. A denotes the set of actions, and the action $a \in A$ is a continuous vector and has the same dimension as the item. The ranking score of item i can be obtained by the dot product item of action a and item i.
- P. $P(s_{t+1} \mid s_t, a_t)$ represents the probability of performing the conversion of a_t to s_{t+1} under state s_t. If the user u ignores the recommended item, then $s_{t+1} = s_t$ and vice versa s_{t+1} will be updated.
- $r_t = R(s_t, a_t)$. The user will give feedback based on the items recommended by the recommending agent, providing rewards to the recommending agent through the reward function R.
- γ. $\gamma \in [0, 1]$ weighs the importance of current and future returns.

4   MAS-DRLRC Model

According to the formal representation of the MDP, the goal of MAS-DRLRC is to train the recommender agent to learn a policy π_θ such that recommending items to any user u at any time step t yields the maximum expected discounted cumulative reward G_t.

$$G_t \triangleq \max_{\pi_\theta} \mathbb{E}_{\pi_\theta} \sum_{j=0}^{T} \gamma^j R(s_{t+j}, a_{t+j}) \tag{1}$$

As shown in Fig. 2, MAS-DRLRC is based on the DDPG method to learn the recommended policy, so an Actor network and a Critic network, as well as the corresponding target network and state representation model, need to be carefully designed.

(1) The Actor network. The Actor network $\pi_\theta(\cdot \mid s_t)$ takes as input the state s_t of the current time step t and outputs a continuous vector a_t with the same size dimension as the item. a_t does not directly recommend an item but acts as a ranking vector, and the dot product of a_t and item i_j is able to obtain the ranking score of item i_j:

$$\text{scor}_{tj} = a_t i_j^T \tag{2}$$

The ranking vector a_t dot product with all candidate items, to generate their own ranking score, recommend agent according to the item's ranking score the top K item will be recommended to the user.

(2) The Critic network, The Critic network $Q_\omega(s_t, a_t)$ is used as a state-action value function to map the state s_t and action a_t at the current time step t as inputs to a real value that measures the cumulative discount gain of performing action a_t at the current state s_t. $Q_\omega(s_t, a_t)$, the cumulative discounted benefit of executing action a_t under the current state s_t, and at the same time provides the gradient signal for the Actor network and updates the Actor network parameters.

$$\nabla J(\theta) = \frac{1}{N} \sum_j \nabla Q_\omega(s, a) \Big|_{s=s_j, a=\pi_\theta(s_j)} \nabla_\theta \pi_\theta(s) \Big|_{s=s_j} \tag{3}$$

Using the chain gradient rule in Eq. 3 above, the batch gradient ascent is able to update the Actor network parameters θ. In addition, in order to avoid the failure of the Actor to converge, the Critic network is updated with a time series difference and a fixed target network by minimizing the loss function of the Critic network L Critic network parameters ω:

$$L = \frac{1}{N} \sum_j (y_j - Q_\omega(s_j, a_j))^2 \tag{4}$$

where $y_j = r_j + \lambda Q_{\omega'}(s_{j+1}, \pi_{\theta'}(s_{j+1}))$, $Q_{\omega'}$ and $\pi_{\theta'}$ denote the target network of Critic network and Actor, respectively.

(3) State representation is a crucial aspect of the MAS-DRLRC model as both the Actor and Critic networks require it as input to construct necessary information features of the user. However, traditional recommendation systems based on DRL often construct user state representations with user and item independent feature embedding, which fails to leverage the power of heterogeneous information networks. Therefore, the MAS-DRLRC model aims to enhance the user state representation by constructing a structured representation of users and items using a heterogeneous information network.

To achieve this, the MAS-DRLRC model incorporates a Graph Attention Representation Module (GAM) and an Attention State Representation Module (ASRM) in the state representation model, as depicted in Fig. 2. The GAM generates structured representations of users and items using the heterogeneous information network, which enables exploration of the potential relationships between users and items, as well as between users themselves.

On the other hand, the ASRM module models the sequential information in the state and adjusts the weights of different item information using the attention mechanism. This helps generate personalized state representations of users by emphasizing the most relevant item information at any given time.

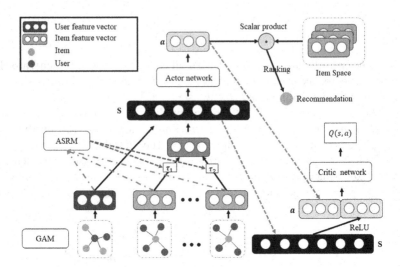

Fig. 2. MASDRLRC Framework

The combination of both GAM and ASRM in the state representation model enhances the user state representation, making it more effective in capturing the complex relationships and patterns between users and items.

In the graph attention representation module, users and items are first mapped into a low-dimensional vector space with $e_c^u \in \mathbb{R}^d$ and $e_j^i \in \mathbb{R}^d$ denote the original node features of user u_c and item i_j in the heterogeneous information network G, respectively. Since the deep reinforcement learning algorithm learns the recommendation strategy through the interaction between the agent and the user, it is impractical to construct the state representation through the complete heterogeneous information network in each recommendation. Therefore, the graph attention representation module aggregates the neighborhood information in the sub-graph $G_f(u_c)$ with the user as the central node or the sub-graph $G_f(i_j)$ with the item as the central node to generate a graph-aware user g_c^u and item g_j^i structured representation which is able to generate its own feature vector using the neighbor node information. This approach not only simplifies the training of the DRL model but also prevents redundant training and information transfer among nodes, resulting in a reduction of training time. Moreover, to minimize the impact of noisy neighbors who may be trusted but not similar, an attention mechanism is utilized in the graph attention representation module to assess the trustworthiness of neighbors based on user and user's neighbor feature vectors and assign weights accordingly. Ideally, less relevant neighbor nodes will be assigned smaller weights, while important neighbor nodes will be assigned larger weights.

Using the example of generating user characteristics g_c^u, a structured representation of users and items is generated as follows:

$$\alpha_{u_c\beta} = \frac{\exp\left(\sigma\left(W_\alpha^T\left[e_c^u \oplus e_\beta^\bullet\right] + b_\alpha\right)\right)}{\sum_{v \in N_1(u_c)} \exp\left(\sigma\left(W_\alpha^T\left[e_c^u \oplus e_v^\bullet\right] + b_\alpha\right)\right)} \tag{5}$$

where $W_\alpha \in \mathbb{R}^{2d}$ and $b_\alpha \in \mathbb{R}^1$ are trainable weights and biases, respectively, $\oplus$ denotes concat function, and σ is the activation function. In order to improve the calculation efficiency, MAS-DRLRC samples L neighbor nodes uniformly and randomly from the sub-graph $G_1(u_c)$ as neighborhood information, $N_1^+(u_c)$ denotes all nodes within the sub-graph $G_1(u_c)$, which includes itself as well as neighbor nodes, and $N_1(u_c)$ denotes a subset of $N_1^+(u_c)$, and the number of nodes is L. Please note that $N_1(u_c)$ during the training of every iteration from $N_1^+(u_c)$ in random sampling, when $L > |N_1^+(u_c)|$, $N_1(u_c)$ for fixed sample. Since $G_1(u_c)$ contains both project nodes and user nodes, for a clearer representation, $\bullet$ is represented as u or i depending on the node properties. The calculated $\alpha_{u_c v}$ is able to assign appropriate weights to the corresponding nodes, and finally, the final g_c^u representation is obtained by aggregating Eq. 6.

$$g_c^u = \sigma\left(\sum_{v \in N_1(u_c)} \alpha_{u_c v} e_v^\bullet\right) \tag{6}$$

Therefore this module improves the personalized representation of the state by selectively paying attention to different historical items according to the target users. Specifically, different weights are assigned to the items in h_t by the attention mechanism, and then the feature representation of h_t is generated by weighted summation i_{att}. The attention mechanism assigns weights to different historical interaction items based on the user structured representation, and the same items will have different weights under different user characteristics, which enhances the personalized representation of the state. The calculation process is shown in Eq. 7.

$$\tau_{u_c z} = \frac{\exp\left(\sigma\left(W_\tau\left[g_c^u g_z^i\right] + b_\tau\right)\right)}{\sum_{v \in h_t} \exp\left(\sigma\left(W_\tau\left[g_c^u g_v^i\right] + b_\tau\right)\right)} \tag{7}$$

A vector with the same dimension size as the items are generated by aggregating Eq. 8 and the weights $\tau_{u_c g}$.

$$i_{att} = \sum_{v \in h_t} \tau_{u_c v} g_v^i \tag{8}$$

In addition, Eq. 8 compresses the feature vectors in h_t to reduce the dimensionality of the state representation and to eliminate the effect of overfitting due to the location factor in h_t. i_{att} not only contains the features of the history records but also achieves selective attention to the interaction history items according to the recommended users.

The final user state is represented as $S_t = [g_c^u \oplus i_{att}]$, which is stitched together from the structured representation of the user and the vector of historical item aggregation, not only incorporating the user's neighborhood information but also selectively focusing on different items, highlighting the personalized representation of the state.

5   Evaluation

5.1   Parameter Setting and Performance Comparison

To evaluate the performance of MAS-DRLRC, random, BPR [5], NeuMF [6], DRR [7], DRN [8], and GraphRec [9] are used for comparison. Among them, the random method randomly selects K items from the set of candidate items as the top-ranked recommendation items. BPR learns the potential representations of users and items and is a Bayesian personality ranking algorithm. NeuMF is a deep learning-based recommendation algorithm for handling implicit feedback through a combination of neural networks and traditional matrix decomposition. DRR is an interactive deep reinforcement learning-based DRR is an interactive recommendation algorithm based on deep reinforcement learning, which carefully learns user states to learn recommendation strategies. DRN uses a Deep Q-Network network to build an interactive recommendation system framework and uses a competitive gradient descent algorithm (DBGDA) for online training. graphRec uses graph neural network approach for the social recommendation.

For each dataset, the ratio of training, validation, and test sets is divided into 8 : 1 : 1. For a fair comparison, the baseline algorithm optimizes the parameters by the validation set, the MAS-DRLRC embedding size $d = 32$, the neural network hidden layer node size 256, the learning rate 0.001, the discount factor $\gamma = 0.8$, the experience pool size 20000, the batch update size 256, reward r is the size of user feedback on the top ranked item and focus only on the top $K = 10$ ranked items.

Table 1. Performance comparison of all methods under cold-start and warm-start

Model	LastFM		Ciao		Epinions	
	$HR@10$	$NDCG@10$	$HR@10$	$NDCG@10$	$HR@10$	$NDCG@10$
Random	0.100	0.045	0.100	0.045	0.100	0.045
BPR(warm)	0.545	0.410	0.395	0.271	0.476	0.411
NeuMF(warm)	0.591	0.419	0.422	0.293	0.493	0.396
GraphRec(warm)	0.613	0.422	0.447	0.253	0.522	0.410
DRR(warm)	0.513	0.395	0.289	0.167	0.435	0.402
MAS-DRLRC(warm)	**0.636**	**0.423**	**0.452**	**0.310**	**0.572**	**0.419**
BPR(cold)	0.679	0.469	0.445	0.255	0.512	0.415
NeuMF(cold)	0.690	0.477	0.459	0.267	0.536	0.407
GraphRec(cold)	0.676	0.471	0.461	0.279	0.548	0.413
DRR(cold)	0.682	0.471	0.463	0.297	0.592	0.420
MAS-DRLRC(cold)	**0.719**	**0.535**	**0.469**	**0.317**	**0.632**	**0.426**

MAS-DRLRC is compared with the baseline algorithm. Tables 1 show the performance comparison of all algorithms under hot and cold starts with $HR@10$ and $NDCG@10$ metrics. The proposed MAS-DRLRC algorithm outperforms the other algorithms under both cold and hot starts in all data sets. The cold-start metrics have a decreasing trend compared to the warm-start metrics, because the reinforcement learning-based recommendation algorithm requires more data for training than the traditional recommendation algorithm, resulting in a serious decrease in DRR metrics under cold-start, but the MAS-DRLRC algorithm and GraphRec mitigate the effect of data sparsity with the help of neighborhood information in the heterogeneous information network, and in addition, the MAS-DRLRC algorithm shows the optimal performance.

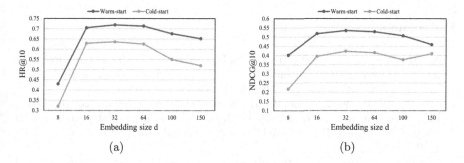

(a)   (b)

Fig. 3. Parameter study on Embedding Size d on the LastFM.

5.2   Impact of Embedding Size

This section analyzes the impact of d on MAS-DRLRC by varying the size d of the user and item embedding vectors. $d \in 8, 16, 32, 64, 100, 150$ to examine how the performance of MAS-DRLRC varies. The comparison results are shown in Fig. 3. The recommended performance increases and then decreases, and the recommended performance reaches its peak when $d = 32$, and MAS-DRLRC has the best performance. When $d = 8, 16$, the difference in structured representations is too large to fully describe the corresponding features due to the small dimensionality, and when $d = 100, 150$, the dimensionality is too large to make the user and item salient features too smooth or Insufficient training makes the user and item representations insufficiently trained to result in a continuous decrease in recommendation accuracy.

6   Conclusion

This chapter proposes a novel multi-layer attentional social recommendation method (MAS-DRLRC) based on deep reinforcement learning. The proposed method utilizes a heterogeneous information network that incorporates social network and user-item bipartite graph to construct structured representations of users and items. It further leverages attention mechanisms to adjust the weights of neighborhood information, and thus selectively attend to relevant items for different users using external attention mechanisms. Additionally, the proposed method captures the dynamic changes of user preferences through deep reinforcement learning methods. The experimental results demonstrate that MAS-DRLRC effectively addresses the cold-start and data sparsity problems, and improves the accuracy of recommendations. In future work, the integration of knowledge graph information into the heterogeneous information network can potentially enhance recommendation accuracy by considering the relationship between nodes for a more precise structured representation of users and items.

References

1. Xie, R., Zhang, S., Wang, R., Xia, F., Lin, L.: Hierarchical reinforcement learning for integrated recommendation. In: Proceedings of the AAAI Conference on Artificial Intelligence, vol. 35, pp. 4521–4528 (2021)
2. Lei, Y., Pei, H., Yan, H., Li, W.: Reinforcement learning based recommendation with graph convolutional q-network. In: Proceedings of the 43rd International ACM SIGIR Conference on Research and Development in Information Retrieval, pp. 1757–1760 (2020)
3. Liu, F., et al.: State representation modeling for deep reinforcement learning based recommendation. Knowl.-Based Syst. **205**, 106170 (2020)
4. Xin, X., Karatzoglou, A., Arapakis, I., Jose, J.M.: Self-supervised reinforcement learning for recommender systems. In: Proceedings of the 43rd International ACM SIGIR Conference on Research and Development in Information Retrieval, pp. 931–940 (2020)
5. Rendle, S., Freudenthaler, C., Gantner, Z., Schmidt-Thieme, L.: Bpr: Bayesian personalized ranking from implicit feedback. arXiv preprint arXiv:1205.2618 (2012)
6. He, X., Liao, L., Zhang, H., Nie, L., Hu, X., Chua, T.-S.: Neural collaborative filtering. In: Proceedings of the 26th International Conference on World Wide Web, pp. 173–182 (2017)
7. Liu, F., et al.: Deep reinforcement learning based recommendation with explicit user-item interactions modeling. arXiv preprint arXiv:1810.12027 (2018)
8. Zheng, G., e al.: DRN: a deep reinforcement learning framework for news recommendation. In: Proceedings of the 2018 World Wide Web Conference, pp. 167–176 (2018)
9. Fan, W., et al.: Graph neural networks for social recommendation. In: The World Wide Web Conference, pp. 417–426 (2019)

SPOAHA: Spark Program Optimizer Based on Artificial Hummingbird Algorithm

Miao Wang, Jiteng Zhen, Yupeng Ma, Xu Huang, and Hong Zhang(✉)

School of Cyber Security and Computer, Hebei University, Baoding 071002, China
{wm,hzhang}@hbu.edu.cn,
{20201205054,20201202075,20207014040}@stumail.hbu.edu.cn

Abstract. In this era of the Internet of Things (IoT), a large number of sensor devices collect and generate various sensing data over time. It is very essential to mine fresh information by analyzing large amounts of data, predict the future, and make correct decisions. Therefore, a growing number of data-intensive computing frameworks have been proposed, such as Hadoop, Spark, Flink, etc. Rather than reading and writing files to disks, Spark processes data with a memory-based computing framework to improve the performance, which has attracted more attention from researchers. However, due to a wealth of operators provided by Spark, a certain application can be implemented in various ways, which also show big differences in performance. Therefore, tuning a Spark application is a very error-prone and time-consuming process, and requires developers to have a deep understanding of Spark's operating principles and characteristics. In this paper, we summarize a series of rules such as operator reordering and operator replacement to design and implement a Spark program optimizer, called SPOAHA, based on the artificial Hummingbird algorithm. Experimental results show that without changing the semantics of the original program, the optimized program dramatically reduces the amount of data involved in the shuffling period, and speeds up the execution time by up to 2.7×.

Keywords: Spark · Big Data · Program Optimization · Artificial Hummingbird Algorithm

1 Introduction

The challenge of gaining insights from the Internet of Things (IoT) is considered one of the most exciting and critical opportunities in academia and industry. As the number of applications that need to be processed increases, the analysis of big data streams from sensors and devices is bound to become a key area of data mining research [4]. Since it becomes difficult to process these massive data by traditional database management tools, more and more data-intensive computing frameworks have been proposed, such as MapReduce [5], Apache Hadoop [7], Apache Spark [22], Apache Flink [6], and so on.

Z. Jin et al. (Eds.): KSEM 2023, LNAI 14119, pp. 317–331, 2023.
https://doi.org/10.1007/978-3-031-40289-0_26

Apache Spark is a popular open-source, distributed processing system for handling large data sets. Compared with other computing frameworks, Spark uses RDD (Resilient Distributed Dataset) to store intermediate data based on memory and applies a dependency graph, called Lineage, for fault-tolerance, which significantly improves the efficiency of data processing and analysis [21]. Meanwhile, it contains a wealth of RDD operators that make Spark more flexible for data processing.

At present, the Spark optimization of most scholars from academia to industry mainly focus on the framework itself, such as memory optimization, scheduling optimization, parameter configuration optimization, and shuffling process optimization, but there are still few theoretical and experimental studies on Spark operators. We have done a lot of experiments to explore the different characteristics of Spark operators based on the theory of [9,11,18]. We discover that:

- The change of some operators' order does not affect the semantics of the original program, but the performances are different before and after the change.
- The replacement of operators with the same semantics also has a large influence on the application's performance.

For applying operator replacement and reordering to a Spark program, it is necessary to analyze interrelationship of adjacent operators that can be optimized. Of course, the highest performance for a Spark Program is to examine the entire program to ensure that locations satisfying operator replacement and reordering criteria are all considered. Yet, the temporal complexity necessitates the adoption of a meta-heuristic algorithm [2].

Biomimetic algorithms to tackle diverse engineering challenges have gained the greatest popularity in recent years and has proven to be incredibly effective. In this paper, we propose a Spark program optimizer based on the artificial Hummingbird algorithm, called SPOAHA. It can optimize the Spark program by our pre-designed performance model [23]. The contributions to this paper are summarized as follows:

- We formulate a set of reasonable classification standards based on the function and scope of operators and design the classifier component to reduce the complexity of application modeling.
- We summarize a series of operator reordering and operator replacement rules. Applying these rules can effectively improve the performance of applications, especially in terms of data transfer and execution time.
- We employ a variant artificial Hummingbird algorithm to find a better execution plan for an Spark application. It can accurately generate operator orders that comply with the replacement rules in a short period, and notify the optimized program to the developer or programmer in the form of message.

The remaining structure of this paper is as follows. In Sect. 2, we introduce the related work for Spark optimization. Then we discuss our design and implementation of SPOAHA in Sect. 3. In Sect. 4, we show experimental results by different operator optimization rules. At last, we conclude remarks and future works in Sect. 5.

2 Related Work

At present, the biggest challenge we face is not how to collect data, but how to use this data quickly and effectively to maximize its value [13]. Therefore, massively distributed computing frameworks were developed. Due to Spark's efficiency, versatility, and ease of use, it is deeply attracted by researchers from academia to industry for its optimization [16]. Here, we introduce the related work from two aspects: the programming optimization and the framework optimization:

Optimizations in Spark programming: HighSpark [9] puts forward some development principles such as avoiding the creation of repeated RDDs, persisting RDDs that reuse many times, and optimizing data structures. But it is demanding for developers, even with high-level experience, to optimize programs according to these principles. Catalyst [1] is a scalable query optimizer of Spark-SQL, which supports optimization based on features of the Scala programming language. It embeds optimization rules, data sources, and data types into the Scala programming language to offer benefits such as automatic optimization and letting users write complex pipelines. RIOS [12] is an adaptive query optimization technique for Spark that leverages the batch execution strategy to derive a better plan by masking the collection of data statistics with data scans. However, these two optimizers only support DataFrame and DataSet APIs, rather than RDD APIs. Although TaBOS [17] summarizes some optimization rules, it is difficult to implement due to the complexity.

Optimizations in Spark framework: Several researches construct performance models to explore the impact of different factors on Spark application performance, such as parameter configuration, system resources, etc. [10,14,15]. Herodotou et al. [8] study the existing methods of parameter tuning in batch and streaming data processing systems, summarize them into six categories, and summarize the advantages and disadvantages of each category. Wang et al. [19] propose an optimization method for automatically tuning configuration parameters of Spark based on binary classification and multi-classification. Cheng et al. [3] employ a new approach based on Adaboost to build a set of performance models to predict the performance of Spark applications under different configurations. The work of MEMTUNE [20] is to use DAG information to prefetch the data needed in the next stage to overlap calculation with I/O. The above methods are mainly aimed at the optimization of the framework itself and do not take into consideration the theory and performance of Spark operators.

3 Design and Implementation

In this section, we introduce the entire life cycle of SPOAHA in detail. We simplify the complexity of rules by classifying operators. In order to find out which part of the source program needs to be optimized, we formulate a series of equivalent criteria. Then, we employ the artificial hummingbird algorithm to detect the alternative Spark programs for optimization and adopt our pre-designed performance model [23] to decide which alternative program is the optimal one. The system architecture of SPOAHA is shown in Fig. 1. The source program of a spark program is used as an input, and the outputs are the optimized program and the operation log. It mainly consists of four components:

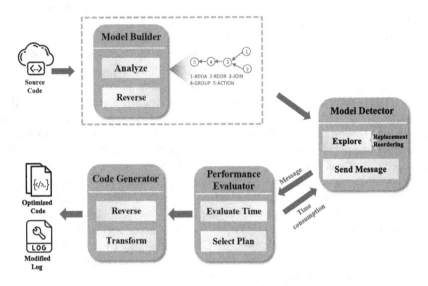

Fig. 1. Architecture of SPOAHA

Model Builder: The Model Builder is the component to transform the source code into a format that can be analyzed by the artificial hummingbird model. It mainly consists of two steps: parsing and reversal. Parsing is to analyze the attributes of each operator operation. Reversal is the process of outputting the parsed program in reverse order, so that the Checker module traces back for the alternative reordering. After that, the whole program is transformed into a format that can be recognized by the Model Detector later.

Model Detector: The model detector is used to detect alternative execution plans based on replacement rules generated by the artificial hummingbird algorithm, consisting of a series of operations. The rules are mainly divided into two types: operator reordering and operator replacemenTt. Section 3.3 will introduce them in detail. The artificial hummingbird model detector gives the corresponding optional plan if a part of the program sequence obeys one of the replacement rules. How to evaluate the program based on the message is implemented in the Performance Evaluator.

Performance Evaluator: Performance Evaluator is to evaluate the execution time of each executing plan and decide the optimized one based on our pre-designed performance model, called Hedgehog [23]. Hedgehog is an end-to-end performance model for Spark, which is easy to use with low overhead.

Code Generator: The optimized program output by the Performance Evaluator is in reverse order and cannot be recognized by the Spark engine. Therefore, the reverse operation is performed on it first, and then it is transformed back into the Spark executable source code.

3.1 Operator Classification

In order to formulate rules and model spark applications, we divide operators into nine categories according to their functions and scopes, as shown in Table 1. Here, we use $A.Map^E$ to explain the notions. In $A.Map^E$, "A" denotes the operational RDD with a key-value pair format, and "E" represents the data attribute that the Map operation affects, which can be "Key" or "Value".

Table 1. Exemplified classification of operations

Category	Notation	Examples in Apache Spark
Map	$A.Map^E$	map,mapValues
Filter	$A.Filte^E$	distinct,filter
Join	$A.Join^E$	join,leftOuterJoin,rightOuterJoin,fullOuterJoin
Group	$A.Group^E$	groupByKey,reduceByKey,combineByKey,foldByKey, aggregateByKey
Sort	$A.Sort^E$	sortBy,sortByKey
Set	$A.Set^E(B)$	union,intersection,sustract
Partitions	$A.Partitons^E$	repartition,coalese
Action	$A.Action^E$	reduce,collect,take,fold,aggregate
Others	$A.Others^E$	parallelize,textFile,sample

The Map class is a unary transforming operation that works on a key-value paired RDD and produces a new RDD. The Filter class is to generally reduce the number of input RDD's elements and leave the key-values that satisfy the filter criteria. The reduction ratio is related to the input data set and the user-defined filter function, but the value of each key-value does not change. The Join class is used to combine values from two RDDs based on join criteria. The Group class aggregates the same key data together to apply an aggregation function, such as summation, maximum, average, etc. The Sort class sorts the data in a specific order, and the number and values of output elements remain the same. The Set class contains the classic set operations, such as intersection, union, or subtraction on two data sets. The Partitions class is used to change the number of partitions for one RDD. Then the number and values of key-value pairs are the same as before. The Action class is a kind of action operator in Spark, used to trigger the execution of the calculation and return the result of a job.

3.2 Rules

By analyzing the characteristics of Spark operators and experimental tests, we summarize two types of rewriting rules: Operator reordering and Operator replacement. When defining the rules, we make full use of the operator classification in Sect. 3.1, which simplifies the complexity of the rules.

Operator Reordering. Predicate pushdown is a classic optimization rule in SQL systems that pushes the filter operation down before operations like "join" to reduce the amount of data transferred significantly. Similarly, in Spark program, without changing the semantics of the program, pushing operators like "filter" to the position as close to the data source as possible can effectively reduce the volume of data processed by the downstream operator as well as the overall program consumption time. Especially in the process of shuffling, the reduction of intermediate data transmitted across a network of computing nodes is very necessary. By observing the functions and features of Spark operators, we find that there are two operators, "filter" and "distinct", that are available to implement the predicate pushdown optimization. Table 2 shows the equivalence conditions for reordering these two operators with others.

Table 2. Equivalence criterion for operator reordering

Idx	Equivalence Formulae	Condition
1	$Op^{E1}.filter^{E2}=filter^{E2}.Op^{E1}$	$Op \in \{Sort, Partitions\}$
2	$A.Op^{E1}(B).filter^{E2}=A.filter^{E2}.Op^{E1}(B.filter^{E2})$	$Op=Set$
3	$Op^{E1}.filter^{E2}=filter^{E2}.Op^{E1}$	$Op \in \{Group, mapValues\} \wedge E2=K$
4	$A.Op^{E1}(B).filter^{E2}=A.filter^{E2}.Op^{E1}(B.filter^{E2})$	$Op=Join \wedge E2=K$
5	$A.Op^{E1}(B).filter^{E2}=A.filter^{E2}.Op^{E1}(B)$	$Op=Join \wedge E2=VA$
6	$A.Op^{E1}(B).filter^{E2}=A.Op^{E1}(B.filter^{E2})$	$Op=Join \wedge E2=VB$
7	$Op^{E1}.filter^{E2}=filter^{E2}.Op^{E1}$	$Op=map \wedge (E1 \wedge E2=\varnothing)$
8	$Op^{E}.distinct = distinct.Op^{E}$	$Op \in \{Map, Sort, Partitions\}$
9	$A.Op^{E}(B).distinct=A.distinct.Op^{E}(B.distinct).distinct$	$Op=union$
10	$A.Op^{E}(B)=A.distinct.Op^{E}(B.distinct)$	$OP=intersection$

Operator Replacement. Spark provides a wealth of operation operators, which brings great flexibility in developing applications. As a result, there exist a variety of executing plans organized by a sequence of operations to program an application, but each of these arrangements achieves different performance. Hence, it is painful for a developer to select appropriate operations. To solve this problem, we summarize a series of operator replacement rules, shown in Table 3.

Table 3. Replacement criteria

Idx	Original Formulae	Equivalence Formulae
1	groupByKey.mapValues (v=>v.sum)	reduceByKey((v1,v2)=>v1+v2)
2	groupByKey.mapValues (v=>v.product)	reduceByKey((v1,v2)=>v1*v2)
3	groupByKey.mapValues (v=>v.max)	reduceByKey((v1,v2)=>Max(v1,v2))
4	groupByKey.mapValues (v=>v.min)	reduceByKey((v1,v2)=>Min(v1,v2))
5	groupByKey.mapValues (v=>v.sum/v.size)	combineByKey(v=>(v,1), (acc:(Int,Int),v)=>(acc._1+v,acc._2+1), (acc1:(Int,Int),acc2:(Int,Int))=> (acc._1+acc2._1,acc1._2+acc2._2)) .mapValues(v=>v._1/v._2)
6	groupByKey.mapValues (v=>v.fold(init)(f))	foldByKey(init)(f)
7	groupByKey.mapValues (v=>v.aggregate(init)(f1,f2))	aggregateByKey (init)(f1,f2)
8	map(f(x)).map(g(x))	map(g(f(x)))
9	filter(f(x)).filter(g(x))	filter(f(x)&&g(x))

3.3 Artificial Hummingbird Model

The artificial hummingbird algorithm [24] was inspired by hummingbirds' flight abilities, memory powers, and foraging strategies. In contrast to other birds, hummingbirds are able to achieve three different flight postures: axial, diagonal and omnidirectional, shown in Fig. 2. Hummingbirds have an amazing memory, being able to remember the location of each flower, nectar-refilling rate, and the time of the last visit. Hummingbirds forage in three ways: guided foraging, territorial foraging, and migration foraging.

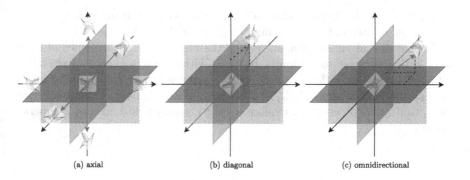

(a) axial   (b) diagonal   (c) omnidirectional

Fig. 2. Three flight behaviors of hummingbirds

In our hummingbird algorithm, the hummingbird's food source is the sequence of operators and the nectar-refilling rate denotes the execution time of the sequence. The number of hummingbirds is n, and the length of the Spark program is L_{opr}. During initialization, we set the random number $L_{opr}/3$ from 0 to $L_{opr} - 1$ for each hummingbird. Then according to the rules shown in Table 2 and Table 3, we replace or reorder the operators at the subscript of the random number.

Three flight attitudes in our algorithm are equiprobable. Meanwhile, guided foraging and territorial foraging are equiprobable. The choice of the two foraging modes are represented by Eq. 1:

$$V_i = \begin{cases} tar_i + a \times D \times (tar_i - x_i) & r < 1/2 \\ x_i + b \times D \times x_i & r \geq 1/2 \end{cases} \quad (1)$$

V_i stands for the candidate sequence of operators, tar_i for the target sequence of operators, x_i for the current sequence of operators, i for the index of hummingbird, a, b for random numbers from the standard normal distribution, D for the direction switch vector, and r for a random decimal number.

We regards three flight postures as using only replacement rules, only reordering rules, or both replacement and reordering rules.

We compare the execution time of each potential sequence of operators to the execution time of the current sequence of operators during the guided foraging and territorial foraging phases, and determine the hummingbird's sequence of operators in the next iteration, shown in Eq. 2.

$$x_i(t+1) = \begin{cases} V_i(t+1) & f(x_i(t)) > f(V_i(t+1)) \\ x_i(t) & f(x_i(t)) \leq f(V_i(t+1)) \end{cases} \quad (2)$$

where $f(\cdot)$ is the function that calculates the execution time, and $x_i(t)$ is the sequence of operators for the i_{th} hummingbird of the t_{th} iteration.

During the migration foraging phase, the hummingbird's sequence of operators with the worst execution is replaced with a new sequence of operators obtained by resetting the initial operator sequence to prevent trapping into a local optimum after every $L_{opr}/10$ iterations. With the help of this technique, the optimization process can explore a bigger search field and find a superior answer.

Algorithm 1. Improved artificial hummingbird algorithm

Require: $SparkProgrammtype[L_{opr}](prog), max_i teration$
Ensure: Optimized SparkProgram
1: Initialize all the birds
   // using Tables 2 and 3
2: **while** $t \leq max\_iteration$ **do**
3:   **for** i_{th} bird from $1 \leftarrow n$ **do**
4:     **if** $rand \leq 1/2$ **then**
5:       Follow guided foraging.
6:       **if** $r < 1/3$ **then**
7:         Follow axial flight.
8:       **else if** $r \leq 2/3$ **then**
9:         Follow omnidirectional.
10:      **else**
11:        Follow diagonal flight.
12:      **end if**
13:    **else**
14:      Follow territorial foraging.
15:      **if** $r < 1/3$ **then**
16:        Follow axial flight.
17:      **else if** $r \leq 2/3$ **then**
18:        Follow omnidirectional.
19:      **else**
20:        Follow diagonal flight.
21:      **end if**
22:    **end if**
23:    **if** $mod(t, L_{opr}/10)$ **then**
24:      Follow migration foraging.
25:      Initialize the worst bird.
         //using Tables 2 and 3
26:    **end if**
27: **end for**
28: Update positions
29: $t = t + 1$
30: **end while**
    Return the best fitness value

Algorithm 1 shows our approach to construct the model checker in detail. Since we classify Spark operators into nine categories, we declare a new symbolic type, mtype, defined as mtype = {Map, Filter, Join, Group, Sort, Set, Partitions, Action, Others}. We model Spark program into an operation array of "mtype", and load the operator replacement and reordering rules in Table 2 and Table 3. Then the Model Detector executes the hummingbird optimization algorithm based on operator replacement and reordering rules. During the iterations of the artificial Hummingbird algorithm, each candidate plan is evaluated by the Performance Evaluator to select the optimal program.

4   Experiments

In this section, we describe the experiments to evaluate the performance of the operator reordering and replacement rules for the Spark application. We design a number of classic scenarios to compare the execution time and the shuffling data of the optimized program with the original program.

4.1   Experimental Results

Scenario 1: In order to evaluate the performance of "filter" and "join" reordering, we consider a scenario for counting the number of illegal parking service requests at each busy hour, using the 311 service request dataset. From Table 4, "FrequencyRDD" represents the number of 311 service requests per hour, in which the Key is the hour of the request time, and the value is the number of service requests. Figure 3 shows the execution time before and after the reordering optimization of this Spark program. The optimized reordering can gain improvement from 28.5% on 6 GB to 40% on 3 GB compared with the naive job. This is because pushing the "filter" forward can dramatically remove unnecessary data and speed up the execution of the Spark program. Figure 4 shows the amount of shuffling data before and after the program optimization. The optimized Spark job reduces the amount of shuffling data by 94% on average when varying the input data size from 3 GB to 12 GB.

Table 4. Filter and join reordering

Type	Spark program
Naive	FrequencyRDD=NYServiceRDD.map(hour, 1).reduceByKey(v1+v2)
	NYServiceRDD.join(FrequencyRDD).filter(RequestCount>100000)
	.filter(EventType=="IllegalParking")
Optimized	FrequencyRDD=NYServiceRDD.map(hour, 1).reduceByKey(v1+v2)
	NYServiceRDD.filter(eventType=="IllegalParking")
	.join(FrequencyRDD).filter(RequestCount>100000)

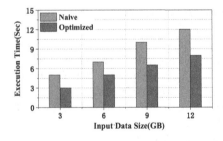

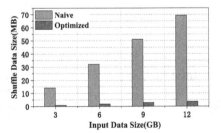

Fig. 3. Execution time with different input data size in Scenario 1

Fig. 4. Shuffling data size when varying the input data size in Scenario 1

Scenario 2: We evaluate the performance improvement of "filter"(E=Key) and "groupByKey" reordering. In this scenario, we count the number of each word in the Wikipedia dataset, and the word must be contained in the list of an English dictionary, as shown in Table 5. Since the scope type of the "filter" operator is "Key" rather than "value", the "filter" behind the "groupByKey" operator can be immediately moved forward according to Rule 3 in Table 2. Figure 5 shows the improvement in the execution time of the optimized program with the input data size varying from 4 GB to 16 GB, which is from 26.6% on 8 GB to 42.4% on 4 GB. The performance improvement is related to the reduction of the amount of shuffling data. That is the more the amount of shuffling data is reduced, the more the execution time of the program is decreased. Figure 6 demonstrates the shuffling data size of the optimized program and the naive program when the input data size is changed from 4 GB to 16 GB. When the input data size is 4 GB, the reduction of the transferring data during the shuffling process is the biggest, which is 62.5%, so that the corresponding improvement of the optimized program is the largest, which is 42.4%. On the contrary, for the input data size of 8 GB, the improvement of 26.6% is the lowest due to the smallest reduction of the shuffling data (41.9%).

Scenario 3: We design a case to sort the words in the Wikipedia dataset by the number of occurrences, requiring the length of each word to be greater than 10, to evaluate the performance of the "filter" consecutively forward moves in a Spark program, shown in Table 6. In this scenario, we consider the input data size of 20 GB to show the performance of the naive program and the other

Table 5. Filter and groupByKey reordering

Type	Spark program
Naive	broadWordSet= SparkContext.broadcast(wordSet)
	WikiRDD.groupByKey().filter(broadWordSet.contains(Key))
	.mapValues(iterator.sum)
Optimized	broadWordSet= SparkContext.broadcast(wordSet)
	WikiRDD.filter(broadWordSet.contains(Key)).groupByKey()
	.mapValues(iterator.sum)

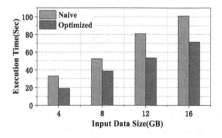 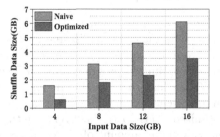

Fig. 5. Execution time with different input data size in Scenario 2

Fig. 6. Shuffling data size when varying the input data size in Scenario 2

328   M. Wang et al.

three optimized programs in Fig. 7. The improvements of the execution time are respectively 21.1%, 60.5%, and 63.3% for pushing the "filter" operator consecutive forward once, twice, and three times. The amount of shuffling data during "reduceByKey" and "sortBy" is illustrated in Fig. 8. Among these reorderings, when the order of "filter" and "reduceByKey" is exchanged, the amount of data transferring across computing nodes during "reduceByKey" is extremely reduced by 80.6%, which is also the reason for the largest performance gain in the execution time of the second forward. The overall improvement of the three consecutive reorderings is 63.3%, which also indicates that it is the most effective to move the "filter" operator as close as possible to the data source.

Table 6. Filter moves forward multiple times

Type	Spark program
Naive	WikiRDD.map(word,1).reduceByKey(v1+v2).sortBy(value) .filter(wordLenth>10)
Optimized One	WikiRDD.map(word,1).reduceByKey(v1+v2).filter(wordLenth>10) .sortBy(value)
Optimized Two	WikiRDD.map(word,1).filter(wordLenth>10).reduceByKey(v1+v2) .sortBy(value)
Optimized Three	WikiRDD.filter(wordLenth>10).map(word,1).reduceByKey(v1+v2) .sortBy(value)

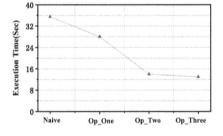

Fig. 7. Execution time of each optimization in Scenario 3   **Fig. 8.** Shuffling data size in different stages in Scenario 3

Scenario 4: We evaluate the effect of replacing "groupByKey" with "reduceByKey" by using the Wikipedia data set to count the number of occurrences of each word. In Table 7, the naive program employs "groupByKey" for summation, but the optimized program uses "reduceByKey" for summation instead. From Fig. 9, we find that, as the amount of input data increases, the performance improvement becomes larger and larger. When the input data size is 100 GB the optimized job is 2.7 times faster than the naive. Figure 10 reveals the reason that the gap of the amount of data during shuffling also becomes bigger when the input data size increases. The "reduceByKey" operation can merge data with

Table 7. Replace groupByKey with reduceByKey

Type	Spark program
Naive	WikiRDD.groupByKey().mapValues(iterator.sum)
Optimized	WikiRDD.reduceByKey(v1+v2)

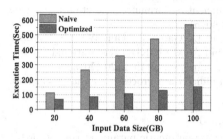 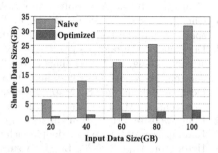

Fig. 9. Execution time with different input data size in Scenario 4

Fig. 10. Shuffling data size when varying the input data size in Scenario 4

the same key in each partition before shuffling to reduce data transferring and avoid memory overflow.

5 Conclusions and Future Work

In this article, we design and implement a Spark program optimizer based on the artificial hummingbird model. The optimizer employs our pre-designed performance model to optimize Spark programs, which is very helpful not only for beginners to learn the principles of spark operators, but also for experts to reconstruct Spark programs efficiently. We first classify operators according to their theories and characteristics, and then summarize a series of reordering and replacing rules. We model the Spark program into an operation array and employ the artificial hummingbird model to detect the operator replacement and reordering rules for optimization. We evaluate the performance of these rules on several scenarios, which show that the optimized program outperforms the naive program in every scenario.

In the future, we consider designing a dynamic detection tool to profile the program more elaborately so that we can add more complicated rules, such as caching the reused RDD, replacing "map" with "mapPartitions", replacing "aggregate" with "treeAggregate", and so on.

Acknowledgement. This work is supported by Hebei Natural Science Foundation of China [No. F2019201361].

References

1. Armbrust, M., et al.: Spark SQL: relational data processing in spark. In: Proceedings of the 2015 ACM SIGMOD International Conference on Management of Data, pp. 1383–1394 (2015)
2. Beheshti, Z., Shamsuddin, S.M.H.: A review of population-based meta-heuristic algorithms. Int. J. Adv. Soft Comput. Appl 5(1), 1–35 (2013)
3. Cheng, G., Ying, S., Wang, B., Li, Y.: Efficient performance prediction for apache spark. J. Parallel Distrib. Comput. 149, 40–51 (2021)
4. De Francisci Morales, G., Bifet, A., Khan, L., Gama, J., Fan, W.: IoT big data stream mining. In: Proceedings of the 22nd ACM SIGKDD International Conference on Knowledge Discovery and Data Mining, pp. 2119–2120 (2016)
5. Dean, J., Ghemawat, S.: Mapreduce: simplified data processing on large clusters. Commun. ACM 51(1), 107–113 (2008)
6. Flink: website. https://flink.apache.org/
7. Hadoop: website. http://hadoop.apache.org/
8. Herodotou, H., Chen, Y., Lu, J.: A survey on automatic parameter tuning for big data processing systems. ACM Comput. Surv. (CSUR) 53(2), 1–37 (2020)
9. Karau, H., Warren, R.: High Performance Spark: Best Practices for Scaling and Optimizing Apache Spark. O'Reilly Media, Inc., Sebastopol (2017)
10. Li, M., Tan, J., Wang, Y., Zhang, L., Salapura, V.: SparkBench: a comprehensive benchmarking suite for in memory data analytic platform spark. In: Proceedings of the 12th ACM International Conference on Computing Frontiers, pp. 1–8. ACM (2015)
11. Li, X.: Spark performance tuning guide. https://tech.meituan.com/2016/04/29/spark-tuning-basic.html (2016)
12. Li, Y., Li, M., Ding, L., Interlandi, M.: Rios: Runtime integrated optimizer for spark. In: Proceedings of the ACM Symposium on Cloud Computing, pp. 275–287 (2018)
13. Mothe, R., Tharun Reddy, S., Vijay Kumar, B., Rajeshwar Rao, A., Chythanya, K.R.: A review on big data analytics in Internet of Things (IoT) and Its roles, applications and challenges. In: Kumar, A., Senatore, S., Gunjan, V.K. (eds.) ICDSMLA 2020. LNEE, vol. 783, pp. 765–773. Springer, Singapore (2022). https://doi.org/10.1007/978-981-16-3690-5_70
14. Nguyen, N., Khan, M.M.H., Albayram, Y., Wang, K.: Understanding the influence of configuration settings: an execution model-driven framework for apache spark platform. In: 2017 IEEE 10th International Conference on Cloud Computing (CLOUD), pp. 802–807. IEEE (2017)
15. Ousterhout, K., Rasti, R., Ratnasamy, S., Shenker, S., Chun, B.G.: Making sense of performance in data analytics frameworks. In: 12th {USENIX} Symposium on Networked Systems Design and Implementation ({NSDI} 15), pp. 293–307 (2015)
16. Salloum, S., Dautov, R., Chen, X., Peng, P.X., Huang, J.Z.: Big data analytics on apache spark. Int. J. Data Sci. Anal. 1(3), 145–164 (2016)
17. Shmeis, Z., Jaber, M.: A rewrite-based optimizer for spark. Futur. Gener. Comput. Syst. 98, 586–599 (2019)
18. Spark: website. http://spark.apache.org/
19. Wang, G., Xu, J., He, B.: A novel method for tuning configuration parameters of spark based on machine learning. In: 2016 IEEE 18th International Conference on High Performance Computing and Communications; IEEE 14th International Conference on Smart City; IEEE 2nd International Conference on Data Science and Systems (HPCC/SmartCity/DSS), pp. 586–593. IEEE (2016)

20. Xu, L., Li, M., Zhang, L., Butt, A.R., Wang, Y., Hu, Z.Z.: Memtune: dynamic memory management for in-memory data analytic platforms. In: 2016 IEEE International Parallel and Distributed Processing Symposium (IPDPS), pp. 383–392. IEEE (2016)
21. Zaharia, M., et al.: Resilient distributed datasets: a fault-tolerant abstraction for in-memory cluster computing. In: 9th {USENIX} Symposium on Networked Systems Design and Implementation ({NSDI} 12), pp. 15–28 (2012)
22. Zaharia, M., et al.: Apache spark: a unified engine for big data processing. Commun. ACM 59(11), 56–65 (2016)
23. Zhang, H., Huang, H., Wang, L.: MRapid: an efficient short job optimizer on Hadoop. In: 2017 IEEE International Parallel and Distributed Processing Symposium (IPDPS)., pp. 459–468. IEEE (2017)
24. Zhao, W., Wang, L., Mirjalili, S.: Artificial hummingbird algorithm: a new bio-inspired optimizer with its engineering applications. Comput. Methods Appl. Mech. Eng. 388, 114194 (2022)

TGKT-Based Personalized Learning Path Recommendation with Reinforcement Learning

Zhanxuan Chen[1], Zhengyang Wu[1,2(✉)], Yong Tang[1,2], and Jinwei Zhou[1]

[1] School of Computer Science, South China Normal University,
Guangzhou 510631, Guangdong, China
{czxuan,wuzhengyang,ytang,jinweiz}@m.scnu.edu.cn
[2] Pazhou Lab, Guangzhou 510330, Guangdong, China

Abstract. In recent years, emerging technologies represented by artificial intelligence have been widely applied in education, and online learning has transcended the limitations of time and space. How to recommend personalized learning paths for learners based on their characteristics has become a new issue. However, in the existing researches on personalized learning path recommendation, many researchers have not fully considered or only mined the initial personalized features of learners, and the process of learning path recommendations does not have good interpretability. In order to solve these issues, this paper proposes a model named TGKT-RL, in which we combine temporal convolutional network and graph attention network into the knowledge tracing model and use it as the environment of the reinforcement learning model. At the same time, we set learning goals for learners and adjust recommendation policy based on the states and rewards during the simulated learning process, ultimately recommending a personalized learning path. We conduct a series of experiments on two public knowledge tracing datasets, and the results show that our method achieves good performance and has good interpretability.

Keywords: Personalized learning path recommendation ·
Reinforcement learning · Knowledge tracing · Temporal convolutional
network · Graph attention network

1 Introduction

Online education has developed rapidly in recent years. Compared with offline education, online education provides great convenience and diverse resources, but there are also some obvious problems, such as unreasonable resources allocation and lack of targeting for learners. A large number of scholars at home and abroad have conducted research on the above problems and proposed different solutions, and personalized learning path recommendation is one of the mainstream directions of research. Personalized learning path recommendation refers

Z. Jin et al. (Eds.): KSEM 2023, LNAI 14119, pp. 332–346, 2023.
https://doi.org/10.1007/978-3-031-40289-0_27

to consider comprehensively of the differences in the learning ability, knowledge background, learning objectives, etc. of the target learner, tailoring a learning path that conforms to educational laws and can achieve the learner's learning objectives, and can also detect the learner's learning status in real-time [23].

However, in the existing researches on personalized learning path recommendation, most researchers tried to generate a complete learning path after mining the learners' personalized features only once. Although this kind of method is simple and direct, the researchers overlooked the learners' learning process. In fact, the learners' personalized features may change during the learning process, so the static recommendation process may not meet the actual complex educational environment. Meanwhile, in the process of mining personalized features of learners, many researchers overlooked the potential relationships of learning resources and the temporal features of the learning process, resulting in a lack of interpretability of the final recommended learning paths. In addition, in the process of learning path recommendation, many researchers focused on recommending learning resources based on learners' personalized features, but overlooked that learners have different learning objectives during the learning process. It is more in line with the actual educational scenario to recommend comprehensively based on the learner's dynamic personalized features and learning objectives.

To this end, we utilizes knowledge tracing technology and integrates temporal convolutional network (TCN) and graph attention network (GAT) to model learners' learning situations based on their historical learning data, which can better dynamically mine personalized features of learners. Besides, in order to better simulate the process of recommending learning resources in actual education scenario, we use an Actor-Critic based reinforcement learning (RL) method to train an agent to recommend personalized learning paths that are more interpretable. The main contributions of this paper are as follows:

- A deep knowledge tracing model TGKT based on TCN and GAT to extract learners' knowledge states and model their learning situations, which can learn the temporal features of long-term historical data, reduce information omissions, and better capture the potential relationships between learning resources, thereby more accurately mining the dynamic personalized features of learners.
- A personalized learning path recommendation model TGKT-RL, using Soft Actor-Critic reinforcement learning method to simulate the actual learning process with learners' goals. At the same time, the recommendation policy is adjusted based on changes of knowledge states from global perspective and changes of knowledge skills from local perspective during the training process, ultimately recommending personalized learning paths for learners.
- Demonstration of the effectiveness and interpretability of our model TGKT-RL through multiple experiments.

2   Related Work

2.1   Mining Personalized Features of Learners

In order to address the personalized learning needs of learners, the first step is to mine the learning style or motivation of the target learners based on their prior knowledge or historical learning data [23]. Zhu et al. considered the learners' knowledge background as a dimension of features [25]. Nabizadeh et al. considered learners' time constraints when mining personalized features [9]. Item response theory (IRT) is a very common theoretical model in educational measurement, and Nabizadeh et al. also mined learners' learning ability based on IRT [8]. Liu et al. used the deep knowledge tracing model to capture learners' latent learning abilities, and then measured their learning achievements at specific stages [6]. However, the authors' assumption that learners' mastery of learning resources will improve after each practice, which does not conform to actual situation.

2.2   Knowledge Tracing Based on Deep Learning

Piech et al. [14] proposed deep knowledge tracing (DKT) based on recurrent neural network (RNN) to predict learners' performance. However, RNN is prone to gradient vanishing problem for longer sequences and cannot utilize input information from a long time ago. Subsequently, some researchers incorporated additional information [5,10,13,18,24] into the above model to further improve the knowledge tracing model. Besides, TCN is also used to learn long-term interactive information [7,16,21]. In addition, many researchers also used graph structures to learn more potential relationships [11,19,22].

2.3   Personalized Learning Path Recommendation

Some researchers used graph theory [17], knowledge graphs [2] and other methods to recommend effective learning paths for students based on their learning style, goals, background, needs, etc. Rafsanjan [15], Nabizadeh [8] and others considered time constraints and used item response theory to recommend paths that maximize scores within a given time. In addition, the mastery of knowledge and the selection of learning resources by learners during the learning process can also be seen as an evolutionary process, therefore many researchers had begun to consider personalized learning path recommendation from the perspective of evolutionary algorithms [12,20]. Some researchers also used reinforcement learning methods to recommend learning paths, such as CAI et al. [1] who simulated the learning requirement for knowledge acquisition in actual learning process and used the A2C algorithm to recommend personalized learning paths while Ai et al. [3] who used the TRPO algorithm to learn exercise recommendation policy for personalized math assignments recommendation. However, they both overlooked the learners' learning objectives and just applied reinforcement learning methods, resulting in insufficient interpretability of the recommendations.

Although the different methods discussed above have their own advantages, they either fail to effectively mine learners' personalized features, or overlook learners' learning goals and just simply apply some recommendation methods in the process of recommending personalized learning paths, resulting in insufficient interpretability of the recommendations. Compared to this, our model utilizes a deep knowledge tracing model based on temporal convolutional network and graph attention network to extract students' knowledge states, which can capture the features of time and learning resources and then dynamically mine personalized features of learners. Furthermore, we consider the learners' goals, changes in knowledge states and mastery degree of knowledge skills to comprehensively obtain a personalized learning path in the process of recommendation, thereby improving the interpretability.

3   Problem Definition

Our problem can be divided into two parts: knowledge tracing and personalized learning path recommendation. Knowledge tracing takes a series of interactions between student and questions as input, and outputs the prediction of student's performance to the next question. Personalized learning path recommendation [23] generates a sequence of knowledge components according to individual differences in learning preferences, goals, etc. Table 1 shows some important symbols, and the following section provides a more detailed explanation of their meanings.

Table 1. A summary of notations.

Notation	Description
X	the learning records of learner
Q	the universal set of questions
SK	the universal set of knowledge skills
q_i	the ith question(represented as $q_{i,t}$ when time step t is involved)
a_i	the answer of the ith question(represented as $a_{i,t}$ when time step t is involved)
k_j	the jth knowledge skill
p_t	the probability of answering correctly the question $q_{i,t}$ at time step t
G_{kl}	the graph for knowledge learning
h_{goal}	the learning goal of learner

Definition 1 (Knowledge Tracing).

$$KT_{s,t}\left(X_{<t}, q_{i,t}\right) \overset{def}{=} p\left(a_{i,t} = 1 \mid X_{<t}, q_{i,t}\right) = f_{KT}\left(X_{<t}, q_{i,t}\right)$$

$p\left(a_{i,t} = 1 \mid X_{<t}, q_{i,t}\right)$ *denotes that the probability of* $a_{i,t} = 1$ *under the conditions of* $X_{<t}$ *and* $q_{i,t}$. $X_{<t}$ *denotes the learning record* $\{x_1, x_2, \ldots, x_{t-1}\}$ *of the learner before time step* t *while* $x_i = \{q_i, a_i\}$ *denotes the historical learning record. Besides,* $q_i \in Q$ *denotes that the question* q_i *belongs to the universal set*

Q of questions and $a_i \in \{0, 1\}$ denotes the answer of question q_i. In summary, $KT_{s,t}$ predicts the probability of the learner s answers the question correctly based on the learning record and f_{KT} denotes the knowledge tracing model.

Definition 2 (Graph for Knowledge Learning).

$$G_{kl} \overset{def}{=} \left\{ q_i, r_{(q_i,k_j)}, k_j | q_i \in Q, k_j \in SK \right\}$$

We first define the set of questions and knowledge skills as $Q = (q_1, q_2, \ldots, q_n)$ and $SK = (k_1, k_2, \ldots, k_m)$, where n and m respectively denote the number of questions and knowledge skills. In the actual learning process, one skill k_j usually related to many questions while each question corresponds to one or more knowledge skills. In order to explore the potential information, we construct a knowledge learning graph G_{kl}, where $r_{(q_i,k_j)}$ denotes whether question q_i and knowledge skill k_j is related.

Definition 3 (Personalized Learning Path Recommendation).

$$LP(G_{kl}, q_{i,t}) \overset{def}{=} path(G_{kl}, q_{i,t})$$

The learning path $LP(G_{kl}, q_{i,t})$ denotes the path from q_1 in the knowledge graph G_{kl} at time step t, it can also be expressed as:

$$LP(G_{kl}, q_{i,t}) = \{q_{1,t}, q_{2,t+1}, \ldots, q_{i,t+\omega} \mid q_i \in Q\}$$

$$LPR(G_{kl}, h_t, h_{goal}) = f_{LPR}(G_{kl}, h_t, h_{goal})$$

$LPR(G_{kl}, h_t, h_{goal})$ denotes the learning path recommended by model $f_{LPR}(G_{kl}, h_t, h_{goal})$ based on the knowledge graph G_{kl}, according to the learning status h_t and the learning goal h_{goal} of the learner. $f_{LPR}(G_{kl}, h_t, h_{goal}) = q_{i,t+1} \in Q$, that means the question $q_{i,t+1}$ is dynamically recommended according to the learning status and the goal of the learner.

4 Methodology

In this section, we first introduce the structure of our model TGKT-RL, and then introduce the two network structures of the model respectively.

4.1 The Whole Architecture of Our Model

Our main approach is to model the learning process of learners through knowledge tracing, by constructing a learner simulator, and then generating personalized learning paths through reinforcement learning.

We train our model TGKT-RL in two parts: one is the Knowledge Tracing Network (KTN), and the other is the Learning Path Recommendation Network (LPRN). The specific model structure is shown as Fig. 1:

The KTN models the learner's learning situation based on the learner's historical learning records. The LPRN trains a reinforcement learning agent to

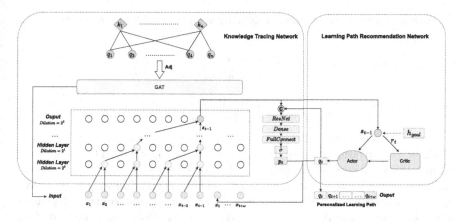

Fig. 1. The architecture of our model TGKT-RL.

recommend personalized exercise $q_{i,t}$ based on the knowledge state s_{t-1} obtained from KTN at time step $t-1$. The KTN then predicts the probability p_t of answering correctly to the question $q_{i,t}$ recommended by the LPRN and provides a new knowledge state s_t at time step t. Then the Actor adjusts its recommendation policy based on the state and the reward given by the Critic in the LPRN, gradually recommending more suitable and personalized exercises for the learner.

4.2 Knowledge Tracing Network (KTN)

As shown in Fig. 1, the KTN includes Embedding, Graph Attention Network and Temporal Convolution Network, which are responsible for the vectorization of relational dependencies of the learning records and the extraction of knowledge states.

To build our model, we need to construct the knowledge learning graph G_{kl} at first as Definition 2, then we use GAT to learn the relationship between nodes through self-attention mechanism, and calculate the weights between nodes based on these relationships. Then, we aggregate the neighbor skill nodes of each question node and obtain the feature vectors of them accordingly. Finally we can get the set of feature vectors of the question nodes $h = \{h_1, h_2, \ldots, h_n\}$ which is used to improve the question representation, where n denotes the number of question nodes in G_{kl}.

After that we need to vectorize all the data. Assuming that Q and SK denotes the universal set of questions and knowledge skills, then question q_i can be denoted as a vector $e_{q_i} \in \mathbb{R}^d$ and the answer a_i can be denoted as a vector $e_{a_i} \in \{0,1\}^d$, and the learning record $X_{<t}$ is denoted as a set connected by knowledge question vectors and answer vectors and the corresponding question feature vectors as follows:

$$E_{X<t} = \big(\{x_1, x_2, \ldots, x_{t-1}\} \mid x_i = e_{q_i} \oplus e_{\Delta t(q_i)} \oplus e_{a_i} \oplus h_i\big) \tag{1}$$

In order to reflect the temporal changes, we define the temporal vector $e_{\Delta t(q_i)}$ in this paper as follows:

$$e_{q_i} = f_{q2e} \left(\begin{pmatrix} \text{onehot}(i) \cdot (1 - e_{a_i}) \\ \text{onehot}(i) \cdot e_{a_i} \end{pmatrix} \right) \tag{2}$$

$$e_{\Delta t(q_i)} = \begin{pmatrix} \log \Delta t. (1 - e_{a_i}) \\ \log \Delta t \cdot e_{a_i} \end{pmatrix} \tag{3}$$

where f_{q2e} denotes the knowledge questions transformation function.

After vectorization, the input sequence will be input into TCN in order to extract the knowledge states as Fig. 1. The structure of TCN mainly uses one-dimensional Fully Convolutional Network (1D FCN) and Causal Dilated Convolution to observe longer input sequences and capture long-term time dependencies. FCN can ensure that the input and output lengths remain the same from layer to layer in the network, and therefore each input has a corresponding output at each time step. By incorporating causal convolution, the network's output at time step t depends solely on the input prior to time t, preventing any leakage of information from the future. However, causal convolution requires a very deep network for the long learning record of learners. To solve this problem, TCN uses dilated convolution to avoid the network depth from being too deep, where d is the dilated factor, which can increase the receptive field exponentially. Finally, we can obtain the knowledge state matrix $S_t \in \mathbb{R}^{N \times d}$ at each time step, where N is the total number of learning records, and $s_t \in \mathbb{R}^d$ denotes the knowledge state at time step t which is also used as the input of the LPRN.

In the LPRN, the Actor recommends the question $q_{i,t}$ at time step t based on the state s_{t-1} and policy. At this point, we concatenate the embedding of $q_{i,t}$ with s_{t-1}, and the concatenation result will be input into Residual Network, Dense Convolutional Network and fully connected network. Finally, we proceed through the sigmoid activation layer and obtain the prediction value p_t for question $q_{i,t}$ as follows:

$$p_t = \text{sigmoid}\left([s_{t-1}, e_{q_{i,t}}]\right) \tag{4}$$

The main role of Residual Network and Dense Convolutional Network is to enable the model to better extract the features of input information, thereby enhancing the expression ability of neural network and improving the performance of our model, finally improving the prediction accuracy.

The loss function of the KTN is calculated as follows:

$$\mathcal{L} = -\sum_{t=1}^{N} (a_{i,t} \log p_t + (1 - a_{i,t}) \log (1 - p_t)) \tag{5}$$

where a_i represents the true label.

To obtain the next state s_t, we estimate the answer $a_{i,t}$ to the question $q_{i,t}$ based on the prediction value p_t. If $p_t \geq 0.5$, then $a_{i,t}=1$, otherwise $a_{i,t}=0$. Then, we combine the question and the corresponding answer as $x_t = \{q_{i,t}, a_{i,t}\}$ which means the learning record at time step t, and add it into the historical learning record $\{x_1, x_2, \ldots, x_t\}$ after re-vectorization. Finally, we obtain the knowledge state s_t at time step t through TCN processing again.

4.3   Learning Path Recommendation Network (LPRN)

The LPRN is a reinforcement learning network. The actual training needs to train the KTN based on historical data at first. the KTN is used as the reinforcement learning environment to provide knowledge states at each time step and participate in the training of LPRN in order to train an agent to recommend personalized exercises.

We model the recommendation process as a Partially Observable Markov Decision Process (POMDP), where the state is the learner's latent knowledge state obtained from the KTN and the action is the recommendation of an exercise. The training process can be referred to Fig. 2.

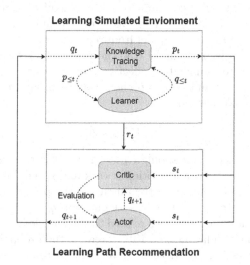

Fig. 2. Learning Path Recommendation training process.

Before the start of training, we set a target knowledge state in advance as $h_{goal} = \{p_{k_1}, p_{k_2}, \ldots, p_{k_n} \mid p_{k_i} \in [0, 1]\}$ to represent the mastery degree of each knowledge skill k_i learner wants to achieve. After knowledge state generated at each time step, we need to compare it with h_{goal} as follows:

$$C_t = h_{goal} - s_t = \{d_{k_1}, d_{k_2}, \ldots, d_{k_n}\} \tag{6}$$

where d_{k_i} denotes the difference between the current knowledge state and the target knowledge state of skill k_i. If $|C_t - \epsilon| \to 0$, then the reinforcement learning network training is completed, and the exercises sequence generated by the LPRN is our recommended personalized learning path. Otherwise, it is necessary to further train the LPRN. At this point, we consider a global change stability degree F_t of all historical knowledge states $\{s_1, s_2, \ldots, s_t\}$ to measure whether the knowledge states change stably, and we will consider it as part of the reward which is beneficial to achieving our target, as follows:

$$F_t = X(s_1, s_2, \ldots, s_t) \tag{7}$$

To compare the difference in knowledge mastery degree of skill k_i before and after the recommendation at time step t, the difference can be formalized as:

$$A_t = \begin{cases} \frac{p_{k_i,t} - p_{k_i,t-1}}{n_{k_i,t}}, p_{k_i,t} - p_{k_i,t-1} > 0 \\ p_{k_i,t} - p_{k_i,t-1}, p_{k_i,t} - p_{k_i,t-1} \le 0 \end{cases} \tag{8}$$

where k_i denotes the skill related to the latest recommended exercise $q_{i,t}$, $p_{k_i,t}$ denotes the probability of answering correctly of skill k_i at time step t, $n_{k_i,t}$ denotes the number of times skill k_i has been recommended at time step t. The difference A_t can avoid the model from repeatedly recommending the same skills with high rewards. For our LPRN, the reward function is defined as the reward obtained by recommending effective and suitable exercises. Therefore, we consider Eqs. (6), (7) and (8) comprehensively to design the reward function. This process can be formalized as:

$$r_t = Y(C_t, F_t, A_t) \tag{9}$$

where $Y(C_t, F_t, A_t)$ denotes mapping C_t, F_t, A_t to $[0,1]$ through MLP. Then s_t will be input into the Actor and Critic network and r_t will be input into Critic network responsible for evaluating the quality of the policy made by the Actor at last time step. Actor predicts the next question $q_{i,t+1}$ based on s_t and the policy, where we select the questions related to the knowledge skills with $d_{k_i} < 0$ in Eq. (6) for recommendation, and KTN predicts the probability of answering correctly to the question $q_{i,t+1}$, then we add the learning record at time step $t+1$ to the historical learning record sequence as input for KTN to obtain the knowledge state s_{t+1} at next time step, so as to form a training closed loop.

The termination condition of reinforcement learning network is that when the state $s_{t+\omega}$ generated at time step $t+\omega$ has reached our initial target h_{goal}, that is $|C_{t+\omega} - \epsilon| \to 0$, then we can get the personalized learning path LP recommended by the model as follows:

$$LP = \{q_{1,t}, q_{2,t+1}, \ldots, q_{i,t+\omega} \mid q_i \in Q\} \tag{10}$$

In this paper, we apply an reinforcement method Soft Actor-Critic [4] to solve our problem, in which the gradient formulas of APN (Actor Policy Network) [represented by LPR in this paper] and CVN (Critic Value Network) are as follows:

$$\begin{aligned} \widehat{\nabla}_\theta J_{CVN}(\theta) =& \nabla_\theta f_{\theta:CVN}(q_{i,t}, s_t, h_{goal})(f_{\theta:CVN}(q_{i,t}, s_t, h_{goal}) \\ & - (r_t + gamma(f_{\bar\theta:CVN}(q_{i,t+1}, s_{t+1}, h_{goal}) \\ & - \alpha \log(f_{\emptyset:LPR}(q_{i,t+1} \mid G_{kl}, s_{t+1}, h_{goal}))))) \end{aligned} \tag{11}$$

$$\widehat{\nabla}_{\emptyset} J_{LPR}(\emptyset) = \nabla_{\emptyset} \alpha \log \left(f_{\emptyset:LPR} \left(q_{i,t} \mid G_{kl}, s_t, h_{goal} \right) \right)$$

$$+ \left(\nabla_{q_{i,t}} \alpha \log \left(f_{\emptyset:LPR} \left(q_{i,t} \mid G_{kl}, s_t, h_{goal} \right) \right) \right) \quad (12)$$

$$- \nabla_{q_{i,t}} f_{\theta:CVN} \left(q_{i,t}, s_t, h_{goal} \right) \right) \nabla_{\emptyset} f_{\emptyset} \left(\epsilon_t, s_t \right)$$

The specific training process can be referred to Algorithm 1:

Algorithm 1. Learning Path Recommendation training process with Soft Actor-Critic

Input: KTN (Knowledge Tracing Network), APN (Actor Policy Network), CVN (Critic Value Network), X_0, q_0, G_{kl}, s_0, h_{goal}, θ_1, θ_2, $\emptyset$, D, T
Output: f_{LPR}
1: Init(APN,CVN)   //Initialize the APN,CVN network parameters
2: **for** each iteration **do**
3:     **for** each step $t=1$ to T **do**
4:         $q_{i,t} = f_{LPR} \left(G_{kl}, s_{t-1}, h_{goal} \right)$ //action
5:         $p \left(a_i = 1 \right) = f_{KT} \left(X_{<t}, q_{i,t} \right)$
6:         $X \leftarrow X \cup \{(q_{i,t}, a_i)\}$
7:         $s_t = \varphi_{ss} \left(X_{<t}, \varphi_{sk} \left(X_{<t} \right) \right)$ //state
8:         $C_t = h_{goal} - s_t$
9:         $F_t = f \left(s_1, s_2, \ldots, s_t \right)$
10:        $A_t = \omega \left(p_{k_i,t}, p_{k_i,t-1} \right)$
11:        $r_t = \varphi \left(C_t, F_t, A_t \right)$ //reward
12:        $D \leftarrow D \cup \{(s_{t-1}, q_{i,t}, r_t, s_t)\}$ //Replay Buffer
13:    **end for**
14:    **for** each gradient step **do**
15:        $\theta_i \leftarrow \theta_i - \mu_{CVN} \widehat{\nabla}_{\theta_i} J_{CVN} \left(\theta_i \right)$ $for\ i \in \{1,2\}$
16:        $\emptyset \leftarrow \emptyset - \mu_{LPR} \widehat{\nabla}_{\emptyset} J_{LPR}(\emptyset)$
17:        $\theta_i \leftarrow \tau \theta_i + (1 - \tau)\bar{\theta}_i$ $for\ i \in \{1,2\}$
18:    **end for**
19: **end for**
20: **return** f_{LPR}

---

5 Experiment

In this section, we will demonstrate the effectiveness and advantages of our model TGKT-RL through extensive experiments. Specifically, we will compare the performance of our model on two real datasets and explore the diversity of the model's recommendation results as well as the changes in knowledge mastery degree during the process. Furthermore, we will conduct ablation studies to observe the rationality of different reward settings in reinforcement learning.

5.1 Datasets

In order to better train our model in the experiments, we conduct experiments on two widely used datasets. The statistics of these datasets are shown in Table 2, and the details are as follows:

- **ASSIST09**[1] collects teaching data from the ASSISTments online teaching
  system from 2009 to 2010, including math topics for grades 4–10. After removing invalid data, the dataset includes 3,852 students, 167 skills, 17,737 exercises and 282,619 records.
- **ASSIST12**[2] collects teaching data from the ASSISTments online teaching
  system during the school year 2012–2013. In this dataset each exercise is
  related to one skill but one skill related to more than one exercise. After
  removing invalid data, the dataset includes 27,485 students, 265 skills, 53,065
  exercises and 2,709,436 records.

Table 2. Datasets Statistics.

Items	ASSIST09	ASSIST12
# students	3852	27485
# exercises	17737	53065
# skills	167	265
# records	282619	2709436

5.2 Baselines

To evaluate the recommendation performance of our model, we introduce two
baselines and the details of the baselines are as follows:

- **Greedy Algorithm** follows a strategy of local optimal solution, that is, at
  each step it simulates all recommended skills and selects the recommended
  skill that can provide the learner with higher mastery degree after learning.
- **Random Algorithm** considers the learner's state simulated by the knowledge tracing environment and generates a random learning path by randomly
  selecting knowledge skill at each step, in order to find potential optimal solutions.

5.3 Performance

We conduct multiple rounds of experiments and take the average value as the
result. For the above two datasets, we set the learning rate of KTN to 0.001.
In the LPRN, considering the actual learning situation of learners, we set the
maximum learning length of each experiment to 200 to avoid learners being
trapped in a too long learning process. The three metrics we compare are average
of reward, total mastery degree and total running time. The average of reward is

[1] https://sites.google.com/site/assistmentsdata/home/2009-2010-assistment-data/skill-builder-data-2009-2010.
[2] https://sites.google.com/site/assistmentsdata/datasets/2012-13-school-data-with-affect.

the average value of each recommendation round of reward, with a higher average reward indicating better help for learners' knowledge state improvement. Total mastery level represents the sum of predicted probabilities for all knowledge skills of learners, with a higher total mastery level indicating better overall learning outcomes for learners.

Table 3. Comparison of result on different datasets.

Algorithm	Average of reward		Total mastery degree		Total running time(s)	
	ASSIST09	ASSIST12	ASSIST09	ASSIST12	ASSIST09	ASSIST12
MODEL	0.705	0.694	72.454	69.350	4827.64	7203.26
GA	0.733	0.719	74.646	71.167	15274.16	22853.15
RA	0.647	0.622	61.324	57.839	240.41	337.93

The experiment results are shown as Table 3, which demonstrate that our method has better performance in terms of average reward and total mastery level on both ASSIST09 and ASSIST12 datasets compared to the random algorithm. The greedy algorithm performs slightly better as it considers all possible actions at each step, but only at the cost of a large amount of running time. It can be seen that our method significantly reduces running time compared to the greedy algorithm, while its performance in terms of average reward and total mastery degree on both datasets is close to that of the greedy algorithm. Therefore, considering the effectiveness and running cost comprehensively, our method is practical and effective.

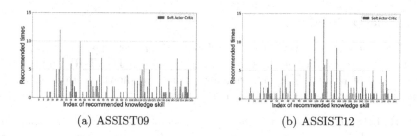

(a) ASSIST09   (b) ASSIST12

Fig. 3. Diversity analysis of the recommended skills in a learning path.

To avoid excessive repetition of recommending same knowledge skills in a personalized learning path, we count the recommended times of each knowledge skill in the two datasets. As shown in Fig. 3, the horizontal axis represents the index of the recommended knowledge skill while the vertical axis represents the number of times each skill was recommended. It is worth noting that some knowledge skills have never been recommended, which may be due to missing data in the corresponding sequences of learners in the original dataset or the limited of maximum learning length. However, the entire recommendation process covers the vast majority of knowledge skills, making the recommended learning path more diversified under the premise of a maximum learning length of 200 for learners.

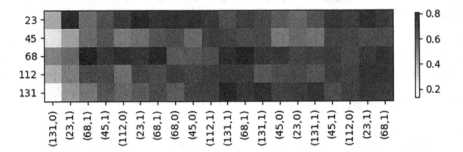

Fig. 4. The knowledge state prediction of one student.

Figure 4 shows the changes in predicted knowledge states for five skills (ID: 23, 45, 68, 112, and 131). The horizontal axis represents the recommended knowledge skills and the predicted answers while the vertical axis represents the index of the five skills. The depth of blue indicates the mastery level of the knowledge skill, with darker colors indicating higher mastery levels. At the initial stage, the mastery level of each skill is low, but after a period of practice, the learner's relevant knowledge state gradually improves. Although there may be some fluctuations during the training process, the learner's final knowledge state can reach a high and relatively stable level.

5.4 Ablation Study

In order to verify the effectiveness of different reward settings in the LPRN, we conduct ablation studies on three variants of our model TGKT-RL and compare the average of reward. The performance results are shown in Table 4 and the details of the three settings are listed as follows:

- **TGKT-RL-C_t** removes the difference between the knowledge state s_t at time step t and the pre-set target knowledge state h_{goal} during each recommendation round.
- **TGKT-RL-F_t** removes the global change stability degree F_t for each recommendation round, we only focus on the current knowledge state s_t at time step t.
- **TGKT-RL-A_t** removes the difference of the mastery degree and recommended times of the recommended knowledge skills before and after each round of recommendation

From Table 4 we have the following findings: our model TGKT-RL, which considers all aspects of reward, achieves the best performance, which shows the effectiveness of the comprehensive reward settings. Moreover, we observe that

Table 4. Results of ablation study on two datasets.

Model	ASSIST09	ASSIST12
TGKT-RL -C_t	0.6766	0.6693
TGKT-RL -F_t	0.6512	0.6480
TGKT-RL -A_t	0.5652	0.5878
TGKT-RL	**0.7053**	**0.6935**

TGKT-RL-C_t performs better than other variants, indicating that taking into account the difference between the knowledge state and the pre-set target knowledge state h_{goal} during each recommendation round can better help us select knowledge skills that are far from the target for recommendation, thereby rapidly improving the learners' knowledge mastery degree. Additionally, the performance of TGKT-RL-F_t suggests that considering the global change stability degree F_t can enhance the stability and effectiveness of recommendation. Comparing the results of TGKT-RL-A_t with our model, the worst performance proves that it's not negligible to consider the difference in mastery degree of the recommended knowledge skills before and after each recommendation, which is also beneficial for timely adjusting the reinforcement learning policy, therefore enhancing the rationality and effectiveness of recommendation.

6 Conclusion

In this paper, we propose a personalized learning path recommendation model TGKT-RL which is based on knowledge tracing and reinforcement learning. By constructing KTN to model learners' learning process and applying it for dynamic knowledge tracing. Then, we construct LPRN to recommend personalized exercises based on learners' goals and learning outcomes, and dynamically adjust the recommendation policy according to the states and rewards during the process, and finally obtain a personalized learning path. The results on the two real datasets show that our method achieve better comprehensive performance, which can significantly improve the effectiveness and in line with learners' actual learning situation. In addition, we also conduct ablation studies to verify the effectiveness of different reward settings in the LPRN. One of the limitations of our study is that we just conduct a single task for reinforcement learning, while considering multi-task reinforcement learning may be better suited to the actual learning situation. We will continue to work on this issue in the future.

References

1. Ai, F., et al.: Concept-aware deep knowledge tracing and exercise recommendation in an online learning system. (2019)
2. Bian, C.L., Wang, D.L., Liu, S.Y., Lu, W.G., Dong, J.Y.: Adaptive learning path recommendation based on graph theory and an improved immune algorithm. KSII Trans. Internet Inf. Syst. **13**, 2277–2298 (2019)

3. Cai, D., Zhang, Y., Dai, B.: Learning path recommendation based on knowledge tracing model and reinforcement learning. In: ICCC, pp. 1881–1885 (2019)
4. Christodoulou, P.: Soft actor-critic for discrete action settings. CoRR abs/1910.07207 (2019)
5. Ghosh, A., Heffernan, N., Lan, A.S.: Context-aware attentive knowledge tracing. In: Proceedings of the 26th ACM SIGKDD International Conference on Knowledge Discovery & Data Mining, pp. 2330–2339 (2020)
6. Liu, Q., Tong, S., Liu, C., Zhao, H., Chen, E., Ma, H.: Exploiting cognitive structure for adaptive learning. In: SIGKDD, pp. 627–635 (2019)
7. Ma, R., et al.: Dtkt: an improved deep temporal convolutional network for knowledge tracing. In: ICCSE, pp. 794–799 (2021)
8. Nabizadeh, A.H., et al.: Adaptive learning path recommender approach using auxiliary learning objects. Comput. Educ. **147**, 103777 (2020)
9. Nabizadeh, A.H., Jorge, A.M., Leal, J.P.: RUTICO: recommending successful learning paths under time constraints. In: UMAP, pp. 153–158 (2017)
10. Nagatani, K., et al.: Augmenting knowledge tracing by considering forgetting behavior. In: WWW, pp. 3101–3107 (2019)
11. Nakagawa, H., Iwasawa, Y., Matsuo, Y.: Graph-based knowledge tracing: modeling student proficiency using graph neural network. In: WIC, pp. 156–163 (2019)
12. Niknam, M., Thulasiraman, P.: LPR: a bio-inspired intelligent learning path recommendation system based on meaningful learning theory. Educ. Inf. Technol. **25**, 3797–3819 (2020)
13. Pandey, S., Karypis, G.: A self-attentive model for knowledge tracing. arXiv preprint arXiv:1907.06837 (2019)
14. Piech, C., et al.: Deep knowledge tracing. In: Advances in Neural Information Processing Systems, vol. 28, pp. 505–513 (2015)
15. Rafsanjani, A.H.N.: A long term goal recommender approach for learning environments. In: 11th International Conference on Web Information Systems and Technologies (2018)
16. Shao, X., Zhang, M.: Temporal convolutional knowledge tracing model with attention mechanism. J. Comput. Appl. **43**, 343-348 (2022)
17. Shi, D., et al.: A learning path recommendation model based on a multidimensional knowledge graph framework for e-learning. Knowl. Based Syst. **195**, 105618 (2020)
18. Shin, D., Shim, Y., Yu, H., Lee, S., Kim, B., Choi, Y.: SAINT+: integrating temporal features for EdNet correctness prediction. In: LAK, pp. 490–496 (2021)
19. Song, X., Li, J., Tang, Y., Zhao, T., Chen, Y.: JKT: a joint graph convolutional network based deep knowledge tracing. Inf. Sci. **580**, 510–523 (2021)
20. Vanitha, V., Krishnan, P.: A modified ant colony algorithm for personalized learning path construction. J. Intell. Fuzzy Syst. **37**, 6785–6800 (2019)
21. Wang, C., et al.: TCN-KT: a temporal convolutional knowledge tracking model fusion of personal basis and forgetting. Appl. Res. Comput. **2022** (039–005) (2022)
22. Yang, Y., et al.: Gikt: a graph-based interaction model for knowledge tracing. In: PKDD, pp. 299–315 (2021)
23. Yun, Y., Dai, H., Zhang, Y., Shang, X., Li, Z.: A survey of personalized learning path recommendation. J. Softw. **33**(12), 4590–4615 (2021)
24. Zhang, J., Shi, X., King, I., Yeung, D.Y.: Dynamic key-value memory networks for knowledge tracing. In: WWW, pp. 765–774 (2017)
25. Zhu, H., et al.: A multi-constraint learning path recommendation algorithm based on knowledge map. Knowl. Based Syst. **143**, 102–114 (2018)

Fusion High-Order Information with Nonnegative Matrix Factorization Based Community Infomax for Community Detection

Ying Li[1], Guohua Chen[2,3(✉)], Yong Tang[1], and Nini Zhang[1]

[1] School of Computer Science, South China Normal University, Guangzhou, China
{liying,ytang,zhangnini}@m.scnu.edu.cn
[2] Network Center, South China Normal University, Guangzhou, China
chengh@m.scnu.edu.cn
[3] Pazhou Lab, Guangzhou, China

Abstract. Community detection plays an important role in understanding the structures and functions of complex networks. Due to their simplicity, flexibility, effectiveness, and better interpretability, Nonnegative Matrix Factorization (NMF)-based methods have been widely employed for community detection. However, most existing NMF-based community detection algorithms are shallow methods and their performance is limited when facing complex real-world networks. On the other view, the high-order information of the graph can provide more abundant structure information for community detection. Considering those questions, we propose a novel high-order NMF-based community detection method called HGI-NMF, which is composed of three modules: multi-hops graph attention encoders, graph-level mutual information, and NMF-based community mutual information. This approach first encodes the high-order graph structure with an attention encoder and then uses the readout function, discriminator and graph, and community-level mutual information to jointly optimize our model. The experimental results show that our model outperforms state-of-the-art community detection methods.

Keywords: Community detection · Nonnegative matrix factorization · Graph neural networks · Mutal information

1 Introduction

Nowadays, various real-world complex interaction systems are ubiquitous in nature which can be characterized by complex networks, such as social networks, citation networks, biological neural networks and so on. These networks often consist of functional units, which manifest in the form of communities. Community detection is a kind of method to find the clusters of vertices which have similar characteristics. In specific, community detection take as inputs the network topology and network attributes and output a set of communities that can

© The Author(s), under exclusive license to Springer Nature Switzerland AG 2023
Z. Jin et al. (Eds.): KSEM 2023, LNAI 14119, pp. 347–359, 2023.
https://doi.org/10.1007/978-3-031-40289-0_28

be either disjoint or overlapping, where nodes in the same community connect to each other more densely than those in different community [9,26].

In the past decades, various methods for community detection have been proposed, include modularity optimization based methods [38], stochastic block model based methods [1], clustering based method [6,17], statistical inference and so on. Recently, NMF-based community detection methods are widely used as an effective clustering model [14,18,23,34,40,41]. The purpose of NMF is to decompose the adjacency matrix of a network into two low-dimensional representations, and one of which can be interpreted as a node-community membership matrix. NMF-based community detection has exhibited its unique advantages, the existing NMF-based community detection approaches are all shallow methods. They assume that the original networks could be directly reconstructed using a linear combination of community features. Considering the complicated and various nonlinear features of real-world networks, it is highly possible that the mapping between the original network and the community membership space contains rather complex structural information, which cannot be well learned and interpreted by classic NMF-based community detection approaches.

In recent years, graph neural network(GNN) proposed to deal with unstructured graph data and achieved huge success in many domains. The aim of GNN is learning a function which can map every node into a low-dimension vector space with graph implicit structure information [8,12,29]. The high-order structure information of graph and the attribute information of nodes play important roles on graph embedding which can provide more information for community discovery. However, due to the aggregation strategy of current graph neural network models, model need to propagate multiple times in every training steps. In other words, traditional graph neural network stacking multiple message propagate layer to acquire high level graph structure information. Due to the limitation of the number of hidden layers of graph neural network and over-smooth problem [16,19,32,37], most graph neural networks cannot obtain high level embedding features of nodes.

Motivated by the above-mentioned analyses, in this article we propose a novel high-order NMF-based community detection method called HGI-NMF, which can learn high order community structure information. We use a multi-hop graph attention encoder to get latent representations for each node in the attributed graph. After that we perform GNMF method on nodes representation vectors to get community division matrix, and get the community summary and graph summary representations via a readout operation. A discriminator is applied to calculate the probabilities of nodes belonging to different communities. The multi-hop graph attention encoder and the discriminator are jointly optimized so that the model can learn topology information, node attribute information, and higher-order information simultaneously. At last, we use other method like MLP on the learned node representations to assign the node to correspond community. We conduct extensive experiments to demonstrate the effectiveness of HGI-NMF. Experiment results show that the representation learned by HGI-NMF can outperform most strong baseline and state-of-the-art community detection methods in Normalized Mutual Information (NMI) and Adjusted Rand Index (ARI), and Accuracy (ACC) on three well-known citation network.

Our contributions are summarized as follows:

- We proposed a new model for community detection, which can learn low-dimension nodes representation with node attribute and higher-order graph structure and community information at the same time.
- We design a new NMF-based community mutual information method on attributed graphs to help learn the community related node representations. This method can help model learn the community partition directly.
- We perform experiments on three citation network, and compare our model with several benchmark methods. Experiment results demonstrate the effectiveness and efficiency of our model.

The rest of this paper is organized as follows. We first briefly review the related work in Sect. 2, and then respectively detail the proposed method HGI-NMF and report the experiment results in Sects. 3 and 4. Finally, we conclude this paper in Sect. 5.

2 Relate Work

2.1 NMF-Based Community Detection Method

Nonnegative Matrix Factorization is a classical low-rank matrix factorization model for dimensionality reduction and feature extraction [14]. The method aims to decompose the feature matrix W into two matrices ($U \in \mathbb{R}^{n \times k}$ and $P \in \mathbb{R}^{k \times n}$) following nonnegative constraints that $U \geq 0$ and $P \geq 0$. The matrix U corresponds to the mapping between the given network and the community membership space. Each column in the matrix $P = [p_{ij}]$ indicates the community membership for each node (v_i, c_j) in the probability of p_{ij}. Due to the nonnegativity constraint, every data sample can be represented as an additive linear combination of the basis features in the basis matrix, and the coefficients are from the corresponding vector in the coefficient matrix. NMF-based community detection methods is applicable for disjoint and overlapping community detection and have good interpretability.

As pioneers, Psorakis et al. [23] presented a powerful interpretability probabilistic approach, which utilizes a Bayesian nonnegative matrix factorization model to extract community information from a network for overlapping community detection. Recently, various NMF-based community detection methods have been proposed by extending the basic NMF. Kuang et al. [13] and others [20,42] developed a symmetric NMF-based methods, which decompose the second power of the normalized adjacency matrix based on symmetric nonnegative matrix factorization. Some research [18,36,39] incorporate semi-supervised NMF method into community detection. For example, Liu et al. [18] combine semi-supervised NMF and graph regularization with the pairwise constraints; Wu et al. [36] proposed a pairwise constraint propagation-induced SymmNMF-based semi-supervised clustering method, which can learn the similarity and assignment matrices adaptively and simultaneously. Cai et al. [3] and other works [10] developed a graph regularization based NMF approach (graph regularized NMF) for parts-based data representation, which constructs an affinity graph to encode the geometrical information and seeks a matrix factorization to preserve the graph structure. With the development of graph neural network, some researcher try to combine NMF-based community detection method with graph representation learning, such as Wang et al. [34] proposed a modularized nonnegative matrix factorization model to incorporate the community structure into network embedding. Rozemberczki et al. [24] proposed a NMF-based graph-embedding algorithm to learns community structures and node embeddings simultaneously. Ma et al. [21] and Li et al. [15] proposed nonnegative matrix factorization frameworks to detect communities dynamic graph and hypergraph respectively.

2.2   Graph Neural Networks

Early GNNs studies concentrated on the recurrent graph neural networks (RecGNNs) [7,25]. Those methods learned the node's representations by iteratively propagating neighbor information until a stable fixed point is reached. This process is computationally expensive and all node's representations are learned with the shared weights which means the nodes with similar neighbor could not well recognized. Though RecGNNs are not preformed well in some tasks, the idea of message passing still inherited by the later works. Inspired by the success of CNNs and RecGNNs, many methods introduce CNNs on a 2D grid to general graphs, which called graph convolutional neural networks (GCNNs). GCNNs defines a convolution operation on graphs and can learn graph representation by iteratively aggregate the features from neighbors, which include [2,11,12,22].

Graph attention neural networks [29] incorporate attention mechanisms into GNNs by assigning different importance to nodes of the same neighborhood at the feature aggregation step. Based on this work, other attention-based GNNs have been proposed, including GaAN [43], HAN [35], GeniePath [19] and so on. Wang et al. [33] consider power series expansion for the attention matrix inverse and geometric distribution decay factor to aggregation multi-hop neighbor information which is not very efficiency and blocked by the size of graph adjacency matrix. Zhang et al. [44] convert graph to multiple linkless subgraphs with top-k intimacy sampling approach.

There are quite a number of works on GNNs. However, rare of them considered the community information in real-world graphs.

3   Method

Give a network $G = (\mathcal{V}, \mathcal{E}, \mathcal{X})$, where $\mathcal{V}$ is the set of nodes and $\mathcal{E}$ is the set of edges. $N = |V|$ and $M = |E|$ means the number of nodes and edges respectively. Then we use $A \in \mathbb{R}^{N \times N}$ to denote the adjacency matrix of graph G and $X \in \mathcal{R}^{N \times F}$ to denote the node's feature matrix, where F is the features dimension.

In this article, our work aims at learning an encoder $f : \mathbb{R}^{N \times F} \to \mathbb{R}^{N \times d}$ that can map the node feature into a low-dimensional space $\mathbb{R}^d$, where d is usually far less than F, and then use other method like MLP to assign each node into its community. We denote the initial feature of node v_i as h_i, and use vector representation matrix $X = (h_1, h_2, \cdots, h_N)^T$ to denote the representations of all nodes (Fig. 1).

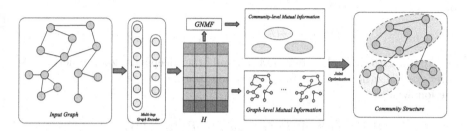

Fig. 1. Architecture of d HGI-NMF.

3.1   Graph Attention Networks with High-Order Information

For the given adjacency matrix A and feature matrix X as inputs, the graph encoder aims to encode the high-order graph structure information into the low-dimension embedding representation for every node in graph G. Graph attention network use attention mechanism to aggregate the node's first-order neighbor information. At each layer l, a vector message is computed for each edge (v_i, v_j). The attention score s of an edge (v_i, v_j) is computed by the following:

$$s_{i,j}^{(l)} = LeakyReLU \left(\alpha^{(l)} tanh(W^{(l)} h_i^{(l)} \| W^{(l)} h_j^{(l)}) \right) \tag{1}$$

where $W^{(l)} \in \mathbb{R}^{d \times d}$ and $\alpha^{(l)} \in R^{1 \times 2d}$ are the trainable weights. $h_i \in \mathbb{R}^d$ represents the embedding of node i at ith layer.

Applying Eq. 1 on each edge of the graph G , we obtain an attention score matrix $S^{(l)}$:

$$S_{i,j}^{(l)} = \begin{cases} s_{i,j}^{(l)}, & (v_i, v_j) \in G \\ 0, & othervise. \end{cases} \tag{2}$$

Subsequently we obtain the attention matrix $\mathcal{A}^{(l)}$ by performing row-wised softmax over the score matrix $S^{(l)}$: $\mathcal{A}^{(l)} = softmax(S^{(l)})$. $\mathcal{A}_{ij}$ denotes the attention value at layer l when aggregating message from node j to node i.

In order to learning high-order graph topology information, one traditional ideal is aggregate all possible multi-hop information:

$$AttDiffusion(\mathcal{A}^{(l)}, H^{(l)}, \Theta) = \mathcal{A}^{(l)} H^{(l)}$$

$$\hat{H}^{(l+1)} = \sum_{i=0}^{\infty} \theta_i AttDiffusion(\mathcal{A}^{(l),i}, H^{(l)}, \Theta) \tag{3}$$

where $\mathcal{A}^{(l),i} = \underbrace{\mathcal{A}^{(l)} \cdot \mathcal{A}^{(l)} \cdots \mathcal{A}^{(l)}}_{i}$ is i power of l layer attention matrix, θ_i is the information decay factor and $\theta_i > \theta_{i+1}$ and θ is the set of parameters. Due to computing the powers of the attention matrix, the information aggregate method compute by Eq. 3 may be prohibitively expensive. To resolve this bottleneck, we apply a approximate computation which first propose by MAGNA [33]. They approximate $\mathcal{A}^{(l)}H^{(l)}$ with a sequence $Z^{(}K)$ which converges to the true value of $\mathcal{A}^{(l)}H^{(l)}$ as $K \to \infty$:

$$Z^{(0)} = H^{(l)}, Z^{(K+1)} = (1 - \alpha)\mathcal{A}Z^{(k)} + \alpha Z^{(0)} \tag{4}$$

Applid with multiple attention head and other deep aggregation method like layer normalization and residual connection, the final node feature update rule are follow:

$$\hat{H}^{(l)} = \left(||_{i=1}^{M} AttDiffusion(\mathcal{A}^{(l)}, H^{(l)}, \Theta_i)\right) W_o$$
$$\hat{H}^{(l+1)} = \hat{H}^{(l)} + H^{(l)} \tag{5}$$
$$H^{(l+1)} = W_2^{(l)} ReLU\left(W_1^{(l)} LayerNorm(\hat{H}^{(l+1)})\right) + \hat{H}^{(l+1)}$$

where W_1, W_2, W_o are trainable weight matrix.

3.2   Graph and Community Level Summary

With the node embedding H learned via multi-hop graph attention encoder, we introduce a readout operation to get the community-level summary vectors for each community and graph-level summary for the graph. For convenience, we refer it as community representation and graph representation in the following. Community representation summarize the obtained node embeddings of corresponding community members, thus reflects their distribution. We utilize a community representation matrix C to denote representations of all communities, where C_i is the representation of the ith community.

In order to get C, we first need to identify the members of each community. In this part, we apply GNMF community detection method which produces a soft assignment of the nodes to communities. The goal of GNMF is denote as:

$$L_{GNMF} = ||H - UV^T||^2 + \lambda Tr(V^T LV) \tag{6}$$

where the matrix U means community belonging matrix and $Tr(\cdot)$ denotes the trace of a matrix.

Then we use a readout function $\mathcal{R}$ to get graph summary representation according to node representations H and community summary representation according to both H and corresponding community belonging relationships U.

We simply use the mean-pooling operation for all node's features within the same community since mean learns distributions:

$$s_{c_i} = \mathcal{R}(\varepsilon(H,A),U) = \sigma(\frac{1}{|c_i|} \sum_{j \in c_i} h_j)$$

$$s_g = \mathcal{R}(\varepsilon(H,A)) = \sigma(\frac{1}{N} \sum_{i=1}^{N} h_i)$$

(7)

where $\varepsilon(\cdot)$ indicate the graph neural network which introduced in Sect. 3.1.

3.3 Mutual Infomax Learning

Graph-Level Mutual Infomax. Two random variables X and Y's mutual information is defined as:

$$I(X;Y) = H(X) - H(X|Y) = \int_{XY} log \frac{dP_{XY}}{dP_X \times dP_Y} dP_{XY}$$

(8)

where $H(X)$ indicates the entropy of X; $H(X|Y)$ indicates the entropy bought by Y when X is given, P_{XY} represents the joint distribution of X and Y, and P_X and P_Y are the corresponding marginal distribution of X and Y.

Following DGI [30], the basic idea of training the network encoder with the InfoMax principle is to maximize the mutual information between nodes' patch representation h_i (local) and the representation of graph summary s. This training strategy encourages the encoder the aggregate more graph-level informaion for a node, and the noise information in a node's vicinity should not be encoded. However, calculating the mutual information of continuous vectors precisely is difficult. The Jensen-Shannon MI estimator is frequently used to maximize MI's lower bound between the joint distribution and the marginal products. A discriminator is developed and employs a typical binary cross-entropy (BCE) loss across samples from the (positive) joint distribution and the (negative) product of marginals. The general objective is defined as:

$$\mathcal{L}_{graph} = \frac{1}{N+M} \left(\sum_{i=1}^{N} \mathbb{E}_{(A,X)}[log\mathcal{D}(h_i,s_g)] + \sum_{j=1}^{M} \mathbb{E}_{(\tilde{A},\tilde{X})}[log\mathcal{D}(\tilde{h}_i,s_g)] \right)$$

(9)

where s_g is the presentation of graph summary present in Eq. 7. $\mathcal{D}(h_i,s_i) = \sigma(h_i^T W s_i)$ is the discriminator that provides the likelihood score assigned to this path-summary pair.

354 Y. Li et al.

Community-Level Mutual Infomax. In this part, we are represent the proxy for mutual information between community representation and node representation. We denote the discriminator of community-level is $\mathcal{D}_c(h_i, s_{c_i})$, therefore $\mathcal{D}_c(h_i, s_{c_i})$ is the probability that node v_i belongs to community c_j. $\mathcal{D}_c(h_i, s_{c_i})$ should be higher for node-community pairs that exists belonging relationship, and lower for those that do not exist such relationship. In our work, we use the Euclidean distance between node and community representation to reflect the probability of the node belongs to the corresponding community. The shorter the distance, the greater the probability that the node belongs to the community:

$$\mathcal{D}_c(h_i, s_{c_j}) = 1 - \sigma\left(\sqrt{\sum_{l \in d}(h_{il} - c_{jl})^2}\right) \tag{10}$$

where σ is a row-wise softmax function that is used to convert distance into probabilities.

We use the community assignment to treat nodes as positive and negative samples at the same time. We assume that each community can be viewed as an independent distribution, and edges can be viewed as been generated by these distributions. Therefore, a node can be regarded as a positive sample of the corresponding community as well as a negative sample of other communities. The mutual information between node vector and the corresponding community representation should be high, while that with other community representations should be low. The matrices of positive and negative samples can be formulated as:

$$\begin{aligned} \mathcal{D}^+ &= \mathcal{D} \circ U \\ \mathcal{D}^- &= \mathcal{D} - \mathcal{D}^+ \end{aligned} \tag{11}$$

where $\circ$ is Hadamard product operation. Follow with loss fuction proposed by DGI, The discrimination objective between communities and nodes is defined as:

$$\mathcal{L}_{comm} = \frac{1}{NM}\left(\sum_{i=1}^{N}\mathbb{E}_{(A,X)}[log\mathcal{D}^+(h_i, s_i)] + \sum_{j \neq i}\mathbb{E}_{(\tilde{A},\tilde{X})}[log\mathcal{D}^-(\tilde{h}_i, s_j)]\right) \tag{12}$$

Therefore, overall objective is in conjunction with the graph-level and community-level objective:

$$\mathcal{L} = \mathcal{L}_{graph} + \lambda\mathcal{L}_{comm} \tag{13}$$

where λ is a parameter that determines each component's importance.

4 Experiments

4.1 Datasets

In this part, we select 3 real-world citation networks, including Cora, Citeseer, and Pubmed. For citation network, node corresponds to a paper and edges are citation links between two papers. Each node has a class label which represents the topic associated with the paper. For the sake of simplicity, the number of communities k on each network is set to be the number of node labels. The basic information of real-world networks is shown in Table 1.

Table 1. Summary of the real-world datasets used in our experiments.

	Cora	Citeseer	Pubmed
Nodes	2708	3327	19717
Edges	5278	4552	44338
Feature	1433	3703	500
Communities	7	6	3

4.2 Comparison Models

Our proposed method in this paper is a NMF-based community detection method powered by high-order graph attention networks. For fair comparison, we select seven representative NMF-based community detection algorithms and five graph representation learning based community detection models as our baselines.

The NMF-based community detection methods include: Fundamental low-rank matrix fraction method(NMF); Symmetric NMF(SNMF); Variant NMF(O-NMF) which enforcing orthogonal constraints on community membership matrix U. HPNMF [40] based on symmetric NMF with graph regularized constraint; Deep Autoencoder NMF(DANMF) [41] based on deep NMF with deep auto encode decode component component; Modularized NMF(M-NMF) [34] which propose a unified framework to jointly optimize NMF-based representation learning model and modularity-based community detection model. NSED [27] which similar to DANMF but every encode/decode component is based on shallow NMF with only one layer factorization structure.

And graph representation learning method are follows: DNGR [4], a deep learning based method. It first constructs the high-dimensional positive point-wise mutual information matrix representations and then applies the stacked denoising autoencoder to obtain node representations. DAEGC [31] is a goal-directed graph clustering approach employing an attention network to encode the importance of the neighboring nodes to a target node and decoder is trained to reconstruct the graph structure. vGraph [28], a probabilistic generative model to learn community membership and node representation collaboratively. AGC [45] is an adaptive graph convolution method for attributed graph clustering that exploits high-order graph convolution to capture global cluster structure and adaptively selects the appropriate order for different graphs.

Table 2. Performance Comparison on datasets

	Cora			CiteSeer			Pubmed		
	ACC	ARI	NMI	ACC	ARI	NMI	ACC	ARI	NMI
NMF	0.417	0.214	0.265	0.287	0.059	0.081	0.513	0.097	0.160
OMNF	0.381	0.196	0.241	0.333	0.082	0.142	0.557	0.158	0.158
SMNF	0.437	0.192	0.319	0.362	0.091	0.152	0.534	0.137	0.183
HPMNF	0.402	0.186	0.289	0.345	0.080	0.135	0.507	0.096	0.151
DAMNF	0.549	0.319	0.411	0.424	0.134	0.183	0.639	0.256	0.222
M-NMF	0.164	0.0002	0.035	0.189	0.0007	0.003	0.339	0.0001	0.0002
NSED	0.423	0.178	0.292	0.344	0.086	0.149	0.520	0.125	0.172
DNGR	0.419	0.142	0.318	0.326	0.044	0.180	0.458	0.054	0.155
vGraph	0.287	0.312	0.345	0.293	0.067	0.103	0.260	0.185	0.224
AGC	0.689	0.462	0.536	0.670	0.402	0.411	0.697	0.281	0.316
DAEGC	0.704	0.496	0.528	0.672	0.410	0.397	0.671	0.287	0.266
Ours	**0.719**	**0.512**	**0.596**	**0.693**	**0.421**	**0.430**	**0.701**	**0.293**	**0.367**

4.3   Evaluation Metrics

In this paper, we apply three widely used metrics normalized mutual information (NMI), adjusted rand index (ARI) and clustering accuracy (Accuracy) to evaluate the performance of community detection. Detailed definitions for these metrics can be found in [5].

4.4   Experiments Results

In the community detection task, we compare the performance of our model with other well known community detection methods. Table 2 shows the performance of our model and other fifteen baseline methods evaluated by NMI, ACC and ARI, where the bold values indicate the best performance. Every results in this table are the average of 20 different runs.

As shown in Table 2, the framework we proposed in this paper are perform better than all the other methods on three datasets by ACC, ARI and MNI metrics simultaneously, which shows its effectiveness in the community detection task. The results illustrate that, on one hand, owing to combination of the high-order network topology and NMF-based community information, HGI-NMF method outperforms those approaches using topology alone graph representation methods, such as DeepWalk, DAEGC and others. On the other hand, we can observe that the graph representation learning methods like DAEGC, VGAE, AGC and our method perform much better than other NMF-based methods and graph representation algorithms. This observation demonstrates that the joint learning of NMF-based community information with graph neural network is effective and can better encode the community-related graph information on attributed graphs.

4.5 Ablation Study

We perform an ablation study to understand the importance of each design choice of our framework based on the NMI result of three datasets with diverse characteristics. Specifically, we wants to know the influence of the component in our model including high-order graph attention encoder, community-level and graph-level mutual information.

We can observe from Table 3 that each component is critical for our model. The row 5 "Only Graph MI" in Table 3 means delete multi-hop graph encoder and community mutual information. In this circumstance, this model is theoretically equal with DGI. Combine with row 1 and 2, we can notice that compare with original DGI model, incorporate high-order information and community information are contribute the superior performance of HGI-NMF over previous models. Examining the row 2, row 3 and row 4 of this table, we can see that high-order graph structure information is more critical than other components, which indicate that we should put more attention on high-order graph structure information in the future study.

Table 3. The NMI results of ablation study on three datasets

Module	Cora	CiteSeer	Pubmed
Full model	0.596	0.430	0.367
- Multi-hop GNN	0.557	0.395	0.314
- Community MI	0.574	0.417	0.355
- Graph MI	0.562	0.401	0.326
Only Graph MI	0.475	0.342	0.268

5 Conclusion

In this article we propose a new model called HGI-NMF which aims to combine high-order graph attention encoder, graph mutual information, NMF-based community mutual information to achieve better performance. The graph mutual information and community mutual information are jointly optimized to simultaneously obtain both graph embedding and community detection result. Experiment results show that our model can get better community detection results than other baseline, including NMF-based community detection methods and graph representation learning methods.

Acknowledgements. This work was supported in part by the National Natural Science Foundation of China under grants U1811263.

References

1. Abbe, E.: Community detection and stochastic block models: recent developments. J. Mach. Learn. Res. **18**, 1–86 (2017)
2. Atwood, J., Towsley, D.: Diffusion-convolutional neural networks. In: NeurIPS, pp. 1993–2001 (2016)
3. Cai, D., He, X., Han, J., Huang, T.S.: Graph regularized nonnegative matrix factorization for data representation. TPAMI **33**(8), 1548–1560 (2011)
4. Cao, S., Lu, W., Xu, Q.: Deep neural networks for learning graph representations. In: AAAI, pp. 1145–1152 (2016)
5. Chakraborty, T., Dalmia, A., Mukherjee, A., Ganguly, N.: Metrics for community analysis: a survey. ACM Comput. Surv. **50**(4), 1–37 (2017)
6. Fanuel, M., Alaiz, C.M., Suykens, J.A.: Magnetic eigenmaps for community detection in directed networks. Phys. Rev. E **95**(2), 022302 (2017)
7. Gori, M., Monfardini, G., Scarselli, F.: A new model for learning in graph domains. In: IJCNN, vol. 2, pp. 729–734 (2005)
8. Hamilton, W.L., Ying, Z., Leskovec, J.: Inductive representation learning on large graphs. In: NeurIPS, pp. 1024–1034 (2017)
9. Javed, M.A., Younis, M.S., Latif, S., Qadir, J., Baig, A.: Community detection in networks: a multidisciplinary review. J. Netw. Comput. Appl. **108**, 87–111 (2018)
10. Jin, H., Yu, W., Li, S.: Graph regularized nonnegative matrix tri-factorization for overlapping community detection. Phys. A **515**, 376–387 (2019)
11. Kejani, M.T., Dornaika, F., Talebi, H.: Graph convolution networks with manifold regularization for semi-supervised learning. Neural Netw. **127**, 160–167 (2020)
12. Kipf, T.N., Welling, M.: Semi-supervised classification with graph convolutional networks. In: ICLR (2017)
13. Kuang, D., Park, H., Ding, C.H.Q.: Symmetric nonnegative matrix factorization for graph clustering. In: SDM, pp. 106–117 (2012)
14. Lee, D.D., Seung, H.S.: Learning the parts of objects by non-negative matrix factorization. Nature **401**(6755), 788–791 (1999)
15. Li, P., Huang, L., Wang, C., Lai, J.: EdMot: an edge enhancement approach for motif-aware community detection. In: KDD, pp. 479–487 (2019)
16. Li, Q., Han, Z., Wu, X.: Deeper insights into graph convolutional networks for semi-supervised learning. In: AAAI, pp. 3538–3545 (2018)
17. Li, Y., He, K., Bindel, D., Hopcroft, J.E.: Uncovering the small community structure in large networks: a local spectral approach. In: WWW, pp. 658–668 (2015)
18. Liu, X., Wang, W., He, D., Jiao, P., Jin, D., Cannistraci, C.V.: Semi-supervised community detection based on non-negative matrix factorization with node popularity. Inf. Sci. **381**, 304–321 (2017)
19. Liu, Z., et al.: GeniePath: graph neural networks with adaptive receptive paths. In: AAAI, vol. 33, pp. 4424–4431 (2019)
20. Luo, X., Liu, Z., Jin, L., Zhou, Y., Zhou, M.: Symmetric nonnegative matrix factorization-based community detection models and their convergence analysis. TNNLS **33**(3), 1203–1215 (2022)
21. Ma, X., Dong, D.: Evolutionary nonnegative matrix factorization algorithms for community detection in dynamic networks. TKDE **29**(5), 1045–1058 (2017)
22. Niepert, M., Ahmed, M., Kutzkov, K.: Learning convolutional neural networks for graphs. In: ICML, vol. 48, pp. 2014–2023 (2016)
23. Psorakis, I., Roberts, S., Ebden, M., Sheldon, B.: Overlapping community detection using Bayesian non-negative matrix factorization. Phys. Rev. E **83**(6), 066114 (2011)

24. Rozemberczki, B., Davies, R., Sarkar, R., Sutton, C.: GEMSEC: graph embedding with self clustering. In: ASONAM, pp. 65–72 (2019)
25. Scarselli, F., Gori, M., Tsoi, A.C., Hagenbuchner, M., Monfardini, G.: The graph neural network model. IEEE Trans. Neural Networks **20**(1), 61–80 (2009)
26. Su, X., et al.: A comprehensive survey on community detection with deep learning. TNNLS, 1–21 (2022)
27. Sun, B., Shen, H., Gao, J., Ouyang, W., Cheng, X.: A non-negative symmetric encoder-decoder approach for community detection. In: CIKM, pp. 597–606 (2017)
28. Sun, F., Qu, M., Hoffmann, J., Huang, C., Tang, J.: vGraph: a generative model for joint community detection and node representation learning. In: NeurIPS, pp. 512–522 (2019)
29. Velickovic, P., Cucurull, G., Casanova, A., Romero, A., Liò, P., Bengio, Y.: Graph attention networks. In: ICLR (2018)
30. Velickovic, P., Fedus, W., Hamilton, W.L., Liò, P., Bengio, Y., Hjelm, R.D.: Deep graph infomax. In: ICLR (2019)
31. Wang, C., Pan, S., Hu, R., Long, G., Jiang, J., Zhang, C.: Attributed graph clustering: a deep attentional embedding approach. In: IJCAI, pp. 3670–3676 (2019)
32. Wang, G., Ying, R., Huang, J., Leskovec, J.: Improving graph attention networks with large margin-based constraints. arXiv preprint: arXiv:1910.11945 (2019)
33. Wang, G., Ying, R., Huang, J., Leskovec, J.: Multi-hop attention graph neural networks. In: IJCAI, pp. 3089–3096 (2021)
34. Wang, X., Cui, P., Wang, J., Pei, J., Zhu, W., Yang, S.: Community preserving network embedding. In: AAAI, pp. 203–209 (2017)
35. Wang, X., et al.: Heterogeneous graph attention network. In: WWW, pp. 2022–2032 (2019)
36. Wu, W., Jia, Y., Kwong, S., Hou, J.: Pairwise constraint propagation-induced symmetric nonnegative matrix factorization. TNNLS **29**(12), 6348–6361 (2018)
37. Xu, K., Hu, W., Leskovec, J., Jegelka, S.: How powerful are graph neural networks? In: ICLR (2019)
38. Yang, L., Cao, X., He, D., Wang, C., Wang, X., Zhang, W.: Modularity based community detection with deep learning. In: IJCAI, pp. 2252–2258 (2016)
39. Yang, L., Cao, X., Jin, D., Wang, X., Meng, D.: A unified semi-supervised community detection framework using latent space graph regularization. IEEE Trans. Cybern. **45**(11), 2585–2598 (2015)
40. Ye, F., Chen, C., Wen, Z., Zheng, Z., Chen, W., Zhou, Y.: Homophily preserving community detection. TNNLS **31**(8), 2903–2915 (2020)
41. Ye, F., Chen, C., Zheng, Z.: Deep autoencoder-like nonnegative matrix factorization for community detection. In: CIKM, pp. 1393–1402 (2018)
42. Ye, F., Chen, C., Zheng, Z., Li, R., Yu, J.X.: Discrete overlapping community detection with pseudo supervision. In: ICDM, pp. 708–717 (2019)
43. Zhang, J., Shi, X., Xie, J., Ma, H., King, I., Yeung, D.: GaAN: gated attention networks for learning on large and Spatio temporal graphs. In: UAI, pp. 339–349 (2018)
44. Zhang, J., Zhang, H., Xia, C., Sun, L.: Graph-BERT: only attention is needed for learning graph representations. CoRR abs/2001.05140 (2020)
45. Zhang, X., Liu, H., Li, Q., Wu, X.: Attributed graph clustering via adaptive graph convolution. In: IJCAI, pp. 4327–4333 (2019)

Multi-task Learning Based Skin Segmentation

Taizhe Tan[1,2](✉) and Zhenghao Shan[1]

[1] School of Computer Science and Technology, Guangdong University of Technology,
Guangzhou 510006, China
969313709@qq.com
[2] Heyuan Bay Area Digital Economy Technology Innovation Center,
Heyuan 517001, China

Abstract. Skin segmentation is a critical task in computer vision that has diverse applications in several fields such as biometrics, medical imaging, and video surveillance. Despite its importance, the acquisition of high-quality data remains a significant challenge in skin segmentation research. In this paper, we propose a novel skin segmentation algorithm for single-person images by utilizing a dual-task neural network built on the multi-task learning framework. Specifically, the algorithm employs an encoder-decoder architecture consisting of a shared backbone, two dynamic encoders, and a decoder. The dynamic encoders use dynamic convolution to extract more spatial location information, while the decoder utilizes a query-based dual-task approach that allows each task to utilize the information generated by the other one efficiently. The experimental results indicate that the proposed skin segmentation algorithm outperforms or matches the current state-of-the-art techniques on the benchmark test set.

Keywords: Skin segmentation · query-based · multi-task learning · encoder-decoder · deep learning

1 Introduction

As a semantic segmentation technique, skin segmentation refers to the identification and separation of skin pixels from an image [1]. Skin segmentation serves as a critical component in various areas of image analysis, for instance, skin segmentation plays a major role in identifying nude bodies in pornographic content detection online [2]. However, the low specificity of skin and significant variation in different human races continue to pose challenges for accurate skin segmentation. Relying on color information alone has proven challenging due to numerous internal and external factors that impact the appearance of skin pixels in images. While early segmentation methods relied on low-level visual features at the pixel level [3]. In recent years, deep learning approaches, such as Full Convolutional Networks (FCNs) [4], encoder-decoder architectures (e.g., U-Net [5]),

© The Author(s), under exclusive license to Springer Nature Switzerland AG 2023
Z. Jin et al. (Eds.): KSEM 2023, LNAI 14119, pp. 360–369, 2023.
https://doi.org/10.1007/978-3-031-40289-0_29

Transformer-based semantic segmentation algorithms (e.g., Swin-Transformer [6]), achieved superior results in multi-object segmentation.

However, these techniques suffer from limitations caused by annotated skin data. In addition to this, collecting a massive dataset of human skin is both expensive and time-consuming. To address this, researchers proposed a novel approach that leverages the human portrait as weak semantic supervision in skin segmentation tasks [7]. However, the method adds the output from one encoder to the other encoder as a weaker supervised signal resulting in a stepwise training process. Therefore, we find that an end-to-end approach using a query-based dual-task learning approach in the decoding process would better exploit mutual information among tasks.

Our network comprises an encoder-decoder architecture that employs a shared backbone network to generate a shared feature map from input images. This shared feature map is then processed by two distinct dynamic encoders and distillation decoders to obtain prediction results for skin and portrait tasks. The dynamic convolutional networks inspired us to use two independent dynamic encoders on the initial features extracted by the backbone network to facilitate the separation of task-related features. Dynamic convolution increases model expressiveness without increasing network depth and width, highlighting relevant information regions for the current task. To improve task interaction, we feed the skin features and portrait features obtained from the previous dynamic encoding to the information interaction module. The generated features are passed into the distillation module containing a multi-headed attention operation, where they are combined to create the final features. Our approach allows the network to adaptively focus on valuable features from its task while using information from another task when decoding. Notably, the distillation module employs transformer-based methods, which integrates global modeling capabilities that are not present in convolutional neural networks. While it may encounter difficulties in focusing on task-specific features since the query, key, and value are all computed based on the same features. Thanks to the specific inductive bias, CNN-based models can capture the content of multiple tasks in the local domain better. To overcome these limitations, the proposed approach combines a CNN-based model with a transformer-based model to balance model effectiveness and learning efficiency. Since a single dataset may not contain annotations for all tasks, the dataset used in this study has only one type of annotation.

2   Related Work

2.1   Skin Segmentation Algorithm Based on Deep Learning

deep learning-based techniques have exhibited substantial progress in effectiveness. A U-net-based approach is proposed by the authors in literature [8]. This approach reduces the dependence on color information and instead utilizes rich semantic information. While literature [9] includes an architecture improvement to U-Net through the inclusion of large-scale contextual features, larger convolutional kernels in skin detection. In literature [7] presents a semi-supervised methodology that uses similar datasets and a dual-task full convolutional network.

2.2 Multi-task Learning

Multi-task learning applications range from portrait matting [10] to instance segmentation and semantic segmentation. These approaches can be classified as Encoder-focused or Decoder-focused, depending on where the task interaction occurs. In the Encoder-focused architecture [11], the task's features are shared before the feature input independent task exclusive head, i.e., in the encoding phase. On the other hand, the Decoder-focused architecture [12] shares or exchanges information mainly in the decoding phase.

2.3 Dynamic Convolution and Transformer

Dynamic Convolution. Dynamic convolutional networks aim to generate various convolutional kernels and utilize them to convolve input features. One study presented CondConv [13], a network based on conditional parametric convolution, which parameterizes the convolution kernel as a linear combination of multiple specialist knowledge to increase model capacity. Furthermore, another study extended CondConv and introduced ODConv [14], a dynamic convolution-based network that employs multidimensional attention mechanism through a parallel strategy to achieve full-dimensional dynamics. In this paper, we incorporate dynamic convolution as a crucial step in the coding process to extract local information more effectively.

Transformer. The concept of applying Transformer directly to image domains was introduced by Visual Transformer (ViT) [15]. Then a lot of related work [16]) emerged. Moreover, query-based target detection framework has significantly evolved, where DETR [16] proposed a new method to depict it as a query-based direct set prediction problem, and subsequent work [17] accomplished a parallel performance to state-of-the-art detectors.

3 Method

The task of skin segmentation and portrait segmentation share similarities while providing complementary information. During network training, portrait segmentation served as a regularizer for skin segmentation. As shown in Fig. 1, the network architecture uses an encoder-decoder structure, where input images are processed through a backbone network, generating features of multiple scales which are then upsampled to the same size and concatenated. Two dynamic encoders not sharing parameters were then used to dynamically extract the features, which were concatenated and fed into the distillation decoder as queries to decode the encoded information. Finally, the obtained features were input separately to the task header, resulting in the prediction.

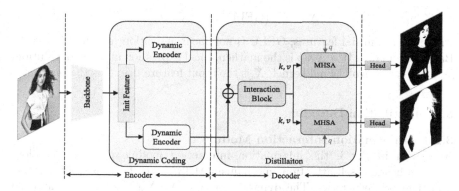

Fig. 1. An overview of our model, which comprises dynamic encoder and distillation decoder.

3.1 Dynamic Coding

The dynamic coding module serves to perform dynamic extraction of skin features and is constructed upon ODConv [14] We utilize this feature in the dynamic encoding module to conduct dynamic convolution operations on the initial shared features.

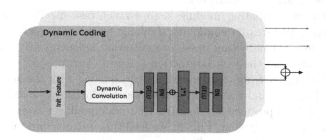

Fig. 2. Dynamic Encoder.

As shown in Fig. 1, the purpose of this module is to decouple spatially coupled features through feature extraction on the space domain. Consequently, to ensure complete decoupling, as shown in Fig. 2, the features proceed through a module consisting 1×1 convolution. These extracted dynamic features undergo a series of operations, including GELU activation layer, BatchNorm, residual connection, convolution, GELU activation layer, and BatchNorm. Subsequently, the obtained features are adjusted in dimension: $bchw \longrightarrow b(hw)c$ to facilitate computation in ensuing modules. Afterward, as queries, they are input into the distillation decoder, the whole process can be formulated as follows:

$$\bar{X} = X_f + BN\left(\text{GELU}\left(O\left(X_f\right)\right)\right) \tag{1}$$

$$X = \text{BN}\left(\text{GELU}\left(W \times \bar{X} + b\right)\right) \tag{2}$$

where X_f are initial features, GELU is nonlinear activation function, BN is the BatchNorm layer, $W \times X + b$ is the mathematical expression of 1×1 convolution, W is a 1×1 convolutional kernel, $\bar{X}$ is the input feature map, b is the bias term.

3.2   Distillation Decoding

3.2.1   Information Interaction Module

As shown in Fig. 3, the information interaction module primarily employs a multi-headed self-attention mechanism(MHSA) to facilitate information exchange between tasks. The dynamic features $X_s, X_p(N \times C)$ are combined in the channel dimension to form a hybridized feature matrix $(N \times 2C')$. Subsequently, a MHSA operation is conducted on the mixed feature matrix to derive a task interaction matrix $\hat{X}$. The obtained matrix is then passed through a linear and normalization layer. This entire process is mathematically represented as follows:

$$X' = Concat(X_s, X_p) \tag{3}$$

$$\hat{X} = MHSA(Q, K, V) \tag{4}$$

3.2.2   Task Distillation Module

The aim of task distillation module is to extract task-specific features from task interaction features by employing dynamic features as queries in MHSA. We achieve this by conducting layer normalization independently on both the dynamic features and the task interaction features. This process enables us to generate a task query from the dynamic features, along with the key and value from the task interaction features. We then perform MHSA calculations on the resulting Q, K, V to produce new features that undergo linear layer and residual operations for size adjustment. Finally, we feed this features into task header to generate the final prediction results.

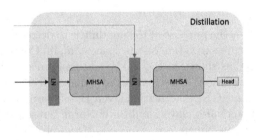

Fig. 3. Distillation

3.3 Loss Function

As stated previously, data samples possess solely skin-based annotations, an effective supervision method is leveraged by calculating their cross-entropy loss between the annotations M_s and outputs O_s. Similarly, data samples with portrait annotations undergo the same approach. Consequently, our loss function encompasses the summation of these two cross-entropy losses and is formulated as follows:

$$L_{ce} = L_{ce}(O_s, M_s) + L_{ce}(O_p, M_p) \tag{5}$$

4 Experimental Results

4.1 Datasets and Implementation Details

The methodology employed in this study involved the utilization of PyTorch on an NVIDIA GeForce GTX 2080Ti, with the Adam optimizer being implemented and an initial learning rate of 1e-4 set. The training process lasted for 15 generations, which spanned a total of 30 h. To train the proposed method, The datasets used are as follows. The visual skin segmentation dataset, consisting of 46,775 high-quality images, was used for skin segmentation. The SuperviselyPersonDataset dataset, containing 5,711 images, was used for the portrait dataset. Additionally, the pratheepan face dataset containing 78 images with annotations, was utilized as a benchmark. All the aforementioned datasets are publicly available.

Table 1. Segmentation results on the VSS dataset.

Method	Precision	Recall	F1-score
SegNet [18]	80.77%	79.98%	80.37%
UNet [5]	82.54%	85.64%	84.70%
DSNet [19]	85.61%	85.11%	85.36%
Our Method	**94.44%**	**86.02%**	**90.03%**

4.2 Result

Table 1 and Fig. 4 provides a comprehensive analysis of the proposed method in comparison to other prominent approaches on the VSS dataset. The results show that our method outperforms other skin segmentation methods on all measures. Furthermore, in Table 2 and Fig. 5, we have also compared our network with other methods on the Pratheepan Face dataset. The results show that our method outperforms the other methods in both Recall and iou metrics, while second to sota method in precision.

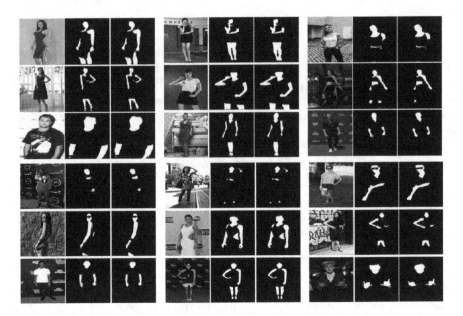

Fig. 4. The proposed method segmentation results on VSS dataset, the first column is the original image, the second column is the label, and the third column is the predicted result.

4.3   Ablation Study

To validate the effect of each module, a thorough evaluation of each module was conducted. The results in Table 3 indicate that both the dynamic encoder and distillation modules exhibit favorable outcomes. Notably, the distillation module appears to exert a greater influence on the performance. This observation can be attributed to the requirement of acquiring task interaction information.

Table 2. Segmentation results on the Pratheepan.

Method	Precision	Recall	IoU
Thresholding [20]	65.31%	89.58%	60.20%
GMM [21]	62.36%	91.50%	85.50%
UNet [5]	93.42%	90.91%	85.50%
ResNet50 [22]	92.19%	90.72%	84.33%
SOTA [7]	**95.23%**	92.08%	87.90%
Our Method	94.48%	**94.27%**	**88.75%**

Table 3. Ablation experiments on the Pratheepan.

Method	Precision	Recall	F1-score
baseline [23]	93.51%	83.93%	88.46%
w/dynamic conv	93.85%	84.83%	89.11%
w/distill	92.85%	**86.43%**	89.53%
Our Method	**94.44%**	86.02%	**90.03%**

Fig. 5. Segmentation results on the Pratheepan, the first column is the original image, the second column is the label, and the third column is the predicted result.

5 Conclusion

This study presents a novel multi-task based skin segmentation method. the method leverages the similarity between the portrait segmentation task and the skin segmentation task, which enhances the network's performance without requiring an increase in the skin annotation dataset. The proposed network generates segmentation results for both tasks using a single image as the input. To extract richer features, the network encoder employs dynamic coding while the decoder utilizes a Query-based distillation module, combining the benefits convolutions and transformers. Empirical results demonstrate that the proposed method surpasses other existing methods. However, the attention mechanism requires significant computational resources. Therefore, future research should focus on reducing the computational memory requirements and designing lighter and more efficient network structures.

References

1. Naji, S., Jalab, H.A., Kareem, S.A.: A survey on skin detection in colored images. Artif. Intell. Rev., 1–47 (2019)
2. Maidhof, C., Hashemifard, K., Offermann, J., Ziee, M., Flórez-Revuelta, F.: Underneath your clothes: a social and technological perspective on nudity in the context of AAL technology. In: Proceedings of the 15th International Conference on PErvasive Technologies Related to Assistive Environments (2022)
3. Hsieh, I.-S., Fan, K.-C., Lin, C.: A statistic approach to the detection of human faces in color nature scene. Pattern Recognit. **35**, 1583–1596 (2002)
4. Shelhamer, E., Long, J., Darrell, T.: Fully convolutional networks for semantic segmentation. In: 2015 IEEE Conference on Computer Vision and Pattern Recognition (CVPR), pp. 3431–3440 (2014)
5. Ronneberger, O., Fischer, P., Brox, T.: U-Net: convolutional networks for biomedical image segmentation. In: Navab, N., Hornegger, J., Wells, W.M., Frangi, A.F. (eds.) MICCAI 2015. LNCS, vol. 9351, pp. 234–241. Springer, Cham (2015). https://doi.org/10.1007/978-3-319-24574-4_28
6. Liu, Z., et al.: Swin transformer: hierarchical vision transformer using shifted windows. In: 2021 IEEE/CVF International Conference on Computer Vision (ICCV), pp. 9992–10002 (2021)
7. He, Y., et al.: Semi- supervised skin detection by network with mutual guidance. In: 2019 IEEE/CVF International Conference on Computer Vision (ICCV), pp. 2111–2120 (2019)
8. Xu, H., Sarkar, A., Abbott, A.L.: Color invariant skin segmentation. In: 2022 IEEE/CVF Conference on Computer Vision and Pattern Recognition Workshops (CVPRW), pp. 2905–2914 (2022)
9. Tarasiewicz, T., Nalepa, J., Kawulok, M.: Skinny: a lightweight U-Net for skin detection and segmentation. In: 2020 IEEE International Conference on Image Processing (ICIP), pp. 2386–2390 (2020)
10. Li, J., Ma, S., Zhang, J., Tao, D.: Privacy-preserving portrait matting. In: Proceedings of the 29th ACM International Conference on Multimedia (2021)
11. Sener, O., Koltun, V.: Multi-task learning as multi-objective optimization. In: Neural Information Processing Systems (2018)
12. Vandenhende, S., Georgoulis, S., Van Gool, L.: MTI-Net: multi-scale task interaction networks for multi-task learning. In: Vedaldi, A., Bischof, H., Brox, T., Frahm, J.-M. (eds.) ECCV 2020. LNCS, vol. 12349, pp. 527–543. Springer, Cham (2020). https://doi.org/10.1007/978-3-030-58548-8_31
13. Yang, B., Bender, G., Le, Q.V., Ngiam, J.: CondConv: conditionally parameterized convolutions for efficient inference. In: Neural Information Processing Systems (2019)
14. Li, C., Zhou, A., Yao, A.: Omni-dimensional dynamic convolution. arXiv preprint: arXiv:2209.07947 (2022)
15. Dosovitskiy, A., et al.: An image is worth 16x16 words: transformers for image recognition at scale. arXiv abs/2010.11929 (2020)
16. Carion, N., Massa, F., Synnaeve, G., Usunier, N., Kirillov, A., Zagoruyko, S.: End-to-end object detection with transformers. In: Vedaldi, A., Bischof, H., Brox, T., Frahm, J.-M. (eds.) ECCV 2020. LNCS, vol. 12346, pp. 213–229. Springer, Cham (2020). https://doi.org/10.1007/978-3-030-58452-8_13
17. Gao, P., Zheng, M., Wang, X., Dai, J., Li, H.: Fast convergence of DETR with spatially modulated co-attention. In: 2021 IEEE/CVF International Conference on Computer Vision (ICCV), pp. 3601–3610 (2021)

18. Badrinarayanan, V., Kendall, A., Cipolla, R.: SegNet: a deep convolutional encoder-decoder architecture for image segmentation. IEEE Trans. Pattern Anal. Mach. Intell. **39**, 2481–2495 (2015)
19. Hasan, M.K., Dahal, L., Samarakoon, P.N., Tushar, F.I., Marly, R.M.: DSNet: Automatic Dermoscopic skin lesion segmentation. Comput. Biol. Med. **120**, 103738 (2019)
20. Kovac, J., Peer, P., Solina, F.: Human skin color clustering for face detection. In: The IEEE Region 8 EUROCON 2003. Computer as a Tool, vol. 2, pp. 144–1482 (2003)
21. Jones, M.J., Rehg, J.M.: Statistical color models with application to skin detection. Int. J. Comput. Vision **46**, 81–96 (1999)
22. He, K., Zhang, X., Ren, S., Sun, J.: Deep residual learning for image recognition. In: 2016 IEEE Conference on Computer Vision and Pattern Recognition (CVPR), pp. 770–778 (2015)
23. Liu, Z., et al.: Swin transformer v2: Scaling up capacity and resolution. In: 2022 IEEE/CVF Conference on Computer Vision and Pattern Recognition (CVPR), pp. 11999–12009 (2021)

User Feedback-Based Counterfactual Data Augmentation for Sequential Recommendation

Haiyang Wang[1], Yan Chu[1(✉)] , Hui Ning[1], Zhengkui Wang[2] ,
and Wen Shan[3]

[1] Harbin Engineering University, Harbin 150001, China
chuyan@hrbeu.edu.cn
[2] InfoComm Technology Cluster, Singapore Institute of Technology,
Singapore, Singapore
zhengkui.wang@singaporetech.edu.sg
[3] Singapore University of Social Sciences, Singapore, Singapore
viviensw@suss.edu.sg

Abstract. The sequential recommendation is a prominent task that aims to provide accurate recommendations by leveraging users' historical behavior. However, the challenge of data sparsity poses a significant obstacle in achieving effective sequential recommendations. In this paper, we propose a User Feedback-based Counterfactual data augmentation method for Sequential Recommendation (UFC4-SRec) to address this challenge. Our approach focuses on expanding the dataset for sequential recommendation tasks by employing counterfactual inference techniques. The UFC4-SRec method consists of two main components: a counterfactual generator and a recommender. The counterfactual generator is responsible for generating counterfactual examples based on users' feedback. By incorporating users' preferences for items, the generated counterfactual data are designed to be closer to their actual preferences. On the other hand, the recommender employs various sequential recommendation models to provide recommendation results. To guide the counterfactual generator, the recommender imitates reinforcement learning by computing reward values based on the quality of the generated data. To evaluate the effectiveness of our method, we conduct experiments on three real-world datasets. The experimental results demonstrate that our UFC4-SRec approach significantly improves the performance of sequential recommendation tasks. Moreover, it effectively addresses the data sparsity problem commonly encountered in sequential recommendations.

Keywords: Sequential Recommendation · Data Sparsity · Counterfactual Data Augmentation · Reinforcement Learning · Recommendation Systems

Supported by Fundamental Research Funds for the Central Universities under Grant. 3072022TS0601, National Key Laboratory Foundation of Underwater Measurement and Control Technology, and International Exchange Program of Harbin Engineering University for Innovation-oriented Talents Cultivation.

1 Introduction

With the widespread use of online platforms and information explosion, sequential recommendation tasks play an important role in improving user satisfaction and platform efficiency. The sequential recommendation aims to provide personalized recommendations to users based on their historical interactions and behaviors, considering their actions' temporal dynamics and sequential dependencies. It has been successfully applied to various fields such as e-commerce, news recommendation, and video streaming [1].

However, one of the major challenges for sequential recommendation tasks is the data sparsity problem [2]. Users do not interact with sufficient items, so accurate user profiles can not be built. This makes it difficult to provide personalized recommendations to users, especially for new or inactive users. To address this challenge, researchers have explored various data augmentation techniques [3–5]. Several researchers have proposed using counterfactual inference methods to enhance data augmentation in sequential recommendation tasks [6]. They attempt to model user behavior through counterfactual analysis to infer how users would act in different scenarios that do not occur in reality.

Although these approaches have shown good results in improving recommendation performance, they focus mainly on the attribute information of items and ignore users' feedback, which is one of the important influencing factors of recommendation results, and methods that ignore user feedback may fail to correctly reflect users' tendencies in some aspects. To address this issue, we propose a counterfactual data enhancement method based on users' feedback applicable to sequential recommendation tasks. Counterfactual data are generated for users' feedback, focusing on the changes in the recommendation sequence after users' feedback on an item is changed, and generating diverse and accurate counterfactual data.

The main contributions of our paper are summarized as follows:

(1) We propose a User Feedback-based Counterfactual data augmentation method for Sequential Recommendation, UFC4SRec. We set up a reward value imitating reinforcement learning to guide the generation of counterfactual data.
(2) We conduct extensive experiments on three realistic datasets to validate the effectiveness of our approach on different models.

Section 2 shows related work on counterfactual inference and data augmentation. Section 3 presents the method UFC4SRec. Section 4 and Sect. 5 provide the experimental evaluations and conclusions, respectively.

2 Related Work

Various attempts have been made to address the data sparsity problem for sequential recommendation tasks. Ni et al. [5] introduced generative adversarial networks and designed a sequence enhancement module and a comparison GAN module to implement data-level and model-level enhancements. Li et al. [3] proposed an attention-based sequence-to-sequence generation model to address the sparsity of the training set by making the check-in records uniformly distributed problem.

Counterfactual reasoning, an important approach to causal reasoning, has unique advantages in data augmentation and is therefore widely used in data augmentation methods. Liu et al. [7] proposed a data augmentation method for neural machine translation by generating path-specific counterfactual aligned phrases to create an augmented corpus of parallel translations. Temraz et al. [8] proposed a data augmentation method for class imbalanced datasets by adaptively combining existing instances in the dataset using actual feature values rather than interpolation between instances.

Naturally, some researchers have also attempted to use counterfactual reasoning methods to address the data sparsity issue in the sequential recommendation. Chen et al. [9] designed a sampler model and an anchoring model to build a counterfactual data augmentation framework, generating high-quality sequences of user behaviors through the sampler model, while the anchoring model is responsible for training based on the original and newly generated samples. McInerney et al. [10] proposed a counterfactual estimator that allows for an asymptotically unbiased approach with low variance in sequential interactions in the rewards.

However, existing counterfactual data augmentation methods mostly consider item attributes and ignore the role of users' feedback. In fact, users' feedback contains users' true preferences towards items and is one of the important influencing factors of recommendation results. Therefore, we believe that incorporating users' feedback into the counterfactual data augmentation framework can improve the performance of recommendation algorithms.

3   UFC4SRec

3.1   Framework Overview

Counterfactual reasoning has been applied to address the problem of data sparsity in sequential recommendation [6]. Counterfactual data can be generated by setting up counterfactual questions on item attributes. However, users' feedback has been difficult to quantify and model in previous works, which is an important factor in recommendation results. To address this, we propose the counterfactual data augmentation based on users' feedback for Sequential Recommendation. After generating counterfactual examples, instead of having the generator itself judge whether the example conforms to the distribution of real data, the example is fed into a recommender model. We design a method imitating reinforcement learning to calculate a reward value when the recommender model computes the recommendation result for the input data. The higher the reward values are, the more the generated counterfactual data do conform to the real distribution. The task of the counterfactual generator is to generate counterfactual examples that can receive a higher reward value. Our framework is illustrated in Fig. 1.

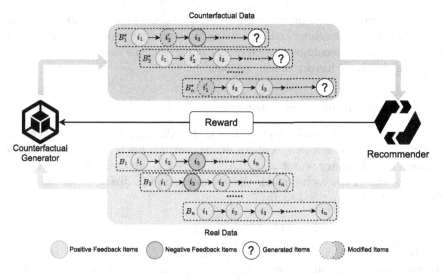

Fig. 1. The Framework of UFC4SRec.

The **Real Dataset**, which consists of a set of recommendation sequences, is fed into the **Recommender** to train the recommendation model and the **Counterfactual Generator** is to generate counterfactual data. The counterfactual generator reverses the preference of a certain item in the historical behavior sequence, such as from liking to disliking. At this point, the last item in the sequence will also change due to the change in historical behavior. The counterfactual generator's task is to find the accurate last item that meets the distribution of the real dataset. After finding the last item, complete **Counterfactual Data** are generated. The generated counterfactual data are fed into the recommender, which give the **Reward** value to evaluate the quality of the generated example. The counterfactual generator's task is to generate counterfactual examples that can receive higher reward values. By generating high-quality counterfactual examples, data augmentation for sequential recommendation tasks can be achieved.

3.2 Sequential Recommendation Rank Score

Suppose there is a user set $U = u_1, u_2, \cdots, u_{|U|}$ and an item set $V = v_1, v_2, \cdots, v_{|V|}$. User u_i has interacted with a series of historical items $H_i = v_1^i, v_2^i, \cdots, v_n^i$. The feedback corresponding to these historical items is $B_i = b_1^i, b_2^i, \cdots, b_n^i$. If the user likes the item, then $b_t^i = 1$; if the user does not like the item, then $b_t^i = 0$. The ranking score r_{ij} of user u_i on item v_j predicted by the sequential recommendation model f based on H_i and B_i can be expressed as:

$$r_{ij} = f(H_i, B_i, v_j) \tag{1}$$

The recommendation model predicts user preferences and generates a recommendation list by ranking candidate items in descending order of ranking score r_{ij}. The sequential recommendation model can predict the user's recent behavior based on the user's history of interactions.

3.3   Counterfactual Generator

To generate counterfactual data based on user feedback, the first step of the generator is to determine which feedback of the user u_i's historical items should be changed [11]. A binary vector $\Delta_i = 0, 1^{|B_i|}$ is used to represent the intervention, where the size of the vector equals the size of the user feedback vector B_i. Then, the intervention is applied to B_i:

$$B_i^* = (1 - B_i) \odot \Delta_i + B_i \odot (1 - \Delta_i) \tag{2}$$

For each $\delta_t \in \Delta_i$, if $\delta_t = 1$, the corresponding feedback is reversed; otherwise, the feedback remains unchanged. For example, if $B_i = [0, 1, 1]$ and $\Delta_i = [1, 1, 0]$, it means that the feedback of the user on the first and second items should be flipped, and thus $B_i^* = [1, 0, 1]$. To determine which feedback should be changed, an optimization function is designed for Δ_i as follows:

$$\Delta_i = \mathrm{argmin}_{(\Delta_i)} \parallel \Delta_i \parallel_0 + \alpha \bullet \mathcal{R}(v_{(n+1)} \mid H_i, B_i^*) \tag{3}$$

The zero norms $\parallel \Delta_i \parallel_0$ of the intervention vector Δ_i in Eq. (2) represents the amount of feedback change, where α is a hyperparameter and v_{n+1} is the embedding vector of the next item with its ground-truth information. $\mathcal{R}(v_{n+1} \mid H_i, B_i^*)$ is the ranking score of user u_i on item v_{n+1} under the counterfactual user feedback B_i^*, where B_i^* is obtained by applying interventions to the original feedback vector B_i using the binary vector $\Delta_i = 0, 1^{|B_i|}$. For each $\delta_t \in \Delta_i$, if $\delta_t = 1$, the corresponding feedback is reversed; otherwise, the feedback remains unchanged. For example, if $B_i = [0, 1, 1]$ and $\Delta_i = [1, 1, 0]$, it means that the feedback on the first and second items should be reversed, so $B_i^* = [1, 0, 1]$. To decide which feedback should be changed, an optimization function is designed for Δ_i as shown in Eq. (2). The first term aims to minimize the amount of intervened feedback between the original and counterfactual data, while the second term tries to find explicit feedback that can change the output sequence, i.e., the ranking score of item v_{n+1} under counterfactual feedback B_i^* decreases, making the new item appear as an output.

To obtain the next item, given the historical interactions H_i and intervened feedback B_i^*, the generator is used to derive the next item $\hat{v}_{n+1}$ that the user may interact with:

$$\hat{v}_{n+1} = \mathrm{argmax}_{v \in I} \mathcal{R}(v \mid H_i, B_i^*) \tag{4}$$

To obtain the next new item, the generator is fed with the historical items H_i and the intervened feedback B_i^* to derive the next item $\hat{v}_{n+1}$ that the user might interact with. Here, I is a set of items in the dataset, which can be the entire item set V or another set involving prior knowledge. Finally, an explicit counterfactual sequence is generated as $(H_i, B_i^\star, \hat{v}_{n+1})$, where the model $\mathcal{A}$ is trained on the augmented training dataset together with the original sequence $(H_i, B_i^\star, v_{n+1})$.

3.4   Recommender-Based Rewards

It is common to combine the generation process of counterfactual data with reinforcement learning, and our idea is similar [12]. To effectively explore large modification spaces and generate high-quality counterfactual interactions, the counterfactual generator in UFC4SRec needs to meet two requirements. First, the generator should accurately identify the most critical items that affect the final recommendation results, rather than randomly modifying the behavior sequence. Second, the generated counterfactual examples should conform as closely as possible to the real distribution. Considering these two aspects, two rewards are designed for the counterfactual generator in UFC4SRec based on the feedback signal of the recommendation system to guide the generation of counterfactual interactions.

Information-Based Reward. The first reward is inspired by the principle of information bottleneck [13], which models the relationship between the input x, the output y, and the input representation z. Its goal is to optimize the trade-off between accuracy $I(z; y)$ and compactness $I(z; x)$, which can be defined as follows:

$$\mathcal{L}_{IB} = -I(z; y) + \beta I(z; x) \tag{5}$$

where $I(.)$ represents the mutual information between two random variables, $I(z; y)$ is the accuracy term, $I(z; x)$ is the compression term, and β is the Lagrange multiplier. This loss attempts to generate accurate predictions by minimizing redundant information in the representation z [14].

According to the description in Sect. 3.4, the input features are denoted as $x = (u, \Delta_i)$, the input representation as $z = (H_i, B_i^\star, v_{n+1})$, and y represents whether user u interacts with item i, where $y \in 0, 1$. When the counterfactual generator generates new interaction items, the new input representation z can be obtained based on Eq. (4) as $z = (H_i, B_i^\star, \hat{v}_{n+1})$. Then, the information bottleneck can be utilized to guide the modification process by encouraging actions that lead to better item representations. To achieve this goal, the first term $I(z; y)$ should be maximized, which enables z to find i that has the largest impact on the result, and the second term $I(z; x)$ should also be maximized, which allows z to better fit the distribution of the original data. Formally, based on Eq. (5), the information-based reward can be represented as:

$$R_{IB} \sim I(z; y) - \beta I(z; x) \tag{6}$$

As it is difficult to directly calculate $I(z; y)$ and $I(z; x)$, the lower bound of the accuracy term $I(z; y)$ and the upper bound of the compression term $I(z; x)$

are used as the information-based reward $R_I B$. For the first term $I(z; y)$, we have $I(z; y) = H_P(y) - H_P(y|z)$, where $H(\cdot)$ represents the entropy of $p(\cdot)$. Since $H_P(y)$ is a constant, it can be ignored. Then, the lower bound is further derived as:

$$
\begin{aligned}
I(z, y) &\geq -H_P(y|z) \\
&= \iint p(y, z) \log p(y|z) dy dz \\
&\geq \iint p(y, z) \log q(y|z) dz dy \\
&= -H_{p,q}(y|z)
\end{aligned}
\tag{7}
$$

The term $q(y|z)$ is an estimate of $p(y|z)$, and the parameters of the classifier are denoted by θ, such as weight matrices or embedding parameters. Therefore, cross-entropy can be used as a proxy for the first term.

For the second term, $I(z; x)$, according to the definition of mutual information and the Gibbs inequality, the following inequality holds:

$$
\begin{aligned}
I(z; x) &= \mathbb{E}_X[D_{KL}(p(z|x)\|p(z))] \\
&\leq \mathbb{E}_X[D_{KL}(p(z|x)\|q(z))]
\end{aligned}
\tag{8}
$$

where $q(z)$ is a variational distribution. Following the information-theoretic counterfactual variational information bottleneck [15], the posterior $p(z|x) = N(\mu(x), diag(\sigma^2(x)))$ is assumed to be a Gaussian distribution, and the prior $q(z) = N(0, I)$ is a standard Gaussian variable distribution. If $\sigma(x)$ is fixed as a zero matrix, z will be reduced to a deterministic embedding. Then, the rewritten upper bound is obtained:

$$
\mathbb{E}_X[D_{KL}(p(z|x)\|q(z))] = \frac{1}{2}\|\mu(x)\|^2 + \frac{1}{2}\sum_d(\sigma_d^2 - \log \sigma_d^2 - 1)
\tag{9}
$$

This means that for a deterministic embedding z, the upper bound can be modeled by directly computing the $l2$-norm of the embedding vector z. Therefore, the information-based reward can be computed as:

$$
R_{IB} = -H_{p,q}(y|z) - \beta\|\mu(x)\|^2
\tag{10}
$$

Prediction-Based Reward. The second type of reward is based on the prediction difference between factual and counterfactual interactions, known as a prediction-based reward. It helps the counterfactual generator to generate counterfactual data that better conforms to the real data distribution. Specifically, given a real interaction sequence and a counterfactual interaction sequence, the recommendation system evaluates them by assigning recommendation scores to both sequences. If there is a large difference between the scores of the two sequences, it indicates that the generated counterfactual data is of poor quality. On the contrary, the smaller the score difference between the two, the higher the quality of the generated counterfactual data. Based on this idea, a prediction-based reward function can be designed for the counterfactual generator:

$$R_{PD} = \log \left(\sigma \left(H_i^\top B_i - H_i^\top B_i^* \right) \right) \tag{11}$$

where $\sigma\left(\cdot\right)$ is the sigmoid function. Finally, a combination of information-based rewards and prediction-based rewards is used as the final reward:

$$R = \gamma R_{IB} + (1 - \gamma)R_{PD} \tag{12}$$

where γ is a balancing parameter, and its effect on the results will be discussed in Sect. 4.4.

When the counterfactual generator performs modification operations, it will receive corresponding rewards according to Eq. (12). By maximizing this reward, the counterfactual generator is encouraged to generate high-quality counterfactual interactions.

4   Experiments and Analysis

4.1   Dataset and Metrics

UFC4SRec was tested on a publicly available real data set.

ML100K [16] MovieLens-100K is a standard dataset for recommendation system research that contains 100,000 movie ratings data, rated by 943 users for 1,682 movies.

Amazon [17] The Movies & TV and Electronics datasets from the Amazon e-commerce dataset are selected for the experiment. The Movies & TV contains 123,961 users, 50,053 products, and 1,697,533 product ratings. The Electronics contains 192,404 users, 63,002 products, and 1,689,188 product ratings.

In the experiments, we use the Hit Rate (HR@K) and the Normalized Discounted Cumulative Gain (NDCG@K) at rank K to evaluate the recommendation performance.

4.2   Parameter Settings

In the experiments, all methods use the ReLU function as the activation function, the embedding size is set to 32, and a mini-batch is used to optimize the methods with a batch size of 64. Grid search is performed for hyperparameters: the learning rate is searched among $[0.0001, 0.001, 0.01, 0.1]$, and α is searched among $[10^{-3}, 10^{-2}, 10^{-1}, 1, 10^1, 10^2, 10^3]$, and finally is set to 10.

4.3   Results and Analysis

To validate the effectiveness of the UFC4SRec, the following baseline models are used.

(1) STAMP [18] is a sequential recommendation model based on an attention mechanism that captures users' long-term and short-term recommendation preferences.

Table 1. Results on three data sets.

Dataset	Method	HR@5	HR@10	NDCG@5	NDCG@10
ML100K	STAMP	0.503	0.665	0.352	0.402
	CASR-STAMP	0.511	0.676	0.351	0.406
	UFC4SRec-STAMP	**0.519**	**0.681**	**0.362**	**0.414**
	GRU4Rec	0.502	0.672	0.340	0.403
	CASR-GRU4Rec	0.509	0.680	0.349	0.411
	UFC4SRec-GRU4Rec	**0.517**	**0.688**	**0.363**	**0.426**
	SASRec	0.508	0.678	0.348	0.411
	CASR-SASRec	0.518	0.685	0.357	0.415
	UFC4SRec-SASRec	**0.529**	**0.697**	**0.371**	**0.423**
	NCR	0.514	0.680	0.359	0.412
	CASR-NCR	0.518	0.689	0.362	0.419
	UFC4SRec-NCR	**0.529**	**0.701**	**0.373**	**0.429**
Movies & TV	STAMP	0.521	0.657	0.406	0.427
	CASR-STAMP	0.532	0.661	0.412	0.445
	UFC4SRec-STAMP	**0.547**	**0.681**	**0.429**	**0.452**
	GRU4Rec	0.538	0.661	0.411	0.431
	CASR-GRU4Rec	0.542	0.671	0.414	0.453
	UFC4SRec-GRU4Rec	**0.551**	**0.689**	**0.423**	**0.461**
	SASRec	0.543	0.667	0.412	0.456
	CASR-SASRec	0.549	0.673	0.420	0.461
	UFC4SRec-SASRec	**0.558**	**0.690**	**0.432**	**0.473**
	NCR	0.551	0.673	0.415	0.457
	CASR-NCR	0.555	0.682	0.417	0.458
	UFC4SRec-NCR	**0.563**	**0.695**	**0.429**	**0.469**
Electronics	STAMP	0.412	0.542	0.301	0.341
	CASR-STAMP	0.425	0.553	0.307	0.349
	UFC4SRec-STAMP	**0.442**	**0.563**	**0.323**	**0.359**
	GRU4Rec	0.432	0.554	0.312	0.354
	CASR-GRU4Rec	0.447	0.560	0.326	0.369
	UFC4SRec-GRU4Rec	**0.468**	**0.579**	**0.341**	**0.382**
	SASRec	0.439	0.558	0.322	0.357
	CASR-SASRec	0.450	0.575	0.335	0.365
	UFC4SRec-SASRec	**0.468**	**0.587**	**0.351**	**0.385**
	NCR	0.441	0.557	0.332	0.366
	CASR-NCR	0.451	0.569	0.339	0.374
	UFC4SRec-NCR	**0.463**	**0.580**	**0.349**	**0.387**

(2) GRU4Rec [19] is a Recurrent Neural Network based on the sequential recommendation model.
(3) SASRec [20] is a sequential recommendation model based on a self-attentive
mechanism.
(4) NCR [21] is a sequential recommendation model based on neurological reasoning that captures the logical relationship between user-item interactions
for recommendations.
(5) CASR [9] is a counterfactual data augmentation method based on item
attributes.

CASR and UFC4SRec can be applied to the STAMP, GRU4Rec, SASRec,
and NCR models as data augmentation methods. Table 1 shows the results of
the four baseline models on the datasets without data augmentation, with data
augmentation using CASR, and with data augmentation using UFC4SRec.

If "X" represents one of the four sequentially recommended models, "CASR-
X" represents the results of model X on the data set enhanced with CASR,
and "UFC4SRec-X" represents the results of model X on the dataset enhanced
with data using UFC4SRec. The best results are shown in bold. The results
show that the models trained on the dataset with data augmentation using our
method perform better. Specifically, the hit rate of UFC4SRec is on average
1.5% higher than that of CASR and 3% higher than that of the case without
data enhancement.

The trend of the reward value with the number of iterations is shown in
Fig. 2. It can be seen that the reward feedback value grows rapidly and stabilizes gradually on all three datasets, indicating that the counterfactual generator
learns the ability to steadily generate suitable counterfactual examples for the
model with the feedback from the recommender, and can generate stable and
usable counterfactual examples for the model.

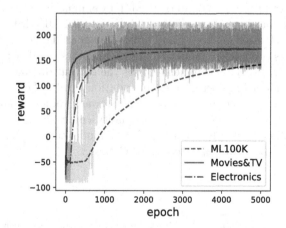

Fig. 2. Reward values on the three datasets.

4.4 Hyperparameter Analysis

The balancing parameter γ is to adjust the share of the two rewards in the total rewards. We tested different values of γ on all three data sets, and the results are shown in Fig. 3. From the results, we can conclude that γ performs best at around 0.5. It indicates that both reward values play a positive role in the quality of the counterfactual examples generated by the counterfactual generator. Therefore it is necessary to set both reward values.

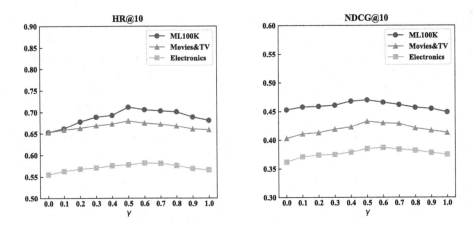

Fig. 3. The effect of γ values on the results.

5 Conclusions

In this paper, we propose a counterfactual data enhancement method based on users' feedback for sequential recommendation tasks, UFC4SRec, which constructs a counterfactual generator and a recommender. The counterfactual generator constructs counterfactual data by targeting users' feedback that expresses user satisfaction, and the recommender uses the current popular sequential recommendation model to generate recommendation results. Feedback values are also extracted in the recommender to design reward values to guide the counterfactual generator and generate better-quality counterfactual examples. The experiments validate that the recommendation model can achieve better results when trained on the data generated by UFC4SRec.

References

1. Cheng, M., Liu, Z., Liu, Q., Ge, S., Chen, E.: Towards automatic discovering of deep hybrid network architecture for sequential recommendation. In: Proceedings of the ACM Web Conference 2022, WWW 2022, pp. 1923–1932 (2022)

2. Bian, S., Zhao, W.X., Wang, J., Wen, J.R.: A relevant and diverse retrieval-enhanced data augmentation framework for sequential recommendation. In: Proceedings of the 31st ACM International Conference on Information & Knowledge Management, CIKM 2022, pp. 2923–2932 (2022)
3. Li, Y., Luo, Y., Zhang, Z., Sadiq, S., Cui, P.: Context-aware attention-based data augmentation for POI recommendation. In: 2019 IEEE 35th International Conference on Data Engineering Workshops (ICDEW), pp. 177–184 (2019)
4. Jiang, S., et al.: Explainable text classification via attentive and targeted mixing data augmentation. In: IJCAI, vol. 2023, pp. 2562–2575 (2023)
5. Ni, S., Zhou, W., Wen, J., Hu, L., Qiao, S.: Enhancing sequential recommendation with contrastive generative adversarial network. Inf. Process. Manag. **60**(3), 103331 (2023)
6. Chen, X., et al.: Data augmented sequential recommendation based on counterfactual thinking. IEEE Trans. Knowl. Data Eng., 1–14 (2022)
7. Liu, Q., Kusner, M., Blunsom, P.: Counterfactual data augmentation for neural machine translation. In: Proceedings of the 2021 Conference of the North American Chapter of the Association for Computational Linguistics: Human Language Technologies, pp. 187–197. Association for Computational Linguistics (2021)
8. Temraz, M.: Solving the class imbalance problem using a counterfactual method for data augmentation. Mach. Learn. Appl. **9**, 100375 (2022)
9. Wang, Z., et al.: Counterfactual Data-Augmented Sequential Recommendation. In: Proceedings of the 44th International ACM SIGIR Conference on Research and Development in Information Retrieval, SIGIR 2021, pp. 347–356 (2021)
10. McInerney, J., Brost, B., Chandar, P., Mehrotra, R., Carterette, B.: Counterfactual evaluation of slate recommendations with sequential reward interactions. In: Proceedings of the 26th ACM SIGKDD International Conference on Knowledge Discovery & Data Mining, KDD 2020, pp. 1779–1788 (2020)
11. Ji, J., et al.: Counterfactual collaborative reasoning. In: Proceedings of the Sixteenth ACM International Conference on Web Search and Data Mining, WSDM 2023, pp. 249–257 (2023)
12. Mu, S., Li, Y., Zhao, W.X., Wang, J., Ding, B.: Alleviating spurious correlations in knowledge-aware recommendations through counterfactual generator. In: Proceedings of the 45th International ACM SIGIR Conference on Research and Development in Information Retrieval, SIGIR 2022, pp. 1401–1411 (2022)
13. Tishby, N., Pereira, F.C., Bialek, W.: The information bottleneck method. arXiv e-prints p. physics/0004057 (2000), aDS Bibcode: 2000physics...4057T
14. Alemi, A.A., Fischer, I., Dillon, J.V.: Deep variational information bottleneck. In: International Conference on Learning Representations. ICLR 2017 (2017)
15. Wang, Z., Chen, X., Wen, R., Huang, S.L., Kuruoglu, E., Zheng, Y.: Information theoretic counterfactual learning from missing-not-at-random feedback. In: Advances in Neural Information Processing Systems, vol. 33, pp. 1854–1864 (2020)
16. Harper, F.M., Konstan, J.A.: The MovieLens datasets: history and context. ACM Trans. Interact. Intell. Syst. **5**(4), 1–19 (2015)
17. Ni, J., Li, J.: Justifying recommendations using distantly-labeled reviews and fine-grained aspects. In: Proceedings of the 2019 Conference on Empirical Methods in Natural Language Processing and the 9th International Joint Conference on Natural Language Processing (EMNLP-IJCNLP), pp. 188–197 (2019)
18. Liu, Q., Zeng, Y., Mokhosi, R., Zhang, H.: STAMP: short-term attention/memory priority model for session-based recommendation. In: Proceedings of the 24th ACM SIGKDD International Conference on Knowledge Discovery & Data Mining, KDD 2018, pp. 1831–1839 (2018)

19. Hidasi, B., Karatzoglou, A., Baltrunas, L., Tikk, D.: Session-based recommendations with recurrent neural networks (2016). arXiv:1511.06939
20. Kang, W.C., McAuley, J.: Self-attentive sequential recommendation. In: 2018 IEEE International Conference on Data Mining (ICDM), pp. 197–206 (2018)
21. Chen, H., Shi, S., Li, Y., Zhang, Y.: Neural collaborative reasoning. In: Proceedings of the Web Conference 2021, WWW 2021, pp. 1516–1527 (2021)

Citation Recommendation Based on Knowledge Graph and Multi-task Learning

Jing Wan(✉), Minghui Yuan, Danya Wang, and Yao Fu

Beijing University of Chemical Technology, Beijing 100029, China
{wanj,llolitaY,2019210509,2017200813}@mail.buct.edu.cn

Abstract. The Citation Recommendation aims to address the problem of academic information overload by filtering and suggesting relevant references for researchers. Traditional content-based citation recommendation methods may not be comprehensive enough to extract paper attributes that are essential for evaluating paper content similarity. To better use the abundant attributes and interaction information, the knowledge graph is introduced to recommendation system recently. We construct a multi-task learning-based model for citation recommendation that incorporates a knowledge graph, consisting of two primary tasks: citation recommendation and knowledge graph link prediction. To identify the interactions between papers, we propose a pseudo-interaction matrix in the citation recommendation task. The knowledge graph link prediction task aids in identifying paper attribute information and enhancing representation. By automatically merging and sharing low-level features, exploring feature similarity, and enhancing the performance of both tasks, the multi-task learning framework can improve the final recommendation result significantly. Multiple experiments on the academic paper datasets AMiner and DBLP verify the effectiveness of our proposed model.

Keywords: Citation recommendation · Knowledge graph · Multi-task learning · Stacked Denoising Autoencoder · Link prediction

1 Introduction

The development of internet technology has led to an exponential increase in network information, resulting in the problem of "information overload". Recommendation systems have emerged as a solution to filter and recommend relevant information. In academia, the issue of "academic information overload" also exists. Researchers have increasingly encountered the challenge of locating appropriate and accessible reference articles from a vast amount of academic literature that is relevant to their research fields. As a result, the introduction of recommendation systems for citation recommendation in academia has become an urgent matter.

Z. Jin et al. (Eds.): KSEM 2023, LNAI 14119, pp. 383–398, 2023.
https://doi.org/10.1007/978-3-031-40289-0_31

The citation recommendation process involves academic papers that are rich in content and information. As a result, content-based (CB) citation recommendation methods were more prevalent in the early days. These models rely on the content of papers, including their titles, abstracts, keywords, and context to generate recommendations [7,13]. However, content-based citation recommendation models typically rely on calculating text similarity, which may not be comprehensive enough for mining paper attributes. When citing references, researchers consider various aspects, and relying solely on paper content for similarity calculation may overlook important attributes, like the authority of the paper [3].

Researchers have addressed this issue by incorporating knowledge graphs (KGs), which offer rich attribute information to supplement the recommendations. In particular, with the maturity of knowledge graph embedding (KGE) technology, it has been applied to citation recommendation with promising results. Some efforts use multiple mechanisms, such as the TransR model [32] and the semantic matching model [31]. KGE typically incorporates attribute structure features obtained from the KG through splicing and fusion to enhance item representations. However, this approach of adding features for each item may lead to overfitting [20].

Some works adopt a multi-task learning framework to solve these problems. Wang et al. [27] treated recommend systems and knowledge graph feature learning as two distinct yet related tasks, and then utilized a multi-task learning framework to integrate features and make recommendations. This method extracts auxiliary information from external knowledge, such as knowledge graph, and utilizes a multi-task learning model to learn item features and high-level interactions between entities in the graph. These approaches allow for the exploration of potential interaction characteristics between items in the recommendation system.

Inspired by the above research, we adopt a multi-task learning approach that includes the citation recommendation task and graph link prediction task. Our model transforms the link prediction task into the prediction of citation relations. It adds additional information to enhance feature description and embedding features to prevent overfitting. The citation recommendation task specifically involves constructing a pseudo-interaction matrix to mine other attribute characteristics of papers, such as the number of citations and impact factors, which can reflect the authority of the article to a certain extent. Moreover, our multi-task model uses the feature similarity of the two tasks to share features, thereby improving their performance and enhancing the final recommendation results. Our contributions of this paper are as follows:

(1) A citation recommendation model based on a knowledge graph and multi-task learning is proposed, the KG link prediction task for predicting citation relations is designed to assist the citation recommendation task, and multi-task learning is performed via feature sharing.
(2) We construct a pseudo-interaction matrix to extract potential interaction features between papers by using a stack-type noise reduction autoencoder. Then, we fuse the interaction features with the paper text features extracted by a convolutional neural network (CNN).

(3) We conduct experiments on the AMiner and DBLP datasets, the results of which prove the effectiveness of the method proposed in this paper.

2 Related Work

2.1 Citation Recommendation

Citation recommendation is a common strategy used by recommendation systems to deal with "academic information overload", and its implementation method is similar to that of recommendation models. The current citation recommendation models can be classified into CB models, collaborative filtering-based (CF) models, graph-based (GB) models, and hybrid models [1]. The CB models capture the relationship between papers by extracting the papers' content information. Bhagavatula et al. [4] viewed the citation recommendation problem as a two-stage filtering and sorting process, looked for its neighbors as candidate recommendation objects, and used the reference discriminant model to obtain the ranking results. Färber et al. [7] proposed a model that categorizes potential citation contexts. However, CB models suffer from insufficient attribute feature mining. CF models such as that of Hu et al. [11] use the dual citation relationship between authors and papers to develop recommendations. Although they can use the citation relationship to recommend references for researchers, the amount of literature is enormous, and the CF model suffers from the cold start problem. Altaf et al. [2] proposed using heterogeneous graphs to hierarchically learn the representations of papers and paper datasets for the recommendation task. However, GB models can easily cause high computational complexity due to the large number of papers. Therefore, hybrid models have been proposed by researchers. Yadav et al. [30] defined the "popularity" of a paper and combined it with semantic similarity to obtain recommendation results to compensate for the shortcomings of the above single method.

The citation recommendation task of our work explores the potential interactions between papers, fuses the interaction features with the text features obtained from the paper content, and combines them with other auxiliary information for further research.

2.2 Knowledge Graph

The knowledge graph is a large-scale network structure composed of a large number of entities and their relations. The methods that introduce KGs into the recommendation model can be divided into recommendations based on ontology and recommendations based on linked open data (LOD) [29]. The former methods usually obtain finer-grained feature representations and then combine them with other methods. Kethavarapu et al. [15] created a dynamic ontology and calculated the similarity for the recommendation. However, ontology construction is manual, and its generalization ability is insufficient. Recommendations based on LOD extract features by leveraging the connection relations between entities to generate more interpretable results. Medrek et al. [17] automatically extracted metadata links to datasets to further mine information. Oramas et al. [18] built named entity links and word disambiguation links combined with recommendation engines to improve accuracy. Although the above methods can automatically mine hidden features, they face the challenge of constructing a complete knowledge base. Tang et al. [23] combined the content of a paper with the knowledge graph and employed graph convolutional networks to model the high-level graph connections and achieve recommendations.

The knowledge graph link prediction task in our work uses the semantic matching model to predict cited papers based on the knowledge graph, which is constructed from the paper datasets.

2.3   Multi-task Learning

Multi-task learning can train the required model by sharing information among multiple related tasks, resulting in improved generalization performance for the target task [5]. The current multi-task learning methods generally include feature learning methods, low-rank methods, task clustering methods, task relation learning methods, and decomposition methods [34]. Hassani et al. [9] introduced an unsupervised multi-task model to learn features jointly. Su et al. [22] proposed using low-rank attribute embedding combined with multi-task learning for recognition. Wang et al. [28] realized multi-task learning through joint tensor decomposition of a recommendation task and a content modeling task based on user preferences to improve recommendation interpretation.

We consider mining the papers' features of the previous two tasks and jointly sharing them to enhance the performances of both tasks. Thus improving the effectiveness of the final citation recommendation.

3   Problem Formulation

We regard the citing paper and candidate papers in the citation recommendation as the "user" and "item" in the common recommendation task, denoted as y and x, respectively. For each paper y, the set of candidate cited papers is known, denoted as $X = \left\{ x^{(1)}, x^{(2)}, \cdots, x^{(i)}, \cdots, x^{(m)} \right\}$, where m is the number of papers.

We construct the paper knowledge graph G, composed of entity-relation-entity triplets (e_h, e_r, e_t). Here e_h, e_r and e_t of each triplet represent the paper entity, attribute, and attribute value, respectively. For instance, *(KGAT: Knowledge Graph Attention Network for Recommendation, paper.year, 2019)* indicates that the publication year of this paper is 2019.

Given the citing paper y, the candidate cited paper $x^{(i)}$ and the knowledge graph G, we extract the features of y and $x^{(i)}$, and combine them with the additional information obtained from knowledge graph G. According to the citation preference, we calculate the preference $score(y; x^{(i)})$ of paper y on candidate cited paper $x^{(i)}$. Finally, we rank the scores and generate the final citation recommendation list.

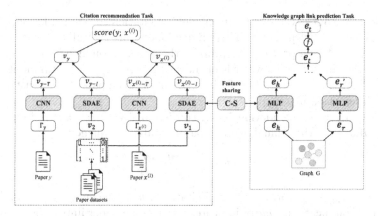

Fig. 1. The framework of our model includes three parts: a citation recommendation task, a knowledge graph link prediction task, and a feature sharing module.

4 KMCR Model

The overall knowledge graph and multi-task learning-based model for citation recommendation (KMCR) is shown in Fig. 1. The model is composed of three parts: a citation recommendation task module, a knowledge graph link prediction task module, and a feature sharing module.

The left side is the citation recommendation task module. This module takes the citing paper y and candidate cited paper $x^{(i)}$ as inputs, then constructs a pseudo-interaction matrix between the papers to extract the initial interaction feature v and the initial text feature Γ. Then, the final interaction feature $v_{(*-I)}$ and text feature $v_{(*-T)}$ are fed into the fusion operator, which outputs the citation probability.

The right side is the knowledge graph link prediction task module. This module uses the knowledge graph G to obtain the head entity feature e_h and relation feature e_r of the paper. The obtained features are then fed into a multi-layer perceptron model (MLP) and output the predicted tail entity $e_{t'}$, which is then supervised by the real tail entity e_t.

In the middle of the figure is the feature sharing module. This module enables sharing of features between the citation recommendation task and the knowledge graph link prediction task through a cross-sharing network [27].

4.1 Citation Recommendation

In the citation recommendation task, we first construct a pseudo-interaction matrix and extract the interaction features between papers. Then, we extract the text features of papers based on their content. Finally, we fuse the interaction features and text features of the papers to obtain their respective feature representations, and then calculate the paper citation preference score for recommendation.

Pseudo-Interaction Matrix. In the field of citation recommendation, papers with high citation frequency and high impact factor are typically given priority in the recommendation process. We propose the paper recommendation index and compare the subject and keywords of the citing paper y and the candidate cited paper $x^{(i)}$. By mining the potential interaction between papers, we construct the pseudo-interaction matrix.

The paper recommendation index consists of two index terms $index_1$ and $index_2$. $index_1$ is the annual average paper citation frequency:

$$index_1 = \frac{n_{citation}}{(y_e - y_c)} \tag{1}$$

where $n_{citation}$ is the total number of citations, y_e is the current year, and y_c is the year of publication. $index_2$ indicates the average paper impact factor, which is the average of the journal's impact factors (Chinese Academy of Sciences) over the past five years. We utilize the Z-score to standardize $index_1$ and $index_2$:

$$z^* = \frac{(z - \mu)}{\sigma} \tag{2}$$

where z^* is the value standardized by the Z-score, z is the specific sample data value, μ and σ are the sample data average value and standard deviation, respectively.

With the weight parameters, the recommendation index of each paper is as follows:

$$index = w_1 \times index_1' + w_2 \times index_2' \tag{3}$$

where w_1 and w_2 are the paper recommendation index weight parameters.

In addition, the citation relation between papers is set as $p(y; x^{(i)})$; if paper y cites paper $x^{(i)}$, $p(y; x^{(i)}) = 1$; otherwise, $p(y; x^{(i)}) = 0$.

We construct the pseudo-interaction matrix $I \in R^{m \times m}$ where m is the number of papers. If $p(y; x^{(i)}) = 1$, the corresponding row value of paper y and the corresponding column of paper $x^{(i)}$ is 1, otherwise, it will be 0.

According to the statistical results, we set the recommendation index threshold as 3. When the recommendation index of paper $x^{(i)}$ exceeds the threshold, if it has the same subject as that of paper y and contains two or more similar keywords, let $p(y; x^{(i)}) = 1$; otherwise, let $p(y; x^{(i)}) = 0$.

For a paper $x^{(i)}$ whose recommendation index is lower than the threshold, if it belongs to the same discipline as paper y and contains four or more similar keywords, we also let $p(y; x^{(i)}) = 1$; otherwise, let $p(y; x^{(i)}) = 0$.

Interaction Feature Embedding. We explore the potential interactions between papers and extract interaction features. Based on the matrix I, we denote the row vector and column vector of I as the initial interaction features of paper y and $x^{(i)}$. Then we use the dropout method to add noise to the interaction features. The results are denoted as v_1 and v_2, respectively.

The corrupted data, which contains added noise, is treated as an observable value and used as the input for the stacked denoising autoencoder (SDAE) for initialization. After L-layer network encoding and decoding, the reconstructed output representations v_1' and v_2' are obtained, respectively. We refer to the formula proposed by Wang et al. [25]. For the cited paper, the SDAE encoding and decoding output interaction features are as follows:

$$v \sim N(v_1^L, \lambda_n^{-1} I_L) \tag{4}$$

where v_1^L is the output interaction feature vector of the $L - th$ layer of the SDAE, λ_n is the model hyperparameter in the $L - th$ hidden layer, and $N(\cdot)$ is the Gaussian distribution.

By reducing the reconstruction error between the output of the last SDAE layer and the interaction feature, we extract the final interaction features of the citing paper and the candidate paper, denoted respectively as v_{y-I} and $v_{x^{(i)}-I}$.

Text Feature Embedding. We employ the CNN model to extract content features from the title and abstract of a paper [16].

We use the GloVe model that pretrained on large-scale general data to vectorize each sentence containing words in the text of the paper to generate a text vector representation matrix $T_{1:n} \in R^{d_w \times n}$, where n is the number of words. Then, we design the filter $h \in R^{d_w \times k}$ to perform a sliding convolution operation on the sentence-level feature matrix, where k is the filter window size and $k < n$, we formulate each sub-matrix $T_{i:i+k-1}$ to extract features as follows:

$$conv_i^h = f_c(h * T_{i:i+k-1} + b_c), (i = 1, \cdots, n + 1 - k) \tag{5}$$

where $f_c(\cdot)$ is the nonlinear activation function, $*$ is the convolution operation, and b_c is the relative deviation. Therefore, we use a filter to convolve the text vector matrix to obtain $n + 1 - k$ corresponding features as follows:

$$Conv^h = [conv_1^h conv_2^h \cdots conv_{n+k-1}^h] \tag{6}$$

We utilize the maximum pooling method to obtain the convolution result by filtering the sentence content. The content feature is as follows:

$$v_t = max \left\{ Conv^h \right\} \tag{7}$$

We splice all low-dimensional text features v_t to obtain the feature expression of all the content in the text. Finally, we extract the text feature vector v_T through the fully connected layer. The text features of paper y and cited paper $x^{(i)}$ are denoted as v_{y-T}, $v_{x^{(i)}-T}$, respectively.

Feature Fusion. After concatenating the interaction features with the text features. We obtain the final feature representation vectors of paper y and cited paper $x^{(i)}$, then utilize the pair-wise method for cited paper $x^{(i)}$ to measure the citation preference of paper y:

$$score_{CR}(y; x^{(i)}) = \sigma(v_y v_{x^{(i)}}^T) \tag{8}$$

On this basis, we calculate the set of preference scores for all papers $x^{(i)}$ of paper y and generate a list of results for citation recommendations.

4.2 Paper Knowledge Graph Link Prediction

Paper Knowledge Graph. To fully utilize the additional attributes, we create a knowledge graph based on each paper. For each article selected in the dataset, we choose 3 to 5 attributes and generate corresponding triplets to construct the paper's attribute knowledge graph as comprehensively as possible. The attributes selected for generating corresponding triplets in the dataset are the paper's author, year of publication, citation frequency, journal identifier, and reference citation, respectively.

We train the link prediction problem in the knowledge graph as a separate task model and use multi-task learning during training, along with the citation recommendation task. The KGE method can also better prevent the model from overfitting the training data [20].

Knowledge Graph Link Prediction. We use the semantic matching model method based on the MLP to predict the tail entity in the KG. The head entity $e_h \in R^{d_k}$ and the relationship $e_r \in R^{d_k}$ are sent to MLP layers to obtain the high-level features e'_h and e'_r. Then, the constructed prediction model can be used to obtain the tail entity e'_t:

$$e'_t = M^l \left(\begin{bmatrix} e'_h \\ e'_r \end{bmatrix} \right) \tag{9}$$

where $M^l(\cdot)$ is a function of the l-layer MLP network.

We minimize the similarity between the tail entity vector and the predicted tail entity vector, and obtain the loss function of this module for joint training:

$$score_{kg}(h,r,t') = f_k(e_t, e'_t) \tag{10}$$

$$Loss_{KG} = - \sum_{(h,r,t) \in G} score_{kg}(h,r,t) + \sum_{(h,r,t') \notin G} score_{kg}(h,r,t') \tag{11}$$

where $f_k(\cdot)$ is the similarity function, which maximizes the $score_{kg}(h,r,t')$ by narrowing the gap between the predicted triplet and the true triplet, which completes the tail entity's link prediction task model training.

4.3 Feature Sharing Module

We jointly learn the above two tasks through feature sharing. Proposed by Wang et al. [27], we use the cross&compress unit and design a cross-sharing model in our citation recommendation task to achieve feature sharing, as in Fig. 2.

After obtaining the interaction feature v_1^l and entity feature e_h^l of the candidate papers, we define feature vector cross fusion using matrix inner product:

$$Q^l = (v_1^l)^T e_h^l = \begin{pmatrix} v_1^{l(1)} e_h^{l(1)} & \cdots & v_1^{l(1)} e_h^{l(d_k)} \\ \vdots & \ddots & \vdots \\ v_1^{l(d_I)} e_h^{l(1)} & \cdots & v_1^{l(d_I)} e_h^{l(d_k)} \end{pmatrix} \tag{12}$$

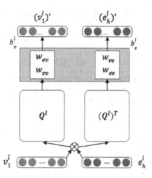

Fig. 2. Cross-sharing network model.

We take the interaction feature $v_1^l \in R^{d_I}$ of the candidate paper outputted by the $l - th$ layer of SDAE, and the corresponding paper entity feature $e_h^l \in R^{d_k}$ outputted by the $l - th$ layer of MLP. Through the vector inner product, we obtain the cross matrix $Q^l \in R^{d_I x d_k}$. The element $v_1^{l(i)} e_h^{l(j)}$ ($i \in \{1, 2, ..., d_I\}$, $j \in \{1, 2, ..., d_I\}$) in the matrix represents the cross interaction between features from different task models. Then, we perform feature conversion by setting the shared weights w_{**} and deviation b_*^l to reseparate the cross matrix, resulting in new interaction features $(v_1^l)'$ and new paper entity features $(e_h^l)'$ of the cited paper:

$$\left(v_1^l\right)' = Q^l w_{vv} + Q^l w_{ev} + b_v^l \tag{13}$$

$$\left(e_h^l\right)' = (Q^l)^T w_{ee} + (Q^l)^T w_{ve} + b_e^l \tag{14}$$

We denote the new interaction feature of the candidate paper obtained through the cross-sharing network as $\left(v_{x^{(i)}-I}\right)'$. It is then used as the input, as mentioned in the citation recommendation task, to output the final candidate paper feature representation $v_{x^{(i)}}'$. Through the layer-by-layer network model transmission, the candidate papers' feature representations in the recommendation model are improved. We formulate the final score and loss function of citation recommendation module is:

$$score(y; x^{(i)}) = \sigma(v_y(v_{x^{(i)}}')^T) \tag{15}$$

$$Loss_{CR} = \sum_{k=1}^{m_y} \sum_{i=1}^{m_{x^i}} CrossEntropy(score(y_k; x^{(i)}), p(y_k; x^{(i)})) \tag{16}$$

where the m_y indicates the number of original papers y in the training set, and m_{x^i} indicates the number of candidate papers x^i in the training set.

In this way, the multi-task joint training method is used instead of feature embedding methods. The overall loss function is as follows:

$$Loss_{KMCR} = Loss_{CR} + \lambda_1 Loss_{KG} + \lambda_2 \|W\|_2 \tag{17}$$

where W is the parameter matrix in the cross-sharing network. The λ_1 and λ_2 are weight parameters.

Table 1. The statistical results by processing datasets

Datasets	AMiner	DBLP
Papers	83,564	47,963
Citations	402,839	328,253
Triplets	818,657	547,653

5 Experiments

5.1 Datasets

Two paper datasets, AMiner [24] and DBLP [21], are selected for experimental verification. The AMiner dataset is a part of academic paper data from the Open Academic Graph (OAG 1.0) released by Tang et al. It also consists of approximately 166 million academic papers and related metadata from the Microsoft Academic Graph (MAG). DBLP is also a commonly used paper dataset for academic paper research, containing published academic research results in computer-related fields. We filter out older and rarely cited papers, as well as those that lack the five essential attributes, from the two datasets during the data processing phase. As presented in Table 1, after performing data cleaning and other preprocessing operations, we obtained the datasets that were used in the experiments through statistical analysis.

5.2 Experimental Setup

In the model proposed in this paper, we utilize the pretrained word vector from the GloVe model to initialize the text paper content and use the method in paper [20] to negatively sample the paper data during training.

In the recommendation index, we set w_1 and w_2 to 0.35 and 0.65, respectively. We set the interaction feature dimension to 100 and the number of hidden layers of the SDAE is 3. The word embedding dimension is 300. We use 8 filters and the sliding window is $\{2, 3, 4, 5\}$. We run our model in 10 epochs with a batch size of 32. All the paper data in each dataset are divided into a training set and a test set at a ratio of 7:3.

In addition, this experiment uses the recall rate (Recall) and the normalized discounted cumulative gain (NDCG) to evaluate the results. The Recall calculation formula is:

$$Recall@k = \frac{1}{N} \sum_{i=1}^{N} \frac{\mid R_c \bigcap R_r \mid}{\mid R_c \mid} \tag{18}$$

where N is the total number of samples in the test set, R_c represents the actual recommendation pair, and R_r represents the generated recommendation list.

Table 2. Results of citation recommendation on several datasets.

Dataset	Model	Recall@10	NDCG@10
AMiner	BM25	0.0694	0.1014
	NPM	0.3243	0.2671
	KMCR	**0.3386**	**0.4122**
DBLP	BM25	0.0812	0.1035
	NPM	0.3446	0.2557
	CRM	0.2426*	0.2057*
	CTM	0.2693*	0.2314*
	ASL (2020)	0.3742*	0.3052*
	RDL (2017)	0.2810*	0.2382*
	DC2V (2020)	0.4037*	0.2684*
	H-d2v (2018)	0.2132*	0.1314*
	KMCR	**0.3413**	**0.4182**

Note: * indicates the results retrieved from other papers.

NDCG measures the relevance and ranking of recommended items in the actual recommendation list. The NDCG calculation formula is:

$$NDCG@k = \frac{1}{N} \sum_{j=1}^{N} (\sum_{i=1}^{k} \frac{2^{r_i} - 1}{log_2(i+1)} / IDCG@k) \qquad (19)$$

where k is the number of recommended items in the recommendation list, and r_i represents the relevant score of the $i-th$ result in the generated recommendation list, if the two are related, $r_i = 1$; otherwise, $r_i = 0$.

5.3 Experimental Results

Comparison with Baselines. The baseline models we compared including BM25 [19], NPM [14], CRM [10], CTM [12], ASL [6], RDL [26], DocCit2V [33] and Hyperdoc2vec [8]. The top-K recommendation results of the experiments on the two datasets are presented in Table 2, Fig. 3 and Fig. 4.

Table 2 demonstrates the comparisons of the results based on Recall@k and NDCG@k evaluation metrics. Our KMCR model generally outperforms the baselines in most cases. Specifically, for NDCG@10, our results improved by 54.32% and 37.02% over the best baseline results in the two datasets, indicating that our model represents a significant improvement.

More detailed experimental results diagrams are shown in Fig. 3 and Fig. 4. Figure 3-(a) presents a comparison of the Recall@k results between the KMCR model and the baselines when generating recommendation lists of varying lengths on the AMiner dataset. Figure 3-(b) is a comparison of the NDCG@k results. The results in Fig. 4 are the comparison results of Recall@k and NDCG@k obtained by experiments on the DBLP dataset. The results more intuitively demonstrate that our model consistently outperforms the baseline as the number of recommended citations increases.

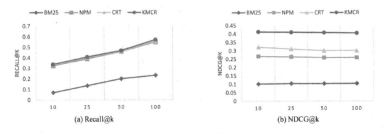

Fig. 3. Validation of KMCR on Aminer dataset.

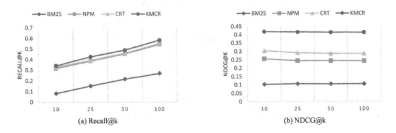

Fig. 4. Validation of KMCR on DBLP dataset.

Comparison with KMCR Variants. We further compared KMCR with its three variants to demonstrate the efficacy of our tasks

- CRT: CRT is the citation recommendation task we proposed. It integrates and recommends features according to the interaction features and text features in the paper.
- CRT w/o-I model: The interaction features are randomly initialized. And combined with the text features in CRT.
- CRT w/o-T model: We only use the interaction features from the SDAE in CRT.

Impact of CRT and KG Link Prediction Task. Figures 3 and 4 show that both the KMCR model and CRT model perform best among all methods on the two datasets.

It can also be seen that the KMCR method can obtain better Recall@k and NDCG@k results in two datasets, and is always better than the CRT model. The experimental results show that embedding the attribute features of the paper entities in the KG into the citation recommendation model can generate better recommendation results, proving the effectiveness of the multi-task learning citation recommendation method proposed in this paper, which integrates multiple pieces of additional information.

Table 3. Results of Variants.

Dataset	Model	Recall@10	NDCG@10
AMiner	CRT w/o-I	0.3288	0.3190
	CRT w/o-T	0.2313	0.2026
	CRT	**0.3324**	**0.3217**
	KMCR	**0.3386**	**0.4122**
DBLP	CRT w/o-I	0.2957	0.2723
	CRT w/o-T	0.2737	0.2583
	CRT	**0.3281**	**0.3042**
	KMCR	**0.3413**	**0.4182**

Impact of Interaction Features in CRT. As shown in Table 3, for the CRT w/o-I model randomly initializing the interaction features, the results of Recall@10 and NDCG@10 obtained in the top-K recommendation are lower than those of the CRT model. The results show that in the process of extracting interaction features, mining the potential interactions between the papers using a pseudo-interaction matrix can be more accurate. The interaction feature of papers also indirectly proves the effectiveness of the rule-based potential interaction mining method between papers proposed in this paper.

Impact of Text Feature in CRT. The validity verification of text feature embedding is shown in Table 3. The results of the CRT w/o-T model and the CTR model on the AMiner and DBLP datasets are compared. It can be seen that the lack of text features will significantly affect the accuracy of the recommended citation.

Additionally, comparing the results obtained on the two datasets, it is found that the lack of text features has a more significant impact on the AMiner than on the DBLP. In our opinion, since the AMiner dataset has a larger number and variety of papers, makes it has higher sparsity in the interaction feature matrix. Therefore, Text features are particularly important in this case.

The results also verify that the fusion of text features proposed in this paper strengthens the expression of a paper and enhances the importance of citation recommendation effects.

6 Conclusions

We proposed a KMCR model to address the insufficient paper attribute mining in citation recommendation tasks and ease of overfitting when introducing KGs. By constructing a pseudo-interaction matrix, we extracted the potential interaction features between papers. We fused them with the text features of a given paper to calculate the preference score between the citing paper and the candidate cited paper to complete the recommendation task. For the paper dataset used in the experiment, we constructed a paper knowledge graph to mine features. We performed feature sharing and joint learning for the citation recommendation task, based on feature fusion and the knowledge graph link prediction task. Our model significantly improved the generalization performance of the citation recommendation task.

References

1. Ali, Z., Ullah, I., Khan, A., Ullah Jan, A., Muhammad, K.: An overview and evaluation of citation recommendation models. Scientometrics **126**(5), 4083–4119 (2021). https://doi.org/10.1007/s11192-021-03909-y
2. Altaf, B., Akujuobi, U., Yu, L., Zhang, X.: Dataset recommendation via variational graph autoencoder. In: 2019 IEEE International Conference on Data Mining (ICDM), pp. 11–20. IEEE, New York (2019)
3. Bai, X., Wang, M., Lee, I., Yang, Z., Kong, X., Xia, F.: Scientific paper recommendation: a survey. IEEE Access **7**, 9324–9339 (2019)
4. Bhagavatula, C., Feldman, S., Power, R., Ammar, W.: Content-based citation recommendation. In: Proceedings of NAACL, pp. 238–251. Association for Computational Linguistics, Stroudsburg (2018)
5. Caruana, R.: Multitask learning. Mach. Learn. **28**(1), 41–75 (1997)
6. Dai, T., Zhu, L., Wang, Y., Carley, K.M.: Attentive stacked denoising autoencoder with BI-LSTM for personalized context-aware citation recommendation. IEEE/ACM Trans. Audio, Speech, Lang. Process. **28**, 553–568 (2020)
7. Färber, M., Thiemann, A., Jatowt, A.: To cite, or not to cite? detecting citation contexts in text. In: Pasi, G., Piwowarski, B., Azzopardi, L., Hanbury, A. (eds.) ECIR 2018. LNCS, vol. 10772, pp. 598–603. Springer, Cham (2018). https://doi.org/10.1007/978-3-319-76941-7_50
8. Han, J., Song, Y., Zhao, W.X., Shi, S., Zhang, H.: hyperdoc2vec: distributed representations of hypertext documents. In: Proceedings of ACL, pp. 2384–2394. Association for Computational Linguistics, Stroudsburg (2018)
9. Hassani, K., Haley, M.: Unsupervised multi-task feature learning on point clouds. In: Proceedings of ICCV, pp. 8159–8170. IEEE, New York (2019)
10. He, Q., Pei, J., Kifer, D., Mitra, P., Giles, L.: Context-aware citation recommendation. In: Proceedings of WWW, pp. 421–430. Association for Computing Machinery, New York (2010)
11. Hu, D., Ma, H., Liu, Y., He, X.: Scientific paper recommendation using author's dual role citation relationship. In: Shi, Z., Vadera, S., Chang, E. (eds.) IIP 2020. IAICT, vol. 581, pp. 121–132. Springer, Cham (2020). https://doi.org/10.1007/978-3-030-46931-3_12
12. Huang, W., Kataria, S., Caragea, C., Mitra, P., Giles, C.L., Rokach, L.: Recommending citations: translating papers into references. In: Proceedings of CIKM, pp. 1910–1914. Association for Computing Machinery, New York (2012)
13. Huang, W., Wu, Z., Liang, C., Mitra, P., Giles, C.: A neural probabilistic model for context based citation recommendation. In: Proceedings of AAAI, vol. 29 (2015)
14. Huang, W., Wu, Z., Liang, C., Mitra, P., Giles, C.L.: A neural probabilistic model for context based citation recommendation. In: Proceedings of AAAI, pp. 2404–2410. AAAI Press, Palo Alto, CA (2015)
15. Kethavarapu, U.P.K., Saraswathi, S.: Concept based dynamic ontology creation for job recommendation system. In: International Conference on Computational Modelling and Security, pp. 915–921. Elsevier, Amsterdam (2016)

16. Kim, Y.: Convolutional neural networks for sentence classification. In: Proceedings of EMNLP, Association for Computational Linguistics, Doha (2014)
17. Medrek, J., Otto, C., Ewerth, R.: Recommending scientific videos based on metadata enrichment using linked open data. In: Méndez, E., Crestani, F., Ribeiro, C., David, G., Lopes, J.C. (eds.) TPDL 2018. LNCS, vol. 11057, pp. 286–292. Springer, Cham (2018). https://doi.org/10.1007/978-3-030-00066-0_25
18. Oramas, S., Ostuni, V.C., Noia, T.D., Serra, X., Sciascio, E.D.: Sound and music recommendation with knowledge graphs. ACM Trans. Intell. Syst. Technol. (TIST) **8**(2), 1–21 (2016)
19. Robertson, S.E., Walker, S.: Some simple effective approximations to the 2-poisson model for probabilistic weighted retrieval. In: In: Croft, B.W., van Rijsbergen, C.J. (eds) SIGIR 1994, pp. 232–241. Springer, London (1994). https://doi.org/10.1007/978-1-4471-2099-5_24
20. Rossi, A., Barbosa, D., Firmani, D., Matinata, A., Merialdo, P.: Knowledge graph embedding for link prediction: a comparative analysis. ACM Trans. Knowl. Disc. Data (TKDD) **15**(2), 1–49 (2021)
21. Sinha, A., et al.: An overview of microsoft academic service (MAS) and applications. In: Proceedings of WWW, pp. 243–246. Association for Computing Machinery, New York (2015)
22. Su, C., Yang, F., Zhang, S., Tian, Q., Davis, L.S., Gao, W.: Multi-task learning with low rank attribute embedding for person re-identification. In: Proceedings of ICCV, pp. 3739–3747. IEEE, New York (2015)
23. Tang, H., Liu, B., Qian, J.: Content-based and knowledge graph-based paper recommendation: exploring user preferences with the knowledge graphs for scientific paper recommendation. Concurr. Comput.: Pract. Exper. **33**(13) (2021). https://doi.org/10.1002/cpe.6227
24. Tang, J., Zhang, J., Yao, L., Li, J., Zhang, L., Su, Z.: ArnetMiner: extraction and mining of academic social networks. In: Proceedings of KDD, pp. 990–998. Association for Computing Machinery, New York (2008)
25. Wang, H., Shi, X., Yeung, D.Y.: Relational stacked denoising autoencoder for tag recommendation. In: Proceedings of AAAI, pp. 3052–3058. AAAI Press, Palo Alto, CA (2015)
26. Wang, H., Shi, X., Yeung, D.Y.: Relational deep learning: A deep latent variable model for link prediction. In: Proceedings of AAAI, pp. 2688–2694. AAAI Press, Palo Alto, CA (2017)
27. Wang, H., Zhang, F., Zhao, M., Li, W., Xie, X., Guo, M.: Multi-task feature learning for knowledge graph enhanced recommendation. In: Proceedings of WWW, pp. 2000–2010. Association for Computing Machinery, New York (2019)
28. Wang, N., Wang, H., Jia, Y., Yin, Y.: Explainable recommendation via multi-task learning in opinionated text data. In: Proceedings of SIGIR, pp. 165–174. Association for Computing Machinery, New York (2018)
29. Xu, Z., Mao, C., Wang, X., Xu, W., Ye, L.: Improving network-based Top-N recommendation with background knowledge from linked open data. In: U, L.H., Xie, H. (eds.) APWeb-WAIM 2018. LNCS, vol. 11268, pp. 174–187. Springer, Cham (2018). https://doi.org/10.1007/978-3-030-01298-4_16
30. Yadav, P., Remala, N., Pervin, N.: Reccite: a hybrid approach to recommend potential papers. In: Proceedings of IEEE BigData, pp. 2956–2964. IEEE, New York (2019)
31. Yang, B., Yih, W.T., He, X., Gao, J., Deng, L.: Embedding entities and relations for learning and inference in knowledge bases. In: Proceedings of the International Conference on Learning Representations. abs/1412.6575 (2015)

32. Zhang, F., Yuan, N.J., Lian, D., Xie, X., Ma, W.Y.: Collaborative knowledge base embedding for recommender systems. In: Proceedings of KDD, pp. 353–362. Association for Computing Machinery, New York (2016)
33. Zhang, Y., Ma, Q.: Doccit2vec: citation recommendation via embedding of content and structural contexts. IEEE Access 8, 115865–115875 (2020)
34. Zhang, Y., Yang, Q.: A survey on multi-task learning. IEEE Trans. Knowl. Data Eng. 34(12), 5586–5609 (2022)

A Pairing Enhancement Approach for Aspect Sentiment Triplet Extraction

Fan Yang, Mian Zhang, Gongzhen Hu, and Xiabing Zhou[(✉)]

School of Computer Science and Technology, Soochow University, Suzhou, China
{fyangoct,mzhang2,gzhu}@stu.suda.edu.cn, zhouxiabing@suda.edu.cn

Abstract. Aspect Sentiment Triplet Extraction (ASTE) aims to extract the triplet of an aspect term, an opinion term, and their corresponding sentiment polarity from the review texts. Due to the complexity of language and the existence of multiple aspect terms and opinion terms in a single sentence, current models often confuse the connections between an aspect term and the opinion term describing it. To address this issue, we propose a pairing enhancement approach for ASTE, which incorporates contrastive learning during the training stage to inject aspect-opinion pairing knowledge into the triplet extraction model. Experimental results demonstrate that our approach performs well on four ASTE datasets (i.e., 14lap, 14res, 15res and 16res) compared to several related classical and state-of-the-art triplet extraction methods. Moreover, ablation studies conduct an analysis and verify the advantage of contrastive learning over other pairing enhancement approaches.

Keywords: Contrastive learning · Aspect sentiment triplet extraction · Generative model

1 Introduction

Aspect-based Sentiment Analysis (ABSA) is an aggregation of several fine-grained sentiment analysis tasks, which involves identifying various aspect-level sentiment elements, including aspect terms, aspect categories, opinion terms, and sentiment polarities [18]. Aspect Sentiment Triplet Extraction (ASTE) is a recently proposed subtask of ABSA by Peng et al. [7], aiming to extract sentiment triplets consisting of an aspect, an opinion, and their corresponding sentiment polarity. Figure 1 shows an example of ASTE.

Given the strong relevance between the subtasks of ABSA, several studies focus on designing unified generation templates and leveraging pre-trained sequence-to-sequence language models to perform multiple tasks simultaneously [14,19]. Such methods offer a relatively simple way to generate triplets end-to-end without any modifying of the pre-trained models. However, they often fail to match aspects with their corresponding opinions accurately in sentences containing multiple aspects or opinions. This results in poor performance of the triplet extraction task. As demonstrated in Fig. 1, the review text contains three

Z. Jin et al. (Eds.): KSEM 2023, LNAI 14119, pp. 399–410, 2023.
https://doi.org/10.1007/978-3-031-40289-0_32

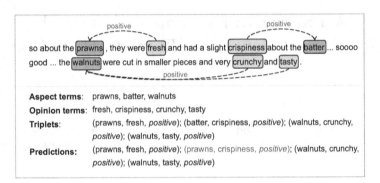

Fig. 1. An example of ASTE. The prediction results are generated by [19].

aspect terms and four opinion terms. Specifically, the opinion term *"crispiness"* is used to describe the aspect term *"batter"*. However, since the model does not consider constraining the pairing process when generating triples, it mistakenly matches *"crispiness"* with *"prawns"*.

To address this issue, we propose a novel pairing information enhancement approach for ASTE in training stage, where we adopt contrastive learning [16,17] to explicitly inject aspect-opinion pairing knowledge into ASTE model. Specifically, we first design descriptions about the pairing information between the aspect and opinion terms and encode the descriptions with an independent encoder. Then, the dense representations of the aspect-opinion pairs are extracted from the encoding outputs of the triplet extraction model. At last, we leverage the contrastive learning objective to push together the matched (mismatched) aspect and opinion and the description of *pair* (*unpair*) in the same vector space, while pushing away the matched (mismatched) against the description of *unpair* (*pair*). Experimental results show that our approach performs well on four ASTE datasets (e.g., 14lap, 14res, 15res, 16res) compared to several related classical and state-of-the-art triplet extraction methods. Moreover, ablation studies further confirm the effectiveness and advantage of our approach in enhancing the pairing ability of the model. These findings suggest that it is crucial to improve the pairing ability when aiming to enhance the performance of triplet extraction models, and our approach achieves this effectively.

To summarize, our main contributions include the following:

- We propose a pairing information enhancement approach for the ASTE task, which has proven to be successful in improving the performance of triplet extraction by enhancing the pairing process.
- Given the effectiveness of contrastive learning in semantic representation learning, we apply it between the pair type description embeddings and term pair embeddings, which enables the triple extraction models to obtain semantic knowledge related to pair matching. To the best of our knowledge, this is the first work to optimize the pair-matching process for ASTE via contrastive learning.

- Experimental results on four ASTE datasets show that our methods outperforms the state-of-the-art triplet extraction approaches.

2 Related Work

Span-based models are one of the effective methods for extracting triplets [2,12]. Additionally, machine reading comprehension is also used to solve the triplet extraction problem [1]. The aforementioned studies are all pipeline-based, which can potentially lead to error propagation. However, joint learning-based approaches can solve this problem well. Some researchers design unified annotation schemes, such as the position-aware tagging scheme [13] and the grid tagging scheme (GTS) [11]. Other researchers adopt generative frameworks to mine the rich label semantics deeply. Mukherjee et al. [6] extended the encoder-decoder architecture with a pointer network-based decoding framework. Zhang et al. [19] employed the pre-trained T5 model as the generation model, and imported annotation-style and extraction-style modeling paradigms. Han et al. [14] exploited BART to solve all ABSA subtasks in an end-to-end framework. The approach of employing pre-trained sequence-to-sequence language models to generate triplets is relatively simple, much of the research focuses on designing a unified generative template to satisfy multiple ABSA tasks. However, due to the complexity of language and the existence of multiple aspects and opinions in a single sentence, these models often confuse the connections.

3 Method

Our new approach that leverages contrastive learning to explicitly inject pairing knowledge into the triplet extraction model includes three main steps: (1) we extract the dense representations of the terms from the encoding outputs of the triplet extraction model; (2) we design descriptions that indicate whether an aspect term and opinion term match and encode them with an independent encoder; (3) based on the description embeddings and pair embeddings, we adopt contrastive learning objective to enhance the ability of the model to pair aspect and opinion terms. Figure 2 provides an overview of the proposed approach.

3.1 Task Formulation

Given an input sentence $X = \{x_1, ..., x_n\}$ with n words, the goal of ASTE model is to extract a set of triplets $T = \{(a, o, s)_i\}_{i=1}^{|T|}$ from X, where a and o denote aspect term and opinion term, respectively. The sentiment polarity s of the given aspect can be *positive, neutral* or *negative*.

3.2 Triplet Extraction

Following the framework proposed by Zhang et al. [19], we leverage the T5 [10], an encoder-decoder-based model pre-trained on a multi-task mixture of

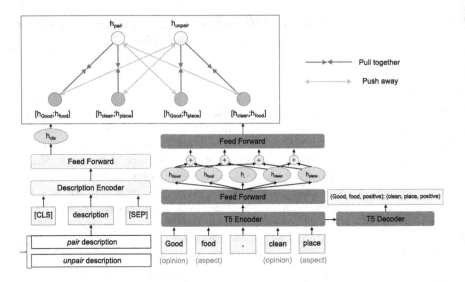

Fig. 2. The overall architecture of our approach. The description encoder and T5 encoder are used to encode the description of whether a pair is matched and the input text, respectively. We use the vector corresponding to [CLS] as the description representation. We apply pooling and concatenation operations to obtain the final term pair representations from the text encoder. By contrastive learning, we minimize the distance between the description corresponding to *pair* and true term pairs and maximize it with false term pairs.

unsupervised and supervised tasks, to formulate the triplet extraction task in a generative manner. Traditional methods use task-specific classification networks to model and predict sentiment terms and tendencies. These methods make predictions in a discriminative manner and use the class indices as labels, which often ignores the rich semantics within the labels. In contrast, generative methods decode a single sequence that contains triplets, including aspects, opinions, and sentiment polarities, enabling a deeper exploration of the semantics, thus providing a more effective solution to the triplet extraction problem.

Encoder. The T5 encoder is used to encode the input review text X into the hidden representation $\mathbf{H}^e$, which contains the semantics of X:

$$\mathbf{H}^e = \text{T5Encoder}(x_1, ..., x_n), \tag{1}$$

where $\mathbf{H}^e \in \mathbb{R}^{n \times d}$, and d is the hidden dimension.

Decoder. Following Zhang et al. [19], the output paradigm is divided into annotation style and extraction style. For annotation style, each aspect term is annotated with its corresponding opinion terms and sentiment polarity, i.e., [aspect | opinion | sentiment polarity]. For extraction style, the target is the triplets concatenation outputs. An example is shown below:

- **Input**: Nice keyboard, battery and screen work ok.

- **Target (Annotation-style)**: Nice [keyboard | positive | Nice], [battery | neutral | ok] and [screen | neutral | ok] work ok.
- **Target (Extraction-style)**: (keyborad, Nice, positive); (battery, ok, neutral); (screen, ok, neutral).

To generate the outputs defined above, the T5 decoder takes the encoder outputs $\mathbf{H}^e$ and the previous decoder outputs $Y_{<t}$ as inputs to get current decoder output $\mathbf{h}_t^d$. Then, $\mathbf{h}_t^d$ is passed through a fully connected softmax layer and mapped to the vocabulary distribution:

$$\mathbf{h}_t^d = \text{T5Decoder}(\mathbf{H}^e, Y_{<t}), \qquad (2)$$

$$P_t = \text{softmax}(\mathbf{W}_v \mathbf{h}_t^d + \mathbf{b}_v), \qquad (3)$$

where $\mathbf{h}_t^d \in \mathbb{R}^d$, $\mathbf{W}_v$ and $\mathbf{b}_v$ are learnable parameters.

Triplet Generation Objective. We utilize the cross-entropy function to calculate the loss:

$$\mathcal{L}_e = -\sum_i^n y_i \log(P_i) + (1 - y_i) log(1 - P_i), \qquad (4)$$

where y_i is the ground truth label, representing the aspect term, opinion term, sentiment label or other component in the target output.

3.3 Pair Contrastive Learning

Description Embeddings. We define $\mathcal{D} = \{D_{pair}, D_{unpair}\}$ as the set of descriptions indicating whether the aspect terms and opinion terms match, derived from prototypical instances. Given a description D_k with m words, we employ BERT [4] to learn the sequence representation:

$$\mathbf{h}_{[\text{CLS}]}^{D_k} = \text{BERT}(\{d_1, ..., d_m\}), \qquad (5)$$

where $\mathbf{h}_{[\text{CLS}]}$ is the output of BERT corresponding to [CLS]. Then, a linear layer is used to obtain the final representation for the description D_k.

$$\mathbf{d}_k = \mathbf{W_d} \mathbf{h}_{[\text{CLS}]}^{D_k} + \mathbf{b_d}, \qquad (6)$$

where $\mathbf{d}_k \in \mathbb{R}^d$, $\mathbf{W_d}$ and $\mathbf{b_d}$ are learnable parameters.

Term Pair Embeddings. To generate positive and negative pair instances, according to the position index $I \in \{0, ..., n\}$ of aspects and opinions in the input X, we first extract the dense representations of the aspect terms $\mathbf{h}_a$ and opinion terms $\mathbf{h}_o$ from the encoding outputs $\mathbf{H}^e$:

$$\mathbf{h}_a = f(\mathbf{H}^e[I_{a_{start}} : I_{a_{end}}]), \qquad (7)$$

$$\mathbf{h}_o = f(\mathbf{H}^e[I_{o_{start}} : I_{o_{end}}]), \qquad (8)$$

where $\mathbf{h}_a, \mathbf{h}_o \in \mathbb{R}^d$ is the dense representation of aspect terms and opinion terms. f: $\mathbb{R}^{d \times n} \to \mathbb{R}^{d \times 1}$ is a average pooling function that maps n output vectors to 1 representative vector. Then, we perform a linear function on the concatenation of $\mathbf{h}_a$ and $\mathbf{h}_o$:

$$\mathbf{h}_c = \mathbf{W_s}(\mathbf{h}_a \oplus \mathbf{h}_o) + \mathbf{b_s}, \tag{9}$$

where $\mathbf{h}_c \in \mathbb{R}^d$ is the final representation of term pairs, $\mathbf{W_s}$ and $\mathbf{b_s}$ are learnable parameters.

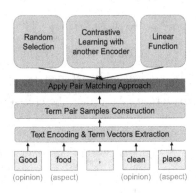

Fig. 3. Application of different pairing information enhancement approaches on the triplet extraction model.

Contrastive Learning Objective. To implement pairing information enhancement, we test three approaches to match the known aspect terms and opinion terms, namely random selection, linear function and contrastive learning. The framework is shown in Fig. 3. The experimental results are presented in Sect. 4.6. In the end, we chose contrastive learning with the best performance.

During contrastive learning, we force the representation of *pair* and *unpair* descriptions d_k to be similar with the positive aspect-opinion term pairs, and to be dissimilar with the negative term pairs:

$$\mathcal{L}_c = -log \frac{e^{sim(\mathbf{h}_c, \mathbf{d}_k)/\tau}}{e^{sim(\mathbf{h}_c, \mathbf{d}_k)/\tau} + \sum_{\mathbf{h}' \in \mathbf{H}_k^-} e^{sim(\mathbf{h}', \mathbf{d}_k)/\tau}}, \tag{10}$$

where the pair corresponding to $\mathbf{h}_c$ belongs to pair type D_k, $\mathbf{h}'$ is the set of all negative pairs, $\mathbf{d}_k$ is the pair type description, and τ is the temperature coefficient. Since the descriptions represent the central point of *pair* (*unpair*), they contain rich pairing-related semantic information. By employing contrastive learning, the pair composed of aspect and opinion extracted by T5 can learn this information, thus facilitating the extraction of valuable features for pairing. Consequently, this enables the generation of more accurate triplets.

3.4 Training

Finally, we combine the above loss functions to form the loss objective of our approach:

$$\mathcal{L} = \alpha\mathcal{L}_e + \beta\mathcal{L}_c, \tag{11}$$

where α and β are scalar hyperparameters.

4 Experiments

4.1 Experimental Setup

We evaluate our approach on ASTE-Data-V2 released by Xu et al. [13], which includes three datasets of restaurant domain (i.e., 14res, 15res, and 16res) and one dataset of laptop domain (i.e., 14lap). These datasets originally come from SemEval Challenges [5,8,9]. The statistics are shown in Table 1, each dataset contains numerous examples of multi-aspect terms, multi-opinion terms, as well as combinations of both multi-aspect and multi-opinion terms.

Table 1. The statistics of ASTE-Data-V2. ($\square$, $\circ$, $\heartsuit$, and $\Diamond$ denote the number of sentences, triplets containing more than one aspect, triplets containing more than one opinion, and triplets containing more than one aspect and opinion, respectively.)

Dataset	14lap				14res				15res				16res			
	$\square$	$\circ$	$\heartsuit$	$\Diamond$	$\square$	$\circ$	$\heartsuit$	$\Diamond$	$\square$	$\circ$	$\heartsuit$	$\Diamond$	$\square$	$\circ$	$\heartsuit$	$\Diamond$
train	906	265	274	178	1266	533	557	429	605	183	239	155	857	244	319	210
val	219	59	69	42	310	123	132	98	148	49	64	41	210	65	77	50
test	328	103	111	70	492	228	245	187	322	82	98	68	326	91	119	76

4.2 Implementation Details

We implement our approach based on GAS [19] repository and follow their work to choose T5 [10] as the pre-trained language model. We employ the prediction normalization strategy presented by GAS. The description encoder is initialized using BERT-base-cased[1]. The output size of the linear layer is set to 128, and the initial temperature parameter is 0.07. Our model is trained using the AdamW optimizer with a learning rate of 3e-4. We apply a dropout rate of 0.5 and a batch size of 16, and the model is trained up to 20 epochs. The weights for the loss function are set to $\alpha = 0.9$ and $\beta = 0.1$. We use F1 scores to evaluate the triplet extraction performance. We report the average score of five runs.

---

[1] https://huggingface.co/bert-base-cased.

4.3 Baselines

We compare the performance of our approach with the following baselines:

- **Peng-two-stage** [7], a two-stage framework, which extracted aspect-sentiment pairs and opinion terms in the first stage, followed by Cartesian product pairing and classification in the second stage.
- **GTS-BERT** [11], a unified grid tagging scheme, which designed an inference strategy to exploit mutual indications between different opinion factors.
- **S³E²** [3], a model based on vanilla GTS and represented semantic and syntactic relations between word pairs by a graph neural network to enhance the triplet extraction performance.
- **BMRC** [1], a method that converted the ASTE task into a multi-turn machine reading comprehension (MRC) task with well-designed queries.
- **ASTE-RL** [15], a model that treated the aspects and opinions as arguments of sentiment in a hierarchical reinforcement learning framework.
- **BART-ABSA** [14], a generative method that converted the ASTE task into the index generation problem through the BART model.
- **GAS** [19], a method that employed the T5 model as the generation model, and imported annotation style and extraction style modeling paradigms.

4.4 Main Results

The experimental results on ASTE-Data-V2 are shown in Table 2. To make a fair comparison with GAS [19], we implement our approach on both extraction style and annotation style output templates. It is worth noting that our approach outperforms other studies among all the baselines considered. On the 14lap, 14res, 15res, and 16res datasets in extraction style, our approach achieves an F1 score increase of 0.90%, 0.37%, 0.68%, and 1.28%, respectively, compared to GAS. Similarly, for annotation style, we also increase the F1 scores by 7.19%, 3.17%, 2.52%, and 2.29%, respectively. These results indicate that enhancing pairing information is essential for solving the ASTE task, while the training process of vanilla T5 does not consider controlling aspect-opinion pairing, introducing contrastive learning enables the model to learn such information.

4.5 Effectiveness of Pairing Information Enhancement

To prove that the improved performance of triplet extraction shown in Table 2 is indeed due to the enhancement of pairing tasks, that is, contrastive learning is effective for improving the pairing accuracy, we conduct experiments on the Aspect Opinion Pair Extraction (AOPE) task. Table 3 displays the results with and without employing contrastive learning. The table illustrates that the pairing performance has significantly improved with the introduction of contrastive learning, regardless of the annotation style or extraction style. This highlights the importance of implementing pairing information enhancement.

Table 2. Benchmark evaluation results on ASTE-Data-V2 (F1-score, %). All baseline results are from the original papers.

	14lap	14res	15res	16res
Peng-two-stage	42.87	51.46	52.32	54.21
GTS-BERT	54.36	67.50	60.15	67.93
S^3E^2	52.01	66.74	58.66	66.87
BMRC	58.18	68.64	58.79	67.35
ASTE-RL	59.50	69.61	62.72	68.42
BART-ABSA	58.69	65.25	59.26	67.62
GAS-extraction	60.78	72.16	62.10	70.10
Ours-extraction	**61.68**	**72.53**	62.78	**71.38**
GAS-annotation	54.31	69.30	61.02	68.65
Ours-annotation	61.50	72.47	**63.54**	70.94

Table 3. Ablation study on Aspect Opinion Pair Extraction (AOPE), "CL" represents contrastive learning (F1-score, %).

	14lap	14res	15res	16res
Ours-extraction	**69.05**	**74.74**	**67.27**	74.50
w/o CL	68.08	74.12	67.19	**74.54**
Ours-annotation	**69.84**	**75.50**	**71.22**	**76.40**
w/o CL	69.55	75.15	67.93	75.42

4.6 Comparison of Pairing Strategies

To demonstrate the advantage of contrastive learning in enhancing pairing information, we conduct a comparison with random selection and linear function-based pairing methods, the comparison framework is illustrated in the Fig. 3. In order to increase the controllability of the results and minimize the interference caused by extraction results on the final metrics, we assume that the aspects and opinions in the input sequence are already known, and only focus on evaluating the effectiveness of pairing. As shown in Table 4, contrastive learning outperforms the other two methods. Random selection performs worst because it does not introduce any prior knowledge. In addition, method based on linear function shows an significant improvement over random pairing, but still not as good as contrastive learning, demonstrating the superiority of contrastive learning in learning the information of whether to pair.

4.7 Pair Feature Visualization

To offer a more comprehensible illustration of the impact of contrastive learning on the pair representations, we present Fig. 4, which shows the changes in pair

Table 4. Comparison results of different pairing strategies (F1-score, %).

	14lap	14res	15res	16res
random selection	47.52	49.71	47.69	48.52
linear function	81.93	89.27	89.80	90.82
contrastive learning	**84.18**	**90.51**	**91.42**	**91.49**

representations before and after training on four datasets. In this figure, the black and red points represent the central points of true and false pairs, respectively. These points correspond to the vectors obtained from pair descriptions. The green and pink points represent true and false pair sample vectors from the input sequences. Before training, the sample vectors are mixed and are difficult to distinguish with low discrimination. However, after training, they are separated into two distinct clusters and dispersed around their respective centers, forming a relatively clear boundary. This boundary is determined by features learned from contrastive learning, which enables the vectors of centers to be similar with the corresponding positive term pairs, and dissimilar with the negative ones. This result suggests that the introduction of contrastive learning allows different pair samples to learn the semantic features specific to their corresponding types.

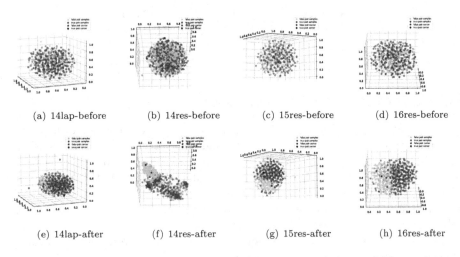

(a) 14lap-before   (b) 14res-before   (c) 15res-before   (d) 16res-before

(e) 14lap-after   (f) 14res-after   (g) 15res-after   (h) 16res-after

Fig. 4. Visualization of pair representations of four datasets before and after training.

4.8   Case Study

Table 5 presents the representative generated results by GAS and our approach. In the first example, the term "crispiness" is used to describe "batter", but GAS mistakenly matches this opinion term with "prawns". In the second example, although GAS correctly extracts the aspect terms "runs" and "fans", it also extracts the non-opinion term "huge bonus", resulting in incorrect matching relations. The first two examples indicate that our approach produces fewer pairing errors than the previous vanilla T5-based method. In the third example, GAS generates redundant matches, while our approach do not suffer from this problem but has some errors in boundary detection. We believe that future work could attempt to correct these boundary errors.

Table 5. Case study.

Review	Ground-truth	GAS	Ours
so about the prawns, they were fresh and had a slight crispiness about the batter ... soooo good ... the walnuts were cut in smaller pieces and very crunchy and tasty.	(prawns, fresh, positive) (batter, crispiness, positive) (walnuts, crunchy, positive) (walnuts, tasty, positive)	(prawns, fresh, positive) **(prawns, crispiness, positive)** (winters, crunchy, positive) (winters, tasty, positive)	(prawns, fresh, positive) (batter, crispiness, positive) (walnuts, crunchy, positive) (walnuts, tasty, positive)
The Mac mini is about 8x smaller than my old computer which is a huge bonus and runs very quiet, actually the fans aren't audible unlike my old pc	(runs, quiet, positive) (fans, aren't audible, positive)	**(runs, huge bonus, positive)** **(fans, quiet, positive)**	(runs, quiet, positive) (fans, aren't audible, positive)
BEST spicy tuna roll, great asian salad.	(asian salad, great, positive) (spicy tuna roll, BEST, positive) /	(spicy tuna roll, BEST, positive) (spicy tuna roll, great, positive) (asian salad, great, positive)	**(tuna roll, BEST, positive)** (asian salad, great, positive) /

5 Conclusion

In this paper, we propose a pairing information enhancement approach for Aspect Sentiment Triplet Extraction (ASTE), which incorporates contrastive learning during the training stage of the triplet extraction model. We introduce contrastive learning objectives based on the pair description vectors and pair sample vectors to enhance the ability of model to pair aspect terms and opinion terms. Experimental results demonstrate that our approach performs well on four ASTE datasets compared to several related classical and state-of-the-art triplet extraction methods. Future directions include: incorporating additional pair knowledge; applications to other ABSA tasks.

Acknowledgements. The work is supported by National Nature Science Foundation of China (No. 62176174).

References

1. Chen, S., Wang, Y., Liu, J., Wang, Y.: Bidirectional machine reading comprehension for aspect sentiment triplet extraction. In: Proceedings of the AAAI Conference on Artificial Intelligence, vol. 35, pp. 12666–12674 (2021)
2. Chen, Y., Keming, C., Sun, X., Zhang, Z.: A span-level bidirectional network for aspect sentiment triplet extraction. In: Proceedings of the 2022 Conference on Empirical Methods in Natural Language Processing, pp. 4300–4309 (2022)
3. Chen, Z., Huang, H., Liu, B., Shi, X., Jin, H.: Semantic and syntactic enhanced aspect sentiment triplet extraction. arXiv preprint arXiv:2106.03315 (2021)

4. Devlin, J., Chang, M.W., Lee, K., Toutanova, K.: Bert: pre-training of deep bidirectional transformers for language understanding. In: Proceedings of the 2019 Conference of the North American Chapter of the Association for Computational Linguistics: Human Language Technologies, Volume 1 (Long and Short Papers), pp. 4171–4186 (2019)
5. Kirange, D., Deshmukh, R.R., Kirange, M.: Aspect based sentiment analysis semeval-2014 task 4. Asian J. Comput. Sci. Inf. Technol. **4**(8), 72–75 (2014)
6. Mukherjee, R., Nayak, T., Butala, Y., Bhattacharya, S., Goyal, P.: Paste: a tagging-free decoding framework using pointer networks for aspect sentiment triplet extraction. In: Proceedings of the 2021 Conference on Empirical Methods in Natural Language Processing, pp. 9279–9291 (2021)
7. Peng, H., Xu, L., Bing, L., Huang, F., Lu, W., Si, L.: Knowing what, how and why: a near complete solution for aspect-based sentiment analysis. In: Proceedings of the AAAI Conference on Artificial Intelligence, vol. 34, pp. 8600–8607 (2020)
8. Pontiki, M., et al.: Semeval-2016 task 5: aspect based sentiment analysis. In: International Workshop on Semantic Evaluation, pp. 19–30 (2016)
9. Pontiki, M., Galanis, D., Papageorgiou, H., Manandhar, S., Androutsopoulos, I.: Semeval-2015 task 12: aspect based sentiment analysis. In: Proceedings of the 9th International Workshop on Semantic Evaluation (SemEval 2015), pp. 486–495 (2015)
10. Raffel, C., et al.: Exploring the limits of transfer learning with a unified text-to-text transformer. J. Mach. Learn. Res. **21**(1), 5485–5551 (2020)
11. Wu, Z., Ying, C., Zhao, F., Fan, Z., Dai, X., Xia, R.: Grid tagging scheme for aspect-oriented fine-grained opinion extraction. In: Findings of the Association for Computational Linguistics: EMNLP 2020, pp. 2576–2585 (2020)
12. Xu, L., Chia, Y.K., Bing, L.: Learning span-level interactions for aspect sentiment triplet extraction. arXiv preprint arXiv:2107.12214 (2021)
13. Xu, L., Li, H., Lu, W., Bing, L.: Position-aware tagging for aspect sentiment triplet extraction. In: Proceedings of the 2020 Conference on Empirical Methods in Natural Language Processing (EMNLP), pp. 2339–2349 (2020)
14. Yan, H., Dai, J., Ji, T., Qiu, X., Zhang, Z.: A unified generative framework for aspect-based sentiment analysis. In: Proceedings of the 59th Annual Meeting of the Association for Computational Linguistics and the 11th International Joint Conference on Natural Language Processing (Volume 1: Long Papers), pp. 2416–2429 (2021)
15. Yu Bai Jian, S., Nayak, T., Majumder, N., Poria, S.: Aspect sentiment triplet extraction using reinforcement learning. In: Proceedings of the 30th ACM International Conference on Information & Knowledge Management, pp. 3603–3607 (2021)
16. Zhang, S., Cheng, H., Gao, J., Poon, H.: Optimizing bi-encoder for named entity recognition via contrastive learning. arXiv preprint arXiv:2208.14565 (2022)
17. Zhang, S., et al.: Knowledge-rich self-supervision for biomedical entity linking. In: Findings of the Association for Computational Linguistics: EMNLP 2022, pp. 868–880 (2022)
18. Zhang, W., Deng, Y., Li, X., Yuan, Y., Bing, L., Lam, W.: Aspect sentiment quad prediction as paraphrase generation. In: Proceedings of the 2021 Conference on Empirical Methods in Natural Language Processing, pp. 9209–9219 (2021)
19. Zhang, W., Li, X., Deng, Y., Bing, L., Lam, W.: Towards generative aspect-based sentiment analysis. In: Proceedings of the 59th Annual Meeting of the Association for Computational Linguistics and the 11th International Joint Conference on Natural Language Processing (Volume 2: Short Papers), pp. 504–510 (2021)

The Minimal Negated Model Semantics of Assumable Logic Programs

Shutao Zhang$^{(\boxtimes)}$ and Zhizheng Zhang

Southeast University, Nanjing, Jiangsu, China
{shutao_zhang,seu_zzz}@seu.edu.cn

Abstract. Assumable Logic Programming (ALP) extends the regular logic programs with an assumption operator **C**. The intuition of **C**p is that it is acceptable to assume p unless it is forced not to. This paper presents the minimal negated model semantics, a new semantics of ALP, where the minimal negated set is defined to formalize this intuition. The assumptions in this set must be negated, and the ones outside are considered acceptable. This paper also discusses the relationship between the minimal negated model semantics and the stable model semantics. This new semantics provides new insight into assumable logic programming.

Keywords: Stable Model Semantics · Assumable Logic Programming · Minimal Negated Model · Reverse Reduct

1 Introduction

For a logic-based intelligent agent, making assumptions is essential for constructing the belief of possible worlds and making decisions [3,4,7]. Various methods and tools have been proposed in the decades, including Assumption-based Truth Maintenance System [8], Probabilistic Assumption-based Reasoning [9,10], Default Logic [12,13], Answer Set Programming and its extensions [1,2,5,6].

For assumption-based reasoning, Assumable Logic Programming (ALP) is proposed [15]. Compared with Answer Set Programs, the ALP programs provide a more powerful tool by adding an assumption **C**p in rules' bodies. This operator is used to represent assumptions, defaults, and exceptions that characterize common sense with the capability of making assumptions. An assumption **C**p can be read as "it is acceptable to assume p is true" or "assume p," and $\neg$**C**p can be read as "it is not acceptable to assume p is true" or "can not assume p."

Example 1. Consider an ALP program.

$$innocent(X) \leftarrow suspect(X), \mathbf{C}innocent(X).$$
$$guilty(X) \leftarrow suspect(X), \neg\mathbf{C}innocent(X).$$
$$\leftarrow innocent(X), guilty(X). \tag{1}$$
$$guilty(X) \leftarrow witnessed(X, Y), suspect(X).$$
$$suspect(tom).$$

This work was supported by the Pre-research Key Laboratory Fund for Equipment (Grant No. 6142101210205).

Z. Jin et al. (Eds.): KSEM 2023, LNAI 14119, pp. 411–422, 2023.
https://doi.org/10.1007/978-3-031-40289-0_33

This program can be informally read as follows. Assuming the innocence of a suspect is acceptable, then he is believed to be innocent; if it is not acceptable, then he is believed to be guilty. A suspect can not be both innocent and guilty. If someone witnesses a suspect's crime, then the suspect is guilty. Additionally, Tom is a suspect.

Three principles are fundamental for a reasoning agent of ALP programs.

Satisfied Principle For every rule in an ALP program, if its body is believed and its assumptions are acceptable, then the agent should believe the head of this rule.
Consistent Principle The agent must not accept contradictions.
Rational Principle The agent should not believe a literal unless forced to; it should accept an assumption unless it is forced not to.

By the above principles, a rational reasoner of this program should discover that assuming Tom is innocent is consistent with the given knowledge. With this assumption, it can be derived that Tom is innocent. Meanwhile, since there is no reason to reject this assumption, the reasoner should not negate the innocence of Tom and believe Tom is guilty. Overall, the reasoner has such a consequence: believe $innocence(tom)$ under the assumption $innocence(tom)$.

Based on these principles, the stable model semantics for ALP is introduced [15]. This semantics formalizes the rational principle for assumptions as maximizing the set of assumption literals that do not cause conflicts. Another natural and intuitive interpretation of this principle is to minimize the set of assumption literals that will cause conflicts. This interpretation seems to be a dual of the one in the stable model semantics. From this observation, the following questions can be raised.

1. What is the formal definition of the semantics of ALP under the interpretation of negated assumptions?
2. What is the relationship between the semantics under the two interpretations?

This paper will focus on answering the above two questions. Under the new interpretation, the ALP semantics is called *minimal negated model semantics*.

The rest of this paper is organized as follows. Firstly, Sect. 2 reviews ALP by introducing its syntax and stable model semantics. Then, Sect. 3 introduces the concept of reverse reduct. Based on this concept, the minimal negated models of ALP programs are defined. In a minimal negated model, the calculation of negated assumption literal sets is based on the reverse reduct, which abductively traces the inconsistencies and their causes. Finally, Sect. 4 discusses the relation between minimal negated model semantics and stable model semantics of ALP.

2 Assumable Logic Program and Its Stable Model Semantics

This section reviews the former work of Assumable Logic Programming in [14, 15], including the syntax and stable model semantics of ALP. To fit the discussion in this paper, a few details of the semantics are different from their former descriptions in previous works.

2.1 Syntax of ALP

Within ALP, the *atoms* preserve the same definition as those within traditional logic programs. A *literal* is an atom that may proceed with a negation as failure (NAF) operator $\neg$. Additionally, an ALP rule might contain *assumptions*, which are expressions of the form $\mathbf{C}e$ or $\neg\mathbf{C}e$, where e is a literal and $\mathbf{C}$ is an assumption operator.

An ALP program is a finite set of three kinds of non-disjunctive rules: *regular rules*, *facts*, and *constraints*. A *regular rule* is a rule of the form

$$a \leftarrow b_1, \ldots, b_m, \neg b_{m+1}, \ldots, \neg b_n, \mathbf{C}d_1, \ldots, \mathbf{C}d_j, \neg\mathbf{C}d_{j+1}, \ldots, \neg\mathbf{C}d_k. \tag{2}$$

where a, b_is are atoms, and d_is are literals.

The *fact* and *constraint* are special cases of regular rules. A *fact* is a rule with an empty body. A *constraint* is a rule of the form

$$\leftarrow b_1, \ldots, b_m, \neg b_{m+1}, \ldots, \neg b_n, \mathbf{C}d_1, \ldots, \mathbf{C}d_j, \neg\mathbf{C}d_{j+1}, \ldots, \neg\mathbf{C}d_k. \tag{3}$$

The empty head of a constraint can also be written as $\bot$, which means a conflict.

For convenient description, $body(r)$ can be split into four parts, which are $B^+ = \{b_1, \ldots, b_m\}$, $B^- = \{b_{m+1}, \ldots, b_n\}$, $D^+ = \{d_1, \ldots, d_j\}$, and $D^- = \{d_{j+1}, \ldots, d_k\}$. All three kinds of rules can be abbreviated as the following form

$$H \leftarrow B^+, \neg B^-, \mathbf{C}D^+, \neg\mathbf{C}D^-. \tag{4}$$

where H is a singleton or empty set of atom, B^+ and B^- are sets of atoms, D^+ and D^- are sets of literals. More specifically, we use D^{++} to denote the set of positive literals in D^+, D^{+-} the set of negative literals in D^+, D^{-+} the set of positive literals in D^-, and D^{--} the set of negative literals in D^-.

Let us consider the program (1) in Example 1. For the first two rules r_1 and r_2 in this program, $B^+(r_1) = B^+(r_2) = \{suspect(X)\}$, and $D^+(r_1) = D^-(r_2) = \{innocent(X)\}$. Furthermore, $D^{++}(r_1) = D^{-+}(r_2) = \{innocent(X)\}$.

An ALP program is *ground* if it contains no variables. For an ALP program Π with variables, the non-variable program obtained by grounding is denoted as $gr(\Pi)$, the Herbrand Universe of Π as $HU(\Pi)$, and the Herbrand Base as $HB(\Pi)$. Additionally, the Assumption Base, denoted as $AB(\Pi)$, is the set of literals that occur in the assumptions in $gr(\Pi)$. For instance of the program (1), its Herbrand Base is $\{s(t), i(t), g(t), w(t, t)\}$[1], and its Assumption Base is $\{i(t)\}$.

---

[1] The predicates and terms are abbreviated to their initials.

2.2   Stable Model Semantics

The informal reading of an ALP program involves two kinds of consequences: the acceptable assumptions of literals and the believed atoms. The set of believed atoms is a subset of $HB(\Pi)$, while the set of acceptable assumptions is a subset of $AB(\Pi)$. Therefore, the interpretation of an ALP program is defined as follows.

Definition 1 (Interpretation). *Let Π be a finite ALP program. An interpretation I of Π is a tuple (X, A), where X, called a* belief set, *is a consistent subset of $HB(\Pi)$, and A, called an* acceptable assumption literal set *or an* assumable set *for short, is a consistent subset of $AB(\Pi)$.*

Definition 2 (Satisfaction). *Let (X, A) be an interpretation.*

- *For a ground atom p, (X, A) satisfies p, denoted by $(X, A) \models_A p$, if $p \in X$;*
- *for a ground literal $\neg p$, $(X, A) \models_A \neg p$, if $p \notin X$;*
- *for ground assumptions $\mathbf{C}p$ and $\neg\mathbf{C}\neg p$, $(X, A) \models_A \mathbf{C}p$ and $(X, A) \models_A \neg\mathbf{C}\neg p$ if $p \in A$;*
- *for ground assumptions $\mathbf{C}\neg p$ and $\neg\mathbf{C}p$, $(X, A) \models_A \mathbf{C}\neg p$ and $(X, A) \models_A \neg\mathbf{C}p$ if $p \notin A$.*

For a conjunction T of ground literals and assumptions, $(X, A) \models_A T$ if (X, A) satisfies all literals and assumptions in T. Furthermore, (X, A) satisfies a ground rule $H \leftarrow T$ if $(X, A) \models_A H$ or $(X, A) \not\models_A T$, and (X, A) satisfies a ground ALP program Π if for every rule r in Π, $(X, A) \models_A r$.

Definition 3 (Assumption Reduct). *Let Π be an ALP program, A a consistent subset of $AB(\Pi)$. The* assumption reduct *of Π w.r.t. A, denoted by Π_{as}^A, is a normal logic program without assumptions that obtained from Π by eliminating the assumptions in every rule r of the form (4), such that*

1. if $D^+ \subseteq A$ and $D^- \cap A = \emptyset$, then replace r with r':

$$H \leftarrow B^+, \neg B^-. \tag{5}$$

2. otherwise, remove r.

The assumption reduct Π_{as}^A is the comprehension of Π under the acceptable assumptions represented by A. By computing the stable models of this normal logic program Π_{as}^A, an agent obtains the consequences of Π with A. However, the reasoning agent can only accept a consistent interpretation, defined as follows.

Definition 4 (Consistent Interpretation). *Let Π be an ALP program, X be a set of atoms, and A a consistent set of literal. A is called a* consistent assumable set *of Π if there exists X s.t. $\Pi_{as}^A \cup \{l.|l \in (X \cup A)\}$ is consistent, i.e., $AS(\Pi_{as}^A \cup \{l.|l \in (X \cup A)\}) \neq \emptyset$, and (X, A) is called a* consistent interpretation *of Π.*

Definition 5 (Stable Model). *Let Π be an ALP program, (X, A) an interpretation of Π. (X, A) is a* stable model *of Π if and only if all the following conditions hold.*

1. X is a stable model of Π_{as}^A;
2. (X, A) is a consistent interpretation of Π;
3. for any $A' \supsetneq A$, there does not exist X' such that the above two conditions holds for (X', A').

The collection of all stable models of Π is denoted as $SM(\Pi)$.

This definition reflects the three principles of ALP reasoning mentioned in Sect. 1. The first condition ensures that every rule in Π_{as}^A is derived from a rule in Π whose assumptions are satisfied by A, so the head of r is believed if its body is believed, following the satisfied principle. The second condition guarantees that (X, A) does not cause any contradiction, which meets the consistent principle. The third condition demands the assumption in a stable model to be maximal. In contrast, the first condition requires the belief set to be minimal, which matches the rational principle of ALP reasoning.

Let us consider the program (1) in Example 1. This program has two consistent assumable sets $A_1 = \{i(t)\}$ and $A_2 = \emptyset$. On the one hand, since A_1 is maximal and $\Pi_{as}^{A_1}$ has a stable model $X_1 = \{i(t)\}$, (X_1, A_1) is a stable model of Π. On the other hand, A_2 is not a desired assumable set because of $A_2 \subsetneq A_1$. Therefore, (X_1, A_1) is the unique stable model of Π.

3 The Minimal Negated Model

This section introduces the minimal negated model semantics of ALP programs. This semantics is based on assumption reduct and reverse reduct that establishes the justifications for the belief sets and assumable sets, respectively.

3.1 Reverse Reduct

The reverse reduct is designed to reverse the dependence relationship in an ALP program. Therefore, the causes of inconsistencies can be found by computing the stable models of this reversed program. For easy understanding and convenient description, this section starts with a particular case of ALP with limited syntax, then extends this method to the general case.

A Special Case ALP^N. ALP^N is a subset of ALP without negative literals. An ALP^N program is a finite set of rules of the form.

$$H \leftarrow B^+, \mathbf{C}D^{++}, \neg \mathbf{C}D^{-+}. \tag{6}$$

where H, B^+, D^{++}, and D^{-+} are defined in Sect. 2. In an ALP^N program, the head of a rule is derived by this rule if and only if all atoms and negative assumptions in its body are justified, and the positive assumptions are not negated.

Definition 6 (Reverse Reduct). *Let Π be an ALP^N program, X a consistent set of literals. The reverse reduct of Π w.r.t. X, denoted by Π^X_{rev}, is obtained from Π as follows.*

– *For every rule r in Π of the form (6), replace it with a new rule r_{rev}:*

$$B^+|(D^{++} - H) \leftarrow H, D^{-+}. \tag{7}$$

– *for every atom p in X, add the constraint $\leftarrow p$. into Π^X_{rev}.*

The reverse reduct is aimed to represent the propagation of negated assumptions in an ALP^N program. In the reverse reduct, an atom p means that the assumption of p is negated. For example, let us consider the following program Π.

$$\begin{aligned} q &\leftarrow \mathbf{C}p. \\ &\leftarrow q. \end{aligned} \tag{8}$$

The reversed reduct of this program w.r.t. $\emptyset$ is

$$\begin{aligned} p &\leftarrow q. \\ q&. \end{aligned} \tag{9}$$

The first rule in the reverse reduct means that the assumption of p is negated if the assumption of q is negated. Likely, the reverse reduct of constraint $\leftarrow q$. is a fact q., which means the assumption of q is negated.

By computing the stable model of a reverse reduct[2], an agent calculates the negated assumptions with the belief set for an ALP^N program. For the program (8), its reverse reduct (9) w.r.t. $\emptyset$ has a stable model $\{p, q\}$, which means the assumption of p and q are both negated with the belief set $\emptyset$.

Let us consider a more complex program Π.

$$\begin{aligned} p &\leftarrow \mathbf{C}p, \neg\mathbf{C}s. \\ q &\leftarrow \mathbf{C}q, \neg\mathbf{C}t. \\ &\leftarrow s, t. \end{aligned} \tag{10}$$

With a belief set $X = \{p\}$, the reverse reduct Π^X_{rev} is

$$\begin{aligned} &\leftarrow p, s. \\ &\leftarrow q, t. \\ s&|t. \\ &\leftarrow p. \end{aligned} \tag{11}$$

This reverse reduct has two stable models, $N_1 = \{s\}$ and $N_2 = \{t\}$.

Proposition 1. *Let Π be an ALP^N program. If Π has a stable model (X, A), then $\exists N \in SM(\Pi^X_{rev})$ such that $A = AB(\Pi) - N$.*

---

[2] The reverse reduct of an ALP^N program is an ordinary answer set program, whose stable models are also called "answer sets.".

Let us review the program (10) and its reverse reduct. For the negated set N_1, X is a stable model of $\Pi_{as}^{AB(\Pi)-N_1}$. However, for the negated set N_2, although it is a stable model of Π_{rev}^X, X is not a stable model of $\Pi_{as}^{AB(\Pi)-N_2}$.

To prove Proposition 1, the following lemma is proved first.

Lemma 1. *Let Π be an ALP^N program. If Π is consistent, then $\Pi_{rev}^{\emptyset}$ is consistent.*

Proof. Assume Π is consistent and $(X, A) \in SM(\Pi)$. Since (X, A) is a consistent interpretation of Π, a rule in Π whose assumptions are satisfied by A is also satisfied by $X \cup A$. Let us construct $N = HB(\Pi) - X - A$. Then by emulating the satisfiable conditions of rules of the form (6) and (7), it is evident that every reversed rule in $\Pi_{rev}^{\emptyset}$ satisfies N. Since $\Pi_{rev}^{\emptyset}$ is a disjunctive logic program without negations, this program is also consistent. Lemma 1 is proved.

Proof. (Proposition 1). This proposition is proved by contradiction. Assuming (X, A) is a stable model of Π, but $\forall N \in SM(\Pi_{rev}^X)$, $A \neq AB(\Pi) - N$. Since $A \neq AB(\Pi) - N$, $A \subseteq AB(\Pi)$ and A is maximal, then $\forall N, A \cap N \neq \emptyset$. Therefore, $\Pi' = \Pi_{rev}^X \cup \{\leftarrow p. | p \in A\}$ is inconsistent.

However, since $(X, A) \in SM(\Pi)$, $\Pi_{as}^A \cup \{l. | l \in X \cup A\}$ is consistent and has a stable model X'. Therefore, $\Pi'' = \Pi \cup \{l. | l \in X \cup A\}$ is also consistent since it has a stable model (X', A). According to Lemma 1, since Π'' is consistent, $\Pi' = (\Pi'')_{rev}^{\emptyset}$ is also consistent, which is contrary to our assumption. In summary, Proposition 1 is proved.

Move to ALP

Definition 7 (Reverse Reduct of an ALP program). *Let Π be an arbitrary ALP program. The ALP^N program Π_N is obtained by replacing every occurrence of negative literal $\neg p$ with a new atom np. Then the reverse reduct of Π w.r.t. a consistent atom set X is*

- *add every rules in $(\Pi_N)_{rev}^X$ into Π_{rev}^X.*
- *for every negative literal $\neg p$ that occurs in Π, add the following rule into Π_{rev}^X:*

$$\leftarrow p, np. \tag{12}$$

- *for every negative literal $\neg p$ that occurs in $AB(\Pi)$, add the following rule into Π_{rev}^X:*

$$p | np. \tag{13}$$

In the rest of this paper, $at(N)$ denotes the set of atoms that represent literals in N, e.g., $at(\{p, \neg q\}) = \{p, nq\}$; lit denotes an inverse operator of at.

The additional rules (12) and (13) in Π_{rev}^X are aimed at the implicit negations between opposite literals. For every negative literal $\neg p$ that occurs in Π, it is natural that the reasoner can not negate both the assumption of p and $\neg p$, which is represented by rule (12). Meanwhile, for $\neg p$ in $AB(\Pi)$, the reasoner must negate one of the assumptions of p or $\neg p$, so that the reasoner does not accept a pair of contrary assumptions. Rule (13) represents the above knowledge for negative literals in $AB(\Pi)$.

For example, consider the following ALP program Π.

$$
\begin{aligned}
p &\leftarrow \neg q. \\
q &\leftarrow \neg p. \\
s &\leftarrow p, \mathbf{C}\neg q. \\
&\leftarrow s, t.
\end{aligned}
\tag{14}
$$

Let us consider a belief set $X = \{s, p\}$. According to the definition, Π_{rev}^X is the following disjunctive logic program.

$$
\begin{aligned}
nq &\leftarrow p. & &\leftarrow p, np. \\
np &\leftarrow q. & &\leftarrow q, nq. \\
p|nq &\leftarrow s. & &\leftarrow p. \\
s|t. & & &\leftarrow s. \\
q|nq. & &
\end{aligned}
\tag{15}
$$

Π_{rev}^X has two stable models, $N_1' = \{t, q, np\}$ and $N_2' = \{t, nq\}$, which correspond to $N_1 = \{t, q, \neg p\}$ and $N_2 = \{t, \neg q\}$, respectively. Since the stable models only consider the assumptions in $AB(\Pi) = \{\neg q\}$, the assumable set $AB(\Pi) - N_1$ is preferred over $AB(\Pi) - N_2$. For $A = AB(\Pi) - N_1$, the assumption reduct Π_{as}^A is

$$
\begin{aligned}
p &\leftarrow \neg q. \\
q &\leftarrow \neg p. \\
s &\leftarrow p. \\
&\leftarrow s, t.
\end{aligned}
\tag{16}
$$

Π_{as}^A has two stable models, $X_1 = \{p, s\}$ and $X_2 = \{q\}$, where X_2 does not compatible with the assumable set A. Therefore, $(\{p, s\}, \{\neg q\})$ is a stable model of Π.

There is a counterpart of Proposition 1 for general ALP programs.

Proposition 2. *Let Π be an arbitrary ALP program. If (X, A) is a stable model of Π, then there exists $N \in SM(\Pi_{rev}^X)$, such that $A = AB(\Pi) - N$.*

The proof of this proposition is similar to the proof of Proposition 1.

Lemma 2. *Let Π be an ALP program. If Π is consistent, then $\Pi_{rev}^\emptyset$ is consistent.*

Proof. Assuming (X, A) is a stable model of Π. Constructing $N' = at(HB(\Pi) \cup \neg HB(\Pi)) - at(X \cup A \cup \neg(HB(\Pi) - X))$. By the satisfaction in Definition 2, every rule in $\Pi_{rev}^\emptyset$ is satisfied by N', $\Pi_{rev}^\emptyset$ is satisfiable. Since $\Pi_{rev}^\emptyset$ is a disjunctive logic program without negations, $\Pi_{rev}^\emptyset$ is also consistent.

Proof (Proposition 2). Assuming (X, A) is a stable model of Π, but $\forall N \in SM(\Pi_{rev}^X)$, $A \neq AB(\Pi) - N$. Therefore, $\forall N$ in $lit(SM(\Pi_{rev}^X))$, $\exists l \in A$, s.t. $l \in N$. It means that $\Pi' = \Pi_{rev}^X \cup \{\leftarrow at(l).|l \in A\}$ is inconsistent. However, $\Pi_{as}^A \cup \{l.|l \in (X \cup A)\}$ is consistent, which means $\Pi'' = \Pi \cup \{l.|l \in (X \cup A)\}$ is also consistent. By Lemma 2, $\Pi' = (\Pi'')_{rev}^\emptyset$ should be consistent, which is conflict with the assumption of this proof. In summary, Proposition 2 is proved.

3.2 The Definition of Minimal Negated Models

It is observed that the belief sets can be calculated by solving the assumption reducts w.r.t. assumable sets. In contrast, the negated sets, a counterpart of assumable sets, can be calculated by solving the reverse reducts w.r.t. belief sets.

Definition 8 (Minimal Negated Model). *Let Π be an ALP program, X a set of atoms, and N a set of literals. (X, N) is a minimal negated model of Π iff X is a stable model of $\Pi_{as}^{AB(\Pi)-N}$, and N is a stable model of Π_{rev}^X. The collection of all minimal negated models of Π is denoted as $MM(\Pi)$.*

Take the example of the program (1) in Example 1. This program has two minimal negated models, $(\{guilty(tom), suspect(tom)\}, \{innocent(tom)\})$ and $(\{innocent(tom), suspect(tom)\}, \{guilty(tom), witnessed(tom, tom)\})$.

In Definition 8, X and N are stable models of two regular answer set logic program $\Pi_{as}^{AB(\Pi)-N}$ and Π_{rev}^X, respectively, i.e., X and N can be generated by the least model operation [11]. Therefore, a fixpoint semantics for minimal negated models can be proposed as follow.

Definition 9 (Fixpoint Semantics of Minimal Negated Model). *Let Π be an ALP program. The following operators represent the calculation of belief sets and negated sets:*

- $\Phi(X, N) = LM((\Pi_{as}^{AB(\Pi)-N})_{GL}^X)$, where Π_{GL}^X denotes the GL-reduct of an ASP program Π w.r.t. X, and LM is the least model operator.
- $\Psi(X, N) = LM((\Pi_{rev}^X)_{GL}^{at(N)})$.

Then a minimal negated model of Π is a fixpoint of operator T, which is defined as

$$T(X, N) = (\Phi(X, N), lit(\Psi(X, N))) \qquad (17)$$

4 Relation with Stable Models

This section answers the second question mentioned in Sect. 1. Several results show that for an ALP program, there exists a corresponding minimal negated model for every stable model.

4.1   The Case of General ALP

In a stable model of an ALP program Π, the assumable set is a subset of $AB(\Pi)$. Meanwhile, the negated set in a minimal negated model is a subset of $HB(\Pi) \cup \neg HB(\Pi)$. For the maximal assumable set in a stable model, the set of negated assumption literals in $AB(\Pi)$ is minimized. Therefore, for every stable model of Π, there exists a minimal negated model with corresponding negated assumptions. However, this proposition does not imply its inverse.

Theorem 1 (Main Theorem). *Let Π be an ALP program, and $MM(\Pi)$ be the set of all minimal negated models of Π. An interpretation (X, A) is a stable model of Π iff*

– *there exists $(X, N) \in MM(\Pi)$ such that $A = AB(\Pi) - N$;*
– *there does not exist $(X', N') \in MM(\Pi)$ such that $A \subsetneq AB(\Pi) - N'$.*

Let us consider the program (1) in Example 1. This program has a stable model $M = (\{i(t), s(t)\}, \{i(t)\})$, and two minimal negated models, $M'_1 = (\{i(t), s(t)\}, \{g(t), w(t, t)\})$ and $M'_2 = (\{g(t), s(t)\}, \{i(t)\})$. Since the stable models only consider the assumption literals in $AB(\Pi)$, the corresponding interpretation of M'_1, i.e. M, is preferred over the one of M'_2.

To prove the main theorem, the following lemmas are proved first.

Lemma 3. *Let Π be an ALP program. If (X, N) is a minimal negated model of Π, then $(X, AB(\Pi) - N)$ is a consistent interpretation of Π.*

Proof. Since N is a stable model of Π^X_{rev} and $N \models \neg(X \cup A)$, $\Pi^\emptyset_{rev} \cup \{\leftarrow l. | l \in X \cup A\}$ is satisfiable. For every rule r in Π that contains assumptions, r is removed in Π^A_{as} as long as in $(\Pi^\emptyset_{rev})^N_{GL}$. Therefore, since $\Pi^\emptyset_{rev} \cup \{\leftarrow l. | l \in X \cup A\}$ is satisfiable, its reverse program $\Pi^A_{as} \cup \{l. l \in X \cup A\}$ is also satisfiable.

Lemma 4. *Let Π be an ALP program. If (X, A) is a stable model of Π, then there exists a minimal negated model (X, N) of Π, such that $A = AB(\Pi) - N$.*

Proof. By Proposition 2, if (X, A), then $\exists N \in SM(\Pi^X_{rev})$ s.t. $A = AB(\Pi) - N$. Then by the definition of stable models and minimal negated models $X \in SM(\Pi^{AB(\Pi)-N}_{as})$, (X, N) is a minimal negated model of Π.

Proof (Main Theorem).

– For the if direction, by the definition of assumption reduct and minimal negated models, (X, A) follows the first condition of Definition 5 if its corresponding minimal negated model exists. Furthermore, Lemma 3 indicates that (X, A) is also a consistent interpretation, which follows the second condition of Definition 5. Finally, by the second condition in Theorem 1, A is maximal. Then the third condition of the stable model holds, (X, A) is a stable model of Π.
– For the only if direction, if (X, A) is a stable model of Π, then by Lemma 4, there exists $(X, N) \in MM(\Pi)$ s.t. $A = AB(\Pi) - N$. By the third condition of Definition 5, there does not exist a stable model (X', A') s.t. $A \subsetneq A'$. Therefore, the second condition in Theorem 1 holds for (X, A).

In summary, Theorem 1 is proved.

4.2 Some Special Cases

Let us explore the relationship between these two semantics for some special cases. The first corollary below shows that the minimal negated semantics is a smooth extension of the stable model semantics of the answer set programs.

Corollary 1. *Let Π be an answer set program without disjunction. An interpretation X is a stable model of Π iff there exists a minimal negated model (X, N) of Π.*

Proof. For a consistent answer set program without disjunctions, its reverse reduct is consistent by Proposition 3. However, since an ASP program contains no assumptions, the negated set does not affect its reasoning result.

Now, consider the ALP^N program with only assumptions in the bodies, i.e., a program consists of rules of the form

$$H \leftarrow D^{++}, \neg D^{-+}. \qquad (18)$$

Corollary 2. *Let Π be an ALP^N program that consists of the rules of the form (18). An interpretation (X, A) is a stable model of Π iff $(X, AB(\Pi) - A)$ is a minimal negated model of Π.*

Proof. Let Π be an ALP^N program in which every rule has the form of (18). Then $AB(\Pi) \cup heads(\Pi) = HB(\Pi)$, where $heads(\Pi)$ is the set of all atoms that occur in the heads of rules. The body of a rule can only be satisfied if it is not falsified by a negated set. Therefore, there is a one-one mapping between the stable models and minimal negated models for such a program.

5 Conclusion

This paper introduces a new semantics, the minimal negated model semantics, for ALP that formalized the rational principle of ALP reasoning in a new approach. This semantics is based on the concept of reverse reduct, which is designed for tracing the inconsistencies that cause the negation of assumptions. The reverse reduct provides a justification of the minimal negated assumption sets. By the definition of the reasoning operators, Φ and Ψ, a fixpoint semantics for minimal negated models is also given in this paper. After that, the relationship between the stable model semantics and the minimal negated model semantics is explored. For every stable model of an ALP program, there exists a minimal negated model with the same belief set and a corresponding negated set.

Future works include further investigation of the semantics of ALP. A new algorithm for ALP programs based on reverse reduct and minimal negated model will be developed soon. Besides, inspired by the justification of assumptions in this paper, the research on the well-founded semantics of ALP is already on schedule.

References

1. Balduccini, M., Gelfond, M.: Logic programs with consistency-restoring rules. In: International Symposium on Logical Formalization of Commonsense Reasoning, AAAI 2003 Spring Symposium Series, vol. 102 (2003)
2. Baral, C., Gelfond, M., Rushton, N.: Probabilistic reasoning with answer sets. Theory Pract. Log. Program. **9**(1), 57–144 (2009). https://doi.org/10.1017/S1471068408003645
3. Bondarenko, A., Dung, P.M., Kowalski, R.A., Toni, F.: An abstract, argumentation-theoretic approach to default reasoning. Artif. Intell. **93**, 63–101 (1997)
4. Bondarenko, A., Toni, F., Kowalski, R.A.: An assumption-based framework for non-monotonic reasoning. In: Logic Programming and Non-monotonic Reasoning, Proceedings of the Second International Workshop, Lisbon, Portugal, June 1993, pp. 171–189. MIT Press (1993)
5. Cabalar, P., Kaminski, R., Ostrowski, M., Schaub, T.: An ASP semantics for default reasoning with constraints. In: IJCAI International Joint Conference on Artificial Intelligence 2016-January, pp. 1015–1021 (2016)
6. Gelfond, M., Przymusinska, H., Lifschitz, V., Truszczynski, M., Przymusinska, H., Truszczynski, M.: Disjunctive defaults. In: Proceedings of the 2nd International Conference on Principles of Knowledge Representation and Reasoning (KR 1991), Cambridge, MA, USA, 22–25 April 1991, pp. 230–237. Morgan Kaufmann (1991)
7. Jago, M.: Modelling assumption-based reasoning using contexts. In: Workshop on Context Representation and Reasoning (CRR 2005) (2005)
8. de Kleer, J.: A general labeling algorithm for assumption-based truth maintenance. In: Proceedings of the 7th National Conference on Artificial Intelligence, St. Paul, MN, USA, 21–26 August 1988, pp. 188–192. AAAI Press/The MIT Press (1988)
9. Kohlas, J., Anrig, B., Haenni, R., Monney, P.: Model-based diagnostics and probabilistic assumption-based reasoning. Artif. Intell. **104**(1–2), 71–106 (1998)
10. Kohlas, J., Monney, P.: Probabilistic assumption-based reasoning. In: UAI 1993: Proceedings of the Ninth Annual Conference on Uncertainty in Artificial Intelligence, The Catholic University of America, Providence, Washington, DC, USA, 9–11 July 1993, pp. 485–491. Morgan Kaufmann (1993)
11. Leone, N., Rullo, P., Scarcello, F.: Disjunctive stable models: unfounded sets, fixpoint semantics, and computation. Inf. Comput. **135**(2), 69–112 (1997)
12. Poole, D.: A logical framework for default reasoning. Artif. Intell. **36**(1), 27–47 (1988)
13. Reiter, R.: A logic for default reasoning. Artif. Intell. **13**(1–2), 81–132 (1980)
14. Zhang, S., Zhang, Z., Shen, J.: Constrained default logic programming. In: Proceedings of the International Conference on Logic Programming 2022 Workshops co-located with the 38th International Conference on Logic Programming (ICLP 2022), Haifa, Israel, 31st July–1st August 2022. CEUR Workshop Proceedings, vol. 3193. CEUR-WS.org (2022)
15. Zhang, Z.: Assumable answer set programming. In: Proceedings of the International Conference on Logic Programming 2022 Workshops co-located with the 38th International Conference on Logic Programming (ICLP 2022), Haifa, Israel, 31st July–1st August 2022. CEUR Workshop Proceedings, vol. 3193. CEUR-WS.org (2022)

MT-BICN: Multi-task Balanced Information Cascade Network for Recommendation

Haotian Wu[1]($\boxtimes$) and Yubo Gao[2]($\boxtimes$)

[1] Beijing Jiaotong University, Beijing 100044, China
wu_haotian@bjtu.edu.cn
[2] North University of China, Taiyuan 030051, China
gaoyubo.andrews@gmail.com

Abstract. Multi-task learning (MTL) is a promising research direction in recommender systems, whose prediction accuracy greatly depends on the quality of the modeling of the relationships among tasks. Much of the prior research focus on three tasks: predicting click-through rate (CTR), post-view click-through & conversion rate (CTCVR), and post-click conversion rate (CVR), which rely on inherent user action pattern of impression → click → conversion. Information cascade pattern, represented by Adaptive Information Transfer Multi-task (AITM), attempts to model such sequential dependencies in the feature space close to the output for the first time. However, we observe that the first task in the information cascade model usually tends to be the victim, which is not in line with expectations. To this end, we propose a novel architecture: Multi-task Balanced Information Cascade Network (MT-BICN). We set up both shared experts and task-specific experts for each task to provide a bottom-line guarantee for each task's performance, which largely reduces the risk of each task falling victim to the seesaw phenomenon. Information transfer unit (ITU) is designed and set at the output layer of the top tower to explicitly model the sequential dependencies among tasks. In addition, to further improve the feature extraction capability of the bottom shared experts, task-specific experts, and task towers, we design individual optimization objectives for the BASE model without introducing ITUs, and a balanced marginal constraint to encourage the introduction of ITU to benefit the later tasks without harming the former ones. We conducted extensive experiments on open-source large-scale recommendation datasets from AliExpress. The experimental results show that our approach significantly outperforms the mainstream MTL learning approaches for recommender systems. In addition, the ablation study demonstrates the necessity of designing core modules in MT-BICN.

Keywords: Sequential Dependence · Multi-task Learning · Recommender Systems · Performance Balance

---

H. Wu and Y. Gao—Contributed equally to this work.

1   Introduction

With the booming of e-commerce, information overload has gradually become an increasingly ubiquitous problem, which creates barriers for users of online shopping platforms to access desired items [25]. Recommender system provides an effective solution to this problem. It greatly alleviates the negative effects of information overload by mining users' hidden patterns and matching them with a series of items tailored to their desires [19]. Recommender systems often involve optimizing multiple objectives simultaneously to meet diverse business needs. For example, platforms simultaneously predict click-through rates (CTR) to evaluate the attractiveness of items to users, post-click conversion rate (CVR) to measure the real economic benefits of items or strategies, and user ratings of items to analyze whether the user is motivated to repurchase the items and to guide online shopping platform merchants to improve their strategies [18,24]. It is highly inefficient to construct models for these tasks one by one, so the application of multi-task learning in recommender systems is prompted in both research and application fields [3,10,11,13,25].

Multi-task learning (MTL) is a machine learning paradigm that simultaneously trains data from different tasks to obtain shared representations. One of the most common modeling approaches for MTL is the hard parameter sharing mechanism, which typically sets up a bottom feature extractor shared by all tasks and keeps several task-specific output layers for each task [12]. Although hard parameter sharing methods have been widely used in the field of recommender systems [4,7,23], harmful parameter interference among tasks can significantly affect the performance of hard parameter sharing models. In addition, the hard sharing mechanism cannot effectively capture the differences between tasks and more complex inter-task dependence relationships.

To tackle these challenges, researchers have made numerous effective attempts in recent years to model the relationships among tasks. One important strategy is the Mixture-Experts-Bottom pattern [1,8,13], in which multiple experts are set at the bottom to capture richer shared features. It utilizes task-specific gating networks to aggregate the outputs of multiple experts and feed them to task-specific towers at the top, adaptively modeling the relationships and differences between tasks in this way. However, such Mixture-Experts-Bottom pattern can only transfer shallow representations among tasks [18].

Another branch of the approach [9,17] relies on classical user behavior sequence patterns in the recommender systems: impression → click → conversion [9,18], which can be employed to model the CTR, CVR, and post-view click-through & conversion rate (CTCVR). Specifically, the dependence between CTR and CVR can be formulated as $pCTCVR = pCTR \times pCVR$. Some works [9,15,17] have attempted to exploit this probabilistic transfer relationship to set up loss functions to model the sequence dependence relationship among them explicitly, which are called Probability-Transfer pattern. However, the Probability-Transfer pattern can only rely on the scalar product to transfer simple probability information while ignoring more useful feature representations in the vector space, resulting in a large loss of gain. If any one of the probabilities is not predicted accurately, multiple tasks will be affected [20].

To address this problem, the Information-Cascade pattern, represented by Adaptive Information Transfer Multi-task (AITM) [20] is proposed, which is based on the intuition that the vector space closer to the output layer tends to contain richer and more useful information. It enables the model to adaptively transfer information in the vector space close to the output layer and capture sequential dependence between tasks more effectively by the Adaptive Information Transfer (AIT) module [20]. However, the bottom of the Information-Cascade pattern is still based on the traditional hard sharing mechanism, which largely limits its capability to handle inter-task conflicts. In addition, we observe that the first task in the information cascade pattern usually tends to be a victim. Specifically, in this pattern, the first task in the task sequence does not obtain information from the previous task except the shared feature extractor, which largely affects the first task to benefit from MTL and even makes it a victim, Fig. 1 illustrates our findings, which corroborate this insight. After introducing the information transfer module in the hard parameter sharing model, the performance of the CTCVR task shows different degrees of improvement, however, this improvement seems to be at the sacrifice of the performance of the CTR task. In the impression → click → conversion pattern, the CTR task is the first task in the task sequence. The performance degradation of CTR, a highly important task in recommender systems, is not in line with expectations.

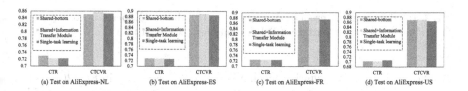

Fig. 1. The Findings on Four AliExpress Datasets

To solve the existing problem for Information-Cascade pattern, we propose a novel architecture: Multi-task Balanced Information Cascade Network (MT-BICN). Besides the shared experts, we set task-specific experts for each task to provide a bottom-line guarantee for each task's performance, which largely reduces the risk of each task becoming a victim of the seesaw phenomenon. In addition, this setup can effectively reduce harmful interference between shared and task-specific knowledge and thus mitigate task conflicts. We set Information Transfer Unit (ITU) in the output layer of the top tower to explicitly model the sequential dependencies between tasks. To further improve the feature extraction capabilities of the bottom shared experts, task-specific experts and task towers, we setup individual optimization objectives for the BASE model without introducing ITUs. What's more, we design a balanced marginal constraint to encourage the introduction of ITU to be beneficial to the later tasks without harming the former tasks. We conducted extensive experiments on four open-source large-scale recommendation datasets from AliExpress. The experimental results demonstrate that our approach significantly outperforms the mainstream MTL methods of recommender systems. The ablation studies prove the necessity of designing the core module in MT-BICN.

2   Related Work

In this section, we present the main MTL works related to our work in four-fold: Hard parameter sharing mechanism, Mixture-Experts-Bottom pattern, Probability-Transfer pattern, and Information-Cascade pattern.

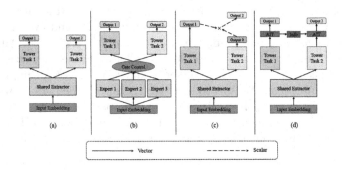

Fig. 2. (a) Hard parameter sharing mechanism. (b) Mixture-Experts-Bottom pattern. (c) Probability-Transfer pattern. (d) Information-Cascade pattern

The hard parameter sharing mechanism [2,7,23], as shown in Fig. 2(a), is the most commonly used MTL structure. It is generally applied by sharing hidden layers among all tasks while keeping several task-specific output layers [12]. The hard sharing mechanism forces all tasks to share a bottom parameter space, which may lead to conflicts and interferences between tasks. As a result, the relationship between tasks may be ignored or weakened, which leads to the degradation of model performance [13].

To address these shortcomings of the hard parameter sharing mechanism, the Mixture-Expert-Bottom pattern (as shown in Fig. 2(b)) attempts to capture richer shared representations by setting multiple experts at the bottom and controlling how expert modules are shared across tasks through gating networks. Tower modules at the top handle each task separately [20]. Multi-gate Mixture-of-Experts (MMOE) [8] is a milestone work under this type of approach, which extends MOE [5] to utilize different input-generated gates for each task to obtain different fusing weights in MTL. In this way, the relationships and differences among tasks are modeled, thus mitigating negative transfer phenomena. Considering that harmful interference between task-specific and shared knowledge still exists in MMOE, Customized Gated Control (CGC) [13] attempts to further mitigate the negative transfer and seesaw phenomena by explicitly dividing task-specific and shared experts to reduce the interference between these two types of knowledge. Multi-gate Mixture-of-Experts with Exclusivity (MMOEEx) [1] is another improvement of MMOE, which is similar to the idea of CGC: allowing some extractors to contribute to specific tasks and others to be shared by all tasks. MMOEEx achieves this by introducing novel exclusivity and exclusion conditions to induce diversity of extractors. However, Mixture-Expert-Bottom pattern is not specially designed for tasks with sequential dependence and there is no information exchange among the top tower modules, which causes the top towers cannot help the task to improve each other [20].

Another branch of methods to model task relationships in MTL is to transfer probabilities in the output layers of different tasks [20] as shown in Fig. 2(c). Entire Space Multi-task Model (ESMM) [9] is a classic model of such type of methods, which learns $pCVR$ implicitly as an intermediate variable between $pCTR$ and $pCTCVR$, based on $pCTCVR = pCTR \times pCVR$, so that $pCVR$ can be derived over the entire input space. ESM^2 [17] expands ESMM to more-task scenarios. Entire Space Counterfactual Multi-task Modelling ($ESCM^2$) [15] is an improved method for ESMM, which employs a counterfactual risk mini-mizer as a regularizer in ESMM to tackle Inherent Estimation Bias issue for CVR estimation and Potential Independence Priority issue for CTCVR estimation. However, Probability-Transfer pattern has two main shortcomings: First, it ignores richer and more useful representations in the vector space close to the output layer and can only transfer simple probability information via the scalar product. Second, inaccurate prediction of any one of the probabilities will harm the performances of multiple tasks [18,20].

The Information-Cascade pattern, as shown in Fig. 2(d), is an improvement at the top tower module of the model level. The Information-Cascade pattern adds information transfer modules that match the order in the task sequence at positions close to the output layer to better exploit the richer representations in vector space and model the sequential dependence among tasks. The Adaptive Information Transfer Multi-task (AITM) framework [20] is a classic work for this type of approach. However, this approach usually focuses excessively on utilizing the information in the top tower modules, while ignoring the fact that the quality of the features extracted by the bottom extractor also affects the quality of the information in the top tower. Conflicts and interferences among tasks can still significantly affect the performance of the information cascade pattern. Besides, the first task in the task sequence does not have access to the information of the previous tasks, so it is vulnerable to being a victim of the seesaw phenomenon [18].

3 Methodology

3.1 Problem Definition

Let $\mathcal{S} = \{x_i, y_i, z_i\}|_{i=1}^{N}$ is the observed dataset, where N is the total number of samples in the observed dataset. x_i denotes the ith sample with multiple fields(e.g. user field, item field) y_i, z_i denote the binary labels of click and conversion to the ith sample respectively. $y = 1$ or $z = 1$ means click or conversion event occurs respectively. $pCTR, pCVR, pCTCVR$ are defined as follows:

1. post-view click-through rate (CTR): $pCTR = p(y = 1|x)$
2. post-click conversion rate (CVR): $pCVR = p(z = 1|y = 1, x)$
3. post-view click- through&conversion rate: $pCTCVR = p(y = 1, z = 1|x)$

3.2 The Structure of Multi-task Balanced Information Cascade Network(MT-BICN)

To explicitly model the sequential dependence among tasks under the premise of balancing the performance of each task, we propose a novel Multi-task Balanced Information Cascade Network (MT-BICN), and Fig. 3 illustrates the structure of MT-BICN. We set task-specific experts for each task, by which the performance of each task is ensured to maintain above a certain level. Shared experts are used to extract common features across tasks. At the output layer of the model, we set up information extractor and information filters (collectively named Information Transfer Unit (ITU)), which are used to learn what information should be transferred and how much information should be transferred to the next task, respectively. To balance each task more efficiently and prevent them from becoming victims in the seesaw phenomenon, we set separate optimization objectives for the base network(denoted as BASE) that does not introduce ITU, as indicated by the black arrows in Fig. 3, and combine them into the total loss. Other than that we propose a novel balanced margin constraint for encouraging the introduction of information transfer unit that does not harm the previous task and benefits the latter task simultaneously.

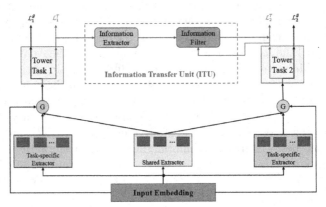

Fig. 3. The structure of Multi-task Balanced Information Cascade Network(MT-BICN). For simplicity, only two adjacent tasks are shown in the figure.

Assuming $\mathbf{x}$ is the input representation, $TE_k^j(\cdot)$ and $SE^m(\cdot)$ represent $j - th$ Expert for task k and $m - th$ Shared-Expert, respectively. The outputs of Task k-specific Extractor (e_k) and Shared Extractor (s) can be formulated as:

$$e_k = [TE_k^1(\mathbf{x}), TE_k^2(\mathbf{x}), \cdots, TE_k^J(\mathbf{x})]^{\mathrm{T}} \qquad (1)$$

$$s = [SE^1(\mathbf{x}), SE^2(\mathbf{x}), \cdots, SE^M(\mathbf{x})]^{\mathrm{T}} \qquad (2)$$

where J is the total number of Task k-specific Experts and M is the total number of Shared Experts. These experts are multiple-layer perceptron (MLP) with ReLU as activation function. G denotes the gating network which is based on a single-layer feed-forward network with Softmax as the activation function and is used to weighted fuse the task-specific features and shared features for each task. The output of gating networks for task k is denoted as $g^k(\mathbf{x})$, which can be calculated as follows:

$$g_k(\mathbf{x}) = w_k(\mathbf{x})S_k(\mathbf{x}) = \mathrm{Softmax}\,(W_k^g \mathbf{x})\, S_k(\mathbf{x}) \qquad (3)$$

$$S_k = [e_k, s]^{\mathrm{T}} \qquad (4)$$

where W_g^k is a trainable parameter matrix with dimension of $(M + J) \times d$, and d is the dimension of input representation. S_k is the selected matrix for task k, which contains the outputs of task k-specific experts and shared experts.

Suppose that $\hat{y}_k^g$ is the output of Tower for task k in the case of BASE, and v_k^t is the output of Tower for task k in the case of BASE with ITU.

$$\hat{y}_k^g = f_k(g_k(\mathbf{x})) \qquad (5)$$

$$v_k^t = f_k(g_k^t(\mathbf{x})) \qquad (6)$$

where $f_k(\cdot)$ represents the MLP structures for task k's tower and $g_k^t(\mathbf{x}$ is the output of gating network in the case of BASE with ITU, whose calculation process is same with BASE. ITU is composed of the information extractor and information filter. Information extractor is a MLP, which is used to capture what information should be transferred between task $k-1$ and task k. Information filter is a self-attention-based module [14], which is used to adaptively control the amount of transferred information. We denote z_{k-1}^t is the output of ITU for task $k - 1$. The output of ITU for task k is denoted as z_k^t, which can be formulated as:

$$z_k^t = \sum_{q \in \{u_{k-1}, v_k^t\}} \phi_1(q)\,\mathrm{Softmax}\left[\frac{\phi_2(q)\cdot\phi_3(q)}{\sqrt{d_k}}\right] \qquad (7)$$
$$u_{k-1} = h_{k-1}\left(v_{k-1}^t\right)$$

where $h_{k-1}(\cdot)$ is the neural network of Information Extractor to learn the transferred information between task $k-1$ and task k and u_{k-1} is the learned transfer information. Inspired by self-attention [14], $\phi_1(\cdot)$, $\phi_2(\cdot)$, $\phi_3(\cdot)$ are three single-layer feed-forward neural networks to map q to different spaces and learn "Value, Query, Key". In this way, transferred information will be adaptively filtered and fed to next task. Previous work has proven the effectiveness of this kind of attention mechanism [20–22]. The prediction probability of each task k in the case of BASE with ITU is denoted as $\hat{y}_k^t$:

$$\hat{y}_k^t = sigmoid(MLP(z_k^t)) \qquad (8)$$

where the MLP is used to project the z_k^t to the output space. $z_k^t = v_k^t (k = 1)$.

3.3 Training Objective

In this study, we consider the dual-task case, as in other mainstream studies of MTL in recommender systems [16].

Loss Function. The loss functions employed in this study are all cross-entropy losses. Suppose that L_1 is the loss for task 1, which can be calculated by:

$$\mathcal{L}_1 = -\frac{1}{N} \sum_{(x,y_1)\in\mathcal{D}} \left[\left(y_1 \log \hat{y}_1^g + (1-y_1)\log\left(1-\hat{y}_1^g\right)\right) + \left(y_1 \log \hat{y}_1^t + (1-y_1)\log\left(1-\hat{y}_1^t\right)\right) \right]$$

(9)

where y_1 are ground-truth labels for task 1, N is the number of samples in the entire sample space $\mathcal{D}$. The calculation process of loss for task 2 ($\mathcal{L}_2$) is same as $\mathcal{L}_1$.

Balanced Margin Constraints. The core of our idea is to effectively model sequential dependencies between tasks explicitly under the premise of balancing each task. Intuitively, the introduction of ITU can benefit the latter task without harming the former task. To force MT-BICN obey this rule, we design a balanced margin constraint for each task, which aims to improve the probabilities of the correct labels. Let balanced margin constraint is $\mathcal{L}^{bmc}$, which can be formulated as:

$$\mathcal{L}^{bmc} = \alpha_1 \times \mathcal{L}_1^{bmc} + \alpha_2 \times \mathcal{L}_2^{bmc}$$

$$= \alpha_1 \times \frac{1}{N} \sum_{x\in\mathcal{D}} \max y_1 \left(\hat{y}_1^t - \hat{y}_1^g, 0\right) + \alpha_2 \times \frac{1}{N} \sum_{x\in\mathcal{D}} \max y_2 \left(\hat{y}_2^g - \hat{y}_2^t, 0\right)$$

(10)

If $\hat{y}_1^t > \hat{y}_1^g$, $\mathcal{L}_1^{bmc}$ will be positive. In this way, those cases where the introduction of ITU causes degradation in Task 1 performance will be penalized and the probabilities of the correct labels will be improved. $\mathcal{L}_2^{bmc}$ encourages Task 2 to benefit from the ITU, that is, it performs better than BASE without introducing the ITU. α_1 and α_2 are hyper-parameters that are used to control the strength of the penalty.

Model Training. The total loss $\mathcal{L}$ can be calculated by weighted summing up the loss functions of BASE, BASE with ITU and balanced margin constraint, that is:

$$\mathcal{L} = \lambda\mathcal{L}_1 + (1-\lambda)\mathcal{L}_2 + \mathcal{L}^{bmc}$$

(11)

where λ is the coefficient balancing the two tasks.

4   Experiments

4.1   Datasets Description and Baselines

The datasets used in this paper are gathered from real-world traffic logs of the search system in AliExpress, which contain item and user data from four countries: Spain (AliExpress-ES), French (AliExpress-FR), Netherlands (AliExpress-NL), and America (AliExpress-US). We compare MT-BICN with competitive baselines of recommender systems:

1. **SingleTask**: Train one MLP model for each task, respectively.
2. **Shared-Bottom** [2]: It is a traditional MTL model with a shared extractor and multiple towers for tasks.
3. **OMoE** [5]: The OMoE with Mixture-Expert-Bottom pattern integrates experts by sharing one gate among all tasks.
4. **MMOE** [8]: MMOE with Mixture-Expert-Bottom pattern introduces multiple expert networks and a gating network for each task, and learns different combinations of expert networks for each task by gating networks.
5. **PLE** [13]: The Progressive Layered Extraction (PLE) with Mixture-Expert-Bottom pattern explicitly separates task-shared experts and task-specific experts, which alleviates the parameter interference.
6. **ESMM** [9]: The ESMM with Probability- Transfer pattern solves the non-end-to-end post-click conversion rate via training on the entire space.
7. **AITM** [20]: The AITM with Information-Cascade pattern models the sequential dependence among tasks by introducing adaptive information transfer module at the top of shared-bottom model
8. **MetaHeac** [25]: The Meta Hybrid Experts and Critics (MetaHeac) is a Meta Learning approach to train a generalized initialization model that learns the connections between different tasks so that it can quickly adapt to new categories of content promotion tasks.
9. **MMOEEx** [1]: MMOEEx with Mixture-Expert-Bottom pattern introduces exclusivity and exclusion conditions in MMOE to induce diversity of extractors.

4.2 Experimental Settings

To evaluate the performance of proposed MT-BICN and baselines we use the standard metric: Area Under ROC (AUC), following the previous studies [9, 13,20]. We repeat each group of experiments 10 times and report the average AUC. The number of task-specific experts and shared experts are both set to 4. Experts and Towers are two-layer MLPs. All the model are trained adopting Adam optimizer [6], with the initial learning rate of $1e-3$. α_1, α_1, λ are set to $1e-6$, $1e-4$ and 0.5, respectively.

4.3 Performance Comparison

Table 1 shows the results of MT-BICN and other competitive MTL baselines in recommender systems on four large-scale open-source datasets. In this section, we provide reasonable discussions about the performance of different models.

We find that the shared-bottom, AITM, and ESMM all suffer from negative transfer or seesaw problems to varying degrees. The introduction of Mixture-Expert-Bottom models and task-specific gate networks effectively captures the differences between tasks and mitigates the negative transfer or seesaw phenomenon. Models such as PLE and MMOEEx that introduce shared private patterns in Mixture-Expert-Bottom models reduce the harmful interference between shared and task-specific knowledge and further alleviate the negative transfer and seesaw phenomenon. In addition, we observe that the CTR AUC of AITM is generally lower than that of the shared bottom, while CTCVR is vice versa. This suggests that AITM's improvement for CTCVR tasks may come at the expense of its performance on CTR tasks. Our proposed MT-BICN effectively addresses this issue and significantly outperforms the baseline models.

Table 1. Performance comparsion of baselines and MT-BICN on 4 recommender systems datasets

Datasets	AliExpress-NL		AliExpress-ES		AliExpress-FR		AliExpress-US	
Methods	CTR	CTCVR	CTR	CTCVR	CTR	CTCVR	CTR	CTCVR
SingleTask	0.7224	0.8529	0.7268	0.8855	0.7241	0.8748	0.7071	0.8658
Shared-Bottom	0.7230	0.8509	0.7288	0.8869	0.7250	0.8714	0.7031	0.8703
OMoE	0.7255	0.8611	0.7254	0.8860	0.7258	0.8781	0.7049	0.8701
MMoE	0.7234	0.8606	0.7285	0.8898	0.7216	0.8811	0.7043	0.8735
PLE	0.7292	0.8641	0.7303	0.8913	0.7276	0.8806	0.7138	0.8743
AITM	0.7229	0.8576	0.7284	0.8905	0.7247	0.8802	0.7025	0.8720
ESMM	0.7243	0.8602	0.7271	0.8892	0.7233	0.8797	0.7062	0.8712
MetaHeac	0.7263	0.8615	0.7299	0.8883	0.7249	0.8813	0.7089	0.8767
MMOEEx	0.7281	0.8625	0.7292	0.8901	0.7265	0.8817	0.7123	0.8735
MT-BICN	**0.7333**	**0.8725**	**0.7349**	**0.8959**	**0.7383**	**0.8858**	**0.7177**	**0.8865**

4.4 Ablation Study

In this section, diverse ablation experiments are conducted to verify the necessity of designing the core components of MT-BICN. "BASE" denotes the model after removing the ITU, the individual optimization objectives and the balanced margin constraint from MT-BICN. "BASE+ITU" denotes the model in which only the ITU is introduced in BASE. "w/o $\mathcal{L}^{bmc}$" denotes the model that removes the balanced margin constraint in the MT-BICN. It adds individual optimization objectives set for the BASE network compared to "BASE+ITU". "w/o $\mathcal{L}_2^{bmc}$" and "w/o $\mathcal{L}_1^{bmc}$" represent the models that remove $\mathcal{L}_2^{bmc}$ and $\mathcal{L}_1^{bmc}$ from the MT-BICN, respectively, and they are employed to evaluate the importance of each component in the balanced margin constraint. The main results of ablation studies are reported in Table 2.

The Necessity of Designing the ITU and Individual Optimization Objectives for BASE Network. To verify the necessity of ITU and setting individual optimization objectives for BASE, we design three variants termed BASE, BASE+ITU, and "w/o $\mathcal{L}^{bmc}$", and their results are shown in Table 2.

We can find that the introduction of ITU improves the effectiveness of BASE on CTR and CTCVR tasks to different degrees. Among them, the improvement effect on the CTCVR task is more significant. One possible reason is that the information of ITU flows from the CTR task tower to the CTCVR task tower, and thus the CTCVR task is easier to benefit from this pattern. In addition, we introduce individual optimization objectives for BASE on the basis of "BASE+ITU". As shown in experimental results for "w/o $\mathcal{L}^{bmc}$", its performance is further improved relative to "BASE+ITU". The individual optimization objectives contribute to improving the performance of each module in the BASE network, which also provides a guarantee for ITU to capture more useful information.

The Necessity of Balanced Margin Constraint and Its Components the necessity of balanced margin constraint and its component, we design three variants named "w/o $\mathcal{L}_2^{bmc}$", "w/o $\mathcal{L}_1^{bmc}$" and "w/o $\mathcal{L}^{bmc}$". We find that deleting any of the components of the balanced margin constraint will cause the performances of the model to degrade even below the variants without the balanced margin constraint, suggesting that adopting $\mathcal{L}_1^{bmc}$ or $\mathcal{L}_2^{bmc}$ alone may exacerbate the imbalance in task performance. In addition to this, we observe that in most cases, the impact of deleting $\mathcal{L}_2^{bmc}$ is greater than that of deleting $\mathcal{L}_1^{bmc}$. One possible reason is that when the performance of BASE is poor, $\mathcal{L}_1^{bmc}$ will be susceptible to output positive penalty terms, which will increase the magnitude of $\mathcal{L}_1^{bmc}$ and lead to an imbalance in multi-task optimization.

Table 2. Ablation studies for core modules of MT-BICN in terms of CTR AUC and CTCVR AUC

Model	CTR AUC				CTCVR AUC			
	NL	ES	FR	US	NL	ES	FR	US
MT-BICN	**0.7333**	**0.7349**	**0.7383**	**0.7177**	**0.8725**	**0.8959**	**0.8858**	**0.8865**
w/o $\mathcal{L}_2^{bmc}$	0.7246	0.7306	0.7279	0.7108	0.8672	0.8904	0.8785	0.8815
w/o $\mathcal{L}_1^{bmc}$	0.7285	0.7319	0.7283	0.7076	0.8679	0.8934	0.8824	0.8831
w/o $\mathcal{L}^{bmc}$	0.7321	0.7328	0.7319	0.7147	0.8707	0.8939	0.8850	0.8832
BASE+ITU	0.7293	0.7329	0.7291	0.7144	0.8662	0.8919	0.8829	0.8807
BASE	0.7292	0.7303	0.7276	0.7138	0.8641	0.8913	0.8806	0.8677

5   Conclusion

To efficiently model the sequential dependence between tasks on the basis of balancing the performance of each task, following the information-cascade pattern, we propose a novel architecture: MT-BICN. We set up both shared experts and task-specific experts for each task to reduce the risk of each task falling victim to the seesaw phenomenon. This setup effectively reduces harmful interference between shared knowledge and task-specific knowledge, thus mitigating task conflicts. ITUs are designed to explicitly model the sequential dependencies between tasks. Furthermore, we propose a novel training approach that sets individual optimization objectives for the BASE model without the introduction of ITUs and balances the performance of two adjacent tasks with balanced marginal constraints. Extensive experiments on open-source large-scale recommendation datasets demonstrate the superiority of the proposed MT-BICN. In addition, the ablation study demonstrates the necessity of designing core modules in MT-BICN. In future work, we should give more consideration to further improving MT-BICN by decoupling the shared feature space from the task-specific feature space or exploring more efficient methods for balancing three or more tasks simultaneously.

References

1. Aoki, R., Tung, F., Oliveira, G.L.: Heterogeneous multi-task learning with expert diversity. IEEE/ACM Trans. Comput. Biol. Bioinf. **19**(6), 3093–3102 (2022)
2. Caruana, R.: Multitask learning. Mach. Learn. **28**, 41–75 (1997)
3. Ding, K., et al.: Mssm: a multiple-level sparse sharing model for efficient multitask learning. In: Proceedings of the 44th International ACM SIGIR Conference on Research and Development in Information Retrieval, pp. 2237–2241 (2021)
4. He, Y., Feng, X., Cheng, C., Ji, G., Guo, Y., Caverlee, J.: Metabalance: improving multi-task recommendations via adapting gradient magnitudes of auxiliary tasks. In: Proceedings of the ACM Web Conference 2022, pp. 2205–2215 (2022)
5. Jacobs, R.A., Jordan, M.I., Nowlan, S.J., Hinton, G.E.: Adaptive mixtures of local experts. Neural Comput. **3**(1), 79–87 (1991)
6. Kingma, D.P., Ba, J.: Adam: a method for stochastic optimization. arXiv preprint arXiv:1412.6980 (2014)
7. Liu, J., Li, X., An, B., Xia, Z., Wang, X.: Multi-faceted hierarchical multi-task learning for recommender systems. In: Proceedings of the 31st ACM International Conference on Information & Knowledge Management, pp. 3332–3341 (2022)
8. Ma, J., Zhao, Z., Yi, X., Chen, J., Hong, L., Chi, E.H.: Modeling task relationships in multi-task learning with multi-gate mixture-of-experts. In: Proceedings of the 24th ACM SIGKDD International Conference on Knowledge Discovery & Data Mining, pp. 1930–1939 (2018)
9. Ma, X., et al.: Entire space multi-task model: an effective approach for estimating post-click conversion rate. In: The 41st International ACM SIGIR Conference on Research & Development in Information Retrieval, pp. 1137–1140 (2018)
10. Ni, Y., et al.: Perceive your users in depth: learning universal user representations from multiple e-commerce tasks. In: Proceedings of the 24th ACM SIGKDD International Conference on Knowledge Discovery & Data Mining, pp. 596–605 (2018)
11. Qin, Z., Cheng, Y., Zhao, Z., Chen, Z., Metzler, D., Qin, J.: Multitask mixture of sequential experts for user activity streams. In: Proceedings of the 26th ACM SIGKDD International Conference on Knowledge Discovery & Data Mining, pp. 3083–3091 (2020)
12. Ruder, S.: An overview of multi-task learning in deep neural networks. arXiv preprint arXiv:1706.05098 (2017)

13. Tang, H., Liu, J., Zhao, M., Gong, X.: Progressive layered extraction (PLE): A novel multi-task learning (MTL) model for personalized recommendations. In: Proceedings of the 14th ACM Conference on Recommender Systems, pp. 269–278 (2020)
14. Vaswani, A., et al.: Attention is all you need. Adv. Neural Inf. Process. Syst. **30** (2017)
15. Wang, H., et al.: Escm2: entire space counterfactual multi-task model for post-click conversion rate estimation. In: Proceedings of the 45th International ACM SIGIR Conference on Research and Development in Information Retrieval, pp. 363–372 (2022)
16. Wang, Y., et al.: Multi-task deep recommender systems: a survey. arXiv preprint arXiv:2302.03525 (2023)
17. Wen, H., et al.: Entire space multi-task modeling via post-click behavior decomposition for conversion rate prediction. In: Proceedings of the 43rd International ACM SIGIR Conference on Research and Development in Information Retrieval, pp. 2377–2386 (2020)
18. Wu, H.: Mncm: multi-level network cascades model for multi-task learning. In: Proceedings of the 31st ACM International Conference on Information & Knowledge Management, pp. 4565–4569 (2022)
19. Wu, L., He, X., Wang, X., Zhang, K., Wang, M.: A survey on accuracy-oriented neural recommendation: from collaborative filtering to information-rich recommendation. IEEE Trans. Know. Data Eng. **35**(5), 4425–4445 (2022)
20. Xi, D., et al.: Modeling the sequential dependence among audience multi-step conversions with multi-task learning in targeted display advertising. In: Proceedings of the 27th ACM SIGKDD Conference on Knowledge Discovery & Data Mining, pp. 3745–3755 (2021)
21. Xi, D., et al.: Modeling the field value variations and field interactions simultaneously for fraud detection. In: Proceedings of the AAAI Conference on Artificial Intelligence, vol. 35, pp. 14957–14965 (2021)
22. Xi, D., et al.: Neural hierarchical factorization machines for user's event sequence analysis. In: Proceedings of the 43rd International ACM SIGIR Conference on Research and Development in Information Retrieval, p. 1893–1896 (2020)
23. Yang, E., et al.: Adatask: a task-aware adaptive learning rate approach to multi-task learning. arXiv preprint arXiv:2211.15055 (2022)
24. Zhang, D., et al.: Ctnocvr: a novelty auxiliary task making the lower-CTR-higher-CVR upper. In: Proceedings of the 45th International ACM SIGIR Conference on Research and Development in Information Retrieval, pp. 2272–2276 (2022)
25. Zhu, Y., et al.: Learning to expand audience via meta hybrid experts and critics for recommendation and advertising. In: Proceedings of the 27th ACM SIGKDD Conference on Knowledge Discovery & Data Mining, pp. 4005–4013 (2021)

Author Index

Printed in the United States
by Baker & Taylor Publisher Services